THE PAPERS OF DANIEL WEBSTER

CHARLES M. WILTSE, EDITOR-IN-CHIEF

SERIES ONE: CORRESPONDENCE

THE UNIVERSITY PRESS

OF NEW ENGLAND

Sponsoring Institutions

BRANDEIS UNIVERSITY

CLARK UNIVERSITY

DARTMOUTH COLLEGE

UNIVERSITY OF NEW HAMPSHIRE

UNIVERSITY OF RHODE ISLAND

UNIVERSITY OF VERMONT

The Papers of
Daniel Webster

Correspondence, Volume 3

1830-1834

CHARLES M. WILTSE, EDITOR

DAVID G. ALLEN, ASSISTANT EDITOR

PUBLISHED FOR

DARTMOUTH COLLEGE BY THE

UNIVERSITY PRESS OF NEW ENGLAND

HANOVER, NEW HAMPSHIRE 1977

*This edition of the Papers of Daniel Webster is published by Dartmouth
College with assistance from the National Historical Publications and
Records Commission and the National Endowment for the Humanities.*

Acknowledgments

Again as in earlier volumes the editors are indebted to libraries and librarians, archives and archivists, and individual collectors too numerous for individual mention. Those to whom our debt is greatest are the National Archives; the Library of Congress, and especially to John McDonough, Manuscript Historian; the Massachusetts Historical Society and its Director, Stephen T. Riley; the New Hampshire Historical Society and its Director, John F. Page. To Baker Library of Dartmouth College our obligation is beyond acknowledgment. The editorial staff of the Webster Papers is housed in Baker, and it is no exaggeration to say that every member of the library's professional staff, without exception, has contributed at need. To name Dean of Libraries Edward Connery Lathem, Reference Librarian Virginia L. Close, Curator of Rare Books and Chief of Special Collections, Walter W. Wright, and Archivist Kenneth C. Cramer is to single out only a top-level sampling.

Equally great is our indebtedness to those who have made this project possible by their generous financial support: Dartmouth College, the National Endowment for the Humanities, and the National Historical Publications and Records Commission. Among individuals, our obligation is great to President John G. Kemeny of Dartmouth College, to Vice President and Dean of the Faculty Leonard M. Rieser, to Professors James M. Cox of the English Department, Louis Morton of the History Department, and Vincent Starzinger of the Department of Government; and to Mr. William B. Durant, Executive Officer to the Faculty of Arts and Sciences, who continues to be financial advisor to the project. At the National Endowment for the Humanities we are especially indebted to Dr. Simone Reagor, Director of the Division of Research Grants. Our obligation to staff members of the National Historical Publications and Records Commission extend in particular to the Commission Chairman, Dr. James B. Rhoads, Archivist of the United States; and to Dr. Frank G. Burke, Executive Director, and Mr. Fred Shelley, his Deputy.

Because this volume covers the period of most intensive controversy over the Second Bank of the United States, it has been read in manuscript by Professor Colin D. Campbell, Dartmouth College specialist in Money and Banking, and by Mr. Clifton B. Luttrell, Assistant Vice President of the Federal Reserve Bank of St. Louis. To each of these, our most cordial thanks are due.

On the staff of the Webster Papers itself the editors of this volume could not have performed their duties as efficiently or as well if they had not been able at all times to call upon the special skills of Diplomatic Editor Kenneth E. Shewmaker, Legal Editor Alfred Konefsky, and Associate Editor Harold D. Moser. Mrs. Mary V. Anstruther, who combines the roles of Secretary and Research Assistant, has consistently performed services above and beyond the call of duty.

Hanover, New Hampshire   C. M. W.

Contents

*For the page number on which each document of
the Papers begins, see the Calendar.*

A section of illustrations follows page 292

Introduction

As the decade of the 1830s opened, the legacy of the Missouri Compromise was all too apparent in Southern hostility to the tariff and in outspoken Northern distaste for slavery. Hypersensitive to the vulnerability of her labor system under any doctrine of majority rule, Vice President Calhoun, now the intellectual leader of the South, had devised an ingenious interpretation of the Constitution that vested in each state under appropriate circumstances the power to nullify acts of the national government. The northern answer came from Daniel Webster in a spectacular debate with Senator Robert Y. Hayne of South Carolina. Already widely known and respected in political circles and by the business community, Webster now emerged as something of a popular hero. His second reply to Hayne was more widely read and more enthusiastically acclaimed than any speech made in either house of Congress up to that time.

The constitutional debate, though its roots lay as deep as America's colonial origins, was precipitated by a move to slow down the settlement of the public lands. The sectional character of the reaction heralded the emergence of a western interest, distinct alike from the older North and South and ready to bargain with either for the advancement of its own special needs. The West required cheap land, just as the manufacturing states needed a protective tariff, and as the slave states demanded a constitution that would leave in their own hands the power to resist any interference with their labor system.

Webster's role as "defender of the Constitution" was reinforced and entrenched by his later debate with Calhoun over the power of the general government to use force to collect the revenues. The question arose after South Carolina late in 1832 had actually nullified the tariff. At the same time his rejection of Clay's compromise, his valiant though futile efforts to gain a recharter for the Bank of the United States, and his losing battle to prevent removal of the government deposits from the Bank endeared him to the already potent world of industry and finance. He stood unequivocally for a strong central government, of which a national bank was a useful and efficient, if not a necessary arm; for the subsidy of American manufactures through tariff protection; for the extension and improvement of internal and external transportation in order to promote indefinitely the expansion of commerce.

It was during the same five-year period from 1830 through 1834 that abolitionist attacks on slavery, and southern resistance to government by a numerical majority both reached crisis proportions. Webster, in his debates with Hayne and Calhoun, in his opposition to tariff reduction for appeasement of the South, and in his support of central power, was the natural leader of the forces of nationalism. On the slavery question his role was less conspicuous. So far as the records survive, he nowhere mentions or alludes to Garrison's *Liberator*, which began publication in Boston in January 1831. He was in regular correspondence with Virginians at the time, yet he has nowhere any comment to make on Nat Turner's rebellion. David Walker lived and wrote in Boston, and died there in 1830 after setting the South aflame with his *Appeal to the Coloured Citizens of the World*, yet Webster's extant correspondence has no word to say of the man or his work. Nor does he mention the American Antislavery Society, founded in 1833 by the Tappan brothers, although he was at that very time dealing with Lewis Tappan in Boston real estate. Asked to state his position on slavery, he did so without demur—and without change from his earliest opinions on that subject. He was against slavery, he would oppose its extension, but it must be left alone where it already existed, protected from interference by the Constitution itself.

A concomitant of the Bank fight was the birth of the second American party system, combining under the ubiquitous Whig banner the otherwise disparate elements of the opposition to Andrew Jackson. In the rise of the Whig party Webster played a decisive, if sometimes a reluctant, part. He had points of agreement with Jackson and major differences with both Clay and Calhoun. But he had by 1834 a clearly evolved concept of the nature of the American Constitutional system, which found a more comfortable home with the Whigs than with the Democrats. What had begun as a power struggle between slave and free states had now become a contest between a political organization depending heavily upon mass support and an opposition that cut across sectional lines— an economic elite seeking to wrest control from numbers.

As in earlier years Webster appeared frequently before the Supreme Court, but the bulk of his cases no longer involved the great constitutional issues that were being debated in the Senate. His court work in this period was most frequently in behalf of his perennial client, the Bank of the United States, and of other corporate mainstays of the business community.

By the close of 1834 Webster stood preeminent among those who upheld the primacy of the Nation over the States, yet he had not offended the South by any overt criticism of slavery, nor the West by opposing either federally sponsored public works or cheap lands for settlers. He was ready to make his first bid for the presidency, more acceptable to the North and East than even the gallant "Harry of the West," and with a legion of friends and supporters the country over.

PLAN OF WORK

From its inception the Papers of Daniel Webster was planned as an integrated project, using both microfilm and letterpress publication. The persistent pressure of time and the steadily rising cost of book publication were important factors in the choice of the dual media, but the overriding consideration was the desire to bring all of Webster together, without abridgment or gloss, for those who were equipped to use it that way, while providing the less dedicated scholar and the general reader with the essential Webster in convenient annotated form. The microfilm edition, in four different groupings, is as complete as the surviving records permit. Webster's correspondence, including letters received as well as letters sent, together with miscellaneous notes, memoranda, briefs, drafts, formal writings, reports, petitions, and business papers have been issued with printed guide and index as *The Papers of Daniel Webster* by University Microfilms, Ann Arbor, Michigan. *The Legal Papers of Daniel Webster*, also issued with guide and alphabetical list of cases by University Microfilms, consists of records drawn primarily from the county courts of New Hampshire and Massachusetts and from the state and lower federal courts in New England. Records of the Department of State and of the Supreme Court are available on film from the National Archives and Records Service of the General Services Administration, but the user must select for himself the reels that may contain Webster material.

The value of this film, including as it does virtually all known Webster papers, cannot be overstated; but its very magnitude makes it unmanageable. It is relatively expensive, requires special equipment to use, is hard on the eyes, and effectively buries the grains of wheat by mixing them unevenly with an enormous amount of chaff. The user of the film, moreover, must decipher for himself often difficult or faded handwriting. He must search out the identity of persons and the nature of events alluded to, and finally he must rely upon his own judgment as to the significance of the given document. In the letterpress edition all this has been done for him, even to the selection of documents in terms of their significance, by editors totally immersed in the time and place and almost as familiar with the central characters as was Webster himself.

The letterpress edition in effect complements and renders more useful these various microfilm collections, whose very existence has made it possible to select more rigorously the documents important enough to be offered to the larger audience reached by the printed book. Each volume of correspondence, moreover, includes a calendar of letters written in the same time period but not selected for publication. For each of these the microfilm frame number is cited, as is volume and page citation for any document now available only in a printed version. Footnote references are also made to the film wherever appropriate. Items found subsequent to publication of the appropriate volume will be calendared at the end of the *Correspondence* Series. For the general reader and for the student of the period rather than of the man, the editors believe the selection of items printed will be ample. The biographer, and the scholar pursuing an in-depth study of some segment of the times, will need the film, to which he will find the printed volumes an indispensable annotated guide.

The letterpress edition is being published in four different series, overlapping in time but not in content, in order to make maximum use of subject matter specialists as technical editors. The edition has been planned in a total of fourteen volumes, of which seven are correspondence, three are legal papers, two are diplomatic papers, and two are speeches and formal writings. The present volume, including the period 1830–1834, is the third of the correspondence series.

EDITORIAL METHOD

Letters and other documents included in this volume are arranged in chronological sequence, irrespective of whether Webster was the writer or the recipient. The only exception is for letters that were sent as enclosures in later correspondence. These have been placed immediately after the document which they accompanied. Date and point of origin have been placed at the upper right of each letter. If all or part of this information has been supplied by the editors, it appears in square brackets, with a question mark if conjecture. The complimentary close, which in the original manuscripts often takes up three or four lines, has been run continuously with the last line of the text.

All letters are reproduced in full except in rare instances where the only surviving text is incomplete or is from a printed source which did not reproduce it in its entirety. Needless to say, texts from printed sources are used only when the original manuscript has not been found, but the letter is of sufficient importance to warrant its inclusion.

The letters themselves have been reproduced in type as nearly as possible the way they were written. Misspellings have been retained without the annoyingly obtrusive "(*sic*)"; and abbreviations and contractions have been allowed to stand unless the editor feels they will not be readily understood by a present-day reader. In such cases the abbreviation has been expanded, with square brackets enclosing the letters supplied. Punctuation, too, has been left as Webster and his correspondents used it, save only that dashes clearly intended as periods are so written. Superscript letters in abbreviations or contractions have been brought down, but a period is supplied only if the last letter of the abbreviation is not the last letter of the word abbreviated. In all other cases, periods, apostrophes, dashes, and other forms of punctuation have been left as Webster and his contemporaries used them. The ampersand, far more frequently used than the spelled out "and," has been retained, but diacritical marks over contractions have been omitted even where the contraction itself is retained.

Canceled words or passages that are obvious slips, immediately corrected, have been left out altogether; those which show some change of thought or attitude or have stylistic or psychological implications have been included between angled brackets. Interlineations by the author have been incorporated into the text, but marginal passages, again if by the author, have been treated as postscripts and placed below the signature.

In order to keep explanatory footnotes to a minimum, general notes have been interspersed from time to time with the letters that constitute the text of the volume. These serve to indicate what Webster was doing at a particular time or to explain a sequence of events that may help to clarify subsequent correspondence. Footnotes are used to identify persons, places, events, situations, problems, or other matters that help to understand the context of a particular reference.

Individuals are identified only once, generally the first time they are mentioned. For the convenience of the reader who may have missed this first reference, the appropriate index entry is printed in bold face type. Well-known individuals—those in the *Dictionary of American Biography* or the *Biographical Directory of the American Congress*—have not been identified at all unless the context seems to require it. For those in the DAB the index entry is marked with an asterisk, and with a dagger for those in the BDAC. The extent of footnoting has been reduced by adding given names and initials in square brackets where text references are to surnames only.

Immediately following each document is an unnumbered note indicating the provenance of the document and if appropriate, giving some information about the writer or recipient. Symbols used in these provenance notes are the standard descriptive symbols and the location symbols developed by the Union Catalog Division of the Library of Congress. Those appearing in the present volume have been listed under Abbreviations and Symbols below.

Webster Chronology, 1830–1834

1830

January 26/27 Webster expounded the nature of the Union in his second reply to Senator Robert Y. Hayne, an exposition that became the classic statement of American nationalism.

February 4/5 Argued before Supreme Court for plaintiff in error in *Carver* v. *Jackson*, one of the Astor land cases.

April 6 Mexico forbade further colonization of Texas by United States citizens, and prohibited importation into Texas of Negro slaves.

April 13 Jefferson's Birthday dinner in Washington, attended by President Jackson and Vice President Calhoun, revealed basic ideological split in Democratic party.

May 27 Jackson took stand against internal improvements by the Federal Government with veto of Maysville Road bill.

May 28 Jackson signed bill to remove eastern Indian tribes to lands west of Mississippi River.

August 3 Webster appeared for the prosecution in the trial of John Francis Knapp for the murder of Captain Joseph White in Salem, Massachusetts.

September 11 Webster had some support for a presidential nomination by an Anti-Masonic convention in Philadelphia, but urged caution on his followers. No nomination was made.

December Webster's first book publication, *Speeches and Forensic Arguments*, edited by his nephew Charles B. Haddock, issued in Boston.

1831

January 1 First issue of the *Liberator*, outspoken antislavery paper edited by William Lloyd Garrison.

February 15	Vice President Calhoun published correspondence relating to Jackson's Florida expedition of 1818, resulting in an irrevocable break with the President.
March 11	Webster argued the Charles River Bridge case before the Supreme Court, with no decision.
March 24	Webster spoke at a public dinner in New York, taking the occasion to contest Calhoun's nullification doctrine.
August 21/25	Nat Turner's rebellion in Southampton, Virginia, intensified sectional differences.
September 26	Anti-Masonic Party Convention in Baltimore nominated William Wirt of Maryland for President and Amos Ellmaker of Pennsylvania for Vice President.
December 12	A National Republican Convention in Baltimore nominated Henry Clay for President and John Sergeant of Pennsylvania for Vice President.

1832

January 9	Webster named to select committee to consider recharter of the Bank of the United States.
January 24/26	Successfully opposed confirmation of Van Buren as Minister to England.
March 3	In *Worcester* v. *Georgia* the Supreme Court decided that the state had no jurisdiction over the Cherokee Indians. The decision was ignored by both Georgia and Jackson.
April 5	Webster submitted a Report on the Apportionment of Representatives under the fifth census, proposing a change in method.
April 23	Webster purchased Marshfield, Massachusetts property that was thereafter his home.
May 31	Democratic National Convention in Baltimore endorsed Jackson for a second term and nominated Van Buren for Vice President.
July 10	Jackson vetoed bill rechartering the Bank of the United States.

July 11   Webster delivered a major speech denouncing Jackson's veto of the bank recharter bill.

July 14   Tariff of 1832 passed, Webster favoring.

October 12   Webster spoke in criticism of the Jackson administration at the state convention of National Republicans, Worcester, Massachusetts.

November 24   South Carolina nullified the Tariffs of 1828 and 1832.

November/ December   Jackson reelected with 219 electoral votes to 49 for Clay and 7 for Wirt.

December 10   Jackson issued a proclamation asserting the supremacy of the National Government and pronouncing Nullification to be rebellion.

December 17   Webster denounced Nullification at a citizens' meeting in Faneuil Hall.

December 28   John C. Calhoun resigned the Vice Presidency of the United States, having been elected Senator from South Carolina.

1833

January 15/16   Webster reelected Senator by Massachusetts legislature, unanimously in Senate, 432 to 46 in House.

February 12   Webster named to select committee to prepare a compromise tariff bill.

February 16   In a major speech in reply to Calhoun, Webster upheld the "Force Bill."

March 2   Jackson signed both the Compromise Tariff, which Webster opposed, and the Force Bill, which he approved.

May 17–July 15   Webster toured New York, Ohio, and Pennsylvania, both to see what was then the "West" and to be seen by it.

September 26   Treasury Secretary Roger B. Taney ordered that government revenue thereafter was to be deposited in certain state banks instead of the Bank of the United

States; disbursements were to continue to be made from the BUS as long as funds remained.

December 2   The 23rd Congress convened, with the opposition, though divided on many issues, numerically superior to the administration forces.

December 4   American Antislavery Society founded by Arthur and Lewis Tappan.

December 16   The Whig Coalition was launched in the Senate where the previous rule was voted down and committees were named by ballot, giving control to the opposition. Webster, at his request, became Chairman of the Committee on Finance.

1834

February 5   Webster's Committee on Finance condemned removal of the deposits from the Bank of the United States.

March 14   Webster argued for the plaintiff in *Wheaton* v. *Peters*, the first copyright case to come before the Supreme Court.

March 28   Webster voted with Senate majority to censure the President for removing the deposits.

April 14   In a Senate speech Clay applied the name "Whigs" to the coalition opposing the administration.

April 15   Jackson formally protested the Senate's resolution of censure.

May 7   Webster spoke against receiving the President's protest.

June 24   Taney's recess appointment as Secretary of the Treasury was rejected by the Senate.

December 17   The Boston *Atlas*, with Webster's knowledge and consent, editorially nominated him for President.

Abbreviations and Symbols

DESCRIPTIVE SYMBOLS

Abstract	Summary of contents, or a portion thereof, of a letter or document
AD	Autograph Document
AD draft	Autograph Document, draft
ADS	Autograph Document Signed
ADS copy	Autograph Document Signed, copied by writer
ADS draft	Autograph Document Signed, draft
AL	Autograph Letter
ALS	Autograph Letter Signed
ALS copy	Autograph Letter Signed, copied by writer
ALS draft	Autograph Letter Signed, draft
AN	Autograph Note
ANS	Autograph Note Signed
Copy	Copy, not by writer
DS	Document Signed
Extract	Copy of a portion of a letter or document
LC	Letterbook Copy
LS	Letter Signed

LOCATION SYMBOLS

CCC	Honnold Library, Claremont, Calif.
CLU	University of California at Los Angeles
CSmH	Henry E. Huntington Library, San Marino, Calif.
CtHC	Hartford Seminary Foundation, Hartford, Conn.
CtY	Yale University
DLC	Library of Congress
DMaM	Marine Corps Museum, Washington, D.C.
DNA	National Archives
GU	University of Georgia, Athens
ICHi	Chicago Historical Society
ICN	Newberry Library, Chicago
InU	Indiana University, Bloomington

KyU	University of Kentucky, Lexington
M	Massachusetts State Library
MAnP	Phillips Academy, Andover, Mass.
MB	Boston Public Library
MBBA	Boston Bar Association
MBBS	Bostonian Society
MBNU	Northeastern University, Boston
MBS	Social Law Library, Boston
MDuHi	Duxbury Rural and Historical Society, Duxbury, Mass.
MH	Harvard University
MH-BA	Harvard Graduate School of Business Administration
MH-L	Harvard Law School
MHi	Massachusetts Historical Society, Boston
MLexHi	Lexington Historical Society, Lexington, Mass.
MNS	Smith College, Northampton, Mass.
MWA	American Antiquarian Society, Worcester, Mass.
MWalB	Brandeis University
MWalK	John F. Kennedy Library, Waltham, Mass.
MWenhHi	Wenham Historical Society and Museum, Wenham, Mass.
MdHi	Maryland Historical Society, Baltimore
MeHi	Maine Historical Society, Portland
MeWC	Colby College, Waterville, Me.
MiD-B	Burton Historical Collection, Detroit Public Library
MiDbEI	Henry Ford Museum, Dearborn, Mich.
MiU	University of Michigan, Ann Arbor
MiU-C	University of Michigan, Henry L. Clements Library
MnHi	Minnesota Historical Society, St. Paul
MnU	University of Minnesota, Minneapolis
MoHi	Missouri Historical Society, Columbia
N	New York State Library, Albany
NBLiHi	Long Island Historical Society, Brooklyn
NBuHi	Buffalo Historical Society
NHi	New-York Historical Society, New York City
NIC	Cornell University
NN	New York Public Library
NNC	Columbia University
NNebgWM	Washington's Headquarters Museum, Newburgh, N.Y.
NNPM	Pierpont Morgan Library, New York City
NNS	New York Society Library, New York City
NPV	Vassar College, Poughkeepsie, N.Y.
NRU	University of Rochester
Nc-Ar	North Carolina State Department of Archives and History, Raleigh

NcD	Duke University
NcU	University of North Carolina, Chapel Hill
NhD	Dartmouth College
NhExP	Phillips Exeter Academy, Exeter, N. H.
NhHi	New Hampshire Historical Society, Concord
NhPoS	Strawbery Banke Collection, Portsmouth, N.H.
NjHi	New Jersey Historical Society, Newark
NjMoHP	Morristown National Historical Park, Morristown, N. J.
NjP	Princeton University
NjR	Rutgers-The State University, New Brunswick, N. J.
OHaBHi	Butler County Historical Society, Hamilton, Ohio
OHi	Ohio Historical Society, Columbus
OClWHi	Western Reserve Historical Society, Cleveland
OMC	Marietta College, Marietta, Ohio
OYMHi	The Arms Museum, Mahoning Valley Historical Society, Youngstown, Ohio
PCarlD	Dickinson College, Carlisle, Pa.
PGC	Gettysburg College, Gettysburg, Pa.
PHC	Haverford College, Haverford, Pa.
PHi	Historical Society of Pennsylvania, Philadelphia
PP	Free Library of Philadelphia
PPAmP	American Philosophical Society, Philadelphia
PPL	Library Company of Philadelphia
PU-S	University of Pennsylvania, Edgar Fahs Smith Memorial Library
PWb	Osterhout Free Library, Wilkes-Barre, Pa.
PWbH	Wyoming Historical and Geological Society, Wilkes-Barre, Pa.
RNHi	Newport Historical Society, Newport, R. I.
RPB	Brown University
ScU	University of South Carolina, Columbia
T	Tennessee State Library and Archives, Nashville
TxU	University of Texas, Austin
ViU	University of Virginia, Charlottesville

SHORT TITLES

Colton, *Henry Clay*	Calvin Colton, ed., *The Private Correspondence of Henry Clay* (New York, 1856).
Correspondence	Charles M. Wiltse and Harold D. Moser, eds., *The Papers of Daniel Webster,*

	Correspondence, vols. 1, 2 (Hanover, 1974, 1976).
Curtis	George Ticknor Curtis, *Life of Daniel Webster* (2 vols., New York, 1870).
Fuess, *Cushing*	Claude Moore Fuess, *The Life of Caleb Cushing* (2 vols., New York, 1923).
McGrane, *Correspondence of Nicholas Biddle*	Reginald C. McGrane, ed., *The Correspondence of Nicholas Biddle dealing with National Affairs, 1807–1844* (Boston and New York, 1919).
Mason, *Memoir and Correspondence*	Robert Means Mason and G. S. Hilliard, eds., *Memoir and Correspondence of Jeremiah Mason* (Cambridge, Mass., 1873).
MHi Proc.	*Proceedings of the Massachusetts Historical Society.*
mDW	Microfilm Edition of the Papers of Daniel Webster (Ann Arbor, 1971). References followed by frame numbers.
mDWs	Microfilm Edition of the Papers of Daniel Webster, Supplementary Reel.
PC	Fletcher Webster, ed., *The Private Correspondence of Daniel Webster* (2 vols., Boston, 1856).
Shanks, *Mangum Papers*	Henry Thomas Shanks, ed., *The Papers of Willie Person Mangum* (5 vols., Raleigh, N.C., 1950–1956).
Speeches and Forensic Arguments	Daniel Webster, *Speeches and Forensic Arguments* (3 vols., Boston, 1830, 1835, 1843).
Van Tyne	Claude H. Van Tyne, ed., *The Letters of Daniel Webster* (New York, 1902).
W & S	James W. McIntyre, ed., *The Writings and Speeches of Daniel Webster* (National Edition, 18 vols., New York, 1903).

THE PAPERS OF DANIEL WEBSTER

CHARLES M. WILTSE, EDITOR-IN-CHIEF

SERIES ONE: CORRESPONDENCE

The Papers, 1830–1834

FROM ELIZA BUCKMINSTER LEE

Rowe Place Jan 1st 1830

My dear friend,

I am perhaps the *last* to *offer* you my congratulations on the late happy event, but I assure [you] I am not the *least* interested, nor the most indifferent of your friends. The date of my letter also reminds me that it is a new-year—and I can add also the wishes of the day; that this year may be as happy as the happiest of your life, and though I have always believed it, every one who has had the pleasure of an acquaintance with Mrs. Webster[1] tells me, that she will make *every year* a year of happiness to you.

I thank you for your letter giving me notice of your marriage. It was deficient in a few important particulars—as to who were the parties—who were the guests, and by whom it was solemnized. You are in truth not a good narrator of what all ladies like to hear, and my imagination must fill up the great deficiencies [in] your letter.

Be so kind as to offer my affectionate regards to your *wife*. Before many months I shall have the pleasure of seeing her in Boston. Give my best love to Julia[2] and believe me always truly yrs.   Eliza Lee

ALS. NhHi. Published in Van Tyne, pp. 576–577.

1. Caroline Le Roy Webster, whom DW had married December 12, 1829.

2. Julia Webster (1818–1848), DW's daughter. After her mother's death in January 1828, Julia had stayed for several months with Mrs. Lee while her father was in Washington.

Few doubted by 1830 that an adequate system of transportation was essential, not only to the growth but to the very existence of the nation. Whether roads, canals, or the new railroads were to be preferred, however, was a matter of lively debate; and whether the federal government, the states, or private enterprise should pay the cost was a matter of bitter controversy. The slaveholding states, to protect their own peculiar institution, were committed to a strict and narrow construction of the Constitution. When the South Carolina Canal and Rail Road Company, organized to divert to Charleston some of the profitable trade in upland cotton then moving by river through the rival port of Savannah, prepared to ask Congress for financial aid, members of the state's own con-

gressional delegation, pleading constitutional scruples, would not present the petition. In the letter below, William Aiken, president of the company, asks Webster to perform this service. Senator Robert Young Hayne transmitted the necessary documents to his New England rival by his letter of January 15, below, and Webster spoke in favor of the proposal three days later, though without success. The 136-mile Charleston and Hamburg Rail-Road was completed in October 1833 with a state loan.

FROM WILLIAM AIKEN

> *Office So. Ca. Canal &*
> *Rail Road Co.*
> Charleston 9th January 1830

Sir,

The Directors of the So. Carolina Canal and Rail Road Co. have instructed me respectfully to request from you the favor to present their Petition[1] to the Senate of the United States, praying the aid of the General Government, in furtherance of the objects of their Institution.

The subject is fully developed in the Petition and Documents accompanying it, which will be presented to you by Genl. [Robert Y.] Hayne of this State and we trust every point of difficulty touching the completion of the work and our ability to effect that object, should the General Government aid the enterprise to the extent prayed for, will be removed by Col. [Abraham] Blanding[2] of this State, at present on a visit to.the City of Washington.

In soliciting your aid in behalf of our Institution, it is due to the Gentlemen who are Senators from our State, to inform you, that objects predicated on constitutional grounds will induce them to oppose the object of our Petition, and some reluctance to present it therefore must be experienced on which we are not inclined to trespass.

The quality of this enterprise as it relates to the Genl. Govt. is obviously calculated to acquire for it, the most indulgent consideration. The purpose is not less to give a particular direction to the produce of this and a Sister State, than to procure for commercial operations, certainty and confidence. The deepening of our Bar, or improving the facilities of our Port would not more certainly advance the interests of the Merchant, than in communicating assurances of a prompt execution of their orders. The present season with almost all the past evidence the uncertainty and losses incident to an exclusive reliance on our Rivers, for the transportation of Produce. For until within a very few days this Harbor has been crowded with Ships, and our Country Warehouses with Cotton: the

Planter and the Merchant incurring heavy charges and deprecating the disappointments and delays to which they are subjected. In a Military point of view the contemplated Road will subserve highly essential objects. The United States Arsenal at Augusta would be rendered more generally and promptly useful, and confer protection when under present circumstances, the emergency would pass, before the relief required from it could be obtained. Still more important would be the facility, of transporting troops from the dense population of the interior to the Atlantic border of our State. These advantages are not unworthy of the patronage of the Genl. Government whether they refer to foreign invasion or domestic insurrection. As a Post Road its benefits will be most extensively conferred, nor will it admit of doubt, that in a much shorter period than works of such magnitude have hitherto been accomplished, it will under the fostering care of the General Government be made to constitute a link of Union with the rising States of the West, attaching them more strongly through the powerful influences of interest to their Atlantic Brethren. These however are subjects on which we will not dilate.

Should you, Sir, approve our purposes, believing that the General Government do legitimately possess the power to aid such works, (of great public utility,) in the way intimated, you will confer an obligation which we shall most sensibly feel, by bestowing on it the acknowledged influences of your attention and talents. We would gratefully add yours to the names of the Patrons of our Infant Institution, and the record of service will be found in the general advantages resulting to our City and State. With sentiments of high consideration, I remain Sir Your most obt. servt.

Wm. Aiken Prest.
So. Ca. Canal & Rail R. Coy

LS. ScU. Published in Curtis, 1: 367–368.

1. Not found, but see "Report on the Charleston and Hamburg Rail-Road," mDW 42624.

2. Blanding (1776–1839; Brown 1796) was born in Massachusetts but moved to South Carolina soon after graduation from college. A successful lawyer, he served in the state legislature and as a commissioner on the State Board of Public Works.

TO SARAH GOODRIDGE

Washington Jan. 11 [10]. 30

Dr Miss Goodrich,

I believe I left Town without paying you for Edward's[1] Portrait. If you will let me know how much I shall send you, I will enclose it. I brought all our little pictures to New York, where they were much approved & admired, especially by our old family friends, Dr. and Mrs [Cyrus] Perkins.[2] Little Grace Everett['s][3] we brought to Washington,—her father was glad to see it.

I hardly know who there is of your profession here now, except Mr [Charles B.] King,[4] and Mr [Chester] Harding—neither of whom have I visited. We hear that the Boston Atheneum has employed Harding to paint a full length portrait of Ch. J. Marshall.[5]

We have been here now abt. ten days, & have just got into comfortable lodgings, with Dr. [Harvey] Lindsley,[6] nearly opposite Dr. [Thomas] Sewall's.[7] The Court commences tomorrow.

I thank you for your congratulations, on a recent occurrence, & hope for an opportunity of making you & this Lady acquainted. Julia is with us, & seems quite happy. I am, with regard, Yrs   D. Webster

ALS. MHi. Dated January 11 but post-marked January 10.

1. Edward Webster (1820–1848; Dartmouth 1841), second son of DW.

2. Perkins (1778–1849; Dartmouth 1800), New York physician.

3. Grace (1827–1836), third child of Charlotte Brooks and Edward Everett.

4. King (1785–1862), American portrait painter, studied art under Benjamin West in London, sharing rooms with Charles Leslie, Washington Allston, and later Thomas Sully.

5. The trustees of the Boston Athenaeum had authorized the portrait some two years earlier but Marshall's agreement was not assured until January 1830. Shortly thereafter Harding accepted the commission, for which he was paid $350 instead of the $200 originally offered.

6. Lindsly (1804–1889; Princeton 1820), Washington, D.C., physician and prominent figure in the American Colonization Society.

7. Sewall (1786–1845; Harvard Medical School 1812), Webster's personal physician in Washington, D.C., and professor of anatomy at the National Medical College.

TO JOSEPH HOPKINSON

Jan. 11 [10]. '30

D Sir

Your communication was timely.[1] We shall tomorrow report a bill, encreasing the salaries of certain of the District Judges,[2] yours, inter alios. Judge [Samuel Rossiter] Betts has been here—& has made a strong representation of the State of the public business, in his Court. The result is, a resolution by the Com[mitt]ee, to report a bill, making it [h]is duty to reside in N. York, & to hold *monthly* Courts—so as to keep up, in the progress to judgment, with the City Court—& to give him a competent salary. Seizing on the occasion we have agreed in Com[mitt]ee, unanimously, to put into the same bill an augmentation of certain other salaries—yours, to 2500.

I think it probable the bill will pass the Senate. What will be its fate in the House, he knows who knows every thing. Believe me, I shall be most happy if this little piece of good can be done—anything bright, in the prospect before us, relieves the eye. Yrs. truly   D. Webster

ALS. PHi. Dated January 11 but postmarked January 10.
  1. Not found.
  2. "An act increasing the terms of the judicial courts of the United States for the southern district of New York and adding to the compensation of several district judges of the United States," 4 *U.S. Statutes at Large* 422.

TO NICHOLAS BIDDLE

Jan. 14 [1830]

D Sir

Mr [Richard] Smith[1] spoke to me last evening, in relation to a question, pending here, relative to the right to take interest for the 64 days. You know what the question is.[2] The Court called it on today. I answered to it, & shall be obliged to proceed with it, shortly. I hope, however, to stave it off till Mr [John] Sergeant comes. Unless he is to be here soon, I will thank you to forward me a copy of an opinion furnished to you on this point by Mr [Horace] Binney.

Little new in Congress. The W[ay]s & M[ean]s in H. R. are, 5-to-2 agt. the President about the renewal of the charter. A Report is expected to be made—but is yet not agreed on.[3] Yrs. truly   D. Webster

ALS. DLC.
  1. Smith, cashier of the Washington branch of the Bank of the United States (BUS). Although the BUS itself was not directly involved at this time, the issue, which concerned the definition of usury, was one in which all banks doing business in the District of Columbia shared an interest. The question had first arisen three years earlier. See DW to Biddle, February 25, 1827, *Correspondence*, 2: 165.
  2. Arguing for the Bank of Washington (not to be confused with the Washington branch of the BUS), Webster contended that the taking of interest for sixty-four days on a sixty-day note was not usury if, as was the custom of banks in the District of Columbia, it was not due and payable until the sixty-fourth day. The Court decided, February 3, 1830, in favor of Webster's client. *Thornton* v. *Bank of Washington*, 3 Peters 36 (1830).
  3. George McDuffie, chairman of the House Committee of Ways and Means, presented a report on April 13, 1830, recommending recharter of the Bank. *Committee Reports*, 21st Cong., 1st sess., Serial 201, Report No. 358.

The nature and extent of the President's power to remove federal officeholders were debated with varying degrees of zeal, learning, and acrimony throughout most of the nineteenth century, but never more vociferously than in Jackson's time. By January of 1830 the names of replacements were being submitted to the Senate in substantial numbers.

*Of the 300 nominations made during the session, 121 were to replace of-
ficeholders who had been removed. Opposition senators protested vigor-
ously but had only limited success in blocking confirmation. Webster
and others who thought as he did went to the historical roots of the prob-
lem in the Constitution itself, and consulted freely with those familiar
with the precedents. Examples of such consultation appear below in
Webster's letter to Hopkinson of January 15, and in Chancellor Kent's
letter to Webster of January 21.*

TO JOSEPH HOPKINSON

friday Eve' [January 15, 1830]
11 oclock

D Sir

While sitting over my fire, every body else having retired, I have
sketched the enclosed very rough draft of a few *propositions*.

I wish you would give them a morning's thinking, & let me know,
within a week, what part of them is orthodox—what het[e]rodox. *Show
them to no other person.* Yrs   D. Webster

ENCLOSURE

That by the Constitution of U. S. the power of appointing to office is
vested in the President & Senate.

That no power of removal, as a separate & distinct power, exists any
where, except in those cases in which it is conferred on the Senate, as a
part of their judgment, in Conviction on impeachment.

That in other cases, & where the tenure of office is not fixed, by the
Constitution or laws, the power of removal exists only as consequential
to the power of appointment.

That tho' an office, of the kind last mentioned be full, the appointment
of another person to the same office supersedes the commission & authority of the incumbent by legal & necessary consequence.

That according to the true intent & meaning of the Constitution, the
President alone does not possess the power of removal from office; in as
much as no such power is expressly given to him by the Constitution, nor
is any where recognized in it; nor any provision made to guard it from
abuse; nor any provision for recording its exercise.

That one main end, designed by the institution of the Senate, was to
provide a salutary & substantial check to the power of the President, in
the matter of appointments to office;—& that a construction which acknowledges in the President an uncontrolled power of removal, & of thus
procuring vacancies, essentially impairs the strength & value of that

check, & tends to a dangerous enlargement of influence by the patronage of office.

That a general indiscriminate removal from office, of any grade, without the imputation of misconduct, & on the avowed ground of gratifying personal & party friends, is hostile to the spirit of the Constitution, & dangerous to the peace, prosperity, & permanency of the Govt.

ALS, with AD draft enclosure. PHi.   mDW 8342.
Hopkinson replied on January 19. See

FROM ROBERT YOUNG HAYNE

Washington 15th January 1830.

Sir.

I have this day received a letter from the President of the "South Carolina Canal and Rail Road Company," in which I am requested "to deliver to the Hon: Daniel Webster, the Petition with the accompanying documents, which were transmitted to you, as we shall simultaneously solicit his interference in our behalf."

In compliance with this request, I herewith transmit you the Memorial of the Company praying "a subscription on the part of the United States, for 2500. shares of the capital stock of said company."[1] As I presume you have received a communication from the Company[2] indicating their views and wishes,—it is of course unnecessary, for me to enter into any explanations. It may be proper, however, to state, that on receiving the memorial of the company a short time since, with a request to present it to the Senate, I deemed it my duty to inform the petitioners, that as I believed their application to be at variance, with *the principles* for which the State of South Carolina was contending, in relation to the powers of the federal government, (and which her legislature had on several recent occasions, *solemnly avowed*,)—I should consider it, my duty, on presenting the memorial, to accompany it with *such explanations*, as would prevent the compromitment of my own principles, or those of the State, and submitting to the company whether under these circumstances, they would desire me to present their memorial,—declaring at the same time, my determination in that <respect> event to comply with their instructions. The answer to this communication, just received, shews that the company have preferred, another, and as they presume a more favorable channel through which to present their claims to the Senate; and in obedience to their directions, I now send you the Papers. I have the honor to be Sir very respectfully your obt. Servt.

Robt. Y. Hayne

ALS. MeHi. The wide-ranging debate on Foot's Resolution had already begun, but neither Hayne nor Webster had yet entered the contest. See p. 16, below.

1. Not found.
2. See above, William Aiken to DW, January 9, 1830.

FROM JOSEPH HEALY

Washington N. H. January 18.
1830

Confidential
Dear Sir,

During the period which has elapsed since I saw you at Washington, on the 4th of March last, (where we both witnessed a triumph, which, I shall always believe was the effect of a delusion) events have transpired in this, your native State, apparently disastrous, and certainly hostile to our mutual and ardent desires: one of which, the sudden death of your lamented Brother, is peculiarly afflictive to you. It must, however, afford you some consolation to reflect that, even his political enemies, who have dreaded his influence, and who have been so active in poisoning the publick mind with falsehood, concerning him, are, now he is gone, ready to do justice to his character, and seem to mourn the loss of so valuable a Citizen.

The Election, then pending in this State, terminated different from our expectation. When I reached Boston, I saw Mr. [John] Wallace [, Jr.].,[1] one of the Candidates for Congress, who told me, that the result, so far as he had heard, was unfavorable, but still hoping that the returns from the whole State would show a different result from the few, he had then seen, I did not write to you, at that time; and finding afterwards, that the state of the vote was known at Boston as soon as I could know it myself, I concluded, you would get the information, from the publick prints earlier than I could give it to you and so I did not write you at all.

The triumph of the Jackson party in this State, last March, has made them more insolent and overbearing than ever. All who have not gone for the *Hero* are to be forever proscribed, and would be immolated, if they had the power. But, tho cast down, we are not discouraged. We intend never to submit, quietly, to the present proscriptive course, pursued by those in power. We yet *love liberty and hate oppression*, and are preparing to martial our strength for another Campaign, in March. Our whole delegation in Congress, save one, are against us, and their influence will be exerted to sustain themselves in power. In this state of things, we need the aid of all our friends. It is one common cause the cause of our whole Country. Every heart, with American feelings, beats in unison. Can you and will you lend a helping hand? Some facts, with their illustrations, from your ready and experienced pen, may do great good: these may be communicated *directly* to the presses in this State, or *indirectly* through the medium of myself, should you prefer it.

Nothing, in my judgement, is wanting to insure success and bring N. H. right again, but a *knowledge* of her own true interest. The people will act right, when rightly informed.

I am aware that your time and mind are severely taxed with official and professional business, but still hope that a portion of both will be devoted to the principle request, made in this communication.

I hope you are enjoying excellent health, and that your recent conjugal connexion will sweeten all your future days; and that to these blessings, may be added *one more, dear to your heart*, the peace & prosperity of our beloved Country. With respect and esteem your sincere friend   Joseph Healy

ALS. DLC. Healy (1776–1861), recently a member of Congress from New Hampshire, was at this time on the Governor's Council.
    1. Wallace (1781–1837), from Web-ster's native Hillsborough County, New Hampshire, had served in various state offices but was unsuccessful in his bid for a seat in Congress.

FROM JAMES KENT

New York Jany. 21. 1830.

Dear Sir,

I ought to have replied earlier to your letter of the fifteenth Instant,[1] but I have been diverted by a number of perplexing avocations, each of them, singly, petty in its nature, but conjointly such things make up the sum of the life of ordinary minds; and now to the purpose. I beg leave to decline any opinion on the question you state; first, I have not time to do it justice and render any thing I would say worthy of you; second, I am not going to undertake to instruct a Senatorial Statesman, who has thought on the subject infinitely more than I have, for it comes officially before him.

Hamilton in the Federalist No 77[2] was of the opinion that the President could not remove without the consent of the Senate. I heard the question debated in the summer of 1789, and [James] Madison, [Egbert] Benson, [Fisher] Ames, [John] Laurance &c were in favor of the right of removal by the President, and such has been the opinion ever since and the practice. I thought they were right, because, I then thought this side uniformly right. Mr. [Alexander] White of Virginia was strenuously opposed to that construction. You will find the discussion in Fenno's U. S. Gazeteer for July or August or September 1789.[3] Mr. Madison reason[s] technically like a Lawyer. Now when I come to think on the subject with my confirmed wary views of things, I pause and doubt of the construction, on account of the word *advice*. That word is pregnant with meaning, and means something beyond *consent* to nominations, or it would not have been inserted. The consent (so it might be argued) applies to the individual named. The advice to the measure itself which draws to it the whole ground of the interference. Again it is a great and general principle in all Jurisprudence that when there is no positive provision in the case regulating the principle, the power that appoints is the power to determine the pleasure of the appointment and the limitation. It is the power to reappoint, and the power to appoint and reappoint, when all else is silent, is the power to remove. I begin to have a strong suspicion that Hamilton was right, as he always was on public questions. On the other hand it is too late to call the Presidents power in question, after a declaratory act of Congress[4] and an acquiescence of half a century. We should hurt the reputation of our Government with the world, and we are accused already of the Republican tendency of reducing all Executive power into the legislative, and making Congress a national Convention. That the President grossly abuses the power of removal is manifest, but it is the evil Genius of Democracy to be the sport of factions. Hamilton said in the Federalist, in his speeches, and a hundred times to me, that faction would ruin us; and our Government had not sufficient balance and energy to resist the propensity to them, and to controul their *tyranny* and their profligacy. All theories of Government that suppose the mass of the people virtuous and able, and willing to act virtuously are plainly Utopian and *will remain so* until the return of the Saturnian age. Yours very sincerely   James Kent.

P.S. I never heard of any such book written by Mr. Wells,[5] and I don't believe he ever wrote any such.

Copy. DLC. Published in *PC*, 1: 486–487.

1. Not found.

2. Numbered 76 in the original newspaper publication, the essay appears as number 77 in the McLean edition of 1788, where most modern editors have retained it.

3. The debate Kent presumably heard centered around the establishment of executive departments and took place mainly on May 19 and June 16, 1789. It was on the latter date that White entered his objection to the removal power, although William Smith of South Carolina had said much the same thing on May 19. Since Kent makes no reference to Smith, it is possible that he heard only the June 16 portion of the discussion and did not refresh his memory by reexamining his sources. See *Annals of Congress*, 1st Cong., 1st sess., pp. 383–399, 473–498.

4. Acts establishing the Departments of State, Treasury, and War, 1 *U.S. Statutes at Large* 28–29, 49–50, 65–67. All three acts provide for continuity of administration in the event that "the said principal officer shall

be removed from office by the President of the United States." Taking note of the ambiguity, Congress, in 1820, had specifically given to the President the power to remove district attorneys, collectors of customs, naval officers, and others. 3 *U.S. Statutes at Large* 582. In the first volume of his *Commentaries*, published in 1826, Kent had affirmed the removal power: "This question has never been made the subject of judicial discussion; and the construction given to the constitution in 1789, has continued to rest on this loose incidental declaratory opinion of congress, and the sense and practice of government since that time. It may now be considered as firmly and definitively settled, and there is good sense and practical utility in the construction" (James Kent, *Commentaries on American Law*, 4 vols., New York, 1826–1830, 1: 289–290).

5. Not identified.

FROM JOSEPH E. SPRAGUE

Council Chamber Boston
January 31, 1830

My dear Sir

I wrote you sometime since on a Subject you had previously mentioned to me and have not as yet been apprized that my letter reached you.[1] From its character I feel some solicitude to know if it arrived safe. It was addressed to you some ten days before you left Boston. There's a petition of mine before your committee which I hope may be acted upon as early as can be.[2]

Neither of these subjects however have induced me to write you at this time. You have been pleased heretofore to compliment me on my knowledge of the politics of New England and my skill in giving them a proper direction. <If> So far as I understand at all the politics of New England and am <at all> skilled in their direction I have no hesitation in saying that the Boston Patriot[3] is the most powerfull enginge which can be used to direct the politics of Massachusetts, New Hampshire Maine & Vermont and it has a most powerfull influence in Many other states. Thousands & Thousands of *old Republicans* as they are styled read this as Holy Writ and they read nothing else. Those of this description in the four states I have named who are influenced by this press are sufficient to control the politics of those states. That I entertained this opinion of the Patriot is not new to you as I mentioned it to you in May when you first proposed to me to remove to Boston. You then thought we could not get the control of that press. Yesterday, however, J[ohn] B[razer] Davis[4] (I never had spoken to him in any way on the subject) called on me at the Council Chamber and offered to sell to me the whole establishment. He was willing to be concerned himself <one sixth> in the property without any commission with the paper or he was willing to hold half of it and do all the business of the paper and give to me the sole and entire control of the editorial Department. The price he said of the whole establishment would be about thirty thousand Dollars. He gave for his third eight thousand. The [New England] Palladium sold for about twenty thousand & the [Daily] Centinel for more. I suppose the price would not be lower if so low as twenty four thousand dollars. This press is too important in my opinion to be the property of an individual and ought to be under the control of the Party. If our friends mean to sustain themselves in New England they ought not to suffer the present opportunity to possess this press to escape them. If they purchase it, they may command my services as an editor at a moderate rate. I think I can get along with Davis as half owner very well. But if there should be a wish to have the paper entirely out of its present hands I have no doubt Mr [Warwick] Palfray would leave the Register⁵ and take charge of it with me. The gross receipts of [the] establishment are from 16 to 18000 Dollars. The expenses about 12000. The net income 4500 Dollars. If you should form a company to purchase it you could easily give it a much more extended circulation. Since the first of January they have 75 new subscribers & 19 have stopped making a gain in three weeks without any exertion of 56. Of these 23 were for the daily Paper and only one daily discontinued. They have eleven hundred subscribers to the daily paper and two thousand nine hundred to the semi-weekly; four thousand in the whole. Mr Davis communication to me is to be considered as private as the nature of the subject will admit and I have promised to inform [him] what can be done so soon as I can hear from Washington. With great respect Your obedient Servant   Jos. E. Sprague

ALS. DLC. Sprague (1782–1852; Harvard 1804) was an attorney whose public activities included terms in the Massachusetts General Court, on the Executive Council, and as postmaster of Salem.

1. Not found.

2. Not found.

3. *Boston Patriot & Mercantile Advertiser.* The paper merged as of January 1, 1832, with the *Daily Adver-*tiser to form the *Daily Advertiser & Patriot,* but was still generally known as the *Patriot.* See also DW to [Edward Everett], August 25, 1831, below.

4. Davis (1798–1832; Harvard 1815), lawyer and editor, represented Boston in the state legislature and was an aid to Governor Levi Lincoln.

5. Palfray (1787–1838), editor of the Salem *Essex Register.*

TO [HENRY WILLIS KINSMAN]

[Washington January 1830]

Memo—As to notes &c—

On your list—
Jno Wells¹—700—Jan. 18/21—
    renew for 500—blank note sent—

(for 4 mos, if so may be)
Nathan Hale—750—Jan. 19/22—
  renew for 500—blank note sent
    (for 4 mos, if so may be)
Charles Thacher,[2] 400—Jan 7. 29—Feb. 1—
  renew, say, for 300—blank note sent—
  —[renew for such time as to bring me home, if so may be)
J[ames] W[illiam] Paige[3] 2500—Jan. 28/31—
  renew for 2000—note sent—

These, I think, are all, for Jany, on yr list.

There is one, (with Mr W.)

600 I[saac] P. D[avis][4]—due Jan. 18/21—which I should like to have renewed, in whole or in part—& send blank note.

These renewals, &c, you must keep a minute of—& also, it will be well to make out & send to me an accurate list of all notes &c used since I left home, so as that both with you & with me we may have exact lists of payables.

I have duly read all the papers in the Tenessee cause. Mr. [Felix] Grundy having become a member of the Senate, I thought I had better not argue the cause agt. him[5] & have therefore transferred the fee & the papers to Mr [David Bayard] Ogden.   D. W.

ALS. Dr. Gurdon S. Pulford, Palo Alto, Calif. Kinsman (1803–1859; Dartmouth 1822), native of Portland, had read law in Webster's office. He became Webster's legal associate when Alexander Bliss died suddenly in 1827.

1. Welles (1764–1855), Boston merchant, served in both houses of the Massachusetts legislature and on the Governor's Council, and was president of the City Council of Boston.

2. Commission merchant at 42 India Wharf.

3. Paige (1792–1868), half brother of Grace Fletcher Webster and prominent Boston merchant.

4. Davis (1771–1855), Boston manufacturer and businessman, and close friend of Webster.

5. *James Boyce's Executors* v. *Felix Grundy*, 3 Peters 210 (1830).

Webster's activities in behalf of the Adams administration, and the publicity attending his appearances before the Supreme Court, had made him a nationally known figure even before his spectacular debate with Senator Robert Y. Hayne in January 1830. His entry into the debate may well have been "quite unexpected" as he wrote to Jeremiah Mason on February 27 (see below); but he was thoroughly prepared and had in fact been on the lookout for a year past for just such a platform from which to say precisely what he said in his second reply on January 26 and 27. In his first reply on January 20 he adroitly turned the question of public land settlement posed by the original resolution of Senator Samuel Augustus Foot of Connecticut into an examination of the nature of the federal union. In his second he was answering not Hayne but Vice President John Caldwell Calhoun, whose Exposition and Protest *had been published by the South Carolina legislature in December 1828. With special reference to the Tariff of 1828, the* Exposition *advanced the doctrine that a state might exercise her original sovereignty to arrest the enforcement within her borders, or "nullify" any act of the general government which she held to be unconstitutional. Webster had known since he first read Calhoun's pamphlet that it must be answered; and he had known almost as long that he was the one to do it.*

Acutely conscious as he was of the historical importance of the debate, and alert to every nuance of its more immediate political impact, Webster worked over the text of his argument for almost a month before he permitted its publication. There is ample testimony from those who heard the debate that he was in no sense correcting or enlarging upon his theme for the eyes of history; he was laboring to create with the written word the same awesome effect he had created when the words were spoken in the Senate chamber. The first reply, which was in fact no reply at all, but a challenge, appeared in the National Intelligencer *on February 2, but the second reply was not published for another three weeks. It came at last in three installments in the* Intelligencer *for February 23, 25, and 27.*

The reaction was immediate and so overwhelming as to surpass even Webster's own fondest hopes. The first reply restored New England's pride and renewed her sense of accomplishment; but out of the second emerged a nation, transcending any federation of local sovereignties and standing as a potential equal in the nineteenth-century world of national states. Webster had not so much created a theory as he had articulated in plain, understandable language concepts that were already rooted in the consciousness of a growing body of Americans. He put into memorable and eternally quotable language what most, apart from those committed to the intellectual defense of slavery, deep in their hearts believed.

A sampling of the laudatory letters that poured in appears below. The chorus of praise, including voices even from the South, would have stirred the ambition of a man less vain than Daniel Webster.

FROM NICHOLAS BIDDLE

Phila. Feby 3. 1830

My dear Sir,

I thank you for your news of the victory about the 64 days.[1] I hear a great deal from all quarters about your later triumph. Mr [John] Sergeant leaves Phila tomorrow.

I wish you could give a gentle impulse to the Com[mitt]ee of Ways & Means. I am afraid that there may be some new combination of parties or factions in which the Bank may be embroiled in spite of itself, & I think that it would have a better chance of justice before the new fusion. With great regard Yrs   N Biddle

ALS. DLC.
1. *Thornton* v. *Bank of Washington*, 3 Peters 36 (1830).

FROM JEREMIAH EVARTS

Boston, Feb. 6, 1830.

Dear Sir,

The late effort, which you made in the Senate, is a subject of universal congratulation here, so far as I see. Among the reasons, which I, and numbers of those whom I meet, find for rejoicing in this effort, it is not the least, that the way seems prepared, by the discussion, for your taking, with decisive effect, a leading part in the Indian question.

Some of your personal, and many of your political friends have said, that there never was a subject better fitted to your habits of thinking and speaking, than the present controversy between the southern states, and the southern Indians. I should esteem it a favor of Providence, not less to yourself than to the weak and suffering party, if your powers could be strongly enlisted in this service. I hope the main discussion will not come on, till after the Supreme Court shall have risen, which I suppose will be before the middle of March.

These few sentences are merely an introduction of the subject. I shall endeavor to write at greater length in a few days. I am, Sir, Yours very respectfully,   Jerh. Evarts

ALS. DLC.

FROM HENRY ALEXANDER SCAMMELL DEARBORN

Brinley Place, Roxbury
Feby. 19. 1830.

My Dear Sir,

I enclose a communication I wrote a few weeks since for the Patriot, on the purchase of the Canadas.[1] I have no doubt it can be done, for we can afford to give 100,000,000 of dollars for it, and that is a sum England would not refuse, and I doubt whether she would half of it. The revenue of Quebec, Halifax St. Johns & the other ports, would yield an income, more than sufficient, to pay the interest in the largest price named, and with the immense domains of the crown, create a sinking-fund amply sufficient to liquidate the debt, in a few years.

Besides settling, *for ever*, all the great questions, which are now subjects of negociation, it would give us the whole supply of the West Indies, restore to [us] the timber trade to England,—for we should have only the Baltic to compete with. The timber trade from the Colonies to Great Britain is immense & carried on chiefly in ships owned in England, & if we hold the country it will require an increased navigation to carry on all that transportation, as well as that of the West Indies, which will give an immense impetus to our commerce.

In a political point of view, we should gain, *here in the North*, eight Senators & a proportional number of representatives, as four states would soon be formed, of New Brunswick, Nova Scotia, Lower & Upper Canada, and we want this to counterbalance the growing states of the northwest.

In describing the statesman, who should manage such a negociation, I had in "my minds eye" a *Senator* from *New England*. Little minds, may start at this gigantic project; but I do not appeal to politicians, to whom a *county* is an empire, and a *state* the universe; let them glory in their conceptions of the *vast*, & perish as unremembered as the bustle which they make, about the petty concerns of their *constituents*. Constituents,—a word ever in the mouth of demagogues, but does not belong to the nomenclature of a great legislator,—to the man who represents the *whole* country, the union. God knows that the constituents,—the people of congressional districts, have representatives *enough*, but the Republic has *few*. Look at the host of names borne on the rolls of Congress, since the adoption of the constitution & these *agents* of *constituents*, make up the great mass; the really & truly able representatives of the *nation*; those who will live through all time; whose names are identified with the history of the United States, scarcely amount to a dozen; all the others are as *unknown* as their *constituents*.

I am looking out with deep respect for your speeches. With the highest respect your most obt. servt.   H. Dearborn

ALS. NhHi.   1. Enclosure not found.

TO JEREMIAH MASON

Washington, February 27, 1830

Dear Sir,

The press has sent abroad all I said in the late debate, and you will have seen it. I have paid what attention I could to the reporter's notes;

but, in the midst of other pressing engagements, I have not made either speech what it ought to be; but let them go. The whole matter was quite unexpected. I was busy with the court, and paying no attention to the debate which was going on sluggishly in the Senate, without exciting any interest. Happening to have nothing to do for the moment, in court, I went into the Senate, and Mr. Hayne, so it turned out, just then rose. When he sat down, my friends said he must be answered, and I thought so too, and being thus got in, thought I must go through. It is singular enough, though perhaps not unaccountable, that the feeling of this little public is all on our side. I may say to you that I never before spoke in the hearing of an audience so excited, so eager, and so sympathetic.

The appointments are not yet acted on, though I am expecting them to be taken up daily. [Isaac] Hill's chance[1] is just about even. It depends on a single vote, or two at most, and they keep their own counsels, so that we shall never know till the time of voting comes. [John P.] Decatur's chance[2] is not equal. I think he will be rejected. I have some hopes that all the printers will be thrown out; but there is no certainty about it. Calhoun is forming a party against Van Buren, and as the President is supposed to be Van Buren's man, the Vice-President has great difficulty to separate his opposition to Van Buren from opposition to the President. Our idea is to let them pretty much alone; by no means to act a secondary part to either. We never can and never must support either.

While they are thus arranging themselves for battle, that is, Calhoun and Van Buren, there are two considerations which are likely to be overlooked, or disregarded by them, and which are material to be considered. 1. The probability that General Jackson will run again; that that is his present purpose, I am quite sure. 2. The extraordinary power of this anti-Masonic party, especially in Pennsylvania.

Judge Story has been ill, so as to be out of court for three or four days. He is now well again. Mr. Justice [Henry] Baldwin is thought to give promise of being a very good judge. The other new judge [John McLean], I fear, has his head turned too much to politics.

I have been written to, to go to New Hampshire to try a cause against you next August, brought by Mrs. [John W.] Mellen v. Dover Company.[3] Where is the August court holden? I suppose up at the Lakes. If it were an easy and plain case on our side, I might be willing to go; but I have some of your pounding in my bones yet, and don't care about any more till that wears out. Yours ever truly, with regards to your family,

Daniel Webster.

Text from PC, 1: 488–489. Original not found.

1. Hill was nominated on February

4 to be second comptroller of the Treasury. After various postponements, the nomination was rejected

on April 12 by a vote of 33 to 15.

2. Decatur, brother of the hapless commodore, had been nominated on January 13 to be collector of customs at Portsmouth, New Hampshire, replacing Timothy Upham, removed. The nomination, which had been engineered by Isaac Hill, produced a split between the Hill and Woodbury factions in the New Hampshire democracy. See Donald B. Cole, *Jack-sonian Democracy in New Hampshire, 1800–1851* (Cambridge, 1970), pp. 88, 92. Decatur was rejected by the Senate on March 29 with only one vote—Dickerson of New Jersey—in his favor.

3. Although the case appears on the 1831 docket of the Strafford County Court, Webster is not listed as counsel. See Mason to DW, March 8, 1830, below.

FROM HENRY RIDGLEY WARFIELD

Frederick Town 1st. March 1830

My Dear Sir—

Your letter of the 25th. ult[im]o.[1] I have received—also two copies of your first speech on Mr. Foots resolution for which I thank you. One of the speeches I presented to the Chief Justice of this district [John Buchanan], who is also the Chief Justice of our State. He speaks of it in terms of high commendation—he is what I sincerely think every virtuous, intelligent and true friend to this country ought to be,—your friend.

No subject, which for years past has been agitated in congress has awakened more interest or excited more curiosity than the debate on the above mentioned resolution, owing mainly to subjects introduced, but which certainly have no possible connection with the question to which the resolution points. It is almost the only topic of political discussion. The news papers of the day are in great demand. But the detached form in which your views are therein presented takes much from the gratification of the perusal. It gives me real pleasure to assure you that many of the best informed among the late supporters of General Jackson liberally extend to you merited applause. It is distinctly understood here that General Jackson will not again be before us for the Presidency and many of his most prominent supporters in the late contest, have not yet decided on their course. As to their ultimate decision, I have no certain grounds of conjecture, but it is obvious that the course lately pursued by the friends of Mr. Calhoun has greatly blighted his prospects here. As to myself and I believe I can speak with equal certainty of *Every man* who acted with me, on the last contest for the Presidency, that there is no diminution in their attachment to Mr. Clay, nor will there be a change of opinion unless for some cause which has not yet been before the public.

I believe I might be tempted to Enter more fully into political matters, if our District Court was not in session and I had more leisure. But as my time at present is employed in Professional avocations I must decline it. You will oblige me by forwarding me copies of your first & second speech on the resolution referred to. They will be extremely acceptable to my Friends in this Town and to Country Gentlemen who are here as Jurors. I will only add that it is the fixed determination of the Friends of Mr Clay hereafter zealously to contest every inch of ground, —This state is indisputably with him. It was lost at the last Election by gross, palpable negligence in this very County.

The Idea of uniting the Jackson party in this state in support of *any individual* is perfectly preposterous. They are at this moment virtually dissolved—or as the cynical old [John Randolph of] Rhoanoke would say, "blown sky high"—"sky high sir"[2] With sincere Esteem faithfully yrs.   Henry R. Warfield

ALS. DLC.
1. Not found.
2. The quoted phrase was used by Randolph in his attack on the Pana-ma Mission in 1826. See William Cabell Bruce, *John Randolph of Roanoke 1773–1833* (New York, 1922), 1: 509.

TO JEREMIAH MASON

Washington Mar. 2. 1830

D Sir

I see in the Boston Statesman, of Feb. 26—or 27, a renewal of an old story, told a year or two ago, about a letter said to be written by me to Mr. [Charles Humphrey] Atherton, relative to the Hartford Convention.[1] If I remember, when the story was told before, your name had something to do with it.

I have no recollection of any letter to Mr Atherton, on the subject, either by you & me, or by me singly. If you could inquire of Mr Atherton, & learn whether any letter of any kind was written to him, by us, or either of us, *without communicating to him that you do it at my request*, I should be glad to know what he has to say abt. it. But I do not incline to inquire, myself, nor that you should inquire, in my name or behalf.

We have no news here, since I wrote you last. Appointments, not acted on. We have seen an acct. of your Portsmo[uth] Town Meeting,— the letters, &c.—[2]

I believe Mr Bell can find no originals here.[3] Yrs truly   D Webster

ALS. MH. Published in Mason, *Memoir and Correspondence*, p. 330.
1. The *Statesman*, a Democratic paper devoted to the interests of David Henshaw, reported on February 27 that there had been a statement in a New York paper several years before that New Hampshire Federalist

Charles H. Atherton had received a letter from Webster "advising and requesting him to get elected a delegate to the Hartford Convention." In Atherton's published reply, discussed below (Mason to DW, May [March] 13, 1830, note 2), he acknowledged receiving such a letter, but not from Webster.

2. The allusion to the Portsmouth town meeting concerns the political repercussions of Jackson's appointment of John P. Decatur to be collector of customs. The "letters, etc.," is probably a reference to the charges against Timothy Upham, discussed in footnote 3, following.

3. The reference is to a controversy involving Timothy Upham, then National Republican candidate for governor of New Hampshire, who had been removed by Jackson from his post—collector of customs in Portsmouth. On February 15 Isaac Hill's *New Hampshire Patriot* charged that

Upham, in collusion "with leading Federalists," had smuggled goods to and from British provinces during the Embargo and Non-Intercourse periods. The *Portsmouth Journal* countered on March 6, asserting that the documents produced by Hill in support of his charge had been pronounced forgeries "by all who saw them" excepting only the Hill Democrats. The "originals" that Webster reports cannot be found in Washington would be originals of these documents. "Mr. Bell" is probably Senator Samuel Bell of New Hampshire, but may be James Bell (1804–1857), a Portsmouth attorney who sometimes collaborated on legal matters with both Mason and Webster. See Charles H. Bell, *The Bench and Bar of New Hampshire* (Boston and New York, 1894), pp. 190–192; Mason to DW, February 8, 1830, mDW 8415; and Mason to DW, March 8, 1830, below.

TO CHARLES BRICKETT HADDOCK

Washington Mar. 4. 1830

Dear Charles,

I recd duly yrs of the 17 of Feb.[1] Affairs at Salisbury may as well remain as they are till I get home. We will then endeavor to meet, in that region, & settle some arrangement. I am glad Mrs [Achsah Pollard] W[ebster][2] & the children are with you, & pray you to remember me to them. We ourselves are all well.

As to my *"works,"* if a book is to be made, I should think the following might be selected.

1   Plymo. Discourse. I think this the best of my efforts
2   Bunker Hill
3   Adams & Jefferson
4   Greek Speech
5.   Tariff Speech, of 1824
6.   Panama Mission
7.   Bank Speech
8.   Currency Speech, 1816 (which I have caused to be copied, & now
                                             send; but have not read a word of, since
                                             it was deliv'd.[)]

Two Speeches of this
Session.[3]
Speech Revolutionary
Officers.

Dinner Speech, Boston[4]
Faneuil Hall, election Speech[5]

(There are two of these, pretty much
alike—I do not know which is best—but
one shd. be printed.[)][6]

If any law speeches be printed, I think the following are the best
D. College.
Steam Boat.
Prescott's defence (but I have never read this. I have quite forgotten
it.[)]
You speak of the *Dedham* speech. I do not know what you refer to. I
defended Judge [Samuel] Haven, on an Indictment, growing out of an
ecclesiastical dispute at Dedham—but the speech was never published
to my knowledge.[7]
The address to the Mechanics Ass: might be rigged up, & put in for
variety.
I doubt whether there is any thing readable, in what I sd. in Convention—those debates might be looked to. I doubt whether it will be worth
while to begin the work till I get home. A good deal of care should be
bestowed upon it; & such a publication, at the present moment, will
have so many bearings, that it must be well considered what it should
contain. We can have no family *Memoir*—as to biographical notices, if
any they must be exceedingly brief. If, however, it is matter of importance to the printers, to begin earlier, you may let me know. The picture
is by Stewart[8]—it is at Mr I[saac] P. Davis'. I suppose he would suffer
it to be used, by a distinguished engraver if it were thot. best to have
an engraving.
If I could pick up what I said, year before last, to yr boys,[9] & what I
said last yr, to those of Amherst,[10] they could be put together, & make
something which would eke out variety. With regards to yr family Yrs
                              D Webster

One vol, would be enough, in all conscience.

ALS. NhD. Published in *PC*, 1: 490–
491.
    1. Not found.
    2. Achsah Pollard (1801–1896) of
Concord, New Hampshire, married
Ezekiel Webster, then four years a
widower, on August 2, 1825.
    3. Although Webster writes here in
parallel columns, the context and the

ultimate contents of the volume being
compiled seem to indicate that the
"Two Speeches of this Session" are
not intended to be the two speeches
noted in the adjacent space. The only
speeches of the 1829–1830 session of
Congress actually reprinted are the
two replies to Hayne, which are not
otherwise mentioned in the letter, but

which he most certainly did not mean to omit.

4. Speech in Faneuil Hall, June 5, 1828, at a public dinner given him by the Citizens of Boston, as a mark of respect for his public services.

5. Speech delivered at a meeting of Citizens of Boston, held in Faneuil Hall on the evening of April 3, 1825, preparatory to the general election in Massachusetts.

6. The first of these was on January 12, 1827, in the House of Representatives. The second, and the one chosen by Haddock, was delivered in the Senate on April 25, 1828, on a bill for the "relief of the Surviving Officers of the Revolution."

7. Haven (1771–1847; Harvard 1789), Norfolk County judge and registrar of deeds, had written a pamphlet upholding a faction of the Dedham church congregation which had disagreed with the selection of a new minister and had seceded, taking with them the portable assets of the church. The new minister sued Haven for libel, but no indictment was returned by the Norfolk County grand jury. Later in the year (1819) a Middlesex County grand jury at Cambridge did indict but Haven was acquitted. Webster defended Haven against the first attempt to indict, but not at the trial.

8. The frontispiece actually used in *Speeches and Forensic Arguments* resembles the Gilbert Stuart portrait (see *Correspondence*, 1, Figure 11), but it was actually drawn from life and engraved by James Barton Longacre, sometime between April and November 1830. See Isaac P. Davis to Thomas Sully, April 26, 1830, *Pennsylvania Magazine of History and Biography*, 22 (1898): 246–247. The portrait is reproduced in the illustration section of this volume.

9. Speech at Dartmouth College, July 21, 1828, W & S, 13: 31–34.

10. No text has been found, but the remarks were apparently combined with the Dartmouth address above, as Webster suggested, in an undated abstract, "Remarks on Education," mDW 8267, printed in W & S, 13: 106–107.

FROM SAMUEL ATKINSON

Wheeling March 5th 1830

Dear Sir

I have seen & read your late speeches in the senate. I hope you will deem this a sufficient apology for my asking the favor of you to send me them in the pamphlet form. At a time when the public mind was *sane* (and the period of its arrival will not be retarded by the late discussion in the senate) the author, would be deemed, at least a *candidate* for, if not altogether worthy, of the first office in the gift of the american people. We have fallen upon strange times. The charm is broken. There is too much of the reality of fact, perhaps, to justify me in saying that I fancy I hear the cotton cables of the south cracking snapping & parting while the bulwarks of the nation are safely moored with the hemp of Kentucky & the North. I have not time at this moment to say anything more than that you ought to visit the Western Country. You have many friends here—real friends. No Bentons among them. Your obt Sert   S. Atkinson

ALS. DLC. Atkinson (1788–1851; Brown 1813) came from Boscawen, New Hampshire, where his brother Daniel Clark read law in Webster's office. Samuel Atkinson settled first in Chillicothe, Ohio, then Wheeling, and finally Pataskala, Ohio. At the time of his death he was warden of the Ohio state penitentiary.

TO JOHN HAMPDEN PLEASANTS

Washington Mar 6. 1830

Private & Confidential
Dear Sir

Soon after I had posted a speech to you this morning, I recd yours of the 4th inst.[1] I am glad you have written to me, on general accounts; I need not say how much I am gratified to learn there are *some* in Va. who think of my efforts without disrespect. To tell you the truth, I have sometimes felt, that while political foes have dealt to me, in yr good state, a large measure of abuse, political friends have not always interposed a shield, under circumstances, when, perhaps it might have been expected by one engaged in the same general public cause. But I have no hard feeling, in this respect. I know there were reasons, why some of us should bear abuse, without expecting to be defended. That time, I hope, has gone by. At any rate, I shd. not hope to find myself in such a condition again. I am willing to correspond with you, freely, but *in entire & sacred confidence.* Thro life, thus far, I have been as much guarded as possible agt. the accidents of the Post office & other accidents attending confidential correspondence. Nevertheless, the times require occasional confidence, & that some hazards be run. I am willing, therefore, to write you an occasional letter—knowing that I shall be safe, even if I had secrets to communicate, which will not often be the case. I shall be glad to hear from you often, you may rely on confidence on my side.

At present, there is not much to be said, growing out of the state of things here. The more objectionable nominations have not yet been acted on. It is quite uncertain how they will be disposed of. The Senate will be so nearly equally divided, that a vote or two will decide sundry nominations, & no one can say how those votes may be given. There will be close voting, certainly, in several cases. I agree with you, it is a balanced question, whether more good will flow from the rejection than from the confirmation. It wd. disappoint individuals, doubtless; but would it not, on the whole, rather strengthen the Admin to send [Isaac] Hill, [Amos] Kendall[2] &c home?

As to future operations, the general idea here seems to be this:—to bring forward no candidate this year—tho' doubtless, the general impression is that Mr C[lay] stands first & foremost in the ranks of those who wd. desire a change. I do not think there is the least abatement of the respect & confidence entertained for him. As to the other Western Gentleman, whom you mention, he must not be thought of, *for he is not with us.* Depend upon it, there is a negotiation in train to bring him out as V P. to run on the Ticket with Mr Calhoun. In my opinion, he has very little weight or influence in the Country, & that is fast declining.[3] Our friends in the west will quit him, of course, if in that event, as he must give up their interests.

I wish now to say, that two things are not to be omitted, when we speculate on the future.

First, that Genl. Jackson will certainly be considered again, if he live & be well; I say *certainly*, I mean only that I have no doubt of it.

Second, that we cannot now foresee what events will follow from what is passing in Penna & New York, on the subject of *Anti-Masonry.* This matter, be assured, is not to be disregarded.

In the meantime, it seems to me our course must be this.

—Expose the selfishness & *pretence* of the men in power, as much as possible; taking care to let the *ministers* be made responsible, for at least their full share. The acts will be theirs, in most cases; & therefore they·ought to be responsible for them, themselves.

—Show ourselves uniform, & just, by acting according to our principles; & opposing only such measures as deserve no support.

—As to *Tariff subjects*, we of the north must hold on where we are. And as to Internal Improvements, we, also, must go, temperately & cautiously for them also.

—Agree in all measures having in view the payt. of the debt.

—<Finally> To hold ourselves absolutely aloof from Mr. Van B. & Mr C[alhoun] & be ready to act for ourselves when the proper time comes—& to maintain our own men, & defend our own friends—

—Finally, cultivate a truly national spirit—go for great ends, & hold up the necessity of the Union &c.

AL draft. NhHi. Published in *PC*, 1: 491–493.

1. Published in part in Curtis, 1: 370.

2. Kendall was narrowly confirmed as fourth auditor of the Treasury on May 10, 1830, when Vice President Calhoun broke a 24 to 24 tie in favor of his appointment.

3. The reference is to Associate Justice John McLean of Ohio, whose friendship and support of Calhoun went back more than a decade. By 1830, however, McLean was viewed more as a rival than a political ally. Francis P. Weisenburger, *The Life of John McLean: A Politician on the United States Supreme Court* (Columbus, Ohio, 1937), pp. 72–73.

TO AMOS LAWRENCE

Washington March 8. 1830

Dear Sir

I thank you, very sincerely, for your very kind & friendly letter.[1] The sacrifices made in being here, & the mortifications sometimes experienced, are amply compensated by the consciousness that my friends at home feel that I have done some little service to our New England.

I pray you to remember [me], with very true regard to Mrs L. & believe me, Very faithfully & gratefully Yrs   D Webster

ALS. MLexHi. Published in William R. Lawrence, *Extracts from the Diary and Correspondence of the late Amos Lawrence* (Boston, 1855), pp. 97–98.
1. Amos Lawrence to DW, March 3, 1830, mDW 8474.

FROM JEREMIAH MASON

Portsmouth March 8th. 1830

Dear Sir,

Not being on good terms with Mr. [Charles H.] Atherton, & not liking to write him on the subject you mention, I have requested Robert Means[1] to make the desired enquiries. If anything ᴗan be ascertained from him, I think it can be done better by conversation than by writing. When I know the result I will inform you. I have no recollection of ever writing to him on the subject alluded to.

I have read your last speech with great delight. It was sent me in pamphlet form from Boston. My expectation was highly raised, & I can truly say it has been fully satisfied. Your defence of N England is all that could be desired, & you have been most fortunate in effecting it, without polluting your own hands with any of the filth, that was so abundantly collected round you. But the constitutional argument is of vastly greater importance. I have read that with great attention, & think it unanswerable. If I mistake not, it cannot fail of producing a sensible effect even in S. Carolina. If Col Hains [Robert Y. Hayne] answer is received as the true construction of the Constitution, our government is at an end. The sophistical Virginia resolutions of 1798 afford the only support of this wild doctrine. Mr. Madison, by adopting your gloss upon his resolutions, might atone for all his political sins, & confer a greater benefit on his Country than he has done by the labour of a long life. But of his doing this, I fear there is no hope.

This is our election day. Col [Timothy] Upham has a majority of about one hundred in this town. I do not know the exact number. We have succeeded in choosing five anti Jackson representatives. Strong hopes are entertained of an anti Jackson House of Reps. This is important as a senator of U. S. is to be chosen. Uphams chance for Governor is thought to be tolerable. The forged papers lately returned by Hill from Washington have done much for him about here.[2] If they have been as efficient in other parts of the State he is elected. The papers were lately brought here, & pronounced to be forgeries by all who saw them, except *Isaac Waldron*[3] & *Elisha Whidden*.[4] Waldron is supposed to have the promise of [John P.] Decatur's place, in case he should be rejected by the Senate.

The suit of Mrs. [John W.] Mellen agt. the Dover Man[ufacturin]g Co. must I believe end in nothing. If there be any thing to argue in it, it must be a mere question of law; which I think cannot come on at the next Term, which is to be held at Gilford. If you are inclined to come again to the old County of Strafford to argue a cause, you had best be engaged for the Def[endan]ts, who are able & will be willing, if the case raises any question, to pay you good fees. The Pl[aintif]f has, I believe, spent all her money already. I think you had best not engage before I see you. Affectionately yours   J. Mason

ALS. NhHi. Published in *PC*, 1: 494–496.

1. New Hampshire lawyer (1786–1842; Bowdoin 1807), Means received his legal training in the office of Charles H. Atherton and was Mason's brother-in-law. Charles H. Bell, *The Bench and Bar of New Hampshire* (Boston and New York, 1894), p. 509.

2. See above, DW to Mason, March 2, note 3.

3. Waldron (1774–1843) was at this time a director, and later president, of the Portsmouth Commercial Bank, one of the administration's "pet" banks of 1833.

4. Whidden, a Portsmouth merchant in West Indian goods.

FROM GEORGE HAY

Oak Hill, near Aldie Loudon
March 10. 1830

Dear Sir

If your late speeches, growing out of Foote's resolution or amendment, have been printed in the pamphlet form, as I presume they have and am sure they ought, you will greatly oblige me, by sending me a copy.

That a state has a right, derived not from the constitution, but from the eternal & universal principle of self preservation, to withdraw from the Union, and to declare the political compact void, is a point about which I have never doubted: while I have been almost as clear that events, justifying such a declaration never will take place. Nor have I any doubt on this point, that a state retaining its position in the Union, has no right to oppose by legislation and force, the execution of a law of the U. S. altho persuaded—convinced—to demonstration of the unconstitutionality of such law. Col. H[ayne]'s idea of the power of a state to suspend the operation of a law, until the majority appeal, and procure a decision in their favor, is visionary. I beg your pardon. I want to know your ideas, and I am without ceremony, obtruding mine upon you. But as I have begun, I will trespass on your time & patience, with two suggestions, and two only. The first is, that a citizen of a state, acting in conformity to a *law* of that State, which law opposes force to the execution of a public & general law of the U. S. cannot be guilty of treason. I should not readily undertake to prove this negative proposition to be true. I do not think that I could prove it: indeed I should find it the easier task, to prove the contrary: but yet my mind clings to this negative proposition, with all the tenacity of deliberate conviction. This subject deserves your consideration & that of Congress, and deserves it *now*.

My second suggestion relates to what I conceive to be a defect or rather an omission in your speech. You have not presented a view of the exact position in which a seceding state, and the other states, will stand as to each other. Will not the latter retain possession, by right, of all the forts, dock yards, &c. over which they have by cession, exclusive jurisdiction, within the limits of the seceding state? And will they not have a right, upon the clearest principle of national law, to which alone the seceding state can *now* appeal, to adopt such measures and all such measures as will prevent the seceding state, from making its own act, the instrument of incalculable injury to the other states? If you should speak again on this subject, "look over and down the precipice," and tell us what is to be found there. These ulterior speculations, might be extremely useful.

I give you my word that when I took up my pen, I meant only to ask you for a copy of your speeches. I did not intend to trouble you with a single remark, and I beg that in answer to this you will do no more than to inclose to me the copy required. With great respect, Yr. ob. sv.

Geo. Hay

ALS. DLC.

FROM HENRY BOND

Philadelphia March 11th. 1830

Honored and dear Sir,

I have received your speech of the 26th of January, for which I return you many thanks. I am so sensible of being influenced by feelings of partiality in forming an estimate of the value of your performances, that I cannot suppose they will be equally gratifying to indifferent persons as they are to myself. I cannot, however, recollect an instance, when the appearance of a new work by a popular author, or any new discovery or remarkable event has been such a general topic of conversation among intelligent gentlemen, as your last speech. Often have I heard it said by those, whose opinion, in such a case, is worth listening to, that they never read any other speech with so much interest and pleasure. I sometimes hear the question asked, will Mr. Webster speak again in this debate? Some say *they hope not*; that *he ought not*; that *he has said enough*; and the reason I hear assigned for such an opinion is, that this speech has raised you to your culmination, and that if you should make another speech, you would not be able to retain extreme elevation. Others, who, I think, understand your powers and principles of action better, differ from them. They think the point upon which you stand, instead of being an isolated peak, is on a broad *plateau*, where there is some room for action and motion without necessarily descending.

Besides, it is thought the immense importance of some of the principles brought into discussion must make you overlook the chance of your not equalling yourself; that the attention of the public is now so much attracted to the constitutional questions in debate, and such efforts are making both in Congress and out of it to disseminate unsound and dangerous doctrines, that an immense responsibility rests upon you, especially when it is considered how much you have it in your power to influence, enlighten and direct the public sentiment. You have rendered the position you have taken impregnable and they would now be glad to see you demolish all the preparations to approach it. Little as I have said, I fear you will consider me presumptuous in saying so much, and therefore conclude by assuring you, that to the admiration which I entertain in common with others, I join that attachment which delights in every thing pertaining to your welfare, Henry Bond

ALS. NhHi. Bond (1790–1859; Dartmouth 1813, Medical School 1817) was a prominent Philadelphia physician.

TO GEORGE HAY

Washington March 12. 1830,

Dear Sir,

I have great pleasure in complying with your request to send you my speech, in pamphlet form.

The two suggestions which you make, in your letter,[1] and to which you ask my attention, are of the first importance. I will state, in few words my opinion on them.

The first is, that a citizen of a state, acting in conformity to a *law* of that state, which law appears [opposes?] force to a public and general law of the United States, cannot be guilty of treason.

I must confess I dissent entirely from this proposition; it appears to me incapable of being maintained, and with you, I am happy to find, it is rather a proposition to which your mind clings, by its usual habit of thinking, than one to be supported by argument.

To your second suggestion, I will observe that it is true, that in my speech I have not presented a view of the exact position, in which a seceding state, and the other states, would stand as to each other.

My reason is, the constitution presents no such view, and provides for [no] such case. It does not contemplate its own destruction. You may well ask, what will become of property of the U. S. such as forts &c in the seceding state. It might also be well asked, if one state shall secede, and then another, on whom will the public debt rest, and the other duties of Government, such as the Indian Annuities, stipulations in treaties with foreign nations &c?

It is plain to me, My Dear Sir, that secession is Revolution. It may be more or less violent: it may be bloody or not bloody: but it is fundamental change of political system: it is Revolution: and the constitution does not provide for Revolution. As in other cases, so in this. Revolution, if it comes, must bring its own law with it.

That it may not come at all, is the fervent prayer of, Dear Sir, Your most obt. sevt. Danl Webster

LS. MiDbEI.   1. See above.

During the 1829–1830 session of Congress, Webster received numerous letters, some like the one below from Noah Worcester, enclosing petitions asking Congress to intervene to protect the rights of the southern Indians. The removal of the Indians to lands beyond the Mississippi held a high place among Jackson's policies, and the necessary legislation was passed at this session, over opposition led by various missionary groups. The writer of the letter was personally well known to Webster. His brother Thomas was pastor of the Salisbury, New Hampshire, Congregational Church which Webster had attended; and his nephew, Samuel Austin Worcester, then a missionary among the Cherokees, was soon to go down in history as the plaintiff in error in Worcester v. Georgia, *a case that gave John Marshall yet another opportunity to affirm the supremacy of the nation over the states (6 Peters 515 [1832]).*

Another who wrote cogently upon the subject was Jeremiah Evarts, whose letter of February 6, 1830, appears above. Webster was certainly familiar with Evarts' essays on "the present crisis in the condition of the American Indians" which had recently appeared in the National Intelligencer.*Throughout the controversy over Indian removal, however, Webster took a less active part than many of his constituents hoped for. He introduced the petitions sent to him, but did not participate in debate on the Indian Removal Bill. He voted in favor of an amendment, soundly beaten, that would have guaranteed protection of the tribes pending removal, but the vote on final passage is not recorded.*

FROM NOAH WORCESTER

Brighton March 12. 1830

Dear Sir,

I inclose to you a concise Memorial,[1] signed by a number of the leading men in this town, relating to the all important question which now agitates the country. We might probably have obtained the signatures of nearly all the legal voters in this place, but this was deemed unnecessary. I have had some doubts as to the expediency of sending any more Memorials from this state at so late a period. But not knowing what would be best in that particular, a few names have been obtained in compliance with the opinion and wishes of the Meeting held at Boston from all parts of the state, whose Memorial you have probably received.[2] As you will be much better able to judge of the expediency of presenting the inclosed than the subscribers can be at such a distance from the capital, they submit it entirely to your judgement.

I have read, Sir, with great pleasure your several replies to Mr. Hayne. The argument on the sovereignty of the several states was much needed. It appears to me not only correct but invincible. In my opinion it was a happy circumstance that you had occasion to discuss that question prior to entering on the Georgia controversy. You have sapped the Georgia principles without naming them. Admitting the correctness of your argument, Georgia has not a foot of ground left on which she can justify her pretensions, or her late proceedings, in regard to the Chérokees, or their lands. Great is the confidence which the people of this state place in yourself and Mr [Edward] Everett, in regard to the cause in which they feel so deeply interested. What you have already done seems to them a pledge, that the cause of justice and mercy will not be less for the want of an able advocate. Never before, I suspect, were you called to plead a cause in which the honor of the nation and the interests of humanity were more deeply concerned than they are in the controversy between Georgia and the Cherokees. I might perhaps more properly say *between Georgia and the United States.* It is my prayer that your life and health may be preserved through the arduous struggle, and for many years yet to come; and that, in pleading the cause now pending, you may be enabled to answer the raised hopes and expectations of your constituents and your friends. Yours affectionately   N. Worcester

P.S. Should the principles and the spirit of the Georgia politicians be adopted and cherished by the slaves of that state, what but the horrors of St Domingo must be the consequences?

ALS. NhD.

1. "Memorial of the inhabitants of Brighton, Mass., asking for protection of the southern Indians," mDW 43020, presented in the United States Senate by Webster on March 23, 1830.

2. "Memorial of sundry citizens of Massachusetts praying that the Southern Indians may be protected in their rights & privileges," mDW 42996, presented by Webster in the United States Senate on March 1, 1830.

FROM JEREMIAH MASON

Portsmouth, May [March] 13, 1830

Dear Sir,

I send you inclosed a letter from Robert Means[1] in answer to my request to him to inquire of Mr. [Charles H.] Atherton respecting the newspaper story of your advising him to join the Hartford Convention. I suppose you have seen his voluntary disavowal in the Boston papers[2] of your having made any such application.

Vast numbers of your speech have been published, and they seem to be producing a strong impression. Were it not for the depraved condition of political morality, I should entertain hopes that the present discussion in the Senate would produce great and permanent alterations in public opinion. It must doubtless have considerable effect. I hope Governor [Samuel] Bell will answer [Levi] Woodbury's miserable trash. Indeed, I do not see how he can in justice to himself avoid doing it.

Our election is lost, as you have probably seen by the newspapers. The falsehoods and forgeries against [Timothy] Upham were contradicted as speedily as they could be, but there was not time for the contradiction to have its full effect, except in the immediate vicinity of this place.

It is believed that if the election had come on a fortnight later Upham would have carried it. As it is, both Senate and House will have majorities of Jacksonians. It is not certain, however, that Woodbury or (in the case of his being otherwise provided for) [Isaac] Hill will be elected to the Senate of the United States.[3] It is quite possible that some other Jackson man may step in before them. . . . Yours as ever,   J. M.

Text from Mason, *Memoir and Correspondence*, pp. 330–331, which is incomplete, and where the letter is misdated May 13. Original not found.

1. Not found; subsequently returned to Mason. See DW to Mason, March 19, 1830, below. For background see above, DW to Mason, March 2, 1830, and Mason to DW, March 8, 1830.

2. Atherton's letter, dated March 1, was addressed to the editor of the *Boston Statesman*, but was quickly reprinted in other papers (for example, the *Boston Courier*, March 8, 1830). It was in response to the *Statesman's* story of February 27, which asserted that in 1814 Atherton had received a letter from Webster, advising him "to get up a meeting in the county of Hillsborough, for the purpose of electing delegates to the Hartford Convention." According to Atherton, he had received such a letter not from Webster "but from a person living in a part of the state, very remote from him, and with whom I have no knowledge or belief, that Mr. Webster had any communication either written or verbal in relation to the Hartford Convention, or the choosing of a delegate to the same. Nor have I any knowledge from any source whatever, that Mr. Webster was a promoter of that Convention, took any interest in it, or was desirous of having any delegate chosen to it." But compare DW to William Sullivan, October 17, 1814 (first letter), *Correspondence*, 1: 170.

3. In June Hill won the contested New Hampshire seat in the United States Senate over Woodbury by 117 to 22 in the General Court and 9 to 3 in the state Senate.

FROM [ISAAC PARKER]

[March 13, 1830]

I say a few words on a separate sheet, thinking it possible you may have occasion to show the other.[1]

I don't think I ever knew so undivided an opinion on any subject, as upon the high merits of your speech. At first some few thought you passed over the attack upon the Hartford Convention too slightly but those most interested in that question, thought your peculiar position justified you in avoiding any more particular defensive remarks on that subject. Indeed I think had your speech come out entire at first, there would have been no grumbling.

ALS. DLC.   1. Not found.

FROM JACOB HALL AND SAMUEL AUSTIN, JR.

Boston March 17 1830

Sir.

At a meeting of "The Friends of the present administration of this Commonwealth" at the Chamber of the Common Council last evening, "for the purpose of choosing a County Committee, & transacting such other business as might come before them."

Hon Jacob Hall was appointed chairman [and] S. Austin, Jr. Secy.

On this occasion, the following resolutions were put, & carried unanimously.

"Resolved. That this meeting entertain a deep & grateful sense of the distinguished services of the Hon Daniel Webster, in the Senate of the United States."

"Resolved. That the Chairman & Secy. communicate this vote to the Hon Mr Webster at Washington."

In performing the duty assigned us, permit us to assure you, of our full concurrence in the sentiments of the meeting, & our pleasure in being the organ of its communication.

We have the honor to be Sir, Your obed Sevts

> Jacob Hall, Chairman
> to the Meeting
> S. Austin, Jr. Secy.

ALS. DLC. Hall was a state senator from Boston and an active Anti-Mason; Austin was a Boston merchant and shipowner.

FROM LEVI LINCOLN

Worcester, March 17, 1830.

My Dear Sir

I cannot consent to forward the accompanying official papers[1] without improving the same opportunity to express to you my grateful sense of your kind recollection and attention, in transmitting various documents during the present session of Congress, and especially copies of your speeches on Mr. Foote's resolution. As a New-England man, I thank you for the able defence of this much-abused part of the country; as a citizen of Massachusetts, I thank you for the vindication of her character for patriotism, for attachment to the Federal Union, for services, sacrifices, and undeviating and devoted regard to the interest of a common cause and country—and as a Republican—ay, and as an *old-fashioned Jefferson* Republican, too! I feel the weight of obligation to you for asserting the consistency of principle and the integrity of purpose with which we oppose despotism in every shape, and however exercised—whether from a foreign source or under the abuse of domestic authority. If any thing can rouse the people of the United States to a sense of their danger, and a timely protection of themselves and their free institutions, it must be the appeals to their intelligence and virtue which have been addressed to them from the Senate-chamber. I pray God they may be effectual. They have awakened attention, and there must be safety in the result. . . . With great respect and esteem, most truly, Your obedient and obliged servant, Levi Lincoln.

Text from Curtis, 1: 370–371. Origi-   1. Not found.
nal not found.

TO JEREMIAH MASON

Washington Mar. 19. '30

My Dear Sir

I return Mr. [Robert] M[ean]'s Letter. Mr. [Charles H.] A[therton] did quite as well in his letter to the Statesman, as could be expected.[1]

We have not yet acted on the N. H. nominations. I know not whether to decide to reject them, or not. [John P.] Decatur & [Samuel] Cushman are in great danger—but would they be succeeded by any body better? And if Hill should be rejected, should we not have him in the Senate?[2]

Appearances in various parts of the Country indicate dissatisfaction with the present state of things. The stock of patronage is exhausted, & many are left unprovided for; & they are looking out for other parties, & other leaders. It is admitted, I believe by most, that Mr. Clay is gaining rapidly in the west. Kentucky is doubtless strong for him, & as agt. any body but Genl Jackson, he would take nearly all the western votes. In the meantime, the *Anti masonic* party, steadily encreasing in N York, is breaking out like an Irish rebellion in Pennsylvania. It goes on with a force, that subdues all other feeling. These things put party calculation at defiance. The party here are obviously very much alarmed. The Admin Senators are understood to have held a *Caucus*, three nights ago, & endeavored to unite & rally. Something more of tone & decision has been since visible. It may become, *perhaps*, the confirmation of all the appointments. As to measures, they are irreconcilable. They can not stir agt. the Tariff. As a means of union,—& a necessary means—they seem now resolved to keep the present President in office thro a second term. He now intends to hold on, beyond all doubt. Here again, accidents to his life or health, would produce quite a new state of things. So that, on the whole, I do not think there has been a period in our time when one could see less of the future than the present.

I thank you for your civil saying abt. my speech. It has made much more *talk* than it deserves, owing to the topic, & to the times. I hope it is doing some good at the South, where, I have reason to think, it is very generally circulated & read. Yrs very sincerely   D Webster

☞ having cut my thumb, I write even worse than usual.

ALS. MHi. Published in Mason, *Mem-*   where it is misdated 1835.
oir and Correspondence, pp. 357–358,   1. See above, Mason to DW, March

13, 1830, note 2.

2. Both Decatur and Cushman were rejected by the Senate ten days later. Isaac Hill was rejected as second comptroller of the Treasury on April 12, 1830, but as Webster predicted, he was elected to the Senate.

FROM WILLIAM SULLIVAN

Boston March 23d. 1830.

Dear Sir,

I have not done justice to you, or myself, in not having sooner acknowledged the favor conferred by you, in sending to me your speeches on Mr. Foots resolution. The delay enables me to speak confidently of public opinion on your achievements;—an opinion, not formed under sudden impulses, but with good judgment, and full means of using it. This opinion appears to me to be, that your speeches, on this occasion, not only excel all former ones, made by you, but by every other man, in our own country:—and that out of it, we must go back to the days of [Edmund] Burke[, William Pitt, First Earl of] Chatham &c to find objects of comparison. This is the opinion of the Club; and some of its members, you know, are judges,—and very good ones. Its seems to me, that the most *valuable* quality of these Speeches, is, that they teach the citizens in general, what their relation to the federal Government is; —and in a manner so comprehensible, and satisfactory, that every one not only assents, but is surprized, that the doctrine should not have been familiar to him;—and even that the same train of thought should not have occurred in his own mind. It is a pleasure to your friends here, to be able to infer, from the effect produced in different parts of the Union, that an individual, even, without the aid of war, and great public excitement, can raise himself to an elevation, on which he may be viewed from all parts of an extensive empire, with an honorable national pride. This is something to set off against *military* delusion.

I presume we have here, as you have in Washington many groundless assertions, and items of news. Of late, the rumors have turned on new coalitions; the latest is, I think, to this effect;—that Mr. V. B: and yourself have come to an understanding;—but, whether with the consent, and appropriation of Mr. Clay, or without consulting him, rumor seems not to know.

The election pending here, is of considerable importance; but I do not find that any influential, and discreet men are attempting to give it a proper direction. The representation of this county in the Senate is of much importance, the coming year, on account of the valuation.

The Court are sitting and will continue to sit about a fortnight longer. They have a great deal to do;—and more than four men can properly do. The subjects, apart from home politics, most spoken of here, are the discouraging state of things in England;—the want of talent in the public men there;—some persons intimating that great changes must soon occur; and the continuance of similar embarrassments in this region. I do not hear any one speak of changes for the better or even of the hope of them.

As to mere town news,—Mr Thorndike[1] is said to be much indisposed. Mr. [Andrew] Ritchie is to review Jefferson's works.[2] Alex[ander Hill] E[verett] is said to have become proprietor of the N[orth] A[merican] R[eview].[3] Mr. [Harrison Gray] Otis has been well enough to dine with the "Young Fish," lately. Mr. [David?] Sears[4] and family are coming home in this spring. My own family are well;—I noticed, last evening, that some of them, were very busy in making extracts from the poets, on small slips of paper, to be deposited in cornu copia of the confectioners, for future use.

It is a cold snowy day;—and from the Northeast;—and one of those days in which one must plunge into business, or pleasure, within doors, to escape the misery of feeling what is going on without. An excellent day it might be made around a table with six or 8 congenial minds, with something fit thereon, for use. Formerly, when the wind was damp, and eastwardly, a small piece of salmon, and a brant, a piece, for six, in a snug room, with something liquid that could tell of the last century, had a tendency to make one forget which way the wind was. Whether the times are so bad that the like effects would not follow from such causes, is a point, which I should be willing to test by actual experiment.

I beg leave to tender my best respects to Mrs. Webster;—if you should know when the ladies of Boston may expect the pleasure of seeing her among them, and should tell me of it, I should be glad to be the medium of such news. With great regard, respect (and thankfulness, as your fellow citizen) Your obliged friend   Wm. Sullivan

ALS. NhHi. Published in *PC*, 1: 497–499.

1. Probably Israel Thorndike, Sr. (1755–1832).

2. Ritchie (1782–1862; Harvard 1802), Boston businessman and social friend of both Webster and Sullivan. His unsigned review of Thomas Jefferson Randolph, ed., *Memoir, Correspondence and Miscellanies, from the Papers of Thomas Jefferson* (Charlottesville, 1829), appeared in the *North American Review* for April 1830.

3. On March 10, 1830, Alexander H. Everett bought the controlling interest in the *North American Review* from Jared Sparks, whom he succeeded as editor.

4. Sears (1787–1871; Harvard 1807), prominent merchant, land speculator, and social leader of Boston.

FROM DANIEL FLETCHER WEBSTER

Hopkinton March 23d. 1830.

My Dear Father.

I have not written you the last week, because I have had nothing to say to you, except that I progress in my studies, and am quite well, and send love, which would hardly fill a sheet of paper.

Mr [Samuel B.] Walcott[1] has gone to Boston. He went a week ago last Sunday. Mrs W. is a[t] Salem and expects to be confined there. Mr W. goes to Court every term at Concord and Worcester and Cambridge, and seems to have his hands full. We have had most beautiful weather till to day; when to our utter astonishment, we woke and found the ground already covered, and the snows coming down quite fast. It now blows and snows like December.

I never knew what the constitution really was, till your last short speech. I thought it was a compact between states. I like that last reply better than all the rest; for it comes out so á propos, and *conclusive* that Mr H[ayne] has nothing more to say. It is the "Cou[p] de Grace." It winds him up; as we boys used to say. I saw in the papers that the Postmaster had made a new construction of the franking law to suit the occasion.[2] I do not know how it is; but it seems to me to be as plain an usurpation, or misuse of power as ever was. However, they can only do so three years longer.

Uncle [James] William [Paige] went to New York some time ago, and I do not know whether he has yet returned. I need very much a new suit of clothes. I have had but one coat, very cheap coat, this year, which is of very poor material, and did not last so long as it ought; and I want a good coat occasionally.

The tailors here are not good, and I thought that I might perhaps, go to Boston, in the evening stage, and back again the day after. I could get Measured and get the cloth, and have them sent up to me; that is if Uncle is at home. If you will permit this; and let Julia write to me about it, I will ask Uncle. I would not trouble you about this; but I am really in need. I shall not lose time, as I can make it up in two lessons. Please give my love to Mother, and Julia, and I remain Your ever affectionate Son   D F Webster

ALS. NhHi. Published in part in Van Tyne, p. 151. Daniel Fletcher Webster (1813–1865; Harvard 1833), Webster's oldest son and oldest living child, was at this time preparing to enter Harvard.

1. Walcott (1795–1854; Harvard 1819) tutored Fletcher Webster for Harvard. He had studied law in Webster's office and was admitted to the Suffolk bar in 1824, but moved to Hopkinton, Massachusetts, where he

served in many local offices.

2. Postmaster General William Taylor Barry had ruled, just in time to interfere with the distribution of Webster's reply to Hayne, that packets heavier than two ounces could not be franked.

FROM GEORGE HAY

Oak Hill, near Aldie—Loudon
Mar 24 1830

Dear Sir

I received from the Secretary of the Senate [Walter Lowrie], the pamphlet, which I had taken the liberty to ask for; and in a few days afterwards, your letter of the 12th inst.[1] which I beg you to remember was *not* asked for. On the contrary, I intreated you, I think, to take no trouble on yourself except that of forwarding the speech required. But in defiance of this admonition, and of the laborious duties, legislative and forensic in which you are engaged, but which I am happy to learn are not so heavy as to disturb your repose, you have honored me with a notice of the topics which I had unexpectedly, as well as hastily and briefly touched. I feel myself therefore bound, even on the principles of ordinary Civility, to reply to your letter: and to tell the plain truth, I am very glad to be so bound. But on your account, I shall discharge my obligation, at the least possible expence to you of time or patience.

The following propositions are the result of my Solitary reflections on the constitutional matter presented for consideration by your speech: of which by the bye I would say something extremely Civil, if I did not see that, quite as much in that way has been already said, as you could possibly wish to hear.

1st proposition—that the *people* of the U. S. ordained and established our present government: but that the people of each State, in adopting it, acted for themselves, separately as a sovereign and independent people in their original and not in their organized political character.

2d—that whether the government be considered as a compact or a grant of power or partly one and partly the other each State in the Union acting in the same character in which it acted when it adopted the Constitution, had a right, not derived from the constitution, but from the eternal & universal principles of self preservation, to secede, at its discretion, from the Union—

3. that when this secession has been declared & announced, the relations between the seceding state and those which adhere to the Union, depend entirely on the law of nature and nations: and the inhabitants of the seceding state, cease to be citizens of the United States, or of any one of them.

4. that there is no middle course, between Secession and acquiescence; and that therefore when a state in its existing organized capacity, undertakes to oppose force to the execution of a general law of the U. S. force so exerted is treason. I say this with great reluctance—multa gemens—but unless the law of the U. S. thus opposed, is declared by the Courts of the U. S. to be unconstitutional, the conclusion is inevitable. Where the fact of secession has been proclaimed, or is notorious, the question of treason, of course cannot arise.

5. that the forts, arsenals, magazines[,] dockyards, &c. &c. within the limits of the seceding state, the scites of which have been ceded to the U. S. remain the property of the U. S.—: and that the U. S. have a claim on the state so seceding, for its proportion of the debts due by the [illegible]

6. that the states remaining united have a right to adopt such measures as will be adequate to prevent the seceding state from so availing itself of the act of Secession, and of its local position, as to frustrate their laws, of trade or revenue, or laws providing for the general defence & safety.

7. that it is the right, and the duty of the U. S. Judiciary to decide and declare, in all cases arising under the constitution, or laws of the U. S. &c. &c. regularly brought before it, what the law is: <and> that in performing this duty they must ex necessitate rei, discard all laws of the U. S. not warranted by the constitution, and all state constitutions and state laws, repugnant to the constitution or any law of the U. S. made in pursuance thereof: and that this decision is constitutionally binding on all the states so long as they remain members of the Union.
(29. March. I expected to have concluded this letter on the day on which it was commenced but the rheumatism has now come upon me for the first time in my life, with a force which has rendered me almost insensible of the blessing of my long exemption.—)

But this is not the quarter from which our greatest danger is to come. This Union is not to be destroyed or impaired by men who complain, however acrimoniously or turbulently, of violations of the constitution, or of laws, that are partial and oppressive. Laws injurious to liberty, all, in time, will unite to repeal; and laws, that are partial, and *oppressive* because they are partial, can never be carried fully into effect. This is a sort of cutaneous eruption, which however painful to the patient or distressing to the family, is topical and reaches no farther. The disease which *I*, dread, is of a far more formidable character. It touches the vitals of our system. It is the corruption of the public mind and morals, by means placed by the Constitution in the hands of the Executive for far different purposes. When men are dismissed from offices, high and low, not for delinquency public or private, but for exercising the right and performing the duty of an honest and independent voter: when men are put into office, not for any public service, or private virtue, but as a reward for their well timed devotion to the C. Magistrate: when the independence of the press is assailed, not openly, and manfully by legislation in face of day, but by bestowing offices on editors the most profligate and audacious: when the presidential election is converted into a perpetual appeal to the meanest and most sordid passions of the human heart, and calls into activity and notice, the meanest & basest of mankind: when we see all this, and much more than all this, we feel grief, and shame, and mortification, in all their varieties of bitterness: but when we learn, or have cause to apprehend that the Senate of the U. S. will not exert their constitutional authority, to its uttermost extent, for the suppression of these evils, I blush for the character, & tremble for the permanence of republican institutions.

I believe that there is not a word of what I have written to day, that has any relation to the point, to which my reply was to be directed. In parliamentary language, it is entirely out of order. But as Senators of the U. S. are not very fastidious on the subject of relevancy in debate, I hope you will have the goodness to excuse me, especially as I promise to do so no more—unless you should favor me with another speech in pamphlet form and another letter. I am, with very high respect Yr. mo: ob: svt. Geo: Hay

P.S. If Mr. W. can conveniently lay his hand on the Nat[ional] Int[elligencer] 21-March 1822—4th. page. 2d. col. 2d. paragraph from the bottom, he will see that the main question in this discussion is not new to G. H.[2] As to the main point, in Cohens [v. Virginia] case, G H has not changed his opinion; but he is now thoroughly persuaded, that the doctrine of the S[upreme] C[ourt], whether true or not is essential to the preservation of this Union.

ALS. NjP.

1. See above.

2. The paragraph referred to is part of a three-and-a-half-column review of *Cohens* v. *Virginia* (6 Wheaton 430 [1821]), signed "A Member of the Legislature of Virginia in 1820"—by this evidence, George Hay. In his argument, Hay repels any implication that the state of Virginia did, or could, "make legislative war against any federal act or sentence founded on a construction of the constitution which she condemns." He held the Supreme Court to have improperly taken jurisdiction in the *Cohens* case, but applauded the state for nevertheless carrying out the Court's decision.

FROM CHARLES TAIT

Claiborne (Ala) Mch. 24th. 1830

Dear Sir

I had the pleasure by the last mail to receive your second speech on Mr. Foot's resolution, for which you will please accept my best thanks. It is gratifying for me to be thus recollected in my retirement, in a remote corner of our extensive but common country.

I had read in the Intelli[gence]r with great interest the debate on Mr. F[oot']s Re[solutio]n in the senate, and feel a deep conviction of the danger of the new doctrines now urged with ability & zeal in the councils of the nation. I hope your able & eloquent argument will be generally read. I think it cannot be read without a salutary effect. Your views of the powers of this Govt. and the *means* of its interpretation & I may say of presentation appear to me to be sound & must ultimately prevail. If not there will be, sooner or later, an end of this Union. Let the power of the States be prescribed but let not the powers of the Genl. Govt. be destroyed or abridged. With my best wishes for your welfare I have the honor to be Your obt. Sert.   C. Tait

ALS. NhD.

FROM NATHAN DANE

Beverly, March 26th. 1830

Dear Sir,

I have received your second speech on the motion of Mr Foot, respecting the public lands, for which I thank you. You recollect you ascribed to me the formation of the ordinance of the Old Congress of July 13th. 1787. Since writing you last,[1] I have seen Mr [Thomas Hart] Benton's speech on the subject,[2] in the National Intelligencer of March 6th, 1830, in which, I find, on no authority, he ascribes its formation, in substance to Mr Jefferson; that is, that Mr. Jefferson formed an ordinance in 1784, & he seems to infer, from that the Ordinance of '87 was taken or copied. This inference of Benton's, has not the least foundation, as thus appears. Mr Jefferson's resolve or plan, (not ordinance,) of April 23d 1784,[3] is contained in two pages & a half; is a mere incipient plan, in no manner matured for practice, as may be seen. The ordinance of July, 1787,[4] contains eight pages; is in itself a complete system, & finished for practice; and what is very material, there cannot be found in it more than twenty lines taken from Jefferson's plan, & these worded differently. In fact, his plan & this ordinance, are totally different, in size, in style, in form, & in principle. Probably not one person in a thousand knows or suspects this essential difference, or those who read, or are told what Benton has said, nor do I see it much noticed in the debates. Ought not this difference to be made known? Mr Benton's assertion, so groundless, extorts from me the above, & the following exposition, in defence of those who have long ascribed to me the formation.

I observe Mr. Benton & Mr. Hayne both assert, you failed in your proof of the part you ascribed to me. Does that part stand as you wish it to remain? I remember you once asked me for some account of this ordinance, & that I gave you an account in a few words, & referred to the 7th. Vol. of my Abridgment, chap. 223.[5] If then I had, in the least, anticipated what has taken place, I should have given you a much fuller account. As in the endless debate, you may have an opportunity, in a note or otherwise, to use further evidence, I will state a small portion.

1. As I am the only member of Congress living who had any concern in forming, or in passing this ordinance, no living testimony is to be expected.

2. In the North American Review of July, 1826, pages 1 to 41, is a review of my "General Abridgment," &c., of American law. In page 40, it is said, I "was the framer of the celebrated ordinance of Congress of 1787." At present, it is enough to add this fact, stated in the Inaugural Discourse of Judge Story, page 58.[6] Neither of these, it seems, Mr. Hayne has read, and he could only find me in that *aged* (& really harmless) convention, which so unnecessarily excited fear & alarm, as history will be able to show.

Generally, when persons have asked me questions respecting the ordinance, I have referred to the ordinance itself, as evidently being the work of a Massachusetts lawyer, on the face of it. I now make the same reference, and to its style found in my Abridgment, &c.

3d. When I mention the formation of this ordinance, it is proper to explain. It consists of three parts. 1st, The titles to estates, real & personal, by deed, by will, & by descent; also personal by delivery. These titles occupy the first part of the ordinance, not a page, evidently, selected from the laws of Massachusetts, except it omits the double share of the oldest son. These titles were made to take root in the first & early settlements, in 400,000 square miles. Such titles so taking root, we well know, are, in their nature, in no small degree *permanent*; so, vastly important. I believe these were the first titles to property, completely republican, in Federal America; being in no part whatever feudal or monarchical. In my 9th Vol. chap. 223 continued, titles, &c., in the several States, may be seen the dregs of feudality, continued to this day, in a majority of our States. 2d. It consists of the *temporary* parts that ceased with the territorial condition; which in the age of a nation soon pass away; &

hence are not *important*. These parts occupy about 4 pages. They designate the officers, their qualifications, appointments, duties, oaths, &c., & a temporary legislature. Neither those parts, nor the titles, were in Jefferson's plan, as you will see. The 3d part, about three pages, consists of the 6 *fundamental articles of compact*, expressly made *permanent*, & *to endure for ever*, so the most important & valuable part of the ordinance. These, & the titles to estates, I have ever considered the parts of the ordinance that give it, its peculiar character & value; & never the *temporary* parts, of short duration. Hence, whenever I have written or spoken of its formation, I have mainly referred to these titles & articles; not to the *temporary* parts, in the forming of which, in part, in 1786, Mr. [Charles] Pinckney, myself, and, I think, [Melancton] Smith, took a part. So little was done with the report of 1786, that only a few lines of it were entered in the Journals. I think the files, if to be found, will show that report was re-formed, and temporary parts added to it, by the committee of '87; and that I then added the titles & 6 articles—5 of them before the report of 1787 was printed, & the 6th article after, as below.[7]

4th. As the *slave* article has ever principally attracted the public attention, I have as you will see, ever been careful to give Mr. Jefferson & Mr. [Rufus] King their full credit in regard to it. I find in the Missouri contest, 10 years ago, the slave owners, in Congress, condemned the six articles generally, & Mr [Charles] Pinckney, one of the committee of 1786, added, they were an attempt to establish a *compact*, where none could exist, for want of proper parties. This objection, & also, the one stating the ordinance was an *usurpation*, led me to add pages 442, beginning *remarks* to page 450, in which I labored much to prove it was no usurpation, & that the articles of compact were valid. They may be referred to, as in them may be seen the style of the ordinance, though written 34 years after that was. Slave owners will not claim as Mr. Pinckney's work, what he condemned. Careful to give Mr. J. & Mr. K. full credit in pages 443, 446, 7th Vol. I noticed Mr. Jefferson's plan of '84, & gave him credit for his attempt to exclude slavery after the year 1800. I may now add, he left it to take root about 17 years; so his exclusion was far short of the 6th article in the ordinance. p[age] 446, I noticed the motion (Mr King's) of March 16, 1785, & admitted it to be a motion to exclude slavery, as fully as in the 6th article. I now think I admitted too much. He moved to exclude slavery only from *the States*, described in the resolve of Congress, of April 23, 1784, Jefferson's resolve, & to be added to it. It was very doubtful whether the word, *States*, in that resolve, included any more territory, than the individual State ceded; & whether the word *States* included preceding *territorial condition*. Some thought his motion meant only *future* exclusion, as did

Mr. Jefferson's plan clearly; therefore, in forming the ordinance of '87, all about states, in his plan, was excluded, as was nearly all his plan, as inspection will prove, and that ordinance made, in a few plain words, to include "the territory of the United States northwest of the river Ohio" —all made for the purposes of temporary government, one district— and the 6th article excludes slavery forever from "the said territory." One part of my claim to the slave article, I now, for the first time, state. In April, 1820, (Missouri contest,) search was made for the original manuscript of the ordinance of '87. Daniel Bent's[8] answer was, "that no written draft could be found"—but there was found attached to the printed ordinance, in my handwriting, the sixth article, as it now is— that is, the slave article. So this article was made a part of the ordinance, solely by the care of him, who says Mr. Benton no more formed the ordinance of '87 than he did. I have Bent's certificate, &c.

5. In pages 389, 390, sec. 3. 7th Vol. I mention the ordinance of '87 was framed, mainly, from the laws of Massachusetts. This appears on the fact of it; meaning the titles to estates, and nearly all the 6 articles, the *permanent* & important parts of it, & some other parts; & in order to take the credit of it to Massachusetts, I added, "this ordinance (formed by the author, &c.) was framed," &c. I then had no idea it was ever claimed as the draft of any other person. Mr. Jefferson I never thought of. In the Missouri contest, Mr. [William] Grayson was mentioned as the author, but as he never was on any committee in the case, nor wrote a word of it, the mention of him was deemed an idle affair. We say, & properly, Mr. Jefferson was the author of the Declaration of Independence, (or formed it, as you observe,) yet he no more than collected the important parts, & put them together. If any lawyer will critically examine the laws & constitutions of the several States, as they were in 1787, he will find the titles, 6 articles, &c. were not to be found any where else, so well as in Massachusetts, and by one, who in '87, had been engaged several years in revising her laws. See N[orth] A[merican] Review, July, 1826, pages 40–41. I have never claimed *originality*, except in regard to the clause against impairing contracts, & perhaps the *Indian* article, part of the 3d article, including, also, religion, morality, knowledge, schools, &c.

6th. The style of the ordinance. Since the year 1782, books & records show my writings, especially in the forms of statutes. My law writings have been extensively published—and often on important subjects, the first draft has been reduced half or more. This process naturally ends in a studied, compressed style, rather hard. Had I room I could refer to numerous parts of my writings, published & not published, to show this style—and this is the style of the ordinance, courteously denominated in the discourse mentioned "a sententious skilfulness of expression." But in a letter already long, only a few cases can be referred to. I go back to 1785, and refer to my statement of the great land titles in Maine, published by the legislature in a pamphlet[9]—some statutes revised on subjects of importance from 1782 to 1801[10]—my Rules & Cases, and Notes, in the American precedents, &c[11]—my defence of Harvard University against the claims of West Boston Bridge, not published, but to be found, no doubt, in the files of the University—my argument in Kilham v. Ward & al., 2 Vol. Mass. Reports[12]—Introduction of my Abridgment—Summary view of executory estates, ch. 114. art. 31— State rights & sovereignty, chap. 143. especially ch. 187—and this chapter continued in the (supplement) 9th Vol., though written 42 years after the ordinance was. It is believed, in these, & other cases, the style of the ordinance can be found.

I am surprised Senators, Benton & Hayne, attempt to place Mr. Jefferson's fame, in any part, on his meagre, inadequate plan of '84. If his exalted reputation rests on no better foundation than this, will it be immortal? I can account for their bold assertions, only on the supposition they had never read his plan.

Thus far I have felt it a duty to state the above facts and matters in the more durable form of writing, for several reasons—one, for the defence of my most respectable & best friends, who long have, publicly, ascribed to me the formation of this ordinance; &, especially, for your defence, who have generously and ably repelled the attacks & sneers, which have mainly produced this letter.

I will only add that, in the years 1784, '85, '86, & '87, the Eastern members in the Old Congress, really thought they were preparing the North Western Territory, principally, for New England settlers; and to them the 3d. & 6th. articles of compact more especially had reference; therefore, when North Carolina ceded her western territory, & requested this ordinance to be extended to it, except the *slave* article that exception had my full assent, because slavery had taken root in it, and it was then probable, it would be settled, principally, by slave owners.

If Mr. Hayne had been as careful to read all the H[artford] Convention did, as he seems to have been to spy out matter of accusation, he would, I think, have seen its liberality towards slave owners in proposing they yield their slave votes, solely on the ground *of their own generosity*, not on any claim of *right* whatever; & if he & Mr. Benton had better noticed the two plans of surveys & sales of the public lands, they would, I think, have hid the southern one under the table, a plan but a little better than that of Mr. Jefferson. So had Mr. Hayne thought a little more of Congress's exercise of *unlimited* power to make new states at pleasure, on any purchased territory, he never would, I believe, have reproached that convention for proposing to restrain such *unlimited*, tremendous power. If Mr. H. can properly advocate, as he does, such *unlimited* power, why may not others advocate power in Congress to make roads & canals, a power far less *unlimited*? Yours sincerely,

N. Dane

LS. MHi. Published in *MHi Proc.*, 1st Series (1867–1869), pp. 475–480.

1. Not found.

2. *Register of Debates*, 21st Cong., 1st sess., pp. 95–119.

3. Worthington C. Ford, et al., eds., *Journals of the Continental Congress* (Washington, D.C. 1904–1937), 26: 275–279. There were few changes between Jefferson's plan and the Ordinance of 1784.

4. *Journals of the Continental Congress*, 32: 334–343.

5. *A general abridgement and digest of American law, with occasional notes and comments* (9 vols., Boston, 1823–1829).

6. Joseph Story, *A discourse pronounced upon the inauguration of the author, as Dane professor of law in Harvard University, on the twenty-fifth day of August, 1829* (Boston, 1829).

7. See *Journals of the Continental Congress*, 30: 131–132; 32: 238–241.

8. Probably Daniel Brent, chief clerk of the State Department.

9. The reference is probably to the "Statement of the Kennebeck Claims" of June 15, 1785, which was authorized by a committee made up of Samuel Phillips, Jr., Nathaniel Wells, and Nathan Dane. See *Documentary History of Maine* (24 vols., Portland, 1869–1916), 21: 72–119.

10. Dane, George R. Minot, and John Davis, eds., *Laws of the Commonwealth from 1780 to the end of 1800* (Boston, 1801).

11. *American Precedents of Declarations* (Boston, 1801), anonymously authored by Joseph Story, Benoni Perham, and apparently Nathan Dane.

12. *Asa Kilham* v. *Benjamin Ward, Jun. et al.*, 2 Massachusetts Reports 236.

TO [ISAAC P. DAVIS]

Washington March 29, '30

My Dear Sir

I perceive the Booksellers are threatening to afflict the community with a book, made up of my speeches. This offence is one, for which they are answerable only to the public, & to their own pockets. But it seems further intended, that I shall be compelled to lend my *countenance* to the undertaking. To this, I demur. By an advertisement which happened to catch my eye in the Nat[ional] Int[elligencer] this morning,[1] it would seem that the Book is to have a head in it, from [Gilbert] Stuarts picture. This without my consent; & I suppose it only said, subject to a tacit condition, that such consent should be first had & obtained. I have written the proposed publishers,[2] on the subject. The object of this is merely to repeat to you the substance of what I have said to them. If they insist, first on making the book, which I suspect they had better not do, & secondly on having a head in it, which I do not at all desire they should, but prefer much they should not, I am willing to take the proper course to have a correct & handsome engraving, from Stuart's picture, or from one to be made by [Chester] Harding.³ I am agt. all *lithographic* things. As yet, *I* have not consented that any body should make an engraving from Stuarts.

You will see the proposed publishers easily, & can learn from them my wishes more at large. I should like your *own* opinion, whether to have an engraving from Stuart, or to give Harding a sitting, for that purpose.

Mrs W[ebster] will leave me in about three weeks, for N York. I shall hasten thither, & thence to Boston, the moment the session closes. I hope to be home by the 25th of May. If I should, we must, once more, wet a line together, in Mashpee. Remember me kindly to Mrs D—& believe me truly Yrs   D. Webster

ALS. NhHi. Published in *PC*, 1: 499–500.

1. The advertisement also appeared in the triweekly edition of the *National Intelligencer* for March 30.

2. Presumably Benjamin Perkins and Theophilus Rogers Marvin of Boston, who later published the volume. The letter referred to has not been found; but see DW to Perkins & Marvin, March 30, mDWs.

3. See above, DW to Charles Brickett Haddock, March 4, 1830, note 8.

FROM BENJAMIN ESTILL

Abingdon 4th. April 1830

Dear Sir.

I thank you for having sent me your speech on Mr. Foots resolution; but I thank you more for having made it, for having prostrated, I trust forever, that mischievous nonsense called Carolina doctrine, and taught its arrogant supporter, a lesson of humility, which neither he nor his party are likely soon to forget. The violent Jacksonians here, rail at the speech, and speaker, in good round terms; a certain proof of their own estimate of their merit, and in my opinion, a higher compliment to both, than the judgment of the candid of all parties, who admit that Mr. Haine was completely prostrated in the debate. I do not wonder that the individual filling the chair, to use his own phraze, winced so much during your remarks; I only wonder at his impudence in pretending to consistency in his opinions: He who as late as 1823 was understood to be an ultra latitudinarian, and who in 1825 in C[arolina], is reported to have said that the Virginia doctrines of Strict construction were with slight modification the true doctrines. He who, whilst Mr. [John] Randolph was violating all the decencies of debate, in calling the President a northern puritan, & his secretary of State, a western blackleg,[1] had no power to call him to order or to preserve order, yet whilst Mr [David] Barton was lashing his colleague [Thomas Hart Benton] and others of that party, made the notable discovery that he had power to call a member to order, which he accordingly exercised, in calling Mr Barton to order, and reminding him that he was using expressions inadmissible in a deliberative body. I remember that in Mr. Randolphs case, he sheltered himself under a construction of the rules of the senate. Have they been since altered? If they have not, then I should like to see by what process of sophistry, he can reconcile his two decisions, and support his claim to consistency. By the by, I think you great men, are morbidly sensitive, on this subject of consistency, so much so that you seem to regard inconsistency in political opinion, as the unpardonable sin in a Statesman. Now I regard change of opinion as the highest proof of integrity in a Statesman, if not the only proof of it; and I think no man need blush to acknowledge that he has profited by experience, and that he grows wiser as he grows older. In a government like ours, confessedly of experiment, there seems to me more reason to expect the Statesman to change his opinions, & that frequently, than under any other; and yet, I should think such change of sentiment, no reproach under the oldest & best understood government; and to be candid, the first moment at which I was able to feel the slightest respect for the Hon. Mr [Thomas] Chilton was, when he honestly announced, that he had been duped by the slang of the day, coalition, reform, &c.[2] I had supposed that with the ballance of that pack he was more knave than fool. That he was using an odious and often refuted calumny like the ballance of his party, to ride into power, and even his celebrated reform resolution I had supposed (for I never saw the man) was merely ad captandum. But now he convinces me that he was an honest dupe, and he entitles himself in some degree, [to] respect by honestly announcing the fact, and refusing longer to be a tool of the party.

Pray present to our friend Mr [Asher] Rob[b]ins, the kindest regard of Mrs E & myself and remind him that it gives us great pleasure to hear from him. And we pray you to accept for yourself our best wishes for your prosperity & happiness.   Benjamin Estill

ALS. NhD. The name is spelled with one "l" in BDAC but the spelling of the signature is followed here.

1. *Register of Debates*, 19th Cong., 1st sess., p. 398.

2. Chilton, from Elizabethtown, Kentucky, was elected to Congress in 1826 as a Jacksonian, pledged to reduce what he regarded as the excessive expenditures of the Adams administration. After three years of failure to achieve this goal, he an-

nounced himself "a friend of HENRY CLAY," and charged the Democrats with being more extravagant than the National Republicans. *National Intelligencer*, March 27, 1830.

TO JEREMIAH MASON

Wednesday Eve' April 14 [1830]

D Sir

A feeble attempt was made to day to reconsider [Isaac] Hill's nomination,[1] but as the rejection had been notified to the President, it was held to be out of order. His game, I think, is finished here. The President has the power, I suppose, of nominating him again; tho' he will hardly be advised to do that, & it would do no good, if he should do so. Nothing could get him thro the Senate, for any office. The rejection has produced a strong sensation here for so small a thing. The poor N. H. members especially are wofully mortified. H[enry] H[ubbard], I learn was heard to say he would rather have lost the whole N. H. Election. [Amos] Kendall's fate & [Mordecai Manuel] Noahs not yet decided. They are both doubtful. I incline to think they will both depend on the casting vote of the V[ice] P[resident.][2]

There was a great party dinner, yesterday, as you will see. The object was to recompose & reconstruct the party, on the old Jefferson platform. The thing did not go off well. Many, very many of the party found themselves taken in. *All the Penna. members, having seen, before dinner, what the toasts were, took themselves off!*[3]

I think we shall see some schism grow out of it. McDuffies Report on the Bank Subject, is not yet printed.[4] It is said to be a stiff negative to the President.

I am tired with the session, & wish myself safely in N. E. Yrs truly

D Webster

How will Mr H[ill] appear, should he be prefered for a seat in the Senate, since ⅔rds of its members have so significantly manifested their opinion of him. *If he were to come there, they could not speak to him.*

Copy. NhHi. Published in Van Tyne, pp. 152–153.

1. Hill's nomination as second comptroller of the Treasury had been rejected on April 12. On the fourteenth a motion to reconsider was ruled out of order by the presiding senator, John Forsyth of Georgia.

2. Action on Kendall and Noah was postponed at this time, but Webster's analysis ultimately proved correct. Kendall was confirmed as fourth auditor on May 10, and Noah as surveyor of the Port of New York on May 28, both by the casting vote of the Vice President.

3. The much publicized Jefferson's birthday dinner, held at Brown's Hotel on April 13. The Pennsylvania members withdrew when they saw

that the prepared toasts were strongly antitariff. Jackson's toast and Calhoun's rejoinder added to the impression of dissention in the party.

4. *Committee Reports*, 21st Cong.,

1st sess., Serial 201, Report No. 358, presented on April 13, 1830 by George McDuffie, chairman of the Committee of Ways and Means.

FROM JOSEPH LANIER WILLIAMS

Knoxville T. April 14th [1830]

Dear Sir—

I have had the pleasure of reading, four or five times over, your Second Speech on Foot's Resolution. Two or three copies, you have sent to my father, Jno. Williams. Pursuant to his advice, I have read the Speech as often as I tell you, not after the usual mode of reading such productions, but for the purpose of studying it. From the Federalist, I have derived some fixed conceptions of the structure of our government; but I now candidly confess that, previously to my seeing the *constitutional* portion of your Second Speech, I was comparatively ignorant on the subject. I consider it the most gigantic argument that was ever made— and, especially, the most inimitably luminous and conclusive exposition of our constitution that has ever been given to the world. These remarks, I presume to make for your own inspection inasmuch as I insist upon them, behind your back, whenever the subject is mentioned. And it may not here be superfluous to say that my opinion is the opinion of nine-tenths of the gentlemen of Ten[nessee]. By gentlemen, I, of course, don't mean, either ragamuffins, fashionable Editors, brawling pettifoggers, or street demagogues. These being, necessarily, Jackson men to the spirit, all think the other way. The copies you sent my father were the first that reached Knoxville. They were subsequently sent by Lewis Williams, Mr [Robert Perkins] Letcher, and other members of Congress. We understood them as intended, not for our own reading only, but for the reading of as many of the community as practicable. Accordingly, we gave them circulation. *Each* copy, by this time, has probably been read by as many as fifty different gentlemen, all capable of understanding it for themselves. They are yet circulating as currently as at first; and there is now a great demand for them. Such is the cause of my addressing you this letter—to procure a few more of them. Will you be so good as to send me, as soon as convenient, a few additional copies? After they have circulated thro' a number of hands, I reclaim them and start them thro' a new channel of circulation, so as not to let them get too far beyond my reach. This has been my habit; and I purpose continuing it. If you should feel any delicacy about franking some of them to me at this place, you could get Lewis Williams to do it. We would have a new edition of the pamphlet stricken off at this place, but its necessary bulk renders that impracticable.

Mr Hayne was rendered deservedly ridiculous by his *classic* illustrations. In the classics, he must be, either *rusty* or superficial. Even I could not but feel contempt for his *right-wrong* application of Banquo's ghost. He must have been made ashamed of this blunder, by your reply; for, from what I have seen of him in the private and social circle at Washington, I judge him to be a man of a good deal of sensibility.[1] And from some personal observation of his senatorial demeanor, I had come to the conclusion that he had some moderation and modesty in his composition; but his late wanton and, to me, disgusting exhibitions, have permanently eradicated all such favorable impressions. Benton! "Alas poor Yorick."—Verbum sat—You treated *him*, quite judiciously. 'Twas right to hand him over to [David] Barton.[2] The latter had his tools ready at hand and knew well the material he was to work upon. Benton must be some thing more than ordinary to be able to hold his head up in the Senate after being afraid to hear Barton deliver his speech and after then seeing it in the prints of the Union. Don't you consider this a very well-timed and brilliant thing of the kind? I think it even as much so as it is original and eccentric. It seems to have made him very conspicuous in the nation as a satirist and independent politician; and the trimming he gave one of our Senators had made him particularly conspicuous in this State. This castigation is merciless and beyond every thing I have ever seen. And *we* in Ten[nessee] know well the accuracy of his delineations of Judge [Hugh Lawson] White. If he had been intimately associated with the Judge, for forty years, in the business of life, he *could not* have given us a portrait of more exact similitude to the original. As a satirist Barton must now stand above the outre nymph [John Randolph] of Roanoke. The latter equals him only in bitterness—and makes a stroke only now and then, which, unassociated with his manner, sometimes so little takes effect as scarcely to cut thro' the skin while Barton is equally as original in his mode of thinking and style of expression— makes continually one stroke after another, always gashing to the bone.

Since I am just thro' one sheet of paper and have thus determined to give you a long epistle, let me ask you a question or two, relative to Judge White and his Indian Report.[3] Did you ever see any thing to equal, in wantonness and insolent contempt of the understandings of others, that part of his Report which says, substantially, that the clause in the constitution giving congress power to regulate commerce or intercourse with the Indian tribes, has reference, not to any Indians residing *within* the chartered limits of the States, but to those only residing *without*? I may grossly misunderstand this branch of the subject; but it does seem to me that this is abominable doctrine. No distinction is made in the constitution with regard to the residence of the Indians; and the Indians with whom, as I understand, we had any intercourse at the time of establishing the constitution, all resided *within* the limits of the States. The latter being the fact would seem to leave no doubt that the "regulating commerce" clause had in contemplation those Indians residing *within* the limits of the States. If I have correctly informed myself, it was not until after the purchase of Louisiana that we had intercourse with Indians residing within our territories and *without* the limits of the States. If it be a fact, as I believe, that, at the time the constitution was formed, there were *no* Indians *in* the U. States *except* those who resided *within* the chartered limits of the States, the futility and stupid folly of the Report is, as I conceive, at once exposed. The doctrine of the Report seems to be condemned by the uniform *practice* of the government. If this be not the case, what becomes of almost all our treaties? Are they not then, null and void? If the "regulating commerce" clause in the constitution has, according to the Report, reference only to those Indians *out of* the limits of the States; and if, as is the fact, most of our territory, acquired by treaty with Indians, has been acquired by treaty stipulations with Indians residing *within* the limits of the States; is it not palpable that, in said treaties, the President & Senate, under this clause, were not a competent contracting party? The Report would seem to be making the President & Senate as having uniformly mistaken the meaning of the constitution—as having uniformly acquired territory by stipulating with those whom they had no right to stipulate with. This, it seems to me, involves too much of an absurdity. And will you believe that this very doctrine is the one which this very Judge White used to ridicule and reprobate? A most astonishing obliquity seems to have attended him on all occasions when the interest of the Indians was involved. Some years since, he, as an advocate, received considerable fees from some Cherokees, to sustain their claim to reservations of land under the treaties of '17 & '19. On those treaties and on the guarantee in one of the treaties referred to in his late Report, he rested the validity of his clients' claim. He procured decisions in their favour. So soon, however, as these causes were disposed of, it was so contrived that he was employed to advocate the other side of the question. For this service, he received large fees; and, in some instances, he actually defeated the reservation claims and yet this Judge White is the man who, when here in Ten[nessee] is, ever industrious in denouncing you, not only by the word of his own mouth, but thro' Haiskell [Frederick S. Heiskell],[4] his standing receptacle of filth, and thro' his numberless other retailers of falsehood and scandal, for your alleged abandonment of avowed principles. In enumerating your political villanies, he generally refers to your Tariff speech in '24 and your vote on the Tariff of '28—and on this point, he reaches the climax of his accustomed invective. If he was not—as Barton appropriately says he is—the congenial compeer of Duff Green, he would not be guilty of the meanness, when here in Ten[nessee] of reiterating that charge against you, after your conclusively satisfactory explanation of your course. And now I should rejoice to see you sunder into atoms his Report, when the Bill is called up for discussion. I have taken the liberty of addressing you this long letter inasmuch as, while at Washington, I have so far had the pleasure of your acquaintance as to share your personal civilities. With the highest respect & esteem, I have the honor to be Yr' Obt Servt

Joseph L. Williams

P.S. I was in the Cherokee nation the other day; and while there, I heard some conversation about Judge White's Bill proposing to send the Indians, nolens volens, West of the Mississippi. Col [Gideon] Morgan,[5] a white man and very intelligent head of an Indian family told me that it was expressly upon White's written, and he thought, published, opinion, that the Cherokees founded their present government on that spot. For unquestionable authority Morgan referred me to Jno. Ross, one of the Head Men of the Cherokee Nation—this too, but a few years before his Indian Report in the Senate! What miserable prostitution to the purposes of the witless old goat—*the purpled ass*—of the White Palace! Would it be improper for some of you no[r]thern Senators to call upon him, in debate, to say whether he had not transmitted to John Ross, the opinion referred to?

ALS. DLC.

1. In Hayne's second speech, he makes Banquo's ghost refer to the "murdered" Adams-Clay coalition of North and West. He was describing the North's rising anxiety over the possibility of a similar alliance between South and West, offered by Benton as the debate on Foot's Resolution got under way. Webster made short work of Hayne's metaphor, noting that Banquo returned to haunt his enemies, not his friends. It was, he pointed out, "at those who had begun with caresses, and ended with foul and treacherous murder, that the gory locks were shaken!"

2. Barton's speech, begun on February 9, was more an attack on his Missouri colleague than a discussion of the point at issue. *Register of Debates*, 21st Cong., 1st sess., pp. 146–159.

3. *Senate Documents*, 21st Cong., 1st sess., Serial 193, Report No. 61. The bitterness of Williams' attack on Senator White underscores the fratricidal in-fighting of Tennessee politics. Senator White was Joseph Williams' uncle, but at this time still a

Jacksonian. Williams' father, John
Williams, had been displaced in the
Senate by Jackson himself, who then
passed the seat on to White, Williams' brother-in-law.

4. Publisher of the *Knoxville
Register* and a political intimate of
White and Jackson.
5. Not otherwise identified.

FROM JOSEPH STORY

Cambridge April 17. 1830

My dear Sir

I was truly comforted by your kind letter, which I received a day or two ago.[1] As soon as I recovered from the severe fatigues of my long & boisterous passage in the Sound, (perilous, withall) & had escaped from the throng of kind friends that called on me, I was about writing you. But an entire new direction was given to my thoughts by the horrible murder of old Captn [Joseph] White at Salem.[2] You are aware that he died childless & that his principal heirs are Mr Stephen White[3] & my sisters children.[4] It is altogether the most mysterious & dreadful affair that I ever heard of. "Truth is stranger than fiction" has been often said. I never knew any case, which so completely illustrated the truth of the remark as this. Not the slightest trace has as yet been found by which to detect the assassins, (for I am satisfied there was more than one) & we are yet in a darkness rendered still darker by the utter defeat of every conjecture. I have been obliged to go to Salem several times, & every thing there seems in inextricable confusion. I never knew such an universal panic. It is not confined to Salem, or Boston, but seems to pervade the whole community. We are all astounded & looking to know from what quarter the next blow will come. There is a universal dread & sense of insecurity, as if we lived in the midst of a Banditti.

I am satisfied the object was plunder, though it was not probably found, having been removed some time before from the house. It was a deep scheme, by persons who were adept in their vocation & irretrievably wicked, damned spirits. Its success is astonishing. Its malicious deliberation unparalled.

Mr White left a Will. He has given many legacies to his relatives; but the bulk of his fortune goes to Mr Stephen White, who will get from 150 to 200 thousand dollars. Three of my Neices will receive about 25,000 each. But of this no more.

I have been in several circles of our friends since my return, all of whom speak in the most gratifying terms of your Speeches. The first effect has not in any degree subsided; admiration & respect seem to have assumed a permanent mastery over all the meaner views of the doubters & the grumblers. There never was a triumph more complete

& to all appearance more undisputed. I hear, however, that at the South there is a little rally; but I suspect it is a feint.

I met Mr [William Hickling] Prescott the other day & I know you will be pleased to know that he thinks most highly of your speeches, deeming them all that we could wish & as sound as they are striking. His praise is worth much, for it is considerate & slow.

In respect to the Circuit Court I have no objection to any adjournment, which will suit the convenience of the Bar. If *after* the R Island court it will be agreeable to me. Arrange, as you think best on this subject remembering only, that our hot weather begins soon after the 20th of June.

All your friends ˙are impatient to see *Mr* Webster, & above all *Mrs Webster*; & I am quite sure she will be doubly welcomed *home*, for we are quite bent upon making her give up all thoughts that she has any other home than Boston. And Mrs Story & myself are anxious to prove to her, that Cambridge is not more than three miles from town, & a good deal more pleasant & quiet than Pennsylvania Avenue.

I have talked a little with the Saints about a certain thing.[5] They are satisfied with my views, to wait events, & agree that it is not well to say a word until a movement shall be made else where. N England never seemed <disposed> less inclined to quarrel with her own than now; but she will be wise & frugal of her resources.

The rejection of [Isaac] Hill has given, I believe, general satisfaction. If followed up by others of a like cast, it will do the Admin more good, than any of their measures. Are the reports of the [Jefferson] Birth Day Dinner arrangements & Developments mere gossip, or true?

I write you in great haste, being hard driven by business but always Most truly Your friend   Joseph Story

P.S. Remember me most kindly to Mr [Nathaniel] Silsbee & his family— & to Mrs Webster & Julia. Forget not my admonition about your self. Work & think as little as practicable for the present.

ALS. NhHi. Published in Van Tyne, pp. 153–155.

1. DW to Joseph Story, April 10, 1830, mDW 8651.

2. Born August 23, 1748, Joseph White had been a shipmaster, but soon became a wealthy merchant in Salem.

3. Born in Salem on July 10, 1778, Stephen White, a nephew of the murdered man, married Harriet, the daughter of Elisha and Mehitable Story of Marblehead. She died in 1827, and White moved to Boston about 1830. While living in Salem, White was an enterprising merchant and had been elected to the state legislature several times. He soon was to become one of Webster's close friends and financial angels.

4. Harriet Story White's children included: Harriet (or Harriette as she generally wrote it) Story, born November 1809, who married James

William Paige of Boston in 1831; Caroline, born June 1811, who married Daniel Fletcher Webster on November 27, 1836; Ellen Marion, born August 1812, who married John

Benjamin Joy; and Joseph, born January 1814, who died in Boston in 1838.

5. Neither the "Saints" nor the "certain thing" have been identified.

TO HENRY CLAY

Washington April 18. 1830

My Dear Sir

We have heard with great pleasure of your safe arrival at your own home, after your interesting trip down the great river; & we all enjoyed, as sincerely as you could have done, the tokens of regard & affection which the good people manifested towards you, at the various points of your tour. More than all, it was gratifying to hear from Mr [Joel Roberts] Poinsett such excellent account of your health.

You see every thing we do here without, I fear deriving much pleasure from any part of it. It will be a session without much *outcome*. The poor Senate is put to hard service, but, in general, takes it all very patiently. It is now said we are to have a renomination of [Isaac] Hill! If that should not be the case, I suppose Mr [Virgil] Maxcy, of Maryland, may likely be nominated to the place—at least, if Mr Calhoun's wishes should prevail. So far as the Senate is concerned, every thing was lost by the elections last year in New-Jersey & Louisiana.

I incline to think there is a good deal of reaction & change, in various places, in the public opinion, as to the merits of the present Administration; but there certainly is far less complaint of the enormous abuse of the power of removal than I expected to see. For my part, if there be no popular rebuke of this practice, I think it seriously endangers the continuance & well being of the govt. We shall make a stand agt. the rest of the printers. If *all* our own friends would go with us, we should reject them all. But the mortification is, that when a case is presented so bad, as that we can get two or three votes from their side, some one of our own friends falls off, & quits us.[1] The chance, in regard to Noah, & your sweet friend Kendall is about even. At worst, we hope to put their confirmation on the Vice President.

The New Orleans Road bill,[2] you perceive, is lost. For my own part, I am tired of struggling for this & similar measures, against Administration influence, & the Administration party. I believe it may be as well to let their own notions prevail, & to let the people see & feel the results to which those notions lead.

The dinner of the 13th was not only a failure, but has given great offense. The Penna members, having, before dinner, obtained a sight of the *toasts*, seceded in a body. It is said *they* talk of a dinner. The object of those who originated the proceeding of the 13th was to give a *state right anti Tariff* tone & character to the whole party. It was to found the party on *Southern* principles, & such principles as should exclude, not only their avowed political opponents, but Mr. Van Buren's friends also.

The President means to be re elected. He *has* meant so, all along. Seeing this, V. B. has been endeavoring to make a merit of persuading him to do so, on the ground of its being necessary to keep the party together. Calhoun is more than half reconciled to it from two considerations; first, he hardly feels as confident as he has done, of his own present strength; second, he regards the chance of *succession*, in seven years, as pretty important. If any thing should prevent Genl J. from being a candidate for re election, my hopes would now be exceeding strong of beating both V. B. & C. How it will be expedient for us to act, in case the present incumbent should actually be candidate again, we can better determine hereafter. My own firm belief is, that if we were to let the Administration, this session & the next, have their own way, & follow out their own principles, they would be so unpopular as that the Genl. could not possibly be re elected. I do not mean by this, that we should let them disturb the Tariff; or injure any other existing interest; still less, that we should, in the slightest degree, vote or act against our own principles. All these being safe, & all existing interests preserved, I still think if we leave to them to decide on *new* measures, of internal improvement &c, according to *their* own will, they will soon find what the sense of the people is. But I forbear further *talk*.

I pray you to make my most sincere regards to Mrs Clay, & to believe me always cordially & truly Yrs   D. Webster

I sent you a copy of my Speech. I send now two or three more, for any friends in yr neighborhood who may wish to read so long a story.

ALS. DLC. Published in Colton, *Henry Clay*, pp. 259–260 (in part).

1. The reference is to a reprinting of the public documents proposed by Gales and Seaton. A resolution providing for a subscription to the series by the secretary of the Senate had been passed on January 29. A motion to postpone the subscription was tabled on February 1, but was amended on the twenty-fourth to the effect that an appropriation for the purpose must first be made, and that proposals from other printers must be heard. The amended resolution was still being debated when this letter was written. The original resolution was finally repealed on May 17, but in the following session the subscription to Gales and Seaton was approved by both houses. The resulting reprint is familiar as *American State Papers*.

2. A bill to construct a national road from Buffalo to New Orleans by way of Washington was defeated in the House 105 to 88 on April 14.

TO NATHAN HALE

Washington April 24. 1830

Dr. Sir,

I fear we shall have an Impeachment here[1]—& if so, I should [like] to have, as a book containing some useful matter on such subjects, *Prescott's Trial.*[2] Will you look up, & send me a copy of that trial. Mark it for me, on an inside envelope—put on an outside envelope, & address it to "Walter Lowrie Esqr., Secretary of the Senate, Washington" Yrs truly   Danl Webster

ALS. MHi.

1. James Hawkins Peck, federal district court judge in Missouri, was impeached by the House in April 1830, but the actual trial before the Senate did not take place until the next session of Congress. It lasted from December 13, 1830, to January 31, 1831, when Peck was aquitted. The charges against Peck had been accumulating for some time. See DW to Charles Miner, March 24, 1827, *Correspondence*, 2: 173–174.

2. *Trial by Impeachment of James Prescott, Probate Judge* (Boston, 1821). Prescott, a probate judge in Middlesex County, Massachusetts, was impeached in 1821 on fifteen articles which included charges of indiscretion in accepting fees and acting as a consultant in cases pending before his own court. The trial lasted from February 6 to April 27, 1821, at which time Prescott was found guilty on three of the articles and removed from office. Webster, along with such other noted lawyers as George Blake and Samuel Hoar, served as counsel for Prescott. Webster's argument in Prescott's defense was published later in 1830 in his *Speeches and Forensic Arguments*, pp. 138–169.

TO WILLIAM PLUMER, JR.

Washington April 24. 1830

Dear Sir

I thank you for your kind letter of the 27 April [March].[1] If my speech has done, or shall do, the slightest good, I shall be sufficiently gratified. It was, in the strictest sense, unexpected, & occasional; yet I am willing to confess, that having the occasion thus forced upon me, I did the best I could, under its pressure. The *subject* & the *times* have given it a degree of circulation, to which its own merits could not have entitled it. Connected with this subject, *one* good thing—excellent, & most important—will ere long be made known. At present, it is locked up in confidence. All I can say is, & I wd. not have that repeated, except perhaps to yr father, that the world will one day—perhaps not a distant one—know *Mr Madison's* sentiments on these constitutional questions, fully & precisely; together with his understanding of the Va. Resolutions of 1797–8.[2]

It will be an important paper.

It is now thought, that pains are taking to *sound* the Senate, with a view of ascertaining the expediency of a *renomination* of Isaac Hill. No doubt, a great effort will be made. I hope, not with success. I never shall believe he can either get *thro'* the Senate, or get *into* it, till I see it.

It is difficult to get copies of the Executive Journal. I have obtained one, this session, for Ch[ancellor James] Kent. If *possible*, I will hunt up another set for you; but if not this year, have little doubt I can do it next. If I can get it, will see it sent, in a safe manner.

It seems now to be understood that the actual Incumbent of the Presidency intends to stand for a reelection. This disappoints more than one.

If that should not happen, I hesitate not to say I think Mr Clay's chance much the best. He is evidently gaining, in the west, & among the political men here. What will be advisable, if Genl. J. should be again candidate, cannot now be decided.

I shall be happy to hear from you, as often as you will confer that favor. Have the goodness to present my regards to your father, & believe me, with much sincere respect, Yrs   Danl Webster

ALS. MB. Published in part in Peter Harvey, *Reminiscences and Anecdotes of Daniel Webster* (Boston, 1877), pp. 155–156.

1. Not found.

2. Webster was undoubtedly aware of the recent exchange between Madison and Edward Everett. See Madison to Everett, April 8 and 17, 1830, Everett Papers, MHi. Madison thought the debates on Foot's Resolution had "thrown lights on some constitutional questions" but had also shown "errors which have their sources in an oblivion of explanatory circumstances, and in the silent innovations of time on the meaning of words & phrases." He then sent Everett a copy of "a sketch" of his "views" originally requested by Hayne which was subsequently published with only minor changes in the *North American Review*, 31 (August 1830): 537–546.

TO JOHN WOODS

Washington April 24. 1830

My Dear Sir,

I thank you for your very kind letter of the 31 March,[1] & am glad to hear so favorable an account of the state of public opinion & feeling in your quarter. As much may be said, I think, of the tone of things here. Our friend Mr Clay appears to me be growing every day more & more strong in the hopes & confidence of the County; & I cannot but think that whenever a change takes place, he is most likely to succeed to the Executive Chair. In New England he has a very firm hold on public opinion.

It seems difficult, at present, to take any step to make him a candidate, more distinctly than he is such already. It is yet a good while to the election; & my own opinion is, that he gains by every hour that elapses before a new controversy begins.

I regret, very much, that I am again disappointed in my hopes of seeing Ohio. The session will be long, & is likely to be still further protracted by an *Impeachment*.[2] All these things will keep me to so late a period, that if I visit the west, it will be mid summer before I see N. E. Next year is the short session. Nothing extraordinary occurring to prevent, I intend going over the mountains, on the rising of the Supreme Court, say abt. April 1st, & passing 3 or 4 weeks in Western Penna & Ohio.

I thank [you] for your civil commendation of my speech. It gratifies me to find that it has circulation in your State.

As often as you have leisure, it will give me much pleasure to hear from you, & to keep up & cherish our acquaintance. I am, Dr Sir, with regard, Yrs truly   Danl Webster

ALS. NhHi.
1. Not found.
2. Of Judge James H. Peck. See

above, DW to Hale, April 24, 1830, note 1.

FROM HENRY CLAY

Ashland, 29th April, 1830.
My Dear Sir:

I received to-day your very acceptable favor of the 18th instant.[1] The copies of the speech to which it refers have not been received, but probably will come safe to hand. If they do not, it is to be hoped that the seed may not fall on barren ground. I congratulate you on the very great addition which you have made during the present session to your previous high reputation. Your speeches, and particularly that in reply to Mr. Hayne, are the theme of praise from every tongue; and I have shared in the delight which all have felt. I trust that they will do much good. It is a great consolation to the honest patriot that, whatever may be his own fate, his principles will stand, and his country, sooner or later, derive the benefit of their illustration and establishment. To that consolation you will be eminently entitled.

I have attentively observed the course of measures and events in and out of Congress. If all shall not have been, much will be, done to bring the public mind back to soberness and truth; and I yet see no cause of despair. It is greatly to be regretted that the Senate has not better fulfilled its high duties incident to the power of appointment. It ought to have rejected all nominations made to supply persons dismissed for political cause; all to replace those whom they approved at the last session; most of the printers, and most of the members of Congress. If it has left undone some things which it ought to have done, we ought to be thankful for some of its rejections. Those of [Henry] Lee[2] and Hill are especially entitled to the public gratitude; and I hope it will place us under a similar obligation for the rejection of Kendall and Noah.

The importance of rejecting certain nominations does not consist in the exclusion merely of unworthy men from office, although that is far from being a minor object; but it shows that Jackson is not infallible nor invulnerable. The character of an eminent public man resembles a fortification. If every attack is repelled, if no breach on any point be made, he becomes impregnable. But if you once make a breach, no matter how small, the work may be carried. Considering how many of his recommendations in his opening message have failed, or are likely to fail, if to their defeat could be added that of some of his more obnoxious nominations, it seems to me that the effect on the public would be very great. Indeed, whatever may be the result of his nominations not disposed of at the date of your letter, the effect of his miscarriages has been considerable. He still shows game, appears stout and strong; but I think his strength is that of the buck, mortally wounded, who springs boldly forward while he is internally bleeding to death.

In this view of the matter, I must respectfully doubt that policy which would surrender to his party their undisturbed course on any subject respecting which they were believed to be wrong. Success too often sanctions; and their success, in reference to the defeat of the power of internal improvement, for example, would, I fear, tend to produce acquiescence in the surrender of the power. If, indeed, they can defeat, at present, the power, after all proper exertions by our friends, good might result from that. We should have done our duty; and the great body of the nation would then see that it was not our fault that they did not get the benefit of the exercise of the power; and that, if they wished for that, they must support us.

My observation induces me to believe that there is a great reaction in respect to the present administration; and that the exercise of the power of patronage is condemned by a vast number of the Jackson party as well as by our own friends. It is true, as you justly remark, that there is less public disapprobation expressed of the dismissions than could have been expected. But, I believe, nevertheless, that it exists very extensively. I speak confidently on this subject as it regards the valley of the Mississippi.

I have noticed the movements at Harrisburg and Albany. The former, if we are rightly informed, was an abortion; and the latter may, I suppose, be considered as essentially Mr. V. B——'s. That Jackson will be again a candidate is highly probable. If he can unite in his support Virginia, Pennsylvania, and New York, opposition to his election will be vain. If either of those States can be detached from him, he may be beaten. What is the probability of their union? You are better judges at Washington than I can be. My information from the western part of Pennsylvania is very flattering; and something may come out of the late celebration of Mr. Jefferson's birthday.

In considering the expediency of using my name in opposition to General Jackson, I desire that every interest and feeling which I may be supposed to cherish in respect to myself should be entirely discarded. The question ought to be examined and decided exclusively in reference to our cause, and, which is the same thing, the great interests of our country. No personal or private considerations ought to have the smallest influence in its determination. If I could make an honorable retreat from public life, forever, it would cost me much less effort to do so than will be believed.

After saying so much, it is scarcely necessary to add that I shall acquiesce—most cheerfully acquiesce—in whatever line of policy my friends may mark out at Washington.

There are three courses: 1. Assuming that Jackson will be a candidate, to abandon all opposition to his reëlection; 2. To hoist our banner, and proclaim, prior to the close of the present session, our candidate; 3. To wait until the next session of Congress.

I shall not discuss the advantages and disadvantages of each. My friends at Washington are more competent, from their superior information, and more impartial than I am, to compare and weigh them.

Even if the second of the suggested courses should be deemed expedient, the question would not be free from difficulty as to the time when and the place where our candidate should be announced. . . .

I shall be glad to hear from you again before the session closes. I am, ever truly your friend, H. Clay

Text from Curtis, 1: 374–376, which is incomplete. Original not found.

1. See above.

2. Henry Lee of Virginia was rejected 46 to 0 by the Senate on March 11 after having been nominated for United States consul general for the City and Kingdom of Algiers.

TO LOUIS DWIGHT

Washington, May 2, 1830.

Sir,

I have received your letter of the 19th of April,[1] asking my opinion upon several questions, all relative to the subject of imprisonment for debt. I am quite willing to express my general opinions on that interesting subject, although they are not so matured as to be entitled to influence other men's judgments. The existing laws, I think, call loudly for revision and amendment. Your first four questions seek to know what I think of imprisonment for small sums. I am decidedly against it; I would carry the exemption to debts of thirty or forty dollars, at least. Individual instances of evil or hardship might, I am aware, follow from such a change; but I am persuaded the general result would be favorable, in a high degree, to industry, sobriety, and good morals, as well as to personal liberty.

You ask, in the next place, what I think of imprisonment for debt in any case where there is no evidence of fraud. Certainly I am of opinion that there should be no imprisonment for debt, where it appears that no fraud has been practised, or intended, either in contracting the debt or in omitting to pay it. But, then, it seems to me, that, when a man does not fulfill a lawful promise, he ought to show his inability, and to show also that his own conduct has been fair and honest. He ought not to be allowed merely *to say* he cannot pay, and then to call on the creditor to *prove* that his inability is pretended or fraudulent. He ought to show why he does not and cannot fulfil his contract, and to give reasonable evidence that he has not acted fraudulently; and, this being done, his person ought to be held no longer. In the first place, the creditor is entitled to the oath of his debtor, and, in the next place, to satisfactory explanation of any suspicious circumstances.

There are two sorts of fraud, either of which, when proved, ought to prevent a liberation of the person, viz: fraud in contracting the debt, and fraud in concealing, or making way with, the means of payment. And the usual provisions of the bankrupt act ought to be added, that no one should be discharged, who is proved to have lost money in any species of gaming; and I should include, in this class, *all adventures in lotteries.* Having tendered his own oath, and made just explanation of any circumstances of suspicion, if there be such, and not having lost money by gaming, the debtor ought to be discharged at once; which answers another of your questions; for the detention of thirty days, before the oath can be taken, appears to me wholly useless.

You are pleased to ask whether, in my judgment, Christians can, with a good conscience, imprison, either other Christians or infidels. He would be very little of a Christian, I think, who should make a difference, in such a case, and be willing to use a degree of severity towards Jew or Greek, which he would not use towards one of his own faith. Whether conscientious men can imprison anybody for debt, whom they do not believe dishonest or fraudulent, is a question which every man, while the law allows such imprisonment, must decide for himself. In answer to your inquiry, whether I have found it necessary to use such coercion, in regard to debts of my own, I have to say, that I never imprisoned any man for my own debt, under any circumstances; nor have I, in five and twenty years' professional practice, ever recommended it to others, except in cases where there was manifest proof, or violent and unexplained suspicion, of intentional fraud.

Imprisonment for debt, my dear sir, as it is now practised, is, in my judgment, a great evil; and, it seems to me, an effectual remedy for the larger part of the evil is obvious. Nineteen twentieths of the whole of it would be relieved, in my opinion, if imprisonment for *small debts* were to be abolished. That object I believe to be attainable; and to its attainment, I think, the main attention of those who take an interest in the subject should be directed. Small credits are often given, on the confidence of being able to collect the debt by the terrors of the jail; great ones, seldom or never.

Three simple provisions would accomplish all, in my opinion, that may be considered as absolutely required to a just state of the law, respecting imprisonment for a debt in Massachusetts.

1. That no imprisonment should be allowed, when the debts, exclusive of costs, did not amount to $30.

2. That there should be no necessity of imprisonment for thirty days, as preliminary to taking the poor debtor's oath; nor any longer detention than such as is necessary to give parties notice, and time to prepare for examination; and that a convenient number of magistrates, in every county, should, for the purpose of administering the oaths, be appointed by the government; and that such magistrates should be clothed with such further powers as might be thought expedient, in order to enable them to make a thorough investigation of the fairness or fraud of the debtor's conduct.

3. That in cases where the debtor had been discharged, if the creditor would make oath to newly discovered evidence, proving original fraud, or, to his belief, that the debtor had subsequently received property, and concealed or withheld the same from his creditors, it should be competent to such creditor to have investigation of such charge, and, if made

out, to have execution against the person, and if not made out, that the creditor should pay the cost of the proceeding.

Other provisions might doubtless be useful; but if these three alone could be obtained, they would, in a great measure, clear the jails of debtors, and give general satisfaction, I have no doubt, to creditors.

I ought to add that the imprisonment of females in the common jails, for mere debt, is a barbarism which ought not to be tolerated. Instances of such imprisonment, though rare, do yet sometimes occur, under circumstances, that shock every humane mind. In this respect, the law ought, in my judgment, to be altogether reformed.

Printed in *Speeches and Forensic Arguments*, 1: 519–520. Dwight (1793–1854; Yale 1813, Andover Theological Seminary 1819), was the founder in 1825 and secretary until his death of the Prison Discipline Society of Boston. He was especially active in reforming insane asylums and juvenile reform schools. Dwight's printed letter to Webster was part of a general nationwide solicitation for opinion. See *Reports of the Prison Discipline Society, Boston. 1826–1835* (Boston, 1855), 1: 376–395. Webster's response was one of moderation, but more fully developed than many other responses of a similar persuasion. Since the reply was published in his first volume of speeches in 1830, Webster may have viewed the issue as politically popular enough to take a public stand. Van Buren, Webster's strongest rival for the Presidency after Jackson, had been identified with the issue in New York from as early as 1813 when he delivered an opinion on the subject in the Court of Errors. Edward M. Shepard, *Martin Van Buren* (Boston and New York, 1888), pp. 21–23. In the 1820s he advocated its abolition while in the United States Senate. His efforts culminated with passage in January 1828 of a bill to abolish imprisonment under judgments rendered by federal courts for debts not fraudulently incurred. It was several years before a broader bill was passed. See 4 *U.S. Statutes at Large* 467–469, 595. New York Democrats under the leadership of Tammany's Silas Stilwell capitalized on the political potential of the reform in 1831 when they sponsored legislation and succeeded in wiping out debtors' prisons in the state.

1. Printed circular with MS notes for reply and ANS transmittal by DW, mDW 8679.

TO WARREN DUTTON

Washington May 9. 1830

My Dear Sir,

I thank you for your favor of Apr. 19.[1] To receive a letter at Washington which says nothing of business, little of politics, & gives a little honest Boston talk, such as the writer & the reader might hold together, if they were taking a turn in the mall, is quite refreshing. In general, when

I open a letter, the silent question which I put to myself is, who is this, that wants a *cadetship*, or a *midshipman's warrant*, or an *office*, or an *errand done*, at one of the Departments. Now & then, it is true, there is a professional letter, of rather more agreeable contents.

My new wife ran away a fortnight ago, & took Julia with her. She is visiting her friends & leaving her P. P. Cs[2] in New York—so that when I catch up with her, as the boys say at School, she may be ready for transplantation to Boston. When that will be, I cannot exactly tell. Nothing moves here, but time; or, rather, we all keep in motion, without making progress; like that movement among soldiers, which is called *marking time*; when they lift up their feet, & put them down again, without going forward. We have been principally occupied in *marking time*, since the first Monday in Decr. For the next two weeks, we shall have a scene of confusion, some pressing to take up particular measures—some pressing to keep them off. "Indian Bill"—"Tariff"—"Massachusetts Claim"[3] —"Time of adjournment"—a din will come, from all these & twenty more such, enough to split the ear.

The Tariff Bill, (improperly so called) will pass the House & probably the Senate. Our Mass[achusetts] Delegation in the House have greatly distinguished themselves on that measure. They appear to me to have overcome the Southerners, in the judgt of all the impartial. Mr. [Benjamin] Gorham made an excellent speech.[4] It was clear, & strong, & manly. There was less of his peculiar ingenuity than I have witnessed in some former instances, but far more tone for decision, & force, than in any other effort of his, within my knowledge. [John] Davis had immediately preceded him, & necessarily occupied some of his ground.[5] You know little probably of Davis. He is a singularly clear-headed man. You will read his speech with great pleasure; that is, if you ever read, with pleasure, speeches on questions of political economy, & <*questions*> connected with it. For my part, tho' I like the investigation of particular questions, I give up what is called the "Science of political economy." There is no such science. There are no rules, on these subjects, so fixed & invariable, as that their aggregate constitutes a science. I believe I have recently run over twenty volumes—from Adam Smith to Professor [Thomas Roderick] Dew,[6] (of Va.)—& from the whole, if I were to pick out, with one hand, all the mere *truisms*, &, with the other, all the doubtful propositions, little would be left.

On Monday we propose to take up [Amos] Kendall & [Mordecai M.] Noah. My expectation is, they will both be *confirmed*, by the casting vote of the V. P.—if the Senate should be full, as I think it will be. A week ago, I was confident of their rejection; but one man, who was relied on, will yield, I am fearful, to the importunities of friends, & the *dragooning of* Party.[7] We have had a good deal of Debate, in closed Session, on these subjects, sometimes pretty warm. Some of the Speeches, I suppose, will be hereafter published.—none of mine, however. Were it not for the fear of the out door popularity of Genl Jackson, the Senate would have negatived more than half of his nominations. There is a burning fire of discontent, that must, I think some day, break out. When men go so far as to speak warmly against things, which they feel bound to vote for, we may hope they will soon go a little further. No more of politics.

We have now & then a Bostonian or two here. Your Jackson friends would not stay, long enough to see or be seen. Wm Sawyer & [William] Powell Mason[8] are here, bound to Cincinnati. Mr D[aniel] P[inckney] Parker[9] is here also, with his daughter, & so is my countryman, that good citizen of the world, Mr. A[ndrew E.] Belknap.[10]

I am right down homesick. I want to go to Sandwich, with I[saac] P. [Davis]—first having had a look at you all. At any rate, I wish to shift this present scene—to get out of the Pennsylvania Avenue—to hear no more of bills, resolutions, & motions. I never felt more completely weary of a session. If it do not terminate soon, I shall run away & leave it. I pray you to make my very best regards to Mrs Dutton. Yours ever truly

D. Webster

If instead of a letter, I could send you *peas & strawberries* which were very fine on our table yesterday, I think it would be a better offering.

ALS. NhD. Published in part in *PC*, 1: 500–502. Dutton (1774–1857; Yale 1797) was a newspaper editor, Boston lawyer, and state legislator.

1. Not found.

2. Leaving her calling cards; literally, *pour prendre congé*.

3. For services of the Massachusetts militia in the War of 1812, amounting to more than $800,000. *Committee Reports*, 21st Cong., 1st sess., Serial 200, Report No. 223.

4. *Register of Debates*, 21st Cong., 1st sess., p. 896.

5. *Ibid.*, pp. 872–884.

6. Dew (1802–1846), professor of political economy and metaphysics at William and Mary College. His *Lectures on the Restrictive System*

were published in 1829.

7. Probably James Iredell of North Carolina, whose vote on May 10 in favor of Kendall brought about a 24–24 tie, which the Vice President broke in the affirmative. Iredell then voted against the confirmation of Noah, who was rejected 25 to 23.

8. Sawyer (1774–1860; Harvard 1800), New Hampshire lawyer; Mason (1791–1867; Harvard 1811), Boston lawyer.

9. Parker (1781–1850), Boston merchant.

10. Belknap (1779–1858), writer and commercial agent, son of the Reverend Jeremy Belknap, the New Hampshire historian.

TO JOHN EVELYN DENISON

Washington May 10. 1830

I begin, My Dear Sir, by confessing my faults. It is long since I wrote you, & I have no apology, but the evil habit of omitting today that which may be done tomorrow. Let me assure you I never forget you, nor lose sight of you; from the moment when you last wrote me, when you was just going, but did not go, on a little "family party" to India, to the present, whether in office or out, I have kept a wakeful eye upon you. My friend Mr [Richard] Rush spoke of having seen you, in his late visit to England;[1] & I am indebted to you for a copy of your Brother's very sensible & manly dissertation on Confederacies, recd last autumn.[2]

For the four years, (or five, I believe it may be) since I saw you, my own fortunes have been no otherwise remarkable than as I have experienced domestic changes. I am now the husband of another wife.

Some three years ago, our good people thought I had become old & grave enough for a Senator; wherefore they transferred me to that House of Congress. Mr [Benjamin] Gorham became my successor, as Representative for Boston.

Our political affairs, just now, are destitute of any particular interest. We have our party quarrels—our ins & outs—our likes & dislikes—& we change men, & dynasties; but the Government still keeps on, & holds us thus far safely together. Our foreign relations, like those of our neighbors, are very quiet. We should be glad [if] you would let us into your colonial trade, but if you do not, we shall not quarrel with you on that account. Expensive living, heretofore, the great reduction of prices, now, & the vast overstock of supply, of every kind, beyond the demand, produce what we call here *hard times*; & the country is at present divided, in relation both to the cause, & the remedy. A portion of the South lays all the evil to the *Tariff*—the middle states deny this. The former insists on the repeal of all protecting duties; the latter warmly resists it; & the New England States, tho' not originally in favor of the protecting policy, having now become deeply interested in manufacturing establishments, are not inclined to change back again. All New England, or all with few exceptions, voted against the Tariff of 1824. It is now nearly unanimous against repeal or reduction. But I must send you a speech of mine, to explain this; & will relieve you from further detail here—leaving you to be edified by the speech aforesaid.

You will see strong symptoms of *oppugnation* in the South—especially in So. Carolina. There is, however, I trust, no great danger of violent irregularities. The Tariff will not, at present, certainly, be either repealed or reduced.

Your friend Judge Story has been made a Professor at Law, & has gone to live at Cambridge. He & his brothers of the Bench left us a month ago. The Chief Justice, now almost as old as Lord [James] Mansfield at his retirement, enjoys excellent health, & seems to experience no decay of mind or faculties. We shall break up here in all this month, & for one, I shall be very glad to be off. Summer, & sea shore, are a coincidence of time & place, very favorable to my health & enjoyment.

I shall pack up our blue book[3]—a speech or two, of the session—such as I think will best bear reading across the Atlantic—add one of my own —& ask the favor of Mr [Charles Richard] Vaughan[4] to put them, together with this letter, in the way of reaching your hand. When you see Mr [Edward George Geoffrey Smith] Stanley, Mr Wortley [James Archibald Stuart-Wortley], Mr [Henry] Labouchere, & Col. [Robert Kearsley] Dawson, pray assure them that we hold them in fresh remembrance, on this side the globe. Let not my past omissions forfeit me your future kindness. Pray make my most respectful compliments to Lady Charlotte,[5] & believe me ever, My Dear Sir, with sincere & true regard, cordially yrs   Danl Webster

ALS. DLC. Published in Curtis, 1: 376–377. Denison (1800–1873), member of Parliament and future Speaker of the House of Commons, toured the United States in 1824–1825. The friendship then established with Webster was lifelong. Others of the party, mentioned in the letter, were James A. Stuart-Wortley; Edward Stanley, later earl of Derby and prime minister; Henry Labouchere of the House of Baring; and Colonel Robert K. Dawson of the Royal Engineers.

1. Rush had been sent to England by the towns of Alexandria and Georgetown and the city of Washington to negotiate a loan for the Chesapeake and Ohio Canal for $1.5 million dollars. Although unsuccessful in England despite his many personal contacts, Rush finally secured the loan in Holland.

2. George Anthony Denison, fellow at Oriel College, Oxford, had published his prize essay on "the power and stability of federative governments" from a paper originally read at Oxford on July 1, 1829.

3. This refers to the Biennial Register prepared by the Department of State containing the names and other information of all governmental officeholders.

4. Vaughan (1774–1849) was then British minister to the United States.

5. Nee Charlotte Cavendish Bentinck (d. 1873), third daughter of William, fourth duke of Portland.

TO NATHANIEL F. WILLIAMS

May 14 [1830]

Dr Sir

I send back the draft accepted.[1] I do not think there is much, in the rumour you mention. I believe the President is *resolved* on being reelected, & that other persons are obliged, willing or unwillingly, to submit to this course of things;—& to postpone their own pretentions; altho I think Mr Calhoun comes to this conclusion very reluctantly. Yrs always truly

D Webster

ALS. NhD. Williams (1780–1864) was a Baltimore merchant and life-   long supporter of Webster.

1. Not found.

FROM RALPH RANDOLPH GURLEY

Washington May 15th 1830

My Dear Sir,

Having knowledge of your disposition to relieve the unfortunate, may I solicit your charitable attention to the Bearer a very respectable man of colour, who is seeking some aid to redeem his family. You will be glad to know that the Family of *Philip Lee*,[1] in behalf of which I once sought your friendly assistance, are now free & happy.

With the highest respect & esteem, ever your friend & servant

R R Gurley

ALS. NhHi. Published in Van Tyne, pp. 738–739.

1. Not identified.

TO [AMOS LAWRENCE?]

Washington May 22. 30

My Dear Sir,

Your letter[1] gives me an opportunity of talking freely on a subject which has been suggested to me, from various quarters, & about which I have not said much. I am inclined to avail myself of this opportunity to talk *right on*, & give you the whole of my notions, in regard to the matter. *First*—I have heard that the good people of Boston would, some of them, like to shew me some proof of kindness, by a dinner, a ball, or something else.

Second—That the mode or manner is not yet decided, & that all rests, as yet, in intention. Now, I shall open my heart to you, without reserve.

As to a dinner. There seems to me to be insuperable objections to it. I have recd that compliment, once, as you know—two years ago. It wd. therefore be nothing *new*. But, what is more important, *other persons' feelings might be injured*. Our immediate Rep. [Benjamin Gorham] has acquitted himself very ably, in the H. of R.—& done great honor to the State—so has [John] Davis, & so has [Edward] Everett. In truth, our whole Delegation in the H. of R. is uncommonly able, & all *true*. My colleague [Nathaniel Silsbee] too, tho an unpretending man, has been entirely true, & very useful, in more cases & ways than one. Now it would be invidious to select *me*, alone—as the object of any particular expression of regard. I should, myself, feel that it would be, in some measure, *unjust*. I should think they would have a right to feel *hurt*. And further —my friends know *me*—I know *them*. A public dinner would be no additional proof of regard. I am as sure of their good wishes, & esteem, as if they were to give me a dozen dinners, & ring all the bells for a fortnight. Then, *would it do good elsewhere?* I think not. It would necessarily have some political cast, & however prudently it might be conducted, I suspect it could hardly do good abroad. I am, therefore, My Dear Sir, against a dinner—&, indeed, agt all ostentation, & show, & parade. I believe the interest, as well of my constituents, as of myself is likely to be better promoted by abstaining from all such things. I shall see all Boston—& much of the Commonwealth—in the course of summer—& shall have opportunity of seeing & shaking hands with most, or many of those who take an interest in me, or would wish to give me congratulation.

As to a *Ball*, the sun rides too high for that. Let us think of that, in October.

And now I will tell you what may be done—if you & others see fit. If 50 Gent[lemen] are inclined to make a subscription for a peice of plate —say an urn or some such thing—let them do so. One single article, of size to bear an inscription, would probably be better than more smaller ones. Yet, even this last, which is yr suggestion would be perfectly well.[2]

I have thus spoken to you, in confidence, freely & unreservedly. Whatever you & others do or omit, excepting always a dinner, & any thing else that is ostentatious, will be perfectly satisfactory to me. I know you will, some of you at least, be glad to see me—& that, itself, is high gratification. I owe my neighbors infinitely more than they can ever owe me; & I am satisfied, & gratified, & more than compensated, a thousand times, for any labors or efforts of mine, by the consciousness that I am thought to have done some little good. God bless you—Yrs   D. W.

ALS. MHi. Published in *PC*, 1: 502–503, where the recipient is identified as William Sullivan.

1. Not found.

2. In October 1830 Amos Lawrence presented a "small service of plate, as a testimony of my gratitude for your services to the country, in your late efforts in the Senate, especially for your vindication of the character of Massachusetts and of New England." See Lawrence to DW, October 23, 1830, mDW 8970.

TO NATHANIEL F. WILLIAMS

Saturday Eve May 22. 1830

My Dear Sir,

The fate of the Baltimore & Ohio Rail Road bill was decided today in the Senate *by laying the Bill on the Table.* The vote, I understand, was 22 to 19.[1] Mr [Felix] Grundy & Mr [John] McKinley spoke warmly against it, & urged particularly, the inability of the Treasury to bear the charge, considering, among other things, how great a draft on the public money would be made *by the removal of the Indians,* under the provisions of the Bill now pending in the H. R.[2] And yet your two Baltimore members,[3] I believe seem disposed to go for the Indian Bill, & all the enormous expenditure created by it, let what will happen to other objects. Every Jackson man in the Senate voted against the Bill, if I am rightly informed, except Genl. [Samuel] Smith; & every opposition man for it, with one exception.[4] Genl Smith went all lengths for the Indian Bill; & now that appropriation is urged agt. the Rail Road. The time will come, I trust when Peoples' eyes will be opened.

Dr Sir,

If you communicate the foregoing, let it go in yr handwriting—& let not the source be known or traced. I sent to the Boat today a box containing a variety of speeches &c—which I hope you may make good use of. Yrs   D. W.

AL and ANS. NhD.

1. The bill authorized the government to buy stock in the railroad. It was tabled 21 to 19. Webster's form of expression is ambiguous, since he was present and accounted for one of the nineteen negative votes.

2. This bill passed the House on May 26, with amendments accepted by the Senate. As finally approved the act carried an appropriation of $500,000.

3. The two Baltimore members, Elias Brown and Benjamin Chew Howard, did indeed vote in favor of the Indian Removal Bill.

4. Peleg Sprague, National Republican senator from Maine.

TO JAMES BARBOUR

Washington May 24. 1830

Dr Sir,

I take the liberty of sending you a few copies of my speech, & also of Mr [John] Holmes';[1] supposing it possible you might have a neighbor or two, who would willingly receive from you such an Article.

We are breaking up the session, with much better prospects, I think, for the Country, than those with which we commenced it. Unless we are all greatly misinformed, public opinion, in most parts of the country, is turning strongly against the existing Administration. Recent events here will have an important bearing. The Baltimore Rail Road Bill has been killd in the Senate, by a party vote; & it is now expected that the President will *negative* the Maysville Turnpike Bill. These things place the administration in hostility to Internal Improvement; & as the particular measures are both highly interesting, the first to Maryland & all the West, & the other to Kentucky, & Ohio, they will certainly *tell*, before the people. This truth is perceived clearly, & felt deeply, by the President's friends in the H. of R. I should not be at all surprised, if the conduct of the President & his friends, on these two measures, should be the means, with Heaven's blessing, of preventing the passage of the Indian Bill. I am, Dr Sir, with entire regard, Yrs   Danl Webster

ALS. NN.
1. The second reply to Hayne had only recently been published in pamphlet form. Holmes spoke on the same resolution, February 18, 1830.

TO LEVI LINCOLN

Washington May 24. 30

Private & Confidential
Dear Sir

The H. of R. passed the Bill for the payment of our claims, this day, as amended in that House. But this was at so late an hour, that no *quorum* remained in the Senate, & we could not act on the amendment. Indeed I believe the Senate had actually adjourned, for want of a quorum, before the vote was taken in the House. We hope to be able to act on it, on Monday. There is not a little danger that it may yet be defeated, by accident, or by design. We cannot speak of it, therefore, as a thing accomplished.[1] It seems understood, however, that we are to try to concur, with the House, on Monday, & to take the Bill in that shape. We may have opposition—we may have no quorum—or, for other causes, may yet lose the bill. However, we have embargoed all our friends—& hope to keep a majority in both Houses till the bill shall be passed.

The particular object of this letter is to say something to you upon future measures. The Law, if the Bill become a law, will require a re-auditing of the Accounts. To see this done, the Commonwealth will need agents, to push the business at the Department, & get the money. It is likely not to be inconvenient for *me* to take a part, in this agency; & I have no objection to it, since my time is, so much of it, spent here. I should prefer, however, in the event of having any thing to do in the matter, to have an associate; & I have ventured to write this, for purpose of suggesting to you, that if it should seem proper to appoint an agent, or agents, to pursue this claim, under the law, & obtain the money, it would not be disagreeable to Mr [John] Davis & myself to constitute that agency, provided suitable compensation should be allowed. My own notion is, that on hearing of the passage of the law, the Legislature should pass a Resolution, authorizing the Govr. to appoint an agent or agents, to prosecute the claim, attend to the auditing &c, & to agree with such agent to allow them a commission, not exceeding [blank] per cent on the amt. principle & interest, actually recd, in full for their services, & personal expenses. In this way, a fair compensation might be secured, by what would appear a small commission.

I have hazarded this suggestion to you, with Mr Davis' concurrence. You will judge of it, & feel no embarrassment, on our account, if it should be found convenient to give the matter another direction. Our own impression is, that since some agency must be employed, it is better to find a suitable agent, or suitable agents, among those who know, & are known, *here*; who not only understand the principles & merits of the claim, but are in a situation, also, likely to enable them to draw the attention of the accounting Departments steadily to the subject.

I shall leave the City, the very moment this measure is terminated, & hope to see you in eight days from this time. Meantime, I beg to repeat, that as I have made these suggestions very frankly, you will reject them, I hope & trust, as frankly, if they should not coincide with your opinions of expediency & propriety. With entire regard, Yrs   D. Webster

ALS. MHi.

1. The bill to pay the Massachusetts claim was finally enacted on May 31, 1831. 4 *U.S. Statutes at Large* 428. The Massachusetts General Court passed an enabling resolution June 5, 1830, authorizing the governor and council to appoint an agent, something they did later that month. Two of Lincoln's speeches to the General Court on March 10 and May 30, 1831, refer to John Davis as the Commonwealth's agent, but there is no mention of Webster. See *Massachusetts Acts and Resolves, 1828–1831*, pp. 504–505, 602–603.

TO JAMES MADISON

Washington May 24. '30

Dear Sir

I have hitherto forborne to send you a copy of the speech delivered by me on a recent occasion,[1] from an apprehension, that, since the speech referred to opinions supposed by some, but not admitted by others, to have received your approbation in time passed, you might imagine that I expected from you some intimation of what was the truth, on this point. But, altho' I feel reluctant to omit longer to send you the speech, I pray you to be assured, that I do not feel that I have the slightest right to call on you for any expression of opinion, or any remark on former occurrences. I would not, indeed, conceal my anxious concern not to have misunderstood, or misrepresented, the Resolutions[2] which are understood to have recd. your concurrence; nor my full conviction, that on questions of this kind, your opinions are of the greatest possible weight. Nevertheless, there is nothing which gives me a right to expect from you any suggestion or remark.

I avail myself gladly of this opportunity to present my most respectful and grateful remembrance to Mrs Madison, and to tender to you renewed assurances of my highest respect, and most fervent good wishes.

Danl Webster

ALS. NhD.
1. The second reply to Hayne.
2. The Kentucky Resolutions of

1798 and the Virginia Resolutions of 1799, the former written by Jefferson, the latter by Madison.

FROM JAMES MADISON

Montp[ellie]r May 27. 1830

Dear Sir

I recd. by the mail of yesterday, your favor of the 24th.[1] accompanied by a copy of your late speech, for which I return my thanks. I had before recd. more than one copy from other sources; and had read the speech with a full sense of its powerful bearing on the subjects discussed, and particularly its overwhelming effect on the nullifying doctrine of S. Carolina. Altho I have not concealed my opinions of that doctrine, and of the use made of the proceedings of Virg[ini]a* in 1798–99, I have been unwilling to make a public exhibition of them, as well from the consideration that it might appear obtrusive as that it might enlist me as a newspaper Polemic, and lay me under an obligation to correct errors in other cases in which I was concerned, or by my silence admit that they were not errors. I had however been led by a letter from a distinguished champion of the new doctrine, to explain my views of the subject somewhat at large and in an answer, afterwards to a letter from Mr. Everett to enclose a copy of them.[2] For a particular reason assigned to Mr. E. I asked the favor of him not to regard it as for public use. Taking it for granted that you are in friendship with him, I beg leave to refer you to that communication, as an economy for my pen. The reference will remove the scruple he might otherwise feel in submitting it to your perusal.

The actual System of Govt. for the U. S. is so unexampled in its origin, so complex in its structure, and so peculiar in some of its features, that in describing it the political vocabulary does not furnish terms sufficiently distinctive & appropriate, without a detailed resort to the facts of the case. With that aid I have endeavored to sketch the System, which I understand to constitute the people of the several States one people for certain purposes with a Government competent to the effectuation of them.

Mrs. M. joins in the acknowledg[men]ts & sincere return of your friendly recollections, with the addition of the respects & good wishes wch. we pray may be tendered to Mrs. Webster

* neither the term nullifying nor nullification is in the Resolutions of Virginia; nor is either of them in the Resolutions of Kentucky of 1798 drawn by Mr. Jefferson. The Resolutions of that State in 1799 in which the word nullification appears, were not drawn by him, as is shown by the last paragraph of his letter to W. C. Nicholas. See Vol. 3 of his Correspondence, p. 429.[3]

AL draft. DLC. Published in *Letters and Other Writings of James Madison* (4 vols., Philadelphia, 1865), 4: 84–85.

1. See above.

2. Madison to Hayne, April 4, 1830, Gaillard Hunt, ed., *The Writings of James Madison* (9 vols., New York, 1900–1910), 9: 383–394n. With appropriate but minor changes the same letter, dated August 1830, formed the conclusion of a lengthy review of "Speeches made in the Senate of the United States, on occasion of the Resolutions offered by Mr. Foot, on the Subject of the Public Lands, during the First Session of the Twenty-first Congress," in the *North American Review*, 31 (October 1830): 462–546. The letter was probably solicited by Alexander H. Everett, then owner and editor of the *Review*. See Irving Brant, *James Madison* (6 vols., Indianapolis, 1941–

1961), 6: 479. While he repudiates nullification, Madison holds the Constitution to be a form of compact between the States, an interpretation rejected by Webster, and bluntly denied by Joseph Story in the first volume of his *Commentaries on the Constitution of the United States* (Boston, 1833), 279–343.

3. Thomas Jefferson to Wilson C. Nicholas, September 5, 1799, in Thomas Jefferson Randolph, ed., *Memoir, Correspondence, and Miscellanies, from the Papers of Thomas Jefferson* (2d ed.; Boston and New York, 1830), 3: 429. For a reappraisal of Jefferson's role in this matter, see Adrienne Koch and Harry Ammon, "The Virginia and Kentucky Resolutions: An Episode in Jefferson's and Madison's Defense of Civil Liberties," *William and Mary Quarterly*, 3d Series, 5 (April 1948): 168–169.

TO HENRY CLAY

Washington May 29. 1830

My Dear Sir

We are all with the foot in the stirrup, & are not leaving in a very *composed* state. The passage of the Indian Bill,[1] & the rejection of the Maysville Turnpike Bill[2] have occasioned unusual excitement. The quarrel, yesterday, between Stansbury [William Stanbery] & others, who voted for the Bill, & [James Knox] Polk, [John] Bell &c, was very warm.[3] There is more ill blood raised, I should think, than would easily be quieted again.

We think all recent occurrences have been quite favorable, & that the present prospect is cheering. We have had no *formal* meeting. After much consideration, that idea was given up. We found it difficult to assemble a *few friends*, without giving offence; or a *great number* without the danger of attracting too much notice. We have had, however, a very full & free interchange of opinions, for the last three weeks, & are all harmonious in purpose & design, and in good spirits. We incline to think no formal nomination at present advisable, tho' friends press us to such a measure from divers quarters of the country. It has seemed to me, on the whole, that a formal nomination here would not be *popular enough* in its character & origin, to do good. It would be immediately proclaimed to be the act of your friends, acting *at your instance*. It would excite jealousies, on the one hand, which are now fast dying away, &, on the other, check discontents & schisms, among our opponents, from which much is now to be hoped. Such is our view.

I am much pressed to assent to a nomination of you by the Mass. Legislature now in session. But to this, I steadily object; on the ground, that every body knows we are perfectly safe & strong in Massachusetts, & a nomination, there, would only raise the cry of *coalition revived*. It has seemed to me the proper scene for the first formal action is *Maryland*. Her Legislature is elected in October. Our friends have the utmost confidence they shall carry the State. Indeed there can be little doubt of it. In that event, the Maryland Legislature, next Decr, will occupy a position, from which they can speak to advantage. Without detail, you will see, I think, at once, many advantages in a nomination from this quarter. None could be more favorable, unless it be N York, or Penna, neither of which, I fear, is as likely to be so soon ready for it.

I hope you will think that under all circumstances, we have done wisely, in doing nothing.

If you run agt. Genl Jackson, there will be an election, by the Electors —; &, as you justly state, Gen J. will be chosen, unless either Va. Penna. or New York can be detached from him. Of the three, I have, at present, most hope of N York, & least of Va. Late occurrences will strengthen Gen J. in Va & weaken him, much, in Penna, & perhaps also in New York. I am in hopes that working men, "Anti Masons," & "Anti-Auction men"[4] &c &c &c will break down the Regency. This we shall know in October. If it should turn out so, N. Y. will then open a very fair field. For myself, I recon on recent events as having *ensured* us Maryland, Ohio, Kentucky, & Indiana. This is one very good *breadth*. South of it, I looked for nothing but Louisiana; every thing north of it is worth a contest.

I hope your friends at the west keep a steady regard to Missouri. I am told there is good chance, or some chance, of Mr [David] Barton's reelection. This is matter of very great importance; nothing, indeed, is more momentous to the country, than the approaching election of Senators to the next Congress.

On the whole, My Dear Sir, I think a crisis is arriving, or rather *has arrived*. I think you cannot be kept back from the contest. The *people* will bring you out, *nolens volens. Let them do it*. I advise you, as you will be much watched, *to stay at home*; or, if you wish to travel, visit your old friends in Va. We should all be glad to see you, at the North, *but not now*. You will hear from the north,—every town & village in it—on the *4th. of July*. Parties must, now necessarily, be sorted out, anew; & the great ground of difference will be Tariff & Int. Improvements. You are necessarily at the head of one party, & Gen J. will be, if he is not already, identified with the other. The question will be put to the Country. Let the Country decide it.

I had intended to say a word about myself, but it would be to make a long letter still longer. When I came here, it was my purpose to follow your example, (parva componere magnis) & to vacate my seat, at the end of this session. Events have suspended the execution of that purpose. How I shall think of it when I get home, I do not know. I pray kind remembrance to Mrs Clay, & beg to assure you of my unaltered regard & attachment.   Danl Webster

ALs. DLC. Published in Colton, *Henry Clay*, pp. 274–276.

1. The Senate had concurred with House amendments to the Indian Bill on May 26.

2. Jackson vetoed the Maysville and Lexington Turnpike Road Bill on May 27. The following day the House failed to override the veto.

3. *Register of Debates*, 21st Cong., 1st sess., p. 1140.

4. The "Anti-Auction men" were those who opposed the system of disposing of imported goods at auction, a system believed to favor the foreign over the American merchant. According to a memorial from sundry "Merchants and Mechanics of Boston" sent to Webster earlier in the year, foreign goods were imported into the United States to an annual value of $85,000,000, one half to three fourths of which were "disposed of by sales at auction" (mDW 42654).

FROM HENRY CLAY

Ashland 7th. June 1830

My dear Sir

Your favor of the 29th. Ulto. is duly recd.[1] The decision of my friends at Washington to stand still for the present, and to leave the first movement to Maryland was best, under all circumstances. Their opinion that

I should go no where for political effect is in conformity to my judgment and to my principles. I could not have gone every where that I was pressed to go, and dissatisfaction might have been given at places which I did not visit. I think further that you are right in supposing considerations of policy to be opposed to a nomination at present in Massachusetts. To me personally it would be highly gratifying, but then the question is not what is most agreeable, but what is most expedient.

The exercise of the Veto on the Maysville bill has produced uncommon excitement in K[entucky]. I have not yet heard from other States. Prior to it, the public discontent with Mr. [George Matier] Bibb[2] broke out in violent forms; and in the neighbouring village of Lexington most of the respectable, and some of the least worthy of Jackson's supporters have openly renounced their faith.

We shall attack the Veto, by proposing an amendment of the Constitution to restrict it so as to require a majority of all the members elected to each branch of the Congress, instead of two thirds, subsequently to pass the bill. I think such a amendment right; otherwise I would discountenance it. It is conformable to the analogy of many of the State Constitutions, including our own; and it is in the spirit of our institutions.

The policy of such an attack is obvious. The other party will, of course, defend it, and we shall get the weathergage of them. We will put them on the Aristocratic bench, and more than balance the account of their proposition to amend the Constitution in regard to the P[residential] election.[3]

You will consider how far it may be right and expedient, in proper time, to co-operate in this object.

The Maysville road leads entirely across that third part of K[entucky] which was most favorable to Jackson. You can imagine then what effect must be produced by this event. We were safe before. Now, I think, we may be considered as absolutely certain; and we shall send you some good and true man (I hope [John Jordan] Crittenden, or [Robert P.] Letcher) in place of [John] Rowan.

From all other parts of the West information continues to be good.

I wish you were now in the H. or R. but I doubt whether you ought to return to it. You need make no change to advance your fame. You may rest entirely satisfied with what you have. The example to which you refer is not precisely in point. I had never served in the H. of R. and I was about 32. You have served long there and you are 48.

I am happy to tell you that the very best effects have been produced by your vote and that of our N. England friends generally for the Maysville road. It will not be forgotten.

To guard against the treachery of the P. Office, if you write me, put your letters under cover to James Harper (Lexington).[4] To whom should I address mine? Ever Yrs' Cordially   H. Clay

ALS. NhHi. Published in *PC*, 1: 504–505.

1. See above.

2. Senator Bibb of Kentucky, on May 15, had voted against the Maysville Road Bill.

3. In his first annual message, Jackson had proposed "such an amendment of the Constitution as may remove all intermediate agency in the election of President and Vice President . . . . In connexion with such an amendment, it would seem advisable to limit the service of the Chief Magistrate to a single term of four or six years." Jackson suggested "a provision disqualifying for [appointive] office the Representatives in Congress" whose votes may have determined the outcome of a Presidential election. 21st Cong., 1st sess., *House Journal*, Serial 194, p. 16.

4. Cashier of the Lexington branch of the Bank of the United States.

RECORD OF PAYMENT FROM HERMAN LE ROY TO DANIEL WEBSTER

July 21. 1830. I have now recd the Cash payment of five thousand Dollars, making up the sum of twenty five thousand Dollars, as stipulated by H[erman] Le Roy Esqr. before my marriage, to be advanced to me to be settled on his daughter, my wife. I am to complete the settlement, according to the original understanding, so soon as Counsel can conveniently prepare the necessary instrument.[1]

Danl Webster

ADS. NN. Herman Le Roy (1758–1841), father of the second Mrs. Webster, was a well-known and reasonably affluent merchant in New York.

1. The indenture referred to, dated December 10, 1830 (in mDW 39835-308 and mDWs) is between Webster and Caroline, his wife, parties of the first part, and Herman and Daniel Le Roy, respectively his father-in-law and brother-in-law, parties of the second part. By its terms, Webster acknowledges receipt of $25,000 as his wife's marriage portion, $10,000 on the day of the marriage, $10,000 in the month of July then next ensuing, and the remaining $5,000 at Herman Le Roy's convenience. In return Webster conveyed to the Le Roys, for the benefit of Caroline and her children, "the said Webster's Mansion House situate on Summer Street in said Boston and the Yard and Garden adjoining containing five thousand and thirty feet of land, with the Coach House and other buildings thereon."

The first trial of John Francis (Frank) Knapp for the murder of Captain Joseph White of Salem—see above, Story to DW, April 17—began on August 3 and ended with a hung jury ten days later. In the second trial, lasting from August 14 to August 18, Webster secured a conviction. He had entered the case as special prosecutor at the solicitation of Stephen

White, nephew and heir of the murdered man, and with the encourage-
ment of the attorney general of the Commonwealth; more persuasive
than these facts, and transcending even the $1,000 fee White offered
(mDW 39732), was the long-standing friendship between Webster and
White's brother-in-law, Joseph Story. He was undoubtedly also intrigued
by the legal problems posed. Chief Justice Isaac Parker, presiding over
the trial, had ruled ten years earlier (Commonwealth v. *Phillips, 16 Mas-*
sachusetts 423, 1820) that where no principal in a crime is convicted,
there can be no conviction of an accessory. In the Salem case the princi-
pal, Richard Crowninshield, alleged to have done the actual killing, had
taken his own life in his jail cell, leaving only accessories to be tried. By
Judge Parker's charge to the grand jury, however, the terms "principal"
and "accessory" were so defined that Frank Knapp could now be tried as
a principal, although his brother, Joseph J. Knapp, Jr. and George Crown-
inshield, brother of Richard, remained accessories. The trial was already
in progress when Parker died of apoplexy on July 25, an event that
caused postponement until August 3.

It was at this point that Webster joined the prosecution. Although the
trial had already resumed, he was still seeking, as the following letter to
Story shows, to resolve the legal questions involved.

TO JOSEPH STORY

Friday Morning Aug 6 [1830]
Salem

Dear Sir,

If we prove [John] F[rancis, "Frank"] Knapp a *conspirator*, in the plan
of the murder, as one who was deeply concerned in it, & *it does not ap-*
pear that any accessary part was assigned to him, such as to pay, procure weapons, or other like thing, and the murder is found to have been
committed by the conspirators, or some of them, but no direct proof who
was, or who was not present, is not F[rank] Knapp to be deemed a *prin-*
cipal, unless *he* can prove himself so remote from the locus in quo as to
shew him an accessary only? Suppose two men are overheard to propose
to kill a third by poison—they go together to a shop to buy arsenik—the
man is found poisoned, & with arsenik, & killed;—are not both, *neces-*
sarily, to be regarded as principals, unless one can prove that the other
actually administered the poison, *he* being not present.

I pray you, collect your thoughts, on this point—look to the cases, if
convenient—& I will send to you—or, more probably see you, on Sunday.

I have not found a letter from you here[1]—tho' I have daily applied at
the P. Office. But we have got along, on the point suggested to you the
other day, very well. Yrs   D Webster

ALS. MHi. Published in *MHi Proc.*,
2d Series, 14 (1900–1901): 407–408.
  1. Only one other piece of corre-
spondence on this subject has been found in the Webster papers. See
Stephen White to DW, December 17,
1830, below.

FROM WILLIAM WALLACE IRWIN

Philada. Friday night 17 Septr.
1830

Dear Sir

After a laborious session of one week the convention adjourned this evening *sine die*.[1] The gentlemanly & honorable manner in which Mr. [Francis] Granger conducted himself as the presiding officer, has gained for him the respect & confidence of every Delegate. Amongst the various subjects which were brought before the Convention, many of them of a delicate nature, it was surprising to find a unanimity of sentiment prevailing, which augurs well for the cause, & must ensure its success.

The following resolution has been adopted nem. con.

"Resolved That we recommend to the people of the United States opposed to the masonic Institution, to send Delegates to a National Convention to be held in the City of Baltimore on 26th. day of Septr. 1831 to nominate Candidates for the Offices of President & vice President of the U. S. &c."

There was scarcely a doubt expressed as to the expediency of taking up candidates. The only question was as to the proper time for nominating. When this question was agitated I deemed it, upon mature reflection, judicious to follow your advice, & therefore did not urge an immediate nomination. It also appeared to me unsafe to mention *publicly* my preference, especially as the name of no other gentleman was mentioned, or even alluded to, before the Convention.[2] But from conversation with the members, *out of doors*, I am induced to believe that the prospect is favorable.

It would have afforded me much pleasure, to have given you a detailed account of our proceedings, as well as of other matters, but my time has been so incessantly occupied with my duties as a Delegate, that I have found it out of my power. I intend leaving this city for Pittsburgh on Sunday, & upon my return home I shall endeavour to give whatever information I am possessed of. Be pleased to present my respects to your Lady, & believe me to be Very truly your's   W W Irwin

ALS. NhD.
  1. The National Anti-Masonic convention occurred in Philadelphia on September 11, 1830.

  2. Irwin was prepared actively to support Webster's nomination, whenever he should give the word, but Webster himself, though clearly

receptive, seems to have been somewhat cautious. The word was not

given. See Irwin to DW, August 25,
1830, mDW 8936.

TO JOSEPH STORY

Boston Sep: 18. 1830

My Dear Sir

From the accounts which I have recd of the state of your health, I
have supposed it hardly probable you would go to Wiscassett. I am a little interested to know how this may be, as Mr [William R.] Gray[1] desires
me to go down, for a cause in which his family is interested;[2]—and I
should not think of going unless you are to be there.

My sincere advice to you, My Dear Sir, is *not to go*. The weather is
cold, & you may in some degree, expose yourself, even with the utmost
care. Your health is everything, to yourself, your friends & the public;—
& all things else must yield to it. You must allow me to repeat, what I
have said to you *ore tenus*, that I have felt great concern about you, ever
since I saw what degree of labor you was bestowing on this Law School.
There is a limit, to what the strongest can do. I pray you, be persuaded
to *diminish your labors*. I beg this of you, out of the depths of my regard
& affection. *For all our sakes', spare yourself.*

Mr [Henry Willis] Kinsman will bring back information from you, abt.
your attending the Maine Circuit. If you are not perfectly well, do not
go. It is of no consequence, that you were not at Portland, in May. All
pressing business was done then, & will be done now, without you. I am
Dear Sir, with the utmost attachment, Yrs   D. Webster

ALS. MHi. Published in *MHi Proc.*,
2d Series, 14 (1900–1901): 408.
    1. Gray (1783–1831; Harvard 1800)
was a Boston shipowner and merchant, and the son of William Gray
of Salem and Boston.
    2. The case was *Seth Spring et al.*

v. *William R. Gray et al., Executors of
William Gray*, 22 Federal Cases 978
(October Term, 1830). Webster also
argued the case when it came before
the United States Supreme Court (6
Peters 151, 1832).

TO NATHANIEL F. WILLIAMS

Boston Oct. 20. 1830

My Dear Sir

Maryland has *electrified* us all.[1] Never, certainly, was there a more decisive, or a more gratifying triumph of the cause of public virtue & patriotism. We all feel strongly encreased hopes, of the whole Republic,
from this noble & admirable example.

I do not disapprove of the idea of a Convention in your State to nominate Mr. Clay. On the contrary, I think it might do good; more especially

if good news should come from Ohio. A nomination, by Maryland, would be a very good following up of the Maryland election, & of the Ohio election, if that also should terminate favorably.[2]

There is one idea I wish to suggest, confidentially. Some of our meetings, & many of our Newspapers make, as I think, an injudicious use of Mr Clay's name. They mean well, but they give their opinions & principles too much of a *personal cast*. We should be both for men & measures. We ought to act, as that if death should deprive us of Mr Clay tomorrow, we might still know where we are, & be in a condition to hold on, upon our objects. Our Adversaries run entirely into this notion of a personal party. With them, every thing is Jackson. Let us keep Mr Clay at our head, but let us remember also that we are contending for great principles. If you have a convention you should remember not to forget Genl. [Ezekiel Forman] Chambers, & such of your members in the other House as have deserved well. Men, you know, can only be kept in good spirits, even in a good cause, by mutual cheering, & respectful remembrance, on proper occasions. I hope the Convention will put forth an address, of the usual ability of your Maryland paper. It wd. do much good.

We have a warm election before us here—but not one of doubtful issue. Yrs truly   D. Webster

Give my congratulations to the Editors of the Patriot[3] & Marylander[4]—I have seen their papers. They have been conducted in a manner worthy the cause—& of the success which has attended it.

ALS. NhD.

1. The Maryland election held on October 4, 1830, returned an anti-administration governor and council by a large majority, and a state legislature in which the lower house was dominated by sixty-four anti-Jackson members as against sixteen Jackson members. See above, DW to Clay, May 29, 1830.

2. Clay supporters in Ohio won the governorship and control of the state Senate by a narrow margin, the lower house of the legislature more de-cisively. These Ohio victories were overshadowed, however, by an intra-party struggle going on in Kentucky.

3. The *Baltimore Patriot & Mercantile Advertiser* had been edited since its founding in 1813 by Isaac Munroe (1784–1859), previously editor of the *Boston Patriot*.

4. *The Commercial Chronicle and Daily Marylander* was edited by Sheppard C. Leakin (1790–1867) and Samuel Barnes, former editor of the Baltimore *Whig* and of the Frederick *Political Examiner*.

FROM JOSIAH STODDARD JOHNSTON

Phila. Nov. 6th 1830

My dear Sir

We owe you our acknowledgements for the noble efforts you have made in Boston & for the signal triumph you have obtained for us.[1] I am glad you have put things right in that quarter—for the South rely much upon the disaffected in the north to sustain them in separate assaults they meditate agt. particular interests under the Tarif—& they will draw considerable support from the Jackson members of Maine & N. Hampshire.

I have it from good authority that a very serious & angry correspondence has taken place between the President & Vice President, relative to the propositions & discussions in the Cabinet touching the Generals conduct in Florida—Which has terminated in a rupture. History has in this, at length been put right. A letter has been obtained from [William Harris] Crawford through [John] Forsythe, by the address of [James Alexander] Hamilton [of] N. York, that has set the General right—& which has also set him upon righting himself.[2] This will produce an entire Union among the Crawford party in the South in favor of Van Buren & will leave Calhoun & his friends alone with all the odium of disunion & Nullification upon their heads. There is much jealousy & distrust in the Cabinet & rumor speaks loud of the contemplated changes, but no one knows where the blow will fall. The President is not strong enough to leave out the partizans of Calhoun. They will not consent to his being the Candidate for the Vice Presidency—they will put no more of his friends into office—they will get clear of those they have as fast as possible—& they will supersede Duff Green. What part will Calhoun take in this quasi war?

It is said [John MacPherson] Berrien has taken part openly with the Mail Contractors agt. The P[ost] M[aster] General [William T. Barry] & I know personally the state of feeling between them.[3]

You must be with us at the meeting of Congress. Present my Kind regards to Mrs. Webster. Yours with great esteem   J. S. Johnston

ALS. NhD.

1. On November 1 protariff Nathan Appleton had defeated Henry Lee for a seat in Congress, with active support from Webster.

2. The Jackson-Calhoun controversy went back to the first Seminole War when Calhoun had been secretary of war and Jackson had taken possession of a Spanish fort in Florida against direct orders. In cabinet discussions, Calhoun had favored official action against the headstrong general, but had been overruled. In order to bring William H. Crawford, who had also been a member of Monroe's cabinet, into the Jackson party, it became necessary to eliminate Calhoun, and to this end James A. Hamilton of New York, son of Alexander Hamilton and a Van Buren lieutenant, procured through John Forsyth early in 1828 a statement from Crawford as to Calhoun's position in the old controversy. The South Carolinian was still needed to win the election of 1828, and so the document had been temporarily buried. It was exhumed in May 1830 and shown to Jackson, who promptly demanded an explanation from his Vice President. The unseemly contro-

versy was the talk of Washington at the time Johnston wrote. The exchanges were published early in 1831 in *Niles' Register*, 40 (March 5, 1831): 11–24, 37–40, 41–45, and were reprinted by Richard K. Crallé, ed., *Works of John C. Calhoun* (6 vols., New York, 1851–1855), 6: 349–445.

3. Charges of favoritism, sweeping dismissals, faulty bookkeeping, and under-the-table payments by Barry continued throughout his six years as postmaster general under Jackson and periodically brought on congressional investigations in 1830–31 and 1834–35.

FROM CALEB CUSHING

Newbury Port November 11th 1830

Sir: —

Confident as I am that Mr Webster would not intentionally do injustice to the humblest individual, I venture to address him, not in reference to the passing controversies of the hour, but for the purpose of removing from his mind the doubt, which I understand he has expressed, as to my sentiments on a great national question.

My opinions, respecting the American System so called, were fixed before that System gained the confidence of the great names of our New England. My own researches on the subject were aided by the advice of a friend, who, if his life had been longer spared to me, might have guided my inexperience through difficulties of another description. In the year 1825 this lamented friend, Mr Oliver Putnam,[1] then laboring under the illness which shortly terminated his life, placed in my hands some manuscripts advocating the protection of domestic industry by duties on imports, out of which, with additions & alterations of my own, I compiled a series of papers, which I published in the United States Literary Gazette, under the title of "The Principles of Political Economy, considered and more particularly in their Application to the Industry & General Interests of the United States."[2] These papers were afterwards republished in a separate form, with the addition of some others maintaining the same tenets, and denominated a "Summary of the Principles of Political Economy."[3]

That after such a distinct profession of political faith my sentiments should be doubted, may grieve, but it does not surprise me. My papers, as they combated the free trade theory on abstract general principles, & did not become identified with any election or other act of the people, soon passed away, it seems, into forgetfulness. Besides, foreign examples had produced an idea that men of letters & of theory must necessarily be adverse to the protecting system, which it was the fashion to condemn as the interested side, in contradistinction to the side of principle.

But such, as unfolded in those papers, were then my opinions, as reasoned out from general principles; & on all occasions since, in public bodies & in conversation, whenever an expression of my views was proper, I have constantly upheld the same doctrines. And it is some consolation to me now, to find that arguments, which in the forgotten Summary of my friend & myself were new, & which were then stigmatized in respectable quarters, as forming a "selfish system," which "all theory & all good sense as well as generous feeling look against though it is still enforced by some statesmen who know not how to defend it by argument" (United St. Literary Gaz. vol IV, p. 271),—it is, I say, some consolation to me to find that precisely such arguments were employed, during the late election in Boston, by friends of the protecting system, "who know how to defend it by argument," and who stand high among the highest for "good sense," for "generous feeling," & for wisdom & experience as "statesmen."

Soliciting of Mr Webster, for myself, only that candid judgment, which he bestows on all others, I remain, With sentiments of the greatest respect, His obedient servant,   C. Cushing

ALS. DLC. Published in Fuess, *Cushing*, 1: 68–69.

1. Putnam (1777–1826), merchant and importer from Newburyport, Massachusetts, retired early to Hampstead, New Hampshire, where he read and wrote many essays on the protective system.

2. *United States Literary Gazette*, 3 (1825): 22–25, 63–68, 143–146, 262–266, 306–309, 344–349, 375–378, 423–426.

3. (Cambridge, Massachusetts, 1826.)

FROM WILLIAM LEETE STONE

New York Dec. 14, 1830.

Dear Sir,

The meeting has been held, and was successful.[1] The fact is, we were driven to this course, at this early time, to prevent a meeting, and a nomination of Clay from a source not very desirable. But it has resulted well. The meeting was the largest and most respectable ever held in this city. David B. Ogden addressed the speech, in a very happy and popular way. The address, which you have seen, was adopted by acclamation, together with the resolutions which you will find in the papers. In these you will perceive we have adopted a middle course respecting a nomination— rather concurring in the recommendations of Clay heretofore made, than making a direct nomination ourselves. There were three to four thousand people at the meeting—our most active and respectable citizens; and there was a spirit abroad—a feeling of enthusiasm—such as I have never before witnessed at any public meeting whatever. The result will be effective in this city and state. The Jackson party had no conception that such a Clay meeting could have been got up in this city. Of course their papers will depreciate it. But of this you may be certain—the effect of this meeting in this community will be prodigious. And we have the most cheering advices from the country. There is a charm in Clay's name, which will be powerful in itself—and we hear from Buffalo that [Peter Buell] Porter has taken the field, and a meeting has been called there—and another will be called soon in Dutchess. In great haste, I am, &c. &c.

William L. Stone

ALS. DLC.

1. The meeting, held December 13 with 2,500 in attendance, was for the purpose of uniting all those in opposition to the Jackson administration, and to place Henry Clay in nomination for the Presidency. *National Intelligencer*, December 18, 1830.

FROM STEPHEN WHITE

Boston December 17 1830

My Dear Sir

Although we are in our household in the very hours of removal, being in the midst of bandboxes and bureaus, paperhangings and paint I cannot omit troubling you with a line to speak of the renewed excitement in Salem regarding the wretched woman Mrs [Mary] B[eckford]. Suspicions, horrible as they are, have almost become certainty. Yesterday she sent me a private message intimating her wish that I should not interfere to obtain a commutation for J[oseph] J[enkins] Knapp Jr. The message said she thought it better he should be hung! Now I know she has been, with her daughter Mrs. [Mary White Beckford] K[napp] and Knapps father to Worcester to prevail on Gov: [Levi] Lincoln to grant a reprieve or commutation, though she herself kept in the back ground by remaining at the tavern incog:; doubtless with a view to induce him to believe she was interceding for him while in truth she seeks his life to smother further investigation.[1] [Franklin] Dexter[2] and [William Howard] Gard[i]ner[3] urged their request to the Govr & Council for a commutation in Frank Knapps case, chiefly on the ground that another person was at the bottom of the whole affair. This the Governor stated to Dr [Gideon] Barstow & Mr [Stephen Clarendon] Phillips,[4] who waited on him to claim the reward for the Committee of Vigilance intending to devote it to the payment of expenses &c. This I know will not take you by surprise for I have long seen where your suspicions pointed but it horrifies me who have always thought her very weak but not very wicked. She must be a very devil.

Joseph [White][5] has just come in from Cambridge and states that Daniel [Fletcher Webster] is quite well. Mr [James William] Paige will have seen you before this gets to Washington as I left him in New York last Sunday on his way to Baltimore. We hope to see him here again next week. Give I beg of you my sincere respects and regards to Mrs: Webster and believe me most truly Your obliged friend   Stephen White

ALS. NhHi.

1. Mrs. Beckford was the niece and housekeeper of the murdered Captain White. Her daughter, Mary White Beckford, had married Joseph Jenkins Knapp, Jr., against the old captain's wishes, and had been disinherited for it. Joseph Knapp was one of the conspirators tried and convicted earlier that year, and was at this time awaiting execution. He was hanged on December 31, 1830.

2. Chief counsel for Joseph Knapp, his brother Frank, and their fellow defendant, George Crowninshield.

3. Gardiner (d. 1882; Harvard 1816), Boston lawyer and son-in-law of Thomas Handasyd Perkins, had been associate defense counsel.

4. Barstow had been chairman and Phillips a member of the Salem Committee of Vigilance organized after Captain White's murder which successfully uncovered evidence that brought the Knapps to trial.

5. Joseph White (1814–1838; Harvard 1833) was the son of Stephen White.

FROM DANIEL FLETCHER WEBSTER

Boston Dec 24. 1830

My Dear Father.

I received your kind letter yesterday,[1] and was very glad to hear from you. I had made no preparations to start, as I hardly expected to go to N. York. I shall be able to get away, Monday. The Commons hall was shut up in Cambridge and every body came away; only two students, I believe in all Cambridge; and therefore I came to the Tremont,[2] to stay. I was here when Uncle [James William Paige] came home. He arrived Thursday afternoon.

I went to see Mr [Josiah] Quincy last Tuesday, to get my circular, and he said he would send it to you; it is nothing but a list of absences and such things. I was quite sick for nearly a week; confined to my bed two days, with a bad cold, and for that reason, I missed several recitations and prayers, which you will see noted on my circular. I send you enclosed my matriculation paper,[3] which I was fortunate enough to get this term; several unfortunate fellows will have to remain, on probation, some months longer. I gave my term bill to Mr [Henry Willis] Kinsman; the amount is $77.03. He said he should have some money the first of January, and would pay it then. I should like to board out of Commons, next term, if I could; the board is much better and not more expensive. My bill at commons this term, is thirty two dollars, and I can get board at the best houses in Cambridge, for thirty five. Besides the walk is rather long, in the middle of winter.

I have read about one hundred pages in Hume, and fifty in Johnson. I have been reading a little book called Maitlands Narrative, giving an account of Buonaparte's conduct, on board the Bellerophon.[4] We have finished the five first books of Tacitus, and begin Excerpta Latina, next term. We have read Œdipus and Medea in Greek, and Trigonometry in Mathematics. These are the principal studies, about which I have been employed this term. I hope to do more next term. Neddy [Edward Webster] sends love to you and Mother. "Ecce signum."

My love to Father and Mother, yours   Edward

Please tell Mother I will answer her letter immediately, give my love and duty to her, and I remain Ever your affectionate son,   D. F. Webster

ALS. NhHi.
  1. Not found.
  2. Tremont House, on Tremont Street at Beacon Street.
  3. The Harvard matriculation certificate of Daniel Fletcher Webster, printed D with MS. insertions, mDW 9074, is enclosed with letter.

4. Frederick Lewis Maitland, *Narrative of the Surrender of Buonaparte and of his residence on board H.M.S. Bellerophon. With a detail of the principal events that occurred in that ship between the 24th of May and the 8th of August 1815* (2d ed.; London, 1826).

TO LEVI LINCOLN

Washington Decr. 25. 1830

Private

My Dear Sir

I thank you for your letter of the 13th Inst.[1] It was to me a source of very sincere regret, that owing to the unexpected avocations, which drew me in many different directions, for the summer, I missed the opportunity of much conference & society with you. In future, I shall take more especial care agt. such a disappointment. On the particular subject to which you allude, I am persuaded there are not two friends in the Commonwealth who think differently, or who doubt the entire propriety, &, indeed, necessity, of your remaining in your present situation.[2] As far as my knowledge extends, there certainly was never a time, when the public feeling *was stronger, or more united.* It seems to me, that unless you have insurmountable private reasons, the course of duty is quite plain. I know that my Colleague [Nathaniel Silsbee], & believe all friends here, entirely concur in this sentiment. For one, I should feel greatly alarmed, were I to hear of your proposing to retire.

The impeachment goes on very slowly,[3] & nothing else is doing at all. There seems a sort of peace, for the moment; owing partly, no doubt, to the real but as yet unacknowledged, discontents & *quarrel*, between the Secretary [of State] & *his* friends, & the V. President, & *his* friends. Van Buren, by the aid of Mr Crawford, & others, has put the President in possession of the facts, relative to Mr Calhouns conduct towards him, in the time of the Seminole War; Mr C. having been, on that occasion, the loudest accuser of the Genl, in Mr Monroe's Cabinet, and decidedly in favor of his *arrest*. Learning these facts, (so the story goes) by a letter from Mr Crawford to Mr Forsythe, the President called on Mr C. for an explanation. A correspondence ensued, &, it is said, that Mr C's last letter was sent back, with a summary answer, *that it was not satisfactory.* Mr C's friends lay all this upon Van Buren.

Our own prospects have some bright spots in them, but are not altogether fair. The elections in Penna. & Missouri, of Senators, are as good as we could expect.[4] We feel uneasy about Kentucky. Local & personal divisions prevail there, to a very great extent. [John J.] Crittenden ought to be chosen Senator, & it was expected he wd. be the Clay Candidate, unless Mr C himself were a candidate. But at the late convention at Frankfort, Mr Benjn. Hardin, who has been esteemed a doubtful politician, came out strongly for Mr Clay, & being a man of talent, & much local influence & connexion, is very likely himself to be a strenuous contender for the situation. In the meantime, the majority of the party is very small. Indeed, there seems to be, I am sorry to say it, something hollow, in Mr Clay's western support. It gives way, in the moment of trial.[5]

It is generally thought here, that the idea of a Nat. Convention is brought forward prematurely.[6] We all think that such a meeting, if held at all, cannot be held until next summer or autumn. Instead of turning our thoughts to these larger subjects, it seems to me more to be our duty, as N. E. men, to endeavor to bring N. E. together again, & unite her in the common cause. I do wish it could be impressed on our friends to correspond with the well disposed in N. H. & M[aine] & try to rouse them to an effort. Nothing can be more absolutely devoted than the ruling politicians in these states to what I consider a dangerous & ruinous course of public measures. Cannot these two States be alarmed, & waked up?

I doubt whether much Legislative business will be done this Session. The President's projects will not find favor. The Tariff will not be disturbed.

For myself, I intend to be very much a Looker on. As you have leisure, I hope you will allow me to hear from you.

We miss [John] Davis[7] Yours, with very sincere & fixed regard.

Danl Webster

ALS. MWA.

1. Not found.
2. As governor of Massachusetts.
3. The impeachment trial of federal district court Judge James H. Peck of Missouri occupied the Senate from December 13, 1830, until January 31, 1831.

4. Pennsylvania had chosen William Wilkins, a moderate Jacksonian with an Old Federalist background, to replace William Marks, also a mod-

erate Democrat, who had defended the Adams administration. In Missouri the outspokenly anti-Jackson David Barton was replaced by Alexander Buckner, who ran as a Democrat but not as a Jacksonian, and who was a supporter of both tariff and internal improvements.

5. The Kentucky legislature, in the winter of 1830–31, was called upon to replace Senator John Rowan. Although both houses had anti-Jackson majorities, Clay's partisans feared they could not elect him. They supported instead Clay's close friend John J. Crittenden, who could have won a dubious victory by voting for himself, which he refused to do. After fifteen ballots the election was postponed. Clay's failure to command the party in his own state led National

Republicans outside Kentucky, like Webster himself, to question his qualities of leadership. When a new legislature met in the fall of 1831, however, Crittenden stepped aside and Clay was triumphantly elected to the Senate seat.

6. A "strictly confidential" circular letter, addressed presumably to leading Massachusetts National Republicans, was dated from Washington, December 27, 1830. It bore the names of Daniel Webster, Edward Everett, John Reed, and Joseph Richardson. The argument, in expanded form, follows the lines of this paragraph in Webster's letter to Lincoln (mDW 9079).

7. Davis did not take his seat in the House for this session of Congress until January 3, 1831.

TO NATHANIEL F. WILLIAMS

Washington Decr. 28. 1830

Dear Sir

My accounts from Kentucky (as late as the 16) leave it highly probable the election of a Senator will be postponed. On the other hand, some of the Jackson K. members here are confident of the election of a *Jackson* Senator. This is sufficiently mortifying. Indeed nothing is more discouraging than these appearances of *hollowness*, in Mr Clay's Western support. Would, that these states go one way, or go the other! Yrs truly

D Webster

ALS. NN.

FROM DANIEL FLETCHER WEBSTER

New York, Jan 3. 1831.

My Dear Father,

I received your kind letter,[1] Saturday, and I was very glad to hear from you and mother. I got safely to New York, after two days passage. We were very much dissapointed, at Providence, as the Bo[at] did not arrive till evening; and we left there at twelve [mid?]night. The passage was quite rough, in the first part of [the] voyage; but, afterwards, it was smooth.

Every one is well here, and Julia is very happy and improved much.

Mrs. [Catherine] Newbold[2] is very kind to her, and Julia is contented.

Private

I am very sorry indeed, that I have not done more this term, in reading those authors of whom you approved, I know I have not done enough. I will not attempt to excuse myself any more, for my negligence; but show you that I will amend for the future, and I hope to meet your approval, at the end of the second term. Mr [Josiah] Quincy told me that I had done very well, and that the government had nothing to say against me. Mr [John] Farrar[3] had the kindness to pay me a compliment. I think, I stand very well with the government, and I know I do with the students. If I apply myself as I hope to do; I may perhaps graduate higher than you seem to expect I shall, from the last term. The chief fault is, my dear father, a restlessness; I cannot stick to the same thing long, a fault of which I am as well aware, as yourself. Time and care will I hope correct this. I am a little troubled with my eyes; which are very weak, and it is almost impossible to read in the evening. I have been to Dr Randall[4] and he gave me a wash, which assists them. I shall go home prepared to study and to give you satisfaction.

I staid from Wednesday to Monday at the Tremont house; the Commons were closed and I knew of no other place to which to go, in town. My bill, including stage fare, was 12. dollars and a half. My funds are plentiful, at present. I gave my term bill to Mr. Kinsman. Julia joins with me in love to you and Mother. I remain your truly affectionate Son,

D F Webster

ALS. NhHi. Published in part in Van Tyne, pp. 580–581.

1. Not found.

2. Sister of Caroline Le Roy, Catherine Augusta Le Roy Newbold (1790–1835) was the widow of Thomas Newbold of Philadelphia.

3. Farrar (1779–1853; Harvard 1803), tutor, 1805–1807, was Hollis Professor of Mathematics and Natural History, 1807–1836.

4. This may refer to either John Randall, a physician, at 5 Winter Street, or Moses Randall, physician and dentist, located at 32 Summer Street, both in Boston.

FROM J[OHN] H[EYSHAM] GIBBON

Philadelphia County, near
Holmesburg Pennsylvania
6th Jany. 1831.

Sir,

I have no privilege to claim in using your valuable time, but permit me to solicit a few moments. I have seen an invitation given by the Russian Government for communications and information upon the Subject of Cholera Morbus. The American Physicians are not included in this invitation, but as the disease frequently occurs among us in the Summer season and our plan of treatment is generally attended with Success—and to speak frankly, I feel some confidence in my acquaintance with it—I have used the liberty of addressing a short essay upon that Subject to the Council of Medicine at St. Petersburgh, as a tribute to the humane intentions of the Government, flattering also myself with the hope of aiding in the relief of human suffering.[1]

However moderate my title to attention may be, yet one has feelings of reputation and honourable emulation in such a case, and I wish, as I have written the treatise to have a fair chance shewn to it. Allow me to enquire of you the mode in which our Government generally communicates with Saint Petersburgh, and if you can inform me how and to whom I can safely transmit half a dozen sheets of letter paper which contain my observations.

I feel perfectly assured that you will consider the information I have troubled you with as *confidential* and I hesitate further to occupy you, except with the offering of my very great respect.   J. H. Gibbon, M.D.

ALS. NhHi. Gibbon (d. 1868; University of Pennsylvania 1813, Medical School 1822) was a Philadelphia physician who subsequently moved to Charlotte, North Carolina. In 1854 he published an article in *DeBow's Review* on the biblical justification of slavery.

1. Congress apparently relied upon European details about the conference as well as observations about the disease. See *House Reports*, 22d Cong., 1st sess., Serial 225, Report No. 226.

FROM NICHOLAS BIDDLE

Philada. Jan: 10. 1831.

My dear Sir,

Can you learn from Mr. [Henry Williams] Dwight, without, of course inquiring as for me, what course the Committee of Ways & Means will take as to the President's fiscal scheme referred to them.[1] Yrs: with great respect   N. Biddle.

LC. DLC.

1. In his second annual message to Congress, December 6, 1830, Jackson had recalled his earlier strictures on the Bank of the United States and suggested a modification that would make the bank a branch of the Treasury, "based on the public and individual deposites, without power to make loans or purchase property, which shall remit the funds of the Government, and the expense of which may be paid, if thought advisable, by allowing its officers to sell bills of exchange to private individuals at a moderate premium." Thus reconstituted, the institution would continue to regulate the currency through its power to reject the notes of state banks not redeemable in specie, but it would be "shorn of the influence" that made it "formidable." *House Journal*, 21st Cong., 2d sess., Serial 205, p. 33. This portion of the message was referred to the Committee of Ways and Means.

TO NICHOLAS BIDDLE

Washington Jan. 15. 1831

Dear Sir

I understand Mr [George] McDuffie has said he would make a Report[1] directly *agt.* the scheme of the Message. But he has not yet, as I can learn, brought the subject before the Com[mitt]ee. Yrs   D Webster.

I have never known in W. such a storm as is now raging.

ALS. DLC.

1. McDuffie never released a report. See DW to Biddle, February 4, 1831, below.

TO ALBERT HALLER TRACY

Washington Jan 15. 1831

My Dear Sir

I am obliged to you for your letter of the 27th Decr.[1] as it gives me pleasure to have an opportunity of exchanging opinions, on the important subject, to which it relates. I must confess, however unwilling I am to come to that conviction, that there is much to lead to the belief, which you express, respecting the chance of Mr Clay's election. No one is more desirous of that event than I am, & it is, therefore, with pain that I feel my hope of witnessing it beginning to be weaker. In my judgment, there is no chance of his success, unless he may calculate *either* on N York, or Penna.; & without both, it would be doubtful. I think there is very little hope, indeed, of Penna.; & if the state of Antimasonic feeling, in New York, be much as you represent it, (& your view on that subject concurs with that of others) the prospect of electing Mr Clay is, indeed, not promising. It is far otherwise.

But, My Dear Sir, I fear it is easier to see the evil of our present condition, than to agree on any thing, as a remedy. What you suggest, is, *I* think, very just; that is, that we should look for something, in which N. Y. Penna. & Ohio, would *agree*; But this may not be readily found; & if it were, it must be something, also, in which the N. E. States, N. Jersey, Delaware & Maryland would *agree also*. The N. E. States, which act with us, are much attached to Mr Clay, for this reason, among others, that he was true to, & suffered with, the late Administration. They might, perhaps, forego this preference, from a sense of necessity, & in favor of some one else, in whose loyalty to the cause, & in whose reliable character they could place confidence. But they would do even this, with regret; & any thing short of this, I am persuaded, they would not do at all.

My view of things is pretty much this. We begin with New York. It is clear, that in that State nothing can be done, but by Anti Masonic strength. If the Antimasons shall not consent to support Mr Clay, it is not possible to give him the votes of that State. Let us suppose, then, that there shall be an Anti Masonic Candidate. If he be a fortunate selection, he will succeed in N York, by Antimasonic strength alone, or by that, aided by the votes of other portions of the People. Here will be secured, 36 votes. One hundred will now be wanting. Mass. Con[necticu]t Vermt. & R. Is. will furnish 34. I do not despair of N. H, & a part, or the whole of Maine; but omitting them, for the present, here are 34 N. E. votes. Now these votes, except perhaps, those of Vt. cannot be obtained by Anti Masonry, *as such*. Yet, I suppose, they might mostly be had for an Antimasonic Candidate, who, for other reasons, should be acceptable to the people in those States. This, therefore, would depend, on the question, who the man is. N. Jersey has a growing Anti Masonic interest, & our other friends, there, are reasonable, & conciliatory; the States of Delaware & Maryland, with little or no Antimasonic feeling, might be persuaded, probably, to go, if it were shewn to be necessary, for an Antimasonic Candidate whom they should like, altho. the latter state would, I think, give up Mr Clay, with *great reluctance*. These three States give 22 votes. Probably Indiana & Louisiana, together ten votes, might be hoped for, 'as willing to go with friends. Here, we have some sixty six votes, exclusive of New York; but we wanted one hundred, or thereabouts. Now, Penn. & N Hampshire, the one with 28, & the other with 8 votes, would help us thro'; & Maine, if she could be obtained, would enable us to bear the loss of Indiana, or Louisiana. Indeed, with N. Hamp. & Maine, we could spare both Louisiana & Indiana.

It is *possible*, therefore, barely possible, to succeed, without either Ken. Missouri, or *Ohio*. I leave them out, for the present, for the same reason; viz, I believe Mr Clay can obtain the votes of each; but if he should be withdrawn, my opinion is they will all go for Genl Jackson. Ohio is a State of great importance, & if we could secure her vote, ours would be easy work; provided the other part of the calculation should not materially disappoint us. But I apprehend difficulty in that. My fear is, that the anti masonic preference in that State might take such a direction, that not only would several of the States, which I have already mentioned, absolutely refuse to follow it, but that she herself would inevitably be thrown into the opposite scale. Indeed I do not know whether it is probable that any Anti Masonic candidate could be named, who should obtain her vote; altho. some of our friends say they should by no means despair.

There is another view, of probabilities, or possibilities, not to be entirely disregarded. If a reconciliation between Anti Masons & Mr C's friends, or their cooperation, could not be accomplished, & the Anti Masons should carry Ohio, N. York, & Penna, or even the two last, what would be the State of things? Probably, no choice by the People. That would give rise to a singular result, as far as we can now judge, viz, that the two greatest States in the Union, would vote, in Congress, agt. the votes of the People of those States. The late elections to Congress, in those States, (N. Y. & Penn) are vastly important, & very unfortunate.[2] In the event that there should be no choice by the People, I should have hopes of the votes of the following States, agt. the present Executive, viz, Vermont, Mass, Cont. R. Island, N. Jersey, Delaware, Maryland, Ohio, Indiana, Missouri, Louisiana, & Kentucky—12 in all. I see not where we are to look for a 13th unless some Delegation should be influenced by the vote of its State. Possibly that might happen.

I have thus stated, My Dear [Sir], at tiresome length, what occurs to me; and as I have run into some particulars, I should be very glad to hear from you farther, & to receive a full disclosure of your views & opinions. We correspond, of course, entirely confidentially. I think it of great importance that the Delegates to the Anti Masonic Nat. Convention should be prudent, wise, & far-seeing men. Such I have no doubt will be appointed in N. Y. Toward the latter end of this month, or about the beginning of the next, something will be settled here, as to the time of holding or as to holding, a Convention of Nat. Repubs. This induces a wish, on my part, to hear from you again, so soon as your [leisure?] may admit. I will thank you, at once, to acknowledge the receipt of this, by a single line; as I shall be anxious to know that it has not miscarried.

You see how K[entucky] stands, as to Senator. We still think here, that [John J.] Crittenden will be chosen. Yrs with very true regard,

Danl. Webster

ALS. NN.
1. Not found.
2. Only about one third of the congressmen elected in 1830 from both states were antiadministration, including Anti-Masonic members who outnumbered the National Republicans, especially in Pennsylvania.

TO [NICHOLAS BIDDLE]

[February 2, 1831]
Wednesday 1 oclock

Private & Confidential
Dear Sir,

Mr [Thomas Hart] Benton is now making his *speech* agt. the Bank.[1] It is intended for circulation, & effect out of doors. Nobody seems ready to decide, what shall be done, when he shall conclude. If his speech be answered, it will bring on a debate, quite prematurely, & likely to last the session. If it be not answered, the *thing* itself will be sent abroad, to

make its impression, without any reply. On the whole, my present inclination of opinion is, to hear him thro & then move to lay his proposition on the table—call for the Ayes & Noes—& try to get a *vote* that
shall *tell* against his speech.

I have endeavored, My Dear Sir, to find time to write something on
this very important subject;—but, truly, I have not been able to detract
sufficient time from my professional labors. If I could afford to study
law cases less & some of the great questions more, I should appear, I
think, to somewhat more advantage, & do a little more for the advancement of useful objects. I sometimes feel this so strongly, as to be on the
very point of relinquishing my situation here to some one who can give
better attention to it. The Bank question, itself, is enough to occupy the
thoughts of a public man, till it shall be settled.

If the Debate proceeds, I will endeavor, if it be possible, to keep my
seat here, & say something;—if it be no more than to shew the side I am
on. I find there is a defect, probably, in our Judicial System, in relation
to the District Courts, in States in which there are no Circuit Courts. In
most of these States, (*Mo.*, *Alabama*, *Louisiana*, *Mississippi*, &c &c)—
the Bank *cannot sue* in U. S. Courts. I sat up last night, quite too late,
in hunting up the various Acts, establishing these Courts;—& have,
today, drawn a Bill to cure the evils. I shall try to get the Jud[iciary]
Com[mittee] to sanction it & if so, will report it tomorrow, & try to get
it thro.[2]

How do you stand with Mr [James] Buchanan, Chairman of Judiciary
Com[mitt]ee in H. of R.

Yrs   D W.

ALS. DLC.
   1. *Register of Debates*, 21st

Cong., 2d sess., pp. 46–78.
   2. See below.

TO [NICHOLAS BIDDLE]

Washington feb 4. 1831

Private

Dear Sir

Our majority on Benton's motion for leave[1] was not so great as it
ought to have been, and as I expected it would be. I suppose the two N.
York Senators [Nathan Sanford and Charles Edward Dudley], Mr [Mah-
lon] Dickerson, & others, favored the motion to bring in, from a fear of
appearing to act discourteously towards a political associate. At first, it
was my intention, not to oppose the leave to bring in, but, as soon as
brought in, to move to lay the thing on the Table. For this motion, we
should doubtless have had a far stronger vote. But the mover made his

speech, not on his Resolution, when brought in, but on the leave to bring in, (which, by the way, I hold to be out of order) & having made his Speech, & brought in his Resolution, he, himself, would have consented to its lying on the Table; so that we should, in that way, have administered no rebuke, nor expressed any dissent at all. As it is, the effect here is very well, as far as I have heard; & several Gent[lemen] who felt bound to vote *for* the leave, feel, I believe, no little spleen on acct. of the dilemma in which the mover placed them.

The Speech will doubtless be published. It was a very shallow, ad captandum thing—capable of affecting no man of sense. I do not think it will do any harm in Missouri. Mr [Henry Sheffie] Geyer, of that State, now here, told me yesterday, as soon as it should be published, he will *review it*, for the benefit of Missouri. Mr Geyer is a very able, & very popular man. He will probably run for Congress, in M—, next August agt. the present member—& probably *with success*. He says the Bank is not unpopular in Missouri; & that the People cannot be excited, on that subject. Two years hence, Mr Benton's time expires. I learn that there is no chance of his reelection; & that probably Mo., in both branches of Congress, will be in favor of *renewal of the Charter*.

I had yesterday some conversation with Mr [George] McDuffie. I believe he does not think it worth while to make another Report. Probably he thinks there is nothing new to be said, except, perhaps, as to the President's new project. I believe it to be Mr McDuffie's clear opinion, that the Bank ought to apply for renewal *next Session*. How does this fall in, with the triennial meeting of the Stockholders?

I have introduced a Bill[2] to cure some defects, in the Jurisdiction of the District Courts, in States where there are no Circuit Courts. The *effect* of this *defect* is to shut you out of their Courts. I hope to get the Bill passed.

I mark this letter *private*. Whatever I write, on the subject of the renewal of the Charter, I wish to have so considered. Yrs truly

D. Webster

ALS. DLC.

1. A majority of 23 to 20 refused leave for the introduction of Benton's resolution that the charter of the Bank of the United States should not be renewed.

2. Senate Bill 142, "Respecting the jurisdiction of certain district courts," mDW 42494.

TO NICHOLAS BIDDLE

feb. 10. [1831]

Dear Sir

Our success has been marvellous. The little *Bill*[1] has actually passed both Houses! In this House—perhaps in the other—the very name of the Bank was not uttered.

It is of the greatest importance in M[iss]o[ur]i Alaba. Louisiana, & Miss—if you send a branch to Natchez.

I learn thro' Mr [John] Sergeant, that it is understood orders have gone to Albany, for instructions agt. the Bank.

I will endeavor to find out how that matter is. Yrs   D Webster

ALS. DLC.
1. See preceding letter to Biddle, note 2.

TO NICHOLAS BIDDLE

Washington Feb. 25. 1831

Dear Sir

I have conversed with Mr [John] Sergeant, on the subject of the appointment of the Govt. Directors. It is, on the whole, best in my judgment to make no point, on that matter, with the President. It seems to me suficient, that you should now write to Mr [Samuel Delucenna] Ingham, acknowledging the receipt of his, enclosing the opinion of the Atty Gen [John M. Berrien];[1] & saying, at the same time, that other Learned Counsel have come to a different conclusion, & endorsing Mr. [Horace] Binney's opinion.[2] But contending, that as the Gentlemen are in office, either as holding over, under their former appointments, or else under the new, it seems not material to discuss the point further.

I see no evil, likely to arise from this. Yrs truly   D. Webster

ALS. DLC.
1. A government director of the BUS, B. W. Richards was appointed by Jackson and confirmed by the Senate in 1830, but later that year he sent the President a letter of resignation. In the opinion by Berrien, February 2, 1831 (*Opinions of Attorneys General of the United States* in *House Executive Documents*, 31st Cong., 2d sess., Serial 602, Doc. 55, pp. 747–749), the attorney general argued that the resignation of Richards did not take effect until the President accepted it or until he appointed a successor. Richards was, consequently, regarded as having been a director at the time of the recent annual election.

2. Biddle received an opinion from Binney sometime between February 12 and 14, and enclosed it in a letter to John Sergeant on the latter date. Sergeant had very likely shown it to Webster in the interim. See Biddle to Sergeant, February 12 and 14, 1831, Biddle Letter Books, DLC.

TO [HENRY WILLIS KINSMAN]

Washington feb. 25. 1831

D. Sir

I write, at this time, to give you a little intimation, respecting my projects, for the next three months.

I have long contemplated a tour to the West, as far as Ohio & Kentucky; & know not when I can better put that purpose into execution, than this Spring. My plan, at present, is this.

To get away from this place, so soon as my Court business will allow —say, abt. Mar. 15. To stay a day or two in Philadelphia—as many in N. York—leave Mrs W. there, & proceed straight to Boston—to be in Boston, say, a little before April 1. Stay in & about Boston three weeks, or 4. Then return to N. York, take Mrs W.—go up by way of her brothers, in the western District of N York—pass into Ohio, &c, go over to Kentucky, & then home by way of Pittsburg & Philadelphia.

The whole journey occupying May, & a considerable part of June.

To arrange this, I must have the C[ircui]t Court p[ost]p[one]d till after the session of the same Court at New York. That is, I mean, so far as I am concerned in that Court. I imagine there will be no difficulty in this. There is no important case, as I [see] at present, except Mr [Joseph] Balchs[1]—& the one I lately wrote you about.[2] Any professional business, which can be performed in April, I shall be willing to attend to, probably.

At present, I would not have you mention this project, to any one. I have written to Mr [James William] Paige, on the matter—& shall give the necessary notice to our domestics.

Many things may occur, to defeat or vary this project—& for this, as well as other reasons, I wish little, indeed nothing, said about it.

We are now in the neighborhood of the [Charles River] Bridge cause. Yrs truly   D. Webster

ALS. NNC.

1. *The General Carrington* v. *Merchants Insurance Company*, unreported federal case, which Webster

later argued in the Supreme Court (8 Peters 495, 1834).

2. Letter not found.

TO NICHOLAS BIDDLE

Saturday Eve'
[February 26, 1831]

Dr Sir

Binney & Winship vs Bank U. S. is decided;[1] judgt below *affirmed*— so all is well, as to this. Yrs   D. Webster

The bill respecting the Jurisdiction of the District Courts was presented to the President *Feb. 19th*. As yet, we have not heard from him.[2] I am a little suspicious he thinks there is meching malicho[3] in it.

ALS. DLC.

1. *John Winship et al.* [Amos and

John Binney] v. *Bank of the United States*, 5 Peters 529 (1831), in which

John Sergeant and Webster argued for the defendant in error.

2. The President signed the bill on this date, 4 *U.S. Statutes at Large* 444, but the action was not reported to the Senate until March 2.

3. "Meching malicho," i.e., "miching malicho," or skulking mischief, from *Hamlet*, Act 3, Scene 2.

Edward Everett, in the following letter to his brother, reveals Webster's political ambivalence toward Clay more clearly than any of the senator's own letters in the period. From early 1830, when the debate with Hayne gave him a nationwide following, until Clay's election to the Senate in November 1831 Webster listened—and sometimes appeared to approve —suggestions that he himself be named to replace Clay as the National Republican Presidential candidate.

Most leaders of the party had accepted Clay as Adams' successor when he entered the cabinet in 1825, and Clay had most certainly so regarded himself. But though his personal popularity remained great, the Kentuckian had serious liabilities. He had been out of public life since March 1829, and in his first attempt to regain his power, by way of the senatorial election in Kentucky in the late fall of 1830, he had faulted badly. As Webster commented in his letter to Levi Lincoln, above, December 25, 1830, there was "something hollow, in Mr Clay's western support. It gives way, in the moment of trial." Even earlier he had seen danger in the "personal cast" Clay's leadership had given to the party, urging that both "men & measures" were needed. Webster to Nathaniel F. Williams, October 20, 1830, above.

Webster's own political fortunes, meanwhile, had risen steadily until his popularity, even outside New England, challenged Clay's. (See, for example, Charles Miner of Pennsylvania to DW, December 31, 1830, mDW 9092.) Yet he remained cautious, even vacillating. He listened receptively to suggestions that he was the only man on whom both Anti-Masons and National Republicans could agree, but he would not allow himself to become too deeply involved with the former group for fear of losing the support of the latter. He gave up plans for a western trip in 1831, ostensibly because it might be misunderstood "in the present state of political ferment." (See DW to John Woods, May 10, 1831, mDW 9455.) In the end he realized that for the sake of his own future he could not afford to break ranks, despite his reluctance to give overt support to Clay. He encouraged the Kentuckian to come to the Senate, where "Every thing is to be debated, as if nothing had ever been settled (October 5, 1831, below); and concurred, seemingly without reservation, in the subsequent nomination of his still unacknowledged rival.

EDWARD EVERETT TO ALEXANDER HILL EVERETT

<Washington> Philadelphia
10 March 1831

My dear Brother,

I received a letter from you a day or two before leaving Washington; but I had not then time to answer it. I reached this place after rather an uncomfortable journey; the road from Washington to Baltimore being very bad; & the weather cold from Baltr. to Philada. I shall stay here a few days to avoid the exposure of going immediately home at this season of the Year, with the heavy cold, which I have upon me.

My note at the U. S. Bank, which you were good enough to endorse for me, is due, I think, on the 16th. It is for $500. I cannot conveniently make arrangements to pay the whole; & I should like to get a renewal of a part of it. I accordingly enclose you a draft on the Bank for $200, & my note for $300 at sixty days; which I presume they will have no objection to discounting. I wish you would offer it as soon as you get this, & write the word to New York, (Care of Davis & Brooks [Davis, Brooks & Company]) if they decline to renew it, which, however, they can scarcely do.

You may have observed, in the National Intelligencer & Journal of the 5th of March, an address to the People of the United States. The history of this paper is rather singular. At the Commencement of the session, we had several meetings, and it was agreed that W[ebster] should prepare a document, to serve as an answer to the President's Message. He produced nothing;—& the time wore away, till toward the close of the session. Some of Mr Clay's friends then resolved that they would have a Manifesto of some kind, & that W. should write it. They applied to him, & intimated in a gentle but intelligible way, that he must write it or would be suspected by Clay's friends in the West of coldness. He consented with seeming alacrity; & produced a paper, substantially that which is published in the Intelligencer of the 5th, but containing no allusion to Clay. On the representation of Judge [Robert Perkins] Letcher, who had held the conversations with W. on the subject & procured him to write the address, the concluding sentences were added in which (without naming him) Clay is kindly alluded to. In this form the paper was published. It is a queer production for a party Manifesto. Addressed to the People of the United States; but not editorially nor accompanied by any body's name. Intended as a nominating document, but so faintly alluding to the person nominated, (if a man can be said to be *nominated* who is not named) that [Robert] Walsh here actually asked me who was alluded to, & whether it was not [John] M'Lean!

Walsh has come out as you see *totis veribus*, against the administration & intends to persevere. He told me he designed to lay out his whole strength in opposing it; & for this purpose should enlarge his sheet at an expense of $4000; & that he was sure the re-election of Genl. Jackson could be defeated. He intimated an equal confidence, that Mr Clay could not be his successor, & appeared to think M'Lean was the man.

But the hour when the mail closes is come & I must back off.

AL. MHi. Everett Papers.

TO JOSEPH GALES & WILLIAM WINSTON SEATON

Mar. 12. [1831]

Messrs G. & S.

I send you all I can remember of my Speech on the Insolvent Debtor Bill, which you, so cruelly, refused me the means of preserving![1] You must make atonement by publishing this as soon as you can. I am going away, Wednesday morning, & should like that this should be my forerunner.

I send also a *paragraph*, respecting Dr. [Thomas] Sewall's Address on Intemperance.[2] I pray you to *adopt it*,—I have tried to make it read like a Nat[ional] In[telligencer] Article. It will do no harm to the public, but in many respects, will do good.

Remember, that much is expected of the Nat. Int. this spring & summer. Let the cry be *"onward."* I should be glad of six minutes talk, Monday or Tuesday. Adieu!

AL. NhD.

1. Webster's speech on this subject, given in the Senate on March 1, 1831, was published in the *National Intelligencer* on March 15. His manuscript notes have not been found.

2. Dr. Thomas Sewall, Webster's personal physician in Washington, had recently published *An address on the effects of intemperance on the intellectual, moral, and physical powers. Delivered before the Washington City temperance society.* Webster's paragraph appeared in the *National Intelligencer* on the same day as his speech.

TO HENRY CLAY

Boston Mar. [April] 4. 1831

Private & Confidential

My Dear Sir

It is a long time since I wrote you. This omission has happened, partly because I have had, at no time, much to say, and partly because what may as well be done tomorrow is often neglected today. Even now, I have little to communicate, & write mainly to cherish remembrances, & keep correspondence alive.

You have seen all that has transpired, at Washington, and in the Country, in the last four months. Your opinions & mine are not likely to be different, on any of these occurrences; and, probably the effect produced by them here, is very similar to that which they have also produced with you. Undoubtedly, the correspondence between the Presidt. & Vice President has lowered them both. It shews feelings & objects so personal—so ambitious—I may even say so *factious*, in some or all the parties, that it creates no small degree of disgust. As I came along home, I witnessed this result strongly, in Baltimore, Philadelphia, & New York. I believe, at this moment, a majority in each of those cities, would be glad of a change in men & measures.

Mr Johnstone[1] went west directly from Philadelphia, & can give you all the particulars, respecting the state of things there. I staid a week with Mrs Webster's friends in N York. You will see what publicly transpired.[2] There is a great deal of good spirit in New York, but it is not, at present, very well put in action. Great objects are, in some measure, lost in local divisions. They are canvassing for a City election, very warmly. I do not expect complete success to those opposed to the present state of things; but I have hopes of a great change, & such as shall give promise of a majority soon. The influence & patronage of those in office, in the Corporation, is too great, I fear, to be overthrown by one effort. There is certainly a great disposition, in the City, to unbind itself from the fetters of Tammany.

As to the State, I have no particular knowledge. The only distinct impression which I recd, was, that the Anti Masons were growing something more mild, towards yourself—& giving a little more hope that they would not, themselves, make a nomination for the Presidency. I think they will find such a nomination very difficult, if success should attend the Kentucky & Maryland elections, in Aug. & Sepr. I need not say to you how much depends on the first of these. If Ken: comes out strong, & decided, I am persuaded a very determined and active spirit will pervade every part of the Country; much beyond any thing yet experienced.

It is an interesting inquiry, *whether Mr Calhoun will be put up for the Presidency.* If he should, would not both he & Genl Jackson be beaten, in Va. & Pa.?—& perhaps N. Carolina? My own opinion, at present, is that Mr. Calhoun *will not be brought forward*, unless, perhaps in S. Carolina, from the evident danger of utter overthrow, to which such a measure would expose the whole party. At the same time, I believe *he* is sanguine enough to make the attempt, if his friends would encourage it.

I faithfully promised [Robert P.] Letcher that I would visit the West, this spring. Tho' I have not yet abandoned the idea, my purpose is shaken a little by the advice of friends here. They say, I could not go to Kentucky, at this moment, without exposing *myself*, & what is of more consequence, my *friends*, to invidious & odious remarks, which might have a bad effect on the public mind. I am quite unwilling to give up the jaunt; not knowing at what other period I may hope to be beyond the mountains. Nevertheless, if there be well founded doubts of the prudence of such a thing, it ought to be omitted. My purpose was to go to Ohio, Ken. & Missouri—but not down the River.

Our annual elections take place today. In a State having so many custom houses & Post Offices, &c &c, the patronage of the Govt. will naturally produce some votes in its favor. But there is no general feeling favorable to the Administration. I suppose this State is as strong as any one in the Union.

At your leisure, I shall hope to hear from you. I wish you could make Letcher or [James] Clark write. If anything occurs to either of them which friends here could be useful in, we should be very glad to hear from them.

Notwithstanding appearances, do not despair of N. Hampshire. I pray most kind remembrance to Mrs. Clay. Yours always truly   D. Webster

Mr. [Apr.] 5. Tuesday. The Election returns, which have come in this morning, shew a great falling off, even of the few Administration votes we had last year. [Levi] Lincoln and [Marcus] Morton are the opposing candidates for Govr. [Thomas L.] Winthrop[3] & [Nathan] Willis[4] for Lt. Govr. Morton & Willis the Jackson Candidates.

ALS. DLC. Misdated March 4 in manuscript. The election referred to was held on Monday, April 4, 1831.

1. Probably Senator Josiah S. Johnston of Louisiana, a close political friend of Clay.

2. The reference is to a public dinner in Webster's honor in New York City March 24, 1831. See James Kent, et al., to Webster, February 23, 1831, mDW 9214; and *National*

Intelligencer, March 29, 1831.

3. Winthrop (1760–1841; Harvard 1780) served as lieutenant governor of Massachusetts from 1826 to 1833. His son, Robert Charles Winthrop, read law in Webster's office.

4. Willis (1763–1851) sat on the Massachusetts Executive Council, 1824–1826, served in the state legislature, 1831–1832, and was often a candidate for lieutenant governor.

TO NATHANIEL F. WILLIAMS

Boston April 6. 1831

My Dear Sir

I enclose an unsealed letter[1] for Mr. William L[eigh] Brent, now residing in your State, formerly member of Congress from Louisiana, which I will thank you to read, & then seal & forward to his address. I do not know exactly where he resides. It is somewhere in the Potoma[c] Counties,[2] perhaps Calvert or St. Marys. If you do not know, you can doubtless easily learn. He is residing on an old family estate. You will see that this is in answer to a letter from him. I am a little fearful, tho' there was little or nothing in his letter to create such an apprehension, that he might feel so much despondency, as to Mr. Clay's success, as to think of the expediency of falling in for somebody else. As far as I see, or can judge, we have only to go right forward, & to bring out Mr. Clay, at the proper time, formally. Indeed he is already prominently & fully before the People. Any wavering, among our friends, would be in the highest degree injurious. Let us see what is done in Kentucky, in August. I have good hopes of an excellent result there. If such should take place, it will animate Mr Clay's friends, in the whole Country.

Pray let me hear from you, occasionally. Remember me kindly to Mr Monroe [Isaac Munroe]. Tell him I thank him for his letter[3] recd. in N York. Yrs very truly   D. Webster

You will see the Administration has few friends in this State.

ALS. NhD.
1. Not found. This is probably the letter Webster refers to in his correspondence with Brent on May 9, 1831 (mDW 9447), in response to an earlier request by Brent "for information and opinions, on political subjects."
2. The term is here used to describe that part of Maryland now called the "Western shore."
3. Probably Munroe to DW, March 19, 1831, mDW 9420.

FROM JOHN SERGEANT

Philada. April 9. 1831.

My dear Sir,

Expressing to Judge [Joseph] Hopkinson last evening my regret that Mr. [Robert] Walsh held back as to Mr. Clay, he told me it was in conformity with your opinion expressed when here. Of course, I said nothing more. But considering the matter again this morning, it has seemed to me that he may perhaps continue in this way longer than you would yourself think justifiable. I think it is time now to concentrate our efforts, as far as possible, to a single point. Judge [John] McLean is here. His friends are not inactive, and I fear they may make an impression, in the end unfavorable to us. There are many of the Jackson men who would more easily slide into a McLean party, than give their support to Mr. Clay, simply because they can call McLean a Jackson man, and therefore are not wandering so far in taking part with him. Then, there are the anti masons, who insist upon having their own way, and no one, I believe, can tell what that way will be. They protest, however, against Mr. Clay—not quite so vehemently as against Genl. Jackson, but still they protest. We must endeavour to bear them down. Neither of them can succeed, and both take from us, because many of these Jackson men, if the thing were brought to a simple issue, would go the whole length at once. A great deal more will suggest itself to you.

If, upon consideration, you should concur in this view, and have occasion to write to Judge Hopkinson or Mr. Walsh, I wish you would so express yourself. It is to be feared that uncertainty as to the candidate may have a bad effect in Kentucky.

Our meeting here, in numbers, composition and spirit, far surpassed our expectations. It has given quite a new tone. We are, undoubtedly, very strong in the City and County of Philadelphia. Of the State, generally, I am not prepared to say any thing but this, that if Genl. Jackson were out of the question, it would certainly go for Mr. Clay. Yrs. very truly   John Sergeant.

ALS. DLC.

FROM AMBROSE SPENCER

Near Albany April 19th. 1831.

My dear Sir,

You will recollect that I promised to write you, when I had the high gratification of seeing you in New York, & partaking of the dinner given to you for your patriotic & unrivalled efforts in defence of the constitution, & I cannot omit saying that on no former occasion during my life, have I been more honored or gra[ti]fied. You will believe me when I say that my motives for attending that dinner, were my high & sincere regard for you, & also to give my support to the doctrines you advanced, & which gave rise to the dinner—little indeed did I expect, because I feel that I do not merit, the delicate, but high compliment paid to me, conjointly with Chancellor Kent; & I beg you to accept the unfeigned assurances of a most grateful heart, that the impression is indelible.

I did myself the pleasure of calling on Mrs. Webster, the last week & gave her some assurance that I should visit Boston during the season, & was pleased to learn that you & she contemplated a visit to this part of the State during the summer & have her promise to see us.

The result of the New York charter election is auspicious[1] & will have great influence on our fall elections—indeed I perceive every where indications of returning sobriety & good sense on the part of the people & am encouraged in the hope & belief that the public will appreciate justly the abominations of the general government.

But my dear Sir, I am pained to tell you, that after several interviews with leading Anti-Masons, if they are correctly informed, & I fear they are, the Anti-Masons in this State will never support Mr. Clay. We know he cannot renounce his masonic principles, without ruin & dishonor, & they say that unless he does he cannot be nominated. Anti-Masonry is gaining rapidly in this State & they feel conscious of their strength & importance. I think they will make nominations in September of Candidates for President & Vice President. Some of them I have reason to believe are favorable to me for the latter office; but I shall remain perfectly passive, being a Mason of the 3d. degree, but not having attended a lodge in more than thirty years—but determined to remain, as I have been, perfectly neutral between the Masons and Anti-Masons.

If three tickets of electors are nominated in this State (the election being by general ticket, & determined by a plurality) I fear that Jackson electors would be chosen. Should that event appear probable, the only course to be pursued to prevent that result, would be for the opponents of Jackson to vote for the Anti-Masonic ticket. This would probably & I think certainly defeat the choice of Jackson electors, & bring the choice into the House. How it would be decided there or whether any choice would take place, depends on the result of elections to be held this spring & summer. I merely give you some loose speculations founded on the present state of things.

Having mentioned my own name to you, who were among the first to suggest the idea, I need scarcely say to you, that I am incapable of playing any deceptive game, or acting at all with a view to my own election. I am as indifferent to the subject as any man can be; if I can be serviceable to the Country, I am nothing loth to be so—but any office, must come unsought by me.

I heartily concur in the election of Mr. Clay, not that I think him the only fit, or even fittest man for the Station of President (for he has erred in Judgment on some very important points) but because he seems to be called for by the great mass of those opposed to Jackson, & union is essential to success. But I should be misunderstood in imputing to him *errors*, I do not mean his general principles of government, but those that are of a personal character; such as his acceptance of the Office of Secretary of State under Mr. Adams, & his duel with [John] Randolph &c &c.

You will I am sure excuse me for thus trespassing on your time. In the hope & expectation of seeing you somewhere or somehow during the summer, believe me most sincerely Yours

A Spencer

ALS. DLC. Published in Curtis, 1: 399–400.

1. In the city election concluded on April 14, anti-Tammany and anti-administration forces between them won almost two thirds of the seats on the Board of Aldermen, and elected about half of the assistant aldermen; thus they had a decided majority of the total.

TO ELISHA WHITTLESEY

Boston May 10 1831

My Dear Sir

I have to thank you for your kind letter of April 4.[1] When I left Washington it was my determination to visit Ohio, this month; but I find my friends here doubt the prudence of such a measure. They think it would raise a *hue & cry*, & might do harm, by possibility, on the eve of the Kentucky election. I have not finally settled the point, with myself; but am quite unwilling to give up the idea. If I should be so fortunate as to be in Ohio, you will be sure both to hear of, & see me. My intention was to see Ohio, pretty extensively; & to buy land enough, either in that State or Indiana, for a farm for one of my boys.

What an explosion at Washington! It took us, as I presume it did you, by perfect surprise. The truth is, public opinion drove out the Cabinet; & if [it] be kept enlightened, it will also change the head. I begin to doubt whether Genl. Jackson can be re-elected. My apprehension is, he will yet retire *from the contest*. A well conducted campaign, next winter, I think, will produce this result, in all probability. Mr V. Buren's present *scheme* is, most likely, to be Vice President; &, in interim, to go to London. Being V. President, death or resignation may make him President. If this plan gets *blown*, the People will defeat it. He cannot be chosen V. P. if the plot be understood.

I am particularly desirous of knowing what effect this breaking up has produced on the Western States. That is, at present, a great point. If the Western elections, the ensuing Autumn, should go strongly for Mr Clay, & the party to which he belongs, I shall have great hopes, internal divisions to the contrary notwithstanding, that *New York* will ultimately give him her vote. If so, there will [be] an end of the reign of selfishness, & incompetency.

Pray let me know how you stand this explosion, in Ohio. Yrs truly

Danl Webster

ALS. OClWHi.   1. Not found.

FROM NOAH WEBSTER

New Haven May 13. 1831

Sir.

If you have preserved the letters I wrote to you three or four years ago, [1827]¹ on the subject of obtaining a new copy-right law, I will thank you to inclose them to me by mail, as I wish to take a copy of them, if you do not object. I will return them without delay.

I wish, Sir, to know from you whether Mr [Robert Y.] Hayne of the Senate introduced as reported the copy right bill, the last session, & made any remarks on it. On the second reading I was present, & am confident not a word was said except by yourself. I have the honor to be with much respect Your Obedt Servt   N Webster

ALS. DLC.
1. Bracketed date insertion by Noah Webster.

TO NOAH WEBSTER

Boston May 16. 1831

Dear Sir

I have looked over my letters for 1827, & find only the enclosed from you.¹ There was, I remember, a more important one, recd about that time, which I presume I have left at Washington, filed away among other papers relating to the Copy right subject, or else have given it to some Com[mitt]ee.²

The recent Copy right Bill was recd from the H. of R. &, in the Senate, was referred, on my motion, to the Jud[iciary] Com[mitt]ee. That Com-[mitt]ee asked me to examine it, & report it to the Senate, if I thought proper. I did so. When it was taken up I explained its provisions, short-ly, & it passed, without a single word being said by any other member. I was anxious, as you know, to introduce amendments, which I deemed very material, but abandoned the purpose, at the suggestion of friends, who feared that any amendment would endanger the final passage of the Bill.³ I am, D Sir, with much regard, Yrs   Danl Webster

P.S. I hope no public use is intended to be made of the Statement, which is written above. I add this, because I have seen some printed accounts of occurrences connected with the Copy right bill in the Senate, which were founded in mistake; but which, nevertheless, I do not wish con-tradicted on my authority. If a good deed is done, I am content, without entering into an exact computation of, or, inquiry into, the agency of different individuals.

ALS. NN.

1. Noah Webster to DW, January 29, 1827, in E. E. F. Skeel, comp., *Notes on the Life of Noah Webster* (2 vols., New York, 1912), 2: 301, inquiring about the progress of the copyright bill before the Judiciary Committee.

2. Probably Noah Webster to DW,

September 30, 1826, in *Correspondence*, 2: 130–132.

3. House Bill 145 entitled "An act to amend the several acts respecting copy-rights" was introduced in the Senate on January 10, passed without amendment on the twenty-ninth, and was signed into law on February 3, 1831.

TO JOSEPH WARREN REVERE

Boston July 6. 1831

My Dear Sir,

I have not been so fortunate as to find you in town, the last two days; & being about to set off on a journey myself, I yesterday saw Mr Abbott Lawrence, & fully explained to him my wishes, respecting the Rail Road subscription.[1] I have told him of your kind suggestions, & desired him to confer with you. You will do me a favor, by seeing him, when you come to town.

With thanks for the interest you take in this business, on my account, I remain, Dear sir, with regard, Your Ob. Sert   Danl. Webster

ALS. MHi. Joseph Warren Revere (1777–1868), oldest surviving son of Paul Revere, was founder of the Revere Copper Company and was involved in numerous businesses in

the Boston area.

1. Probably the Boston and Providence Railroad, of which both Lawrence and Revere were prime movers.

FROM STEPHEN WHITE

New York August 7 1831

My Dear Sir

Caroline, Ellen[1] and myself left the Springs on friday morning. Mr LeRoy[2] and party would depart that afternoon or the following morning and Mrs [Cornelia Le Roy] Edgar[3] on Monday. Our good friend Mr [George] Blake, whose admiration for the New Jersey widow[4] had apparently undergone some diminution, was to be leader of the escort to Lebanon and Boston. Mr Blake and myself, with his man John[5] as a coadjutor, made a critical examination of the Roan Horses and renewed the offer of $375; but the owner was very firm to his price though I think $385 would have purchased them. They would I doubt not have suited your purposes. Our party down river was increased by the company of Gov. [Mahlon] Dickerson of New Jersey who made himself quite agreeable.

Mr. Van Buren, it is now said (and I have it from Mr [Henry Randolph?] Storrs who interrogated him) will not go out in the Potomac but in the packet of 16th. Mr S. said the expense in going by the Frigate for wives &c would be $800—and by the Packet not more than $200.[6]

The day on which you left the Springs I received a letter from Mr. S[tephen] C. Phillips which ought to have been received several days before. Had you been there I should have asked you to look at it, and if I find a private conveyance will send it you for it is somewhat voluminous. The main object was to ascertain whether you continued faithful to the interest of Mr Clay and tho' written by Mr Phillips was, doubtless the expression of the wishes of the Central Committee. On that point I assured him there had, so far as I could ascertain, been no alteration in your opinions or feelings. That on more than one occasion recently I had heard you speak of Mr C. and of his claims in a mode evincive of that disposition. That in my individual judgment our friends should all stand firm for him unless a failure of the Kentucky elections or his death both equally fatal to his success, should call for a new candidate in which event I thought neither yourself or your friends should be unmindful how prominent your claims were when compared with any of those other individual[s]. I then referred him to a letter I wrote Mr [Joseph E.] Sprague, detailing among other facts, the great feeling in your favour uniformly evinced by the prominent individuals of all parties wherever you had been and the strong disposition to create a *constitutional party* and to place you at the head of it. While making these remarks however, I distinctly stated them as the result of views consequent upon the failure of Mr. Clay, who I presumed would be supported manfully until his defeat, if it should unhappily take place, should lead our friends to adopt some other more popular candidate rather than make shipwreck of our hopes by an obstinate support of men instead of principles.

It is my intention to leave here on Wednesday for Boston and on the following day I hope to have the pleasure of visiting Summer Street. Mr Herman Edgar[7] will accompany us. To my great surprise I find no letters for me here not even from Mrs P.[8] who promised to be particularly punctual. With best respects and regards to Mrs W, I am most truly & resp Yours   Stephen White

I enclose Mr Phillips letter, *confidentially*.[9]

Colonel [Samuel Lorenzo] Knapp has just called on me evidently much chagrined at the delay, of a work he has in the press in Boston.[10] Mr. [Nathan] Hale of Boston was here last week who told him the only reason [for] the delay was that he could not get the manuscript which was in the hands of Mr [George] Ticknor. August 9th. The storm has prevented the Steam Boat from going and detained this letter. I am afraid also that it will prevent my going by tomorrows boat as the steady rain hindered my going to Jersey to look after my farm there which I must do before I leave. May I ask the favour of your letting them know that in Bowdoin Street? Most truly Yours devotedly   S. W.

Mr. White has the honour to send his friend Mrs: Webster a proof portrait which is to be a frontispiece of a work now in progress. Harriets letter of last Sunday is just received—Tuesday noon.

ALS. NhHi. Published in part in Van Tyne, pp. 161–162.

1. Caroline, the future Mrs. Fletcher Webster, and Ellen were daughters of Stephen White.

2. Whether this is the elder Herman Le Roy or one of his sons has not been determined.

3. Cornelia Le Roy Edgar (1787–1860), sister of Caroline Le Roy Webster, widow of William Edgar, New York lawyer who died in 1823.

4. Not identified. Blake (1769–1841), Boston lawyer and close personal friend of Webster, had lost his wife in 1826.

5. Not identified.

6. Van Buren, appointed minister to England during the recess of Congress, was preparing to depart for London.

7. Herman Le Roy Edgar (1811–1858), son of Cornelia Le Roy Edgar and nephew of Caroline Webster.

8. Probably the writer's daughter Harriette, who had married Webster's brother-in-law, James W. Paige, on June 14, 1831. The final postscript acknowledges a letter from her.

9. Not found.

10. Knapp (1783–1838; Dartmouth 1804), though he occasionally practiced law, was primarily a journalist and popular writer. During the recent Presidential campaign he had been editor of the Washington *National Journal*, house organ of the Adams administration. His *Memoir of the Life of Daniel Webster* (Boston, Stimpson and Clapp, 1831), was actually printed by Hale, whose comment reported by White indicates that Ticknor reviewed the manuscript. The frontispiece, engraved by W. Hoagland from a sketch by James Frothingham, Jr., is the portrait alluded to in the final postscript of this letter. The *Memoir*, Knapp tells us, is expanded from an earlier "hasty sketch" produced "without looking for a single fact not within the recollection of the writer." Ignatius Loyola Robertson, pseud., *Sketches of Public Characters*, (New York, 1830), pp. 5–29. It has all the attributes of a campaign biography. Webster, of course, was not overtly a candidate at this time, but White's letter leaves little doubt that his supporters were prepared to push him forward, should Clay show any sign of faltering.

FROM WILLIAM WIRT

White Sulphur Springs (Va.)
August 17. 1831.

My dear Sir

I hope this letter will find you disengaged and in one of your sweetest moods, tenses and numbers, because I wish you to be acquainted with the gentleman who will hand it to you—Mr. [Salmon Portland] Chase, of Cincinnati, Ohio, the nephew of Bishop [Philander] Chase, a young member of the bar and in my opinion one of the finest intellectual specimens of your own intellectual country. He wrote the life and character of [Henry] Brougham which appeared in the last number of the North American Review[1] and is full of literature and useful information of all sorts. He can give you a political sketch of the west and of the prospects there before us—*"Nefandum Regina."* I beg my respects to Mrs. W. & remain very truly Yours   Wm. Wirt

ALS. NhHi.
   1. "Life and Character of Henry

Brougham," *North American Review*, 33 (July 1831): 227–261.

FROM ROBERT FIELD STOCKTON

Princeton August 19th 1831

My Dr Sir

We have had recently but little communication on the subject of politics—and this letter may not perhaps be acceptable.

The present posture of public affairs however tempts me to communicate to you some views which I in common with many friends here and at the South entertain. Mr Calhouns friends I presume no longer hope for his success—his last address to the public has in my opinion settled that matter.[1] Mr Clay cannot in my poor opinion succeed. The popularity of Genl Jackson is on the wane. If you can get back to your free trade notions of 1824—to the old Federal doctrine in relation to the Judiciary—and to some point on the subject of internal improvements, where the funds of the nation may be used safely for that purpose, without encouraging the System of "Log rolling" so dangerous to all honest Legislation—your chance is good.[2] Most Truly   R. F. Stockton

ALS. NhD. Published in Curtis, 1: 401.
   1. In late July 1831, Calhoun had published his Fort Hill address in

which he first publicly argued in favor of the doctrine of nullification.
   2. Webster's notes for a reply, dated August 25, appear below.

FROM EDWARD CURTIS

New York August 20th. 1831

Dear Sir—

It is certainly *questionable* whether Mr Clay is the choice of Kentucky for President. The mails of this morning confirm our previous information, that he loses seven of the Congl. Delegation.

A newspaper from Louisville dated the 9th. Inst, which I have just seen, asserts that [Albert Gallatin] Hawes is elected over [Thomas] Chilton by 37 votes, & thus they claim eight members of Congress.

Indiana goes all hollow against him & probably Missouri. Those results coming, as they do, upon the heels of certain events, seem to me to fairly justify the Conclusion that for popularity, Mr Clay is not entitled to be called "the man of the West," any longer. And now that darkness rests upon his political horizon elsewhere all around, how long shall borrowed light illuminate its eastern quarter?

I was happy to learn thro the Doctor [Cyrus Perkins], that you & yours reached home in safety & health, and since that time, I trust you have all enjoyed better opportunities for the practice of breathing and sleeping than has fallen to our lot in this suffering city, for the last two weeks.

If we survive the effects of the hot weather that has been, is now, & may be, Mrs. Curtis & myself intend to take leave of absence for five or six days, and this day week expect to rest in the "Cradle of Liberty." Mrs. Curtis & myself will be wronged, if you do not assure Mrs. Webster of our most grateful remembrance, and tender our kindest compliments to Miss Julia & Daniel. I have the honor to be, My Dear Sir, Your friend,
Edward Curtis.

ALS. DLC.

TO [EDWARD EVERETT]

Boston Aug. 25 1831

Dear Sir

I think the matter of the Patriot[1] of great importance, & will most cheerfully cooperate in all proper measures to effect what is desired. If any thing occurs, to which I can contribute an exertion, please give me notice. The Paper is important; generally, & of particular influence in particular Counties. Yrs truly   D. Webster

I burn all little things like this.

ALS. MHi.
1. The *Boston Patriot* merged with Nathan Hale's *Advertiser* to form the *Boston Daily Advertiser & Patriot* on January 1, 1832. John Brazer Davis, editor of the *Patriot*, was in poor health and had found it increasingly difficult to manage the paper. He died in 1832.

TO ROBERT FIELD STOCKTON

[August 25, 1831]

Answered August 25.[1] Glad to receive his letter. As to getting back, difficulty is not in *my* position, but in that of the country. Country cannot go back—cannot bear violent change. Said at the time (1824) I would not vote to change back again. As to judiciary, never altered my opinion, that it is in danger.

AN. NhD. Published in Curtis, 1: 401.

1. The answer to Stockton's letter of August 19, above, has not been found. Webster did not normally retain copies of outgoing letters, but these notes in Webster's hand are filed with Stockton's letter.

TO [CHARLES MINER]

Boston Aug. 28. 1831

My Dear Sir

I wish I could say any thing encouraging on the highly important Subjects mentioned in your letter of the 20th.[1] The Kentucky election has not turned out to be *quite so bad* as it appeared to be, at the date of your letter; but, still, it is unsatisfactory, & has produced an unfavorable impression in this quarter. Speaking to you in the most confidential manner, I must say, that I concur with you, in the opinion that there is very little chance of electing Mr Clay. I believe we may hope for the vote of Kentucky, yet; but even with that, I do not perceive where we are to find enough others to make a majority. My present impression is, *there is but one chance left to save the country from further & worse misrule*; & that is, to bring forward some man, in whose favor the National Republicans & Anti Masons of Pennsylvania & New York could be induced to unite, so as to secure the votes of those States. With *them*, Ohio, New England, New Jersey, Delaware, Maryland would be able to elect a President. But I fear there is very little prospect of finding such a candidate. You say, that you believe the Anti Masons are intent on pushing Judge [John] McLean. It will never do. Our friends in N. England, & elsewhere, *will never be brought to support him*. As against him, the election of Genl Jackson would be certain. A Gentleman, writing from Philadelphia, says, "Let us put up a candidate, if we make a choice, in whom we have perfect confidence, & if we fail, still, a minority, united on principle, & with a sound head, is a better security to the country than success, in behalf of moderate talents, or doubtful principles." I agree to all this; at the same time that I see the difficulty in finding the man. I confess I do not know him. You are pleased to say, that I possess a portion of the confidence of the conflicting parties. Perhaps it may be so; but I cannot think the country is inclined to bring me forward, & it is certain, that I shall do nothing to bring myself forward. I have little experience in public affairs, & have not been long enough before the Country to produce great general confidence. My only merit is an ardent attachment to the Country, & its constitution of Government; & I am already more than paid for all my efforts, if you, & other good men, think I have done any thing to defend the Constitution, & promote the welfare of the Country. In the favor which those efforts have attracted towards me, I see proofs of a real, substantial, fixed attachment among the People to the Constitution. The great body of the Community is quite sound, on that point. And that is the feeling which we ought to cultivate, & on which we must rely. *If we bring about a change, it will be done by us as a Union Party.*

And now, My Dear Sir, will you tell me, whether, in your judgment, there is any individual, who could so unite the Anti Masonic & Nat. Repub. votes of Penna. as to carry the State agt. Genl. Jackson? I should like much to know your present impressions, on that vital question.

The Anti Masonic Convention, at Baltimore,[2] will have a most responsible part to act. The prosperity of the Country, perhaps the fate of its Government, hangs on their decision. God give them true wisdom, & disinterested patriotism!

I shall be glad to hear from you, at your earliest leisure. Yrs truly

D. Webster

You will of course consider this letter as in the strictest sense confidential. I wish I could see Charles Pinckney's Speech—of 1787—[3]

ALS. PWbH.

1. Not found.

2. The convention was to meet September 26.

3. *Observations on the Plan of Government submitted to the Federal Convention in Philadelphia, on the 28th of May, 1787, by Mr. Charles Pinckney, delegate from the State of* *South Carolina. Delivered at different times in the course of their discussions.* (New York, 1787), and reprinted in Frank Moore, *American Eloquence: A collection of Speeches and Addresses, by the most eminent Orators of America* (2 vols., New York, 1862), 1: 362–370.

TO NATHAN HALE

Marshfield Sep. 5. [1831]

Dr Sir

I think it something of an object that the Anti Masonic Convention, to be holden this month, should not nominate Judge [John] McLean; which I think they are very likely to do. He cannot be chosen, but he might draw off some strength, to the prejudice, now or hereafter, of the good cause. It appears to me there is one view of the case, which has not yet been presented to the public in its proper strength; that is, the impropriety of setting up a member of the Supreme Court as a Candidate for the Presidency. In my opinion, it is very objectionable for various reasons. It inflames popular pre;udice against the Court, in the first place; &, in the next, it more or less weakens confidence in the Tribunal. A judge, looking over popularity, is not likely to inspire the highest degree of confidence & regard. A late writer in the N. Y. Journal of Commerce, in a pretty well written & sensible piece, has brought forward the name of Chief Justice Marshall for the Presidency. Now it appears to me here is a fit occasion to say something, on the general subject, without giving offense to Mr McLean's friends. If you think so pray give us a column in the Daily [Advertiser].[1] Much prejudice [is] already against the judges. The present party in power are willing enough to increase those prejudices; & nothing, I think, would aid their views more, than to have an opportunity to tell the People that hereafter our Presidents are to be taken from the Bench.

I am quite sure, that such are Ch. Jus Marshall's notions, on this subject, that nothing in the world would induce him to be a Candidate. I am, Dr Sir, Very truly, Yrs   D Webster

ALS. MNS.

1. An editorial in this vein, "The Presidency and the Judiciary," appeared in Hale's weekly paper, the *Boston Weekly Messenger*, on September 15, 1831.

FROM CHARLES MINER

West Chester, Pa Sept 8 1831

Dear Sir,

I will speak, as I know it is your pleasure I should, with all possible frankness and sincerity. I concur with you entirely respecting Judge [John] McLean; my opinions of that gentleman were made known to you several years ago. That you may see I suggested not my own opinion but that of a portion of the Anti Masonic party, I enclose the *Star*[1] which will shew you the steps taking in his behalf. Several other papers have placed his name at their head. The Calhoun party, of course, would prefer him. His origin and rise to distinction through the aid of Mr. Calhoun you perfectly understand.[2] I much incline to think there is a *secret understanding* between leaders of the two parties that the Anti Masons should bring forward Mr. McLean for President.

As the influence of Mr [Richard] Rush's exasperating letters[3] is more widely diffused, the hope of Union between the National Republican and Anti Masonic parties to which I have looked with hope in your favour, becomes more faint. You will see how remote it seems when I mention that Thomas Smith Esqr. member of Congress from Delaware Co[unty,

Pennsylvania] in 1816 whom, perhaps, you knew, a liberal gentleman of fortune, 14 years a patron, and a zealous Nat. Repn. discontinued his [subscription to the] Record because I am too Anti Masonic, in as much as I advised an Union of the two parties, pleading that it was necessary to the public welfare.

Our friends here, at length, and against my advice, have resolved to form a Ticket in opposition to that party; I shall go with them, yielding up my individual opinion, and we shall make considerable inroads upon their ranks. I am confident that party is not gaining ground. The *Examiner*, published here by Mr [John Douglas] Perkins,[4] a N. England Clergyman, is abandoned for want of support: Several of their distinguished men have come out for our party. The Press in Delaware Co. is offered to the National Republicans as it cannot much longer exist. In Bucks Co. the A[nti] M[asonic] paper has come out against the Tariff. [Joseph] Ritner their candidate for Governor is really a poor creature and the stirring questions of National concern must, I think, ere long, absorb the party. From the *Star* you will see that Mr. Rush has gained little, by his appeals. Their policy is curious, perhaps cunning. Those who are pledged they are sure of; and all their patronage is thrown out to allure those who sit aloof into their ranks, whom then, like C[adwallader] D[avid] Colden they abandon. While, therefore, the Anti Masonic Association is too important to be passed by without great consideration, I do not myself believe there is danger of its becoming the preponderating influence in this state or in any considerable portion of the Union.

In the mean time, the nomination of Mr. Clay at Pittsburg, General [William] Marks presiding,[5] the result of the western elections being fully known, and the ill advised positiveness with which many papers insist on our having gained victories in those states, render a change of candidate, more difficult and less likely to prove efficatious, than I would have wished. Although I am satisfied, that there is a Majority in Pennsylvania who wish Gen. Jackson removed, there at present seems no reasonable hope of uniting the conflicting factions and concentrating their vote on any one; and I see nothing in the melancholy prospect, but his re-election and prolonged misrule.

A vote, complimentary to Mr. Clay, was passed at our Meeting, but Mr. [William H.] Dillingham,[6] our Delegate to the Baltimore Convention is left free, distinctly so to give his suffrage for whomsoever he may after consultation think best. If there is a reasonable prospect of success with another, as I am satisfied there is none for Mr. Clay, should the selection fall on you, as I presume it would, we shall hail it with pleasure and sustain it with spirit.

After this free exposition of our situation, allow me to add my sincere belief that the Country looks to you as its chiefest Hope. We have presumed in case of Mr. Clays election, that you would be his successor; and should he fail, that the National Republican Interest would forthwith rally round you; as, of course, Mr. C. would never again be brought into the field. But if we must fail, our strength in the west, which, perhaps may, hereafter be made available to an Eastern man, may be better preserved by a generous and spirited support of Mr Clay.

My efforts and influence are too humble to speak of, but such as they are, they are *now* tendered, under the highest sense of devotion to my Country, to aid your other friends, in whatever measure may be deemed wise to rescue the nation from existing degradation and impending ruin. Be assured my dear Sir that I am your faithful friend and Servant

Charles Miner

ALS. NhD.

1. Enclosure missing. Probably the *Gettysburg Star*, variously called the *Anti-Masonic Star*, the *Anti-Masonic Star and Republican Banner*, and the *Star and Adams County Republican Banner* between 1827 and 1832.

2. McLean and Calhoun had become intimate when both served in Congress during the War of 1812. Calhoun was probably responsible for McLean's appointments as commissioner of the General Land Office and later as postmaster general under Monroe, and McLean had been one of Calhoun's earliest supporters for the Presidency, in the campaign of 1824.

3. Rush had written several public letters, including one to the Anti-Masonic Committee of York County, Pennsylvania, May 4, 1831; one to the Boston Anti-Masonic Committee on June 30; and a third, to the Lancaster, Pennsylvania, Anti-Masons, on August 13. In each of these he took a position so outspokenly hostile toward Masonry as to offend Clay's

Masonic partisans and to make virtually impossible any rapprochement between Anti-Masons and National Republicans.

4. Perkins (1769–1847; Yale 1791), Connecticut-born Congregational minister, moved to Lancaster County, Pennsylvania, in 1800 and eventually settled in Coatesville. There he became a Presbyterian and edited the short-lived *Anti-Mason Examiner* from 1829 to September 1831. At that time the paper was taken over by Joseph Painter's West Chester *Register* and became the *Anti-Mason Register and Chester County Examiner*.

5. A National Republican meeting in Pittsburgh, August 27, 1831, unanimously recommended Henry Clay and William Wirt as candidates for President and Vice President, respectively, and instructed their delegates to the national convention to support them.

6. Dillingham (1791–1854), Chester County lawyer and state legislator.

TO NATHAN APPLETON

Sandwich, Sep. 11 [1831]

My Dr Sir

The enclosed is from the keeper of the Hotel, in which we lodged last session.[1] The rooms, are, two rooms on the second story, one pretty large one, in front, one smaller in rear, connected by a door of common size. This largest was Mrs Webster's room to see her friends, & we dined there also, when we had company. The smaller room was used as a study—but we dined in it, when quite alone.—2 rooms, in the story next above, which are comfortable lodging rooms,—& then, rooms still higher up for servants.

These rooms would accomodate two Gentlemen very well—there would be a lodging room, & a reading, or sitting room for each, & break-fast & dinner could be served in the larger, without inconvenience. But they would not well accomodate *three* Gentlemen, without compelling some of them to read & write in their lodging rooms.

My expectation is, that Mrs Webster will join me at W[ashington] about the 10th March. There will be room enough for her. She talks something of bringing her sister, Mrs [Catherine Augusta Le Roy] New-bold with her, but I regard that as too uncertain to be the basis of any calculation.

If Mrs [Maria Theresa Gold] Appleton should accompany you, or join you, there would be room enough, of course, for her. If she should not, & your daughter should visit Washington, arrangements could be made to accomodate her.

Under these circumstances, shall we engage the rooms? The charge is *high*, for us two; but the omission of *corkage* (one dollar per bottle) is a considerable diminution. I have had a colored man as my servant, for many years. The keeper of the Hotel furnishes one good one, & these are enough.

Mr [Benjamin] Gorham can tell you what rooms & lodging would cost at Gadsbys, *corkage* included. Gadsby's rooms are much larger, & hand-somest, & his house much nearer the Capitol. In other respects, at least in some others, I should prefer Barnards. I believe Gadsby's culinary establishment is as good as Barnards.

If you will write me a line to say what you think upon all this, I will give Mr [Frederick] Barnard[2] an answer. For myself, I have no strong opinion, either way. The price is high, for our own lodging & board, while alone, which, so far as my family is concerned, will probably be three months. In general, I have found that somebody wanted the pay, as much as I wanted rooms; & have not engaged them till I arrived. Yet there may be some danger that we shall not find what will well suit us.[3]

I shall remain here some few days longer—you may address me at this place Yrs truly,   D. Webster

It is exceeding warm here today.

ALS. MHi. Published in Van Tyne, pp. 162–163.

1. The Websters stayed at Barnard's Mansion Hotel on Pennsylvania Avenue during the 1830–1831 session.

2. Proprietor of the Mansion Hotel

from 1828 to 1833.

3. Both Webster and Appleton eventually settled on staying at Gadsby's National Hotel on Pennsylvania Avenue for the two sessions Appleton served as congressman.

FROM JAMES BUCHANAN

Lancaster 13 Sep: 1831.

Dear Sir,

I enclose you the copy of a letter which I have addressed to the Secretary of the Treasury,[1] because I have taken the liberty of using your name in it. If you consider the reference incorrect it will afford me pleasure to correct it immediately. In looking over your remarks on the Bill for the relief of Insolvent Debtors[2] I was forcibly struck with the liberal & kind expressions which you used in relation to my exertions in the House. Rest assured that they are duly appreciated by me & that I consider it "praise indeed to be praised by you."

Should your recollection correspond with mine in relation to this Bill, if you thought proper to interfere—a word from you would have a powerful effect in correcting the error into which the Attorney General & Secretary of the Treasury have fallen.[3]

Please to present my most respectful compliments to Mrs. Webster & believe me to be truly yours   James Buchanan

ALS. PCarlD. Published in Curtis, 1: 405.

1. Enclosure missing.

2. Delivered in the Senate, March 1, 1831.

3. The Insolvent Debtors Act had been approved March 2, 1831. In an opinion dated July 28, 1831, Attorney

General Roger Brooke Taney had narrowed the definition of insolvency, restricted the class affected, and prescribed procedure. *Opinions of Attorneys General of the United States*, in *House Executive Documents*, 31st Cong., 2d sess., Serial 602, Doc. No. 55, p. 777.

For a decade, between 1825 and 1835, Webster bought and sold Boston real estate, as speculator investor, or as agent for others. Thomas Wigglesworth (1776–1855), to whom the letter below is addressed, was one of the city's wealthiest merchants. The property referred to was owned by the heirs of Henry Hill, of whom Wigglesworth was one. Webster did in fact buy it two months later, on November 17, for $44,966 (mDW 39757); then, in a matter of days, sold it to Wigglesworth in two parcels, one for $23,964 (mDW 39763), and the other for $9,036 or $33,000 for

*the whole property. (Suffolk County Deed Books, Volume 356, folio 82.)
The apparent loss of $11,966 we may be sure was recovered—profitably
—in some other way.*

*Ths was not Webster's first real estate transaction in the Summer and
High Street section of Boston, nor would it be his last. He had bought his
own house on Summer Street in 1825, shortly after Timothy Williams
and Lewis Tappan had acquired substantial holdings in the area which
they had subdivided into twenty-four house lots. (See* Correspondence, 2:
40–42, *and map facing.) Webster had at that time bought lots 1 and 2,
gradually extending his acquisitions to include lots 3 and 4, and 18 and
19. He also held some small parcels in South Boston, and at Lechmere
Point in Cambridge, but the Summer Street–High Street area was the
center of his real estate activity until it abruptly stopped in the middle
1830s when he began speculating heavily in western lands.*

*Webster's Boston properties undoubtedly constituted a sound invest-
ment. They could always be—and were frequently—mortgaged to provide ready cash, and their value could hardly fail to increase with the
growth of the city. (See Stephen White to DW, March 19, 1832, mDW
9942, and DW to James W. Paige, April 6, 1832, mDW 9981.) Although
the Summer Street property remained residential, it assumed added
worth from the expansion of commercial enterprise nearby. In the larger
area, wharfage was increased, streets were widened and extended, mud
flats were filled in, and by the middle of the decade railroad terminals
were under construction.*

TO [THOMAS WIGGLESWORTH]

Sep. 22nd. [1831]
Thursday noon

My Dear Sir

I have only this moment recd yr obliging note of the 17.[1] I thank you
for making me the offer of the lot, next to me—which I am inclined to
accept. I will see you, on the subject, tomorrow. Yrs truly—   D. Webster

ALS. MHi.   1. Not found.

TO NATHANIEL F. WILLIAMS

Boston Oct. 1 [1831]

Dear Sir

I see that Anti Masonic Convention has nominated Mr [William] Wirt.
For him, personally, I have the truest regard, but I fear his acceptance
of the nomination can only ensure the reelection of the present incum-

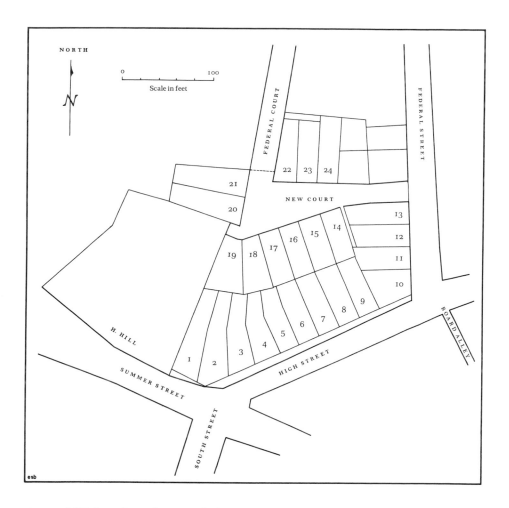

Area of Webster's real estate holdings, Summer Street, Boston

bent. It is a pity—a great pity,—that those who wish a change, cannot agree on a Candidate. We must not flatter ourselves with the hopes of division, on the other side. No Jackson man, but the Genl himself, will receive a vote. Nor will Mr Calhoun receive a vote. If Genl Jackson should be reelected, with a majority of the votes divided between Mr Clay & Mr Wirt, what a spectacle should we exhibit!

May Heaven preserve us! Yrs truly   D. W.

ALS. NhD.

TO HENRY CLAY

Boston, Oct. 5, 1831

My Dear Sir,

Mr [Edward] Everett was kind enough to show me your letter to him, stating the results of the Kentucky Election.

It is doubtless true that some considerable regret was felt in this quarter, that those results were not more strongly in our favor; but, upon the whole, a general satisfaction, as to that matter now prevails, & all think that Kentucky has, at least by a certain, if not by a great majority, declared agt. the present Administration. For my own part, I can say with great truth & sincerity, that I know no political men more deserving the thanks of the Country, than our friends in Kentucky. I have some conception of the obstacles, with which they have had to contend, not for once, but for many times; & their spirit, zeal, & perseverence in maintaining the cause of good Government, place them, in my judgment, in the first class of really patriotic citizens. This opinion I often express; & it gives me always pleasure to express it. Whatever events may come upon us, I feel, for one a debt of gratitude to the good men of Kentucky, for the firmness with which they have breasted a storm, which has threatened, &, I think still threatens, to overturn, not only the interests & institutions, but the Constitution, of the Country.

You must be aware, My Dear Sir, of the strong desire manifested in many parts of the Country, that you should come into the Senate. There is, certainly, a strong feeling of that sort, all along the Atlantic Coast. I learn its existence from private letters, as well as from the Public Newspapers. The wish is entertained here, as earnestly as any where. For myself, I hardly know what my own wishes are; because I suppose Mr [John J.] Crittenden will, of course be thought of again. He has so much talent & fitness for the place, is, according to my apprehension of his character, so true & trustworthy, has done so much for the general good, & been so marked an object, besides, for the opposition & reproach of the

Present Dominant Party at Washington, that I find myself incapable of doing *any thing*, incompatible with his wishes, or expectations. But I know not what his wishes are. Independent of considerations of this kind, the force of which you can weigh infinitely better than I can, I should entirely concur with others, in deeming it most expedient for you to come, now, into the Senate. We are to have an interesting & an arduous session. Every thing is to be attacked. An array is preparing, much more formidable than has ever yet assaulted what we think the leading & important public interests. Not only this Tariff, but the Constitution itself, in its elementary & fundamental provisions, will be assailed with talent, vigor, & union. Every thing is to be debated, as if nothing had ever been settled. You perceive imposing proceedings, under high names, going on in Philadelphia. You see measures adopted *to try the Constitution*, farther South. You see every where, I think, omens of contest, of no ordinary character. At the same time, discouraging things are happening, such as the Baltimore nomination, & *its acceptance*. I assure [you], My Dear Sir, with the prospect of toil & labor which is before me, if honor & conscience were not in the way, I would give my place to another. But *these* dictate to me—or seem to—that, so far as depends on so humble an individual as myself, the crisis must be met. But it would be an infinite gratification to have your aid—or rather your *lead*. I speak in unaffected sincerity & truth, when I say, that I should rejoice, personally, to meet you in the Senate. I am equally sincere in saying that the *cause* would, under present circumstances be materially benefitted by your presence there. I know nothing so likely to be useful. Every thing valuable in the Govt. is to be fought for; & we need your arm, in the fight. At the same time, My Dear Sir, I would not, even thus privately & confidentially to you, say any thing not consistent with delicacy & friendship for Mr Crittenden, for whose character I have great regard, & towards whom you & others have taught me to entertain the feelings of a friend. Wd to God, we could have you both, at this crisis, in the public Councils![1]

There is no material change, in the aspect of things here. Maine continues against us. In N. Hampshire there is a better spirit, & I am far from being without hopes of that State. The *Anti Masons* assembled here yesterday, nominated Mr. [John Quincy] Adams for Govr. agt. Govr. [Levi] Lincoln. I cannot think it possible he should accept the nomination. I have no doubt he will decline it.

I ought to thank you, in your kindness to several friends of mine, who have visited you, in the course of the session. They express themselves highly gratified by your hospitality & good offices.

I pray a most respectful remembrance to Mrs Clay; & hope, that, at some time, on one or the other side of the mountains, Mrs W. may have the pleasure of making her acquaintance. [James] Clark, [Robert P.] Letcher, & [John] Kincaid, I believe are not at great distances from Lexington. If you see them, tender my regards to them. I hope you will let me hear from you, & I am Dr Sir, very truly Yrs   Danl. Webster

ALS. DLC. Published in Colton, *Henry Clay*, pp. 317–319 (incomplete).

1. When the Kentucky legislature met a month later, Crittenden willingly stepped aside to allow Clay a slim margin of victory for the vacant Senate seat. See also above, DW to Levi Lincoln, December 25, 1830, note 5.

FROM AMBROSE SPENCER

Albany Oct. 24. 1831.

Dear Sir.

I am sensible that your professional engagements ingross all your time, & I would not obtrude upon you, did not public interest prompt me to it. It would give me great satisfaction to know whether our opinions coincide upon the course to be adopted as to the next Presidency. I was appointed a delegate to the Baltimore convention by the national republican convention held here in June last. Nothing was done by that body to take from the delegates their freedom of opinion, altho' a resolution was adopted strongly approbatory of the character & qualifications of Mr. Clay. My present opinion is, I shall not attend the convention at Baltimore. It seems to me, to be apparent, that the convention will nominate Mr Clay, taking the News-papers as indices of public opinion. If he should be nominated & accept the nomination our cause is lost, & Genl. Jackson will certainly be re-elected. I am very unwilling to be a party to a course so ruinous to all our hopes; & I am unwilling also to disturb the harmony of the convention by differing from them.

How can Mr Clay's friends deceive themselves by believing he has the least chance of success if Genl. Jackson & Mr [William] Wirt are both in the field? Mr Clay at the utmost can gain but 89 votes, namely Massachusetts, Rhode-Island, Connecticut, New Jersey, Delaware, Maryland, Kentucky, Ohio, Indiana & Louisiana. The remaining votes are to be divided between Genl. Jackson & Mr Wirt. I agree that Mr Wirt would probably obtain only the vote of Vermont, but he would withdraw a sufficient number from those opposed to Genl. Jackson to secure his election by the electoral colleges. Admitting this last opinion to be erroneous, & that there will be a failure to elect a President by the colleges, we know the Representatives of the majority of the States, will vote for him in the House of Representatives.

In my opinion Mr Wirt has gone too far to decline; if however he should, I know enough of the temper & spirit of anti-masonry, to affirm positively, that they will hold another convention, & nominate some one who will not decline. Mr Clay can not be that man. He can not speak his opinions on Masonry & if he could it is too late.

If Mr. Clay would decline before the meeting of the Baltimore convention,[1] or address a letter to that body recommending the nomination of Mr. Wirt & giving his reasons, it seems to me Mr Wirt would receive the votes of all Mr. Clay's friends. He certainly would if they are governed by principle & not devotion to an individual. In that event there is every probability Mr Wirt would be elected. Give him the votes of the States I have mentioned & to this we may confidently add New York & Vermont & he is elected. It is not only my opinion but that of our most considerate & best informed men, that if a union can take place in this State between the Anti-Masons, & those opposed to re-election of Genl. Jackson, they would certainly form a majority of the electors.

I am astonished that an opinion exists that this State will give its vote for Mr Clay should Genl. Jackson & Mr Wirt be candidates. The fact is, Mr Clay in that case would receive comparatively but few votes. Mr Wirt would receive three times more than Mr Clay, but Genl. Jackson would receive more than either, & thus gain the electoral vote of the State. I feel as confident in these facts, as in any future event ever presented to my consideration. The result of the late elections in Vermont, is decisive of the Presidential vote of that state; the Anti-Masons are the largest party now, & one year hence will form the majority; but at all events Mr Clay has nothing to hope from that State.

With respect to Pennsylvania, what I have said of New York, applies to that State. There is already a large body of Anti-Masons there, & it is one of the dogmas of that party, sanctioned by experience, that Anti-Masonry neither goes back nor stands still. There are Anti-Masons enough there, to defeat all hopes of [that] an electoral ticket favorable to Mr. Clay, can be chosen. It is by no means improbable, that the concentration of the Anti-Masonic votes with those opposed to Jackson's re-election, in Mr Wirt, would give him that State. In Virginia too, is there not good hope, that if Genl. Jackson & Mr Wirt are the only candidates, that State may go for the latter. We know there is great defection from Jackson there; Mr Wirt is a Virg[in]ian by birth, & a republican of the Jefferson school, divested of Mr Jefferson's political errors. If Mr Wirt should not command the votes of all Mr Clays friends, this loss will I think be made up, by the votes of many who dislike both Genl. Jackson & Mr. Clay.

Of Mr Wirts high qualifications, I need not say one word to you who know him much more intimately than I do. His nomination was totally unexpected, but ought we not to hail it as a most auspicious event, if he can be the means of defeating the re-election of a man whose administration, has been a curse to the nation?

Now if it is apparent or even probable that Mr Clay can not be elected, but that Mr Wirt can be elected if Mr Clay declines, ought there to be any hesitation in taking measures to produce that result? I feel & acknowledge Mr Clays splendid & patriotic services to the country; & that he has been most cruelly & malignantly persecuted & slandered; & that he has high claims on his country; but what of all this, when the real question is, by what means a weak, wicked & dangerous man shall be defeated. I am for the cause & my Country, & am unwilling from mere personal considerations to sacrifice the cause to the man.

If I am laboring under erroneous impressions, I wish to be undeceived & therefore write you with the utmost freedom & candor. I speak the opinions of many cool & temperate friends of Mr Clay here. If my facts are true it is madness to persist in nominating Mr Clay, & if persisted in the result will be Jackson's re-election.

It is to be feared that Mr Clay is deceived by some of his ardent friends as to the vote of New York, he can not be as to Vermont since their recent election. Is it not possible to lay before Mr Clay a true state of facts, that he may take a course to relieve us from the perplexity we are in? Could he see that his persistence in being a candidate must ensure the re-election of Genl. Jackson, if I rightly estimate him, he would decline in such a way as to transfer his strength to Mr. Wirt.

There are idle speculations, that Mr. Calhoun will be a candidate, & one of the three highest on the electoral tickets. He will not expose his weakness by being a candidate. This is evident from the course of Duff Green—but where is he to gain votes save in S. Carolina?

I could say much more on this all important subject, but I fear your patience will be exhausted in reading this already too long letter.

When you & Mrs. Webster were at Saratoga the last summer, I was quite indisposed, else I certainly would have seen you there. Present me most respectfully & cordially to her & believe me with high respect, Your sincere friend   A Spencer

ALS. NhHi. Published in Van Tyne, pp. 164–167.

1. The National Republican convention met at Baltimore, December 12–16, 1831, at which time Clay was chosen its Presidential nominee by acclamation and John Sergeant, a close friend of Webster, was selected as his running mate.

Baltimore Oct 30th 1831

My Dear Sir,

I had the honor to receive only a few days since your favor addressed to me at Washington.[1] I was absent in Virginia making a short visit to Mr [James] Madison when it arrived at the City. I came over here to attend the Races and have two or three times fallen in with [William] Wirt. I have conversed freely with him about his nomination & he says he accepted it after an unavailing effort to procure its postponement until after the December convention, & after an effort to induce them to support Mr Clay. He says he found both impossible, & accepted it believing that he was the only man who could succeed. The views of his friends are expressed in the enclosed numbers which I have extracted from a paper here.[2] He denies any desertion of Mr Clay, says he never was pledged to him & that he never sought the nomination here. He will not under any circumstances decline & we must so make our calculations. He does not hesitate to declare that the Presidential office ought to be limited to one term, & he should only think of serving that period if elected. The Anti Masonic party will never unite upon Mr Clay, until he unconditionally renounces Masonry, & that he will never do.

I make one suggestion in confidence, supposing the views of this writer 'an old man' to be correct, & that the National Republican & Anti Masonic parties are united would not that party with the accessions made to it the next four years place *you* in a better position to succeed than that afforded by Jackson, or Clays election. The latter would want eight years. Suppose you were to accept the National Republican nomination for Vice President & the Anti Masons were to withdraw Mr [Amos] Ellmaker & unite, you would have a consolidated party in 1836 that would elect you without a question. If Mr Wirt is elected I apprehend that there would be no doubt of your having any place in the Government you would desire.

Without this party there is no prospect of Mr Clays election & in 1836 he would have much less chance.

I think with you the prospects are gloomy without a Union. If you think well of either of these propositions I will set on foot a correspondence with James Wadsworth[3] who is your friend & can bring it about. Your views of these subjects will be received as strictly confidential. The great object of us all is to fall on some practicable scheme to turn out the old Barbarian. With great respect yr mo ob servant   Jos M White

ALS. NhD.

1. Not found.

2. Enclosure missing.

3. Wadsworth (1768–1844), a lead-

ing western New York Anti-Mason from Livingston County, whose son James Samuel (1807–1864) attended Harvard College and worked in Webster's Boston law office.

TO AMBROSE SPENCER

Boston Nov. 16. 1831

Private & Confidential
My Dear Sir

I wrote you a hasty line,[1] some time ago, to acknowledge the receipt of your friendly letter of the 24. of October,[2] & promising to give you my thoughts on the highly important matters, to which it relates.

I incline to think, My Dear Sir, that it may be a wise decision, on your part, with your present opinions, to abstain from attending the Baltimore Convention; for I am convinced you will find there, should you go, very little inclination to support Mr. Wirt's nomination. Indeed if the members of it should vote to support Mr Wirt, unanimously, & Mr Clay should fully concur therein, I think, judging from what I see around me here, we could not induce the People, generally, to vote for him. I am astonished to hear—but I do daily so hear—persons who were never Masons, & who are, in truth, in their sentiments, Anti-Masonic;—that is, they disapprove of secret societies, say, nevertheless, that between Mr Wirt, *standing as he now does*, & Genl Jackson, *they should go for the latter*. This seems strange, but it is true. In this part of the Country, at least in this state, Anti-Masonry as *a sentiment*, is gaining ground; but Anti Masonry, as a political party, or basis of such party, I do not think is gaining. Our people do not feel that Anti Masonry, alone, is a principle broad enough to save the Country, & maintain the Govt. I think, further, that with us, Mr Wirt's nomination has greatly checked the progress of Antimasonry itself. It has caused dissatisfaction, & suspicion, in many, in whom nothing of either existed before. Of your own State you can judge better, but I have been all along apprehensive, that there being no National Republican candidates nominated, generally, throughout N York, very many, who dislike Anti-Masonry, would go over to the Jackson party. I have never thought it possible to get the vote of N York for Mr Wirt—tho' I am a poor judge, of that question. He cannot, I think, obtain any votes in N. E. out of Vermont. He has no chance, at all, in Maryland, Delaware, Ohio, Indiana, or Louisiana. And as to Va. I do not think a respectable ticket could be found for Mr. Wirt, in that State, under present circumstances.

I cannot help thinking, My Dear Sir, that Mr Wirt acted under great mis-information when he accepted the nomination at Baltimore. I believe

I must say, that it is among our misfortunes that Anti Masonry, in this State, has not fallen into the lead of the most prudent & popular persons. Its course, therefore, with us, has not been so satisfactory as it might have been; & for a like cause, I fear Mr Wirt had not before him an accurate view of the <whole> ground, so far as it respected this quarter. As I observed in my former short letter, I believe Mr Wirts nomination has *secured* Genl. Jackson's reelection! I believe he cannot take a vote from Genl. Jackson, but may take a few from Mr Clay; that is, the Vermont votes. But a greater evil resulting from his nomination is, that it greatly discouraged those, who were desirous of producing a change in the Genl Administration, & greatly encouraged the friends of the present President. I hope, indeed, for a different result, but I do not expect it. It is true, the events of the session may produce new aspects of things, & I am willing to anticipate the best.

I have thus, my Dear Sir, freely & in entire & close confidence, expressed my thoughts. You will not find much comfort in them. But let us trust to a kind Providence, & still adhere to the great interests of the Country. We shall at least then deserve success. I do not fear great mischief from acts of Congress. Our most imminent danger, at present, is from the manner in which the appointing power is likely to be exercised. We must pray for long life for all good man in office, & deeming our country yet too young to be ruined, <by bad administration,> we must resist evil, wherever we meet it, & overcome it, if we can. May Heaven prosper us!

It will give me true pleasure to hear from you often—& I may prove myself, a more punctual correspondent, hereafter than on this occasion.

AL draft. NhHi. Published in Van   1. Not found.
Tyne, pp. 167–168.   2. See above.

FROM FRANCIS LIEBER

> Saturday,
> Pearl Street [? Boston]
> [November 19, 1831?]

Sir

Though I am fully aware, how precious your time is, particularly so shortly before the opening of Congress, yet I take the liberty to ask you, whether you would think it worth the while, to give me, in a very succinct statement, the chief arguments against *nullification*? I wish it for my Encyclopaedia, and thought it most advisable to ask at once there for the short article, where I know, I can get it best. According to my custom on religious questions, and sometimes on matters of politics, I shall state what the nullifiers think to be their best arguments, and what their adversaries think in their turn to be in their favor.

The nature of the Americana would not permit me to bestow more than about one page or a little more on the whole article, which I know very well is not the room to elucidate and proove any matter of grave importance, but all I can do is to state *historically* what *is*, the *pro* and *con*, and must leave it to the people to argue. I believe it is only my task to treat such points in a historical point of view. You would much oblige me by an answer.

Present my best compliments to Mrs Webster and believe me Sir most respectfully Your obedt.   Francis Lieber

ALS. NhHi. The date given Lieber's letter is not completely certain. Had Webster written the article on nullification for the *Encyclopaedia Americana*, which he did not, it would have appropriately appeared in volume 9, which was published in 1831, or early 1832 with a backdated time of publication. Webster himself endorsed the letter "Nov.," and the first session of the Twenty-Second Congress met shortly thereafter on December 5, 1831. Webster appears to have left for the South sometime after November 21, so it is likely that Lieber wrote him on Saturday, November 19. Lieber may have wanted to use the occasion as well as the format of his *Encyclopaedia* to present a debate on nullification in light of Calhoun's Fort Hill Address published four months earlier.

In the fall of 1824 while returning to Boston from Cape Cod, Daniel and Grace Webster passed by the farmstead of Captain John Thomas along a back road in Marshfield, in a section of the township called Green Harbor which was within sight of the sea. Attracted by the 300-acre farm and its location, the Websters stopped and talked with Captain Thomas, who invited them to stay for several days. Every summer thereafter they visited the hospitable captain on their way to or from their summer retreat at Sandwich. Some time later, after his second marriage, Webster learned that Thomas' estate was heavily mortgaged and that he was without funds. In 1832, the senator proposed to buy the property under an arrangement whereby Captain and Mrs. Thomas might retain lifetime occupancy.

Even before this arrangement was finalized, Webster took into his employ the captain's two sons, Charles Henry (1807–1894) whom he always referred to as Henry, and Nathaniel Ray (1812–1840), who was always known as Ray. Webster came to rely upon Henry to supervise farming matters and local business, while Ray was often employed in handling matters in the middle states and in Washington.

TO CHARLES HENRY THOMAS

Washington Decr. 17. 1831

Dear Henry,

You will be glad to hear that I arrived here safe, after a cold journey, & a detention of some days at Philadelphia by indisposition. The cold weather still continues, & exceeds all that I have ever experienced in this place.

By Mr Weston,[1] who is now here, I shall send you a sealed package, containing $1000—in bills & check. Mr Weston will know that it contains something *valuable*;—but no more. It will doubtless go safe by him. This is to pay your father. It will be necessary to make some calculations of interest, &c; all which you will do, & pay him off. The contract was, that I was to give 100 Dlls, for a privilege of buying, at 3500, till March. I concluded, so soon after this bargain, to buy, at all events, that when I gave your father the 100 Dollars he seemed unwilling to take it, except as part of the 3500. This shall be just as he thinks right; but to me it seems, equitable, under all the circumstances, that he should receive at least 50 Dollars, in addition to the 3500. He is, indeed, entitled to the whole, & I shall be quite as well satisfied to pay it all, say 3600 in the whole.

Let the deed[2] be carefully & properly made out, & signed, if it be not already done, & fold it up safely in a package, & send it to me here, by mail. It will no doubt come safe. I shall not put it on record, at present; nor is it best to tell more about our matters than is necessary. Let us keep our own secrets.

The frost set in so early, & so strong, that I fear you hardly put out many trees after I saw you. If the ground be not frozen too deep, I should [think] ever-greens, pines &c, might be removed to advantage, on a sled.

Pray let me know how you all do. I left Mrs Webster & Julia well, at N. York, & they were pretty well, when I last heard from them, tho Mrs W. has a little of the influenza.

I hope you will *ride Grey Back*, a good deal. I want to make him a quiet, gentle saddle horse. Show him all the ugly sights of Marshfield, so that he may learn not to start at any thing.

Remember me to the family, & to the Dr. [John Porter] & Ann [Thomas Porter].[3] Yrs truly   Danl Webster

ALS. NhD. Published in *Old-Time New England*, 44 (Fall 1953): 55–56.
1. This may refer to Seth Weston, a Marshfield carpenter, who was a long and close friend of Webster, but it is probably Ezra Weston[, Jr.] (1772–1842), shipbuilder and operator of Duxbury, who was also a friend of the senator and more likely to travel to Washington.

2. See Conveyance of John Thomas' Marshfield farm to Webster, April 23, 1832, mDW 39770.

3. Dr. Porter of Duxbury was a close personal friend of Webster. In 1829 he had married Ann Thomas, daughter of the captain and sister of Charles Henry Thomas, to whom this letter was written.

FROM DANIEL FLETCHER WEBSTER

Cambridge Dec 17th. 1836. [1831]

My Dear Father,

I was very sorry to see that you had been unwell in Philadelphia, I suppose it was only the influenza though; We have all had it here, and the faculty applied to the Corporation for leave to dismiss College, a week sooner than usual, on account of the sickness; but they refused, because, they said, it would make a report and talk, over the country. I am glad they did not, however, as I have no place where I should like to pass three weeks. The vacation will commence next Wednesday. I am going with the [Stephen] Whites to Salem, to pass a day, and think I shall make a visit to Mr [Samuel B.] Walcott. I can take the stage and ride up there, pass a day, and come home by way of Dover.

I have begun German, which twists my mouth into as many shapes as I can possibly screw it. It is much worse to learn than Greek, and in a short time the lessons will require four hours a day. I have learnt Fisher Ames' speech,[1] and should have spoken it last Saturday, but Mr [Edward Tyrrell] Channing excused me on account of hoarseness. It is a very fine extract, and I wish I could do it justice. Edward is doing very well at the Latin School, and he has a part to speak at a public exhibition, next Saturday which I have promised him to come to hear him.

He appears to be very well contented and Uncle [James William Paige] is very kind. We are having a little fuss here about Mayors, Mr [William] Sullivan and [Theodore] Lyman and [Charles] Welles,[2] which last will probably be chosen. You of course know of Mr Elliots [William Harvard Eliot][3] death, but there is another person who I am very sorry to inform you is in danger, that is Dr [John Collins] Warren; he cut his finger while dissecting a subject, and received some of the virus, his arm is in a very bad state, and he fears to lose that. I was never aware before that it was so dangerous. I see there are some dangerous riots in England and especially in Bristol. I wonder what Sir C[harles] Wetherell[4] thinks of it. Mother sent me a little present the other day, I shall write her a letter tomorrow, I will direct it to you as you wished, and you can send it to her and save postage. We are all very well at home and Neddy sends love to you, Your very affectionate son   D. F. Webster

ALS. NhHi. The date appears to have been altered. DFW apparently wrote the correct date, 1831, but a loop was added at the base of the one, probably later.

1. This is presumably Fisher Ames' speech on Jay's Treaty, delivered on April 28, 1796. *Annals of Congress*, 4th Cong., 1st sess., pp. 1239–1263.

2. Welles (1786–1866), Boston Common Council member and alderman, who served as mayor, 1832–1833. Welles thereafter was senior alderman for most of the rest of his life. He became president of the Massachusetts Mutual Fire Insurance Company in 1834.

3. Eliot (1796–1831; Harvard 1815), Boston lawyer and builder of Tremont House, who was also in-

volved in Boston social and cultural affairs. Eliot had been a contender for mayor of Boston until his untimely death in early December 1831.

4. Wetherell (1770–1846), English politician and lawyer, who, because of his stance on the Roman Catholic Emancipation Bill and his vocal opposition to the Reform Bill, was dismissed from the office of attorney-general in the Duke of Wellington's government. Symbolizing reactionary forces in the popular mind, Wetherell made an appearance in Bristol to open the assizes on October 29, 1831, which provoked riots lasting for three days and destroying a considerable part of the city. Leslie Stephen and Sidney Lee, eds., *Dictionary of National Biography* (64 vols., New York, 1885–1903), 60 (1889): 385–387.

TO NICHOLAS BIDDLE

Washington Dec 18. 1831

My Dear Sir

The state of my health, & the severity of the weather have prevented me, since my arrival here, from being much abroad. Nevertheless, I have seen a great number of persons, & conversed with them among other things, respecting the Bank. The result of all these conversations has been a strong confirmation of the opinion which I expressed at Philadelphia that *it is* expedient for the Bank to apply for the renewal of its Charter without delay. I do not meet a Gentleman, hardly, of another opinion; & the little incidents & anecdotes, that occur & circulate among us, all tend to strengthen the impression. Indeed, I am now a good deal inclined to think, that after Genl Jackson's re-election there would be a poor chance for the Bank. I am well informed, that within three days, he has in conversation with several Gentlemen, reiterated his old opinions, somewhat vociferously, & declared them unchangeable.

I have thought, My Dear Sir, the best advice I could give you, is, that you come down here, at once, yourself, & survey the ground. You will have access to men of all parties, & can digest your information, compare opinions & judge discreetly upon the whole matter. In my judgment, this is your true course, & ought to be immediately followed. I am, Dear Sir, always faithfully Yrs   Danl. Webster

ALS. DLC. Published in McGrane, *Correspondence of Nicholas Biddle*, pp. 145–146.

TO JAMES WILLIAM PAIGE

Washington, Tuesday Evening,
January 3, 1832

Dear William,

You will be glad to hear that I am safe back from Annapolis; arrived at sunset this evening, having come across the country and not round by way of Baltimore. We were seven days, all of us, arguing our cause;[1] I used only part of one. It is not yet decided, though we left the judges there, and shall know in a day or two. The controversy is about a narrow pass, which both companies have occasion to occupy on the banks of the Potomac River, at the foot of a perpendicular precipice, where the river breaks through the Catoctin Mountain, one of the ridges of the Alleghany, or part of the Blue Ridge, more properly. There is not room enough for both routes between the river and the foot of the mountain, and neither can take any other course without enormous expense. The canal has the oldest charter, but the railroad located first on this particular spot. The chances of decision are thought to be about even; I incline to think they preponderate a little in our favor.

I pray you say to Mr. [Stephen] White, I thank him for his letter,[2] and shall write him to-morrow. I see Mr. [Thomas] Worcester[3] of Salisbury is dead. Love to Mrs. Paige and Edward [Webster]. Yours, ever truly,

D. W.

Text from *PC*, 1: 513. Original not found.

1. *Chesapeake and Ohio Canal Company* v. *Baltimore and Ohio Railroad Company*, 4 Gill & Johnson 1 (Maryland, 1832). Webster represented the railroad but lost the case.

2. Stephen White to DW, December 15, 1831, mDW 9689.

3. Worcester (1768–1831), minister of the church in Salisbury, New Hampshire, which Webster attended while he lived there.

FROM NICHOLAS BIDDLE

Phil Jan 6th. 1832

My Dear Sir

The memorial of the Bank for the renewal of its charter[1] goes by to-day's mail. In it we argue nothing & discuss nothing, but merely state that the charter is about to expire & that we wish it renewed. You I know have been fearful that we would yield our wishes to the opinions of others, but we have not yielded. Very truly Yrs   N Biddle

LC. DLC.

1. On January 9, 1832, Senator

George Mifflin Dallas of Pennsylvania presented the memorial of the "President, Directors, and Company of the Bank of the United States," requesting that Congress renew the charter for an additional twenty years. The petition is printed in *Register of De-* *bates*, 22d Cong., 1st sess., pp. 53–54. On the same day, George McDuffie presented the memorial in the House of Representatives.

TO NICHOLAS BIDDLE

W[ashington] Jan. 8 [1832]

My Dear Sir

I cannot but think you have done exactly right. Whatever may be the event, it seems to me the path of duty is plain. In my opinion, a failure, this session, if there should be one, will not at all diminish the chances of success, next session.

I suppose the Memorial will make its appearance, in the Senate, thro the V. P.[1] My notion will be to let the Administration's Gentlemen take the Disposition of it, for the present, & see what they will do with it. Yrs truly D Webster

ALS. DLC. Published in McGrane, *Correspondence of Nicholas Biddle,* p. 169.

1. See above, Biddle to DW, January 6, 1832, note 1.

FROM HENRY CLAY

8th. Jan. 32

My dear Sir

You will have learnt that we cannot extract from the Executive its project, in respect to the Tariff. Had we not better therefore assume that sketched in the Treasury Report[1] to be their plan? And to submit our scheme? I incline to think so, and with that view I have prepared the enclosed resolutions,[2] which with the concurrence of Mr. [Nathaniel] Silsbee, yourself, Mr. [Nathan] Appleton and Mr. [John] Davis, I will offer tomorrow. Yrs' faithf'y H. Clay

ALS. NhD.
1. *Executive Documents,* 22d Cong., 1st sess., Serial 216, Doc. No. 3. Secretary McLane recommended a revenue rather than a protective tariff.

2. Enclosure not found. See Webster's comments in DW to Clay, [January 8, 1832], mDW 9783-A. Clay presented a resolution to the Senate on January 10.

TO NICHOLAS BIDDLE

Monday Eve' [January 9, 1832]
7 o'clock

Dr Sir

I wrote you a short line today, in Senate.[1] You will see our Com[mitt]ee is strong eno[ugh] even should Mr [George M.] Dallas' doubts prevail, in his own mind. The question now is, what sort of a report will be best. If I am to have to do in making one, I shall need all sorts of documents. Are you not coming down, yourself? Shall the Bill be brought in, first, in the H. of R.—? What changes, if any may be admitted in the Charter? What shall be the bonus? On these, & other questions, please *speak*.

The vote in H. of R. does not shew real strength. It is *greater*, than is thereby indicated. Many friends tho't a select Com[mitt]ee proper. Most would, if they had seen a proper man, when they looked at the Chair.[2]

—Let us hear— Yrs   D. W.

ALS. DLC.

1. Earlier in the day, Webster had sent to Biddle a list of the senators chosen for the select committee appointed to consider the memorial from the Bank. mDW 9785.

2. Andrew Stevenson of Virginia, Jacksonian Speaker of the House since 1827, had infuriated the opposition by ignoring them in his committee appointments. By a close vote of 100 to 90, the Bank's memorial was referred to the standing Committee on Ways and Means, all seven members of which were putative Democrats. The committee, nevertheless, reported 5 to 2 in favor of recharter.

TO STEPHEN WHITE

Washington Jan. 20 [1832]
In Senate 1 [o'clock]

My dear Sir,

I have recd your letter, of the Eve' of the 18th,[1] & am half frightened to death by the rumor of the cholera's being in Boston. I hope the rumour may turn out to have no foundation; but I look anxiously for the next news.

I write this, while Mr. [Thomas Hart] Benton is going on with a long speech agt. the *Bank*.[2] That will soon be taken up, & will doubtl[ess] produce warm debates. Our Tariff discussion goes on, on Monday. It will last some time. We look for a great effort, in Mr. Clay's final reply.

Our executive business lingers. Mr. Van Buren is not yet disposed of.[3] For one, I see great difficulties, on both sides of that question.

Mr. [Nathan] Appleton's vote, on the Bank question, was well intended. He preferred a Select Com[mitt]ee as the usual more appropriate reference; such as was adopted in the Senate. And probably more of the friends of the Bank would have preferred the same course, if they had not entertained doubts about the manner in which the Com[mitt]ee would have been constituted.

Let me now say, in brief, two or three things, on matters of my own opinion, relative to general political prospects. I say them, pretty much for your own use.

1. I think it not probable,—not an even chance—that A. Jackson will be living, on the first day of [blank in copy]. His constitution appears to me sadly impaired; I see a change since last year.

2. If the President should decease, before the election, the *South* will go for Mr. Calhoun, the North & West for Clay, and N. Y. & Pa. will decide the matter. Those States, or one of them, would, I think be likely to go for Mr. Clay, *unless some event should raise a new sympathy for Mr. Van Buren.*

3. If Genl Jackson is re elected, there is not one chance in ten of his living out his term; & this consideration makes it very important *who is to be Vice President.*

4. I hold it doubtful, whether even if Genl Jackson should be elected, a Vice President of the same party will be chosen. I think there is much probability of a *schism*, on that point, between Va & Pa.—so much for general speculation.

I have told one of the boys just to take the documents on my table, & fold them up. I shall forward them to you. They are of no int[erest] except the report [of Mr. McLane].[4] Yours truly,   D. Webster.

Typed copy. NhD.

1. Not found. The rumor proved unfounded.

2. Benton's speech of January 20 (*Register of Debates*, 22d Cong., 1st sess., pp. 113–144) was his first attack on the Bank since its formal request for recharter. He spoke primarily to resolutions of his own, declaring illegal the "branch drafts" of the BUS and calling for their suppression.

3. The reference is to Van Buren's nomination to be minister to Great Britain, an appointment that the Senate, Webster voting with the majority, denied him.

4. The typed copy from which the text of this letter is derived gives occasional evidence that the transcriber had difficulty with Webster's hand. In the transcription the last four words are "report on the merit," altered here to read "report of Mr. McLane." Senate Document 27, 22d Cong., 1st sess., Serial 212, dated January 13, 1832, is the only public document of the session in print at the time of this letter that Webster might have thought of interest to White. It is a "Report from the Secretary of the Treasury," with the monthly statements of the Bank of the United States, for the year 1831.

The following exchange with John Quincy Adams grew out of Senate executive debates of January 24 and 25 on the nomination of Martin Van Buren as minister to Great Britain. Webster spoke on both days in opposition to the appointment. The debates themselves were published in the Register of Debates, 22 Cong., 1st sess., pp. 1310–1386, *and also in the* National Intelligencer *beginning January 28, after the Senate voted to remove the injunction of secrecy.*

The general charge made against Van Buren was that he had displayed a partisan attitude toward foreign policy in his handling of reciprocity in trade with the British colonies. On March 1, 1823, President Monroe had signed into law a bill providing that if goods imported into the British colonial ports in American vessels were subjected to no other duties than the like goods imported into the same ports "from elsewhere," the President could, by proclamation, establish the same privilege for importations of British colonies into American ports.

Although Britain had already made some concessions, she was unwilling to go so far, and her West Indian ports were soon closed once more to American vessels. So the matter stood until July 20, 1829, when Van Buren, as secretary of state, instructed the American minister in London to seek a settlement by blaming "the acts of the late administration as the cause of forfeiture of privileges which would otherwise be extended to the people of the United States." An act of Congress was presently passed, making the earlier British concessions the basis of a new arrangement. The settlement proved in fact to be mutually satisfactory, but its pointed repudiation of policies of the Adams administration so aroused the opposition senators that, with a little help from Democratic dissidents, Van Buren's nomination was rejected.

TO JOHN QUINCY ADAMS

Tuesday Eve' Jan. 24 [1832]

My Dear Sir,

Does it so happen, that you can, from recollection & without the trouble of any research, refer me to any document, or fact, *anterior to Mr. Monroe's Administration,* shewing that U. S. in their negotiations with England, had preferred a claim to the admission of *our* produce, into the British W. Indies, subject to the same duties, only, as were paid on products of the same kind, imported from the Continental Colonies of G. B.?

I pray you not to give yourself the trouble of research, but if any thing of this kind be in your recollection, it wd. oblige me to have a reference to it. Yours, with entire regard,   Danl Webster

ALS. MHi. Published in Van Tyne, p. 173.

FROM JOHN QUINCY ADAMS

23 [24] Jany 1832

My dear Sir.

The Instructions from President Washington to Mr. Gouverneur Morris of 13. Octr. 1789. ([Thomas B.] Wait's State Papers Vol 10. p. 81.) contains what I understand to be in Substance a demand of free and equal admission to the British West India Islands, in our own Vessels in terms of equal reciprocity.[1]

According to my recollection the same *principle* was constantly adhered to, and was contained in the Instructions to *me* when I was in England. But I have not those Instructions at hand. I do not know that the idea of *consenting* to a discrimination was ever intimated on our part until after Mr Monroe's Administration. I acceded to it with extreme reluctance by the unanimous advice of the members of my Administration, and then without abandoning my own opinion against it. Yours faithfully   J. Q. Adams

ALS. MWalK.

1. "In treating this subject, let it be strongly impressed on your mind, that the privilege of carrying our productions in our vessels to their islands, and bringing in return the productions of those islands to our own ports and markets, is regarded here as of the highest importance; and you will be careful not to countenance any idea of our dispensing with it in a treaty."

FROM AMBROSE SPENCER

Albany Feby 1. 1832.

My dear Sir.

Having just read your speech on Mr Van Buren's nomination,[1] I can not avoid expressing to you my hearty concurrence in every thing you said on that occasion. It is a noble, elevated rebuke of a public functionary, for degrading his Country, & humbling that Country before our proud rival, & it happens most fortunately that he is to be mortified, & rebuked on the very spot, where the degradation took place.

The friends of the rejected, pretend to be highly gratified at the result; but it is all pretence, they are deeply chagrined, & feel in their hearts all the rancour, which can dwell in such bosoms. I hear but one opinion among those opposed to the present national administration, whether Masons or anti-Masons or neutral, that is decided approbation. It would seem impossible for any American to read your remarks, & not approve your course.

It is quite probable, that the Jackson party, will run him as their next Candidate for Governor of this State. The party dare not I think nominate him for the Vice-Presidency. Eno' of Mr. Van Buren. You will recollect that I apprised you long since, that unless there was a concentration of the votes of all opposed to Genl. Jackson, in the support of the same electoral ticket, New York would certainly go for Genl. Jackson. I am still very decidedly of that opinion. If there is any possible chance of defeating Jackson's re-election by the House of Representatives, it would be all important, that measures be taken to induce Mr Clay's friends in this State to unite & support the ticket nominated by the Anti-Masons. To produce that result we shall want the assistance of Mr Clays friends at Washington & in other States. We do believe that if a union is effected we can succeed, but without it there is no hope. Can you tell me, whether in any event, for instance the vetoing the re-incorporation of the bank of the U. S, there is any prospect of Mr Clay's receiving the votes of a majority of the States?

I have all along supposed that the number of Electors was to be according to the last apportionment of representatives. Is this so or not?

I presume Mrs. Webster is with you & I beg you to present to her, my most respectful compliments & to believe me with high respect & esteem Your obedt Servt.   A Spencer

ALS. NhD.

1. At the time he wrote, Spencer had probably read the first of two installments of Webster's speech in the *National Intelligencer*, which ran it in the January 28 and January 31 issues.

The Bank memorial asking for recharter was introduced in the Senate on January 9 by George M. Dallas of Pennsylvania, who at the same time offered a resolution calling for reference to a select committee of five members. Taken by surprise, the administration forces were unable to block the resolution, and the committee was immediately chosen, by ballot. Dallas, with the highest number of votes, became chairman, followed by Webster, Thomas Ewing of Ohio, Robert Y. Hayne of South Carolina, and Josiah S. Johnston of Louisiana. Although Dallas and Hayne were putative Jacksonians, the select committee had an anti-administration majority, and its members were unanimously on the side of the Bank.

Thomas Hart Benton, who had barely lost out in the balloting, offered a new series of resolutions on January 25, adopted on the last day of the month, directing the committee to look into thirteen specific areas of the Bank's operations, including its annual expenses for lawyers' and printers' fees. The select committee was further empowered by the resolutions "to send for persons and papers, and to have oaths administered to witnesses," to hire a clerk "to take minutes of the evidence and to do such writing as the committee may direct." This is the "fresh set of enquiries" alluded to in Biddle's letter, below. Biddle replied in clipped fashion to Benton's thirteen points in a letter to the committee dated February 29, which was published in March. Senate Documents, 22d

Congress, 1st sess. Serial 213, Doc. No. 98. Shortly thereafter the committee reported a bill to renew the Bank's charter.

Frustrated by the pro-Bank committee's limited investigation, and intent on widening the attack, Benton got Georgia Representative Augustin Smith Clayton to offer a resolution calling for an investigation by the House, where the administration had a majority. It was approved on March 14. The resulting committee, reporting at the end of April, was sharply critical of the Bank, but its verdict was not unanimous. A minority report favorable to recharter was signed by John Quincy Adams and by John Goddard Watmough of Pennsylvania. See Reports of Committees, 22 Cong., 1st sess., Serial 227, Report No. 460.

FROM NICHOLAS BIDDLE

Philada. Feby. 2nd 1832

(private)

My dear Sir

I thank you for your speech in secret session, or rather your speeches, which were worthy of you, and of the Country. We are all delighted with it here, and my sole purpose in writing is to tell you this, for I am just closing my evening labors with inditing an answer to your Senate Resolutions about Branch drafts.

I see by to days paper that your Committee have a fresh set of enquiries; In case you mean to notice them at all, I wish you would suggest (as from yourself) to Mr. [George M.] Dallas, to send the budget to me and I will endeavor to answer it forthwith. With great regard, Yrs,

N Biddle

LC. DLC.

FROM JULIA WEBSTER

New York. Feby. 5th. 1831. [1832]

My dear Father,

As it is a rainy afternoon, and I am not going to church, I think I cannot spend my time better than in writing to you. Mother received a letter from you this morning.[1] I think you must want to see her very much, but I shall [be] very sorry when she goes. I was very glad to receive a letter from you,[2] and I should have answered it before, but I have not had time. I wrote a french letter to Cousin Eliza [Buckminster Lee] last week. I went to a German Concert on Friday evening with Mrs. Cambpell White. There are five Bavarians who have just come out from

England, and who sing very well. They have gone to Philadelphia, and I suppose you will see them in Washington.

I have just been writing to Edward to thank him for a pretty pencil that he sent me. Mother had a letter from Aunt Harriet [Story White Paige] yesterday, she said she had a bad cold. Mrs [Cornelia Le Roy] Edgar is much better to-day; but the weather was too unpleasant for her to go down stairs. I am head of my English class. I am studying French history and La Fontaines Fables. I have just got into the second class in french. I hope by the time you come back, that I shall be able to play a few pieces for you on the piano. Tante [Catherine Augusta Le Roy Newbold] expects to move into the new house in April. Mr William Le Roy[3] has determined to live in the western country, I should think it would be much pleasanter for him to be near his brothers. Aunt [Susan Le Roy] Jones'[4] children are better but not out of danger. Mother had a long argument with Mr [David S.] Jones[5] yesterday about your vote in the senate. I believe he did not approve of it, but out of respect to you, he would not oppose it. Mother desires me to give her love to you, and is going to add more for her-self. Mr [Herman] Le Roy[, Sr.?] is getting quite well, he put on a shoe yesterday for the first time in six weeks. Hannah [Cornell Newbold][6] unites with me in a great deal of love to you and believe me ever Dear Father Your affectionate daug[hter]   Julia Webs[ter]

ALS, enclosed with Caroline Le Roy Webster to DW, February 6, 1832. NhHi.

1. Not found
2. Not found.
3. William Le Roy (1795–1888), brother of Caroline Le Roy Webster.
4. Susan Le Roy Jones (1793–1832), fifth child of Herman Le Roy, Sr., and older sister of Caroline Le Roy Webster.

5. Jones (1777–1848; Columbia 1796), corporation counsel for the City of New York, 1813–1816, county judge of Queens County, Long Island, 1840–1843.
6. Hannah (1816–1842), daughter of Catherine Augusta Le Roy and Thomas Newbold.

FROM CAROLINE LE ROY WEBSTER

Monday Morng. Feby. 6. 1832.

Dear Husband

I recd. a kind letter from you yesterday[1]—& to day have recd. two[2]—one private. I thank you kindly for them—but grieve to have the contents of one—but I am sure my dear Mr W. I will not repine—if that will console your loss[3]—& will strive to accommodate my wits accordingly. Dont let it annoy you—it is perhaps for the best you may be compensated in some other way. I shall speak of it to no one—have sent the letter to Papa. I am sorry & truly so to have *offended* you in the slightest way. I will sacredly promise not to do so by a repetition of that sort of jesting. I have no cause to complain—*heaven* knows—nor do I in *earnest*, only out of amusement. I have been a little sick yesterday & am in *bed* to day. Dr [Cyrus] Perkins said he should write you—but on rec[eivin]g your letters —I could not forego. I hope you will consider my apology sufficient & love & forgive me. I have taken a dose of *Senna*—hope to be well tomorrow. The boys are still here. All pretty well—& send a great deal of love. I shall write you fully I hope in a day or two. Dont feel anxious about me. I trust I shall be well again in a day or two—my health has been perfectly good. Ever devotedly your wife   C W.

Julia has gone to school this morng. [illegible]—all love—[4]

ALS. NhHi.
1. Not found.
2. Not found.

3. The allusion is not clear.
4. This line appears on the cover sheet.

FROM WILLIAM BARRON CALHOUN

Boston Feb. 11. 1832.
Dr. Sir,
    At an accidental meeting of several members of the Legislature, a day or two ago, the subject of Slavery in the South was a topic of conversation. It resulted in a request that the gentlemen, who sign the within letter,[1] would obtain the opinion and advice of our Senators and immediate Representatives in Cong. as to the best mode of accomplishing our views.
    We shall be happy to hear from you in regard to this important matter, as soon as your convenience and that of the other gentlemen will allow. With very great respect Yr obt. hbl sert   Wm. B. Calhoun

ALS. DLC.
1. The enclosure is missing, but Webster endorsed Calhoun's letter with the names of its signers: Calhoun, Ira M. Barton (1797–1867), lawyer and Worcester County probate judge, and Thomas Motley (1781–1864), Boston merchant who was the father of the historian John Lothrop Motley.
    Although the substance of the enclosed letter is uncertain, antislavery activity was on the rise in Massachusetts at this time. The most important local event was the formation of William Lloyd Garrison's New England Anti-Slavery Society on January 6, 1832. By March 8 the society had sent to Webster a petition asking for the abolition of slavery in the District of Columbia (mDW 43772), and in the intervening period at least a half-dozen New England and New York communities had sent similar requests to him. An anonymous column on the "Abolition of Slavery" in the *Boston Courier* for February 13, suggesting colonization with financial aid from the federal government, may well have come out of the same "accidental meeting" as the missing enclosure.

Washington Feb. 12. [1832]
Sunday. Eve'

My Dear Sir,

I have your letter of the 6. inst.[1] You will have heard that Mrs Webster has been a good deal unwell; but as my last letters speak favorably, I trust she will be sufficiently recovered to make progress this way, at the appointed time. It seems now to be none too early for you all to be seriously thinking about that same trip. I think you all ought to be here, early in March. The roads, rivers, & canals will now soon be in fine order. Your girls will bring their white <servant> woman, of course.

A white man servant would be an incumbrance.

Judge Clarkson[2] would be quite useful; altho, unless you needed him on the road, you would do very well without any man servant.

I charge myself with the making of all necessary provisions for lodgings, on short notice.

I want to have you say, *when you intend leaving home.* If I know you are on the road, I shall then be sure, that, like Gilpen's hat & wig, you will be here in due time. But I want to get you set out. So much for coming to Washington—& all I have to add, is *come, come.*

We go on here, as usual. You see [George] McDuffie's Report.[3] It will have the effect of uniting the Tariff party, & strengthening it; because it shews there is no medium. We hope to get to a vote on Mr Clay's Resolution, this week. I have little doubt it will pass the Senate.[4]

I think your views about the removal of the Slaves, entirely just. I shall express them, as my own, the first convenient, incidental opportunity; but my opinion is, that, as to any direct measure on the subject, it is better for the southern Gentlemen to take the lead. The case is their's not ours. It is enough, if we are ready to second the movement, & give the money. In the State of Va. opinion is roused, but not yet fixed, & settled. They will have a year of warm controversy, as the question will enter into all their elections.[5]

The Court goes on pretty well. I passed an hour with Judge [Story] today—& found him in good spirits. We have been two or three days arguing an important cause from Cincinnati.[6]

I pray you, kiss the girls' cheeks for me; & give my love to Mrs [James William] Paige, & the Colonel [Thomas Handasyd Perkins]. Yours always faithfully   D. Webster

We are not frighted yet, as the consequence of our rejection of Mr. V[an] B[uren].[7] I think there is no chance of Va. or Pa. going for him.

ALS. NhD.

1. Not found.

2. Not identified.

3. George McDuffie, a Calhoun lieutenant from South Carolina, was then chairman of the Committee on Ways and Means. He had on February 8 reported a bill "to reduce and equalize the duties on imports," arguing against the principle of protection and calling for sweeping reductions in the tariff.

4. On January 10, 1832, Clay had submitted a resolution calling upon the Committee on Finance to report a bill "to abolish the duties on some imported items and to reduce the duties on others." Webster here seems overly optimistic in his assessment of the resolution's future; it did not pass the Senate until March 22 and then only in a heavily amended version.

5. The institution of slavery had been under increasing pressure in Virginia since the state constitutional convention of 1829–1830, climaxed by Nat Turner's rebellion in August 1831. Webster is undoubtedly referring here to the sweeping debate in the state legislature in December 1831 and January 1832. See Theodore M. Whitfield, *Slavery Agitation in Virginia 1829–1832* (Baltimore, 1930). The controversy was resolved in favor of slavery with the publication in December 1832 of Thomas R. Dew's *Review of the Debate in the Virginia Legislature of 1831 and 1832* (Richmond, 1832).

6. *City of Cincinnati* v. *Lessee of Edward White*, 6 Peters 431 (1832).

7. On January 25, 1832, the Senate had rejected Van Buren's appointment as United States minister to Britain, 24 to 23, with the vote of Vice President Calhoun cast to break a manipulated tie.

The apportionment of representation in Congress after each decennial census has always carried political implications. The rearrangement following the Census of 1830 was particularly difficult owing to sharply rising sectional tension and a general westward shift of population. A change of less than a thousand in the ratio of population to representation—that is, in the number of enumerated persons required for each member of the lower house of Congress—might lessen or enlarge the influence of a state in the councils of the nation; or affect the delicate balance among North, South, and West.

Early in January 1832 a select committee of the House reported an apportionment bill which fixed the ratio at 48,000. By a margin of four votes this figure was changed to 44,000 on February 2. It was again changed, to 47,700, before a final passage on February 16, with the Massachusetts delegation unanimous in opposition. Debate on February 14, when the states of Georgia, Kentucky, and New York teamed together to raise the ratio, had been particularly self-serving. That night John Quincy Adams brooded in his diary over "the iniquity of the Apportionment bill, and the disreputable means by which so partial and unjust a distribution of the representation had been effected," seeking some device "to avert

the heavy blow from the State of Massachusetts and from New Eng-
land." The next morning Adams met Webster, who assured him that he
too opposed the apportionment bill in the form in which it then stood.

When the House bill reached the Senate on February 17, Webster
moved that it be referred to a select committee, of which by custom he
became chairman. He realized, however, as he notes in his letter to Levi
Lincoln below, that the majority would overrule him, which they did. The
House bill was reported without amendment. Webster carried his case to
the floor on March 1, after he had received Adams' long letter of Febru-
ary 28, below. He moved an amendment, substituting the ratio of 47,000
for the figure of 47,700 in the bill and adding the provision that each
state having a "major fraction" left over, defined as more than 25,000,
was entitled to an additional representative. Another select committee,
this time of only five members, but again chaired by Webster, reported a
modified version of the amendment, powerfully supported by Webster's
report of April 5. The recommended principle was to assume an optimum
size for the House—Webster suggested 240 members—and to divide the
total population by that figure. The quotient became the ratio in terms of
which representatives were to be apportioned "as near as may be," save
only that no state should be without at least one. The Senate accepted the
new wording, but the House refused to concur; the Senate receded, and
the original House bill became the basis for apportionment in the next
Congress.

TO LEVI LINCOLN
                                                    Washington Feb. 18. 1832.
My Dear Sir

The apportionment Bill which has passed the H. of R.[1] is, as you will
have observed, exceedingly unfavorable to N. England, & especially to
Massachusetts. In the Senate, I moved its reference to a Select Com[mit-
t]ee,[2] which motion prevailed; but the Com[mitt]ee happens to be so constituted, that I entertain little hope of reporting any amendment.[3] We
shall not consent to the present arrangement, however, without a struggle. Its great inequality & injustice call on us loudly for an effort to
change it. The Com[mitt]ee cannot meet till Tuesday, owing to Gentlemen's engagements on other Committees. If a majority shall then be
found in favor of the Bill as it is, it will be at once reported, without
amendment; & I shall then give notice of an intention to call it up, at the
earliest day practicable, & then to propose an amendment.

I believe I shall, in the first place, propose to substitute 44,000 to
47,700, as the former no. was twice voted, in H. of R. & there is reason

to think would now be concurred in. I entertain some small hope that 13 States will go for this No; viz, 6 in N. E., N. J. Pa. Del. Maryd. Louisiana Ohio, Ken. But this is far from certain.

Should this proposition fail, & should we be unable to insert any other no. instead of the one now in the Bill, as the ratio, I think of proposing an amendment, having a complex character; viz, to fix the ratio, say, at 48,000, & allow a Representative for every fraction, where the fraction equals, say, two thirds the No. of the ratio. I believe there is no Constitutional objection to this, & it is a near[er] approach to equality, I think, than can be attained in any other way.

We shall hasten the progress of the measure thro. the Senate as fast as we can, consistently with our object of amendment; well knowing how desirable it must be for the Legislature to know, as early as practicable, the result of our Legislation on this important Subject. I have the honor to be, with very true regard, Your Ob. Servt   Danl Webster

ALS. NhD.

1. House Bill 208, "An act for the apportionment of Representatives among the several States according to the fifth census," passed the House on February 16 by a vote of 130 to 58.

2. *Senate Journal*, 22d Cong., 1st sess., Serial 211, p. 143.

3. The other members of the committee were Alexander Buckner of Missouri, Robert Y. Hayne of South Carolina, William Learned Marcy of New York, John Tipton of Indiana, George M. Dallas of Pennsylvania, and John Forsyth of Georgia. A second select committee, more congenial to Webster's thinking, was appointed on March 28, carrying over Webster, Forsyth, and Hayne, and adding John Middleton Clayton of Delaware and Willie Person Mangum of North Carolina.

FROM DANIEL FLETCHER WEBSTER

Cambridge Feb 25th 1832

My Dear Father,

I received your kind letter to day[1] and rejoice that you were pleased with mine.[2] No more difficulties will occur between myself and Uncle [James William Paige] on account of my conduct towards him I assure you, if I am able to prevent them by circumspection and prudence.

I hope that there is more in me than has yet appeared, for I have done nothing heretofore, and should be very sorry to think that a son of yours was wholly good for nothing; but I fear that people think there is more in me than there really is. I must do all I can to answer their expectations, for it is hard to have expectations raised which can never be fulfilled, yet one ought not to be blamed for not expressing them, when they are not just, and founded upon sufficient grounds.

College matters are the same as they have been, I have reason to think

I have improved greatly since last term and last year. We have a vacation of a fortnight in about four weeks and I am at loss what to do with it. Have you any manner in which you wish me to pass it in particular? I can pass a week very well at Cambridge and a few days with Mr [Samuel B.] Walcott and [Fisher Ames] Harding[3] if you are willing and that will end it pretty much. I have no particular wish one way or another, but leave it entirely to your disposal.

I wrote a letter to Mother the other day in answer to a postscript of her's in one of Julia's letters. Julia wrote a letter in French to Cousin Eliza [Buckminster Lee] a few days ago which was very correct and well written. I hope she is doing well. She has improved a great deal in writing. Edward is studying well, I believe and attends to his books. He has a good deal of taste for speaking and reading. I have no doubt he will be a high scholar.

There is a society here which has been lately formed called the Harvard Union the object of which is to encourage debating and speaking. It is formed by the junction of the Junior and Senior Classes. The first scholars in both founded it. They wish, as much as possible to do away the distinction of Class and therefore have their officers half from each class. The sixth of [or] seventh scholar among the seniors and the best debater has been chosen president and the first scholar secretary; among the Juniors the first scholar also is secretary and I am president. The officers sit alternately on succeeding evenings.

This was an unexpected honour and I must do something to deserve it. It will be my turn soon to deliver an essay before them and I am exceedingly anxious to appear well and talk sense. To this, the choice of a good subject, in which they will all be interested, and upon which I can give some information is mainly necessary. If you can tell me of some one, of which you may happen to think & which I can understand, it will help me very much. I was rather averse at first to join, but thinking afterwards that if I could ever be anything, I could be something *now*, and also that considering my connexions I ought not to be behind hand in such things, I signed my name to the constitution. I hope you will approve of my conduct. All send love to you, my chum desires his regards to y[ou] and I remain ever Your affectionate son

D. Fletcher Webster

ALS. NhHi. Published in part in Van Tyne, pp. 581–582.

1. Not found.

2. DFW to DW, February 9, 1832, mDW 9847.

3. Harding (1811–1846), Harvard classmate of Fletcher's from Dover, Massachusetts. Harding is most likely the "chum" Fletcher refers to in his closing sentence.

FROM JOHN QUINCY ADAMS

House of Representatives U. S.
February [28,] 1832

Dear Sir

In requesting a moment of your attention to the principles to which I have recurred in the discussion upon the apportionment Bill, I beg leave to add one consideration which has impressed itself deeply on my mind but which was not sufficiently disclosed in the debates upon the Bill in the House of Representatives.

The provisions in the Constitution for the formation of the House of Representatives applicable to the question are in these words—

"The House of Representatives shall be composed of Members chosen every second year *by the People* of the several States."

"Representatives and direct taxes shall be apportioned among the several States which may be included within this Union *according to their respective numbers* which shall be determined by adding to the *whole number* of free persons including those bound to service for a term of years, and excluding Indians not taxed, three fifths *of all other persons.*"

Every word of these provisions imports the intention of the Constitution that the *whole people* shall be represented. Every apportionment therefore which leaves a portion of the people totally unrepresented fails to carry into effect the prescription of the Constitution.

The objections of President Washington to the first apportionment Bill presented to him by the two Houses of Congress, were two.

First, referring to the clause of the Constitution requiring that Representatives shall be apportioned among the several States according to their respective numbers, he objected that there was no proportion or divisor which applied to the respective numbers of the States would yield the number and allotment of Representatives proposed by the Bill. Second, referring to the provision of the Constitution, that the number of Representatives shall not exceed one for every thirty thousand, which restriction he considered by the context, and by fair and obvious construction to be applied to the separate and respective numbers of the States: while the Bill had allotted to eight of the States more than one to every thirty thousand.

Let us in the first place observe that notwthstanding both these objections twenty eight members of the House of Representatives, all among the most ardent and ablest supporters of the Administration voted again in favor of the Bill, and only thirty three members against it.

Then, with regard to the first objection, it applies with equal force to the Bill which has now passed the House of Representatives. There is no proportion or divisor which applied to the respective numbers of the

States would yield the number and allotment of Representatives proposed by the Bill. If therefore that objection was valid against that Bill it is valid against this Bill.

With regard to the second objection, it will probably never apply to any Bill proposed at this time or hereafter.

I submit to your consideration the following very simple plan for a Representation of the whole People, and which will be applicable to all future apportionments as well as the present.

It is to assume the ratio of 50000 for the apportionment, and then to add one member for the fraction of every State. The Apportionment will give 226 Members to which the addition of 24 Members will make a House of 250 Members.

The numbers of the respective States will be—

Maine	8
New Hampshire	6
Massachusetts	13
Rhode Island	2
Connecticut	6
Vermont	6
New York	39
New Jersey	7
Pennsylvania	27
Delaware	2
Maryland	9
Virginia	21
North Carolina	13
South Carolina	10
Georgia	9
Kentucky	13
Tennessee	13
Ohio	19
Indiana	7
Mississippi	3
Illinois	4
Louisiana	4
Missouri	3
Alabama	6
=	250

If this allotment is liable to the first objection made by General Washington to the apportionment in the Bill which he returned to the House of Representatives it is no more so than the Bill now before the Senate. There is now no common proportion or divisor, which applied to the respective States will yield the number of Representatives allotted to them. The Bill before the Senate gives to the State of Georgia one member for every 47756 of its population, and to the State of Delaware only one member for a population of 75432.

The only difference of principle between the Bill now before the Senate and that which I would propose, is, that in the present bill the departure from a common divisor consists in an unrepresented fraction of different amount in each State but equal in the whole to 475,478 persons, while in my proposal the same departure would consist in an excess of representation, so distributed however as to result in an inequality between the different States much less than that in the present Bill between the States of Delaware and of Georgia.

To the second objection of President Washington the plan which I propose will under no apportionment ever likely to be proposed hereafter be liable, even upon his construction of the terms of the Constitution.

I have assumed the ratio of 50,000 only by way of illustration and because it would be in the present instance in my own opinion preferable to any other number; but the principle will adapt itself to any other number which might be deemed preferable by others. It has the double advantage of giving a Representation of the whole people, and of placing the numbers of which the House shall be composed always within the discretion of the Legislature. Take for instance the ratio of 60,000 which would give a House of 186 Members, and then by the addition for the fractions it would amount to 210. Take the ratio of 41000, and a House of 277 Members with the addition of 24 for the fractions would make 301. Ten years hence the same principle will be equally applicable to any increased ratio which may be then be deemed expedient, the whole people will still be represented and the numbers of the House still restricted within the discretionary judgment of Congress. One of the great evils of leaving unrepresented fractions is that they must necessarily increase with every increase of the ratio. With a ratio of 100,000 every State might have an unrepresented fraction of 99,999 and the amount of unrepresented fractions might be more than two millions. Accept my most respectful Salutations   [J. Q. Adams]

P.S. By the ratio of 50,000 in the plan proposed I perceive Virginia would still lose one member of her present Representation. So she does by the Bill which has passed the House, and for which a Majority of her members voted. Nor could the apportionment have been carried without their votes. Still to avoid the evil as I esteem it of her losing a Member I would assume the ratio of 48000 which with the additional 24 for the fractions would make a House of 261 Members only two more than a ratio of 44000 would give *without* representation of the fractions.

LC. MHi. Two other copies of this letter exist. One copy, NhHi, mDW 9886, contains a number of important inaccuracies, having been apparently copied in haste from the original letter sent to Webster. The other, an AL, MHi, mDW 9907, from the Everett Papers, contains only minor differences in punctuation and capitalization. The NhHi copy is dated February 28, 1832, and is signed.

TO HIRAM KETCHUM

Washington Mar. 5. 1832

Private

Dear Sir

A very large publication is ordered of the opinion of the Court, in the Cherokee case,[1] for circulation. You intimated that you & your friends had funds, for such like objects. Pray send $300 to Mr [Theodore] Frelinghuysen, or Mr [Samuel] Prentiss, of Vermont. I hope Gentlemen in Boston will furnish a similar amount.

It is contemplated to print 20,000 or 30,000 copies, in Pamphlet form, & to circulate them as widely as possible in the S[outh] and W[est]. Yrs.

D. Webster

P.S. If, on receipt of this, you can authorize me to draw on you for $300, it will answer all the purposes.

ALS. NhD. Attorney and counselor at 50 Wall Street in New York, Ketchum was a close personal friend and later a leader of the Webster Whigs in the city.

1. *Samuel A. Worcester* v. *State of Georgia*, 6 Peters 515 (1832). Marshall's opinion for the Court appeared in the March 10 issue of the *National Intelligencer.*

FROM AMBROSE SPENCER

Albany March 14th. 1832.

My Dear Sir.

Believing that it would be gratifying to you to be informed of the probable effect which passing events have produced on the public mind, I can no longer refrain from writing to you.

I know that your time is so occupied that you have scarcely leisure to read a letter, much less to write to your numerous correspondents & I can therefore hope for no answer.

I am happy in being able to assure you, that the prospects of a complete & thorough union, of all those who were in this state opposed to Genl. Jackson becomes daily more cheering. The leading anti-Masons perceive, that their paramount duty now is, to save their country from disunion & ruin. The reversal of the Judgment in the case of the Missionaries, the high probability, if not certainty that Georgia will resist the mandate of the S. Court of the U. S. & the probability that Genl. Jackson, in his weak unreasoning obstinacy, will refuse to take care that the laws be faithfully executed, or will act inefficiently, present a crisis, which causes all men, who have anything at stake, & who are not blindly given up to party feelings, to pause & enquire how these calamities which threaten us, may be avoided & surmounted.

The opinion is a common one with several of the leading anti-Masons with whom I have conversed, that they ought to, & will nominate an electoral ticket, satisfactory to the friends of Mr. Clay. That is in the decided anti-Masonic Counties, they must conform to the public opinion in their nominations, but in those parts of the State where anti-Masonry has made but little progress, they will nominate men who have taken no part in the excitement, & who will be cheerfully supported by Mr. Clay's friends. For instance in N. York, Col. [Nicholas] Fish, Chancellor [James] Kent, & Col. [John] Trumbull[1] have been named to me, as men whom the anti-Masons will select.

I do entertain the opinion, that N. York will be united in her electoral vote against Jackson, & in that event, it is the belief of our friends that we shall succeed. At no time for the last two years, have I had greater hopes than now, that this State will do its duty.

It is in your power & Mr. Clays to effect much in softening & conciliating anti-Masonry. There are three or four anti-Masonic members of Congress, who deserve your attention, from their standing in their party, & their talents. I allude to Messrs. [Frederick] Whittles[e]y, Bates Cooke, [John Allen] Collier & [Phineas Lyman] Tracy. I recommend that you & Mr. Clay see these gentlemen & converse freely with them. They can give you information that you want & can be instrumental in doing away prejudice to Mr Clay.

I perceive Genl. [Erastus] Root has given offense by his remarks in relation to the bank.[2] He is a known malcontent, hates Van Buren & the Albany regency & by his late temperance course, has become a more respectable man. Can you not see him? Great caution is to be observed, for tho' a pretty independent & honest man, he is very jealous & naturally a radical.

Will a final mandate issue from the S. Court to deliver the Missionaries, during the present term? If not is it not all important to collect & embody, proof if such exists, that Genl. Jackson declares he will not aid in enforcing this judgment & mandate of the Court? It seems to me very important, if he has made the declarations imputed to him, that the proof of them should be spread before the public, in an authentic shape. The effect of fastening upon him such declarations, would be incalculably great. But I weary you with my tediousness. Believe me most truly Yours   A Spencer

p.s. I have read your dinner speech with admiration & delight.[3]

ALS. DLC.

1. The reference is assumed to be to the painter of the Revolution, whose murals were then hanging in the Rotunda of the Capitol. Trumbull was living in New York at this time, sharing the Federalist heritage and the political conservatism of Fish and Kent. See "City of New York," *National Intelligencer*, September 29, 1832. The New York State Anti-Masonic convention, meeting at Utica on June 21, 1832, named Kent as elector-at-large for the Presidential ticket.

2. *Register of Debates*, 22d Cong., 1st sess., pp. 1888, 2036–2042, and especially 2069–2075, February 28,

March 7–8, 1832.
  3. "The Character of Washington," speech delivered at a public dinner in honor of Washington's Centennial,

February 22, 1832. The speech appeared in the *National Intelligencer* on March 6, 1832.

FROM BELLAMY STORER

Cincinnati March. 19. 1832

My dear Sir—

You will perceive that we are all highly pleased with the decisions in our City cause, as the opinion is published at length in our news papers.[1] For the very flattering manner in which you have noticed the part I took in the matter I cannot now express my feelings. I can only say that hereafter I hope to deserve more fully the commendations you have bestowed. I have enclosed a letter to Mr. [William Thomas] Carroll,[2] and one to Mr [Richard] Peters,[3] which I will thank you to hand to them.

The decision in the Cherokees cause, is the all absorbing subject, upon which we speculate: I say speculate, for we cannot anticipate any certain result. One thing is certain, if the judgment of the Court is not carried into immediate effect, the whole west will be in a flame. The subject is one that affects the whole moral sentiment of her people, and as in 1819.20, Ohio presented an unbroken opposition to the extension of slavery, when the Missouri question, was discussed, she will now, throw all her influence, accumulated as it is, into the scale of sectional justice, & national honour. We view the principles of union as virtually dissolved, should the Executive refuse to do its duty; and resting hitherto, as we have done on the virtue, & intelligence of our citizens, we shall struggle for our constitutional privileges, and be among the last to surrender them.

Hope, however, for better things. The darkest hour is seen to be immediately before day-break, and we may yet have, and Heaven grant us may have, the glorious light of liberty & law preserved to us.

What has been the issue of the other city cause?[4] [Thomas] Ewing gave me assurances that he should dismiss it. I am anxious to know, what has been done with it.

You will see in one of the late numbers of [Charles] Hammond's paper,[5] that he cavils at your apportionment system. He tells me he wants to converse with you on the subject, and sometimes talks of going on to the city. He is firm, and true to the cause, but his course is not strictly prudent, politically considered. He is independent, and sometimes too credulous, but withal as honest noble spirited a man as there is in the universe. He has published Mr Clays speeches at length, and on the

Van Buren rejection, he has spoken with the freedom of a sound and gifted mind.

Our people say here by a tremendous majority, do not disturb the *tariff*, for trade has made too many bankrupts already—and unless the importations of British goods are checked, one half the mercantile community will be insolvent. The auctioneers are all supplied, even to the Rocky Mountains, and every petty auction room is full to repletion, of British fabrics to be sold at any price.

They also say recharter the Bank, or we shall go back in all our improvements. On this subject, I am positive there is no difference of opinion in this place. In a population of 32,000 there are not I am satisfied fifty opponents of the institution.

By the way, you promised my wife a volume of your debates & speeches. She will regard the compliment as highly as I should do. Very truly & sincerely Your friend   Bellamy Storer

ALS. NhD.

1. Webster and Storer had recently argued before the Supreme Court on behalf of the city, *Cincinnati v. The Lessee of Edward White*, 6 Peters 431 (1832).

2. Carroll was clerk of the United States Supreme Court from 1827 to 1862.

3. Peters (1779–1848), reporter of the United States Supreme Court as successor to Henry Wheaton. He compiled sixteen volumes of reports between 1828 and 1842.

4. Storer refers here to another case, *Lessee of Edward White* v. *Cincinnati*, Appellate Case file #1675, which was never argued before the Supreme Court. On March 13, 1832, Webster had made a motion and by the consent of opposing counsel Ewing, the writ of error was dismissed.

5. The *Daily Cincinnati Gazette*.

TO CHARLES HENRY THOMAS

Washington Mar. 23. 1832

Dear Henry,

I have recd. a letter from you today,[1] saying that two of my important letters have come safe to hand. I hope, by this time the rest have also come safe to your hand. Mr Gassett [Daniel Bassett][2] is mistaken, about the release of the mortgage. There must be a quitclaim,[3] or else he must go to Plymouth, and sign a receipt on the margin of the *record*. This would be much more troublesome to Mr. Bassett than to sign a quitclaim. Mr [Ebenezer] Gay,[4] or any other Lawyer, will inform Mr Bassett that according to the law of Massachusetts, as now understood, a mortgage can be effectually released only by quitclaim, or by receipt on the margin of the Record.

As to trees, I am afraid only of your making *one mistake*; that is, that *you will not set out enough.* If you will set out *enough*, I will agree not to complain.

Three, Four, five, or six trees may be set together, in a clump. Sometimes a single tree is handsome; indeed, often.

I think it would do very well to set out a good many trees along the south side of the garden wall, & in the N. E. corner of the land bo[ugh]t of Mr Wright⁵—especially of pines, oaks, & other hardy trees, so as to make a cluster, which, in time, may keep off the cold north & East wind from the more tender shrubbery, some of which must be planted along among the trees on the avenue. Something like a little grove, put up there in the corner, to keep the wind off the avenue, will be a nice thing.

I am sorry labour is high, that is, I am sorry for my own sake, tho' glad for the laborer's. But after this spring, we shall have nothing, or but little, to do, in the way of improvement. I think you are right to plough the land, in front of the House.

Take care that the wall, at the gate makes a handsome curve; & along that curve, inside, trees should be planted, great & small, & perhaps a few strong & pretty large ones, ashes, horse chesnuts, & sycamores should be placed *out* side, & well secured.

I congratulate *Hugh*,⁶ on the addition to his family.

So no more at present.   D. W.

ALS. MHi.

1. Not found.

2. Bassett (1787–1848), a master shipwright who lived in Hingham, and brother-in-law of Charles Henry Thomas.

3. See DW to Thomas, January 7, 1832, mDW 9772, and enclosure.

4. Gay (c. 1771–1842, Harvard 1789), lawyer in Boston for several years and afterward of Hingham, who also served as a member of the Massachusetts Senate.

5. This is probably Charles Wright, father of Porter Wright, who owned land adjoining Webster's Marshfield estate.

6. Not identified.

FROM THEODORE DWIGHT

New York April 5th 1832

My dear Sir,

Hearing nothing from any of my friends at Washington, on the state of public opinion, as it regards the decision of the Supreme Court in the Cherokee case, nor what is to be expected in any emergencies that may grow out of that decision, I feel somewhat at a loss what is the proper course to be pursued, or the proper doctrine to be inculcated. I am strongly impressed with the idea, that an attempt ought to be made before long, to rouse the feelings of the country in Support of the Judiciary, or in other words, of the constitution. But I have no other guide than my own judgment, & that is so nearly worn out, that it is not to be trusted, especially in a difficult case. It is obvious to me, & was so before the appearance of the long-winded article in the Globe,[1] that it will be but a very short time before the leading Jackson papers, all over the country, will come out in favour of Georgia, & against the court. They will approach that point by degrees; but I am satisfied they will come to it in the end, & probably in a short time. As soon as that takes place, in my judgment, it will be the duty of those who favour the constitution, & consider it as worth preservation, to make an effort for that purpose, and it appears to me, if the necessary pains are taken, & in the right manner, a sufficient number of our countrymen can be roused to the support of the Judiciary, & the discomfiture of the man, & his myrmidons, who are obviously bent on sacrificing both the constitution & the union.

I cannot but believe, that when the point is ascertained, that Georgia will resist the execution of the sentence of the Court, & General Jackson refuses to enforce it, that a majority of the people of the country will support the constitution. In a struggle for this purpose, they will have the advantage of standing on clear, distinct constitutional ground, while their opponents will as distinctly be placed on unconstitutional ground, in direct hostility to the Judicial branch of the government, & as aiming to subvert the main pillar of the constitution. And in vindication of their conduct, they will have no other apology to offer, than their interested & servile devotion to *a man*, instead of their country.

In opposing General Jackson, as a candidate for the chief magistracy, at the next election, according to my judgment, the attack upon him should be principally upon this ground. When he was up at the former election, *we* prophesied that he would violate the constitution. Those predictions are not only fulfilled, but he is in a fair way to destroy it. In such a warfare there is nothing complex, nothing difficult to be understood, or felt. And if the country will not rally in support of the union, if that is of less value than the election of General Jackson, & the succession of Van Buren, in my opinion, it is of but little importance how soon the matter is settled.

.I have written an article on the present state of things, more for the purpose of seeing how it would look on paper than anything else; for it is not my wish to become a principal in such a warfare. And tho' I lay no claim to the character of a "Hero," I am most truly a *veteran*, & am sick of politics. Several of my friends have examined the article, & are desirous of seeing it in print. If I conclude to publish it, you will see it in our paper.[2] It will disclose, to some extent, the manner in which I think General Jackson may be attacked.

It is said there are some symptoms of discord & dissension in the seat

of the Beast—Albany. How the fact is I do not know. But it will be difficult to disaffect such a voracious party, to such a degree as to run the
risk of forfeiting their share of *the spoils* in the event of *a victory*. I am
very respectfully, & with great sincerity, your very obedt. sevt—

Theodore Dwight

ALS. DLC.
   1. "The Indian Question An Examination of the Cherokee Question," *Washington Globe*, March 31,
1832.
   2. The *New York Daily Advertiser*.

FROM HARRISON GRAY OTIS

Boston April 11. 1832

My dear Sir

The late movements in the Senate on the subject of the Tariff have
occasioned much alarm and anxiety among all classes of manufacturers
in this region. The extinguisher apparently put upon Mr [Henry] Clay's
motion by Mr [William] Wilkins,[1] and the disposal of the report of the
Committee on the motion of Mr [George M.] Dallas,[2] have put every
body here at fault in attempting to fathom the policy. To the sense of
many it has the bad odour of defection from the American System-party,
on calculation of political results. This is not my opinion, having too
much respect for their characters to indulge it and being also incapable
of discerning wherein the political leaders of either party can find their
account in deserting the cause. This is perhaps because I am not in the
"esoterics" of either. It is however certain that the opinion prevails and
gathers strength. The Pennsylvania delegation are considered as holding
the game in their hands but ready to throw up the cards. The sensation
is deep and working mischief. Conversations are already held among
the woolen and cotton proprietors of holding themselves ready to join
the south, and offering to go back to the tariff of 1816, on the first demonstration of a disposition to tamper with the system at their expense,
and I have reason to believe an agent will appear at Washington forthwith with instructions to that effect. They contend that they can do better under that act (injurious as reverting to it would prove) than under
any of the fanciful theories, as yet proposed as substitutes for the existing protection; better than the iron fabricators, who by that act had I
believe a protection of nine dollars per ton. The tendency of this jealousy and of discoursing upon and digesting such projects requires no
explanation to you. Among allied forces the interval between talking of
separation and effecting it is short, and is generally shortened if it come
to the knowledge of the enemy that secession is a subject of debate with
the Allies. What a fine spectacle would the United States exhibit, with

the friends of the American System divided by a schism, underbidding each other to propitiate So Carolina, and she refusing to take them at any price fixed for the sacrifice of their principles! And to this some persons here are strongly inclined to fear it will come at last. It passes my comprehension to imagine, what advantage can be anticipated to any part of the country friendly to the system from permitting a continuance of exposure to this danger of the jealousies which are taking root. To put this question at rest would be I should think to remove a block of stumbling from the paths of the political aspirants on both sides, and to do this by a prompt strait forward course would not only bring whatever of inflamation is destined to be the consequence to a head, with the least possible aggravation of danger from previous fever, but afford light and strength to undertake the cure whether by cataplasm or lancet; or to endure what might not be cured. It must be an egregious illusion to presume that the disaffection in South Carolina will be soothed by any concession not pregnant with ruin to our country. More than two years since I became convinced that the leading men in that country would urge the people to Nullification, which is synonymous with insurrection and revolt. I believe that such is the hallucination and excitement of those fire-eating enthusiasts, & such their miscalculations of the demands of chivalry and honour, such I may add their sincere though erroneous conviction of interest, that they will if possible spur the horse over the precipice. To say nothing of what they threaten, (and it is a mistake to suppose them braggarts and blusterers) in their speeches and written tirades, many of them are desirous in their hearts of being "a nation" by themselves or with such of the plantation states, as would join them, and do not disguise that their sympathies and fellow feeling are more congenial with those of the British nation than with those of their sister states. An English officer of rank told me that two winters ago, he dined on a plantation with a large party 16 or 18 of the most opulent and respectable persons there; who avowed or agreed to the avowal of the opinion by others, that they did not know "what good they had gained by a separation from Great Britain," that the whole advantage rested with the Yankees, and that they wished it had never happened. This conversation was addressed to him as an English officer without reserve and was continued in the same strain. A very distinguish'd South Carolina planter also told me last summer that the Governor said to him, that if his friends and he could not carry their object (nullification or renouncement of protection) "he should be forced to quit the State through very shame." Nor do I see how it is possible to doubt the seriousness and firmness of purpose in these men. Human nature everywhere under similar circumstances displays the same characteristics. The Esprit de Corps (or rather the Esprit de Clan, I believe there is no French for it) is the same "spiritual body" whether seeking whom he may devour in the pine barrens and cotton fields of the South or on the bleak highlands of Scotia. And there will often be found Balmerinos and Kilmarnocks ready to impute the physical defects of their soil & other things to the Union, and to fight first and reason afterward to get disentangled. A "Row" of some sort is therefore to be expected. I perceive two modes only by which it may per chance be averted. There may not be a majority of the people ready for extremes by the time the leaders are "ready." Or Congress may truckle to them by some watergruel compromise equivalent to an abandonment of the system or to a pledge of future abandonment, which is worse—such a compromise as they may claim for a victory. Now the most probable and I believe the only mode to prevent the majority from committing themselves, is for the American party in Congress to display firmness, vigour, union—to do what is right—to adopt substantially Mr Clays resolution—a feature of which is contained in the reported bill—to reduce the duties to some considerable amount, and to let it be understood that if revolt must come, Congress while it would deplore, would be ready to meet it. But seriously as I anticipate commotion at the South in some shape, and firmly as I think it should be met, nobody can entertain more gloomy fears for the consequences, nor would do more to prevent it, if indeed anything can be done without impairing the *principles* of the Protective System. I should be willing as a general principle that measures considered as grievances by any considerable portion of our people which disturb their comfort and portend resistance, should be yielded at any sacrifice short of imposing greater grievance upon the residue. Here then is the difficulty. Experience, circumstances, events prove manifestly that the great manufacturing interests are not steadily protected even at present rates. They ask however for no more than they enjoy. Will the adversary consent to their retaining so much? If yea, the mode is not important. If no, there is an end to protection. Protection is an integer—or if you please a "unit." It is not a subject of apportionment or graduation. Its basis is the amount of duty that will enable the domestic manufacturer to supply the market at prices *somewhat* cheaper than can be afforded by the foreign manufacturer. With this aid he will gradually furnish the entire supply and at length supplant the foreigner. Without it the foreigners will inevitably supplant him. But of all projects that of a *gradual* reduction of duties at certain periods is the most exceptionable and pernicious. It is an incentive to the foreigner to prepare himself for augmenting his supplies *at the prospective periods*, and a discouragement to the native fabricator compelling him to contract his supplies at the same rate. It is presuming that certain conditions and capacities will exist by a given day, which depend on circumstances beyond his ken or control. Should these take place—Should he be competent to stand or go alone at any future period, it will be time enough then to diminish the duties. Should they not so turn out, he must be injured and probably ruined. A prospective reduction of duties in order to place those whose goods have arrived with those whose goods are in transitu, may sometimes be proper, just and expedient, but is wholly inapplicable to a system intended for protection. I cannot persuade myself that any compromise will be listened to by the gentlemen from S Carolina on the admission of these principles. To compromit according to your Namesakes dictionary is a very different notion from that implied in the verb to compromise. We may do the one ex parte, through fear or force, but the other requires the consent of two parties; and to do gratuitously for the sake of appeasing an angry opponent what he will not agree to receive as satisfactory is only to compromit ones self and encourage ulterior pretensions without gaining a single advantage.. It is however possible that a change of the manner of levying the duties might reconcile some of the moderate of your opponents. I was never pleased with the principle of *minimums*. It sounds in fiction, is artificial and devoid of desireable simplicity. Whether it may be safely dispensed with, I am not sufficiently practical to determine. The woolen proprietors say it is the only checkmate to fraud. But if it be renounced, more than a 25 per cent duty must be laid or there is an "end of your worsted." I believe that with 33 1/3 per cent ad valorem, on a fair (not oppressive) valuation in this market—making the duties payable in cash on delivery from the public stores at the pleasure of the consignee—repealing the duties on drugs, it would be better to change the system, if thereby proselytes could be gained and angry passions assuaged. The coarse wool I suppose you cannot touch, without a great cry from those who would most be hurt by a diminished duty. If otherwise, so much the better. However you must do as well as you can—but we are all afraid that some unseen power will throw you all in the wind, and that from that wind will come storms. I am very respectfully with great esteem Yrs   H G Otis

ALS. NhHi.

1. On January 10, Clay submitted a resolution to abolish the tariff on articles not in competition with those "made or produced within the United States," excepting wines and silks whose duties he sought to have reduced. Hayne, on January 16, proposed to amend Clay's resolution so as to reduce all duties to the revenue level within a "reasonable period of time." The amendment was defeated, but was revived on March 22 by William Wilkins, debate continuing until June. This was the incident to which Otis refers. *Senate Journal*, 22d Cong., 1st sess., Serial 211, p. 201. The tariff bill which was ulti-

mately enacted came in late June from the House Committee on Manufactures headed by John Quincy Adams and was passed in the Senate the following month.

2. The motion was made after Dickerson had made his report and presented a bill on March 30, al-

though it was the bill and not the report which Dallas moved to table *Senate Journal*, 22d Cong., 1st sess. Serial 211, p. 218. The report is printed in *Senate Documents*, 22d Cong., 1st sess., Serial 214, Doc. No. 116.

FROM JAMES KENT

New York April 22d 1832

Dear sir

Since the short Note I wrote to you yesterday,[1] I have recollected & examined a document in Point. It is to be found in the *Journals of the House of Assembly of New York for 1791*, pa. 26, & what makes it the more weighty with me is; that *I was present as a Member of Assembly & agreed to the Report* & the apportionment was made accordingly. What a far Retrospect!

The constitution of N Y. of 1777 directed the Senators (being 24) to be apportioned among the four great districts according to the number of Electors *"as near as may be."* The assembly was likewise to be *"justly apportioned"* to the *Number of Electors* in each County on the return of each census. The Report made by my Friend C[ornelius] I. Bogert[2] (who died last January) stated that the Electors of Senators were so many & of Assembly so many & that the Senate was to consist of 24 & the Assembly of 70, but that "the quota was imperfect by reason of the fractional parts or remainders over in each County, & it became necessary to adopt some rule by which these parts might be adjusted, & the Committee were of opinion it was most agreeable *to the Spirit of the Constitution* that when any Senatorial district, or any County had a remainder or Surplus of Electors *exceeding one half of the given ratio*—(ratio was 817 for Senate & 554 for Assembly) such County or such district should be entitled to an additional Member, & when such remainder was less than half it should be rejected."

Upon that rule the County of Suffolk had an additional member for its surplus was above half of 554 & the County of Clinton having a Surplus or rather having a Body of Electors less than half viz: 176!! It had no member & was *quoad hoc* doomed to vote with the adjoining County of Washington for seven years longer. Yours Sincerely   James Kent

ALS. NN.

1. Kent had written to Webster the day before about the select Senate committee report on the apportion-

ment of representation (*Senate Documents*, 22d Cong., 1st sess., Serial 214, Doc. No. 119), and had agreed that Webster's plan caused "no In-

fraction of any rule in the Constitution, but a conformity to its Spirit &
Equity (which is Equality) in the
amendment." mDW 10009.

    2. Bogert (c. 1754–1832, Columbia
1776), a Federalist lawyer who repre-

sented the city and county of New
York in the New York Assembly in
1791. He made the committee report
summarized by Kent on January 21,
1791.

FROM JOSEPH TINKER BUCKINGHAM

Boston, May 11, 1832

Dear Sir,

    Since you left here, I have endeavored to think of some one, able and
disposed [to] give us [a] helping hand in the mode you mentioned, at
our last conversation. But I do not believe there is a young lawyer in the
city who is both able and willing. There are scribblers enough, but weak
and superficial. There are some strong enough, but they are either too
busy or too lazy. E[dmund] Kimball[1] can write and talk better than any
lawyer of his age; but Kimball is sour. I suppose he has been disappointed, and though he detests Jackson and all his party, yet he could
not be prevailed on to write, or hardly to vote, to save us all from per-
dition.

    I received your complimentary note after you had left the place.[2] I
wrote the article to which it refers immediately after our last interview,
and my object in part was to show you, that I could write with some
touches of vitality—as in former years, when you have also been
pleased to approve my efforts, and I have been vain enough to believe
that they have been of some value to *our party* as well as to yourself
personally. But, I have been more than half inclined to follow the example of Kimball, and let those fight the battle who are sure to enjoy the
spoils, let who will gain the victory. Not that I ask or wish for political
promotion, or greater notoriety than I know [I] can obtain as the editor
of the Courier. My ambition *has been* to get rich—that I found impossible, and *now* my ambition *is* to educate my children—and pretty
numerous they are—that they may stand a better chance than I have
had to pick up a share of the *honors* and *emoluments* for which every
body runs the gauntlet. To lay up money or any species of property is
out of the question with me. I have never owned a dollar that I did not
earn by severe and constant labor either of the mind or the body, and the
little income which now falls into my hands is barely adequate to the
call of my family. I have therefore deemed it my duty to be as tame and
as passive as one can be with decency to make friends of the *Mammon
of unrighteousness*. What encouragement have I to do better than my
neighbors? I mean, to write better? If I wielded the pen of Burke or of

Junius, it would be of no profit. You and half a dozen others might thank me, and think that good might come of it; but unless it had the sanction of Mr. [Nathan] Hale's name it would fall still-born from the press. There is a clannish spirit in this city and vicinity which is in nothing more manifest than the opinions respecting the Press. Do you imagine that you could persuade T[homas] H[andasyd] Perkins, William Prescott, George Bond,³ D[aniel] P. Parker, Lem[uel] Shaw, the Lowells, the Cabots, the Amories, and five hundred others that I might name to believe that any other paper than the Daily Advertiser is worth patronizing? Not one of them; and the feeling—if it be a *feeling*—is communicated to thousands of others, their friends acquaintances, and dependants. If I were to write and publish in the Courier the best argument you ever made in your life, unless these gentlemen had a hint that it was borrowed, they would turn up their aristocratic noses as they would if compelled to swallow an apothecaries' shop.

I have been exceedingly plain in my expressions; you may say, impertinent; but I thought it due to you, in consequence of our last conversation, to let you know distinctly my views and feelings, touching the Boston Press. *There is no encouragement* for one—for *me*—to attempt to elevate its character. It would cost me labor and money, and I should be sneered at as a *mechanic* by the aristocracy, and laughed at by professional contemporaries as a *fool*, for entering with zeal into a political warfare where I have everything to lose and nothing to gain.

Still I feel the blood of New England tingling in my fingers when I take hold of the papers devoted to the present administration. Though somewhat in years, and rather patriarchal in other respects, I am willing still to work for the cause—I am proud to work for the cause—but I do not want to work *alone*; and if, when my work is done, it does not circulate among the people—if its distribution is restricted by the pitiful sentiment to which I have ascribed the narrow circulation, what do I accomplish? Nothing.

With respect to getting up a new paper, such as you suggested, I do not believe, if it were practicable to set it a going that much good could be accomplished. To gain a circulation, a paper *must* contain a little of every thing. If it be devoted entirely to politics, business men will not take it, nor any other class of men whom you would have affected by it. I do not think it is in my power to make a paper *intrinsically* any better for country circulation than that I now publish. I have sent you one that you may see how it is made up, and of what materials. As I told you, on Monday, there are near two thousand subscribers—a much better foundation than a new subscription but I have never solicited subscriptions, nor taken any extraordinary measures to increase the circulation. No doubt it might be much increased. I will cheerfully listen to any advice from you tending to increase its usefulness, or if any thing can be made of the establishment to the greater advantage of the cause, by placing it in other hands, it can be purchased for a much less sum than would be needed to get another as well established.

I have much more to say on this subject, but here is as much as you will feel disposed to read, and perhaps more than I should have written for my own credit. It is superfluous to say that is intended to be confidential, for you would hardly have it known that you had *such* a correspondent.

I believe my love for *New-England* is no less than yours—Would to Heaven my ability to display it were equal. I believe that my desire to serve *you* personally is no less than his who loves you most. If I be not truly yours, I am not   J. T. B.

ALS. DLC.

1. Kimball (1793–1873; Harvard 1814), lawyer on Court Street who had been admitted to the Suffolk bar in October 1817 after having studied in Webster's office during the previous year. See mDW 2087.

2. Not found.

3. Bond (1788–1842), a leading Boston merchant in the well-known firm of Whitwell and Bond.

After Webster's letter to Biddle, printed below, there was little written communication between the two men for the next two months. During this crucial period when the Bank Recharter Bill was before both houses, Biddle at the urging of Webster and others friendly to the Bank resided in Washington where his knowledge of the institution and his political skill could be and were used to great advantage. Biddle arrived in Washington on May 20 and returned to Philadelphia on June 12, but at Webster's urgent request returned a week and a half later and remained until about July 4, after passage of the bill in the House.

TO NICHOLAS BIDDLE

Washington
Monday Eve' May 14. 1832

Private

My Dear Sir,

I spoke to Mr [George M.] Dallas, this morning, on the subject of bringing up the Bank question. He said, as he understood the matter, the Bill was to originate in H. of R. Accordingly, I consulted Mr [George] McDuffie; & I found that he was altogether of opinion that the proceeding should begin in *the Senate*. He says he is going to call up the Tariff, immediately, in H. of R. & cannot act upon the Bank until that matter is finished. Since seeing Mr. McDuffie, I have not been able to see Mr Dallas, but shall see him in the morning, & will write you again. My own opinion is, that if anything is to be done or attempted, this session, it must begin in the Senate, and that Wednesday, the 23rd instant, is the latest day for calling it up.

Mr McDuffie authorises me to say to you, that, in his opinion, your presence here will be nearly indispensable. He thinks, that, for two reasons, you ought to be present at the discussion. First, to give information, as it may be needed; second, as a proper respect to Congress, on so important an occasion. I certainly agree with him, altogether.

I will try to write you again, tomorrow. We hear of another assault, this P. M. made by a Major [Morgan A.] Heard, on Mr [Thomas Dickens] Arnold of the H. of R.[1] Yrs truly   Danl Webster

ALS. DLC.

1. Heard, a former army officer, assaulted Congressman Thomas D. Arnold of Tennessee outside the Capitol after the adjournment of the House. Their personal feud had been reported in both the *Globe* and *National Intelligencer* only days before. The incident culminated in Heard's firing a pistol at his antagonist and severely though not fatally wounding him. The antagonism grew out of Heard's personal dislike of Arnold's role in the House trial of Sam Houston for contempt and breach of privilege. Houston had assaulted Congressman William Stanbery of Ohio on April 13 and had been convicted of the charges by the House on the day Webster wrote this letter.

FROM JEREMIAH MASON

Boston May 27. 1832

My dear Sir

Letters from Washington, stating the unanimity of the Committee of the House of Reps. on manufactures, with the exception of Mr [John Strode] Barbour, in reporting a Bill,[1] in accordance with the views of the Secy. of the Treasury,[2] has created great alarm. Those, best informed on the subject, are united in opinion, that such a Bill, if passed, will prove fatal to the wollen manufactures. They think that no rate of ad valorem duties can be safely substituted for the minimum duties. While the foreign wollen trade shall continue in the hands of foreigners, & often the manufacturers, who can readily furnish such inventories, & other evidence of the cost of the articles imported, as they please, no vigilance in the custom house officers could detect & prevent frauds.

Under the present administration, it cannot be imputed that much pains will be taken to prevent known frauds. The best conducted wollen factories have been maintained with great difficulty. Taken all together they have probably since 1824 been a loss to their owners, equal to the amount of the interest of the money, employed in them. The one, I till lately was interested in, proved much worse than this. There was a loss, besides interest, of a part of the capital. Increased skill now affords better prospects. But the present Bill, if enacted, will, I think, turn many of them into cotton factories, & cause others to be abandoned.

The wollen manufactory directly interests a larger portion of the people of the U. States than any other. All the wool growers are directly interested. If this be sacrificed, what ground of hope can there be that other branches, less important & not so directly affecting the interests of great numbers, will not successively experience the same fate. It seems now to be better understood than formerly that the ruin of one branch of industry, or of one kind of property, must unavoidably disturb & injure all the rest.

I thought the New York convention[3] took the only safe ground, which was to defend the whole system. This unites all its friends. It must be defended on this ground or not at all. Alterations & modifications, not materially affecting the principle of protection, are of course to be admitted. Let the wool growers & wollen manufacturers be now sacrificed, & it is idle for the cotton manufacturers to expect, when attacked, to have their aid. The only security is in the union of all the friends of the protective system. For this end all the interests must be faithfully protected. The whole line must be protected or the battle will be lost.

Besides I do not see what is to be gained by yielding up this essential part of the system. As I understand the case the enemies of the protection of manufactures deny that government has the right to attempt it. This is certainly the ground assumed by their leaders, & a dissolution of the union is threatened as the penalty for the exercise of this right. The right is not, in the opinion of a vast majority of the nation of a doubtful nature. To attain it was certainly among the chief inducements to form the government. A great majority deem the exercise of it essential to their welfare, & as far as it has been exercised the results have been emminently successful. Immense interests are involved. Under such circumstances to yield a part, in hopes of appeasing the violence of the opposers, seems to me to be an indication of weakness & folly. This yielding will not satisfy or appease your opponents, but encourage them to reitterated assaults, till the whole system shall be abandoned. It will be early enough to yield a part, & to modify, when there shall be reasonable ground to expect that the doing so will produce satisfaction, & lessen the violence of opposition. I do not believe that yielding, at the present time, would produce that effect. On the contrary I think it would encourage opposition & increase its violence. Such is ordinarily the effect of yielding to unprovoked & unjustifiable threats. I would do nothing to increase the hopes of the Southern States that the exercise of the power in question would be abandoned. The due exercise of it is in my opinion not only essential to welfare of the Country, but to very existence of the union. Without it the government would not be worth preserving, & such, I believe, would on trial be found to be the opinion of all the Northern & Eastern States. The abandonment of the exercise of this power would immediately overwhelm N. England with poverty & ruin.

I do not pretend to calculate the effect of the passing this Bill on the approaching Presidential election. In process of time, I have no doubt, it would render its advocates unpopular & odious. But as the operation of it, is probably suspend[ed] to a future day, the effects would not be felt by the people till after the election will be over. If any thing less than public suffering & calamity can awaken the people to a sense of their true interests, it would seem that the unprincipled conduct & mischievous attempts of the present Administration would do it. General Jackson has sufficiently explained what he means by a judicious tariff.

A number of gentlemen, & Mr A[bbott] Lawrence among the rest, are about setting out for Washington to explain & enforce their views on the pending measure. I am as ever faithfully yours   J. Mason

ALS. MHi. Published in Mason, *Memoir and Correspondence*, pp. 337–340 (and duplicated on pp. 350–352).

1. Adams presented the report of the committee and the bill (H.R. 584) on May 23. *Committee Reports*, 22d Cong., 1st sess., Serial 228, Report No. 481. For Barbour's remarks, see *Register of Debates*, 22d Cong., 1st sess., pp. 3091–3092.

2. In response to a House resolution of January 19, 1832, the secretary of the treasury was "requested to collect such facts and information as may be in his power, of the extent and condition, generally, of the manufacturers of wool, cotton, hemp, iron, sugar, salt and such other articles as are manufactured to a considerable extent in the United States"

and "to accompany it with such a tariff of duties upon imports as, in his opinion, may be best adapted to the advancement of public interest." McLane complied with the resolution, and his report and proposed bill were received in the House on April 27. *Executive Documents*, 22d Cong., 1st sess., Serial 220, Doc. No. 222. The bill from John Quincy Adams' Committee of Manufactures was based on McLane's recommendations.

3. Mason's refence is to a "Memorial of the New York Convention [of the Friends of Domestic Industry], to the Congress of the United States. Presented March 26, 1832, and referred to the Committee on Manufactures." *Niles' Register*, 42 (1832, addendum): 17–39.

TO JOSEPH GALES & WILLIAM WINSTON SEATON

[June 3, 1832]

Dear Messrs G[ale]s & S[eaton]

I am troublesome—but I want to see my Speech No. 2.[1] once more. I have another small *addendum*. If it be not in type soon, it will be large, since it grows, like a cucumber.   D.W.

ALS. NhD.
    1. This is Webster's second speech for renewal of the charter of the Bank of the United States which he delivered in the Senate on May 28,

1832. See *Register of Debates*, 22d Cong., 1st sess., pp. 981–985. The speech appeared subsequently in the *National Intelligencer* on June 9, 1832.

TO NICHOLAS BIDDLE

Tuesday Eve'
[June 12, 1832]

Dear Sir

    The enemies of the Bank attempted a Stratagem upon it, this morning, as you will see; but it failed. The vote [to] lay it on the table (reject) was lost by a maj'ty of 23.[1]—Nine members were absent, of whom 7 are said to be friends of the Bank. There is now some talk of acting upon the Bill, without sending it to any Com[mitt]ee at all. Some conversation, I learn, on this point, was interchanged between members this Eve'. I do not yet know the result, but I should not be at all surprised if the fate of the Bank should be decided, before the week is out. I think you would do well to return hither, as soon as possible. Mr [Erastus] Root is a good deal uneasy, abt. his amendment.[2] If it were not for his wishes, in that regard, I think the friends of the Bank would, nearly all, agree to take the Bill as it is. Yrs ever truly   D. Webster

ALS. DLC.
    1. The motion to table the bill was defeated 111 to 88. The bill had just passed the Senate the day before.
    2. Root had that day expressed his dislike for the bill in its present form on the House floor. (*Register of Debates*, 22d Cong., 1st sess., p. 3455), but was not specific about an amendment. Earlier in the session he had proposed five amendments which included provisions for the creation of

additional bank stock, eleven government directors on a board of twenty-five, wider acceptance of Bank bills and notes throughout the system, and the right of states to tax branches "as they do their own banks" in lieu of a bonus. *Ibid.*, p. 1888 (February 28, 1832). Root may have also been interested in an amendment about Bank branches in New York state, concurred in by the Senate after House passage on July 3.

FROM HARRISON GRAY OTIS

Boston June 12 1832

Dear Sir,

    I am quite obliged to you for your note from the Congressional ephemeris,[1] and consider it a great favor in you to have given me a few minutes from the scanty allowance of leisure which you can command, to inform me how the land lies. Should the bill reported by the Com[mitt]ee of Manufactures pass with Mr [John] Davis' amendments,[2] it will be a great achievement. All will be secured that the friends of the system can reasonably expect and I believe all which at present their interest requires. A great point will be gained by uniting all who are in favor of the principle and differ only about the mode, and by "estopping" such men as Mr [John Quincy] Adams and others who think with him from denying that any concession has been made. It will be also a great advantage to afford to those who favor the views of the nullifiers but who through fear or doubt are not prepared to proceed to extremes, ground for halting where they are, and it is perhaps a consideration of some weight, that as the bill is fashioned upon the frame of the Administration (though essentially variant in some respects) they may be more inclined to defend its provisions and if it works well to claim it as "their thunder." So that I can not but confide, that the bill accompanied with the mitigation of the whole revenue system to the amount of eight millions, must produce a favorable impression on the public mind, and that the nullifiers will be left "in a hole by themselves." Still they will too probably proceed to some extravagant, and perhaps overt opposition to the law, the danger or inconvenience consequent on which will be in the inverse ratio of the force of public opinion manifested against it. The only interest sacrificed by the bill, is one that will affect a concern into which for my sins I have been drawn.[3] But I am content to look for my indemnity in the comfort and security and stability that would result to the business and affairs of one part of the Country, when Government shall refrain for any considerable time from attempting movere quieta. As to the minimum System, as provided for woolens by the act of 1828, though I felt restrained from inveighing against it, by the zeal and tenaciousness of some of our friends in its favor, it ever appeared to me a fictitious sort of legislation, and on many accounts liable to objections.

If the Bank Bill passes, I have ever thought, it will either be signed by the President or *permitted* to become a law. When McClean [Louis McLane] came into office, he was apprised of the Presidents hostility to the Bank, and the latter must also have understood that his Secretary was in favor of it, and that he was to be permitted to avow his approbation of it in his Report. The Message professes to leave the question to the decision of Congress. Now these must be the strangest animals that ever formed a cabinet, if they did so with an understanding that the responsible head of the department of finance should recommend a measure as important if not essential to the orderly adminisn. of the finances, which if adopted by Congress, his Chieftain should be at liberty to veto.

It implies a measure of base sycophancy on one part, and of insulting treachery on the other, in which it would seem neither could ultimately find his account. I therefore think he will hold his breath and down with the potation. Yet he said, about the time I was in Wash[ingto]n, "They mean to try me with their Bank Charter I'm ready for them." After all my dear Sir, there will be no peace or security for us, untill you buy up the Virginia negroes & send them off. If Virginia could be whitewashed she could say with St Paul, "now I am a man I put off childish things," and pour ces autres, they could do us no harm. I do believe, perhaps too fondly that a proposition to this end coming from the North, and managd with judgment and address and introduced with such a speech as I could make, if I was somebody that I wont name; however unfavorably it might be receivd at first, by those whose interest it would chiefly promote would ultimately obtain, and prove to be the most feasible and felicitous of all schemes that have been or can be devised for saving this Confederacy. So please to remember after I am dead, & you see this project realized after all "Old Otis was not so raving about this matter as he appeared to be.["] I am with the highest respect & esteem Dr Sir yr obed

H G Otis

ALS. DLC. Excerpt published in Samuel Eliot Morison, *Life and Letters of Harrison Gray Otis* (2 vols., Boston, 1913), 2: 266.

1. DW to Otis, June 8, 1832, mDW 10104.

2. Davis gave a speech on the Adams Tariff Bill on June 6 (*Register of Debates*, 22d Cong., 1st sess., pp. 3298–3318). at the end of which he proposed an amendment involving a series of changes in Section 2, paragraph 2 concerning imported manufactured wool. Essentially, Davis wanted lower duties on all milled and fulled cloths made wholly of wool, but raised the ad valorem rates for nearly every other category of woolen products. He also asked for stricter enforcement by appraisers against fraudulent valuations of the covered goods in his proposed changes.

3. This allusion may refer to Otis' considerable interests in cotton and woolen manufacturing in Massachusetts which he turned to after his defeat in the governor's race in 1823. During that election he made his role in the Hartford Convention the principal campaign issue.

FROM JOHN MARSHALL

Richmond June 16th. 1832

My dear Sir

I thank you very sincerely for the copy with which you have favored me of your speeches on the bill for renewing the charter of the bank of The United States.[1] I need not say that I consider an accommodation of the tariff question itself as scarcely more interesting to our country than the passage of that bill. Your argument presents the subject in its strongest point of view, and to me seems unanswerable. Mr [Thomas] Ritchie in his Enquirer informs the people of Virginia that Mr. [Littleton Waller] Tazewell has refuted you completely. This he may have done in the opinion of Mr. Ritchie. I have not seen Mr. Tazewell's speech[2] and do not understand from the Enquirer whether his refutation applies to your speech in favor of the bill or to that against the amendment offered by Mr. [Gabriel] Moor[e].[3] By the way, your argument against that amendment is founded on an idea which is to me quite novel. I had often heard it advanced that the states have no constitutional power to establish banks of circulation, but never that Congress might not introduce into the charter a restraining principle which might prohibit branches altogether, or require the assent of a state to their introduction; or a principle which might subject them to state taxation. This may be considered not as granting power of taxation to a state, for a state possesses that power; but as withdrawing a bar which the constitution opposes to the exercise of this power over a franchise created by Congress for national purposes, unless the constitution of the franchise, in its creation, has this quality engrafted on it. I however am far from undertaking to dissent from your proposition. I only say it is new, and I ponder on it. With great and respectful esteem I am your obed J Marshall

I only meant to express my obligation for your attention and I have betrayed myself into the politics of the day.

ALS. NhHi. Published in *PC*, 1: 518–519, but misdated as June 6.

1. Webster delivered his two speeches on the Bank Renewal Bill on May 25 and 28. See *Register of Debates*, 22d Cong., 1st sess., pp. 954–964, 981–988.

2. Tazewell's speech on the Moore amendment was delivered on May 28, but the text was unreported in the *Register of Debates*.

3. The Moore amendment, which was presented to the Senate on May 26, proposed that branches of the Bank of the United States should not be located in a state without its permission and that every branch was liable to state taxation as were state banks.

FROM BELLAMY STORER

Cincinnati June. 19. 1832

My dear Sir,

I have read your remarks in the Senate, on the Bank bill, with great pleasure; and the copies you forwarded to me, my friends will read and retain with equal satisfaction. Your observations on the subject of Bank circulation, are so clear, and yet so orthodox, that no unprejudiced mind can refuse to admit their force. We have seen in this region already, the effects of overtrading in the capital of state Banks. I say overtrading, because these institutions by excessive issues of paper, have converted what should have been a safe medium of exchange, an honest representation of the precious metals, to new merchandise: and in the scramble for profit, the great mass of the people have been made the dupes of covert scoundrels, or *uncommitted* politicians. I thank Heaven, that there is some prospect of a change—would that it might be thorough, and permanent.

Your views on the power of the States to incorporate Banks, were new to me. They have afforded, however a theme for reflection, and study, that I shall hereafter pursue with pleasure. What will be the fate of the Bill in the House? From the indications exhibited in the presentation of the Bill, I have strong hope that it will speedily pass its several stages: But the consent of the Executive! here, I fear the worst. If the Bill does not pass into a law, the immediate effect in the whole west will be disastrous beyond measure. Fire, flood & tempest have never produced a tithe of the desolation, that must follow the refusal to renew the charter of the Bank. I am confident no man in Ohio can be sustained, who votes to postpone the immediate consideration of the Bill.

You will perceive that no electoral ticket has as yet been published, by the friends of Mr Clay—and his opponents have taken occasion from this circumstance to predict that none will be agreed on. This you will readily regard as preposterous. Measures, I learn, will be taken in July to prepare a ticket—and if the anti-masonic votes can be united in its support, it will, beyond question, succeed.

Your friends, Mr. & Mrs. Lowell[1] passed thro this place, during the late session of our Supreme Court. I regret that the illness of Mrs Storer prevented me from extending toward them the attentions I should have been pleased to have bestowed. I am gratified, however, that my wifes health, has now materially improved, and I had flattered myself, pardon the expression of my great personal regard for you, that your name would have been borne in my family, but Heaven has sent me another daughter.

Will you remember me to Mrs W. Truly, your friend   B Storer

Shall I trouble you to send me the minority Bank report & its accompanying documents?

ALS. NhD.   1. Not identified.

TO JEREMIAH MASON

Washington June 23rd 1832

My Dear Sir

I duly recd. your letter, ten days ago.[1] Mr. Biddle, when he wrote you, requested me to send you copies of the Report[2] which I promised to do; but in truth, I had none to send, nor did we, any of us, get more than one copy, until two days ago, when Mr [Samuel] Bell, as he informs me, sent you one.

I have today recd. yr second letter,[3] & it has caused me to finish a duty, which I commenced yesterday, that is to write you, on the Subject of your first.

I have reflected a good deal, & spoke to several friends, Mr. Bell, Mr Clay, Mr. A Lawrence, & others, as to the necessity which the *Globe* may be supposed to have imposed on you to answer its slanders.[4] On the whole, the result of opinion is that there is no immediate occasion for your appearance in print. The abuse of the Globe, on this point, will hardly affect the interest or fate of the Bank, in its present crisis; & if it should, its mischief would be accomplished before your statement could appear. My own impression is, that, after the adjournment of Congress, let the question go which way it may, *it will be expedient* for you, at your leisure, to make a suitable publication. I think it may probably be expected. No doubt, the authority on which the Globe proceeds, is Mr. Woodbury, Mr. Hill, Mr. Hubbard, &c &c or some of them.

In the H. of R. the Tariff Bill will probably be engrossed or rejected to day—I know not which. If it comes here, we shall try, 1st. to amend, & second, if we cannot amend, to postpone the whole subject—our majority, at best, will be small & feeble. Party absorbs every thing; N. York, (her politicians) are obviously willing to sell the Tariff, or any thing else, for the sake of making Mr. V. B. Vice President.

We shall know in a few days, what the end is to be. The H. of R. will probably take up the Bank Bill, Monday or Tuesday. I think it will pass that House; but the prevailing impression is, that the President will return the Bill, with his objections. Yrs truly   Danl Webster

Copy. NhHi. Published in Mason, *Memoir and Correspondence*, pp. 340–341 and 352–353.

1. Not found.

2. "Bank of the United States," *Committee Reports*, 22d Cong., 1st sess., Serial 227, Report No. 460.

3. Not found.

4. Webster is referring to a series of articles which appeared in the *Globe* during the second week in June regarding accusations made against Mason while he served as president of the Portsmouth branch of the Bank of the United States in 1829. This situation has been discussed in Volume 2 of this series, pp. 357–360, but see also Donald B. Cole, *Jacksonian Democracy in New Hampshire, 1800–1850* (Cambridge, 1970), pp. 108–117. Mason and Webster may have had in mind a specific article like the unsigned and undated letter to Francis P. Blair which appeared in the June 9 edition.

The controversy received national

attention in 1832 after John Quincy Adams made his minority report on the Bank renewal bill. Adams complained that the majority report failed to discuss the controversy even though it was "more deserving of the attention of Congress, and of the nation, than any other part of the papers commented upon in the report." "Bank of the United States," *Committee Reports*, p. 393. Subsequently, Adams reproduced the correspond-

ence relating to the affair in the documents accompanying his report. The *National Intelligencer* attempted to side with Mason against national political interference in an article entitled "A Political Revelation" on June 7 and reproduced the documents, but the *Globe* persisted in denouncing Mason and his activities in a series of articles from June 8 to June 15.

TO [STEPHEN WHITE]

Washington June 28. 1832

My Dear Sir,

The Tariff bill was engrossed yesterday, in the H. of R. & will probably *pass* today. It contains many good, & some bad things, & was carried in the House by a strangely mixed vote. Many Gentlemen, south of the Potomac River voted *for it*, as did Mr [John Quincy] Adams, & Mr [Nathan] Appleton, & others; Jno. Davis, Mr [Rufus] Choate & al voted *against* it.[1] Its great objection is, that it leaves the *broad clothes* unprotected. In this respect, we shall try to *mend it*—& I have hopes of success. One thing seems certain—if this bill passes, *nullification* is at an end. There are too many southern votes *for it*, to admit the idea of its being *nullified* by southern votes. If we can make the bill what it ought to be, in regard to woolen clothes, it will do much good. Some other things must be attended to. Say to Mr P. I. [Isaac P.?] Davis, that I do not draw back from attention to drawbacks; that I am bound, by strong cords, to the interest of cordage. *Lead* goes very heavily, in the present Bill; but my ever vigilant colleague will look out, for Salem, & all its interests, urban & suburban. In some other particulars we shall try our hand at amendments. Let us hope for the best, & be prepared for the worst.

The Bank subject will now come up shortly, in the H. of R. where I expect it will pass; *but my opinion is, the President will veto it.* He will put it on the ground of *pre-maturity*—& say, that there is coming, seasonably, a new Congress, under a new Census, &c. But, for the present, he will *veto*. This, *I fully believe*. In the end, the B[an]k will *be reincorporated*. It has an inherent *popularity*, that will & must carry it thro'—tho' it will not get thro this time. This is *my private opinion*; but you must not make it *public*.

I suppose my wife is this day in Boston. I pray you, take good care of her. Give my love to Mr & Mrs [James William] P[aige] & shew him this letter. & give my love also to the damsels.[2] Yrs, ever & a day

D Webster

ALS. NhHi. Published in part in *PC*, 1: 519–520.

1. The bill had been engrossed on June 27 by a vote of 121 to 65, and was passed on this day, 132 to 65. The four Massachusetts representa-tives Webster refers to did not change their votes on final passage.

2. Stephen White's other daugh-ters, Caroline (1811–1886), and Ellen (1812–1861).

TO ISAAC P. DAVIS

Washington, June 30th. [1832]

Dear Sir,

I have recd your letters,[1] & am paying all due attention to the subject of *cordage*. I have drawn an amendment, like Genl. [Henry Alexander Scammell] Dearborns in effect,[2] & sent it to the Com[mitt]ee, to whom the tariff bill is referred. I have spoken to four out of five of the com-[mitt]ee, & I have no doubt they will report the desired amendment, & that it will pass. Depend upon it, I shall follow it up. It will not be either overlooked or *overwhelmed* by cries for the "question," "question."

I am almost worn out—& am getting to be as thin as a hatchell[3]—I sigh for the sea side—& for repose. The H. of R. will probably go to work on the Bank today, & soon settle it, one way, or the other. Probably they will pass it; & probably, too *as I think*, the President will place his *negative upon it*. Others think otherwise. We shall see. Yrs truly,

D. Webster

ALS. NhHi. Published in *PC*, 1: 505.

1. Not found.

2. Dearborn had written to Harri-son Gray Otis in January and ex-plained what he hoped to accom-plish: "As to hemp, & iron we shall endeavor to so amend our law, as to allow a draw back, on all, which goes into the construction of our vesels, as well as on cordage made in the U. S. & exported, & I think it possible the duty may be reduced on Hemp; if not, that on imported cordage will be increased." January 7, 1832, Otis Papers, MHi. The duty on hemp was indeed reduced from $60 to $40 a ton, but no duty on cordage was imposed.

3. A hatchel is a comblike instru-ment used in dressing flax and hemp.

TO ISAAC P. DAVIS

Washington, July 2d 1832

Dr Sir,

The Chairman of the [Senate] Committee of Manufactures [Mahlon

Dickerson] has this morning reported the Tariff Bill, with sundry amendments.

The most important of these amendments, I will endeavor to state, substantially.

On woolen cloths, it is proposed, instead of a general duty of 50 per centum ad valorem, two *minimums* are recommended, one of 50 cents; and one of $2.50; and a duty of 35 per centum ad valorem; no change proposed respecting plains, Kerseys, or Kendall cottons.

The duty on blankets, hosiery, carpetting, (except Brussels &c) raised from 25 per centum to 30; Brussells, Wilton, and Venitian carpeting all put at 40 cents, the square yard; bockings put in with flannels and *no* flannels to pay less than 50 per cent, ad valorem.

Sail duck to pay 8 cents the square yard.

Cotton bagging, instead of 3½ cents, to pay 4 cents a square yard.

On felt hats, 30 cents each, on silks, from Europe, 6 per cent ad valorem, instead of 10; leaving Chinese silks, at 10.

Tea and coffee, to be free articles; cordage, tarred, or untarred, to remain as it is, by existing laws; and no Drawback to be allowed on quantities less than five tons.

All duties on Wines, to be reduced one half, after March, 1834.

Nothing in the act to be construed, so as to reduce the duties on copperas, red & white lead,[1] and certain enumerated chemicals, as they now exist by law. The section (the 4th) which proposes to abolish so much of existing laws as requires an addition of ten per centum, on the value of goods, etc. to be struck out.

There are minor amendments, but these are the principal one[s]. Yours always truly   Danl Webster

The amendments, also, contain provisions in favor of straw hats, grass baskets, mathematical Instruments, &c &c.[2]

LS with insertions in DW's hand. MWalB. Webster probably sent similar form letters to other important constituents.

1. This phrase inserted in DW's hand.

2. This sentence added in DW's hand.

TO ABRAHAM VAN VECHTEN

Washington July 2. 1832

Private & confidential

My Dear Sir

I have been much gratified by the receipt of your letter of the 27th June, relative to the recent nomination of Electors, in New York.[1] Indeed, I had already suggested to a friend, before the receipt of your letter, that I would take the freedom to write you, on the same subject. We look on that nomination as being, on the whole, propitious to the great cause of the Country, under existing circumstances, & we all wish it success. I can say to you, in entire confidence, that there is a perfectly good understanding between Mr Clay, & Mr Wirt; & that they had a free & friendly conversation, in regard to the political state of the Country, when Mr Wirt was here; that it is generally understood, here that Mr Wirt would be glad of an opportunity to make public his wishes, that the whole <power> voice of all opposed to the re election of Genl Jackson should be united for Mr Clay; & that such an opportunity is looked for, & is not unlikely to occur, before the day of giving the votes.

I will only add, that every day brings grounds for <fresh> increased hopes of success, if we can but unite. We hear, today, of a great defection, among the Presidents friends, in Kentucky,[2] & understand it is likely to be contagious, along the Ohio River.

The Tariff bill will pass, amended, in some respects. The Bank Bill will pass the House, much as it passed the Senate, probably; but it is generally believed, & I have no doubt it will be found true, that the President will negative it.

This will affect Penna.;—but how deeply, I cannot say.

On the whole, we think all depends on N York. We cannot doubt, if the great State goes right, <all will go> the general result will be right. We therefore respectfully, but earnestly, beg of all good men in your State that they will make one *great* effort to save the Country. I am, Dr Sir, with mo true regard, Yrs

AL draft. NhHi. Published in Van Tyne, p. 175.

1. mDW 10144, in which Van Vechten discusses the electoral ticket of the New York Anti-Masons, a ticket selected "with a view of conciliating the national republicans."

2. Webster's remarks were made in light of a story carried in the *National Intelligencer* the following day, entitled "Great Political Re-action," concerning forty "Seceders from Jacksonism" who called a public meeting in Louisville to give support to Clay and Sergeant and "denounced in strong terms the mal practices of the present Administration." Like Webster, the *National Intelligencer* saw this as "an astonishing change in public sentiment in that part of the country," that augured "a salutary re-action in other quarters." Neither the names of the "Seceders" nor the circumstances which caused their shift were recounted in the article.

TO [NICHOLAS BIDDLE]

[c. July 4, 1832]

Private.

I should be exceedingly glad to raise the sum of 10,000 or 12,000

Dollars, in Phila. for a time, not unreasonably long, if such a thing were practicable, without making it a Bank transaction. I am interested in some valuable real estate, in Boston, which I went home, in May, to sell, but was too late for the season, & it may now be a year before an opportunity arrives of disposing of it advantageously. This is one cause, for desiring the possession of some pecuniary funds. One other is, that before there shall be another discussion of the Bank question, a new Com[mitt]ee, or another examination of lists &c, the little notes of mine, at the B[oston] Branch, may be diminished, or extinguished, if I remain in Congress.

Under these circumstances, I make a suggestion to you of what wd. suit me.

Two years from the first day of next month, nothing happening, Mr [John] Connell[1] will be indebted to me, by agreement, $5,000 certain, & probably as much more. I should like to get 10. or 12 th[ousa]n[d] Dlls—give my note, or notes, therefor payable to my own order, & indorsed by me; with an order on Mr Connell, (accepted) as a collateral, to pay to the holder of it, whatever might be due to me, on our agreement.

These notes need not all be made of so long date, as to Aug. 1834. Say, 4 notes of 2,500 each, at 6.12.18. & 24 mo's from Aug. 1. 1832. I need not know the holders; the notes may be made payable at B. U. S. Philadelphia; &, in regard to them, I can say, they will, all & each, be paid punctually if I live, & if I do not, there will be assets for their discharge.

All this, perhaps, is equally unreasonable, & impracticable. Such is very much my own opinion. But I have ventured to ask you to con it over, a few minutes. When you have done so, if you see no way of bringing the thing about, *sine labore*, just tear up this letter, & throw the pieces over the side of the Boat, & say, & think nothing more of it. On the other hand, if it should strike you differently, please signify it, in a short note, either addressed to me here, or to be recd. on my reaching Philadelphia. In that case, I would stay a day, in Phila. to arrange the matter; but unless detained by some such occasion, my extreme impatience to reach home will induce me to forego the pleasure of a visit, even of a day, in that or any City, this side of Boston. If you write to me, it will only be necessary for you to say, that you should be glad to see me, on my way home. If any other form would be preferable, it can be adopted.

AL. DLC.

1. Probably the merchant John Connell, located at 330 Chestnut Street, Philadelphia, who became a director of the United States Bank of Pennsylvania in 1838.

TO NICHOLAS BIDDLE

½ past 11 oclock
[July 10, 1832]

Dr Sir

The *Veto* came in this morning.[1] It is a monstrous long paper, & *goes the whole—*

It goes agt. the constitution[al]ity, in effect;

  against the utility & expediency;

  against the time, as premature;

  against the foreign stockholders;

  against refusing the taxing power to states

  &c &c &c.—

It contains the essence of Mr [Thomas Hart] Benton & Mr [Hugh Lawson] Whites speech[es] about the drain of specie from west to East.[2]

It extinguishes all hope of a reincorporation of the Bank under the present President. Yrs D. W.

ALS. DLC.

1. *Senate Journal*, 22d Cong., 1st sess., Serial 211, pp. 433–446.

2. Benton's views were most notably stated in his "branch draft" speech of January 20, 1832 (*Register of Debates*, 22d Cong., 1st sess., pp. 113–144), though reiterated throughout the Bank war debates, while White made similar remarks on June 7 and 8 (*ibid.*, pp. 1052, 1054).

FROM JAMES WATSON WEBB

New York July 13, 1832

(Private)

Dear Sir

We have said nothing this morning on the *weak* veto of the President nor will we until B[iddle] has time to act. For my part I am determined if B. does not act, to let the paper continue its present course with a notice that I have placed the <editorial> political department under Mr. [Mordecai M.] Noah, and intend myself to vote for *Henry Clay*. This is due to my own character for consistency. The state is literally *in our hands* and B. and those concerned, have not *nerve* enough to act. If you can influence him not a moment should be lost. Our silence this morning checked the fall of stock. Our movement will raise or depress it *five per cent.* Yours Respectfully, J. W. Webb.

ALS. DLC.

TO [JOSEPH STORY]

Saturday Morning, July 21. [1832]
Boston

My Dear Sir

I came to town last Eve', & go off this morning, at 8 o'clock, to *Marsh-*

field. I shall stay there some days, & intend, during that period, to correct the notes of my Speech on the *Veto* Message. You have seen that message. My wish is, to give a full answer to its *trash*, on the Constitutional question. That is Taney's work.[1] The argument, you perceive, is, that *some* powers of the Bank are not *necessary*, & so, not Constitutional. Now, My Dear Sir, the object of this is, to request you to turn to the message, read this part of it, & give me, in a letter of three pages, a close & conclusive confutation, in your way, of all its nonsense, in this particular. It will take you less than half an hour. Pray direct it to me at *Marshfield*, & let me have it, if possible, in two or three days. If you could get it into the Boston P. Office, by 4 oclock Monday, P. M. In that case, I shall receive it on Tuesday, which will be in season.

When I come to town, I shall come & see you. I have been unwell, for three weeks—quite run down. I am going to the sea coast, for the purpose of recruiting. Yrs always   Danl Webster

ALS. MHi. Published in *MHi Proc.*, 2d Series, 14 (1900–1901): 408–409.

1. Attorney General Roger B. Taney's role in drafting the veto message has been seriously questioned by Lynn L. Marshall in "The Authorship of Jackson's Bank Veto Message," *Mississippi Valley Historical Review*, 50 (December 1963): 466–

477. Amos Kendall's draft of the message was revised by many, including Andrew Jackson Donelson, Levi Woodbury, Roger B. Taney, and Jackson himself, but there is nothing in the constitutional arguments, Marshall suggests, that was not already known to Kendall, who shaped and designed the message.

FROM JOHN MARSHALL

Happy Creek. Aug 24th 1832.

Dear Sir

My friend Mr William Randolph[1] is a candidate for the office of Sergeant at Arms of the Senate, which is understood to be vacant, & has requested me to make him known to you. He filled that office in the late convention of Virginia with so much propriety as to justify my confidence in saying that he is entirely competent to its duties, and will give entire satisfaction to the Senate, should he be fortunate enough to receive the appointment.

Mr. Randolph is a Gentleman of the best connections who inherited a handsome fortune, which has passed from him without any fault on his part which can in the most remote degree affect his character, & on his correct character and deportment in office the senate may, I am persuaded place entire reliance. I presume that you will receive many applications, to someone of whom you may feel a preference. I have only to say that if in the progress of the election, a contest should arise between Mr Randolph & some person for whom you feel no preference, you cannot bestow your patronage on a more deserving man. With great respect and esteem I am dear Sir your obdt. Ser   J Marshall

Copy. NhHi.

1. Probably William Fitzhugh Randolph of Millwood, Frederick (now Clark) County, Virginia, who contested unsuccessfully. In 1833 the post of Senate sergeant-at-arms was held by Mountjoy Bayly of Virginia, and within two years his assistant, John Shackford of New Hampshire, was elevated to the position.

FROM HENRY CLAY

Ashland 27th. Aug. 1832

Dear Sir

Our Kentucky elections have terminated in the election of the Jackson Candidate [John Breathitt][1] for Governor by a majority of 1260 votes, the N[ational] Republican Candidate for Lieut. Governor [James Turner Morehead] by a majority of 2516 votes, and in 60 out of the 100 members that compose our H. of Representatives, as well as in securing in the Senate, where the majority was against us last year, a majority of 22 out of the 38 members composing that body.

We have been so often mortified with the issue of elections in this state, that I do not know whether you will take any interest in the causes of our recent partial defeat. They were 1st. the employment of extraordinary means by the Jackson party, within and without the State. On this point all their efforts were brought to bear; and every species of influence was exercised. The patronage and the means of that party were profusely used. 2ndly, An irruption of Tennessee voters who came to the polls in some of our border counties. Last year official returns of all the voters, in all the counties, were made to form a basis for the periodical adjustment of the ratio of our representation. In some of those border counties, at the recent election, I understand that the *Jackson majorities*, exceeded the whole number of the voters according to those returns. But we should have been able to resist successfully the joint effect of both the above causes, if it had not been for a third, which operated most extensively. Our candidate was a Presbyterian, and against that sect most deep rooted, and inveterate prejudices exist, the weight of which had not been sufficiently estimated when he was selected. Owing to this latter cause, I believe we lost not less than probably three thousand votes.

But it is less important to dwell on the past and incurable event of our Governors election than to look forward and provide against future disaster. The spirit of our friends is unbroken, their zeal is increased in warmth, and they are full of confidence of success in November. What is more encouraging, they are already engaged in the best plans to secure success. Far from being disheartened, their recent partial defeat arouses them to exertion more vigorous than ever, and the exceptionable means employed by their opponents have fired their indignation. I think there is much reason to hope that the late event will lead to more certain success in November than if we had carried the eléction of the Governor by such a majority as the other side has obtained.

What is most absorbing of public attention at this time is the Bank Veto. On that subject our opponents have been much more industrious in the circulation of documents, than the friends of the institution. The President's message and Benton's rodomontade have been scattered in countless thousands, and time enough to affect the election; whilst on the other side, but little reached us before the election, except Mr Clay's speech,[2] which had a limited circulation, as it arrived only at the moment of the election. A clear, intelligible, popular statement of the case, with a just account of the certain effects of the overthrow of the Bank is much needed.

I hope that our friends abroad will see in our election that the bad issue of it has been neutralized by the good; and that they will derive from it fresh motives to spare no exertions to save the Country. I remain always Faithfully Your friend   H. Clay

P.S. Whilst it would be indiscreet to publish this letter with my name, I request you to show it to Messrs. Dearborne [Henry Alexander Scammell Dearborn], Everetts [Edward Everett], or any other particular friends.   H. C.

Why has not your Speech on the Veto been published at length?   C.

LS with postscript in Clay's hand. DLC. Published in Van Tyne, pp. 176–178.

1. Breathitt (1786–1834), lawyer and legislator who served as lieutenant governor of Kentucky for four years before being elected governor in 1832.

2. Clay spoke in opposition to the veto in the Senate on July 12 after Webster's speech of July 11. Benton followed Clay, provoking the Kentucky senator into debate on the 13th. See *Register of Debates*, 22d Cong., 1st sess., pp. 1265–1274, 1293–1296. Clay himself would hardly have written the sentence in this form. The letter was probably dictated, with a free transcription by the amanuensis.

TO NICHOLAS BIDDLE

Boston Sep. 24. 1832

Private

D. Sir.

Having been thro' last week wandering along the sea side, I found my *speech*, in a Boston newspaper. I read it over, corrected some few errors of the press, & sent it to the Messrs G[ales] & S[eaton]. On coming to town yesterday, I found the same *work* in a pamphlet, sent me, as I presume from Washington.[1] I am afraid the speech is too *forensic*, too much in the manner of legal argument, for general reading, or extensive usefulness. I enclose the letter, from Mr. [Samuel P.] Lyman,[2] that you may, if you think it worth while, cause proper communications to be made in that quarter.

Our good people of Mass. hold a Nat. Repub. Convention at Worcester, the 11th. of October. I am a delegate, & if I do not change my present purpose, shall attend the meeting. If no one else shall be disposed to take a general, view of the merits of the Administration, & the present state of the Country, I think I shall make some few remarks on those topics.[3]

My health is tolerably well restored. My wanderings by the sea side very much over. I am at *home*; & as I do not know that I may expect the pleasure of *seeing* you, it will be the next good thing to *hear* from you. Yrs truly   D. Webster

ALS. DLC.

1. As many as five separate editions of Webster's speech of July 11, 1832, on the President's veto of the Recharter Bill were published. The one referred to here was published in Philadelphia. See Biddle to DW, September 27, 1832, below.

2. Lyman (1804–1869), Utica and Albany lawyer, journalist, and speculator in western lands and in railroad development. He was heavily committed to the Erie Railroad. Entering politics as an Anti-Mason, he became one of Webster's strongest supporters in New York State. He was a close friend of Thurlow Weed, and as will appear in a later volume attempted unsuccessfully to mediate between the Weed and Fillmore factions in the Whig Party. See Harriet A. Weed, ed., *Autobiography of Thurlow Weed* (2 vols., Boston, 1884), 1: 438; Robert J. Rayback, *Millard Fillmore* (Buffalo, 1959), pp. 279–280.

Immediately after Webster's death in 1852, Lyman assembled various newspaper pieces he had written and published them, together with some new material, as *Life and Memorials of Daniel Webster from the New-York Daily Times* (2 vols., New York, 1852).

Lyman's letter of September 11, 1832 (mDWs), encouraged Webster to publish his speech on the President's veto as soon as possible. He explained that there was a "great necessity of some high authority to counteract the effect which, the profuse distribution of the veto, is producing upon the voters in this State. A copy of it is put into the hands of everyone who can read: and I am sorry to add, its contents are inducing many well-disposed, but less informed men, to favour the re-election of Andrew Jackson."

3. See Biddle to DW, October 4, 1832, note 3, below.

TO NICHOLAS BIDDLE

Boston Sep. 24. 1832.

Private

My Dear Sir

As the period approaches for the appointment of the Directors of the

Office [of the Bank of the United States] in this City, I take the liberty
of calling your attention to the subject. It is of a good deal of importance. The opinion, which I expressed to you at Washington is confirmed,
by all that I have seen & heard here. In short, it has become indispensable, I think, to make some change in the organization of the Board. It
is fully expected that some change will be made; & I fear, a good deal of
dissatisfaction would be manifested, if that expectation should be disappointed. It is unpleasant to go into particulars, on such a subject, because it would be necessary to speak of individuals, all worthy & respectable. It has occurred to me, that the most discreet course would be,
for Mr. Copperthwait [Joseph Cowperthwaite],[1] or some other Gentleman connected with the Bank, to take occasion to make a visit to this
place. He will then have an opportunity to converse with Gentlemen,
most respectable for character & most concerned in the Commercial
business of the place; & will thus be enabled to recommend such measures as appear likely to give satisfaction to the Commercial Community.
There is, at present, much complaint. This is *particularly* unpleasant, at
this juncture, & in this place, where the general feeling toward the Bank
is naturally inclined to be highly favorable. I am quite certain, My Dear
Sir, you will dispose of the subject, wisely; but I cannot conclude without repeating, that, in its *various bearings*, much importance belongs to
it. Yrs truly   Danl. Webster

ALS. DLC.

1. Cowperthwaite was second as- sistant cashier of the Bank of the United States at this time.

FROM NICHOLAS BIDDLE

Phila. Septr 27. 1832

My dear Sir

I have this morning received your favors of the 24th inst.[1] The Speech
was printed here under my own eye—which I thought best. It has been
reprinted largely in various papers, and the press is at work with it in
the shape of a pamphlet (which I sent to you) and also in numbers of
the National Gazette extra. It is reported to be very effic[acious] very
much sought after and very greedily devoured, and, what. is important
in these cholera times, easily digested. Mr. [Joseph] Cowperthwait
showed me a letter from Mr [Samuel] Frothingham[2] received this morning, requesting some copies of it. I have requested him to forward some
—and to tell Mr. Frothingham to print an edition of it at Boston. I wish
you would make that edition of it as large as may be, and cause them
to circulate thro' New Hampshire and Maine and parts adjacent.

On the subject of your other letter I will get Mr Cowperthwait who knows every body in Boston to make a visit and sound round all the depths and sho[als]—and it will be very hard if we cannot adjust that who[le] matter satisfactorily.

I pray you to go to Worcester, and being there, take your proper position and "come out" as the phrase is. Our Pennsylvania matters are doing very well, all the auspices denote the election of [Joseph] Ritner. With great regard Yrs   N. Biddle

LC. DLC.
1. Both are printed above.
2. Cashier of the Boston branch of the Bank of the United States; later president of the State Bank of Boston.

TO NICHOLAS BIDDLE

Boston Oct. 1. 1832

Private
My Dr. Sir

I recd yrs of the 27th. on Saturday Eve'.¹ Mr [Samuel] F[rothingham] has spoken to the printer, & the paper [i.e., speech] will be published & circulated, forthwith. From letters recd. from Kentucky, I get the impression that something of this kind is much needed in that quarter.

By yesterday's mail I sent a manuscript to Washington, for the Int[elligencer]. It is half official—half Editorial—half ambiguous, as to its origin (a creature with 3 halves)—but it is addressed to the People of U. S. & does not lack for plain statement, & perhaps hard words. It will probably appear about the end of this week.²

Since I am so far in for it, I believe I shall go to Worcester next week, & even make another speech. Albany has surprised us; Philadelphia delighted us.³ Heaven defend the right. Yrs   D. W.

ALS. DLC.
1. See above.
2. "To the People of the United States," *National Intelligencer*, October 6, 1832.
3. In the recent Albany election anti-Jackson charter officers for the city were elected in four of the five wards, while in Philadelphia anti-Jacksonians were overwhelmingly approved as inspectors of elections, an office the election to which contemporaries regarded as a test of the general election later that fall.

FROM NICHOLAS BIDDLE

Phila. Oct. 4th 1832

My Dear Sir

I have just received yours of the 1st. inst.¹ The manifesto from the

South I shall expect tomorrow.[2] Mr. F[rothingham] the Cashier writes that he proposes an edition of the Speech of 5,000 copies. Had you not better say 10 or 15 or 20 thousand? Mr. F. has been instructed, or will be this day, to follow your counsels as to that matter. When you make a speech at W[orcester], make it strong—and moreover have it ready to print *before* you speak it—and then get Mr. F to print any number of thousands you may deem expedient[3]—that is to say if there is any thing in it about the Bank, as that brings it within my chartered limits. The west has been & will continue to be saturated with good materials.

I flatter myself that Philada. deserves the applause of her sister Boston. With great regard Yrs   N Biddle

LC. DLC.
1. See above.
2. This probably refers to Calhoun's vigorous statement in support of nullification which was written as a letter to Governor James Hamilton, Jr., and published in mid-September. See DW to James Kent, October 29, 1832, below.

3. Webster did have the speech ready for publication shortly after he had delivered the address on October 12. It appeared in both the *Boston Weekly Messenger* and the *Boston Courier* on October 18, and in the *National Intelligencer* on October 23 and 25.

TO HENRY CLAY

Boston Oct. 22. 1832

My Dear Sir
The first accounts from the election in Penna. put us in very good spirits, in this quarter. We began to hope that a substantial change of opinion was about taking place, in the middle States. The later returns from that State have not quite sustained that first impression; nevertheless, they leave Penna. quite as well, indeed better, than I had looked for. But we are thrown sadly back by Ohio. We did not expect a rebuff, from that quarter. On the favorable intelligence from Penna, our friends in Maine, & even in N. Hampshire, took new courage, & were ready to make new exertions. But for the dispiriting result in Ohio, I should have had strong hopes of Maine, & *some* hopes of N. Hamp. As it [is], we do not entirely despair of Maine. Private letters from N York speak with confidence of that State. My own opinion is, that the Anti-Jackson ticket will prevail there. Of Penna, as of all west & south, you are a better judge than I can be. In our own state, we seem quite safe. It is rumoured, that the Jackson Gentlemen & the Anti-Masons, in the Legislature, will unite, next January, to give my place to Mr [John Quincy] Adams. I hardly credit the probability of any such Union, & still

less the probability of his assent to an operation, of that kind. There is no reason to doubt, moreover, that the National Republicans will have a decisive majority, in the Legislature. Our meeting at Worcester was a good one, full of spirit & good feeling.

If you have any thing good to say of Ohio, pray let us hear it. And as to Missouri, what is the prospect there? Is her Legislature changed?

I pray you, remember me most kindly to Mrs Clay; & believe ever cordially, Yours   Danl Webster

ALS. ViU.

1. Webster's views on the progress of the 1832 campaign were derived from the *Boston Courier* published that day, which presented a very optimistic account of the Pennsylvania elections, primarily from the results of contests in Philadelphia, and a gloomy forecast of Ohio, from which no results had been received at all. The final outcomes in these states were more mixed, but the potential strength of the National Republican electoral ticket in either state never materialized.

The nullification controversy occupies considerably less space in Webster's correspondence than might be expected, but the constitutional issue had been in his mind since he first read Calhoun's South Carolina Exposition and Protest *of 1828. His first refutation of the dogma came in January 1830, in his second reply to Hayne, but the matter did not end there. In July 1831 Calhoun expanded upon the theme in his Fort Hill address, and gave it perhaps its definitive expression in a letter addressed to Governor James Hamilton, Jr., dated August 28, 1832, some six weeks after the tariff of 1832 had become law. It was this letter, published in mid-September, that Webster felt must be answered. As he says in the following letter to Chancellor Kent, he would not have time to prepare a reply before the November election, but he hoped to complete it during that month.*

Events were moving too rapidly for so leisurely a mode of argument. Even before Webster's decision to answer Calhoun was reached, South Carolinians had gone to the polls and returned a legislature overwhelmingly controlled by the nullifiers. A hastily summoned special session called for a convention to meet November 19. On the twenty-fourth the tariffs of 1828 and 1832 were declared unconstitutional and the collection of duties imposed by them was forbidden within the state. It was then determined by party caucus that Hayne should be elected governor and Calhoun should fill the Senate seat thus vacated. Webster gave up the project for a critique of nullification by public letter, sure that he and Calhoun would cross swords on that subject before the session ended.

TO JAMES KENT

Boston Oct. 29. 1832

Private & Confidential

My Dear Sir

Mr Calhoun, as you are doubtless aware, has published a labored defence of *nullification*, in the form of a letter to Govr. [James] Hamilton[, Jr].[1] It is far the ablest & most plausible, and therefore the most dangerous vindication of that particular *form of Revolution*, which has yet appeared. In the silence of abler pens, & seeing, as I think I do, that the affairs of this Govt. are rapidly approaching a crisis, I have felt it to be my duty to *answer* Mr Calhoun. And as he adopted the form of a letter, in which to put forth his opinions, I think of giving my answer a similar form. The object of this is, to ask your permission to address my letter *to you*. I propose to *feign* that I have recd a letter from you, calling my attention to Mr Calhoun's publication, & then, in answer to such supposed letter, to proceed to review his whole argument, at some length, not in the style of a *speech*, but in that of cool constitutional & legal discussion. If you feel no repugnance to be thus written to, I will be obliged to you for your assent; on the other hand, if any reasons suggest themselves to your mind, against such a form of publication, another can be readily adopted. I cannot complete the paper before the Election, as I am, at present, a good deal pressed with professional affairs; but I hope to bring it into light in the course of next month.

I have little to say to you, My Dear Sir, upon political subjects. The whole ground is open to you. I trust you will be one of those who will have votes to give, & I devoutly pray you may yet see some way of so uniting the well disposed, as to rescue us from our peril. I am, Dear Sir, with most sincere & true regard, Yours   Danl Webster

ALS. DLC. Published in *PC*, 1: 526–527.

1. Richard K. Crallé, ed., *Works of* *John C. Calhoun* (6 vols., New York, 1853–1855), 5: 144–193.

FROM JAMES KENT

New York October 31. 1832.

(also confidential)

Dear Sir,

I have no objection that you should address in the form of a letter or letters to me your remarks on the Vice Presidents scheme of Nullification, and that you should assume it to be in answer to a letter from me relative to that subject. I shall deem it an honor to be addressed by you while engaged in the investigation of such an interesting subject. The Vice President enclosed one of his pamphlets to me and I read it attentively. It is ingeniously written, but such a construction of the constitution, and such principles as he deduces are visionary and most unsound and sophistical. His repugnance to all solid constitutional Principles would fix a deadly power of destruction in the very vitals of the government.

The crisis is indeed portentous and frightful. We are threatened with destruction all around us, and we seem to be fast losing our original good sense and virtue. The democracy of this city require all their candidates to Congress to give another pledge to support all the measures of the administration. Can anything be more degrading and monstrous? Is the proud House of representatives and the grand inquest of the nation to be composed of such materials?

We are in hopes of carrying the electoral Ticket in which I am included, but the struggle will be tremendous.[1] It will be the great battle of *Armageddon* between the Genius of Liberty and the Spirits of darkness; and suppose we should succeed, what then? Penn. and Vermont if they succeed, will certainly vote for Mr [William] Wirt and then at all events the case goes to the House of Representatives, [where] Jackson will get thirteen states. New York would vote, I presume, either for C[lay] or W[irt] as would best insure success, but Massachusetts, Connecticut, Jersey &c and especially the former will be tenacious and hold out for Clay. I foresee difficulties, if Pennsylvania and New York succeed with their electoral Tickets, and·thus there is no chance for success, but *for every electoral College opposed to Jackson to unite in their candidate*, and I see no possibility of such an Union but upon Wirt.

If we succeed (in our election) I shall take the liberty of writing you again and ask for a free communication of sentiments. If we fail, then indeed we may hang our harps upon the willows or on the witch-elm that shades Saint Fillans Spring!

Your speech at Worcester was admirable for its logic as well as for its fervor and its force. If we are to be saved, we shall largely be indebted to you. Si pergama dextra &c. Adieu, Yours most sincerely

James Kent

Copy. DLC. Published in William Kent, ed., *Memoirs and Letters of James Kent* (Boston, 1898), pp. 209–210.

1. Kent not only served as the head of the Anti-Mason Presidential electoral ticket, but also was approved, as were all other Anti-Masonic electors and the party's candidates for governor and lieutenant governor, by the convention of National Republicans which met in Utica on July 24 and 25, 1832. The National Republicans, however, supported Henry Clay and John Sergeant.

FROM JOHN BROOKS

Princeton Nov 2 1832

Sir

I have complyed with your request for purchasing cattle as follows viz—

Bot. of John L Boylston[1] one dark red bull calf for— it is the same that took the first premium at the last show at Worcester and is said by competent judges to be the best calf ever raised in this neighbourhood	$50.00
one dark Red two year old heifer of John Whitney[2]	40.00
one light red yearling heifer of John Whitney	17 00
one light red two year old heifer of Benjamin Har[r]ington[3]	30.00
two dark red yearlings of Benjamin Har[r]ington	34 00
	171.00

they are all native cattle and are the best selection from the most approved stock both for breed and milk in this Town—the cattle will be at the market in Brighton on the 7 instant in the afternoon ready for delivery to you or any person you may send to receive them.[4] I shall be in Boston about the 15 instant when I will call upon you for the cost of the cattle also for the amount of drift so that you need buy nothing untill you see me untill then I remain most Respectfully yours &c &c

John Brooks

ALS. NhHi. Brooks has not been identified.

1. Boylston (c. 1789–1846), Princeton farmer.

2. Whitney (1792–1846), Princeton farmer.

3. Harrington (b. 1774), Princeton farmer.

4. Across the bottom of the page is the following note in Webster's hand: "Mr. N[athaniel] R[ay] Thomas, the bearer of this, will take care of these cattle for me. Danl Webster"

TO NICHOLAS BIDDLE

Boston Nov. 19. 1832

My Dear Sir,

I recommend the enclosed list of Directors, for the office here. Mr. William Appleton is placed at the head of it, with a view to his being President of the Office. A good deal of attention to the subject, & much conversation with others, have led my own judgment to two results. First that a change in the head of the Office is not only expedient, but absolutely *indispensable*. Second, that Mr. Wm. Appleton is, on the whole, the fittest person now to be made that head. Mr. Appleton, though heretofore not connected especially with the Bank, has been its steady & uni-

form friend, regarding it as a public Institution of great utility. He possesses a safe & accurate judgment in affairs, and is thoroughly acquainted
with the money concerns of the City, & with the men of business in
it. He is of mild manners, & easy of access; of competent fortune & irre-
proachable character. There are other good men,—very good men—who
have been spoken of, & for whom I have true regard, & who, with their
friends, deserve well of the Bank. But in preferring Mr Appleton, I have
done no more than to yield to a sense of duty, & to recommend the person whom I thought, on the whole, most likely to give satisfaction to the
Board at Philadelphia, and to the public here.

You will observe a new name or two, on the list; for instance, R[ob-
ert] G. Shaw.[1] This has been done to extend the circle of the Bank connexion here, & to bring into it persons, not now within it, who are of the
first class of men of business, & also occupy a considerable space in our
Society. The enclosed list has the entire approbation of Mr Abbott Lawrence, with whom I have conferred, except as to his own name. He has
no particular desire to be in the Bank, but probably would be willing to
be a Director, under circumstances agreeable to him. Mr Copperthwait
[Joseph Cowperthwaite] has been recently amongst us, and, as I understand has had a good deal of conversation on the subject. He will be able
to state to you what he learned, or observed. I feel some interest in this
matter, simply because I desire that the respectable part of the public
here may be *satisfied*, with the organization & administration of the Office. I am, Dr. Sir, with the most sincere regard, Yours   Danl. Webster

Private
The truth is, the office must be rid of Mr. G. [Gardiner Greene][2] & of
the *meddlesomeness* of our good friend Mr. P.[3] Somebody must be in the
office, who will be independent of this good man's perpetual presence &
friendly supervision. The truth is, public opinion now regards the office,
not more as a *Bank* than as Messrs *G's & P's* broker's office. They will
kill F. [Samuel Frothingham] if he is not freed from them. His situation
is delicate—especially since the receipt of the official letter, this morning.[4] I have seen him. He is *against* S[amuel] G. P[erkins] for President;[5] thinking, that Mr. P's kind offices, will, in that event, be rather
encreased than diminished. In short, Mr. F. no doubt desires the success of the list I send you; but his <case> situation is peculiar. Mr. P.
is his *surety*. Mr. G. will decline, unless Mr. P. shall prevent it. If Mr. P.
shall think there is no chance to continue Mr G. he will *warmly recommend S. G. P.* That truly good man, Col [Thomas Handasyd] P[erkins]
will no doubt feel a strong wish for S.G.P's success; but he is a sensible
man, and he has already been informed that public opinion here sets in

another direction, I have no doubt he will acquiesce. He, & those who would gladly gratify him, & Mr. *P.* are probably all who will take an interest for S. G. P.

I believe I have now laid the whole matter before you.

P.S. I have again seen Mr. *F.* He is *totally* averse to the appointment of *S.G.P.* & he is tired—tired half to death—with our "excellent friend" Mr. *P.* <He thinks>

William Appleton
David Sears[6]
George Blake
John Borland[7]
Ebenr. Chadwick[8]
J[ames] W[illiam] Paige
George Hallett[9]
Abbott Lawrence
D[aniel] P. Parker
R[esin] D. Shepherd[10]
R[ichard] D. Tucker[11]
Robert G. Shaw
R[ichard] S. Rogers, Salem[12]

ALS with AD enclosure. DLC.

1. Shaw (1776–1853), Boston merchant in the Genoa trade and a land speculator.

2. Greene was president of the Boston branch of the Bank of the United States and had long been involved in bank affairs in Boston, starting with the National Union Bank in 1792. He was treasurer of the Provident Bank for Savings from 1821 to 1823. For other criticism of Greene as branch president, see Nathan Appleton to DW, February 1829, *Correspondence*, 2: 402–404.

3. This is probably John Parker (1757–1840) of Brookline, who was on the board in 1832 but was replaced in the following year. All the men on Webster's list were on the new 1833 board. Four men were removed—Greene, Parker, John Welles, and Israel Munson—and four new men were added—Appleton, Shaw, James W. Paige (Webster's brother-in-law), and George Hallett. Paige and Hallet had previously served as directors. See *Correspondence*, 2: 374–378.

4. The "official letter" was sent by Biddle to Greene on November 15 requesting him and Cashier Frothingham to "forward a list of Directors." In Biddle's letter to Webster that day (mDWs), he asked the senator and Abbott Lawrence to compose their own list "giving such explanations and reasons as may pass immediately from me to the fire near me," and assured him that it would "come to a good result."

5. Samuel G. Perkins (1767–1847), merchant in the Caribbean trade and brother of Thomas Handasyd Perkins.

6. Sears (1787–1871; Harvard 1807), a socially prominent speculator and benefactor, and son of a wealthy Boston merchant.

7. Merchant of Borland and Abbot

Company, 21 Central Wharf, and a director of the Atlas National Bank in 1833.

8. Boston merchant in McClellan and Company, 41 Hancock Street.

9. Merchant on India Wharf, president of the State National Bank in

1823, and treasurer of the Suffolk Saving Bank for Seamen in 1833.

10. Merchant on India Wharf.

11. Merchant on India Wharf involved in some banking activity.

12. Rogers (1792–1836?), Salem merchant and shipowner.

TO LEVI LINCOLN

Boston Decr. 10 [1832]

My Dear Sir,

The general judgment here, as you will have perceived, concurs with yours, as to the postponement of the proposed public meeting. It seems now that the Subject will come, in an official shape, before the Legislature; & I trust it will there receive such a consideration as is required by the honor & character of Massachusetts.[1]

I am prepared, any day, to hear that matters have come to blows in Charleston. The leaders of the nullifiers have placed themselves, in a situation, where retreat is impossible. They can only go forward, try the strength of their party, & the *weakness* of the Govt; & rely on the hope of drawing neighboring States into concurrence with their own measures. I have not the slightest doubt, that both Genl. Jackson & Govr. [James] Hamilto[n,] Jr. fully expect a decision by the sword. I am, Dr Sir, always truly, Your Ob servt   Danl Webster

ALS. MHi.

1. Before the Massachusetts legislature met, a public meeting was held in Faneuil Hall on December 17 "to take into consideration the late proceedings of the Legislature of South-Carolina, and to express their opinions thereon, and to respond to the sentiments expressed in the late

Proclamation of the President of the United States"—the proclamation against the nullifiers, issued on December 10. *Boston Courier*, December 17, 1832. Although the session of Congress opened on December 3, Webster stayed in Boston to attend the meeting. He did not take his seat until December 31.

FROM CHARLES BRICKETT HADDOCK

D[artmouth] Col[lege] Dec. 20th, 1832.

Dear Uncle,

I stopped at Franklin and attended to the subject of. the Lord Lot.[1] Nathan Plummer,[2] and the Gages[3] of Boscawen, had the day before been on & examined the land. Their biggest offer is $500. Mr [Abraham G.] Stevens[4] advises to sell. Mr. [Israel Webster] Kelly[5] thinks $750 ought to be the lowest. Mr [John] Greenough[6] says "The Gages never think of making a bargain unless they see their way clear to make $200." Mr Stevens thinks, that there is little timber on the lot; & that unless you intend to clear it, the present is as good an offer as you will be likely to receive. He wishes to know your reply to Plummer & the Gages as soon as may be convenient.

I conversed with Mr. Adams,[7] of Derry, on the subject of the Derry lands. He thinks the purchase an extraordinary good one—and advises to build a saw, shingle, & clapboard mill on the premises at an expense of $700. Mr Alden[8] of Lebanon, a timber dealer & farmer, is soon to go on & estimate the timber for me. A Canal, connecting the Pond by Folsom's with the river is in contemplation & will be doubtless immediately cut through, which will diminish the land carriage of the lumber about one half. This, while it increases the value of the timber, makes the wood all salable & valuable. As soon as I get Alden's report, I will write you.

The President's Message is as much talked of here, & on the way from Franklin, as the cow, which Danl Webster sent to Professor Hadduck.

We are all well. Mary Ann[9] came home with me. With true regard, Dear Sir, your Nephew   Charles B. Hadduck

ALS. NhD.

1. Webster had apparently sold this lot by 1833. See Memorandum of Real Estate 1825–1833, Corrected to October 1833, below.

2. Plummer (1774–1848), Boscawen farmer and lumber dealer.

3. Richard Gage (1776–1855), proprietor of mills and a lumber business in Boscawen, and William Haseltine Gage (1791–1872), Boscawen farmer engaged also in lumber, woolcarding, and cloth-dressing with his brother Richard.

4. Stevens (1778–1864), overseer for twelve years on Webster's farm, the Elms, in Franklin which the senator had bought from his brother's heirs.

5. Kelly (1778–1857), brother-in-law of Webster's first wife, Grace; a lawyer, sheriff, and judge in the Salisbury area.

6. Greenough (1780–1862), Boscawen store keeper.

7. Not identified.

8. Not identified.

9. Probably Mary Ann Webster (1816–1864), daughter of Ezekiel, who married Professor Edwin David Sanborn of Dartmouth College in 1837.

TO JOSEPH STORY

Philadelphia Decr. 27. [1832]

Dr Sir,

I learn that Judge [Henry] Baldwin has recently manifested an *alienation of mind*. He is now under the hands of medical men, & confined to his own house.[1] It is said to be a decided case.

I believe I have found out the authorship of the Proclamation. It is the work, I have no doubt, of *Mr. [Nicholas Philip] Trist*, a Clerk in the Depart[men]t of State, grandson in law of Mr. Jefferson.[2] He never occurred to me, till his name was mentioned; but I have no doubt it is so; as I know him, well, & know him to be both sound & able, on that point. The discussion of 1830 led to an acquaintance with him, which has since cont[inue]d. He has written other very good things. Don't state this, on my authority. Mr. Clay is yet here. I go on tomorrow. Yrs   D. Webster

ALS. MHi. Published in *MHi Proc.*, 2d Series, 14 (1900–1901): 409.

1. Throughout his tenure as an associate justice of the United States Supreme Court (1830–1844), rumors circulated widely that Judge Baldwin was subject to "temporary derangements." This assumption seems to have been largely unjustified, and originated in his poor health, strained finances, and occasionally eccentric mannerisms. No attempt was ever made to remove him from the bench.

2. Jackson's Nullification Proclamation of December 10, 1832, was largely written by Edward Livingston, the secretary of state. It was a thoroughly nationalistic document, upholding the supremacy of the federal government, repudiating both nullification and secession, and calling upon the people of South Carolina to stay clear of treason.

On December 27, 1832, a little more than two weeks after Jackson's message against the nullifiers, Gulian Crommelin Verplanck of New York introduced a bill to reduce the tariff. Although a one-time Federalist who often did not fully agree with the Democrats, Verplanck had displaced McDuffie as chairman of the House Committee on Ways and Means with administration support, and his bill was understood to be Van Buren's. Its passage would at once quiet the South and give the administration credit for tariff reduction. But southern members opposed the bill. True, it reduced duties generally to the revenue level, adequate to meet the expenses of government, by 1835; but it retained the principle of protection, and it was the power to levy tariffs even more than the duties themselves that was anathema to the South. For to grant that power would be an irrevocable step on the road to the creation of a central government, able and finally willing to abolish slavery.

Webster opposed Verplanck's bill, referred to in the letter below, because its sharp reduction of duties would be, he thought, destructive of New England's economy. But he also opposed Clay's compromise bill; for although it allowed ten years for the gradual reduction of duties to the revenue level, it gave up the principle of protection. Although Webster was a member of the select committee to which the compromise bill was referred in mid-February (the others were Clay, Calhoun, Felix Grundy, John M. Clayton, William Cabell Rives, and George M. Dallas), he never accepted it and opposed it on the floor.

TO HENRY WILLIS KINSMAN

Washington Jan. 1. '33

Dear Sir

I find here two letters from you.[1] In all Bank matters you appear to have done right. The note at Norfolk Bank, must be paid, one half, at the End of the 60 days. Meantime, you must send on, & get Genl. [Henry Alexander Scammell] Dearborn's renewal in season, as I have so many other things to think of here.

You are quite right to accommodate Mr. [Nathan] Hale, with the loan of a few hundred Dollars, whenever he needs it, & you are so lucky as to have the means. As to Master Daniel, you must only see that he is kept within rule. His regular College bills must be paid; but beyond that, ten or fifteen dollars a month must be the extent of his allowance. I never pay any *bill* of his, except regular College bills. All others, he is to pay, with his own money.

I wish I could [send] you some good news from this place; but it is an article not in market. I never saw our friends so desponding. For one, I do not mean to surrender the Constitution, or the great interests of the Union, either to nullification, or to the menace of nullification. But I fear that *party discipline*, operating on members of the Government, will lead to great sacrifices of the public interest. There is danger that Mr. [Gulian C.] Verplan[c]k's proposed bill will pass; & our friends are struck, some by panic, & some by despair. But I trust they will recover their hopes, & that we may yet not let the vessel sink, without a respectable effort to save her. Yrs truly   D. Webster

The Comm[issioner]s under the French Treaty[2] are in session. About 300 Memorials are already filed. They have taken up the first, but not yet decided it.

ALS. NhD.

1. These are Kinsman's two letters of December 27, 1832, referred to in his letterbook, mDW 7475.

2. The treaty of July 4, 1831, was negotiated primarily to settle the claims of American citizens for damages resulting from French actions during the Napoleonic Wars. It also included provisions for the adjustment of French claims against the United States and the reciprocal lowering of tariffs. The treaty was ratified on February 2, 1832, and proclaimed on July 13, 1832. (4 *U.S. Statutes at Large* 574–576.) A commission was established to examine American claims and administer payments in accordance with the treaty provisions. The three commissioners named by the President were George Washington Campbell, of Tennessee; John Kintzing Kane, of Pennsylvania; and Romulus Mitchell Saunders, of North Carolina. They first met officially on August 6, 1832, and were finally adjourned on December 31, 1835. Hunter Miller ed., *Treaties*

and Other International Acts of the   D.C., 1931–1948), 3: 451–461.
United States (8 vols., Washington,

TO WILLIAM SULLIVAN

Washington Jan. 3. 1833

My Dr Sir

I am glad to receive your letter.[1] We are surrounded with difficulties here, of various sorts; & it is not a little uncertain how we shall get out of them.

At the present moment, it would seem, that public opinion, & the stern rebuke by the Executive Government, had, in a great measure, suppressed the immediate danger of Nullification. As far as we see the results of the legislation of S. Carolina, her *laws* limp far behind her *Ordinance*.[2] For aught appears, nothing will interrupt the ordinary collection of duties, after Feb. 1. *unless some individual chuses to try the Nullifying remedy.* If any importer should suffer a seizure to be made, & should endeavor to replevy, under the State process, the Collector would probably *not deliver up* the goods to the Sherriff; nor suffer his own goods to be taken, *in withernam.* This, probably, would bring on a trial of strength.

But our more imminent danger, in my opinion, is, that seizing on the occasion, the Anti-Tariff party will prostrate the whole Tariff system. You will have seen the Bill, reported by Mr. Verplan[c]k. Great & extraordinary efforts are put forth, to push that Bill rapidly thro. Congress. It is likely to be finally acted upon, at least in the H. of R. before the Country can be made to look on it, in its true character. On the other hand, our friends will resist it, of course, & hold on, to the last. A vigorous opposition will at least, it may be hoped, and as I believe, produce the necessity, on the part of the supporters of the measure, to make *some* beneficial amendments in it, before even it can get thro' the H. of R.

Under these circumstances, it seems to me it would be extremely useful, that the Legislature of Massachusetts should express its temperate, but firm opinion, first agt. the doctrine of nullification, second, *on the violation of the public faith*, which would be perpetrated by this *thorough & sudden* prostration of the protective system.

On this ground of *vested interest*, we can make, if well sustained at home, the most efficient stand, agt. the threatened ruin. We mean to occupy this ground, & to make the most of it.

If the Bill were now in the Senate, *it would not pass*: but how far individuals may be brought over by party discipline, in the drill of a month, it is impossible to say.

I do not believe the President, himself, wishes the Bill to pass. E contra, I fancy he would prefer the undivided honor of suppressing nullifi-cation, *now*, & to take his own time, *hereafter*, to remodel the Tariff. But the *Party* push on, fearing the effect of the doctrines of the Proclama-tion, & endeavoring to interpose, & to save Carolina, not by the Procla-mation, but by taking away the Ground of Complaint.

But against this, again, there is some degree of *under current*; because there are *some* who think, that by surrendering the Tariff to the men-aces of nullification, would be voting a triumph to Mr *Calhoun*, at the expense of Mr Van Buren's expectations &c.

I shall be glad to hear from you, & other friends; especially if you can give me any good advice. Yrs ever truly   D. Webster

ALS. MHi. Published in *PC*, 1: 528–529.

1. Not found.

2. The Ordinance of Nullification, adopted in convention on November 19, 1832, but with an effective date of February 1, 1833 (later postponed to March 4), was followed by less radical enabling legislation. Rather than the absolute and compulsory nonpayment of duties called for in the ordinance, the legislation pro-posed a voluntary system based on trial by jury procedure in pronullifi-cation state courts.

TO WARREN DUTTON

Washington Jan. 4. '33

My Dear Sir

You may probably have heard of the breaking out of Judge [Henry] Baldwin's insanity. When I was in Philadelphia, he was under medical treatment, & had become somewhat calm. It was feared, however, that any new excitement would occasion the return of his malady, & on that account, his professional advisers will protest agt. his coming to Wash-ington. He had, however, already begun to talk about packing up his books; & whether he will be here, or not, is quite uncertain.

Judge [William] Johnson, as far as I can learn, is on the mending hand, & I suppose we shall have the pleasure of seeing him in his place. He is said to have pretty much abandoned South Carolina, & to be resid-ing in N. Carolina. The fires of nullification I suppose, he found to be hotter even than his own warm temperament. Judge [Gabriel] Duval is said to be hearty, tho his ability to *hear* causes is not so good as former-ly, however unimpaired may be his capacity for deciding them.

The Chief Justice is understood to be in exceedingly good health, both in the inner & the outer man. Judge [Smith] Thompson is already here, & as well as usual.

I understood at Baltimore that Mr [William] Wirt expected to argue the [Charles River] Bridge cause,[1] again; but do not know whether he has recd. new instructions, to that effect or whether it be his own general inference from circumstances. You will of course keep me informed of any thing which may occur in Boston, respecting that subject.

As to public affairs, I have little to say. They are bad enough. A majority of the H. of R. seems ready to do any thing; & the next House will be no better. The prostration of the system of protection, as a system, seems to me nearly inevitable; but, then, when it is down, we shall begin to build it up again. The People, in many quarters, will not believe it is in danger, till they feel its loss. It may be doubted whether Verplan[c]k's Bill will pass; because it may be doubted whether the President desires to furnish such occasion for triumph to the leaders of nullification. He may, perhaps, be contented with a demonstration of what he shall do hereafter. If he wishes the Bill to pass, it will go thro the House, by an irresistible strength. Nobody can tell whether, sh[oul]d it come to the Senate, it would be passed, postponed, amended, or rejected. At the present moment, however, the prevailing impression is, that it would be postponed. Mr [Mahlon] Dickerson is of this opinion; & his judgment is as good as any ones, in respect to the probable vote of those Senators, whose votes w[oul]d decide the question.

I pray you to remember me to Mrs Dutton. We miss you both. I am, Dear Sir, always & very truly, Yours   Danl Webster

ALS. NhD.

1. This case, which was first argued before the Supreme Court in March 1831, languished on the docket for over six years before being resolved. Although a motion was accepted for reargument in early 1833, nothing was actually done during that term. *Charles River Bridge* v. *Warren Bridge*, 11 Peters 420 (1837).

TO NICHOLAS BIDDLE

Jan. 11. '33

Private

My D Sir

The President nominated today, as Director to fill the Vacancy, Peter Wager[1] (as near as I could hear, & heard). Mr [George M.] Dallas says he is a wine merchant, & tho' perhaps not likely to be a very *efficient* member of yr board, on the other hand not likely to be a *troublesome* one. I wish we had made a stand agt. Mr [John T.] S[ullivan].[2]

What do you say to Mr Peter Wager? You see the fire, kept up between Intelligencer & Globe. I hear little else about the Deposites. I should not be altogether surprised if [the] Com[mitt]ee of W[ays] & M[ean]s should, one of these days, set some inquiry on foot; unless, perhaps, prevented by the arrival of the Stock Certificates. The prevalent disposition of the Com[mitt]ee, as I understand, depends essentially on the vote of Mr [John] Gilmour. Besides not being naturally a very firm man, in temperament, he stands in the situation of a member *not re elected*. Would, that the full weight of responsibility were on his shoulders! He w[oul]d walk the steadier. As it is, there is some chance, I fear tho' I do not know how much, that he will consent to useless & vexatious proceedings. This, however, is but a general impression. I have heard nothing said about it, for some days.

The long Art. in the Globe,[3] I have no doubt, was of Mr C's[4] getting up. Its objects were two. 1. Stock jobbing. 2. To hasten the removal of Deposites for benefit of Manhattan B[an]k.

I see but *two* cases, in which the Bank are interested on the Docket of Supreme Court. Yrs truly   D. W.

I trust Mr. Copperthwaite [Joseph Cowperthwaite] has not forgotten my acceptances, due in Boston abt. three days.[5]

ALS. DLC.

1. Wager (1782–1863), a Philadelphian, was confirmed as a Bank director on February 2, 1833. His renomination for 1834, however, was rejected, together—though by separate votes—with the renominations of Henry Gilpin, Hugh McEldery, and John Sullivan.

2. A government director of the Bank since 1832 who was also from Philadelphia, Sullivan was described by Biddle as "the worst possible character" and "an object of general contempt," and was widely known to have openly transmitted the proceedings of the board to Reuben Whitney, Amos Kendall, and others opposing the Bank in Washington.

3. Biddle was accused of deception, mismanagement, and overextension of the Bank's resources in an article in the *Washington Globe* on January 1, 1833.

4. Probably Churchill Caldom Cambreleng, anti-Bank congressman and active Van Buren supporter from New York City.

5. Endorsement in DW's hand on the cover.

TO [STEPHEN WHITE]

Washington Friday Eve'
Jan. 18. '33

My Dear Sir

I have recd. your letter of Monday, 14th[1]—and am glad to hear there is a probability of some expression of good sentiments by Massachusetts.[2] Such a proceeding will help us. Our prospects here grow daily better. I begin to think our friends have got the mastery of the Tariff, in the H. of R. There may be some renewed effort; but at present the *repealers* are heartless & desponding. This effect has been brought about, first, by the vigorous attack made on the Bill, in Debate. Our own Delegation have behaved most manfully, in this respect. No men could do better. Poor [John] Davis has been sick, it is true, & that is a great draw back; but others have supplied his place. He is getting well, & I hope will be in the House by Monday. The effect has been produced, secondly, by the President's Message of the 16.[3] This has convinced many members that the question with S. Carolina must be *seen thro'*, and that no modification of the Tariff would do any good.

I went into the House, today, after our own adjournment, & several Gentlemen told me they looked on the bill as already a corpse, though they may continue the debate, perhaps, a week longer.

The Message of the 16. has produced a strong sensation. People begin to see, at last, what Nullification is, & what must be done to put it down. It makes them look sober. Mr. Calhoun is highly excited. He acts, as if he felt the whole world to be agt. him. I expect, that, tomorrow, he will move a set of *instructions* to the Com[mit]tee, that is charged with the message. I hardly know what they will be, but I suppose they will comprise the S. C. opinions. Looking upon Mr. C. & the whole party here, as completely prostrate, I confess I feel no disposition to treat them with unnecessary harshness, or censure. Mr. C. will certainly not provoke any thing personal, between himself & me, &, as certainly, I shall forbear from any personal unkindness towards him.

It is now three years, My Dear Sir, since I ventured here, in the face of a most fiery opposition, to maintain sentiments, such as are contained in the Proclamation, & the Message. All the rage of party broke out upon me, for so doing, like an overwhelming flood. Mr. C. himself took a very active part agt. me, (but not more so than the rest) & as I believe, wrote very abusive paragraphs, in the Newspaper. Times, & men, have now changed; tho' as [to] Mr Calhoun, he retains his same opinions, & he sees where they have brought him.

I suppose I shall learn tomorrow who is to be Senator, in my place. One thing I can say with sincerity—*I hope the place will be better filled than it has been.* Mr [Nathaniel] Silsbee has had news of his brother.[4] I a little fear he will go home. Yrs   D. W.

Pray give my love to the Damsels.[5]

Fanny Kemble is here, turning every body's head. I went to see & hear her, last Eve', and paid for it by a tremendous cold. I hear that the Venerable Judges go constantly.

Judge Story has excellent health.

ALS. NhD. Published in the *American Historical Review*, 25 (July 1920): 695–697.

1. Not found.
2. The Massachusetts legislature passed resolutions instructing the state delegation in Congress to thwart efforts to reduce the tariff in conformity with the wishes of the South Carolina nullifiers. See *Senate*

Documents, 22d Cong., 2d sess., Serial 230, Doc. No. 60.

3. The message asked for power to move or abolish ports of entry in which collection of import duties was resisted, and for authority to use military force, if necessary, to collect the revenue.

4. William Silsbee (1779–1833)

was a Salem, Massachusetts, merchant who had been ill for some time with a respiratory ailment. Although he died on January 15, 1833, word of this did not reach Washington until five days later.

5. Caroline and Ellen, Stephen White's daughters.

TO EDWARD EVERETT

[January 26, 1833]

Dr Sir

Do any of yr mess take the Philadelphia Inquirer?—I am told the number recd today contains a Washington letter, giving an account of the result of divers conversations between Mr Clay & Mr Calhoun, &c, &c—& should be glad to see it.[1] Yrs   D. W.

ALS. MHi.

1. On January 25 the *Pennsylvania Inquirer* (later known as the *Philadelphia Inquirer*) published a portion of a letter from a "highly responsible source" which reported that "Mr. Calhoun has informed Mr. Clay and his friends, that if they will arrange a tariff that will *gradually* bring the

receipts of the government within its expenditures, that he will pledge the concurrence of South Carolina, and the withdrawal of the obnoxious ordinance." The correspondent further stated that Clay and his friends had determined to accept this proposition "for the prevention of bloodshed, and the preservation of the Union."

TO JOSEPH HOPKINSON

[January 27, 1833]

Private & Confidential

My Dear Sir,

I write this for the purpose of saying a word on a confidential subject.

There is no sort of doubt that Judge [John] McLean is aiming at the Presidency, & giving his whole heart & mind to that object. He is busy, unless I am mistaken, in Penna. as well as in N. E. & elsewhere. His ground is, a moderate opposition to Genl. Jackson's politics, &c &c. He dislikes the Proclamation, thinks it too strong, & so on. Now, for myself, I should just as soon have Mr V. Buren President, as Judge McLean. The Judge has no firmness, either of political principle, or purpose. His object is to be popular, thro all the means of honest accommodation to the sentiments of others.

But my particular object, at present is, to suggest, whether something ought to be said, seasonably, not agt. the Judge, but against the propriety of his being a Candidate for a great popular office, while yet on the Sup. Bench. The thing strikes me as being very objectionable. He is trying causes, every term, in which States are deeply concerned. Every kind of Constitutional question, as you know, is constantly coming before the Court. Now is [it] right & suitable, that a man who is to judge these questions shall be a candidate before the Nation, for an office, in the highest degree exciting his personal ambition?

If you feel as I do, on this subject, as I cannot doubt you do (we are apt to think alike—& I am proud to know it is so—) what I wish to suggest is, whether Mr. [Robert] W[alsh] could not make a gentle paragraph, in relation to it, which should have a timely & useful effect. It has lately been stated, as matter of rumour, in one of the Albany papers, that Mr. [Mordecai M.] Noah was coming here to set up a paper to support Judge McLean for the Presidency. Could not this be published, with a remark, professing to discredit the rumour, altogether, & giving as ground for disbelief, the improbability that a Judge of the Sup. Court should allow himself to be candidate for the Presidency?

I have now said all I intended. Please *burn* this; & just write me a line, to acknowledge receipt of a letter of this date, as I shall be anxious to know it gets safe to yr hand. I am, with regard, ever truly yrs—

AL. PHi.

FROM CHARLES MINER

Wilkes:Barre Febry 4. 1833

Dear Sir,

I pray you to accept my congratulations, cordial and sincere on your re-election to the Senate; the unanimity, too, in these distracting times of party, was particularly gratifying.[1] "Paul Pry, at Washington" in the "Enquirer," N. Y., places you, I see, next the President at dinner; and intimates a good understanding between you. I earnestly hope, for my Country's sake, it may ever be so. In Gov. [Lewis] Cass and Mr. [Louis] McLane, I have much confidence;[2] and if, to their voices, yours could be heard, without prejudice, at the white House—confidence would be superadded to Hope—for my maxim is never to despair of the Republic. The Report of your Judiciary committee meets my entire approbation, as did your Remarks at the Boston meeting.[3] As a spark from the sun, kindling at the latter, I wrote the following as part of the news boy's verses[4]—the only thing I have written since my removal to this valley. Pardon this intrusion when you are so deeply engaged, and permit me to renew the assurances of my great respect.   Charles Miner

ALS. NhHi.

1. Webster had been elected by the Massachusetts House on January 15, 1833, by a vote of 432 out of 482 members, and unanimously by the Senate the following day.

2. Cass had been appointed secretary of war on December 30, 1831, and McLane treasury secretary on January 13, 1832.

3. Miner is referring to the Revenue Collection Bill, also called the "Force Bill," which had been reported to the Senate on January 21,

1833, by William Wilkins, chairman of the Judiciary Committee. Webster was a prominent member of the committee. The bill had been reprinted in *Niles' Register*, 43 (January 26, 1833): 354–355. The Boston meeting was that of December 17, 1832, at Faneuil Hall where Webster spoke in support of Jackson's Nullification Proclamation. See above, DW to Levi Lincoln, December 10, [1832], note 1.

4. Enclosure missing.

FROM HENRY CLAY

Tuesday 5th Feb. 33.

My Dear Sir

Disappointed in meeting you today in the Senate, I have to adopt this mode of requesting that you will join some of our friends at my lodgings this evening between 7 and 8 oclock to confer on the same subject which engaged our consideration when we lately had a similar meeting. I hope it may suit your convenience to attend. I am faithf[ull]y Yrs

H. Clay

ALS. NhD.

FROM JOSEPH HOPKINSON

Philad. Febr 6. 1833

My dear Sir

I am pleased to hear that you do not mean to come forth in the present debate unless in reply to Mr Calhoun. Why should you? You have nothing more to gain by a Constitutional speech, and it is possible you might fall short of your former effort, unless you were excited by an adequate & important object, that is, the overthrow of the leader of Nullification. If he chooses to abandon the field, & disappoint those who sent him there as their general & their prophet—why let him go. Why should you interrupt his retreat, (which must injure him and his cause), and force him to a contest, where he may, at least, gain some credit for courage and desperate daring. In my opinion, Mr C—will not and *cannot now*, make as good a figure in support of the Sou. Car. metaphysicks— as Mr Hayne did. He cant make as good a speech as that of Hayne. If Mr C. was ever a superior debater, in a *long pull*, to Mr H—which I much doubt, he is now so agitated and confused by passion, so conscious that he is sinking with a sinking cause—that he has lost the respect of the men whose opinions & countenance once gave him consequence and *self respect*—that I am satisfied he will disappoint his present and former friends if he makes the attempt. A main prop he formerly had, which gave much of the consideration to his opinions & much of the persuasion & force to his arguments, was, not their intrinsick superiority, altho' they were always respectable, but the confidence that all had, & that *he had himself*, in the integrity of his purposes and the fair & open character of his means to accomplish them. This charm is gone, & he stands on his *mere strength*, which I have never thought of the first order, altho', I repeat, highly respectable. If he comes out in this debate, you will find him an easier conquest—a Weaker victim than Genl Hayne. You know him well,—better than I do, and if I am mistaken in my estimate of him, you can correct me. The enclosed paragraph is on the same subject I mentioned in my last. I thought a publick hint *to the concerned* might be seasonable.[1] Mo. truly Yrs   Jos. Hopkinson

ALS, with enclosure of a newspaper clipping. MHi.

1. The enclosure, mDW 10568, an editorial from an unidentified newspaper, declared Verplanck's proposal to lower the tariff an attempt to placate South Carolina nullifiers, and argued that it "humiliated and defeated" Jackson's "efforts to sustain the constitutional authority of the United States."

TO JOSEPH HOPKINSON

Washington
feb 7. [1833]
Thursday 3 oclock

Dr Sir

If what I sent you, two or three days ago, should be printed, please have the goodness to send me two or three copies of the paper.[1]

I cannot answer yr questions, in yr last letter.[2] My belief is, that Genl. J. himself wishes the Tariff subject postponed—but political considerations multiply & diversify themselves so much, it is not easy to fathom all men's motives.

Last Eve', it looked very little like passing the Tariff. How it is today, I have not learned. Yrs truly   D. W.

ALS. PHi.

1. Webster's reference is to his letter of February 4, mDW 10551, in which he asked Hopkinson to have published in the *United States Gazette* an "Extract of a letter from Washington" written by "a friend of *ours*."

2. Hopkinson to DW, February 3, 1833, mDW 10544.

Saturday Noon
(9 feby. 1833)

Dr Sir

I recd yr kind letter this morning.[1] All is as it ought to be, in relation to what I sent you. I have recd also a letter from Mr [Elihu] Chauncey.[2] Will you have the goodness to say to him; that his letter has come to hand, & that I shall write him as soon as the pressure of the present moment is over.

You will see a short speech of mine in the Nat[ional] Int[elligencer] of this morning.[3] It has made a little *stir*, here. It explains itself, & I trust you will think it was time—if one may use a homely proverb—to put the saddle on the right horse. I do not often venture to tell a story, in debate, but, on this occasion, the answer of the Yankee Captain was so much to my purpose, I could not avoid it. I have some reason, to think, this morning, that the White House regards it as a *stone very well hone[d]*. The truth is, the President is much in advance of *his own* friends in Congress, on this Carolina subject.

Mr C[alhoun], it was said yesterday, would speak on Monday, or Tuesday. I doubt it. You are Entirely right, about his present condition & present ability. He cannot, I am fully persuaded, make a coherent, able, argumentative speech. I have considered his Resolutions;[4] & if he *should* speak, however little he may have to say, *they* will afford me matter. I rather prefer he should *not* speak; for I am not in very good health, having had a little of rheumatism, to which I have been sometimes subject; but if he should come out, I must of course attempt some reply.

And now, My Dr Sir, I must tell you, *in confidence*, that I am looking, every day for an explosion of another kind. You have seen hints in the Newspapers, that Mr Clay & Mr Calhoun were in negotiation, to settle the Tariff question. Such is still the rumour, & I have no doubt *it is true*. What the precise plan is, or will be, I know not. It is understood Mr C[lay] will agree to almost any thing, in order to settle the question, save the Nullifiers & obtain the credit of *pacification*. You will readily understand, that altho' it may be thought necessary to open this matter, in due season, more or less fully *to me*, yet that *I am not party to the protocols*. On a subject of this sort, it is difficult to say how one will act, till he shall see fully what is proposed. My wish is, *to do nothing this session*; & my determination, which will not be shaken, is, to do nothing, nor suffer any thing to be done, on the Subject of the Tariff, by a *Union of Extremes*. My idea is, that we can uphold the Tariff policy no farther than we can carry Penna., Jersey, & other portions of the Middle States with us; & I

shall join in no policy, which looks to making a tariff *agt. their opinions.*
Do not be surprised, if you should see extraordinary movements, within
a week. Do not be surprised, if a mot[ion] sh[oul]d be made to lay the
pending bill on the table, & take up a plan of Conciliation, proposed by
Messrs C & C! If all this be not done, it will only be *for lack of encouragement.* If you see fit, you may shew this letter to Mr [Elihu] Chauncey;
& there I pray the communication may stop. I foresee, My D Sir, that in
ten days I may [be] called on to act, & to de[c]ide, on highly important
questions. I wish I was where I could enjoy more disinterested & dispas-
sionate advice.

Am I right, in two things?
    1. In preferring to postpone the subject.
    2. In *resolving,* both in the private meetings of friends, & in the Sen-
       ate, if the question come there, to have <no> nothing to do in
       any project of arranging the Tariff, by the aid of the Nullifiers,
       against Penna. Jersey, &c. —?—

I feel conscious of being *right*, on both these points; but shd. be glad
to know what you think of them, but if you wish me to unite with
the Nullifiers, for any thing—even tho' they wd. let me draw the bill myself—you must give me very good reasons. Yrs   D. W.

ALS. PHi.
   1. See above, Hopkinson to DW,
February 6, 1833.
   2. Not found. Chauncey (1779–
1847; Yale 1796) was an influential
Philadelphia lawyer and financier.
Early in the century he had been
editor of the Federalist *Gazette of the
United States* and later a director of
the Bank of Pennsylvania.
   3. Webster spoke in support of the

Revenue Collection Bill on February
8, 1833. *Register of Debates*, 22d
Cong., 2d sess., pp. 409–413.
   4. On January 22 Calhoun submitted three resolutions (*Senate
Documents*, 22d Cong., 2d sess.,
Serial 230, Doc. No. 42) to challenge
the constitutional theory upon which
the Force Bill, reported by the Judiciary Committee the day before, rested.

TO JOSEPH HOPKINSON

Washington
friday Eve' [February 15, 1833]

My Dear friend

I thank you for your kind letters,[1] which I have not today time to answer. You will see I have eno. on my hands. Mr Calhoun spoke today.[2]
As a Constitutional argument, it is too inconsiderable for an answer.
Truly, there is nothing in it. Mr Calhoun may say, *"non sum qualis
eram."* He has an additional hour, tomorrow, & I shall answer him. I
wish not to speak, but it seems unavoidable. Courage! I cannot better

the matter of 1830—nor equal it—but I will try not to show evidence of senility. *I understand the question*; at least, I think so.[3]

You see my Resolutions.[4] I had time to do no more. Yesterday & today, I have been ready with my speech, in explanation, if opportunity had offered. By the principles of those Resolutions, *I shall abide*. Be sure of that.

We are in a great state of excitement. Mr Clay, I think, begins to repent his movement. As far as I <know> learn, he *does not receive the expected support*.

I may say to you, not to be communicated beyond Mr [Elihu] Chauncey & a few friends, that the Select Com[mitt]ee *will not report his Bill*.[5] Mr [Felix] Grundy will go with me & refusing, at least, the *pledge*; and without this *pledge*, I doubt whether Mr Calhoun will take the Bill. We have had some discussion, in Com[mitt]ee, but shall not report till next week.

The Bill for enforcing laws of Revenue &c will pass the Senate, abt. Monday.[6] We should have got on further today, but Mr Calhoun grew so hoarse, he could not speak, & it w[oul]d not have been according to our usage to force him on. I shall finish all I desire to say tomorrow.

I have looked up a great deal of matter; but shall not have time to use a quarter of it. I think *I begin* to understand the Constitution. My Dear Sir, "there were giants in the earth, in those days." This is a day of pigmies—"quorum pars," &c. Nevertheless, I am always, Yrs truly

D. Webster

ALS. PHi.

1. Not found.

2. This was Calhoun's lengthy attack on the Revenue Collection Bill. *Register of Debates*, 22d Cong., 2d sess., pp. 519–553.

3. Webster spoke in reply to Calhoun the following day. *Ibid.*, pp. 554–587.

4. Webster had read several resolutions on the tariff on February 13, accepting the need for lower tariffs to reduce government revenues, but at the same time reasserting the importance of the protective system to American prosperity. *Ibid.*, pp. 483–484.

5. Clay's bill to modify the 1832 tariff, introduced on February 12, 1833, was reported from the select committee on February 19. The only significant amendment was one passed on February 22, providing for home valuation after 1842, when the duties would reach the revenue level. The Senate bill was substituted in the House for the Verplanck bill, and was passed on February 26. The Senate accepted it on March 1 as a House bill, although it was in fact their own.

6. The Force Bill passed the Senate 32 to 1 on February 20, with the entire southern contingent except Tyler walking out of the chamber before the vote. The Force Bill passed the House on March 1, the same day that the tariff compromise passed the Senate. Jackson signed both bills the following day.

TO NATHAN APPLETON

Sunday Eve'
[February 17, 1833]

My Dear Sir

I cannot well say how much I thought of you, or how mournfully, after you left us. You seem to have had an uncommon share of wayfaring hardships, preceding a great, perhaps the greatest of all, domestic afflictions. I have tasted of that cup, & know its bitterness; you have all my condolence.[1]

Yr letter from N.Y. was duly recd, as also yrs from Boston of the 12th.[2] I pray you to make my most kind remembrance to your daughters; they will be doubly dear to you, from the recent occurrence, & you may well esteem them as blessings to be cherished, & to be grateful for.

Mr. Clay came forward with his Bill on Tuesday, as you have seen. It has thrown us into great confusion. I thought it necessary, in the promptest manner, to signify my dissent. The Comm[itt]ee has met, upon the bill, three or four times, but as yet has agreed on nothing.[3] At our last meeting, he, (Mr Clay,) seemed to me to be half sick of his own measure. I meet it, in Com[mitt]ee with unrelenting hostility; so does Mr [George M.] Dallas. Mr [Felix] Grundy would gladly mend it, & turn it into an Administration measure. Mr Calhoun, of course, likes it as it is; & Mr [William C.] Rives will also agree to it, in its original shape. Mr [John M.] Clayton, tho' quite disposed, I think, to go with Mr Clay, will not agree to it, as it is. If Mr Clay himself is satisfied, he can report it as it is, since Mr Grundy will vote for it, if it cannot be amended. I think it quite as likely as any thing, that it will be reported, without amendment, by the votes of Clay, Calhoun, Grundy & Rives. There is no chance for getting it thro the Senate, unamended, nor, probably in any shape. In the meantime, the H. of R. seems to have come to a stand still. It does not look as if there was to be any Tariff, this year. *We shall need you next Session, more than ever.*

I ·have said all I wish on the Nullification matter. It does not seem magnanimous to underrate one's adversary, but, truly, between ourselves, I was greatly disappointed in Mr Calhoun. He has little argument;—at least, so it appeared to me.

Mr [Warren] Dutton, Mr [Erastus] Root, and Mr [Benjamin] Gorham all are here. Mr [Francis Calley?] Gray has taken your rooms. The Senate holds two Sessions a day—and as the Com[mitt]ee on Mr Clays bill meets in the morning, I am kept busy. I am, My Dear Sir, with most true regard, Yrs   Danl Webster

ALS. MHi. Published in Van Tyne, pp. 179–180, where it is dated [February 1833].

1. Appleton had taken a leave of

absence from the House on February 7 in order to return to his critically ill wife, Maria Theresa Gold (1786–1833), in Boston. She died of a lung complication the day before his arrival.

2. Not found.

3. This refers to the select committee on Clay's "compromise" Tariff Bill. The committee, composed of the seven senators mentioned in this letter, was appointed on February 13, 1833. The amended version which it reported on February 21 was unchanged in principle; the only alterations were the addition or subtraction of various relatively minor items from the duty-free list. See *Niles' Register*, 43 (February 23, 1833): 430–431.

FROM HARRISON GRAY OTIS

Boston 18 feby 1833.

My dear Sir,

You may reasonably suppose that your friends here are surprised and puzzled by the Congressional upheaving, and may be willing to compare the impressions made on the minds of your regular or occasional Correspondents. I venture to obtrude myself among the latter, hearing that [Abbott] Lawrence who intended to write you on saturday is somewhat indisposed & presuming therefore, that you will not hear from him by this mail. The prevailing sentiment among the manufacturers here is, I believe that Mr Clays project would secure to them a better protection than they have been led to think it would be possible to obtain from this Congress. That it would enable *the existing establishments*, to indemnify themselves against the consequences of the reduction intended in 1842, by giving them almost a monopoly in the meantime—as the inducements to institute new establishments would be feeble. At the same time it is also considered that the project contains a virtual abdication of the principle of discrimination after 1842 and is therefore obnoxious to all the evils so lucidly stated in your resolutions. You may therefore infer that inasmuch as interest is an overmatch for patriotism, (especially when in alliance with fear,) the mass of those to whom I allude would be more glad than sorry if Clays system should prevail. I certainly am not of that number, and would rather take my chance of events than accede to a dereliction of great principles which would be and is intended to be implied in Mr Clays bill. Were it possible to guard against such implication, I am not prepared to say that under circumstances, which may exist (and of which on the spot you are the best judge) I would not vote for the measure as a *pis aller*. How would it answer then, if this bill or something like it must pass, to propose an Amendment "That nothing in the act should be construed to restrain the right of Congress to vary the provisions of the laws laying duties &c after 1842 if the public interest should require it"—or something equivalent to this provision? It is true that strictly speaking, this would be surplusage, as you cannot bind your successors, but it is equally true that those who construe constructions would call on heaven & earth to witness that a solemn and constitutional pledge had been given, to abandon the discriminating system, in the event of any future attempt to revive it, unless *concluded* by some clause of this description. But these same persons will not hesitate to deny the inference of such pledge as treaty, *whether the clause be in or out of the bill*, should circumstances encourage them to hope for a still further reduction of duties, or for a discrimination unfavorable to the Manufacturing interest after 1842. Some express caveat or protest therefore inserted in the act *might* avail the friends of the System on some future occasion, without exposing them to any assault, from which they can be assured of security without it.

Respecting the details of Mr Clays bill, it would be a great boon to many of your constituents to have the *second* section passed. And a very great injury to have the fourth section.[1] If then the South are indifferent to the first, and the Opponents of the System regardless of the latter, it would be exceedingly despicable that one of these sections should be retained and the other stricken out. The Manufacturers of the *coarse cloths*, have been left to the wolves, by their brethren, and if these will not eat them, pray aid their escape. The introduction of linens and silk, free of duty from on this side the Cape, is *wantonly* calculated to multiply obstructions to the manufacture of Prints and indeed of cottons generally, and to affect unfavorably the India Trade. Mr [Nathan] Appleton will return on the 20th. so as to be in at the death.[2] You certainly have some queer doings. I think I saw "thro' a millstone" with a hole in it, very soon after your meeting. "Now is the winter of our discontent made glorious summer by this Sun of York." Will Shakespear, Will Shakespear, who can think art of thy book. After all he whose "march is on the mountain wave" has the best of it. If you know of such an Admiral, I salute him thro' you. respec[tfully] Yrs   H G Otis.

answer *not* expected—as I used to say when Mayor—I wish *Matthew Carey* would say as much to me.

ALS. NhHi.

1. The second section proposed a repeal of that part of the tariff of July 14, 1832, which placed low-priced woolens in a special category, subject to only a 5 percent duty. The fourth section proposed to exempt linens, silks, and worsteds originating west of the Cape of Good Hope from duties through 1842. *Niles' Register,* 42 (August 11, 1832): 418.

2. This would appear to refer to the imminent conclusion of the second session of the Twenty-second Congress. Appleton returned to Washington on February 25, 1833, and the next day voted with the minority against Clay's "compromise" tariff. Congress was adjourned on Saturday, March 2.

FROM NATHAN APPLETON

Boston Thursday 2 o.clo[ck]
[February 21, 1833]

Dear Sir

The mail having been very late I have only this moment seen Mr Mills[1] with yours of tuesday & the printed table.[2] The protected interests in this quarter would I think all be satisfied with this compromise,—and the making a duty on tea & coffee an accompaniment. A part & parcel of the proposition takes away in a great measure if not wholly the objections which I made in my former letter.[3] If this compromise is pretty sure to be carried in the senate I should hope it might be offered—but there are so many circumstances connected with it of which you can judge best—that I can only say that I think the community will be satisfied with this measure if it can be carried and I am by no means clear that the proposition and failure would do any harm, especially if Mr. Calhoun will agree to it, Yours very truly   N. Appleton

ALS. NhD.   52 Broad Street.
    1. Probably James K. Mills, a Bos-   2. Not found.
ton commission merchant located at   3. Not found.

TO JOSEPH HOPKINSON

Washington. Thursday Eve'
[February 21, 1833]

My Dear Sir

We passed the Revenue Collection bill last eve' at 10 oclock, 33 to 1.[1] Just before the vote, all the known opposers, except Mr Tyler, *retired* from the Senate, Mr Clay had gone out before, & some decided friends of the measure, worn out with fatigue, & not supposing themselves needed, had not been in for the Eve'. Mr Clay has not recorded his vote, either on the Engrossment, or the final passage of the Bill. When present, he has, on incidental questions voted with its friends.

The House quarrelled about its disposition, an hour or two, this morning, but did nothing else. I understand there is very little doubt of its passage, by a large majority.[2] Almost all the members from here north are in favor of the measure, but the Administration leaders are frightened out of their senses. They really have not force to meet the crisis manfully, even with all the power of numbers on their side. I believe, however, that the necessity of the case, & the decision of the President will cause the bill to pass. This latter personage they say is very stiff, & talks warmly to every body. I have only seen him when I went, in turn, to dine at the White house, & then said not a word except about the weather &c, but I hear of his conversation with others.

Today we took up Mr Clay's pretty little Bill, in the Senate. It was pretty soon manifest, as I thought, that he was quite sick of his paternal relation to the little thing, & wd. be glad it were quietly disposed of. However, we spent the morning in talking about it.[3] I have not come out strongly as I intended, either on my own Resolution,[4] or on this Bill. The former I could not get up, without further delaying the Revenue Bill, & on this latter, I have waited thro' today. If the Bill is likely to die an easy death, I do not wish to make a fierce attack upon it, considering that Mr Clay will be here, next session, & that his vote may still be useful, perhaps, in adjusting the Tariff, if he shall have become *cured* of his mania of pacification. On the other hand, I desire to do so much as shall mark my dissent, broadly & distinctly, to the whole principle, & all the details, of this Bill.

I must try to write off my speech, in answer to Mr Calhoun.[5] But when can I do it? These long sessions have worn me out.

I wish you would let Mr [Robert] Walsh know that *I feel sensibly* the kind tone of his paper towards me, & my humble efforts at public service. Tell him, if he does not already know it, that it now seems understood that Mr Livingston stays at home, to see Nullification thro, & that Mr L[evett] Harris goes to France, as Chargé d affair.[6]   Yrs   D. W.

ALS. PHi.

1. Webster was slightly in error; the vote was 32 to 1, with John Tyler the sole recorded dissenter.

2. The bill passed 149 to 47 on March 1, 1833.

3. Clay and Webster were both members of the select committee on the Tariff Bill, which met each morning before the opening of Congress.

4. See above, DW to Joseph Hopkinson, [February 15, 1833], note 4.

5. Here Webster refers to his reply to Calhoun on the Revenue Collection Bill, which he delivered on February 16, 1833. *Register of Debates*, 22d Cong., 2d sess., pp. 553–587.

6. Levett Harris, of New Jersey, was appointed chargé d'affaires to France on March 6, 1833, replacing Nathaniel Niles. Harris' position as head of the French mission was generally regarded as temporary, to be superseded by the eventual appointment of Edward Livingston, then secretary of state, as minister. Livingston resigned from his cabinet post on May 29, 1833, and was appointed minister and envoy extraordinary to France the same day; he arrived in Paris and took charge of the mission on September 30, 1833.

FROM SILAS WRIGHT, JR.

Senate Chamber
Monday morning 25 Feby. [1833]

Dear Sir,

In the afternoon and evening of yesterday I saw most of my friends in the New York delegation in the other House, and after very full conversations with them am inclined to think that it is my duty to vote for the [tariff] bill upon its final reading, unless something in the course of the proceedings hereafter shall change my mind. I give you this information according to my promise and had designed to have done it at your quarters, but company at my room prevented. Yours &c &c,

S. Wright, Jr.

ALS. NhHi. Published in Van Tyne, p. 179.

TO CHARLES HENRY THOMAS

Washington Feb. 26. '33

Dear Henry

I recd yr letter yesterday.[1] I think Mr [Charles?] Baker's[2] price somewhat too high. The land may be worth two thousand dollars, but I do not think it worth more. However, if you think it better to throw away two hundred Dollars, than to be troubled about getting a pasture, you may close with him, & agree to take it, at 2.200. I shall be at home, I trust, in season to be in Marshfield by the first of April; if not, I can send you the money. Let Mr [John?] Ford [, Jr.][3] have a deed in order. If Mr Baker would like any part of the money earlier, you may write to me here, & I will send it to you. I expect to stay here until about the 16th. of March, & then to proceed for home, stopping a few days in N York, where I expect to meet Mrs W.

On receipt of this, you may see Mr Baker, & ascertain whether he will want his money before April, 1st. & let me know.

Among the things forgotten, one was to tell the carpenters to make sundry common *gates*. Three or four will be wanted, in the Spring, & they might as well be made before Spring comes.

I am glad to hear of Ann's health.[4] Pray give my love to her. I shall write her soon, to congratulate her on the occasion. Yrs   D. Webster

ALS. MHi.
  1. Not found.
  2. Probably Charles Baker (c. 1771–1846), Marshfield farmer and neighbor of Webster.
  3. Probably John Ford, Jr. (b. 1796), Marshfield surveyor and justice of the peace.
  4. Ann Thomas Porter, sister of Henry, had given birth to a son, George Keating, on February 9, 1833.

FROM HENRY CLAY

S. Chamber 2d Mar. 33.

My Dear Sir

Will you be at the Senate today? I wish much to see you here. I learnt with surprize and regret this morning that what passed the other day between you and Mr [George] Poindexter is likely to be made the basis of a serious proceeding.[1] I think that ought to be prevented, and it can be prevented honorably to both parties. Do come here if you can. Your friend   H. Clay

ALS. NhD.
1. On February 19, Mississippi Senator George Poindexter verbally assailed Webster, accusing him of treachery and cowardice in his support of Jackson's "Force Bill." Webster refused to reply to Poindexter's charges, and the issues remained dangerously unresolved until March 2, 1833, when Henry Clay instigated a public reconciliation in the Senate between the two men.

FROM JAMES MADISON

Montpellier Mar. 15th 1833

Dear Sir

I return my thanks for the copy of your late very powerful speech in the Senate of the U. S.[1] It crushes "nullification" and must hasten an abandonment of "Secession." But this dodges the blow by confounding the claim to secede at will, with the right of seceding from intolerable oppression. The former answers itself, being a violation without cause, of a faith solemnly pledged. The latter is another name only for revolution, about which there is no theoretic controversy. Its double aspect, nevertheless, with the countenance recd. from certain quarters, is giving it a popular currency here which may influence the approaching elections both for Congress & for the state Legislature. It has gained some advantage also, by mixing itself with the question whether the Constitution of the U. S. was formed by the people or by the States, now under a theoretic discussion, by animated partisans.

It is fortunate when disputed theories, can be decided by undisputed facts. And here the undisputed fact is, that the Constitution was made by the people, but as embodied into the several States, who were parties to it; and therefore made by the States in their highest authoritative capacity. They might, by the same authority; & by the same process, have converted the confederacy, into a mere league or treaty, or continued it with enlarged or abridged powers; or have embodied the people of their respective States into one people, nation or sovereignty; or as they did by a mixed form make them one people, nation or sovereignty, for certain purposes, and not so for others.

The Constitution of the U. S. being established by a competent authority, by that of the sovereign people of the several States who were the parties to it; it remains only to enquire what the Constitution is; and here it speaks for itself: It organizes a government into the usual Legislative Executive and Judiciary Departments; invests it with specified powers; leaving others to the parties to the Constitution, it makes the

Government like other governments to operate directly on the people; and places at its command the needful physical means of executing its powers; and finally proclaims its supremacy and that of the laws made in pursuance of it, over the Constitution & laws of the States; the powers of the Government being exercised, as in other elective & responsible Governments, under the controul of its Constituents, the people & Legislatures of the States; and subject to the Revolutionary rights of the people in extreme cases.

It might have been added, that whilst the Constitution, therefore, is admitted to be in force, its *operation*, in *every respect* must be precisely the *same*, whether its authority be derived from that of the *people*, in the one or the other of the modes, in question; the authority being equally competent in both; and that without an annulment of the Constitution itself its supremacy must be submitted to.

The only distinctive effect between the two modes of forming a Constitution by the authority of the people, is that if formed by them as embodied into separate communities, as in the case of the Constitution of the U. S. a dissolution of the Constitutional Compact would replace them in the condition of separate communities, that being the condition in which they entered into the compact; whereas if formed by the people as one community acting as such by a numerical majority, a dissolution of the compact would reduce them to a state of nature, as so many individual persons. But whilst the constitutional compact remains undissolved, it must be executed according to the forms and provisions specified in the compact. It must not be forgotten, that compact, express, or implied is the vital principle of free Governments as contradistinguished from Governments not free; and that a revolt against this principle, leaves no choice but between anarchy and Despotism.

Such is the Constitution of the United States de jure & de facto; and the name, whatever it be, that may be given to it, can make nothing more or less than what it actually is.

Pardon this hasty effusion, which whether according or not precisely with your ideas, presents, I am aware none that are new to you. With great esteem, and cordial salutation,   James Madison.

AL draft. DLC. The last two short paragraphs and the complimentary close are from the 1851 edition of the *Works of Daniel Webster*, edited by Edward Everett, 1: cvii–cviii, reprinted in PC, 1: 496–497. The printed version omits the paragraphs beginning: "It might have been added . . ." and "The only distinctive effect . . ." although these are included in the *Letters and Other Writings of James Madison* (4 vols., Philadelphia, 1865), 4: 294. There is no evidence that these paragraphs were actually in the letter as received by Webster, even though they were retained in Madison's copy.

1. This was undoubtedly Webster's

"Reply to Calhoun upon the Revenue Collection Bill," delivered in the Senate on February 16, 1833. Notices appeared as early as March 7 in the *National Intelligencer* that the pamphlet was in press, although not actually printed before March 11. In a letter that day, taken to be of that year, Webster wrote to [George M.] Grouard, a fellow New Hampshireman who was then a Washington printer—later foreman of the *Intelligencer*—that "I return the proofs, with more *errata* of the *author*, than of the *Press*" (mDWs). There is talk of an appendix which did not, in fact, exist for this pamphlet speech, but the letter also mentioned Webster's imminent departure from Washington which did take place several days later. Madison must have been among the first recipients of the pamphlet speech, for his response came only four days later. Webster undoubtedly was hoping for the same approbation he had received earlier, in 1830, for his reply to Hayne.

Webster's opposition to Clay's compromise tariff, and his support—indeed his leadership—of the administration forces in behalf of the "Force Bill" brought him for a brief period closer to Jackson than to his own party. The President's proclamation against the nullifiers, prepared by Secretary of State Edward Livingston, followed the doctrine and came very close to the language of the reply to Hayne. As Jackson moved toward Webster's constitutional position, Webster, albeit grudgingly, was driven by his differences with Clay in the direction charted by the Democracy. Van Buren, writing his Autobiography *two decades later, professed to believe that Webster, with Livingston's support, had early in 1833 toyed with the idea of changing parties, and perhaps of accepting a cabinet seat at Jackson's hands (pp. 673–712) More explicit, and certainly less rambling, is Charles W. March, whose* Reminiscences of Congress *(later retitled* Daniel Webster and his Contemporaries) *first appeared in 1850. March says that Jackson, through Livingston, sought Webster's continued support, adding: "That a seat in the cabinet was at the same time proposed to Mr. Webster, on the part of the President, through the same medium of communication, was a belief warmly entertained by some of the nearest friends of both parties" (p. 250). The book went through four editions before Webster's death without contradiction or correction.*

The draft letter to Livingston below seems to lean in the same direction. It was widely known by that date that Livingston was to go as minister to France, but it was probably equally well understood that the State Department had been promised to Louis McLane. The Treasury would thus become vacant, and it is remotely possible that Webster would for a variety of reasons have considered it. It is hardly probable, however, that Jackson would have made the offer, considering Webster's known unwillingness to reduce the tariff, and his recent defense of the

Bank of the United States. The President had, moreover, already deter-
mined to remove the government deposits from the Bank, a decision of
which Webster became aware in a few days (DW to [Biddle], [March
27, 1833], below).

A month after the letter to Livingston was written, Webster reported
to Biddle that he had not heard from the secretary, in a context that im-
plies a primary concern for retaining the government deposits in the
Bank (DW to Biddle, April 21, below). If he still hoped to work with the
Jackson administration, it could only be as the irresistible voice of rea-
son whose mission was to convince the President of his error. Even this
idea was soon abandoned. Webster wrote Lewis Cass on about April 21
(see below) that he would cut short his projected western trip in order to
be at home for Jackson's visit to New England in June. Although he left
on schedule May 17, he gave up any pretense of returning before mid-
July, when there was no longer any possibility of confrontation with the
President.

Webster returned by way of Baltimore, which he reached on July 16,
going the next day to Philadelphia, where the long-awaited meeting with
Livingston took place. The two men continued to New York together on
July 18, by "the 6 o'clock boat of the railroad line" (National Gazette,
July 20, 1833). By that time it was too late for either to influence the
administration. It had probably always been too late for Webster. Liv-
ingston, whose thinking so closely matched his own, was out of the
cabinet and in less than a month would be out of the country. McLane
was already intrenched in the State Department, and the reluctant Wil-
liam John Duane was fighting a losing battle to retain the Treasury.
Though it was not yet official it was evident in financial circles that At-
torney General Roger B. Taney would replace Duane and the deposits
would be removed. There was no longer any place for Daniel Webster
save with the opposition, under Clay's leadership soon to assume the
name of Whigs.

TO [EDWARD LIVINGSTON]

[March 21? 1833]

Confidential

My Dear Sir

I learned that you called at my lodgings on the evening previous to my departure from Washington. It is a source of regret to me, that I was not at home.

It was my intention, My Dear Sir, if circumstances had furnished a convenient opportunity, to say a few words to you, confidentially, before the close of the late session upon subjects interesting to the Country.

Although our political associations have not been identical, yet, from the good understanding, & I hope I may say, mutual respect, which has always existed between us, I flattered myself that <I might venture to propose to you an interchange of opinions, in a private manner> you would not be averse to confidential [interchange], upon topics which must arise, in the course of a short time, & on which public men will be obliged to act. No occasion <for such an interview, however,> seemed to present itself. I am still desirous, however, of such an interview, &, with your permission shall <find some occasion> seek an opportunity to meet with you, before the expiration of many months.

It is generally understood, as you are aware, that we may not have you with us, thro' the summer; but the public seems not to know, (& in that respect I am only as well informed as the Public,) *at what time* yr residence at Washington may be expected to terminate. I should prefer to see you, before your *final departure* from Washington; I do not mean the breaking up of your residence in that City, but the final taking leave of your friends there, if the general expectation is to be realized, by your leaving the Country for a time. I understood from you that you might, perhaps, be at the north, in the early part of the Summer. Should that happen, & should it also be your expectation to be at Washington again, after your excursion to the north, <I will, with your leave, intercept you, some where> a very convenient opportunity will be afforded me of seeing you in the course of your northern journey. But if you are not to return to Washington, it will be only left for me, perhaps, in making a tour which I propose to Ohio, to go by the South, & return by the north, instead of the reverse, as I have hitherto intended. By this change, I shall be able to see you in Washington, provided you should not leave that place earlier than June.

I leave this City in two days, for N. York, where I shall remain till the end of this month. If you will favor me with a line in answer to this, addressed to me in N. [Y.] I shall be glad to receive it. But if any thing should lead you to a desire to postpone any answer which you may think it worth while to make to a later period, please direct [it] to me at Boston.

I will not close this letter, My Dear Sir, without adding, that I find every where, a high & grateful feeling of respect, entertained towards your self, for the part understood to have been performed by you, in late measures so necessary to the honor & well being of the Country, & which have exhibited so much ability & patriotism.[1]

I need not add, that in all this, no one concurs more heartily, than, Sir, Yours &c—

Altered, so far as to propose his coming to N. York by April [1]5—or naming some day in April to meet me.[2]

AL draft. NhHi. Published in Van Tyne, pp. 181–182, who conjectures the recipient is Henry Clay.

1. Webster is referring to Livingston's part in the drafting of Jackson's Nullification Proclamation the previous winter.

2. Endorsement in DW's hand. The alteration referred to is undoubtedly the following passage in DW's hand, bound with the letter in the Webster Papers at NhHi: ". . . but I will add that my expectation of any public benefit, as likely to result from a conversation between us, depends mainly on that conversation taking place, as early as may be. Indeed, I should prefer an opportunity much sooner than June; & will venture to suggest, whether you could not, for the very good reason of a desire for exercise & motion, come to N.Y. for a single day, as early as the middle of April. If you can do so, & will give me seasonable notice, I will meet you."

FROM JOEL ROBERTS POINSETT

Charleston 25th. March 1833

My dear Sir

I received the copy of your speech,[1] which you were so good as to send me, and have read it with great pleasure. It appears to me to be a triumphant refutation of the wild and dangerous speculations of our nullifiers.

No single effort however will suffice to save the Country from the dangers, which threaten it. The leaders of the nullification party are animated with the zeal of fanatics, and are untiring in their efforts to disseminate their doctrines and to destroy the Union. Judging from the past I am convinced it is only by continued and active exertions that they can be controlled and defeated.

Their object is and always has been revolution and secession, and it requires the united counsels and efforts of all good citizens to counteract their designs. The danger to which the union has been exposed by the combination of the interests and passions of the nullifiers is not sufficiently understood. The Disorganisers are banded together, and act with united counsels and united efforts in every State where their influence is felt. We stand alone in this state, supported it is true by public opinion every where; but without any concerted action with those, who are animated by the same feelings and principles as ourselves. If we had been aided in the first instance by the friends of the Union in other states we might have restrained these men within due limits. Cannot we unite the good men in every state for the purpose of preserving our free institutions and counteracting the efforts of the nullifiers, who are associated together to destroy them? Depend upon it that united action is necessary to defeat their machinations. If you have leisure and think this subject worthy your serious consideration I shall be glad to hear from you upon it. I am, Dear sir, With great reg[ard,] Yours faithfully

J. R. Poinsett

ALS. MHi.
    1. Webster's reply to Calhoun, February 16, 1833.

TO [NICHOLAS BIDDLE]

N. York Wed. Morning
[March 27, 1833]

Private
Dear Sir

I have no letter from W[ashington?] yet, but look for one today. Mr. C[ampbell] P[atrick] White went off this morning for *Washington*. I do not know his business; perhaps it is to talk with Mr McLane abt. the Deposites; perhaps, to provide ways & means to pay the debentures. Day before yesterday there was a new attempt in Wall Street to produce an impression that the Deposites wd. be removed. Bets to some amt were made upon the matter. I heard nothing yesterday.

I saw Mr White, for a short time, last Eve', & talked to him of the impropriety & impolicy of this war on the Bank. He *seemed* earnestly to concur.[1] We talked over some other matters abt. state of parties &c, & the prospects of the future. He said he should, on friday, have a full conversation with the President. Mr. W. is kind to me, personally, & not unlikely to concur in correct views, so far as *party* will allow. But he is a strict Disciplinarian of the V. B. School. Yrs truly   D. W.

ALS. DLC.
    1. Campbell Patrick White, a Tammany Hall congressman and former director of the New York branch of the Bank of the United States, was also brother of Robert White, cashier and president of the Manhattan Bank. Not known as an enemy of the Bank of the United States, White's allegiance to anti-Bank Jacksonians appears to have been insured through the selection of the Manhattan Bank as one of the initial "pets" on September 26, 1833.

FROM NATHAN C. BROWNELL, WILLIAM B. BREED, AND STEPHEN WHITNEY

Boston March 27. 1833

(Private)
Dr Sir.

In communicating the accompanying papers, we express the wishes of the Antimasonic members of the Legislature in conjunction with our own, in saying, that if the questions of absorbing public interest, in which you have been engaged, have prevented such an examination of the subject we present to your consideration, as you wish to make, previous to giving your opinion; and if you would wish to inquire further, into the proofs on which the recently developed character and tendency of Freemasonry rest; and the means which Antimasons propose to remove the evil; we earnestly desire that you will defer answering the suggestions made to you, until you feel entirely prepared to do so. This we wish to leave fully to your own discretion & wishes, and in the meantime, the communication made to you, rests entirely with those from whom it proceeds. In discharging this duty, permit us to express the high personal consideration, with whom we are your fellow citizens.

N. C. Brownell
Wm B. Breed
Stephen Whitney

ENCLOSURE: FROM NATHAN C. BROWNELL, WILLIAM B. BREED,
AND STEPHEN WHITNEY

Boston March 27. 1833.

Dr. Sir.

At a full meeting of the Antimasonic members of the Legislature, of Massachusetts, held on the 10th of January 1833, the following resolutions were unanimously adopted.

1. "Resolved, that gross misrepresentations have been circulated by our political opponents, whereby the people were induced to believe that the Antimasonic Republican party, were making an effort to elect Representatives to the General Court, for the purpose of opposing the reelection of Daniel Webster to the Senate of the United States.

2. "Resolved, that in our opinion this artifice of *political* Freemasonry, was not designed to promote the reelection of Mr Webster, but to disaffect his Antimasonic fellow citizens toward him—in the hope of making *him* the friend of Freemasonry, by compelling *Antimasons* to become his opponents.

3. "Resolved, therefore, that the time having arrived when the Antimasonic members of the Legislature, are called upon to express an opinion on the election of a Senator, it is proper that they should now do so, in a manner to justify their own, and the motives of their constituents, and to repel the infamous falsehood, circulated by Freemasonry, without the slightest foundation in truth, or in any opinion ever aroused or intimated, by Antimasons. Wherefore it is

4. "Resolved by the Antimasonic Republican members of the General Court, that we regard our fellow citizen, Daniel Webster, as a man, whose services in the present crisis, belong to the country, and not to a party, and to whose talents and integrity we look with confidence, for a judicious, temperate, and efficient defence of the Union, upon the true principles of the Constitution, as maintained by Washington and his compatriots, and recently enforced in the Proclamation of the President of the United States. That we *expect* from such a man (who does not need either office or party favor to give him consequence or success) a manifestation that he is superior to subserviency to any party, or to any party measures; and that he will practically and fearlessly illustrate his own patriotic declaration, that he will go 'for the country, the whole country, and nothing but the country.' That he will neither hesitate to do justice, by fair and honorable conciliation, to one section of the country, because redress of supposed grievances is demanded in an unconstitutional manner: nor, if that shall fail, shrink from enforcing the laws, and sustaining the true interests of the country, by all constitutional means.

5. "Resolved, That entertaining this opinion of our fellow citizen, we regard him as no more belonging to the *National* Republican party, than to the *Antimasonic* Republican party, and that we deprecate the selfish attempts that have been made, to circumscribe his popularity, and his public usefulness, within the narrow and decreasing limits of the former party.

6. "Resolved that we are fully satisfied that Daniel Webster holds the oaths and the Institution of Freemasonry, in abhorrence and contempt; that he never has interposed his influence to shield Freemasonry from the force of public opinion: that he has avowed and fully believes that 'it ought to come down, it will come down, it *must* come down' and that he has not to our knowledge, said or done, and we feel assured he will not do or say, anything relating to the cause of Antimasonry, of which the Antimasonic party have, or shall have reason to complain.

"Resolved. That Republican Antimasonry, presents the only available basis of union and cooperation, between the *people* of New England, and the *people*, of the great central States, and that *political* Freemasonry, is now the only obstacle to that union, upon which alone a true *national* party can be built up and sustained by the democratic principles of equal rights, constitutional immunities, and the supremacy of the Laws.

"Resolved, therefore, that entertaining these views of our National concerns and of the relation in which our fellow citizen, Daniel Webster, stands to them and to the Antimasonic party, we will cordially and

unanimously give him our support for Senator in the Congress of the United States, for six years, from the 3d of March next."
Signed.

Benjamin Lincoln[1]   Chairman
James Burrage[2]   Secretary.

These resolutions, which were adopted just previous to your reelection to the Senate, by the Legislature, were not transmitted to you at the time; the Antimasonic members of the Legislature, being desirous, under the then alarming crisis of public affairs, to extend to you frankly, their entire support, that you might carry into the National Councils the almost unanimous aprobation of the State you represent. That crisis having passed, at least for the present, the Antimasonic members of the Legislature, at the close of the session, are desirous of communicating to you, the satisfication they derive from finding their expectations of the course you would pursue, as expressed in the above resolutions, in relation to the Constitution and the essential interests of New England, fully realized.

At the time they adopted those resolutions, recommending dignified and just conciliation, a large majority of the Legislature insisted upon no conciliation, and no alteration in the existing laws, relating to the Tariff. We therefore derive an honest satisfaction from the reflection that at that early period, the Antimasonic members of the Legislature expressed expectations, as to the conciliatory and firm course you would pursue, to preserve the union and the laws, which have since been fully answered by the resolutions for the just and moderate protection of the interests of New England, offered by you in the Senate, and by your general course in that Body.

Having thus explained the reasons why the Resolutions adopted at a former meeting in January last, were not forwarded to you officially, at the time, we now take the liberty to do so, when we find you relieved, for the present, from your public duties; and to call your attention mor[e] particularly to the 6th Resolution above communic[a]ted.

The relation in which you now stand to the country, and the manner in which the votes of the Antimasonic members of the Legislature, were given for Senator, with reference to the great interests of the nation, rather than to any party considerations, will, we trust, relieve us from any suspicion from any quarter, of now asking your opinions on this subject, in connexion with any party purposes whatever. At the same time, there is no relation in which you stand to your fellow citizens at this period, which, can be supposed to induce you to express a favorable or unfavorable opinion to the object we have so much at heart; the entire abolition of Freemasonry, and the full establishment of the principle, that secret and oath bound Societies are wholly incompatible with our free Institutions, and ought to be removed, without further delay, by the exercise of all the peaceable and constitutional means in our power. The present time appears to us, the most proper for presenting to your consideration, this subject, and we do so, with the full assurance that you will receive it in that independ[ent] and frank manner, which mark your opinions as a public man.

At the same time we request you to take such time, occasion and mode, as you may deem most proper, to answer this communication, with reference to such disposition of your reply, as you may direct.

With assurances of the highest respect and consideration, we are your fellow citizens.

N. C. Brownell ⎫ Committee of the
Wm B. Breed ⎬ Antimasonic Members
Stephen Whitney ⎭ of the Legislature

ENCLOSURE: FROM NATHAN C. BROWNELL AND JOHN BURRAGE

Boston March 27. 1833

At a meeting of the Antimasonic members of the Legislature, of Massachusetts, held in the State House, on the 27th of March 1833. Hon Nathan C. Brownell, of the Senate, was appointed Chairman, and John Burrage Esqr. of the House, Secretary. A committee for that purpose, having reported a copy of resolutions passed at a former meeting, Jan 10 together with a letter transmitting the same to Hon. Daniel Webster. It was unanimously

Voted, that the same be adopted by this meeting, and that Messrs Brownell of the Senate, and Breed and Whitney of the House, be a committee to forward the letter and resolutions to Mr. Webster, as an expression of the views of the Antimasonic members of the Legislature.

N. C. Brownell ⎫ Chairman
J. Burrage ⎬ Secretary

ALS by Brownell and signed by others, with enclosures: ALS from Brownell and others, March 27, 1833; and DS extract from minutes of a meeting of Anti-Masonic members of the Massachusetts legislature. DLC. Brownell was a Massachusetts state senator from Bristol County; Breed (1791–1833), an Essex County commissioner, served in the Massachusetts House as a representative from Lynn; and Whitney had been a town officer and was currently a state representative from Deerfield.

Although the preceding communications were written in March, Webster may not have seen the resolutions until the middle of the summer. See Benjamin F. Hallett to DW, July 27, 1833, mDW 10996.

1. Lincoln was a dry-goods merchant and state representative from New Bedford.

2. Burrage (1800–1843; Brown 1825) was a lawyer and state representative also from New Bedford.

FROM ELI S. DAVIS

Leesburg Va.
March 27. 1833

Dear Sir,

Wherever I go the people appear pleased at the idea that you are to be substituted as a candidate for the Presidency in lieu of Mr. Clay.

This place is within the Congressional district of Mr. [Charles Fenton] Mercer and where every body went for Mr. Clay, but they say he deceived them by betraying their interest to subserve Calhoun and now they would prefer you. It has been strongly urged by gentlemen of high respectability & influence that our press ought to be located at Washington and that after fixing upon a person to be run as Vice President on the ticket with you as President, a position shd. be immediately taken from which the whole ground of the Union party and the friends of the tariff could be reviewed in a manner so as gradually to unite them in the support of this ticket.

The position I hold in relation to the Union party of the South, and the semi official connextion I hold with the Government at Washington will enable me to act more effectually in bringing about the results desired than perhaps any other person. I am now negotiating with a Mr. Anderson[1] in Washington for a press complete in every respect. If I should conclude to establish the press in Washington I shall either go myself to Boston or send an agent to obtain Subscribers.

Mr. Van Buren who as I before informed you has taken lodgings in the Presidents House sticks as close to the President as a blistering plaster. Of this many [of] Gen: Jacksons friends complain loudly. This letter is written in confidence & is intended only for the eye of your confidential friends. Permit me to renew the assurances of my first & best wishes.   E. S. Davis

ALS. DLC. Little is known about Dr. Eli S. Davis, who launched his Washington, D.C., newspaper, *The Examiner*, on July 4, 1833. Webster was nominated for President in the first edition, and the paper staunchly opposed nullification. It ceased publication later in the year; the last known issue came out on September 5.

1. This may be Robert Anderson, former publisher of the Washington *Columbian Star*. He had discontinued that newspaper in 1826 and moved to Boston where he was employed as a bookbinder.

TO NICHOLAS BIDDLE

N. Y. Thursday 12 oclock
[March 28, 1833]

Dr Sir

I happened to meet Robt. White of the Manhattan Bank yesterday P. M. He spoke in positive terms of the removal of the Deposites, said it *would be done*, &c. &c. Whether he has always talked in this way I know not. His apparently sanguine expectation led me to think it *possible* that his brothers visit to the South might be connected with this matter.

I hope you will not forget to write to Mr [Ralph Isaacs] Ingersoll.[1] I have seen him here, but he has now gone to N. Haven. He regretted not seeing you in Philadelphia. He deserves much respect, for his able & patriotic conduct. Yrs   D. Webster

ALS. DLC. The date could be the following Thursday, April 4, but the letter seems to follow immdiately after the one of [March 27] to Biddle.

1. Ingersoll, a Democratic congressman from Connecticut, had made a strong pro-Bank speech during the final meeting of the House on March 2, 1833. *Register of Debates*, 22d Cong., 2d sess., pp. 1925–1935.

TO JOHN ELLIS WOOL

N York April 1. 1833

My Dear Sir

I had the pleasure on Saturday to receive your very kind letter of the 27th.[1] Your appreciation of my speech [in reply to Calhoun] is grateful.

It was no part of my purpose, in discussing the subjects to which the speech refers, to aim at the reputation of eloquent speaking. I endeavored, only, to explain the Constitution, as well as I could, and in such manner as to be level to common understandings. If I have succeeded, in any considerable degree, in that object, I have accomplished all I wished.

I confess, My Dear Sir, that no political occurrence has ever grieved me, like this Nullification business. It not only disturbed our own domestic tranquillity, but struck a deadly blow at our *character & honor abroad*. This is that part of its effect, which I felt most deeply. Altho I have not had the advantage of being abroad, myself, and of contemplating our country, as she is seen from amidst other nations, yet I am [sure] it must be, as you observed, in our last conversation, you had found it, extremely mortifying to every American in foreign Countries to witness the remarks upon the character of our institutions, which these proceedings of the nullifiers are so well calculated to bring forth.[2] I confess I am slow to forgive the authors of nullification for this dishonor, of their country & its Government. For Mr Calhoun I have formerly entertained very great regard. He appeared to me to be a true friend to his country. His recent conduct seems unaccountable.

I am very glad to learn, My Dr Sir, that you are hereafter to have your headquarters at Washington. I reciprocate, sincerely, the kind sentiments expressed in your letter, & am happy in the prospect of more frequent intercourse, hereafter. If your affairs should take you to the North, in the course of the Summer, I will be obliged to you to give me a little previous notice, as I should like very much to fall in with you. I am, D Sir, with much true regard, Yours   Danl Webster

ALS. NhD.
1. mDW 10807.
2. Wool, as inspector general of

the United States Army, had recently returned from a tour of European military establishments.

FROM BENJAMIN FRANKLIN PERRY

Greenville C[ourt] H[ouse]
April 1 1833

Dear Sir

I have had the honor of receiving from you a copy of your speech in reply to Mr Calhoun on the subject of Nullification for which you will please accept my sincere thanks. This speech, sir, is read with deep interest by the Union party of South Carolina, and by them regarded as the correct exposition of the Constitution. It tears with a giant's hand the cobwebs which the metaphysics of Mr Calhoun have thrown about the doctrine of nullification. As a constitutional argument it will ever remain as the proudest monument of intellectual exertion and power.

I am a member of the State convention and have just returned from its session.[1] In that body I heard expressions and opinions which convinced me that there was and ever had been lurking at the botom of nullification a fixed and settled design to dissolve the Union and set up a Southern Confederacy. The project has been abandoned for the present, in consequence of the disaprobation which it has met with from the other southern states. If they had shown any disposition to aid South Carolina in her unnatural strugle, she would never have accepted of Mr Clays modification of the Tariff.

In the convention we were told by Mr [George] McDuffie and Governor [Robert Y.] Hayne that the contest was not over, but only commenced, and that we must return home and keep up the strugle. Mr [Robert Barnwell] Smith[2] the Attorney General of the State said in his speech to the convention that he despised the Union and had lost all attachment to the U States flag!

The nullifiers are at this time flattering themselves with the hope that there will soon be a contest between Georgia and the U States about the

Indian Lands. Nothing could please them better than for this to happen. If they can get one State to go with them, they would be willing to commence the struggle of disunion.

I was told, in Columbia, during the State convention, by members of Congress that you and Mr [John] Sergeant had instructed the Cherokee Indians to avail themselves of the third section of Wilkins' Bill and renew their suit with Georgia for trespassing upon their lands and having them drawn for by lottery. I do most sincerely hope that no difficulty will occur between the State of Georgia and the U States in consequence of these lands. I should like very much to know from you, if there is any probability of such an event—if the Indians have secured such advice—and if they can a[vail?] themselves of any section of Wilkin[s'] bill—or if there was any section of that Bill intended to apply to Georgia?³

I am, sir, with great respect for your tallents and character and gratitude for your exertions in upholding the constitution of our Country, your most humble servt   B. F. Perry

ALS. NhHi. Published in Curtis, 1: 457–458, but misdated April 10.

1. The South Carolina nullification convention had met in Columbia from March 11 to 18. On March 15 the convention rescinded the Ordinance of Nullification which it had passed the previous November, and on the last day of the session it symbolically nullified the "Force Bill."

2. One of the more radical nullifiers at the convention, Smith had been appointed attorney general in December 1832. In 1837 the Smith family's name was changed to Rhett and subsequently he is generally cited as Robert Barnwell Rhett.

3. Perry refers to the Force Bill reported out by Chairman William Wilkins of the Senate Judiciary Committee on January 21, 1833. For Webster's reply to this query, see DW to Perry, April 27, 1833, below.

TO [NICHOLAS BIDDLE]

N York April 7. 1833

My Dear Sir

I am still lingering here, having been detained by some little professional matters, for the last day or two. I go home tomorrow.

Mr C[ampbell] P[atrick] White returned last Eve' from Washington. I have not been able to have any talk with him abt. the Bank, but I find persons in his connexion are of opinion the deposites will be removed. The price of the stock, however, seems to shew that such is not the general opinion.

I find Mr White to be of opinion that Mr [Edward] Livingston goes abroad in June, (of which there is no doubt) & that Mr [Louis] McLane, *certainly* succeeds him, in the State Department. But he says it is by no means certain who goes into the Treasury; that Mr [Levi] Woodbury says *he* is not going there, &c. He says the talk is, that some person whose name is not yet before the public is likely to fill that place, & he does not know who he is. Mr [William T.] Barry is to go to Spain, but nothing is settled as to his successor.[1]

It strikes me there may be something, possibly, in this idea of bringing forward some man, not yet named, for the Treasury, perhaps Mr [James K.] *Polk*, or Mr [Asbury] Dickens,[2] or some one else. I believe Mr McLane *fears* to remove the Deposites, after the vote of the H. of R;[3] & I am quite afraid that the President has settled it, in his own purpose, as a thing to be done. I have no particular reason, for this impression, but take it up from the general aspect of attendant circumstances. If this be so, the President may be looking out for somebody, willing to do the deed.

I wish you would write me, addressed to Boston, saying whether you have any new information, on grounds of confidence, in the point of the removal.

I think there is a growing opinion here in favor of the renewal of the Charter. Yrs truly   D. Webster

ALS. DLC.

1. Postmaster General Barry had been under attack since 1831 for the handling of affairs in his department. He ultimately resigned to become minister to Spain in April 1835.

2. Dickins (1773–1861) had been chief clerk of the Treasury Department since William H. Crawford's time. He had on a number of occasions been acting secretary, and his Crawford connection made him politically acceptable to the Jacksonians.

3. On March 2, 1833, the House had voted 109 to 46 in favor of Verplanck's resolution "that the government deposites may, in the opinion of this House, be safely continued in the Bank of the United States."

TO [NICHOLAS BIDDLE]

N York April 8 [1833]
Monday Morning

Dr Sir

I had an opportunity last Eve' of seeing Mr C[ampbell] P[atrick] White, & of conversing with him on the Bank Subject. He says, the question about removing the Deposites *is as far from being settled as ever.* I asked him why the Sec. [Louis McLane] did not decide the matter, & put an end to doubt, & to speculation. By all I could gather from his reply, I think it clear that Mr. McLane & Mr. Van Buren are decidedly *agt* the removal, & that the President is still pressing it. A month's longer delay, I should think, would settle the question for this Summer, if no new occurrence should arise.

Mr White says that Mr Jno. R. Livingston[1] of this City has a letter from Mr Edwd. Livingston, in which the latter Gent. expresses an expectation of being in this City, within a few days. Yrs truly

Danl Webster

ALS. DLC.

1. John Robert Livingston (1755–1851), New York businessman and speculator, was an elder brother of Edward Livingston.

FROM NICHOLAS BIDDLE

Phila. April 8. 1833

My dear Sir.

I have received your favor of the 7th inst.[1] I have no information of the intended removal of the deposits, though my opinion is that they will not *dare* to remove them. Nevertheless it is very desirable that whatever is done in the way of pacification should be done soon—for if the deposits are withdrawn, it will be a declaration of war which cannot be recalled.

Mr [Henry] Gilpin told me this morning that he had received a letter from Mr [Edward] Livingston saying that he will be here in a day or two. I presume he is on his way to New York. Very truly yrs   N Biddle

ALS draft. DLC. Published in part in McGrane, *Correspondence of Nicho-* *las Biddle*, p. 202.

1. See above.

FROM MATHEW CAREY

Philada April 9. 1833

Dear Sir

There is nothing doing, nor likely to be done, to disabuse the public mind on the subject of the deplorable infatuation that prevails respecting the protecting system, which will undoubtedly be attacked in each successive session, & will probably be nullified before the period fixed by law for its nullification. The same miserable apathy & parsimony that have laid the foundation of the destruction of the union, still prevail.

Did I understand you to say that Mr [Abbott] Lawrence has expended 1000 Dollrs a year for any length of time in the defence of the protecting system? If so, there must be some egregious error in the affair. You must, I am persuaded, have greatly misunderstood him. Such sums, or half such sums could not have been expended without my knowledge—& I know nothing of them.

From the middle of 1820 till the beginning of 1827, I do not believe, nay I am persuaded, there was not expended in paper & printing, out of Philada. throughout the union, 750 Dollars—& from the beginning of 1827 till the meeting of the New York convention,[1] there was not expended out of Philada. more than about 1000 or 1250 dollars on the same objects. What was expended was chiefly expended in Boston. All I know of, is $200, $250 & $500. It may show the liberality that prevailed, even in Boston, to state a fact. J[onas] B[ond] Brown,[2] one of the few men to have displayed a proper spirit on this subject, in consequence of my importunity, undertook to raise $500 in 1829, & subscribed 100 Dollars himself, & procured a similar subscription from three other persons. He then gave an order for $500 to be expended in printing, calculating that he could easily raise the remaining $100. But in this he was disappointed—as when I saw him here a few months since he had not recd a dollar of it!

Some considerable expense has been incurred it is true, in sending agents to Washington. But even that does not warrant the assumption of the expenditure of Mr Lawrence. I believe that these missionaries went only about three times—& I will suppose six persons went each time—& that their fair expenses were about 150 dollars each. It wd. amount to less than $3000.

It is very true, that when the Manufacturers were aroused out of their lethargic stupor, at the time of the meeting of the N. Y. Convention, large sums were subscribed, amounting to about 5000 Dollars, of which Massachusetts contributed 1500 Dollars—but not one dollar of this large sum was expended to disabuse the South. It was squandered—I say literally squandered on printing thousands and thousands of Reports on Manufactures[3] & four addresses, of which the former were calculated to injure instead of benefiting the cause, as they displayed a prosperity which excited the envy & the jealousy of the southern peoples. I send you two pamphlets of which I offered the one (Prospects, etc.)[4] to the Central C[ommitt]ee at cost, & urged them to publish thousands of the other ["]one of the people["][5] but in vain. They neither bought nor published a copy of either. Had "One of the people" been extensively circulated, say 10,000 copies, to the Southward, Nullification would have been prostrated forever. The pamphlet is irresistible.

But why these details? They are called forth principally by the indignation & scorn I feel at the base treatment I have recd.

Of all the heavy expenses I incurred from March 1819 when I commenced the defence of the protecting system till Decr 1831,—including ten or twelve journeys, of which three cost me 300 Dollars—for postage probably at the least thirty Dollars per annum, for which I never charged or recd a dollar—for paper & printing paid for by me for six years out of that period of nearly twelve years for heavy subscriptions—& various other expenses I neither ask nor expect the reimbursement of a dollar. But my expenses from Jan. 1832, of which I am actually out of pocket at this moment about 570 Dollars, I did expect that a true sense of honour would have led such men as Mr Lawrence, [Asa] Clapp, Mr [Patrick Tracy] Jackson, Mr [Peter H.] Schenck,[6] Mr [Samuel] Richards,[7] &c &c. &c. all wealthy, to have promptly, & cheerfully, & gratefully repaid. But for the honour of human nature I blush to say I have been disappointed. Those overgrown capitalists, in whose defense I have devoted fourteen years with as much zeal and industry & perseverance, as if my temporal & eternal salvation were depending, are not ashamed to shrink from the payment because, as some of them since have said, I was not authorised to incur the expense!!! Sir, if A sees B's house in danger of falling, & in B's absence, or incapacity to buttress it up, undertakes to perform that important service for B. *without being authorised*, B is exonerated from the obligation of reimbursement! Is not this a perfectly analogous case? Would not an individual capable of this shuffling conduct, be regarded as a base man & be shunned by respectable people?

To sum up the whole, I place the matter on this footing. If there be a single honorable man to be found from New Hampshire to Georgia, who on this case being stated to him, viz—that I expended fourteen years of my time in defence of a cause in which I never had the least interest— that my time thus gratuitously given, was worth at least, at a good clerk's wages 1000 Dollars a year—that besides this, I had at my own individual expense, taken ten or twelve expensive journeys—& at the same expense paid postage in this cause, averaging probably thirty Dollars a year (some years 40 or 50)—that I had subscribed liberally in the commencement—that my expenses previous to 1832, were four thousand dollars—that the tariff of 1824 was carried in a great degree, by the conversion of Mr [Rollin Carolas] Mallary by my writing, that in this cause I have incurred the most deadly hostility, &, while I was in business, disgusted & dissatisfied my best customers, who lived principally in the southern states, & moreover, that I most perniciously neglected my business—& finally that men of overgrown wealth, chiefly made by manufactures, & deeply, & vitally interested in manufactures—such men, for instance as Mr. Lawrence, Mr Jackson, Mr Clapp, Mr Schenck, Mr Richards, &c. &c &c. had not only not voluntarily repaid me the trifling sum remaining of my advances in the cause, since Jan 1832 ($570) but had rejected several applications for reimbursement, first painfully trifling with & wounding the feelings of a high minded, independent man to whom they were under such heavy obligations, & who had made such heavy sacrifices in their defence. If, I say, there be a single honourable man to be found who will not pronounce this conduct discreditable & disgraceful to men of wealth, standing in the front ranks of society, then am I as very a Jew as ever came out of Galilee, and as very a negro, as ever was stolen or sold in Monomotapa.[8]

The fact that the above balance of $570 was not drawn from my income, but was a draft on my capital, which I pledge my honour was the case, though it makes the unworthy detention more oppressive to me, does not increase the injustice of the refusal to pay. If I were as rich as William Gray, as Stephen Girard it wd. not change the nature of the case. The money was expended for the benefit and defence of the manufacturers, & would have been highly beneficial to them, had they had the common sense or sound policy to cooperate with me—& it is therefore, I repeat in the fullest sense of the word, a debt of honour.

I hope you will excuse me for addressing this letter to you. It was not my intention, when I began to enter on these details. They do not at all appertain to you, who are no manufacturer. They ought to have been addressed to some of the parties to whose conduct they have reference & whose names are mentioned. And I request the favour of your handing it to some of them. It will save me the necessity of writing to them. Yours, very respectfully, Mathew Carey

ENCLOSURE:

For the [Boston] Courier

In some of the copies of a circular issued, by the subscriber in February there is an egregious error, which those who recd. that circular are requested to correct. In the last column, 4th page, $5000 are stated instead of $500.

Those printers who reset the above, will confer a favour on M Carey

Pray send the above to Mr [Joseph T.] Buckingham

ALS, with ALS enclosure to Joseph T. Buckingham. NhHi.

1. The New York convention of the Friends of Domestic Industry met on October 26, 1831. The permanent committee of the convention, however, assembled periodically thereafter, issuing memorials, reports, and pamphlets into 1833.

2. Brown (c. 1795–1835), a Boston merchant and manufacturer and an indefatigable advocate of the protective tariff.

3. This is probably John Quincy Adams' Committee on Manufactures Report on the Tariff of May 23, 1832.

Committee Reports, 22d Cong., 1st sess., Serial 228, Report No. 481.

4. Probably Carey's *Prospects beyond the Rubicon*, published in eight numbers from December 30, 1832, to January 18, 1833, under the name of "Hamilton," or the second series of two numbers, published on February 11 and 13, 1833.

5. Not identified.

6. A New York merchant located at 33 Pine Street.

7. Richards (1769–1842), Philadelphia merchant and ironmaster.

8. A term formerly given to the extreme southern portion of Africa.

FROM NICHOLAS BIDDLE

Phila. April 10. 1833

Dear Sir;

I wrote to you to day that Mr [Edward] L[ivingston] would be in N. York.[1] I write to you again to say that I think it would be well to see him. The whole question of peace or war lies in the matter of the deposits. If they are withdrawn, it is a declaration of war. It is wiser therefore to begin the work of peace before any irrevocable step is taken.   NB.

ALS draft. DLC. Published in Mc-Grane, *Correspondence of Nicholas*   *Biddle*, p. 205.
1. mDW 10852.

TO SAMUEL JAUDON

Boston April 12. 1833

My Dear Sir,

I mentioned to you, in Philadelphia, that I might have occasion to ask of you the repetition of a kindness, & that when I reached home, I would write you on the subject.

During our connnexion as agents for claims under the Spanish Treaty, & afterwards, before your removal to New Orleans, you occasionally accepted my drafts, when I had occasion for money, as you remember. I am now in such a situation as that a similar friendly accomodation would be useful. In a year & a half, or two years, I hope to be receiving considerable sums, as comm[issio]ns on claims under the French & Neapolitan Treaties, to which claims I am now giving much attention. In the meantime, certain private matters render it convenient that I should anticipate these receipts. If you have no objection, therefore, I should be glad of permission to draw on you. Proper care will of course be taken, in all cases, to see the necessary provision made for your indemnity, & you may be assured that even in the event of accident happening to me, your liability, whatever it might be, would be provided for, out of the fund, now already, in great part *earned*, arising from the comm[issio]ns on the claims.

I pray you to remember me to Mrs Jaudon. We look forward, with much hope & some confidence, to your promised visit, a few months hence. In the meantime, if I can get rid of sundry private & professional Engagements, I intend a trip as far as to the Banks of the Ohio. Yours always with cordial regard,   Danl. Webster

P.S. If instead of drawing myself, I should authorise any other person to draw, I shall of course give you due notice. Formerly, you accepted drafts of mine for as large amounts as $5,000. I do not propose now to draw any bill for a larger amt.

ALS. NHi. Jaudon (1796–1874) served as cashier of the Bank of the United States in Philadelphia. In 1828 he went to New Orleans as cashier of the branch bank there, but returned to his old post in 1832. Mrs. Jaudon was the stepdaughter of Senator Hugh Lawson White of Tennessee.

TO NICHOLAS BIDDLE

Boston April 13. 1833

My Dear Sir

I find every thing going on quite well in the Branch here. It's administration seems entirely satisfactory to the public, & the officers all mutually pleased with one another.[1]

I have repeatedly thought, My Dear Sir, that I would suggest to you, from myself merely, the propriety of increasing Mr. [Samuel] Frothingham's salary. You know all about his diligence, assiduity, & ability. He does nothing, & thinks of nothing, but his duty to the Bank; & having a large family to provide for, he is entitled, I think, to be placed on a fair, perhaps a liberal, scale of allowance.

I suppose you have rules, in these matters, not to be departed from; but if they be such as may allow some augmentation of Mr Frothingham's salary, I think it would be but justice, if it were done. He knows nothing of this letter. Yrs with constant regard,   Danl Webster

ALS. DLC.
1. Note DW's letter to Biddle, November 19, 1832, above.

FROM LEWIS CASS

Washington April 17. 1833

My dear Sir,

I have just received your kind letter,[1] and sincerely thank you for your recollection of me. I think the President will visit New England this season. If he does, he will leave here about the last of May, and he is desirous, that I should accompany him. I shall accordingly do so, and I presume we shall be in Boston not far from the 20th of June. I cannot ask you to postpone your intended journey till after this time, as it might expose you to much inconvenience. Still I will confess to you, that the hope of meeting you and of revisiting with you the scenes and friends of our youth has dwelt upon my mind, since we first conversed together on the subject. Nothing could give me greater pleasures than such an occasion. And if indispensible engagements should so require your absence, at the time, I have mentioned, I shall still look forward at a future day to realize this hope. With sincere regard, I am, my dear sir, Truly your friend   Lew Cass

ALS. NhHi. Published in Curtis, 1: 460–461.
  1. Not found.

TO NICHOLAS BIDDLE

Boston April 21. '33

My Dr Sr

I hear nothing yet, of Mr L[ivingston]. He appears to have been occupied in the inquiry abt. the burning of the Treasury.[1]

A letter went from this quarter, dispatched yesterday, to W[ashington]
from one of the most considerable Jackson men in this State. Its object
was, to shew the inevitable ill effects of *touching the Deposites*; as a
measure, which would create warm opposition at the North, & drive
those, who would willingly support Genl J. in all just measures, back to
the arms of C[lay] & C[alhoun].

I can tell you, further, inter nos, that the President *does* mean to visit
us, & to be here about the 20th. June; but I do not feel authorised to
speak of this, except quietly between ourselves. Yrs   D. Webster

ALS. DLC.   ury building was destroyed by a fire
  1. On March 31, 1833, the Treas-   of suspicious origin.

TO [LEWIS CASS]

[c. April 21, 1833]

I have recd yr letter of [April 17.][1] A journey to the west has long
been in contemplation by me, but I have never yet been able to accomplish it. Every other year the session of Congress has been so far prolonged as to forbid the undertaking, for that reason; & professional
duties have allowed me no leisure, hitherto, in the intervening years. In
addition to these causes, the political state of things has, for some time,
been such, that the motives & objects of such a tour would have been
very likely to be misinterpreted, & misrepresented. In this last respect,
the present moment seems favorable, & [as] I have found myself able
to make the necessary arrangements with my professional engagements,
I have thought it not wise to defer, longer, the execution of that which
has been already a good while postponed.

Nevertheless, I am very unwilling to miss your visit to New England;
& although I might even make that sacrifice, in the hope that you might,
as you suggest, hereafter repeat your visit, I still feel great reluctance in
being from home, when the President comes to Massachusetts. In the
first place, it would give me pleasure to see him, & to extend to him &
his party the hospitalities of my house, as well as to unite with my
friends & neighbors in such manifestations of respect as are due to him.

And in the next place, my absence on such an occasion, when it is known that a visit from him to this part of the Country was intended, may be liable to much misconstruction. I am inclined, therefore, at all events, to [be] at home, by the time the President reaches Boston. My plan has been to return by the first of July, & I shall not be able to accomplish all I intended, & return earlier than that day. But under present circumstances, I shall abridge the extent of my travels, so as to be able to return to Boston by the 20th. of June.

AL draft. NhHi. Published in *PC*, 1: 536–537.
   1. See above.

FROM WILLIAM J. TILLINGHAST, AND OTHERS
Providence April 22. 1833

Respected Sir,

At a meeting in this city on the 19th. instant of persons favorable to the adoption in this state of the Massachusetts mode of Suffrage the subscribers were appointed a committee to report on the subject at a future meeting.

We have since been told by persons interested in preventing such a measure that it would ruin the state and that the best part of the citizens of Massachusetts regret the extension of suffrage in that state and would willingly adopt the R. Island plan were it practicable for them to do so.

Now as the subscribers yield to none in patriotic emotions, we would like to know from high authority if these things are so—for if they are we shall reccommend to the adjourned meeting to abandon their enterprize and sacrafice their own rights <(for none deny the *right*)> on the altar of public good, but if these assertions prove as we suspect they will, to be a slander on our fellow citizens of R. Island and Massachusetts we should also like to know it that we may persevere in what we at present consider a holy cause.

We regret the necessity that has compelled us to trespass on your valuable time, but we fondly anticipate that it cannot deprive you of much of it in answering what appears to us so plain a question, and as our adjourned meeting will be held in a few days we should deem it a lasting favor to receive *at least* a brief answer as soon as your other calls of duty will admit.

The undersigned tho' humble mechanics have seen enough of the world to know that gentlemen who have attained your high eminence are above being "respecter of persons" and we therefore sign our proper names and occupations merely adding that we have addressed similar letters, simultaneously to Hon. John Quincy Adams and Hon. Francis Baylies and hope to receive simultaneous replies.

> respectfully your fellow citizens,
> William J. Tillinghast   Barber
> Lawrence Richards   Blacksmith
> William Mitchell, Shoemaker.
> Seth Luther   Housewright
> William Miller   Currier
> David Brown   Watch and Clock
> Maker

Note. We thought it unnecessary for your information to state that no citizen of R. Island, whatever his standing or whatever duties he may perform to his country can vote for his rulers unless he own a freehold estate worth $134 or [is] the eldest son of such freeholder. But we are confident from what we hear that there is a fire kindling in public opinion in different parts of the state that will consume all the hay and stubble of aristocracy and primogeniture and leave to the land of Roger Williams and Nathaniel Greene the pure gold of democracy and republicanism. 8000 citizens now vote in R. Island. On the Massachusetts mode 20,000 would vote.

ALS by Tillinghast and signed also by others. NhHi. Tillinghast, who sent letters to Webster, Van Buren, and other notables, may have singled out the senator because of his role in the revision of voting qualifications in the Massachusetts Constitutional Convention of 1820–1821. In his speech of December 15, 1820 (*Journal of the Debates and Proceedings in the Convention of Delegates, Chosen to Revise the Constitution of Massachusetts . . . 1820[-] . . . 1821*, Boston, 1853, pp. 304–321, especially pp. 312–315), Webster argued for and won a provision which allowed taxpayers qualified by age, residence, and citizenship to vote in the Commonwealth's elections. The previous constitution, enacted in 1780, had required sixty pounds as qualification for voting in all state elections. By contrast, as Tillinghast's note indicates, Rhode Island continued to operate under its archaic colonial charter which maintained a property qualification, increasingly anachronistic as the state's economy shifted from agriculture to industry. Surprisingly, Webster never answered Tillinghast's inquiry. Tillinghast to Van Buren, May 31, 1833, in Rider Collection of Dorr Manuscripts, vol. 17, John Hay Library, Brown University.

TO BENJAMIN FRANKLIN PERRY

Boston April 27th 1833

My Dear Sir,

I was gratified by the receipt of your letter of the first of this month,[1]

& thank you for the favorable & friendly sentiments which you express, in regard to an effort of mine, at the late Session of Congress, in a cause, which I deemed all important to the Country, and to which, I had already learned, you are as much devoted as myself. I am not at all surprised, My Dear Sir, at the opinions you express, as to the ultimate objects of those who have raised the flag of Nullification. Circumstances, full of meaning, attracted my attention early; and in Decr. 1828, I became thoroughly convinced, that the plan of a Southern Confederacy had been recd with favor, by a great many of the political men of the South, especially of your State. I agree with you also, entirely, in the opinion, that the danger is not over. A systematic & bold attack, now but just begun, will be carried on, I apprehend, against the just & constitutional powers of the Government, and against whatsoever strengthens the Union of the States. For my own part, I look forward to an animated controversy, on these points, for years to come; and if we can sustain *our* side of that controversy, My Dear Sir, with success, as I hope & believe we may, we shall transmit to posterity an inheritance above all price.

I do not apprehend any further difficulty with Georgia.[2] There was not the slightest reference to the Georgia case, in my own mind, nor as far as I know, in that of any other Gentleman, in preparing & passing the Bill for the better collection of the Revenue. It is true, that some of the provisions of that Bill ought, in my judgment, to be permanent. If they had previously existed, the idea of putting the doctrines of Nullification in practice, in the mode recently adopted at least, would probably not have been entertained. I have expected, what I see now publicly announced, that the effort will be to repeal this law, as soon as Congress shall assemble. It is probably expected, that since the occasion has passed by, many will be willing to repeal the law, altho' they were in favor of its passage at the time; & it is hoped, that by the repeal of this Act, it may be considered as decided, that Congress are hereafter to take *no step* to execute any laws, which are resisted by State authority.

The high regard I feel for the patriotic Gentlemen with whom you act, in your own State, and the respect which I have been led to entertain for yourself, induce me, My Dear Sir, to express a wish to hear from you, on the interesting subjects which at present occupy the public attention, whenever your convenience may allow. With friendly salutations I remain Yr ob ser   Danl. Webster

Typescript copy of original in A-Ar. Photocopy not obtainable. An ALS copy in NhHi is misdated April 1, a date firmly on Webster's mind, as the opening sentence indicates. A zero was added to make it April 10 in PC, 1: 534–535, presumably because Fletcher Webster misinterpreted the reason for the obvious error in the copy.

    1. See above.

2. See above, Perry to DW, April 1, 1833.

TO JOEL ROBERTS POINSETT

Boston May 7. 1833

My Dear Sir,

Events have changed the face of things, in some important respects, since the date of your letter to me, vz, Mar. 25.[1] We have passed the Law, for the better collection of the Revenue, & we have, at the same time, removed the occasion for it, by such a modification of the Tariff, as the Nullifiers were willing to accept. I am anxious to know the effect produced by these occurrences, in your State. Judging from the Speeches in the Convention, from the tone of some of the papers, &, more than all, from a letter of Mr Calhoun to some friends,[2] who had invited him to a public dinner, it appears to me that the contest is far from being ended. A repeal of the present law will be proposed, I doubt not, early next session, & a vigorous & persevering effort made to get it out of the Statute Book. This attempt will be made, with the avowed purpose of repudiating the doctrines of the Presidents proclamation, & of establishing the principle, that Congress cannot enforce any law, which a State may chuse to declare unconstitutional.

In short, My Dear Sir, I entirely concur in your views, as expressed in your letter, & think them, substantially, just & applicable now, as well as at the time the letter was written. I hold it an indispensable duty for the friends of Union, every where, to exert themselves for its preservation, & to act in harmony & with concert. The fiercest of the battle has hitherto fallen on the Union party, in your State. They have met the crisis, with manliness, & patriotic spirit. They deserve all praise, & all encouragement. On the other hand, the great majority of the People this way are ardently attached to the Union, themselves, & feel a warm attachment for those, who have elsewhere upheld its interests, & fought its battles, against such fearful odds. Let us cherish this spirit. Let us think, & feel, & act, as if our interest, & our duty, were the same. If I do not mistake, the question of paramount importance in our affairs is likely to be, for some time to come, *the preservation of the Union, or its dissolution;* and no power can decide this question, but that of the People themselves. Let the question be argued—let it be discussed—give the People light, & they will decide right.

I should be glad, My Dr Sir, to hear from you, & especially to learn, as before intimated, what is the tendency of public sentiment, in S. C., since the events of the last session of Congress, & the repeal of the Ordinance. You have occasionally done your northern friends the kindness to visit them in the heat of summer. Is it your purpose to repeat that favor, the present year? I am, Dr Sir, with true regard, Yours

Danl Webster

ALS. NNPM. Published in *W & S*, 16: 672–673.

1. See above.

2. The reference is presumably to Calhoun's letter to certain citizens of

Edgefield, South Carolina, dated March 27, 1833, and reprinted from the *Edgefield Carolinian* in *Niles' Register*, 44 (April 20, 1833): 125–126.

FROM JOSEPH HOPKINSON

Philad. May 12 1833

Dear Sir

I am sorry to give up our Pennsylvania ride; but it is probable that the rout you have now decided on will be more useful—with more variety.[1] As to my son I have another destination for him. This Mr [Levi] Woodbury is a pitiful fellow. Since he refused my application on the ground of no vacancy for Pennsylvania, he has sent a warrant *instanter* to the son of as worthless a profligate as walks our streets—notoriously, so. And he sent it on the single application of the father. But he is one of the *right sort*.

In coming through Penn, I think you should not omit to visit—Chambersburgh[-]Harrisburg-Lancaster-Reading. They are *important points* in the State—with some others—which will occur to you. *Easton* will be out of your way from Pittsburgh, but is well worth a visit.

You have observed that *Slavery & Emancipation* are now to be the tocsin of alarm for the Southern Agitators. Is it possible to get up a phantom that has not appeared even to the most disordered imagination for so many years. The very question has been long since buried & forgotten. We hear no more of Abolition Societies—& st[ate] rights of the South in this property are as much respected in Penna—the center of Anti Slavery—as in Sou. Carolina.

Col. [William] Drayton[2] is so convinced of the persevering designs of these people to disturb & secede from the Union—to go on with their project of a Southern Confederacy, that he is about to remove to this City. Whatever this party may do in Sou. Carolina, I do not believe they can draw any other State into their views. It is so clearly a mere movement of a reckless, personal ambition. Mo[st] truly yours

Jos Hopkinson

If they secede, they will have *Emancipation* in its most terrible form.

ALS. NHi.

1. Webster had discussed a revised route for his western trip in his letter to Hopkinson on May 8 (mDW 10902).

2. Drayton, a Union Democrat from South Carolina who served in Congress from 1825 to 1833, opposed nullification in 1830, and eventually moved to Philadelphia in August 1833, where he was president of the Bank of the United States of Pennsylvania in 1840 and 1841.

FROM BENJAMIN FRANKLIN PERRY

Greenville C[ourt] H[ouse]
May 14th. 1833

My Dear Sir.

I thank you kindly for the letter[1] which I have just had the pleasure of receiving from you, and assure you that I very highly estimate the honor of your correspondence.

I am sincerely glad to hear that you apprehend no further difficulty with Georgia, and that there was no reference whatever to the Indian question in preposing and passing the Bill for the better collection of the revenue. On reflection I think with you that the provisions of that Bill should be permanent and that its repeal at the next session of Congress would be impolitic and of dangerous tendency. The nullification party in South Carolina would boast of it as the triumph of their principles, and the abandonment of that firm and decided stand taken by the General Government for the constitutional enforcement of its laws.

The *revolutionists* of this State, at the head of whom stands Mr. Calhoun, have found it impossible to unite the South, in hostile array against the Federal Government, by means of their exagerated oppressions of the Tariff. I think too they have despaired of success from the Georgia controversy, and see that it is impossible to keep up public excitement by the discussion of that question. But resolute and determined in their purpose, they have seized hold of an other subject, more deeply invol[v]-ing the interest of the whole Southern Country, and hope by the agitation of it to provoke the North and inflame the South. You have no doubt observed the recent movement made by all the nullification presses relative to the slave question. This was done, I have no hesitation in believing at the instance and through the advice of Mr Calhoun, under the impression that it would produce an excitement which might lead to a Southern Convention and ultimately to a confederacy of the slave holding states.

The union party of this state and of all the Southern States are satisfied that there is no disposition on the part of our northern brethren to interfere with the domestic policy of the South. If we thought there was, we would appeal to you my dear sir, as an American citizen, a patriot and a Statesman, to interpose, with the weight of your character and the influence of your great talents, in favour of the South, the Union and the cause of republican Government. Whatever of wrong and of Sin there may be in slavery we are compelled by the force of circumstances to sanction and tolerate. It is an evil which was entailed upon us by our ancestors, and which we cannot remedy, without the ruin of ourselves and the injury of those whom we would think of benefitting. So interwoven is it with our interest, our manners, our climate, and our very being, that no change can ever possibly be effected without a civil commotion, from which the heart of a patriot must turn with horror.

Nothing would please some of the prominent men of South Carolina more than for the subject of emancipation to be discussed in the northern papers and an effort made in Congress to accomplish it. They would then see their wicked prospects brightening, and the darling object of their unhallowed ambition at hand. The honors and high offices of the Federal Government are forever beyond their reach, and hence their only hope of selfish gratification is to *divide* and *reign*. In order to prepare the minds of the people for a Southern confederacy they are daily infusing into their minds the most illiberal and unfounded prejudices against the northern section of our common country.

It would, my dear sir, afford me and the party with whom I am acting, infinite pleasure to hear from you on this important and interesting subject.¹ Since the adjournment of Congress and the dissolu[tion of the] State convention public excitement has in a grea[t] measure subsided, notwithstanding the efforts made to keep it up. I have no doubt that our congressional elections in September next will show an increase of numbers to the Union party, and perhaps one or two additional representatives. With sentiments of profound respect and sincere regard I am yours &c   B. F. Perry

ALS. NhD.
1. See above, DW to Perry, April 27, 1833.

FROM JOHN BOLTON

New York, May 16, 1833.

Dear Sir

It cannot have escaped your observation, that warm discussions are now going on in many of the southern papers, and much agitation is felt or feigned in a portion of the south, on the subject of slavery, and of imputed designs at the north against the security and value of that species of property.

I have been so long and closely connected with Georgia, that I am perhaps more watchful than most others in this quarter of such discussions as these, and having reason moreover to apprehend that, at this particular juncture, the tendency, if not the deliberate aim and purpose, is to excite universal uneasiness and distrust in the slave-holding states, and by consequence, to foment jealousies and heart burnings against the non-slave-holding states, which designing politicians may turn to mischievous account; I have felt desirous since our conversation this morning of obtaining an expression in writing of your views, as to the power of congress on the subject of slaves and slavery, and also as to the existence of any wish or design on the part of the northern men, to interfere in any way with the security or regulation of that species of property.

My immediate object in thus seeking to obtain a written expression of your opinion on these subjects is, that I may communicate it to a distinguished friend of mine in Georgia, who shares in my solicitude in relation thereto, and through him to the public at large. I am, dear sir, with great respect, and esteem, your obedient servant.   JOHN BOLTON.

Text from *Niles' Register*, 44 (June 29, 1833): 295. Original not found. Bolton (1774–1838) was originally a merchant in Savannah and active in the American Bible Society of Georgia. In 1826 he became president of the Delaware and Hudson Canal Company, and later, in 1834, was elected an alderman in New York City. This letter and Webster's reply were first published in the *Savannah Georgian* in May or June 1833, then reprinted in *Niles' Register* on June 29. They appeared in the *Boston Atlas* on August 15, 1835.

TO JOHN BOLTON

New York, May 17th, 1833.

My Dear Sir

I have received your letter of last evening,[1] requesting me to state my opinion of the powers of congress on the subject of slaves and slavery; and of the existence of any wish or design, on the part of northern men, to interfere with the security or regulation of that species of property.

My sentiments on this subject, my dear sir, have been often publicly expressed; but I can have no objection to repeat the declaration of them, if it be thought by you that such a declaration might, in the smallest degree, aid the friends of union and the constitution in the south, in dispelling prejudices which are so industriously fostered, and in quieting agitations so unnecessarily kept alive.

In my opinion, the domestic slavery of the southern states is a subject within the exclusive control of the states themselves; and, this, I am sure, is the opinion of the whole north. Congress has no authority to interfere in the emancipation of slaves, or in the treatment of them in any of the states. This was so resolved by the house of representatives, when congress sat in this city in 1790, on the report of a committee,[2] consisting almost entirely of northern members; and I do not know of an instance of the expression of a different opinion, in either house of congress, since. I cannot say that particular individuals might not possibly be found who suppose that congress may possess some power over the subject, but I do not know any such persons, and if there be any, I am sure they are few. The servitude of so great a portion of the population of the south, is, undoubtedly regarded at the north, as a great evil, moral and political; and the discussions upon it, which have recently taken place in the legislatures of several of the slave-holding states, have been read with very deep interest. But it is regarded, nevertheless, as an evil, the remedy for which lies with those legislatures themselves, to be provided and applied according to *their* own sense of policy and duty. The imputations which you say, and say truly, are constantly made against the north, are, in my opinion, entirely destitute of any just foundation. I have endeavored to repel them, so far as has been in my power, on all proper occasions; and for a fuller expression of my own opinions, both on the power of congress, and on the groundless charges against northern men, I beg leave to refer you to my remarks in the debate on Mr. Foot's resolutions in 1830. I am, my dear sir, with much true regard, your obedient servant,   DAN'L WEBSTER.

Text from *Niles' Register*, 44 (June 29, 1833): 295. Original not found. Published in *W & S*, 12: 210–211.

1. See above.
2. *Annals of Congress*, 1st Cong., 2d sess., pp. 1465–1466, 1523–1525.

FROM JOEL ROBERTS POINSETT

Charleston 24 May 1833

My dear Sir

I received your letter[1] on the subject of the picture and according to your request enclosed ten dollars, which I consider amply sufficient.

There is no doubt that Mr. Calhoun and his followers are using every exertion to keep up the excitement in and out of this state. It is only by agitating, that they can preserve the power they have gained at home, and they build their hopes of future influence on the same foundation. They are now striving to excite the fear & jealousy of the southern people on the slave question and are only to be counteracted by prudent forbearance on the part of the non slave holding states. We have not ventured to write at all even to reply to their bold, impudent and false assertions, or to denounce their wickedness and folly in agitating this most delicate question; we are afraid to move, for we are aware that the interests of the country require this people to be kept tranquil if possible. They have been excited to madness and must be restored to a sound state of mind before we can effect a complete restoration of sound principles. You may be assured, that these men have in view the dissolution of the union and unless we do exert ourselves for its preservation and act with united councils against them they will ultimately succeed. The President has certainly deserved well of his Country. His conduct throughout the whole of this contest has been highly praiseworthy and the principles he has advocated are sound and such as we must sustain. I see by the papers you have passed through New York and are on your Western tour. If I had known sooner of your movements I would have endeavoured to have met you there. I am going to West Point being appointed one of the visitors; but shall be back here on the 4th July and probably remain through the summer as my friends think my absence at this time would discourage the party with which I act. It appears to me important that your papers should assume a conciliatory tone in relation to the slave question. You are bound by the compact to respect that description of property and it is our only hope of safety, and y[et] these reckless men would destroy that hope in order to rescue themselves from the insignifica[nce] into which they will otherwise inevitably fall. [I] do hope our friend Mr. Clay will not sustain Calhoun, or rather will not attempt to do so for [to] support effectually so rotten a fabric is impracticab[le].

We are urging Col. [William] Drayton to be the Candidate for Congress from this district; but he talks of leaving the state. He can not bear to live under a despotism &c[, but] for my own part it is a reason to remain & do battle for the right.

I should be very glad my dear sir to meet you somewhere in the course of the summer. Ever with great regard Yours   J. R. Poinsett

ALS. DLC.
   1. Not found.

MEMORANDUM OF VISIT TO EDWARD LE ROY'S FARM
Tuesday, May 28, [1833]

Arrived at Avon, eve' of 27. On 28th. A. M. visited Mr E. Le Roy's farm. It lies on the Genessee River, north of the road, leading from Avon Bridge, & consists of 1800 acres. The land is of three characters. 1. Flats. This is purely alluvial, low, & level. It is subject to be overflowed. When the County was settled, much of it was prairie. It has great depth of loose soil, vegetable moul[d], & other deposites. On the bank of the river, where the roots of trees are exposed, they are seen six, eight, or ten feet from the surface. The trees still remaining are fine esp[eci]ally elm & white oak, some of them very large. This land is adapted to grazing, but uncertain for wheat. In very dry seasons, wheat has succeeded on it. 2. The *hazel* flat. This is a table of land, rather higher than the last mentioned. It is flat, well covered with wood, undoubtedly, I think alluvial, but an earlier formation. It is not usually overflowed, & is, perhaps, more valuable than the lower flats; as adapted to wheat, as well as grazing. 3. Upland. This seems a peculiar soil. It is full of small stones, & the ground covered with a growth of oaks, of no great size. To the eye, it does not seem to be extraordinary land, but its fertility is very great, especially for wheat & clover. When ploughed little pebbles, stones as they would seem, are turned up, in great plenty; but these crumble, or dissolve, by exposure to the air, & seem to be marl, or a mixture of lime & clay, or some such thing, which I do not exactly know about. This land grows better by cultivation. It will yield two crops of wheat—then one of clover—then one yr pasturage, & then wheat again; all without manure. The only rotation seems to be, from wheat to pasturage, sometimes cropping with the scythe, the first year after wheat.

The lands up & down the River seem much like Mr Le Roys. I saw no difference between his flats, & those at Geneseo. The highland, or upland, near Geneseo, was higher, & seemed to have a heavier original growth.

Mr Le Roy cuts, on his lower flats, 200. or 250 tons of hay. This is housed in small barns, or barracks, standing round on the flats, & is fed out, thence, to the cattle. The cattle live on the meadows, thro' the winter, except working oxen, milch cows &c—and so do the sheep. Mr Le R. winters 100 or 150 head of cattle, & feeds out to them 2 tons of hay a day. This is carried & spread over the field, by a sled, or waggon; so that the growth of the flats is consumed on them. These flats are sometimes plowed, but some of them have not been plowed for 40 yrs, & yet bear good grass. The feed is now abundant.

AD. NhHi. Published in Van Tyne, pp. 660–661, where the date is erroneously conjectured as May 28, 1851. Edward Augustus Le Roy (1804–1865) was the twelfth and youngest child of Herman Le Roy, Sr., and brother of Caroline Le Roy Webster.

TO JOHN G. CAMP, AND OTHERS

Buffalo June 1. 1833

Gentlemen,

I have the honor to acknowledge the receipt of your letter,[1] inviting me, in behalf of the Citizens of Buffalo, to a public dinner. For this manifestation of respect, I tender my sincere and grateful thanks; but, Gentlemen, my stay in the City must necessarily be short, and I feel a strong wish to devote all the time at my command to the examination of its interesting objects, and to an unrestrained and unceremonious intercourse with its citizens.[2] I hope those who have joined in the invitation will find, in this motive, a reason for declining it, not inconsist[ent] with a very true regard for them, or a high estimate of the honor which the invitation confers.

If the citizens of Buffalo have seen any thing to approve, in my attempts to serve the public, I can say, on the other hand, that I have pleasure in the recollection of having supported, with steadiness & zeal, measures important to their local prosperity, as well as to the general interest of the Country. I perceive, with much satisfaction, that the work for the security of your harbour is nearly completed, & that both in its general plan, & in the manner of the execution, it promises to accomplish all that was expected from it. Your local position, Gentleman, is a highly favored one, & your "Infant City" is destined, I doubt not, to reach to great importance. I see the productions of Europe and Asia, and the fruits of interior agriculture, the products of new-discovered or new-wrought Western mines, & the furs of the remote wilderness, already exchanged, every hour, upon your wharfs. To the East, you are connected with the Ocean by a noble work,[3] honorable to the sagacity & public spirit of the People, and an enduring monument to the fame of its distinguished Patron; and to the West, nature opens to you a track of navigation extending a thousand miles into the bosom of a healthy & fertile territory. The quickness, manifested in discerning these advantages, & the spirit by which obstacles to their enjoyment are overcome, shew the intelligence & power of an enlightened people, under the protection & guidance of a well-conducted free Government. By its position, & by the enterprize of its citizens, your City has a bright prospect of participating, largely, in the blessings of that internal Commerce between the States, which is, at once, a main artery of their wealth, & a firm ligament of their Union. With cordial good wishes, I remain, Gentlemen, Your Ob. Sevt.   Danl. Webster

ALS. NBuHi.

1. Not found. Camp was a former military officer involved in the promotion of the Erie Canal, the Buffalo Harbor project, and other internal improvements in western New York.

2. In the course of his stay in Buffalo, Webster spoke informally at the launching of a steamboat named *Daniel Webster* and at a meeting of mechanics and manufacturers. *W & S*, 2: 131–134.

3. The Erie Canal.

FROM HENRY CLAY

Ashland 17th. June 1833.

My dear Sir

The mail brought me today your letter of the 10th.[1] from Columbus and also the intelligence of your safe arrival at Cincinnati. I had been tracing in the papers your progress with much interest.

I regret extremely that you should find us, in so many places, suffering with Cholera. Its visit to Lexington has been frightful. Its mortality there has been exceeded in degree at no other point in the U. S., New Orleans perhaps excepted. The Shops and Stores and principal Hotel have been all closed. The pestilence, within the two or three last days, has considerably declined, and, in a few more, will I think have disappeared. Happily, in a family of about sixty, we have as yet sustained no loss, and are not sure that we have had one case of genuine Cholera.

I shall be mortified and disappointed if you do not visit K[entucky] and Lexington; but I hardly know how to advise you. You will certainly go to Louisville, where there is no danger. At that place, daily intelligence is rec[eive]d from Lexington, and you can hear whether there has been such an abatement of the Cholera as to enable you to visit us without hazard. I hope the state of things will admit of your coming, and I request that you and Mr. [Stephen] White will come directly to Ashland, and any other gentlemen, if there be any other in your party, where, judging from the past, you will be secure, if the disease should even continue to prevail at Lexington. It is not at Frankfort, the principal intermediate point, and where, as every where else, your visit has been anticipated with great pleasure.

As for myself, I shall not leave home for the North until between the 10th. and 15th. July, if I go at all.

Poor [Josiah S.] Johnstons untimely fate has filled me with grief. I fear Mr. [Edward Douglass] White has not survived.[2]

Favor me with a line from Louisville as to your movements; and believe me always faithfully Your friend   H: Clay

P.S. I write in duplicate to Louisville & Cincinnati.

ALS. DLC. Published in Curtis, 1: 462–463.

1. mDW 10963.

2. Johnston, senator from Louisiana, and White, a congressman from that state, were passengers aboard the steamboat *Lioness*, bound from New Orleans to Natchitoches, when an explosion of gunpowder occurred on May 19. The senator was killed, and White was severely, though not fatally, injured.

FROM JOHN TEST

Lawrenceburgh Ind. June 19th 1833

My dear Sir

I have been out, upon what we call, an electioneering campaign, and it was not until to day that I heard, certainly, you were at Cincinnati. It woud. be gratifying to our citizens here, and I need not tell you, peculiarly so to me, if you coud. make it convenient to touch the Shore of Indiana at our place—indeed I can hardly consent that you shoud. return without doing so. You gave me an implied promise some two years ago, you woud. do so, and I feel as though I had a right to insist upon a performance. Our accomodations will be rough and *Houshier*-like, but they will be the frank-offerings of the heart. If you will inform me of the day it woud. suit you to come down, I will endeavour to come up and accompany you. If however it suits the *notions* of the Land of *Steady habits* better, Just land from the Stage or Steam Boat Sans Ceremonie, for I shoud. delight to see you, and so woud. our friends here, under any circumstances, for we are well aware here, that the trappings and gewgaws that popular applause throws around distinguished men, add nothing to their real worth. It woud. however be better, I think, for me to come up and attend you down—write me by return of the mail tomorrow, whether, and when it will suit your convenience to be with us. I woud. have come up to day and seen you, but I found it impossible to do so. Excuse the freedom with which I write, as this is to be considered as a private and friendly communication. Very respectfully your friend   John Test of Ind

ALS. NhD.

TO HENRY CLAY

Chillicothe, June 22d, 1833.

My Dear Sir,

Your kind letter of the 17th[1] was put into my hands at Cincinnati, on the morning of the 20th, just as I was getting into the carriage on my departure for this place. With whatever reluctance, and it was certainly very great, I found it unavoidable that I should give up the Kentucky portion of my journey; since, even though I felt no fear about personal safety, I should yet find those whom I wished to see either in alarm or in affliction. Now that the scourge has departed, as I hope, from your immediate neighborhood, and although Providence has kindly protected your own roof, yet I can well conceive that you must have lost valued friends, and that so terrible a visitation has left a shock which must continue to be felt for some time.

It is my purpose to proceed immediately to Pittsburg, and thence by the shortest route to New York and New England. I find Mr. [Thomas] Ewing here, as well as General [Duncan] M[c]Arthur and other friends. He expresses great pleasure at the escape of your family from the calamity. There is no sickness here, though a case of cholera is reported as having occurred at Portsmouth.

I sincerely hope you will not give up your intended visit to the North. All along the country there is a very general expectation of seeing you, and the disappointment will not be small, should you not come.

I beg you to make my best regards to Mrs. Clay, and say to her, that I will venture to give her my word that if she will visit the North, she will find her tour pleasant and agreeable, and her welcome every where hearty.

Text from Colton, *Henry Clay*, pp. 366–367, in which the complimentary close and signature have been omitted. Original not found.

1. See above.

TO DANIEL FLETCHER WEBSTER

Pittsburg, July 5, 1833.

My Dear Son,

It seems to become doubtful whether I can possibly get home to hear your oration.[1] I regret this, very much indeed, and shall still make every effort in my power to reach Boston in season, but I find so many causes of delay that I cannot say what I may be able to accomplish. I have seldom felt so much concern about anything of the kind as I do upon your success upon that occasion. I pray you spare no pains. Do your best and you will do well enough. It would be a good thing to have printed, if it should be well received. This part of the matter we can see about. I earnestly remind you of the necessity of acting with great caution in regard to all *festivities*. You remember what I said to you on that head and I pray you to forget no part of it. You may ask Mr. [Henry Willis Kinsman][2] for any money which you may have just occasion for. Give my best regards to Mr. Paige's and Mr. White's families. I have not heard from mother and Julia since they arrived at Saratoga. Ever your affectionate father, D. Webster.

Text from Van Tyne, p. 586. Original not found.

1. Fletcher Webster gave the annual class oration on July 16, 1833.

2. Van Tyne leaves a blank for the name, but Kinsman regularly performed this service.

TO EDWARD EVERETT

Monday Morning
[August 5, 1833]

D Sir

Mr [David] Potts [, Jr.], member elect to Congress from Chester Co. Penna. (a distinguished Anti-Mason) is at the Tremont House. If you should be this way, it might be well to leave him a card.

Tomorrow, at 9. or 10. oclock, I will be at leisure in my Office, if you should be in town, & could call, for half an hour. Yrs truly   D. Webster

ALS. MHi

TO EZEKIEL FORMAN CHAMBERS

Boston Aug. 6. 1833

My Dear Sir

I thank you for your obliging letter of the 26th. of July,[1] & for your congratulations on the incidents of my late journey. I owe much to the People of the West, for their kind & hearty [words?] & welcome; & shall not soon [forget] the impression which these have made upon me. And I ought to rejoice, & hope I do, more than for all the testimonials of personal respect, in the prevalance of such an excellent social & political spirit as appears, at the present moment, to pervade that part of the Country which I visited. The feeling in favor of the Union, & the Constitution, & the Government, as it is, is deep, fervid, & general. One cannot say, of course, what miracles party, & discipline, & the skillful plying of all sorts of political machinery may work; but, if left to the course of their own voluntary opinions & preferences, Western N. York, Western Pa, & Ohio are as likely to think & act right, as any portion of the Country. Eastern Pa. I saw little of, except in a few places; & among those I must not omit to particularize the residence of your namesakes & relatives, Chambersburg. It is a beautiful town, filled with most excellent people.

As to the future, the great mass of Western opinion is, I think, quite uncommitted. People talk, & inquire, & discuss; but it does not seem to me that they are pledged, as yet, in fact or form. I found the strength & effect of party organization a good deal less, at the present moment, than I had expected. As to probable *Candidates*, I have no light, except such as is enjoyed by all. My *opinion* is, there will be a Southern Candidate, Mr Calhoun, Mr [Benjamin Watkins] Leigh, or Mr. P[hilip] P[endleton] Barbour, probably the last, & that this Candidate may be very likely to receive a strong support, in the States South of the Potomac, & East of the mountains; that there will also be one, if not two,

Western Candidates, & perhaps, *three*; tho' my impression, at present is, that there will ultimately be but *one*, & that that one will be Judge [John] McLean.

As to your other inquiry, which you do not propose that *I* should answer, perhaps it will be well to put it to *Major Downing*,[2] if you happen to meet with him.

I suppose I may be somewhat singular in supposing that Judge McL. will be the *only* Western Candidate. I do not express the opinion often, or ever, unless *in confidence*; but such *is* my opinion.

On the whole, we are, I think, to wait events, as long as we can; taking care, however, that we do not let the whole Country become committed to other Candidates, before we suggest one of our own, *if we mean to bring one forward at all*. However, on all these subjects we will confer, I trust, early in Decr; and, in the meantime, if you wish to know any thing, which, in your opinion you can better learn from another than from me, please address a letter to Stephen White Esq, Boston, an intelligent & confidential Gentleman. I think, however, it is highly probable you will learn all you wish to know from *Major Downing.*

Mrs Webster thanks you for your kind & friendly remembrances. She contemplates passing the next winter in Washington, & hopes [to have] the pleasure of seeing you often. She sends you all her good wishes, & so does her husband, with his best regards to Mrs Chambers. Yrs, cordially.   Danl. Webster

Is there any danger of your turning Judge? I hope not, for the sake of the Country, & for my own sake.

ALS. NNebgWM.
1. Not found.
2. Webster is referring to "Major Jack Downing," a fictitious character created by Seba Smith (1792–1868). Downing was a rustic Yankee from Maine who came to Washington as a job seeker and ended up as a confidant and counselor of President Jackson. The Downing letters appeared in the *Portland Courier* from January 18, 1830, to 1833 when they

were published together as *The life and writings of Major Jack Downing of Downingville* (Boston, 1833). By the date of this letter Charles Augustus Davis (1797–1867) was writing similar Jack Downing letters to the *New York Daily Advertiser.* Webster's reference could have been to either man. Biddle to DW, August 7, 1833, mDWs, indicates that Webster could to some extent "plant" material for Downing letters.

TO [JOHN RENSHAW THOMSON]

Boston Aug. 6. 1833

My Dear Sir

On my arrival in Boston, a few days after I had the pleasure of exchanging a word with you on the Rail Road, I found your letter of the 12th. of July,[1] enclosing a bank note of 100 Dlls, as a Retainer from the "Delaware & Raritan Canal & Camden & Amboy Rail Road." My family being at Marshfield, I proceeded immediately to that place, & have there been staying ten or twelve days, to recruit from the fatigue of a long journey.

On coming to town, & recurring to your letter, it occurs to me that there may be some difficulty in accepting this Retainer, especially as it is a *general* one, & for all causes. I have understood that some other Rail Road was in contemplation, thro N. Jersey, which may possibly come in competition with this. So I was informed, while in N. York on my way home, & so I have since learned also. And it so happens, that in this new projected road, family friends & connexions of mine are interested, I believe, to some considerable extent. I have not been retained, by those concerned in this new road, but on account of the connexion of Mr [Herman] LeRoy, & other members of his family in it, I feel unwilling to be retained for any opposing interest. If I am in any error, as to the controversies which your company anticipates, or there be any other question, respecting which they would desire my professional advice or aid, I shall very gladly render both.

Under all the circumstances, it has seemed to me to be the proper course to return the Retainer, & leave the matter for the further consideration of your company, in this view.

I pray the most respectful remembrance to Mrs Thompson, & the members of her family, & am, with regard, Your Ob. Servt.

AL draft. NhHi. Published in Van Tyne, pp. 719–720.
1. mDW 10983.

FROM EDWARD EVERETT

Charlestown Massts. 9 Augt. 1833.

(Private)

My dear Sir,

I want to have half an hour's talk with you, on the present state of things, as far as I am concerned, & by way of presenting the case more distinctly, I thought I would lay it before you in writing. You will, of course, let me have your views, *by word of mouth.*

You know the present relative force of the three parties, in the State. At the last election, Gov L[incoln] had less than 2000 majority. The Jackson & Anti M[ason] parties have both increased since then: so that there is no reason to think the Nat[ional] Rep[ublicans]—of themselves—have a majority. We cannot therefore choose a governor *by the*

People, alone. We can unite with the Jackson party & choose [Marcus] Morton. We can unite with the Anti M. & choose a Nat. Rep. acceptable to them, or we can hold on to our separate candidate. I see no motive of policy, in uniting to choose Morton; it is doubtful if our friends generally would agree, & when it was done, I perceive no effect but that of strengthening Mr Van B's interest in Massachusetts. The next step would be the reorganization of the old democratic party, & that places the State in the hands of the Regency. If we hold on to our separate vote, what will be the effect? Considerable difficulties would present themselves in fixing on a candidate. If there be three candidates there will be no choice by the People; the election will go to the General Court, & there our candidate will be chosen. At the same time, however, if there should be three candidates, the Anti M's & Nat. Rep. would be, throughout the election, in collision,—the jealousy and hostility already existing would be embittered,—the A. Ms made more exclusive,—& their co-operation on any future occasion, being repudiated now, would be much more difficult to command. In fact, I think it a pretty important point, to have as few occasions as possible of arraying Nat. Rep. & A. Ms. against each other, & as many as possible of acting together & leaving things quiet. But would there remain three candidates, if the Nat. Rep. reject an alliance with either of the other parties? I think not, & [Benjamin Franklin] Hallet[t] says the Anti Ms will be very apt to unite with the Jackson party & choose Morton, if we will not let them unite with us. What conceivable motive of policy have we to drive the Anti Ms into the Jackson party? Great efforts have been made, on both sides, to produce that result. Judge M's friends have courted the AMs: & H[enry] D[ana] Ward came on a mission from N. York, to persuade his AM brethren, to support Morton, as part of a general policy to give the AM vote to V. B. Hallet[t] is firm against this, but many of his associates are for it; & they all want to vote for a candidate, *who will be chosen.* I have little doubt, that if we will not unite with them, they will unite with the Custom-House party.[1] So that, for the sake of taking the chance of choosing our candidate in the Genl. Court, (which I know we should do, if we could get the matter there), we are *sure* to embitter the *Ams,* even if we succeed; & much more *likely* to drive them to choose Morton. The only remaining course is for the Nat. Rep. to unite with the AMs, in supporting a candidate, & this, for the reasons stated against the other courses, would seem to me obviously the best. It is the only one sure, or even likely, to prevent Morton's election; and it is the only one, which harmonizes with ulterior prospects of vastly greater moment. Now, how is [it] to be arranged? The *Ams* will drop [Samuel] Lathrop & [Timothy] Fuller, (that is they are willing to), with the view of supporting a candidate in union with us. They are willing to continue the present Lt Governor [Samuel Turell Armstrong]. They will nominate Mr [John Quincy] Adams, if he will accept it. He has told me repeatedly he would not; & I think he will stick to that purpose. If he accepts, the Nat. Rep. will have to consider, whether it will be their policy to confirm the nomination. If he declines, I think (to speak unreservedly), that the nomination will be offered to me, if I will say before hand, that I will not reject it. I have been already asked what I would do, & the time is very near at hand, when I must be prepared with a definitive answer, should Mr A (as I think he will) decline. This is the point, on which I wish to be guided by you. Of course I do not accept, unless I am to be supported by the Nat. Rep. party. Could I be chosen handsomely & creditably, I should like it. I am tired of Washington, & strongly disposed at all events to quit. I cannot take my family with me; & I cannot bear to leave them at home. For want of legal training, (or want of something), I really do not do myself justice there. Now I know, as matter of private friendship between us, you would be perfectly willing to gratify me, with any thing reasonable in your power; but I expect you & wish you to act solely on public grounds, including in them, as the most important, your own political position. I do not wish you to encounter one man's dislike nor lose an opportunity of obliging one man, from any reference to me. I was led to think, from your conversations last winter, that you had no views, in reference to the Governorship, to which you attached any interest. But if you have, I shall most cordially acquiesce in them. Neither do I wish or expect you, to take my burdens on your shoulders. If you think it would be better for you, to stand wholly aloof, I shall with equal cordiality approve your doing so;— although, considering your position in the party,—that would prevent my accepting the nomination, as effectually as if you discountenanced it positively. If you think, in reference to myself,—my own peace & character,—considering the clamor that has been raised by the Masonic presses,—I had better have nothing to do with it, I beg you to say so. Should I or any body else be held up for joint support by *Ams* & Nat. Rep. it will perhaps lead the Masonic Nat. Repub. to vote for Morton, but I do not think there would be any danger of the result. [Joseph T.] Buckingham told me the Nat. Rep. party would never sanction an antimasonic nomination; and I judge, from his conversation, that nothing but strong personal kindness prevents him from coming out against me. He intimated that he could not support my nomination. Some of the best Nat. Rep. papers, however, have supported me, among them the Essex Register & Worcester Spy. If you thought it expedient to give a decided sanction & support to the measure, it would go, & that very easily. If not, I should not think of attempting it.

I will only add, that on public grounds, I see no nomination possible, but my own, on which the *Ams* can unite with the Nat. Rep. (Mr Adams' being out of the question) & consequently no other, by which the evils indicated in the first part of this letter can be avoided.

I forgot to say that among twenty other reasons, why I shall submit with a good grace and good will to your decision are these two,—that I know whatever it is it will be dictated by kind feelings—and that as I put myself in my present position, without consulting you, I have not the least claim on you to help me out of it.

This I believe, is the whole case, and you will greatly oblige me, by fixing some time, when you will talk it over with me, before you go to N. H. Ever Yrs   E. E.

ALS copy. MHi.
1. The Henshaw Democrats.

TO SAMUEL P. LYMAN

Boston Aug. 10. 1833

My D Sir

Your letter, addressed to me at LeRoy[, New York], did not find me at that place, but followed me, & was afterwards recd. In like manner, that forwarded thro' Mr [Richard] Rush did not come to my hands, in Philadelphia but was sent hither subsequently by him.[1]

I returned from my journey, July 20th. Its fatigue & exposure brought on a little illness, which induced me to spend a fortnight with my family, on the sea coast. My health is now good, & I expect to be in & about Boston, for the residue of the Summer, & hope to be more attentive to my correspondents than I have been able to be, lately. My journey was an exceedingly agreeable one, & I was much delighted with that part of the Western Country which I saw. An excellent spirit, social & political, at the present moment pervades The People. There is no telling what drill & discipline may effect, but at present the great majority are all constitutional, all liberal, all right. Old political heats seem in a great measure to have subsided, & the public mind is in a very favorable state to receive just impressions, respecting the great public interests of the Country. I think the great State of Ohio will prove herself to be a strong link, in the chain of the National Union.

I remember, with much pleasure, the day or two we passed at Utica, & will thank you to make my grateful acknowledgment to all friends. My friend & fellow traveller, Mr [Stephen] White, informs me that he corresponds with you, which I am gratified to learn.

This is the season for visiting New England. We are, as you know, favored with the company of a good number [of] distant friends, about [co]mmencement week, the last week of this month. If you have leisure & inclination to visit this quarter, I think you would, at that time, see many here whom it would it be pleasing to you to meet. Suppose you take Genl. [John H.] Ostrom[2] with you, & come along.

I shall be glad to hear from you, at your convenience. There are parts of your letters, which I will readily answer, unless Mr White has sufficiently done it. Let me know how that is. Yours with great regard,

D. Webster

ALS. MiU-C.
1. Neither letter found.
2. Ostrom (1794–1845), Utica and

Oneida County officeholder, lawyer, and Utica mayor in 1835.

TO ALBERT HALLER TRACY

Boston Aug. 10. 1833

My Dear Sir,

I returned home, from my long journey, on the 20th. of July, & my family having already gone down to Marshfield, by the sea side, I immediately followed them. For a week or ten days, I was a good deal unwell there; but am now in health, & have come to Boston to resume my chair in the office. On my return, I found your letter of July 20th,[1] respecting our promising young friend, [John William?] Wilgus.[2] I have made inquiries, tho' not so fully as I intend, & find there will be no great difficulty in selecting some suitable place, for his instruction in drawing. I have not yet ascertained the exact expense per quarter, to which he would be subject; but will make further inquiry, & write you again shortly. I will give you a hint—which you may communicate or not to Wilgus' father. Some of our opulent men are accustomed, occasionally, to throw together small sums to make up enough to assist promising young men, in the pursuit of education. A fund, sufficient for 5 or 6 m[onth]s board & tuition, could be very quietly gathered together here, if it should be thought advisable, & would be agreeable to his father. *You* must decide this, upon *your* opinion of the lad's capacity. If you say 'let it be done,' it will be done.

I had, My D Sir, a very agreeable journey, thro' the West, or rather thro' a part of it. I mean the whole part which I visited. It is a fine country, & full of enterprizing People. The prevalent spirit I found to be excellent—far, very far, exceeding my anticipations. Unless the People be cajoled & cheated, they will do *right*, in all political matters.

But I saw nothing, My Dear Sir, to overwhelm or extinguish the remembrance of Buffalo, or to do away the impressions made upon me by the kindness & hospitality of yourself & friends. To yourself, particularly, I feel sincerely grateful, for the kind manner, in which, at the expense of so much of your own time & attention, you made me acquainted with your neighbors. I pray you to remember me, in the most respectful & best manner to Mrs Tracy; & to present my regards, also, to the Gentlemen I saw in Buffalo, as you may happen to meet with them. I believe it is the purpose of my fellow traveller, Mr [Stephen] White, to write you shortly. Yrs with mo. true regard   D Webster

ALS. NN.
  1. Not found.
  2. Probably John William Wilgus (1819–1853), a portrait painter born in Troy, New York, who was a pupil of Samuel F. B. Morse from 1833 to 1836. Wilgus remained in New York City until about 1841 and thereafter lived in Buffalo.

TO EDWARD EVERETT

Aug. 11. [1833]

My D Sir

The contents of yr letter[1] were not surprising to me. Most of its topics, had previously occurred to my mind, from conversation with others, or from reflection, & have formed the anxious subject of my thoughts, for many days. The frankness & confidence with which you address me, are not misplaced. I have been, am, & *shall be* your friend. But I do not feel competent, altogether, to give you advice, on this occasion, such as you ought implicitly to follow. I need further time to think; but, mean while, will state, with honesty & affection, what my present impressions are.

First, then, there is nothing in your letter to the Antimasons[2] which would prevent *me* from voting for you, for any office; & I go further, & say, there is nothing in it which *ought* to prevent the Nat. Repubs from regarding you with their accustomed favor & respect. I shall take pains to say this, every where. At the same time, I regret the publication of the letter, because altho it *ought not*, it *will* produce some degree of unfavorable effects. No man, eminent as you are, but what has enemies & rivals, as well as friends & supporters; and, in addition to this common truth, it is to be remembered, (what we all see) that men are looking out to find reasons *for changing their political relations*; and an important step, taken by a man of standing & influence, will furnish an *occasion* for many such changes.

I repeat, that nothing has occurred to shake my attachment to you, my convictions of your value to the Country, or my readiness to serve your interests.

In the next place, I have no object whatever, as you rightly suppose, connected with the election of Govr. I am pledged for nobody, & have no particular preference. I will add, further, that I wish the Nat. Republicans would support you for the place; &, as I have occasion, I shall so state to friends. But I am afraid it will be difficult to bring about such a result; principally perhaps, from this circumstance, that the parties are rival parties, & that which is the minor insists on going ahead. If it could so have happened, that nothing should have been said or done, until the Nat. Repub: Conv. in October, I entertain no doubt that Convention would have nominated you for Govr., if it had been understood you would like the office. But the Antims meet in *Septr*; should they nominate you, looking to the existing asperities, & to the tone & temper of those papers which would present your nomination to the Public, I think the Nat. Repub. Con. would not follow suit, at least in the *present* state of feeling. Should that state of feeling continue, I think the Nat. Repub. Con. would nominate *John Davis*, or *Wm. B. Calhoun*; probably the latter. In that case, a Govr. would be chosen by the Legislature, &, in all probability the Nat. Repub. candidate would succeed. The end of all which would be, a schism among friends, such as would effectuall[y] destroy the political influence of Massachusetts. The approach of the period for holding the Antimasonic Convention renders it necessary, I presume, for you to determine on your own course soon. My advice, is *to decline the nomination*. I think that is clearly the safer course. You have one office, which the world does not know you are tired of, & which most men would think you would naturally prefer to that of Govr. That is a sufficient reason to the Antims. By so declining, you will disarm your enemies of the means of reproach & calumny, as you would shew that no sinister motives dictated your late movement. In point of reputation, & character, then, you stand intact, on all sides; & will have a loftier position, & more strength, in my opinion, than at any previous period of your life.

As this letter is intended to be, in the strictest sense, confidential, & for your single eye, I will say, that I am informed, from direct sources, that the leading Antims in N. York do not expect to carry their power farther. They do not consider it encreasing; as far as it spread, it produced great majorities; but it stopped at Utica, & there is no appearance of any new start. The principal men do not intend to bring forth a Presidential Candidate of their own—but to select, from those that may be already in the field.

I do not know so much abt. the purposes of Antims in Pennsa.—nor so much about their present strength, or expected progress. Probably, the cause will prosper farther, in some parts of that state, & decline in others. I am suspicious, that the County of Alleghany, (Pittsburg) will reject the Anti-masonic nominations for assembly, in October. They were already warm with electioneering, when I was there.

I do not wonder you are tired of Congress. So am I. But you can hold on for 2 yrs; & should you then be out of public life, for a year or two, long enough to carry your wife to Europe, & to revisit the states of the Union, nothing would be lost. Or you can stay in Congress longer, if you please.

I conclude, my Dear Sir, by saying, that you may rely on the steadiness of my regard & friendship. I think you are an honor to the Country, & entitled to be employed in its highest service, at home or abroad.

One word more. I know you will pay proper, I fear too much, respect, to my advice; & I know you will believe it to be sincere, & religiously honest; but I beseech you, after all, in making up your mind on the questions which may come before you, to pay no regard to any supposed political interest of *mine*.

Do what you think *right*, & for your own *interest*, & that of *the public*. God bless you! Yrs   D Webster

ALS. MHi.
1. See above, Everett to DW, August 9, 1833.
2. Everett to Herman Atwill, in behalf of the Anti-Masonic Committee of Middlesex County, June 29, 1833, Everett Papers, MHi, and printed in the *Boston Courier*, July 18, 1833.

FROM RUFUS CHOATE

Salem 12 Aug. 1833.

Dear Sir

I have hesitated whether I should write to you upon a subject in which you can take very little interest, but in which I take, on my own account, a great deal. It has been intimated that some one has represented to you, that I expressed myself in terms of disrespect & unfriendliness of your self at the dinner of a few of the party on the 4th of July. It would give me inexpressible pain to suppose that you could believe this, lightly as you might regard it; and I cannot suffer the day to pass without assuring you that the representation is wholly false, and—so far as I had the honor to allude to your name, it is the very reverse of the truth.

I was invited to the dinner by those who got it up, and their object was to bring together some of the younger & more effective of the party—to keep ourselves in heart & under arms. The late visit of the Cabinet, it was thought was an electioneering operation of the Vice President, to make an impression, & it was supposed to be well enough to counteract the impression—so far as he was concerned. I doubt whether there was any particular unfriendliness to the President; but it was certainly, & unequivocally an anti-Van Buren Dinner. The specific & immediate object was to keep our own ranks, & to see that none of our number were carried away by the recent flow of good feeling. Our Jackson men have been Van Buren men.

In all I said, addressed by the way to one hundred of as sincere admirers & zealous & decided political friends of yourself as there are in the United States, my sole purpose was to keep up the spirits, & organisation of the party. I went on the ground throughout that the object of the party in power was to secure the succession for V. B.—and that our business was to hang together & prevent it. Every thing was pointed at him—not even at the President at all—& pointed at him as the leading administration Candidate for the Presidency—aspiring to come in as the regular successor—the declared choice & natural head of the existing organization. I feel the absurdity and impertinence of reporting to you a dinner speech—but it is perhaps due to myself to say, that I asked in so many words, whether—just because Mr V. B. was among us—shaking hands with our wives &c. &c.—we should forget our old, tried, trusty *absent friends*—naming yourself & Mr. Clay—& following up those names with the highest possible expression of fervent love & respect. Whoever has troubled himself to give you an account of this matter will remember this if he was present.

It is hardly delicate, for an obvious reason, to say so, but it is also perfectly true, that in speaking of Mr. Clay, I alluded to him as a retired statesman, and toasted him as the setting sun—in Garrick's common lines. I made no allusion whatever, to his coming forward again, & the impression made upon every hearer would be decidedly, that I considered him to have withdrawn from active statesmanship, & an unsuccessful competition—& wished to do him justice as a character of history.

It is hardly possible for me to express the reluctance I have felt to trouble you with this letter. I will bring it to a close by hazarding one assertion, that there is not a man in this nation young or old, who rejoices more than I do, to see this great breaking out of your fame,—& that there is not an audience to whom it would be so unsafe to say any thing cold or disrespectful of yourself, as an audience of National Republicans of Essex. I am Sir With great regard & affection Your obedient servant   Rufus Choate

ALS. DLC. Published in Van Tyne, pp. 184–185.

FROM HENRY ALEXANDER SCAMMELL DEARBORN

> Brinley Place, Roxbury
> August 12. 1833.

My Dear Sir,

I enclose you a draft of the letter I have sent to several gentlemen &

in the course of two days shall have forwarded one to each of the following persons.

Maine. Peleg Sprague & Mr [James] Brook[s]—the editor in Portland.
N. Hamp. S[amuel] Bell
Mass. John Davis & [Isaac Chapman] Bates
Rd Isld. T[ristam] Burges
Connecticut W[illiam] W[olcott] El[l]sworth
Vermont H[oratio] Seymour
N. Jersey T[heodore] Frelinghuysen.
Delaware John M. Clayton
Maryland. Genl [Ezekiel F.] Chambers
Ohio Thomas Ewing
Louisiana G[eorge] A[ugustus] Waggaman & H[enry] A[dams] Bullard
N. York. Govr [Nathaniel] Pitcher and John A. Collier
Penna. Harmar Denny & Col. [John G.] Watmough
Virginia Genl. [Charles Fenton] Mercer
North Carolina Lewis Williams of the House.
Tennessee Th[omas] D. Arnold of the House.

If you will suggest any other names to whom I can write with effect, or any change in the letter, I will cheerfully attend to it. I shall send off all the letters in three days. I enclosed a Courier[1] in each letter. With the highest respect I offer the most friendly salutations.   H. A. S. Dearborn

ENCLOSURE

Brinley Place, Roxbury
August 12. 1833.

My Dear Sir,

From the demonstrations in Virginia & else where it is apparent the Presidential Canvass has been opened, & whether premature or not, it now becomes the duty of every friend to the Constitution & Union to fix on those candidate[s] who will concentrate the votes of all those, of whatever previous party, who are solicitous to perpetuate the republic, in all its vigor & glorious consequences, upon the prosperity of the WHOLE PEOPLE. I enclose a Boston Courier, which contains an article expressive of the views of the national republicans & others in this quarter.

From indications from Ohio Pennsylvania New York, the Union party of the Eastern States, & other parts of the country it is evident that Mr. Webster is looked to as the Candidate who will rally the most powerful party under the battle cry of "THE CONSTITUTION & THE UNION." What is public opinion with you on this momentous subject? Pray write me freely, & let there be an understanding established by correspondence throughout the country as to the course we shall pursue.

We are at a most perilous & momentous epoch in the history of the nation & it requires the zealous & firm cooperation, of all really honest & patriotic men, to preserve & perpetuate the government, in all its purity, efficiency & glory.

I write you with frankness & wish you to deal in the same manner with me.

With sincere esteem & great respect Your most obt. St.

H. A. S. Dearborn

ALS, with ALS draft, dated August 12, 1833, enclosed. NhHi. Published in Van Tyne, pp. 185–186.

1. Dearborn here refers to Joseph T. Buckingham's editorial, "The Presidency—New Parties," which appeared in the August 8 edition of the *Boston Courier*. Mindful that a Presidential campaign was already under way in Virginia and that "a new organization of parties is not only desirable but necessary," the *Courier* cited the "events of the last eight months" as reasons to promote a Unionist party as early as possible. The editorial concluded:

"Let the principles of the President's Proclamation be the principles on which to raise up this new organization. . . . Let . . . the *advocates* of those principles . . . give up all other differences of opinion—let us have no Jacksonians nor National Republicans, as party men—let us have no Freemasons nor Antimasons, no Southrons nor Northmen—but let all be for the principles of the Proclamation, and let the watchword be UNION AND THE CONSTITUTION."

TO [EDWARD EVERETT]

Boston Aug. 13. 1833
Tuesday Morning

D Sir

I had just closed a letter to go to you,[1] to go thro' the P.O. when yrs was recd.[2]

Please send yr draft of address to Univ Men[3] to me, at Marshfield.

I recd. Mr [Dutee Jerauld] Pearce's letter this morning,[4] & have several times tried my hand, at an answer; but have given it up. I am afraid to write any thing. To do him any good, the letter must be shewn, or, in some way *published*; & that wd. produce great evil. I would willing[ly] do Pearce a service. His course has been correct, in Congress, & his ability quite respectable; but interference, in such a matter, if it were right in itself, as it is not, would do him a great deal more hurt than good. If I write at all, it will be merely to express this last sentiment; but I think I shall not write a word. Yrs   D. Webster

ALS. MHi.

1. DW to [Everett], [August 13, 1833], mDW 11077 or 11054.

2. Not found.

3. Everett's "Education of Mankind," an address to the Phi Beta Kappa Society at Yale College, delivered on August 20, 1833, and published in Edward Everett, *Orations*

and Speeches on Various Occasions (Boston, 1836), pp. 378–412.

4. Pearce to DW, August 11, 1833, mDW 11062. Pearce appealed to Webster for aid in his reelection battle against strong, concerted opposition. Webster responded lukewarmly on August 28 (mDWs).

FROM NICHOLAS BIDDLE

Phila. Aug. 13. 1833.

My dear Sir

Altho' we do not feel anxious as to the result of the movements at Washington touching the Bank, still it is thought prudent to prepare for any adverse event and accordingly we have this day given instructions to the Branches to keep their discounts at their present amount—and to shorten the time for which they buy bills of exchange. This will make the institution strong & if any sudden movement is attempted by the Cabinet, proper or improper, we shall be ready. This will, I trust be temporary, as the squall may blow over. With great regard Yo[urs]   N. B.

LC. DLC. Published in McGrane, *Correspondence of Nicholas Biddle*, pp. 214–215.

FROM EDWARD CUTTS, JR.

Portsmouth Aug. 23rd 1833

Dear Sir,

The two sheets accompanying this letter,[1] contain the whole, which I can find, relating to your action in defence of this town during the last war, in the newspapers. The minutes of the proceedings of the Com[mitt]ee of defence on inquiry of Mr [Samuel] Sheafe,[2] I learnt, were delivered to Joseph Seaward[3] the then town clerk. I made an unsuccessful search for it in the town clerk's office, but after a long & painful search in the selectmen's room, I found it, thrown aside as useless, among dust & rubbish. This book is now in my office, but I have engaged to return it, in a short time to the town clerk. I have transcribed most of its contents, wherein your name is particularly connected.

In conversation with Capt Wm. Rice,[4] an active member of the Com[mitt]ee, he remarked that no men were more zealous or more heartily engaged in making preparations for the defence of the town than Mr. Webster & Mr [Jeremiah] Mason. Five of the Com[mitt]ee to wit, Messrs, [John] Goddard,[5] [Edward J.] Long,[6] [Langley] Boardman,[7]

[Charles] Blunt[8] & [Hunking] Penhallow[9] have deceased. From the surviving members of this Com[mitt]ee a very strong statement of the active & able part pursued by you in making preparations for the defence of the town, can doubtless be obtained.[10]

In relation to the Hartford Convention I have taxed my memory & cannot call to my recollection any conversation w[hic]h I ever had with you respecting it.

I have a clear recollection of a conversation which I had on that subject with Mr. [George] Sullivan of Exeter. Mr. S. at that time had the ear of Govr. [John Taylor] Gilman as often as any man. Mr. S. acquainted me, with a conversation w[hic]h the Govr. had holden in his presence with Saml. L. Knapp of Newburyport, then a member of the Mass. legislature & who went to Exeter to induce the Govr. to convene the legislature. Mr. S. was strongly & decidedly opposed to having any thing to do with that convention & I then understood from him that Govr. G. entertained similar views. It is my opinion that when the calling of that convention was first agitated, you was in the western counties in this State & that immediately after your return to Portsm[out]h you proceeded to Washington & that you held no conversation with me respecting it. I have examined my files of letters for the years 1814 & 1815 & tho' I had frequently letters from you during that period the two which are forwarded[11] are the only ones, which contain any allusion to that convention.

It will at all times give me pleasure to serve you in any manner & more especially in vindicating you agst. the charges alluded to in your letter of the 3rd instant.[12] I am, Dear Sir, with great respect, your friend & humble servant   Edw Cutts

ALS. DLC. Cutts (1782–1844; Harvard 1797), was a Portsmouth lawyer.

1. Enclosure missing.

2. Sheafe (c. 1785–1857), a Portsmouth merchant.

3. Seaward (c. 1751–1822), probably a Portsmouth merchant.

4. Rice (d. 1851), a Portsmouth merchant.

5. Goddard (c. 1756–1829), a Portsmouth doctor and merchant, active in town affairs and representative from Portsmouth in the General Court. In 1813 he was elected United States Senator, but refused to serve.

6. Long (d. 1824) of Portsmouth, secretary of the New Hampshire Fire and Marine Insurance Company.

7. Boardman (c. 1775–1833), a Portsmouth cabinet maker.

8. A Portsmouth ship master.

9. A Portsmouth merchant.

10. In addition to those listed in the letter, John L. Parrott, John Haven, and John Bowles were also on the Committee of Defense for Portsmouth. See DW, et al., to John Taylor Gilman, September 3, 1814, mDWs, and *Correspondence*, 1:169–171.

11. No letter from Webster to Cutts during the period has been found alluding to the Hartford Convention.

12. Not found.

TO [EDWARD EVERETT]

Wednesday Eve'
[August 28, 1833]

Dr Sir,

Not seeing the morning Newspaper early, today, it was near noon before I heard of yr return. I send you & yr wife an invitation for tomorrow Eve'.[1] A letter, which I wrote you at Philadelphia,[2] you probably did
not receive. It is of little importance, as I hear Mr [Elihu] Chaunc[e]y is
sick. I hope you will find an opportunity for some conversation with Mr
[Francis] Granger, Mr. [Samuel P.] Lyman, of Utica, & Mr [James
Louis] Petigru. Yrs. truly   D. W.

ALS. MHi.   2. Probably DW to Everett, August
    1. DW to the Everetts, August 29   25, [1833], mDW 11102.
[28], 1833, mDW 11106.

FROM NICHOLAS BIDDLE

Philada. Aug 30th. 1833

My dear Sir

I have received a letter from Mr. J[ohn] S. Barbour who is preparing
the way for resolutions which he intends to offer in the Virginia legislature next winter in favor of the Bank.[1] I wish that you would take that
matter in hand by stirring up our friends in Western Virginia to co-
operate with Mr Barbour. He [you] mentioned when you were here that
you believed that practicable, & the time is approaching when we should
begin. With great regard Yrs.   N Biddle

LC. DLC.   passed the Virginia legislature on
    1. The resolutions as reported by   February 18, 1834. *Niles' Register*,
Barbour of the select committee of   45 (February 22, 1834): 436. The
the Virginia House of Delegates, De-   Virginia senators were instructed and
cember 31, 1833, are printed in   her representatives were requested
Niles' Register, 45 (January 11,   to seek action by Congress to restore
1834): 344. The resolutions, roundly   the deposits to the Bank.
condemning the President's action,

TO SAMUEL JAUDON

Boston Sepr. 26. 1833

Dear Sir

Your letter to Mr F[rothingham] & myself both came safe to hand.[1]
I have now to trouble, I hope not sorely, in the same way. Enclosed is an
acceptance for 5,000 *cancelled*; & two bills for 2,500 to be accepted, as
substitutes. Please do the needful, & return the bills to me; making a
proper memorandum of the exchange.

The explosion has taken place, very much as you predicted.[2] All sensible people here think the Presidents reasons very feeble. As to [Louis] McLane & [Lewis] Cass resigning, I expect no such thing. They have not *character* enough. I hope Mr. [William John] Duane will give us light, on the whole matter.[3] Yrs ever   D. Webster

ALS. NHi.

    1. Not found.

    2. Jackson's announcement of the removal of deposits appeared in the September 20 issue of the *Washington Globe*.

    3. It was uncertain at this time whether Secretary Duane would obey the President's order and remove the deposits. Duane subsequently refused either to remove the deposits or to resign, forcing Jackson to relieve him. Attorney General Roger B. Taney replaced Duane as secretary of the Treasury.

TO JOHN DAVIS

Exeter, Sep. 30. 1833

My D Sir

I came over here today, on professional business; & had intended, before leaving Boston, to write you a single word.

We are not the fashioners of our own fortunes. Our path is often prescribed to us, by a power far greater than ourselves. We must follow the course, which our destinies seem to allot to us; or, in better words, we must yield to those circumstances, with which Providence surrounds us, & follow whither they lead, altho' we might have wished them to be other than they are. It is not unlikely, My Dr Sir, that you may be nominated for Govr. of Massachusetts. If you should be, I see nothing better, on your part, than a resignation to the course of things. I know you desire not the place. For one, I should hardly vote for you, were I in the Convention, because I should feel so much unwillingness to draw you from another sphere. Yet, if the general voice calls you to the head of the Commonwealth, I should rather counsel your obedience to that call; I would not desire greatly to influence your decision; but I write this merely to let you know that if you should incline to accept the nomination, if offered, one friend at least, & he not among the least sincere or the least attached, will approve your determination.

I pray you make my best regards to Mrs Davis Yours always truly
Danl Webster

ALS. MWA. Published in *W & S*, 16: 233–234. Davis went on to win the National Republican gubernatorial nomination; but the results of the general election—with three other candidates, including John Quincy Adams, on the ballot—were indecisive. Adams, running on the Anti-Masonic ticket, came in second to Davis but made great gains for that party at the expense of the National Republicans. The former President eventually withdrew in favor of Da-vis, who was then chosen governor by the state legislature.

FROM BENJAMIN SHURTLEFF

134 Tremont St. Octr 18th 1833

Dear Sir

The Hornless roan heifer is ¼ Bolivar ⅛ Galloway & ⅝ Coelebs' breed i. e. from Coelebs, Jupiter, son of Coelebs by Flora, & Tanner, son of Bolivar by a daughter of Coelebs.

The horned Roan heifer is ¼ Bolivar ¼ Galloway & ½ Coelebs' breed as above.

The Black & White heifer is ½ fill pail of John Breed's[1] stock, bred in & from imported Fill pail ¼ Bolivar and ¼ Coelebs' breed as above.

The Fill pails[2] were imported from Flanders by Col. [Israel] Thorndike & have proved excellent Milkers. Bolivar was imported by Col. [John Hare] Powel having a Pedigree in the Herd book & the heifers from him are very fine Milkers—my son has four of them now in milk. Coelebs & Flora were imported by Cornelius Coolidge[3] & sold to Col. Jaynes.[4] No Pedigree of them is found in the *Herd Book* and although not the most superior milkers, Coelebs has given a fine form & *large* teats to his female progeny.

The Galloways[5] were imported by the late Joseph Barrell[6] & Henry Howell Williams[7] & came into my possession pure & unmixed & give more & better milk of their size than any kind of Stock with which I have been acquainted. See [George] Culley & [Timothy] Pickering on live stock N England Farmer Vol iv page 82[8] Coventry[9] on live stock p. 28 Colonus[10] on Milch Cows N. E. Farmer Vol ix p. 267.

Bolivar's pedigree see N. E. Farmer Vol. vi p. 363 also American Farmer Vol xii p. 90.

Fill pail Mass. Ag. Repository & Journal Vol. v p. 97, 245 197 Vol. vii p. 28 & 29.

Yours respectfully   Benjamin Shurtleff

ALS. NhHi. Shurtleff (1774–1847; Brown 1796, Harvard M.D. 1802) was a Boston physician and father of Nathaniel Bradstreet Shurtleff, Boston mayor and antiquary. Webster had purchased three heifers from Shurtleff at the Brighton fair, October 16, but had lost their pedigrees. See DW to Shurtleff, October 17, 1833, mDW 11169, and to Charles Henry

Thomas, about the same date, mDW 39026.

1. Not identified.
2. "The Hon. Mr. Thorndike has placed at the disposition of the [Massachusetts Agricultural] Society, one bull and one of the cows imported by him the last season from the Low Countries. This breed has been long celebrated for its excellent

qualities for the dairy, in which, if in any thing, our stock of horned cattle is deficient. In reference to this quality, this bull has received the name of *Fill-pail.*" *Massachusetts Agricultural Journal*, 5 (January 1819): 197.

3. Coolidge (c. 1778–1843; Harvard 1798), a Boston merchant who before 1833 had become a building contractor and architect.

4. Not identified.

5. A large, thick, short-legged, mostly hornless variety of cattle, black or brindled in color, originating from Scotland. It was regarded at the time as giving more and richer milk than any other imported stock in proportion to its size and keep.

6. Barrell (d. 1801; Harvard 1783), a Charlestown merchant who resided in Somerville.

7. Probably this refers to the Henry Howell Williams (c. 1767–1832) who lived in Roxbury and died in Colrain, Massachusetts. He and his father of the same name had considerable holdings on Noddle's Island in Boston where they bred cattle.

8. "Colonel Pickering, on Improving the Native Breed of New England Cattle," *New England Farmer and Horticultural Journal*, pp. 81–83, in which Pickering cites as authority George Culley (1735–1813), an important Northumberland agriculturalist, and his influential *Observations on Livestock, containing hints for choosing and improving the best breeds of the most useful kinds of domestic animals* (London, 1786).

9. An anonymous letter writer to Thomas Green Fessenden, the editor of the *Journal*.

10. *Ibid.*

TO JOHN GORHAM PALFREY

At a meeting of the Proprietors of Pews in the Church on Brattle Square duly holden by adjournment on Sunday the twenty-seventh day of October 1833.

Voted unanimously

That the Revd John G. Palfrey be and he hereby is invited to resume the pastoral charge of this Society.

Voted. That the following

gentlemen be a Committee to communicate this invitation to the Revd Mr Palfrey viz

Hon   Daniel Webster
          Abbot Lawrence
          Alexr H. Everett
          Giles Lodge[1]
          George W. Coffin[2]
          James T. Austin
          Harrison G. Otis   Esqrs.

A true Copy from the Records.

attest   Ivers J. Austin[3]—Clerk.

Copy. MH.

1. Lodge, a Boston merchant located at 43 Broad Street.

2. Coffin, the land agent for the

Commonwealth of Massachusetts.
   3. Austin (1808–1889), son of
James Trecothick Austin, graduated
from West Point in 1828, and three
years later was admitted to the Suffolk bar.

TO ISRAEL WEBSTER KELLY

Boston Oct. 28. [1833?]

Dr Sir

I have recd. yr letter of the 23rd inst.[1] Mr [Jeremiah] Gerrish's[2] proposition cannot be accepted. It amounts to little less than *buying* his property, & giving away Dixville. Suppose his two parcels to be worth 4,000, which is higher than you & Capt [Abraham G.] Stevens estimate them, then his proposition only allows 1500 for the Dixville land, which is about 14, or 15 cts pr acre. This will not answer. I would advance 2,000 dollars, if I could get the fair worth of it, & of the Dixville land also, in a good farm; but Mr Gerrish's offer requires more money, & allows next to nothing for Dixville.

Ellen,[3] I have not yet heard from. Yrs   D. Webster

ALS. NhHi.
   1. Not found.
   2. Gerrish (1764–1836), a Boscawen saw mill builder and small manufacturer, was co-owner with Webster of the Dixville township in northern New Hampshire. Gerrish
held two thirds of the property while Webster controlled the other third.
   3. Probably Ellen W. Kelly, Webster's niece and Israel W. Kelly's daughter, who was born in 1809 and married Henry H. Pierce of Winterport, Maine, in 1838.

TO NICHOLAS BIDDLE

Boston Oct. 29. 1833

Private
Dear Sir,

I write this letter, as a private one, & for the purpose of inquiring whether the course for the adoption of the Bank, is yet settled. The removal of the Deposites is a question of great interest to the Government, & as such will doubtless attract the attention of Congress. It is, also, a matter of moment to the Banks, *as one part of their Charter.* In this point of view, it becomes a question whether the Bank should not lay the transaction of removing the Deposites, before Congress.

This, I have no doubt, you have already considered. Yrs   D. Webster

ALS. DLC. Published in McGrane, *Correspondence of Nicholas Biddle,* pp. 216–217.

The following memorandum lists Webster's land dealings, principally in New Hampshire, over the course of the preceding nine years. The document might have been written as early as 1830, but the numerous marginal notes and the last two entries, all written with a finer pen, were probably included about the time Webster sold his Dixville land to Jeremiah Gerrish in late October 1833. See above, DW to Israel W. Kelly, October 28, [1833?]. Since most of these transactions involved obscure local men whose names were likely to appear only in town or local court records, few have been identified.

MEMORANDUM OF REAL ESTATE 1825–1833, CORRECTED TO OCTOBER 1833

vid. post.	One half the Farm in Salisb[ur]y—vid E[zekiel]
	W[ebster']s deed to me of Oct. 6. 1828——5,500
Sold	Farm in Pittsfield, on which Josiah
	White[1] lives—
	Vid David Fogg's deed to me
	Decr. 6. 1825———— 1000——
Sold. vid post.	House & land, in Plymouth,
	N. Hamp—mortgaged to me
	by Danl. Ladd,[2] Sep. 26. 1825.—for 1000——
	vid his deed to me, & S. C. White's
	deed to him.
	He has abandoned right of redemption,
	but whether he has formally quitclaimed,
	I do not know—
Sold. vid post.	Store at Lechmere Point—now occupied by
	Mr Hastings—subject to a Mortgage of 1000—
	Dlls to Mr Taylor—
	bot of S. Hartwell—see Deeds—Mr. [Henry Willis]
	Kinsman knows the circumstances
vid post.	One undivided third part of the Township of
Sold	Dixville; Jeremiah Gerrish owning ⅔rds—
	—excepting a few lots we have sold——
Sold. vid post.	House and Land in Salisbury—mortgaged to me
	by I[srael] W. Kelly— $1000—
	Note & mortgage were sent to E[zekiel] W[ebster]—
	—I.W.K. is ready to quitclaim—

Nov. 24. 1830. Memo.—
        I have sold the land in Plymo, mortgaged
to me by Danl Ladd. The notes for the purchase money
are in the hands of N. P. Noyes Esq. Plymouth—
Oct. 1833. Money due on these notes recd.
        I have also conveyed the land in Salisbury,
mortgaged to me by I[srael] W. Kelley.

Sold

Jereh. Gerrish & myself have made partition of Dixville; vid his deed to me, on file; & we have both agreed not to sell, but with mutual consent, for 5 years.

Octr. 1833. I own the whole farm, in Franklin, formerly Salisbury, having bought out my brothers heirs. I have added several pieces, bought from the estate of Wm. Hadduck.[3] I have sold the Lord's lot, so called being an outlying lot.

Octr. 1833. I have sold the land at Lechmere point to E.A. Hammond, for $3,000. 1000 cash, 2000 in 2 yrs, secured by mortgage. I am to pay Mr Taylors mortgage of 1000

AD. MWalB.

1. White was Webster's brother-in-law, being married to Grace Fletcher Webster's sister Bridget.

2. Probably the Daniel Ladd (b. 1773) who came to Plymouth in 1797 where he was a merchant and inn-

holder until his removal in 1813.

3. Hadduck or Haddock (1769–1828), of Salisbury, was Webster's brother-in-law by his sister Abigail. William was the father of Dartmouth College professor Charles Brickett Haddock.

FROM STEPHEN WHITE

Boston December 4 1833

My Dear Sir

I conclude by this time a letter will *hit* you in Washington. We have not yet heard of your progress farther south than New York, but we hope every day to see your arrival announced in the Intelligencer with more show of truth [than] its former declaration was entitled to. The public papers will tell you of our elections for representatives. Forty are chosen. Mr [John] Davis will probably be elected Governor but it is by no means certain. In the house there will be a large majority of nominal Nat. republicans but many of them will probably be *fence men* and ready to jump in any conceivable direction. Our city nominating committee have adopted as a candidate for Alderman [Josiah] Dunham[1] of South Boston a Jackson man, which is urged by many as an evidence of their abandonment of their distinctive national republican character. The chances are in favour of [Theodore] Lyman rather than [William] Sullivan as Mayor as I think. There is good news from Texas I am told: [José Antonio] Mexia,[2] [Lorenzo de] Zavala[3] & [Antonio López de] St. Anna[4] the first men in the government are principal stockholders in the land grants the conditions of which require all settlers to be Catholics, operating heretofore as a serious obstacle to Colonization. Americans are now by a recent law allowed to settle and another law is proposed to enable foreigners to hold land, which will convert the title of the grants into a fee simple tenure. I mention this as bearing on the value of stock in those companies.

Mr [Henry Willis] Kinsman & myself will address ourselves to the labour of making out my Naples claims as soon as he hears from you when they had better come forward.

I place on the other side a Memo of some enquiries which may lead to advantageous results if made soon.

Money is still severly scarce here. I am told *never more so.*

Ever dear Sir your devoted   Stephen White

Harriet[te Story White Paige] recovers very slowly

A survey and report made by Dr Thomas R. Gedney[5] of the U S Navy of the coast at the entrance of the River Atchafalaya in Louisiana and of the river itself in the office of the Commissioners of the Navy— made within a year—the particular object being to ascertain the quantity of Live Oak growing on Tyger or Tiger Island lying about 20 miles from the mouth of the Atchafalaya, and whether it is easily accessible by vessels for the purpose of taking it off

ALS. NhHi.

1. Dunham (1774–c. 1857), a cordage manufacturer in South Boston.

2. Mexia (d. 1839), Mexican army officer who supported the Texas revolution.

3. Zavala (1788–1836), Mexican landholder in Texas where the *empresarios* obtained colony grants after 1829. Though a general in the Mexican army, Zavala encouraged Texan resistance to Mexico and became vice president of the Republic of Texas.

4. Santa Anna (1795–1876), Mexican general, revolutionist, and president of Mexico, 1833–1835, who attempted to crush the Texas revolution, but was defeated by Sam Houston at San Jacinto on April 21, 1836.

5. Gedney (d. 1857), later lieutenant commander on the United States surveying brig *Washington*, which captured the *Amistad* in 1839.

TO NICHOLAS BIDDLE

Wednesday, 2 oclock.
[December 11, 1833]

Private

Dear sir

I recd. yrs, this morning,[1] & have already seen Mr. [Horace] Binney. We think it best to wait a while.[2]

The Bank defence is eagerly read[3] & I believe gives great satisfation. I have just heard Mr Jno Davis, a cool man, say, it is the most triumphant paper he ever read; & that it ought to be universally read. Other Gentlemen have spoken of it, in terms not less ardent. Yrs truly

D. Webster

ALS. DLC.

1. Biddle to DW, December 9, 1833, mDWs, wherein is contained a copy of the Bank memorial for Congress. Biddle asked for redress of the violation of the stockholders' chartered rights by Jackson's removal of deposits, stated that the Bank had faithfully performed the stipulations of the charter, and argued that Congress, and Congress alone, was the final judge in determining whether the Bank was entitled to the custody of public monies.

2. Binney presented the memorial on December 18, 1833, and it was published in *Register of Debates*, 23d Cong., 1st sess., p. 2207.

3. The *National Intelligencer* published a supplement, dated December 12, 1833, in which is contained the "Report of a Committee of Directors of the Bank of the United States."

Jackson's removal of the government deposits from the Bank of the United States brought into tenuous alliance the disparate elements of the opposition. Henry Clay, titular head of the National Republicans, and John C. Calhoun, theorist and political leader of the Nullifiers, had already formed a union of sorts when the tariff compromise was worked out at the beginning of the year, but Webster's support of the "Force Bill" brought him into vehement conflict with Calhoun, while his opposition to the tariff compromise had separated him from Clay. It was Webster's stand on both of these measures that had brought about an incipient rapprochement with Jackson, the extent of which continued to be a matter of prying speculation to adherents of all parties. Goaded, cajoled, and flattered by Nicholas Biddle, the great triumvirate, each suspicious of the others and each concerned to know how his own personal ambition might be served by this unnatural coalition, displayed their united power when the Twenty-third Congress met in December 1833, by securing committees hostile to the administration.

Committees of the Senate were originally selected by ballot of the senators themselves. The rule was first changed in 1823, when the Eighteenth Congress met in an atmosphere of such bitter sectional and partisan controversy that it was transcended only by giving the power of appointment to the Vice President. Three Congresses later, in 1829, the rule was changed once more because leading Jacksonians did not trust the party loyalty of Vice President Calhoun. This time the appointment of committees was assigned to the President of the Senate pro tem, whose partisanship was presumed beyond question. On motion of Peleg Sprague of Maine, the selection of committees was now returned to the Senate. Calhoun refused any committee assignment, and Clay accepted only the fifth position on Public Lands. Webster, however, actively sought and received chairmanship of the Committee on Finance, to which the key issue of the session would be referred. His margin of

victory, on a third ballot, was 22 votes to 13 for Silas Wright, the ad-
ministration candidate, 2 scattered, and 11 members absent or not vot-
ing. The other four members of the committee, chosen by plurality only,
were John Tyler of Virginia, Thomas Ewing of Ohio, Willie P. Mangum
of North Carolina, and William Wilkins of Pennsylvania. All but Wilkins
opposed Jackson's financial policy.

TO EDWARD EVERETT

friday morning
[December 13, 1833]

Dr Sir,

I think it would be well if you should happen accidentally to fall in
with Mr [Nathaniel] Silsbee, *today.* His feelings, I believe, are quite
right, but it [would] do good to confirm & strengthen them. It would be
a prevailing suggestion (& very properly so) with him, that any promotion of the Chief of the Nullifiers by *our* votes, would appear *extraordinary*, to the people of Mass.

—One idea has occurred to me, which you may suggest, or not, as you
think proper, to Mr C[lay]¹ or to Mr Silsbee. It is this—

I am commencing a new term. If I am to stay here, it wd. be desirable
that I should occupy a place which should connect me with the business
of the Senate, for the future, conspicuously. Such a place is the head of
the Com[mitt]ee of Finance. Supposing *some* alterations, not favorable,
to take place in the Senate, next Congress, still, it is *possible* that the
situation, if now bestowed, might be *retained*. This wd. be no small
advantage.

I hope you have the good pract[ice] of burning, instanter, such notes
as this.

AL. MHi.

1. Faced with a multiple choice of
"C's," the editors have chosen Clay as
most likely in all circumstances. The
Kentuckian, whatever his personal
feelings might then be, would certainly have a stronger partisan interest in seeing Webster at the head of
the Finance Committee than would
Calhoun, Chambers of Maryland, or
Clayton of Delaware, although all of
these were associated with the new
coalition. The allusion in the first
paragraph is probably to a National
Republican offer to make Calhoun
chairman of the Committee on Foreign Relations. Willie P. Mangum,
himself a member of both Finance
and Foreign Relations, says, "Calhoun absolutely refused to go in for
Webster—and altho he (Calhoun)
w'd have been elected at the head of
the Commee. of Foreign Affairs, he
said, as the whole matter seemed to
be a matter of arrangement, that he
wd not accept, and insisted strongly
upon considering it in the light of an
injury, if his friends shd. vote for
him." Mangum to Governor David L.
Swain, December 22, 1833, in
Shanks, *Mangum Papers*, 2:56.

FROM NICHOLAS BIDDLE

Phila. Decr. 15th. 1833.

My dear Sir

I received your favor of the 13th. inst. & after reading it committed it to the flames.[1]

The closing paragraph is one of the highest importance to you as well as to the Country. I only repeat what I have said again & again that the fate of this nation is in the hands of Mr Clay Mr Calhoun & yourself. It is in your power to save us from the misrule of these people in place, but you can only do it while you are united. It is for that reason that every honest man is anxious that you three should not be alienated from each other, and that every thing you all do is watched & canvassed with intense anxiety. You can scarcely imagine how often and how earnestly the few casual phrases which have passed between Mr Clay and yourself have been criticised & weighed, one side in hope, & the other in fear, of finding something to indicate estrangement between you. For all our sakes, do not let this grow into any difficulty. If great talents are sometimes mislead by great passions, there are fortunately still greater talents which can subdue these passions. So let your prudence save the country from the indiscretions of others, if you see any.

Having made my sermon, let me conclude with the best regards of Yrs   N. B.

LC. DLC.
  1. No copy of this letter has been found.

TO [JOSEPH HOPKINSON]

Washington Decr 18 33.

Private

Dear Sir,

Will you do me the favour to read the reasons of the Secretary,[1] of which I send you a copy, and give me your thoughts on one or two topics.

  1st. What is the evidence, or argument, to show, that the power of the Secretary is limited to a case of *danger*; and that it does not spread over the whole wide field of political discretion?

  2d. Are there contracts between Mr [Roger B.] Taney and the State Banks, binding contracts; that is, had he authority to bind the U.S. & had the Directors of the State Banks authority to bind their corporations in this manner?

I do not wish to tax you for a *disquisition* on these points, but am desirous of knowing how they strike you at first sight. An early answer to this will oblige me, though I pray you not to give yourself trouble, nor let this request encroa[ch] on your valuable time. Yours always truly,

Danl Webster

ALS. PHi.
1. "Report from the Secretary of the Treasury, on the removal of the Public Deposites from the Bank of the

United States," *Senate Documents*, 23d Cong., 1st sess., Serial 238, Doc. No. 2.

TO NICHOLAS BIDDLE

Thursday Morning
Decr. 19. 1833

My Dear Sir

I am obliged to you for your sermon, & will hope to profit by it.[1] I mean to keep extremely cool, myself, but I fear the temperature of others will rise, higher & higher. At present, there is no coolness whatever, between those whom you would expect to see acting together. Some little difficulties were found, in arranging the Com[mitt]ees, but they were overcome, by mutual & friendly arrangements.

The President has nominated, for Bank Directors, Jas. A[sheton] Bayard, of Delaware, in place of Saul Alley,[2] of New York, & the three Philadelphia Gentlemen, now Directors,[3] & Mr [Hugh] McEldery,[4] of Baltimore. To Mr Bayard, I suppose nothing can be objected. The other Directors have given a good deal of dissatisfaction, certainly, by their proceedings & their memorial;[5] but I suppose no good is to [be] expected from resisting their re-appointment. Two years ago, I was quite ready to oppose the appointment of two of them; but it was thought better to let them pass, unopposed.

If these persons should be rejected, others, not more fit, might be nominated, or, perhaps, no further nominations made, & an appeal taken to the People, against the Senate, as partizans of the Bank. It appears to me prudent to lay out our whole strength on the *measure*, itself, & to avoid as far as possible, every thing that looks like personal opposition to men, high or low. The less we connect our opinions with personal matters, the more & the greater will be their weight with the public.

I anticipate a warm attack, this morning, on one part of the Secretarys paper, by Mr Clay. He says he shall prove the Secretary has perverted &c, Mr Crawfords opinions &[c].[6] Yrs   D. Webster

ALS. DLC.
1. See above, Biddle to DW, December 15, 1833.
2. Alley was a wealthy New York

merchant. After Bayard declined the appointment, Jackson nominated Alley and he was later confirmed by the Senate.

3. John Sullivan, Henry D. Gilpin, and Peter Wager, all three of whom were rejected, renominated, and again rejected by the Senate.

4. McEldery or McElderry was a Baltimore merchant and frequent member of the Maryland Governor's Council after 1830. Like the three government directors named above, McEldery was renominated after a first rejection by the Senate on February 27, 1834, and was again rejected on May 1.

5. "Memorial of H. D. Gilpin, Peter Wager, John T. Sullivan, and H. McElderry, Government Directors of the United States Bank," *Executive Documents*, 23d Cong., 1st sess., Serial 254, Doc. No. 12, in which they complained of "an organized system of opposition on the part of the majority" of the board in handling the affairs of the Bank.

6. *Register of Debates*, 23d Cong., 1st sess., pp. 51–53. Secretary Taney in his report on the removal of deposits cited, as proof of his contention that he possessed exclusive power to determine when deposits should be removed, a letter of former Treasury Secretary William H. Crawford written to the president of the Mechanics' Bank of New York on February 13, 1817. Crawford wrote that the treasury secretary "will always be disposed to support the credit of the State banks, and will invariably direct transfers from the deposites of the public money in aid of their legitimate exertions to maintain their credit." Critics like Clay argued that Crawford never distinctly asserted the extraordinary and exclusive power over the deposits that Taney attributed to him.

FROM NICHOLAS BIDDLE

Phila. Decem: 20. 1833

My dear Sir

I received this morning your favor of the 19th. inst.—[1]and am rejoiced to hear the state of things in regard to a matter so anxiously watched by the Country.

Touching the nominations I wish to speak, as I always do to you, without reserve. After a great deal of reflection, & I hope, calm reflection, I think most decidedly that these people ought not to be confirmed.

They are people unfit to be there—unfit to associate with the other members—so that their colleagues will not confer with them—or act with them on Committees. Our friends in the Bank are extremely offended with them—it is a serious obstacle to going into the Bank as a Director to be obliged to meet these people, and the whole Board are very anxious to get rid of them.

A more important point is this. They have set themselves up against the rest of the Board whom they denounce—an issue is made up between them. If the Senate confirms them, it sanctions their conduct—it takes part against the Bank. It is the very case of Van Buren's rejection. Such a course would be very disastrous while the Institution is struggling for its existence & wants the support of all its friends. I do not think that the

Senate would lose in public estimation by it. I believe it would gain. I think at this moment when nothing is wanting but a rallying point against the administration, the more manifestations of strength—positive strength, that can be given by the Senate—the better will it be for that body as well as the Country. All our friends unite I believe in this sentiment—as they all hope for the rejection of [Roger B.] Taney & the Govt Directors.

We are not afraid of any change for the worse. You were right two years ago about them—your opinion then is the soundest opinion now.

Think of all these things & believe me Always ẏrs   N. B.

LC. DLC.   1. See above.

TO NICHOLAS BIDDLE

[December 21, 1833]

Private

Dear Sir,

I have thought it proper to write the enclosed letter; to which, however, you need give no attention, if you think it more *prudent* to wait a while. I shall not undertake, professionally, agt. the Bank, whether you answer this, or not. If such things have to go before the *Board*, I should prefer the subject should be *postponed.*—Will you tell me whether you apprehend any danger, from my writing to you, on account of infidelity in the P. Office—& tell me, also, if you are careful to burn *all* letters. Yrs   D. W.

ENCLOSURE: TO NICHOLAS BIDDLE

Washington Decr. 21 1833

Sir

Since I arrived here, I have had an application to be concerned, professionally, against the Bank, which I have declined, of course, although I believe my retainer has not been renewed, or *refreshed*, as usual. If it be wished that my relation to the Bank should be continued, it may be well to send me the usual retainer. Yours with regard,   Danl Webster

ALS, with ALS enclosure, DW to Bid-   *respondence of Nicholas Biddle*, p.
dle, December 21, 1833. DLC. En-   218.
closure published in McGrane, *Cor-*

TO [STEPHEN WHITE]

Boston Decr. 21. [1833]

Dear Sir

I have had an anxious fortnight here, & do not see that the succeeding weeks are likely to be more quiet. The effect of the removal of the Deposites begins to be felt, by the Banks, & by individuals. Meantime, the majority for sustaining the measure, in the House, as far as we can judge at present, is resolute & determined. It is, however, not a large majority. Almost all the *South* will go for the restoration of the Deposites. The weight that bears down any thing, is New York, New Jersey, New Hampshire, & Maine. The Delegation of these States, together, is large, & it is nearly unanimous. Add, too, Tennessee, which is nearly all of a sort. These constitute the main strength of the party, on this question. In the Senate, a majority of 5 or 6 will be against the removal, and in favor of a restoration. But if both Houses should pass a Resolution, such as Mr. [George] McDuffie proposes,[1] it would be *vetoed*; & there is no chance of getting two thirds, unless in consequence of some great shock, to the business of the Country. So that I hardly see where relief is to come from. I came here, as you know, with a strong desire to avoid taking any course, particularly hostile to the Administration. But its conduct, in this business of the Bank, is such that opposition seems unavoidable, whether it avail any thing or not. *What can be done?* Can you think of any thing?

We had a good deal of difficulty in arranging our Com[mitt]ees in the Senate. At one moment, I thought we might break; but at last, friends came to an understanding. On some points, I found it necessary to be decided.

In regard to other matters, not much has been said. The Bank subject absorbs all the attention of every body. I believe it is intended by our friends to postpone the vote, on the motion now pending, for some days, if they can, to see what course things take in the large Cities. It is said *all* the Banks in Philada., *Girard* included, will petition, in all probability, for a restoration.

Our domestic relations have been disturbed by the death of our Landlady.[2] I hope, however, some house keeper will be found, & that we shall get along, without much interruption. We hear today of the Cols [Thomas Handasyd Perkins'] removal to Summer Street, both by your letter[3] & one to him.[4]

I will write you again soon, perhaps on Monday. I fear you suffered much, your way, by the Storm. We have not yet heard. Yrs   D. W.

ALS. DLC.

1. McDuffie had engineered a motion on December 10 by which Taney's report on the removal of deposits was ordered to be referred to a Committee of the Whole House rather than to James K. Polk's pro-Jackson Ways and Means Committee. *House Journal*, 23d Cong., 1st sess., Serial 253, p. 31. Approval of the motion allowed pro-Bank congressmen to debate at length the issue of Presi-

dential authority to remove the deposits. Realizing his mistake, Polk attemped to have the report returned to Ways and Means, and on December 19, McDuffie added a motion on Polk's motion which provided that all public revenue "hereafter collected shall be deposited in the Bank of the United States, in compliance with the public faith, pledged by the charter of the said bank." *Register of Debates*, 23d Cong., 1st sess., p. 2222.

2. Webster's landlady, a Mrs. Thompson, whose boarding house was opposite the Center Market in Washington, died on December 14 after a lengthy illness.

3. Not found.

4. Not found.

FROM ALEXANDER HILL EVERETT

Boston Dec. 24. 1833

Dear Sir

Since I had the pleasure of writing to you[1] we have got through with our municipal Elections the result of which must, I think, have surprised you, and may have some bearing, though I hope not much on general politics. The nomination of Mr [William] Sullivan, though on some accounts very proper was on others rather unfortunate. It was well understood that the Anti-Masons were ready to concur on any candidate not particularly exceptionable to them. Unfortunately Mr. S. by some proceedings in the House of Representatives some years ago and by his recent movements at the Worcester Convention had incurred their dislike and they could not be brought to vote for him. This was pretty well known beforehand by the nominating Convention & some efforts were made to induce other gentlemen—such as Mr. [Samuel T.] Armstrong and Mr J[ohn] C[hipman] Gray,[2]—who, [it] is now thought, would be more agreeable to the A. M.'s to accept the nomination,—but without effect. I am not sure however that any other candidate could have succeeded although some might have obtained a larger vote than Mr. S. did. The Masonic portion of our friends, anticipating that the regular nomination would be made with a view to the concurrence of the A. M.'s, determined to forestall any such movement by coming forward in advance in support of Gen. [Theodore] Lyman. With their support and that of his military friends and a number of independent gentlemen who acted merely from whim or personal preference the General was secure in any event of nearly half the regular voters of our party, who, with the Jackson men to trade theirs, would have carried him in over any opponent. The result affords little or no evidence of any progress of pure Jacksonism but has an indirect tendency to aid that cause;—to what extent the course of future and in some respects contingent events will determine.

The precise strength of parties in our General Court cannot be ascertained with certainty until after the opening as there are a great many new members. It is supposed however that there will be a majority of about fifty in the H. of R's in favour of Mr [John] Davis.

[Richard] Haughton³ did not go on to Washington at the time when it was reported that he intended to go and is still here. His paper has been much more temperate and reasonable since the result of the Election in this city. Indeed the only appearance of waywardness was in a passage in an article purporting to be a letter from Washington containing some not very proper allusions to you. As they were rather obscure and were probably not felt by the public at large it was not thought expedient to give them importance by a formal notice. A gentleman called privately on H[aughton] to inquire into the meaning of it and was told by him that he had read the letter very hastily before he published it and did not perceive that there was any allusion of the kind. It is well understood that the letter was written here by himself.

In preparing an article on Hamilton's Men & Manners in America I have taken occasion to extract for publication in the N. A. Review the passage relating to you.⁴ It is written in an exceedingly favorable tone and comes with more effect in a work which bears throughout the marks of strong prejudice against this country. The papers here, and elsewhere speculate a good deal upon the course of the debates in the Senate, generally with an apparent disposition to support your views as far as they are known. The Courier of today has a very handsome article on that subject.

After the opening of the General Court next week I shall be able to inform you more particularly of the state of parties here. In the mean time, I remain with great respect dear Sir, very truly & faithfully yours

A. H. Everett.

ALS. DLC.

1. Not found.

2. Gray (1793–1881; Harvard 1811), lawyer and perennial member of the Massachusetts House of Representatives or Senate from Boston.

3. Haughton (1799–1841; Yale 1818), senior editor and major owner of the National Republican *Boston Atlas*. Earlier in the year, the *Atlas* had opposed any National Republican–Anti-Masonic coalition behind John Quincy Adams for governor and urged the course that was adopted by the National Republicans in nominating John Davis. The paper became an organ for Webster's Presidential aspirations in the summer of 1834 with the installation of John O. Sargent as associate editor. See Caleb Cushing to DW, August 9, 10, 1834, and DW to Cushing, August 13, 1834, below.

4. Thomas Hamilton (1789–1842), Scottish novelist and traveler. His book, *Men and Manners in America* (Philadelphia, 1833), was reviewed in the *North American Review* in January 1834 (38: 210–270). Everett quoted the passage about Webster in the review (pp. 255–257).

Philada. Dec. 25th 1834 [1833]

My dear Sir

I of course do not wish to see you engaged against the Bank in any case, and should therefore send the refreshment in question at once. But as you leave it to my discretion, I think it better to delay it for a short time—& for a reason which furnishes perhaps the best illustration of the necessity of abating the nuisance which now annoys us. The simple fact—so simple as to be a matter of course, of retaining counsel in a suit would be instantly perverted. If it were done by the Board it would be in the hands of the Editor of the Globe in forty eight hours—if by the Officers of the institution, it would not be there for a week—and the fact would be either immediately announced, or it would be treasured up to be used on the first occasion, when any vote of yours gave displeasure to that gang. The people who would do this are the same people who watch your account and the account of every political antagonist—who paraded in the Globe your visit to my house in the country and the discount to Mr [John] Connell at that time—who take no share in the affairs of the Bank, except to report & misrepresent every transaction of every individual opposed to them. Depend upon it these people should be expelled now that you have the power. Whilst they are here, I think it would be better to delay the matter in question for a short time.

Every body says that the Post Office in Washn. is faithless—but I know nothing—yet I generally have my letters addressed by other hands.

I always and scrupulously burn what I am requested to burn—otherwise not: so that you must dictate your wishes. With great regard Yrs

N. B.

LC. DLC.

Cambridge, December 25, 1833.

My Dear Sir:

I will with great pleasure give you the thoughts, which at present strike me in regard to the questions which you propose for my consideration.[1]

The first question may induce two views, one of which is strictly legal and the other political. In a legal point of view it does not appear to me, that the sixteenth section of the Bank charter[2] involves any other obligation, than that the deposits of the public money shall be made in the United States Bank, unless the Secretary of the Treasury shall otherwise order or direct. But there is no cause assigned for which he may remove, and therefore he has the whole discretion upon the subject as to cause

1. Daniel Webster, drawn and engraved by James B. Longacre, 1830.
Speeches and Forensic Arguments (3 Vols., Boston, 1830–1843), 1
(1830), frontispiece.

2. "Webster Replying to Hayne," by George P. A. Healy, 1851. Faneuil Hall, Boston, Massachusetts.

3. Robert Y. Hayne, engraving by J. B. Forest from an original drawing by J. B. Longacre. James B. Longacre and James Herring, *The National Portrait Gallery of Distinguished Americans* (4 Vols., Philadelphia, 1834–1839), 2 (1835), n.p.

4. Thomas Hart Benton, by Matthew Harris Jouett, c. early 1820s. The Cleveland Museum of Art, Cleveland, Ohio, Gift of Mrs. Otto Miller.

5. (top left) James Kent, by John Wesley Jarvis. Yale University Art Gallery, New Haven, Connecticut, Gift of Benjamin D. Silliman.

6. (top right) Joseph Story, by Chester Harding, c. 1830. Massachusetts Historical Society, Boston, Massachusetts.

7. (bottom left) James Madison, by Asher B. Durand, 1833. New-York Historical Society, New York City, New York.

8. (bottom right) Joseph Hopkinson, by Thomas Sully, 1835. Dartmouth College, Hanover, New Hampshire.

9. Henry Clay, by William James Hubard, 1832. University of Virginia Art Museum, Charlottesville, Virginia.

10. (top left) John McLean, by Thomas Sully, 1831. Pennsylvania Academy of Fine Arts, Philadelphia, Pennsylvania.

11. (top right) John C. Calhoun, by Chester Harding, 1832. The Berkshire Museum, Pittsfield, Massachusetts.

12. (bottom left) William Wirt, by Henry Inman. Boston Athenaeum, Boston, Massachusetts.

13. (bottom right) Martin Van Buren, by Henry Inman, c. 1835. New-York Historical Society, New York City, New York.

14. Horace Binney, by Thomas
Sully, 1833. Theodore F. Jenkins
Law Library Company, Philadel-
phia Bar Association, Philadelphia,
Pennsylvania.

15. John Sergeant, by Thomas
Sully, 1832. Theodore F. Jenkins
Law Library Company, Philadel-
phia Bar Association, Philadelphia,
Pennsylvania.

16. "Bank of the United States, Philadelphia," by William H. Bartlett
and engraved by J. Tingle. Nathaniel P. Willis, *American Scenery; or,
Land, Lake, and River Illustrations of Transatlantic Nature* (2 Vols.,
London and New York, 1837–1838), 2 (1838), facing 73.

17. Nicholas Biddle, by Rembrandt Peale. Brig. General Nicholas Biddle, Philadelphia, Pennsylvania.

18. Joel R. Poinsett, by Thomas Sully, 1840. American Philosophical Society, Philadelphia, Pennsylvania.

19. James Barbour, by Chester Harding. Virginia Museum of Fine Arts, Richmond, Virginia.

20. George McDuffie, by Charles Bird King. Redwood Library and Athenaeum, Newport, Rhode Island.

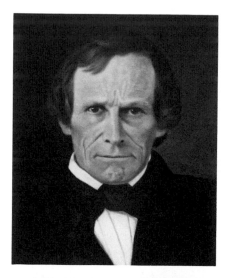

21. (top left) Isaac Hill, by Adna Tenney, 1852. Herbert W. Hill, Hanover, New Hampshire.

22. (top right) Levi Woodbury, by Chester Harding. New Hampshire Historical Society, Concord, New Hampshire.

23. (bottom left) John Davis, by Francis Alexander, c. 1830. Yale University Art Gallery, New Haven, Connecticut, Gift of Chandler Davis.

24. (bottom right) Nathaniel Silsbee, by Chester Harding, 1833. State House, Boston, Massachusetts.

25. Andrew Jackson, by Asher B. Durand, 1835. New-York Historical Society, New York City, New York.

and object, provided only, that he acts *bonâ fide*, and not with intent to evade the provision. I cannot, therefore, as a lawyer, see any ground upon which to place his right, as one limited to the case of danger to the security of the deposits. The law has confided to him a great trust, which it supposes he will perform with fidelity. Both parties have made his discretion the *casus foederis*, and he may act upon his own honest discretion, for any thing I can see in the Act, and he is justified, so far as the terms of the Act are concerned. The only check upon his discretion is, that he must assign the reasons to Congress, who, of course, are thus placed in a situation to revise or review the decision if they please. But I think, (and in this I differ *toto coelo* from Mr. Taney) that it is a purely personal trust in the Secretary, and as much so, as if it had been confided to the Chief Justice of the United States. It has nothing to do with the ordinary duties of his department. The power grows not out of any general authority, given by other laws, but it is, as between these parties, for this purpose, a special umpirage created by the Act, and binding as a part of the contract. It is no answer to say that, if the section had not been there, he might, in virtue of his general authority, have controlled the public funds at his pleasure. *Pro tanto*, this Act modifies and restrains such authority. It is an appeal to him to act, as a special agent selected by both parties, when he decides. I think, then, that the President has not the slightest right to interfere with the business. It is taken out of the sphere of Executive action. It belongs to the Secretary and to him alone, and any interference by the President to control or influence his judgement, much more to deter him from exercising his judgement, is, on the part of the President, a departure from his duty, and if the Secretary acts upon the opinion of the President, and not upon his own, I think he virtually violates the charter and abandons his trust.

So far as to the legal view. But politically, I think the charter manifestly contemplated, and so was understood by all parties, that the deposits should not be withdrawn by the Secretary, except for high and important reasons of state, upon unexpected emergencies, and cases where the action of Congress could not be obtained until after it was necessary to act. The whole history of the charter shows this understanding, and in a political point of view it strikes me as wholly indefensible to remove the deposits, unless some pressing case of this sort is made out. It is curious enough that the Secretary insists that the power belongs to him independently of the Act of Congress, and yet contends, that Congress cannot direct the withdrawal; but he may. How can this be, if he is not the chosen agent of both parties by the contract? Congress may certainly repeal or modify his general powers. I agree with him that Congress could not remove the deposits without his consent; but I think they may require them to be restored without his consent. They may prevent his acting in favor of themselves, but they cannot act against the Bank without his consent, and through him.

As to the other point, I do not know precisely what are all Mr. Taney's arrangements with the State Banks. But supposing them to be that he will permanently make deposits, and they shall be the permanent depositaries of the public funds, upon their agreeing to remit them from place to place as he shall require, and that they shall in some sort be bound for each other, which I merely conjecture, from his report, to be the terms, I should say unhesitatingly, that he has no authority to bind the United States, and that the State Banks had not (as far as I know the nature of their charters) any authority to make such contracts. I am sure the Massachusetts Banks have no such powers. Nor do I believe either the State government or the stockholders would ever assent to such conditions. The State Banks may receive deposits of the United States, as they do those of other Banks. But they cannot make any sort of contract as a consideration of those deposits; they can only contract within the ordinary limits of common banking usages. My views, in short, are these: —

1. The Secretary is the chosen agent or umpire of both parties, as to removal or non-removal.

2. His discretion is not limited to cases of danger to the deposits, but extends over the whole field of political discretion.

3. He must *bonâ fide* exercise it independently and for himself.

4. The President has no right to interfere in the business in any shape.

5. If he does, and the Secretary acts in pursuance of his orders, influence, or control, and without an independent exercise of his own judgment, he violates his trust. It is a wrong to the Bank and to its rights.

6. The State Banks have no proper authority to enter into such contracts, as are stated, and the Secretary has as little right permanently to bind the United States in any arrangements of this sort. It is beside the common duties of his office, and requires express authority.

I write you in very great haste, and merely my first thoughts, being overwhelmed with business, and driven to the top of my speed. Yours always, most affectionately,   Joseph Story.

Text from William W. Story, ed., *Life and Letters of Joseph Story* (2 vols., Boston, 1851), 2: 155–158. Original not found.

1. Evidently Webster wrote Story a letter similar to that to Joseph Hopkinson, December 18, 1833, above. The Story letter has not been found.

2. "*And be it further enacted*, That the deposits of the money of the

United States, in places in which the said bank and branches thereof may be established, shall be made in said bank or branches thereof, unless the Secretary of the Treasury shall at any time otherwise order and direct; in which case the Secretary of the Treasury shall immediately lay before Congress, if in session, and if not, immediately after the commencement of the next session, the reasons of such order or direction." 3 *U.S. Statutes at Law* 274.

FROM JOSEPH HOPKINSON

Philad. Decemb. 27. 1833

My dear Sir

The removal of the Deposites continues to be an encreasing subject of public anxiety, because the belief is universal that the distresses and embarrassments which now affect the operations of every class of our Citizens are owing to that monstrous movement, and that they would cease or be greatly mitigated if the revenue was restored to its lawful place of deposit. A report has currency here, said to come from D[r. Joel Barlow] Sutherland, that a majority of the House will be in favour of this restoration, but that the President will not yield to Congress on this point. Pennsylvania will immediately and vitally feel the effect of the present state of things, as her late loan of 2,000,000—payable in installments of $150,000 monthly cannot be paid by the Contractors, and there is no other fund to satisfy the demands coming in for work done, or to go on with that which must be done. If this pressure should draw from our legislature a vote of instructions to restore the deposits, the effect might be decisive of the question. An attempt will be made by a leading Jackson man in New Jersey, for a similar movement in her legislature.

Altho I think, as I wrote to you, that the Secretary may change the place of deposit for any reason he may choose to act upon, & therefore that the legal efficacy of the act cannot be impaired by the insufficiency of his reasons, yet if he resorts to this extreme measure of his power, for reasons evidently futile & absurd, he becomes an object, most justly, of the severest animadversion & reproach. If his motives were corrupt he would be liable to trial and punishment. Suppose he had said to Congress that he removed the deposites because Mr Biddle is not six feet high—or is not his friend, I presume the removal would be absolute & legal, but how would you deal with the Secretary in such a Case. There is a great deal of feeling here about the re-appointment of the Government Directors, & the expression of opinion very strong against it. You have better means of judging than we, of the course that should be taken. It seems at least to be certain that the attempt to reject them should not be made without a common concert, strong enough to ensure success.

Did you receive my remarks on the *Scire facias*?[1] I think it a strong point of attack and a popular one, if any thing can be popular against General Jackson. We are all puzzled to imagine what has induced [Amos] Kendall to publish his letters to the Brokers in New York.[2] Surely there never was a more bold assumption of power in one holding an official station no higher than an Auditor. He really talks like a Viceroy over the King.

If you can spare a few minutes, let me have a few lines from you, as *confidential as you please.* Can you keep Calhoun quiet, until the Bank is disposed of? If you can sustain the Bank against the President—& pass the land bill in spite of him,[3] the dynasty will explode. All this may be done, and Congress will rise having restored the Constitution to the people, *and be blessed forever.* Yours mo. truly   J. H.

ALS. DLC.

1. Apparently a reference to Hopkinson's reply to Webster's letter of December 18, printed above. The reply has not been found.

2. The letters first appeared in the *New York Standard*, an administration paper, and were thereafter published in *Niles' Register*, 45 (December 28, 1833): 299–300. Kendall's intention in publishing the letters was to show that no collusion existed between the Kitchen Cabinet and certain Wall Street brokers, but critics charged that they demonstrated an intention to crush the Bank by removal of deposits, that the Bank was not insolvent as the Jacksonians had been saying for months, and that the new system operated much less efficiently and at greater cost than had the Bank.

3. On December 10, Clay had reintroduced the land bill vetoed by Jackson the previous session. The bill provided for distribution of revenue from land sales to the states, in proportion to their representation in Congress, without restriction as to use. The intent of the bill was to keep prices high. It was not acted upon at this session of Congress.

FROM STEPHEN WHITE

Boston December 27 1833

My Dear Sir

I have been fully, and painfully aware of the difficulties of your situation and know full well that you must as you say, in yours of 21st instant,[1] have passed an anxious fortnight. The mad pranks of old Andrew under the influence of the Cabinet improper and of his natural recklessness, throws everything into the worst possible position. How we are to get out of it remains to be seen but I cannot but hope you will keep the even tenor of your way and avoid committal as much as possible. There is an excellent article today in the Atlas. I send the paper by this mail.

I do not doubt that tone of feeling will ultimately prevail here. Mr. C[lay] must and will commit himself ere long. He cannot touch pitch without being defiled and the moment the union between himself and Calhoun is more distinctly seen your friends will move here in solid column. [David] Henshaw came home yesterday. He affects to believe that the U. S. Bank, finding the deposites are not to be restored and having great ability to discount, will soon shell out freely and relieve the public distress. I think however from some appearances that he is a good deal frightened notwithstanding his confident tone. The Jackson people here, the best class of them I mean, lament deeply the course taken by the General as tending to drive into opposition those whose talents and influence would otherwise have been a tower of strength to the Administration. I write in great haste but am Ever truly & devotedly Yours

Step. White

ALS. NhHi.   1. See above.

TO CHARLES HENRY THOMAS

Washington Decr. 28 '33

Dear Henry,

I have recd. yr letter of the 22.[1] Am glad you have bought another small piece of wood land. It will be well to embrace such opportunities, when they occur.

I hardly know what to say about the mode of keeping the kelp. If the ground were open, it would be best to spread it, & plough it in, at once. The question is, whether what it loses goes into the earth, or into the *air* —if the latter be the case, then spreading will make the matter worse. Suppose you cover up the heaps, with earth? I incline to think this would be the best mode, but do not know. Perhaps it decays faster, in quantities, than when spread. I am not well enough acquainted with the subject to advise—& must leave it for you, with the best advice you can get. I should think a layer of kelp, & then a layer of earth, would be as likely as any way to preserve it.

Mr [James William] Paige writes me that Mr [John] Welles[2] has sent down the calves. As they are *presents*, they must be well kept. Pray do not let them be checked, in their growth, for want of milk. I suppose you will have milk, plenty, a month or two hence. Meantime, if necessary you must buy another cow in milk—to be wet nurse to the Welles calves. Yrs   D. W.

ALS. MHi.   2. See above, DW to [Henry Willis
    1. Not found.   Kinsman, January 1830], note 1.

TO NICHOLAS BIDDLE

Jan. 2. '34
4 oclock P. M.

Dr Sir,

Mr [Thomas Hart] Benton commenced his Speech today.[1] It was much in his usual style. He stated a vast many things abt. the Bank—in a very round manner—which I do not suppose are correct, & which it is yet an infinite labor for a stranger to set right & explain. He is infinitely laborious—always with the documents—& has ability eno[ugh] to make the most erroneous statements plausible. I wish it were possible that Mr [Samuel] Jaudon, Mr [Joseph] Cowperthwaite, or some other Gentleman, well informed in all these particulars of the Bank operations, could be here, for a week or fortnight. It wd. be of very great utility, in any event. Whether we succeed in restoring the deposites, or not, it is of great importance that, in the progress of the Debates, no unfounded statement agt. the Bank should go unexplained.

This Discussion, it appears to me, must have very great effect on the general question of the rechartering of the Bank. The present distraction & distress ought to be used efficiently for the purpose of carrying home the conviction of the necessity of the Bank, as a permanent measure. In order to this, every misstatement should be corrected, & all false impressions removed; and again, in order to this last, some body is wanted, to be at hand, ready & competent to explain every thing.

I have not seen Mr. [Horace] Binney, since his return. Our duties occupy us. I suppose he is busy, & am sure I am; & the difficulty of frequent interviews prevents me from knowing all that he might tell me.

The Com[mitt]ee [on Finance] have agreed to recommend the appt. of Mr [James A.] Bayard,[2] the next time the senate goes into Executive business. The other Gentlemen will not be reported on, for the present. In conversation with a friend of the Adminis[tration], today, he sd. he supposed their fate would probably depend in the vote the Senate might give on the main question,—an idea, which I did not discountenance.

I am putting my own notions on paper, with some industry—but Heaven only knows when the subject will devolve on my hands. If I have time tomorrow, I will give you a short abstract of what I intend.

Please hand the enclosed[3] to Mr. Cowperthwait, &, if necessary, confer with him, thereupon. Yrs D. Webster

ALS. DLC.

1. *Register of Debates*, 23d Cong., 1st sess., pp. 97–139. Benton continued on January 6 and 7, denounc-ing Clay's resolutions of December 26, which censured the President for assuming "the exercise of a power over the treasury of the United

States, not granted to him by the constitution and laws, and dangerous to the liberties of the people."

2. As a government director of the Bank.

3. Enclosure not found.

TO [NICHOLAS BIDDLE]

Washington
Tuesday. 12 o'clock
[January 7, 1834]

Private

Dear Sir.

I wish to know yr thoughts on a few questions:

1. Does the cause of the Country gain, or lose, by the protraction of the Debate, in the Two Houses?
2. Is it better to delay the decision, than to have it pronounced agt. us?
3. What do you think of the propriety of proposing the <following> enclosed Resolution?[1]

The question is twofold:

   1. As this proceeding would necessarily delay the final vote of the Senate, would it not, in that aspect, be prejudicial?

   2. If we could get a Series of sound, practical opinions, on these points, wd. they not be of value *hereafter*, when the question of renewal shall arise.

Just tell me what you think, of these things.

Mr. [Horace] Binney is expected to speak today.[2]

Yrs   D Webster

ALS. DLC.

1. Enclosure missing. It is not altogether clear whether the resolution referred to was Webster's or someone else's, but the substance of it is discussed in Biddle's reply on January 8, below. Webster was still pursuing his own course on the removal question.

2. *Register of Debates*, 23d Cong., 1st sess., pp. 2320–2364. Binney spoke for three days, starting on January 7, on the removal of deposits.

TO [LEVI LINCOLN]

Washington Jan 8. [1834]

My Dear Sir,

We have recd the account of the manner of filling the [Massachusetts] Senate; & that is our latest intelligence from your quarter. We, of course, considered it a thing settled, that we are to lose Mr [John] Davis,[1] from our circles in this place. He will leave us, with a very high degree of regard, from all parties.

I trust, My Dear Sir, I may flatter myself, that his place will be filled by *yourself*.[2] Hitherto, I have said nothing on this subject to *you*, tho I have conversed on it often, with others. I am sure, there will be no objection to that arrangement—there can be none—unless you raise one yourself. This, I trust, you will not do. I am aware, that your standing & character & the place you have filled, so long, so usefully, & so honorably, fully Entitle you to a seat in the other House of Congress, should such be your choice. It is now six years, as you will remember, since I first expressed to you my sincere wish to see you in that situation. Under present circumstances, I hope you will see no objection to being Mr Davis' successor here, as he is yours, in another place. I desire, at this critical & exigent moment, to see *Massachusetts* as strong here, as it is possible to make her. The country, in my opinion, is in a condition of great danger. It would take an hour to say to you all I think, & all I feel, in regard to that danger; & I will not now venture on it. It will probably be one of "Govr Davis' " first acts to appoint the earliest legal day for the choice of his successor; & I ardently hope to see *you here*, before several of our important questions, now pending, be settled.

I do not know whether we are promoting the public interest by postponing the decision of the deposite question. If there be any chance, (of which I can hardly judge) that external pressure will be so great, as that Congress cannot resist it, then we gain by delay. Otherwise, perhaps, this uncertainty of our present state may be regarded as worse than the worst reality. But, even in this view, what certainty can we arrive at? If the Deposites be not to be restored to the U. S. Bank, *what then? Can Congress adjourn, leaving things where they now are?* Va. is expected to come out agt. [the] Admin[istration] on this point. The Bank of Va. has, by direction of the Stockholders, *rescinded* its contract with the Treasury!³ Mr [Littleton W.] Tazewell is likely to be Gov. of Va. agt. the Administration Candidate. The election was yesterday.⁴

The present state of things in Mass is highly interesting. I feel its importance deeply. Mr [John Quincy] Adams expresses, & I am quite sure he feels it, an *earnest* desire to effect a reconcilation between the N[ational] R[epublican]s & the Anti M[ason]s. *Cannot the thing* be done?

You know Mr Davis' conciliatory sentiments, on that subject. Has it occurred to our friends to consider, how it would do to place one or two Anti Ms in the Council—for the purpose of manifesting a spirit of Union, & to shew that we have no secrets? I submit this thought, quite confidentially, to your reflection. *It is not wholly mine.* I think Mr Bayly [John Bailey], of Dorchester, is, among the Anti Ms, one of those most certain never to join our enemies. But, on this matter, you are likely to know better than myself.

Treat this letter as a conversation between us alone. Yrs truly

D Webster

ALS. MHi.

1. Davis resigned from the House on January 14, 1834, having been elected governor on January 9. See above, DW to Davis, September 30, 1833.

2. Lincoln was subsequently elected to fill the vacancy and took his seat in the House on March 5, 1834.

3. The stockholders of the Bank of Virginia (of whom the state of Virginia was one) rescinded the contract by which it served as a deposit or "pet" bank.

4. Tazewell was elected governor by the Virginia legislature on the second ballot over his closest rival, Edward Watts. Both were antiadministration, and both substantially outpolled Peter Vivian Daniel, the Jackson-Van Buren candidate.

FROM NICHOLAS BIDDLE

Phila. Jany 8. 1834
9 oclock P. M.

My dear Sir

I received a short time ago your favor of the 7th inst.[1] and sit down to give you the best opinion I can—adding that tho' the opinion be suddenly expressed, it has been deliberately formed by reflection on what is passing.

My opinion then is, that the reference, the power to send for persons &c and the Report by the Committee of Finance would not be advisable—would do no good and might do much harm.

As to facts and opinions, the sending for persons and papers would settle nothing—all sorts of opinions—nay all sorts of facts would be presented, and the Report would make no impression on the adverse party. This is not a question like the bullion question of England—to be examined at leisure as the basis of legislation for posterity. It is the incident that is now to be disposed of. Nor do I think it is at all material to the present question whether the Bank has or has not curtailed too rapidly— has made too great preparations to meet its enemies, or has not made enough. That is the question for the Bank and the Stockholders, nor does it necessarily belong to the question between Congress and the Secretary. I should be against all reference. Then as to the advantage of delay:

My opinion is that delay and the protraction of the debate in the Senate [House] would be very useful. Virginia will soon be roused— certainly New Jersey—probably Pennsa.—and all the impulses of popular opinion will be felt in the House.

In the Senate on the contrary, I do not think delay useful. If you can agree in the Senate to any resolution against the removal, the sooner you send it to the House the better.

I believe the true theory of the case is—for the Senate to act as soon as possible and the House to talk as long as possible.

But before the Senate acts, you *must make a Speech*, one of your calm, solid, stern, works, that crushes, like the block of your Quincy Granite, all that it falls on. I want that Jackson & Taney & Benton & all these people should fall by your hand. I wish you to do it for my sake. I wish you to do it for your own.

We are annoyed perpetually by the whispers of exultation which pass among these miserable people that Mr Webster is to come out for them. Only think now of [Reuben M.] Whitney's[2] writing here that it is perfectly settled that you are to leave your friends and go over to this gang. I wish to see some fair occasion on which you can dispel this illusion and demolish the whole concern.

To conclude, I would not refer or make report. I would make a Speech —then pass the resolution—send it to the House, and let them talk 'till they are forced to act by a pressure from abroad. Yrs very truly   N. B.

I enclose a copy of our "status in quo," which represents a very prosperous state of the concern.[3]

———

P.S. After pondering over this whole matter, I thought I would take the advice of our mutual friend Chas Chauncey,[4] so I went down and talked over the whole concern. He concurs entirely with me—and illustrates the insufficiency of sending for information by the fact that the Secretary of our Commonwealth, Mr. [James] Findlay[5] has been spending the holy days in Phila. where he has been eating a course of good dinners, and has gone to Harrisburgh with a firm belief that there is no pecuniary distress in Philadelphia.

LC. DLC.
    1. Printed above.
    2. Whitney (1791–1845), formerly a leading Philadelphia merchant and director of the BUS, was now a Jacksonian and agent for the "pet banks."
    3. Enclosure missing.
    4. Chauncey (1774–1849; Yale 1792), brother of Elihu Chauncey and a prominent Philadelphia lawyer.
    5. Findlay was a one-term Pennsylvania secretary of state from Westmoreland County. He was probably related to former Governor William Findlay.

FROM STEPHEN WHITE

Boston January 9 1834

My Dr Sir

I had the pleasure of receiving your letter of 6th last evening.[1] Today the Senate voted for Governor. Thirty seven votes were polled of which Mr [John] Davis had thirty, [Marcus] Morton four; Blank three. Of the votes for Morton, [William] Foster[2] of Suffolk gave one and three of the six antimasons gave the residue and three voted blank ballots. A committee of both houses was chosen to direct the mode of communicating the election to Mr Davis. A meeting is to be held tomorrow evening to consider the state of trade currency &c. A meeting I mean of the Merchants & Traders of Boston.[3] The object is as I understand it, to adopt certain resolutions prepared, under the authority of a preliminary meeting, by Mr Henry Lee. I signed the call for the meeting. This afternoon Mr [David] Henshaw called on me to state that the object was to promote the views of the Calhoun party, to which, as he said, Lee was strongly attached, and that the tendency was to drive you into strong opposition, by combining opinions of your own friends & Lees adherents, in such manner as to act authoratatively upon you. Many other things, he said, to which I replied that I had reason to know your resolution had been made up to avoid if possible, in the course you should adopt in the Senate, any opposition on mere party or local grounds to the measures of the administration: that the opinions & measures of the nullifiers were of so dangerous & monstrous a character that the preservation of the union and the maintainance of the legitimate power of the general government were with you paramount objects. Nothing, I told him, but such arbitrary and reckless measures as had recently been adopted in the removal of the deposites would shake that resolution, but that I feared, much as you desired to avoid it, you would be driven into uncompromising opposition. He urged many facts to show that the policy adopted by Genl. Jackson would ultimately receive the approbation of Massachusetts and alluded in a mingled tone of exultation and irony to the great accession their party would receive from the mad measures of the Antimasons. He wished me to propose to the meeting a convention of Bank directors to regulate the currency instead of Lees resolutions to restore the deposites or something like it. Of course I shall do no such thing. I told him moderation and a conciliatory course would have secured the acquiescence if not the support of many powerful and patriotic minds but now saw no course but that of decided opposition.

The editor of the Franklin Mercury is a son of the late Wendell Davis.[4] He was a delegate as I hear to the "young mens convention" and there met Duff Green who proposed to him to employ for him a Washington correspondent. This will probably explain why in a National Republican paper such a communication should appear. He has or will be written to on the subject. The money market is easier but still the comodity is exceedingly scarce. General rate 12% per annum. Ever truly yours

Stephen White

I am much gratified to recognize my friend Daniels "writing upon the wall." I hope to have more of it.

ALS. NhHi.

1. Not found.

2. Probably the William Foster (1772–1863) who became the Democratic and Anti-Masonic candidate for lieutenant governor in 1835 and supported Van Buren in 1836.

3. The meeting, originally scheduled for January 10, was postponed until the following day because of crowded conditions in the Old Common Council Room. That night, a large crowd "of all parties" met at Faneuil Hall "to obtain an expression of public sentiment in relation to the existing state of trade, occasioned by the deranged state of the money market." They adopted resolutions (mDW 44628) which Webster presented to the Senate on January 20.

4. Wendell Davis (c. 1776–1831), a former senator and sheriff of Barnstable County, was the brother of Isaac P. Davis. His son, referred to in the letter, was George Thomas Davis (1810–1877; Harvard 1829), a lawyer and newspaper editor in Greenfield, Massachusetts, who served as congressman from 1851 to 1853.

TO CHARLES HENRY THOMAS

In Senate, Jan. 10 1834

Dear Henry,

I recd this morning yrs, written last Sunday,[1] in the storm. We had also a very stormy day here, at the same time. Since then, some days of elegant weather have intervened, are now succeeded, in turn, by sleet & snow. It is probable, that by this time, you have a "white carpet spread all over the ground."

I see by your former letter[2] that you had slain the last beef ox. Fletcher told Edward, that the news from Marshfield was, that the *Bell* had fallen down, & come all to peices, & that the tongue had come out. But Edward remembered the story of killing the *Lion*, & was not to be caught again.

By this time you have recd my letter, with a remittance of $700.[3] It is my purpose to keep you in funds, so that you may push the winter & spring's work *right a head*. I fear we shall have little of your attention after the spring, & nobody knows where you may be next winter.

You seem to think you need more strength of team. In that case, I should think you had better buy a pair of middling sized oxen, such, and in such order, that having done a reasonable share of work, in the winter, & some part of the spring, might be put to pasture & make tolerable beef, by [ne]xt Xmas. This, I think, wd. be more economical than to buy a draft horse. Look round, therefore, for such a pair, if you think best, & buy them. If it should become necessary to buy a little hay, salt or fresh, please to buy it. The oxen must be all *kept well, & worked hard.* That is the only way to get the work done. All good farmers (I am an excellent farmer) instead of sleeping through the long winter, like bears, keep above the snow, & keep moving, & surprise the spring, when spring comes, by showing a great part of spring's work already done. I trust that every time the teams come up they bring loads of kelp, for the land in front of the House; tho' it is not so suitable manure, as some other sorts, for land about to be lain down in grass. I take *muscles* to be better, for that purpose, as being more lasting in their effects. Yet the kelp will help the oats, & the new springing grass; & will have *some* effect the next year. You know we must manure the ploughed land, over by the old orchard, in order to get another crop of corn, for the use of the cattle, as last year. Nothing could be better for this purpose, than kelp; & perhaps instead of dropping them in front of the House, sundry loads had better be taken over there, if the stock holds out on the beach, & you dont get all tired.

I send you a letter from Mr [John] Welles, relative to the calves.[4] It will take you some time to read it. Preserve it. Calves, descended from such renowned ancestors, must be well kept. Give them not only "hay tea," but milk also, & bread & butter too, if necessary. I have written this, while a Genl. is speaking,[5] & I am compelled to sit still; & to this cause you owe so long a letter.

Do not fail to write often. I believe Mrs. W. is about writing to yr mother. Yours always truly   D. Webster

How does the bull grow, & the calf, of last spring? How do the Shurt-liff heifers appear to like Marshfield? I perceive you have reduced the flock of sheep—all right.

ALS. MHi.
   1. Not found.
   2. Not found.
   3. DW to Thomas, January 4, 1834, mDW 11324.

4. Not found.
5. This apparently refers to an un-reported speech probably presented in an executive session of the Senate that met that day.

TO STEPHEN WHITE

Washington Jan 10, 1834

My Dear Sir,

I have not heard from you, for some days, nor have I any late letters from any body in Boston. By our last accounts, you had filled up the Senate. There our accts stop. Many things are transpiring, with you, which excite our attention, but the distance is such that we can hardly communicate our opinions, in season to be useful, even if they were en-titled to any weight. The general impression of friends here, is, & is strong, that a serious effort should be made to bring about a reconcilia-tion between our N[ational] R[epublican] friends, & those of the Anti m[ason]s, who retain their ancient political opinions & principles. I be-lieve we are all ready to express this opinion to all friends, & to urge them, respectfully, upon their consideration. I am sure the new Govr. [John Davis] will go to Massachusetts, under a full conviction of the importance of such efforts, & with a good deal of hope of success from them. I suppose, before you receive this, you will have made the new Council. If not, is there any objection to placing one or two Anti M. gentlemen at the Council board, say Mr. [John] Bailey, or Mr [Timothy] Fuller, or others?[1] Are we not, now to act, on the presumption that the Anti M. party, as a party, is henceforth to lose its identity; & on that ground, is it not wise to leave a wide door for the return of such as may prefer the association of old friends, to that of new ones? I beg to call your attention, earnestly, to this subject. *Somebody* must come forward & take a lead, in measures necessary to effect this reconciliation. Why should not *you* so come forward? Your position is favorable, & I feel little doubt of your success.

We are yet on the Bank. I do not know that things have greatly changed, as to the prospect of final results, since I wrote you last; except that external opinion is growing stronger & stronger. Va is, where you see her—in opposition, but I fear also, joining herself to *nullification*. It is one of the portentous evils of this attack on the Bank, that it disaffects a great part of the South, which, while it suits Jackson, goes right over to Nullification. Mr Calhoun sits here perfectly happy, in all appearance. And well he may so sit. He sees hundreds flocking to his standard, in consequence of these abominable measures.

Nothing seems to me, at present, more probable than that Mr. [Littleton W.] Tazewell will be brought out, as the Southern Candidate for the Presidency; & he will carry the whole South, if Genl. J. goes on, as he is now going, & tries, at the same time to keep his hand under Mr V. B's chin.

I recd. a letter this morning from William [James William Paige],[2] respecting this destructive Construction of the Secretary, on the cotton section of the late act. The subject was brought before the Senate today. You will see Mr Clay's remarks, & mine.[3] It so happens, I told him—it was one of my objections to his bill, that the Sec. *might* so construe it.

Adieu! for today. Always mo. truly Yrs   D. Webster

ALS. NhD.

1. Neither man was placed on the council. In the fall of 1834 Bailey ran as the Anti-Masonic candidate for governor but came in third behind Governor John Davis and Marcus Morton.

2. Not found.

3. *Register of Debates*, 23d Cong., 1st sess., pp. 200–201. Cotton fabrics under the tariff of 1832 were subject to a duty of 25 percent ad valorem with an additional duty in the form of minimums of 30 to 35 cents. The 1833 act provided for a biennial reduction of 10 percent upon all duties imposed by the previous act. Webster had argued at the time that it could

be interpreted to apply to the minimums as well as to the ad valorem
duties. Taney, following McLane's
construction, did indeed so interpret

the act, with the consequence that
duties on cotton fabrics plunged from
80 percent to 24.5 percent ad
valorem.

FROM LEVI LINCOLN

Boston Jany 11 1834
Saturday Evng.

My Dear Sir

I have just received your Friendly Letter of the 8th inst,[1] and altho as
a cautious and timid politician I should take time to consider in what
terms to reply to it, yet as a sincere and confiding Friend, I prefer to
give expression to the feelings and sentiments which it has induced. I
fully concur in your apprehensions of the critical state of our public
affairs. Neither the popular impulse produced by the Presidents tour,
nor the personal intercourse which I had opportunity to hold with another distinguished visitor, has, in any degree, shaken my confidence in
the soundness of those views of general policy, which you did me the
honor to present to my consideration the last spring, at Worcester, and
subsequently in an interview which I had the pleasure to have with you,
in Boston. In reference to my personal attentions to those public Func-
tionaries I endeavoured to discharge the courtesies which were due from
my station, without committing myself, in any respect, to their measures,
or yielding any thing of countenance to their political heresies, or personal aims. I make this remark not because it is at all called for by your
Letter, but that I may be distinctly understood, upon a subject, on which
many have been betrayed into inconsistency of conduct with their professed principles. I hold that the Administration is fast destroying the
peace, prosperity and happiness of this great Nation in the profligate
attempt to secure power in their own hands, and a transmission of it,
to favored and preferred Individuals;—that the Government is to become the *property* of men, and not to be an *Agency* responsible to the
People. In this sentiment, I have looked, with almost a single hope, to
that bold and patriotic spirit of resistance, which has hitherto withstood
the strides of despotism, and from the *Senate* Board sent to the remotest
corners of the Republic, the strains of constitutional law and liberty.

The loss of Mr [John] Davis, in the National Councils, I am well
aware cannot be supplied. Whatever the character, or supposed talents
of another might promise to the too partial anticipations of personal
friendship, his experience, peculiar temperament, and consequent influence are to be supplied by no one. It would certainly not be disagreeable to me, to endeavor, in some poor measure, to discharge the duties

of his place, if my Fellow Citizens should desire it, and my personal and relative duties would permit. But I lament the occasion to say, that I am constrained by a *necessity* paramount to the strongest suggestions of inclination, to suppress all thoughts of succeeding to Mr Davis. My private affairs have become, by neglect, greatly perplexed and embarrassed. With nine years of the vigor of life, I have sacrificed much of the little property, which earlier professional labors had accumulated, and I now go from public office, with impaired means of subsistence, and increased needs of exertion for the support of those who are dependent upon me. In a sense I *must* return to the Bar! It was my intention three years since, and now no alternative, approved upon proper considerations remains to me.

It needs not, My Dear Sir, that with you, I should urge other objections. But I might well add, that my election would be *contested*, and I yet do not hold myself so cheap, as to be willing to solicit popular suffrage. The Administration party could not be expected to acquiesce in my nomination—and the Anti Masons seem determined, that I shall not only be distrusted *in Office*, but that I shall be *followed to retirement*, by their unreasonable and injurious suspicions. The *Advocate* has already denounced the election of Mr Davis as an arranged provision for my accommodation,—and the AntiMasonic Paper at Worcester, has entered a caveat against the *"corrupt Bargain,"* and rallied to the opposition, the well trained and submissive ranks of this *political* party. The hostility of these Men is most unaccountable. I might say, with truth, that not *one* among *them* has labored more earnestly, nor with better effect, than I have honestly done, though by different means, to induce to the abandonment of the Institution of Masonry. This desirable end will yet be accomplished and it will then be seen who have been the most faithful in endeavors to remove this *Rock of Offense* from the Nation. Under present circumstances a *triparte* controversy is to be expected in the District, and he only should become a Candidate, who is willing to risk the humiliation of being brought before the public to be misrepresented and reviled, and to succeed, or be discomfited and ultimately abandoned, on the *chances* of the ballot. But I have troubled you, too far, on this subject of personal reference. As a private Citizen, whatever of capacity or influence I possess is pledged to the vindication of the political principles I possess, and the faithful support of the men in whom I confide.

The pressure produced by the Treasury arrangements is beginning to be severely felt among the whole country, in the *interior* no less than in the *commercial cities*. It will send a note of complaining to Washington, which must penetrate the very recesses of the Palace and cause the selfish and cold blooded misusers of power to quake with fear. Business is at a stand, enterprize repressed, the hand of industry paralyzed. Whether it be the Bank acting in necessary self protection, or operating by measures of vindictive hostility to the Government, the *effect* is the same, and in either case is chargeable upon the gratuitous and profligate policy of the Administration. There is *positively* much distress in the Country, and the most serious apprehensions, that it is to be still greatly aggravated. The merchants have held meetings, and their proceedings, which will shortly be communicated to you, will better express these sentiments, than any language of my own.[2]

The Papers must have anticipated me in any information I could give you of the issue of our Legislative Elections. We look now for the arrival of the *Governor Elect*, upon which, I shall immediately return to Worcester, where I hope to be honored and obliged by such communications from you, from time to time, as your convenience will permit.

The Council, contrary to *usual practise* which postponed the choice, until *after* the qualification of the Governor, was filled on *Friday last*. The only changes are in the substitution of Mr [James] Richardson[3] of Dedham for Mr [Josiah J.] Fiske[4] of Wrentham, Mr [Benjamin] Sheldon[5] of Berkshire for Mr [Henry] *Hubbard*,[6] and in assigning Mr [John R.] Adan's[7] seat vacated by his election to the Senate to Mr [James] Savage.

At the session of the Council *more than a month since*, a Warrant in your favor for $500—was sent to the State Treasury, to be recd on account of fees as Counsel of the Commonwealth in defense against the suit of Rhode Island in the Supreme Court.[8] I particularly requested Mr [Edward D.] Bangs[9] to give you notice of the fact. If the money has not been drawn for, it now awaits your order upon the Treasurer.

With renewed assurances of the most Faithful esteem and respect, most truly, Your obliged Friend and Servant   Levi Lincoln

If Mrs Webster is at Washington, I pray I may be indebted to you, for presenting to her my most respectful regards.

ALS. NhD.

1. See above.

2. See above, Stephen White to DW, January 9, 1834, note 3.

3. Richardson (1771–1858; Harvard 1797), Dedham lawyer.

4. Fiske (1785–1838; Brown 1808), Wrentham lawyer and former state senator.

5. Sheldon (d. 1840; Williams 1806), New Marlborough lawyer.

6. Hubbard (1783–1863), Pittsfield lawyer.

7. Adan (d. 1849; Harvard 1813), Boston lawyer.

8. *Rhode Island* v. *Massachusetts*, 12 Peters 657 (1838), the first in a series of cases involving this controversy.

9. Bangs (1790–1838), secretary of state for the Commonwealth of Massachusetts.

FROM NATHAN APPLETON

Boston 12 Jany 1834.

Dear Sir

We are quite in a quandary and alarm on account of the directions from the Comptroller of the Treasury to the collectors of the customs to enter cotton goods under the law of March 2d. at 24 1/2 per cent duty without regard to the minimum. Is it possible that Mr. [Louis] McLanes circular of 20 April covers up the opinions on which the direction is founded? I cannot find it—although I perceive a half shadow of it. I have written Mr. Clay somewhat at length on the subject—presuming it will be considered his part to make the first movement—which I suppose will be to call for the instructions issued by the treasury department for carrying into effect the law of March 33. But in case of this decision being made by the Secy of the Treasury, right or wrong, it seems to be the general opinion that there is no remedy but by a new explanatory law. In the excited state of parties, I should apprehend considerable delay if not actual difficulty in getting such a bill through the houses. Of course in this state of feeling the subject excites a good deal of solicitude.[1]

It would give me pleasure to hear from you at an odd leisure moment with some of the chit chat of the metropolis. I think you must be both amused & provoked at the liberties the letter writers talk with you. I have been most surprised to see how the editor of the Atlas could pick up a correspond[en]t amongst the nullifiers. I cannot give you the result of the Bank meeting last evening as I did not attend it having an ague in my face. And since yesterday morning we have a regular snow storm. Have you any idea that a change in the majority of the house can be brought about on the subject of the deposites? very truly, Your very ob. st.   N Appleton

My best respects to Mrs. W.

ALS. NhD.

1. The controversy was quickly resolved by new instructions from the Treasury, directing that duties be "calculated on minimum principle," thus cutting the reduction to 10 percent. *Register of Debates*, 23d Cong., 1st sess., pp. 202-203. McLane's letter of April 20, 1833, in which he devised a method for determination of ad valorem equivalents of specific duties, is published in *Senate Documents*, 23d Cong., 1st sess., Serial 239, Doc. No. 43.

TO [HENRY WILLIS KINSMAN]

Washington Jan 13. 1834

Dear Sir

I have recd the enclosed,[1] this morning. It wd. be a good thing, I think, for Mr [Peter Chardon] Brooks to write to Mr Bartlett [William Bartlet], or Mr [Jeremiah] Nelson, on the subject of my letter of yesterday.[2] It may be very probable that all the Newburyport Gentlemen are already engaged to Mr [Caleb] Cushing; if so, it is well. But if unengaged, very probably they wd. sign my paper. Of course, Mr. Brooks will not mention any thing of this letter.

Mr Charles Russell,[3] of New Bedford, has a claim, I believe a large one. You might write to him, saying you are connected with me, & that we should be willing to take the agency of his claim on the same terms as that of others. Yrs   D. Webster

Mr Russell has written me,[4] like many others, to press the indemnity.

ALS. NhHi. Published in Van Tyne, pp. 721–722.

1. Enclosure not found.
2. Probably his letter of January 11, mDW 11354. There Webster indicated that the French Spoliations Bill *"will assuredly pass the Senate,"* and asked Kinsman to make an agreement with Peter Chardon Brooks for the agency of his claims "& ask others to sign it."
3. Russell (1799–1836), a New Bedford merchant.
4. Not found.

FROM JOHN MCLURE

Richmond Jany. 14th 1834

Dr. Sir

Tommorrow or next day we will pass resolutions,[1] of a strong nature disaproving the course of the President in the removal of the Deposits. There is a large majority in favor of denouncing the act[ion] of the Prest. & Sect. so soon as passd. I will forw[ar]d you a copy.

I do assure you the change here is beyond any calculation, that can be expressd. Jacksonism & any hope for Van buren is at an end.

I hope you may get something done in regard to the safety of running Steam boats.[2] [I] would be glad to hear from you respectfully

John McLure

ALS. DLC. McLure (c. 1783–1874) was a Wheeling merchant and manufacturer, and president of the Old North Western Bank of Virginia. He was a Whig member of the Virginia House of Delegates at this time.

1. See above, Biddle to DW, August 30, 1833, note 1.
2. Webster spoke on the subject of steamboat accidents in the Senate on December 23. *Register of Debates*, 23d Cong., 1st sess., pp. 54–57. The Senate then resolved on Webster's motion "that the Committee on Naval Affairs he instructed to inquire into the expediency of passing a law for preventing, as far as may be, accidents to vessels employed in the foreign or coastwise commerce of the United States, from the explosion of steam."

FROM STEPHEN WHITE

Boston January 21 1834 7 P. M.

Dear Sir

I received your note of 15th marked "private"[1] the night before the last. Yesterday at one PM Mr [John] Davis arrived in the City. Last evening I called on him and not finding him at home left my card. Today I have been confined to my desk nearly the whole time and was unable to attend his inauguration which took place this forenoon. I am therefore yet entirely ignorant of the subject to which you allude. Today I got yours of 17th.[2] I am glad you think my haphazard Bank proposition was not *mal appropos*. It sleeps with the Committee (who are well disposed,) waiting events.[3]

You are to deal in your report with the currency question in all its bearings.[4] I venture two or three suggestions—and first, as to the Scarcity of money (sufficiently scarce then) which existed previous to the removal of the deposites. Is it not plain that from the prosperous state of trade and from the enhanced value of almost every species of property consequent thereon, a greater amount of circulating medium was requisite to represent the interchanges and transactions between man and man than was necessary before property acquired this increased value? It is not alone in this country that this is felt to be true. In England by advices, which I have today from Mess. Baring Bro & Co the same thing is taking place. There money is becoming scarce and goods are falling in value "in consequence of the heavy *promlets* (payments) bought at the high prices in August." Bread stuffs are a necessary of life. Money is the lifes blood of commerce. A defecit in the crops of ten, nay of five per cent, drives up the price of bread stuffs fifty per cent. This is admitted even by the most ignorant of the many wiseacres who write on political economy. A like deficiency in the currency, causes a like appreciation in the value of money. A wise government, comprehending this obvious fact, would have foreborne to increase this evil by any rash measures, like that of the removal; but would, if it were indispensible to destroy the Bank have waited until they could assail the Bank without striking through the sides of the people. In your strong and happy method of illustration, such points, if you agree in their truth, will *tell*.

Money with an occasional but rather unimportant variation from day to day is as severely scarce as ever. Last saturday, as they say in the Granite State, *beat all*. From 12 to 16% is the regular rate of discount for the best notes.

Mr. [Henry Willis] Kinsman is confined to his house by sickness. I called to see the *letter* but could not reach him.[5] I try again tomorrow Ever truly yours   Stephen White

I hear Gov. Davis' inaugural address spoken of in high terms. Nothing but necessity would have prevented my hearing it. Bad debts are multiplying and ones affairs require constant vigilance.

ALS. NhHi.

1. Not found.

2. Not found.

3. In the Massachusetts House on January 11 White had moved that the Committee on Banks and Banking consider and report on "the expediency of requesting" the Massachusetts congressional delegation "to use their efforts to procure the passage of a law to charter a new Bank of the United States." The scheme White suggested was designed to accommodate both the jealousy of the states against the existing Bank and the vested interests of its stockholders. Boston *Columbian Centinel*, January 15, 1834.

4. The report referred to can only be that of February 5, 1834, then in preparation, although the documents that constituted its justification— Taney's report giving his reasons for removing the deposits and Clay's resolution pronouncing those reasons to be "unsatisfactory and insufficient"— had not yet been referred to the Finance Committee. Webster probably began work on the business around the first of the year. The Treasury report on the state of the finances was referred to his committee on December 17, and the following day, on Webster's own motion, the appropriate portions of the President's message were also so referred. Debate on removal of the deposits continued from December 26, when Clay's resolution was offered, until February 4, when the treasury secretary's explanation and the Kentucky senator's rejection of it were formally referred to the Committee on Finance. Webster's report, obviously already written, came in the next day.

This sequence of events seems to reflect some of the mutual suspicion and maneuvering for position that went on among the leaders of the Whig coalition at this time. Clay would probably have preferred reference to a select committee, so arranged that the report would come from Calhoun, who as a member of the House had drafted the Bank's charter in the first place; but Webster wanted to make the report, and Biddle wanted Webster to make it. The combination was too powerful to oppose.

5. In his letter to Kinsman of January 11, 1834 (mDW 11354), Webster asked that it be shown to White after Kinsman had arranged to take agency of Peter Chardon Brooks' French claims prior to 1800. Webster thought White "would take pains to get [other] signers" if Brooks made an agreement.

FROM NATHANIEL PRIME

Hell Gate 26th. Jany. 1834

My Dear Sir—

Having been extensively engaged & intimately acquainted with the great financial operations of our Country for the last forty years, and being now wholly retired from the busy scenes of Wall St. to my little farm at Hell Gate, will you allow me in a few words to state what appears to me advisable in the present novel and alarming state of all our Banking Institutions—unless something is done before Congress rise to ward off the approaching evil. In the first place, I have ever considered a National Bank well administered, indispensably necessary, without which we *cannot* at all times sustain a sound currency. A renewal of the present Charter I consider out of the *question*. I would therefore propose a new charter for twenty years, with a capital of $75,000,000—which should embrace the present Bank of 35,000,000. The 24 states, if they chuse, to subscribe 20,000,000 in a state 5 p. ct. stock irredeemable for twenty years. The remaining 20,000,000 by individuals, fairly apportioned among the states. 75 mill[ion] is a less capital in proportion to the present business of our Country, than 35 mill[ion] was in 1816. No bonus, but let the respective states Tax the Capital of any Branch located in their State, the same as they Tax their own Banks. In order to do away constitutional objections, locate the Mother Bank at Washington—to be directed by a Board of Control or Governors composed of seven persons —five to be chosen by the Stockholders and two by the Government. The President of said Board to receive $10,000—per ann[um] and the other six $5,000 each—you must pay well if you would be well served—no one of these Directors to be allowed to vote by Proxy or otherwise,—at an election of the Stockholders. Two thirds of the Branch Directors, to be chosen by the Board of Control—and one third by the State. The Bank to be restricted from dealing in Foreign exchange—except for Government purposes, and the remittances of Dividends. The Bank to be allowed to import Specie and Bullion—and export Bullion only—also to dispose of the State 5 p. Cts. in Europe if they chuse and draw for the proceeds. Restrict the Bank to 3 p. Ct. Dividends half yearly—so far from such a Bank, being injurious to State Banks—it would be their safety in time of great & unexpected pressure—and the growing state of our Country would give them all business enough. I am Dear Sir very respectfully yours   Nathl. Prime

ALS. DLC. Prime was the founder of Prime, Ward, King and Company, New York's leading merchant bank, and was acknowledged as one of the city's five wealthiest men in the early 1830s. He retired from the firm in 1832.

FROM JAMES BLAIR

Capitol U. S. Feby. 1. 1834

My dear sir,

I know you will not, under any circumstances, go for a repeal of the "force bill." Calhoun can not hope for its repeal without your aid. His object, therefore, is only to make an inflamatory Speech, for political, or, rather, *revolutionary*, effect in the South.[1] And as I know you regard the efficiency of fed[era]l Govt, and the preservation of the *Union*, as matters of *paramount* importance,—And a Consideration, Compared with which, the Pub: Deposites, the Bank, the tariff & every Branch of the "American System" dwindle into *insignificance*, I submit to you whether Calhoun ought not to be answered on this great question?[2] If the nullifiers fail in the Senate, the repeal of the force bill may not be agitated in the H of R. And I have been advised to act on the defensive. Your's truly   James Blair.

ALS. DLC.
1. Calhoun did eventually speak on the repealing of the Force Act on April 9. *Register of Debates*, 23d

Cong., 1st sess., pp. 1266–1281.
2. It was Clay rather than Webster who replied to Calhoun, probably by agreement. *Ibid.*, pp. 1281–1284.

TO NATHAN APPLETON

Feb. 2. '34

D Sir

I send you the Documents, which you have requested.[1] I wish I had any thing cheering to say; but Mr [Silas] Wrights budget leaves litttle hope. From all quarters of the Country, however, the complaint appears to grow louder & louder.

It strikes me at present, that the thing most likely to be done, in season to stop the mischief, is to continue the present Bank 3 or 5 yrs, leaving Congress at liberty to make another after 1836.

We look anxiously for the effect which the recent debate in the Senate (Mr. Wright &c) may produce at the north.[2] Yrs   D. Webster

ALS. MHi. Published in Van Tyne, p. 188.
1. Enclosures missing.
2. On January 30 Wright submitted to the Senate resolutions from the New York legislature approving Secretary Taney's course in the removal of

deposits. *Register of Debates*, 23d Cong., 1st sess., pp. 397–405. The high point of the speech was Wright's unequivocal stand in opposing "every bank to be incorporated by Congress" whether it was in Philadelphia, New York, or elsewhere.

FROM HENRY WILLIS KINSMAN

Boston Feby. 3d. 1834

Dear Sir

I this morning had a conversation with Mr. P[eter] C. Brooks about old French claims. He has not yet found the agreement, & seems to doubt the expediency of preparing any agreement at present, because, as he says, it might have an unfavorable effect to call a meeting of the claimants at this time. I told him, that I did not suppose it to be necessary to have any public meeting to accomplish the object; but, that it would answer every purpose to have a paper drawn up & presented to persons interested for their signature, without the formality of any notice to call them together, & I named to him what I thought were reasons for such a course. That, in the three recent Conventions, you had all the nice questions to give opinions upon, & many of them to argue, questions upon which large classes of claims had been decided & that other persons had obtained the benefit of your labours. I told him moreover, that you did not wish to divide the responsibility with any other persons, but wished the whole charge, & would employ, under your immediate direction, such assistance as might be found necessary in preparing papers & memorials, & that in order to make it an object to do this to the neglect of other business, it was important, that you should have the management of all, or nearly all of the claims, from the North, & that therefore it would be well immediately to commence obtaining agencies before any other person should anticipate you, & that it would be convenient for the parties themselves, if solicited by other persons, to be able to say that they had already employed you. I had previously had the same conversation with Mr. Edward Brooks[1] about a fortnight ago. They are both very willing to take any course you may see fit to recommend to secure you the business, & I understood Mr. P. C. B., that he had written you,[2] & should be governed by your answer.

One thing more, Mr Brooks mentioned, that he had heretofore suggested to Edward, that *he* might take charge of these claims himself, but he observed, that he had given up the idea, because it seemed to him, that the attention of one person would be required *here* all the time; in order to prepare the documents & papers, & furnish such proofs as might, from time to time, be called for—and, that, from the character of the books & papers to be consulted, being rather of a confidential nature, no one could so well do this, as Edward, & consequently, that he could not be present at Washington, at the meetings of the Commissioners. As it appeared, from this Statement, that they had at one time entertained the idea of getting up the claims themselves, & that, at any rate, a considerable part of the labour of preparation was to be undertaken by E. Brooks, I thought myself justified in saying for you, that you would recompense him for his services out of your commissions, or make such a deduction from the commissions on his father's claims, as might be thought reasonable under the circumstances—I hope in this I did right.[3]

I do not mean, by repeating what I have said to the Messrs. Brooks to intimate that there was any unwillingness on their part, to assent to your proposition, on the contrary, they were both very well satisfied to employ you, & appear to be desirous to do every thing to forward your views. Mr.

Brooks has had a favorable answer from Mr. Bartlett [William Bartlet], also from Mr. [Henry] Hatch[4] & Mr. [William] Parsons.[5] I am Your:

H. W. Kinsman

ALS. NhHi.

1. Brooks (1793–1878; Harvard 1812), eldest son of Peter Chardon Brooks, Boston lawyer and occasional representative for the city in the Massachusetts legislature.

2. Not found.

3. See Kinsman to DW, January 17,

1834, mDW 11390.

4. Administrator of the estate of Crowell Hatch; possibly the Henry Hatch residing at 23 Orange Place, Boston, but otherwise unidentified.

5. Parsons (1755–1837) was a Boston shipowner and merchant, and brother of Theophilus Parsons.

FROM JOHN BRADFORD WALLACE

Harrisburgh—February 9th. 1834

Dear Sir

I have great pleasure in following a suggestion made to me in Philadelphia a few days ago by Mr E[lihu] Chauncey of giving you information of the state of things here; tho' I have to regret that that state is not more satisfactory than it is. We are merely resting on our arms, waiting for events to help us out—or drive us deeper in. The Governour [George Wolf] seems determined to throw away the glorious opportunity now in his hands of saving the country & elevating himself. He has openly declared his opinion that the removing of the deposites was an unwise measure, but he will not use his influence to have them restored. He certainly wishes the rechartering of the U. S. Bank; but will do nothing to promote it. He justifies himself for the present by the circumstance that proposals are to be received on the 22nd. for that part of our state loan of last year not paid in by S & M Allen—and his apprehension that any movement on his part might have a bad effect on those proposals—or that it might be supposed to have it, and he therefore blamed.[1] If no proposals are made which he can accept, he must take some decisive step. If he recommend the legislature to use their influence in favour of the Bank, they will gladly do it—but there is no certainty that he will do so.[2] I think there is no danger of our doing any harm—tho' no very sanguine ground of hope that we shall do much good. If any indication shall be given of a more decided policy on the part of our state administration, I will immediately inform you of it. Very faithfully Yr friend & ob st

John B. Wallace

ALS. DLC.

1. The day before Wallace wrote to Webster, the Wall Street banking house of S. and M. Allen, which had

offices in Philadelphia and most principal American commercial cities with assets reported in the millions, announced that it had failed. The firm resumed business some weeks later with greatly reduced capital.

2. Although regarded as friendly to the institution, Governor Wolf in a message to the Pennsylvania legisla-

ture on February 26 blamed the Bank for the current financial difficulties of the state. *Niles' Register*, 46 (March 8, 1834): 26–27.

FROM NICHOLAS BIDDLE

Phila. Feby. 10. 1834

My dear Sir,

I have not written to you lately but I follow all your movements with great interest & anxiety: and see every day with great satisfaction that you are going on gloriously.

You have made a report which perfectly demolishes the Sec[retar]y.[1] There is no portion of his political body which is not crushed to pieces under the foundation stone you have laid upon him. There let him lie in peace.

I inclose a letter which I received some time since from Mr [Horace] Binney.[2] Send it back to me when you have read it. Such a testimonial is like a diploma from a University. Even you accustomed as you are to eulogy will not be insensible to the commendation of such a man.

Our Boston friends are a little impatient. We have never asked them to reduce their business—on the contrary their local loans are greater by $100,000 than they were in October. The receipt of the Branch paper moreover to which Mr [Stephen] White objects was one of the best considered & one of the wisest measures I think which could have been adopted. How long it may be continued remains to be decided by circumstances but you may rely on it that when we stop receiving the Branch notes it will be the strongest measure we have yet adopted. In truth while we receive the paper it operates on the community where it is received exactly like so much discount without any charge to the merchants from whom it is received.

I shall devote part of this evening to the demolition of Mr [Benjamin Franklin] Butler's facts by bringing from our files the proofs that from the beginning to the end they have treated these soldiers as pensioners & called their pay pensions. If your Senate Committee does not report on Tuesday they may see my collections which I shall give to Mr [Robert] Walsh tomorrow.[3] Very truly yrs   N Biddle

ALS. DLC.

1. Finance Committee report of February 5, 1834, on the removal of deposits. *Senate Documents*, 23d Cong., 1st sess., Serial 239, Doc. No. 72.

2. Enclosure missing; it was later returned to Biddle (DW to Biddle, February 12, 1834, below).

3. Under the act of June 7, 1832, "for the relief of certain surviving officers and soldiers of the revolu-

tion," the Bank had been made the disbursing agent for the secretary of war. When Biddle was ordered late in January to surrender the pension funds and records to the War Department, in line with Jackson's antibank policy, he refused, against Webster's advice, thereby unnecessarily turning against the Bank the wrath of a whole class of citizens. Attorney General Butler had justified the removal on the ground that the law provided not pensions but pay to Revolutionary veterans. *House Committee Reports*, 23d Cong., 1st sess., Serial 261, Report No. 263 (February 11, 1834), pp. 10–22.

FROM NICHOLAS BIDDLE

Phila Feby 11th. 1834

My dear Sir

I have requested our friend Mr [Joseph] Cowperthwait to go to Washington. He will be very useful to you and to other gentlemen, in consequence of his great familiarity with all the details of our business. I inclose also a statement of our condition in several particulars by which you will be able to compare our reduction of loans with our reduction of deposits.[1] Very respy Yrs   N. B.

LC. DLC.   1. Enclosure missing.

TO NICHOLAS BIDDLE

feb. 12. [1834]

Dr Sir

I am glad if my report is thought to meet the occasion, & the expectations of my friends.

I return Mr [Horace] Binney's letter. His approbation is worth more than most diplomas. What I said on the occasion referred to the world will never know; so that there will be no evidence to disprove his opinion.

The Atty Genls argument is a weak one; it is easy to demolish it, as an argument. But, after all, it is a bad subject to dispute about. The pensioners will not believe that the "Old Soldier" is the cause of keeping back their money. For this reason I have expressed the opinion that it is better to give up the fund & the papers, relying for justification on the official opinion of the Atty Gen, & on the report of a Com[mitt]ee of H of R. If this be not done, the H. of R. will pass a bill removing all the pensions from the Bank; this, the Senate will likely reject, & thus a dispute be created which may last to July; meantime, the clamor will be agt. the Bank, as the author of the wrongs & injuries done the "gallant band" &c &c.

Besides, if the Govt. takes away the money, there will be so much the less ground to require further discounts.

I suppose Mr. [Charles?] Chauncey writes you. I would do so often, but indeed I have time for nothing. Yrs   D Webster

Mr Jaudon has sent me what will do me much good.[1]

ALS. DLC.
   1. The obvious reference is to money, but the communication has not been found.

TO JOHN BRADFORD WALLACE

Washington Feb. 12. '34

My Dear Sir,

I thank you for your letter of the 9th. inst.[1] Every thing from Harrisburg is interesting at the present moment. Indeed I think the future progress of affairs is likely to be very much influenced by what may be done, or omitted there. An opinion prevails that a decisive movement by Govr. [George] Wolfe & your Legislature would affect so many votes in the Penna. Delegation here as would turn the majority in the H. of R.

The Philadelphia Delegation went to the President yesterday. Their reception was any thing but agreeable. The Baltimore Gentlemen are to have an audience today. The common answer will doubtless be given to them, also, which is "go to the man who sits quietly in his armed chair in Philadelphia—he can relieve you" &c &c.

I pray you let me hear from you as often as any thing interesting occurs.

I ought not to omit mentioning the pleasure I had in meeting Mrs. Wallace[2] again, & visiting yr family in Philadelphia. Yours very truly

Danl Webster

ALS. PHi.
   1. See above.
   2. Wallace's wife, Susan, was the sister of Horace Binney, first-term congressman from Philadelphia, lawyer for and now legislative supporter of the Bank of the United States.

TO JOHN GODDARD WATMOUGH

Senate Chamber 1 oclock
[c. February 12, 1834]

My Dr Sir

I have reflected on this pension question, & am of opinion it is expedient to put an end to the controversy.

I have looked at the papers, & have no doubt that the argument is with the Bank; but it is an argument, raised by considering & comparing different Statutes, & which the great mass of the Country will never be able clearly to comprehend; meantime, the administration will make the most & the worst of the subject, for purposes of excitement against the Bank. And I am of opinion that this is not an occasion, fit for a quarrel.

I think, therefore, that it will be wise for Mr. Biddle to give up the funds & Books, placing his justification on grounds like this viz,

That the day of payment is at hand, & extreme inconvenience would arise from disappointing those entitled to it.

That the Atty Genl. has expressed an opinion on the law, favorable to the opinion of the Secretary of War, & a Com[mitt]ee of H. of R. has expressed the same opinion.

That the Bank has no interest, in retaining the fund;

That the Subject is now before Congress, & if Congress shall so see fit, the question may be settled by law, in season for future payments; but is not likely to be able to act, in season for the payment now approaching.

There, My Dear Sir, are but my opinions, not hastily formed indeed, but very hastily expressed. Yrs truly   D. Webster

My dear Sir   I fully concur in these views of Mr. Webster & deem it very important that the course he suggests shd. be followed. Yrs

Benjn. Gorham

ALS, with ALS postscript by Benjamin Gorham. DLC.

FROM NICHOLAS BIDDLE

Phila. Feb 13. 1834

My dear Sir

I have your letter of yesterday.[1] Go on prospering—you are on the right track & I think if you present your plan soon, it will form the rallying point of compromise. I have an idea if you bring forward the project of continuing the charter for three years, the Legislature of Pennsa. may instruct our members of Congress to vote for that specifically.[2]

I note with great care what you say about the pensions & in consequence have gone over the matter again. I am sure I am right in my first view, that this is not the moment to change our position and that we should do nothing until we are shown to be clearly right in the objection, which we may afterwards waive. So if Mr [Horace] Binney reports[3] and the Senate Com[mitte]e reports, we may then say to the Secretary of War, we will pay or we will give up the funds. Mr C[harles] Chauncey is as clear as I am that this is our only course. I have therefore soon to see these two reports, and I will then be as docile as a lamb. I trust also that you will not long postpone raising your banner of compromise. Always yours   N. B.

LC. DLC.

1. Biddle's reference does not seem to fit Webster's letter of February 12, above. It may be to a second letter of the same date, not found.

2. See Biddle to DW, March 15, 1834, note 1, below, for the substance of Webster's Bank Recharter Bill.

3. A minority of the House Committee of Ways and Means—Horace Binney, Benjamin Gorham, and Richard Henry Wilde—submitted their views on the payment of pensioners on February 18. The report was annexed to that of the majority, House Report 263, February 11, 1834.

TO [NICHOLAS BIDDLE]

Monday 1/2 past 12—
[February 17, 1834?]

My Dr Sir,

I recd your letter,[1] yesterday morning, & have showed it to Mr [Horace] Binney. I am sorry he does not appear to think well of our proposed movement. You will have seen Mr [Charles?] Chauncey, & he will have told you of some other things. If Mr C[lay] & Mr C[alhoun] would go along with us, we could carry the compromise Bill thro. the Senate by a strong 2 *thirds* majority. Can you write to any body to talk with Mr Calhoun? Yrs   D. Webster

I understand the news direct from Harrisburg is rather favorable.

ALS. DLC.

1. Webster is probably referring to Biddle's letter of February 14, mDWs, in which the Bank president thought that a plan of "compromise," a Bank charter of four to six years, would be supported at Harrisburg. Webster had suggested a similar solution in a letter above to Nathan Appleton, February 2, 1834.

TO CALEB CUSHING

Washington Feb. 17. 34

My Dear Sir,

I thank you for your friendly letter of the 7th. of this month.[1] My friend, (& yours) Mr [Stephen] White had already informed me of your kind & effective suggestions,[2] in respect to myself & the political course which I have pursued, this Session.

It did not seem to be wise, to begin too soon, or too warmly—& rather to follow, & perhaps hasten, public opinion, than to undertake to give it a premature lead. Opinion seems now to be growing very strong, in many parts of the Country; but it seems to us there is a degree of inactivity, in Mass[achusetts], which we hardly know how to account for. Can nothing be done to make the State *altogether right*, on the great questions now pending? We should all most heartily concur, in an effort to enlighten & animate the public mind. It is mortifying, that out of our 12 Districts, while two are vacant, the member from one other is decidedly against us, & the member from still another not decidedly with us.

Memorials come in upon us, in great numbers, from almost all quarters. I shall feel it my duty to move some measure, if nobody else does, in ten days or a fortnight.

Mr [William] Wirt lies very ill, in this City. His life is not expected, from day to day.[3]

Be kind enough to let me hear from you. Can you give me a list of friends, in Essex North, to whom it would be useful for me to send a little speech of mine—or rather a collection of sundry observations, made at sundry times, on the present absorbing subjects?[4] With true regard, Yours   Danl Webster

ALS. NN. Printed in part in Fuess, *Cushing*, 1: 145–146.

1. Not found.
2. Correspondence not found.
3. Wirt died the following day.
4. Essex North was Cushing's home district, which he had aspired unsuccessfully to represent in the Twenty-second and Twenty-third Congresses. He was not the only antiadministration candidate, and although he won a clear plurality in a three-cornered race, no one received the majority necessary to elect. One special election after another was held, without significant change in the results, until after the ninth trial in March of 1832, Cushing withdrew. Four elections later, in November 1832, after the seat had been vacant for one entire session of Congress, Jeremiah Nelson was elected as a compromise by the united votes of the National Republicans. The contest for the Twenty-third Congress was similar, but this time required only three elections. Opposed by the Anti-Masons, Cushing lost to his democratic rival, Gayton P. Osgood, the congressman "decidedly against us" in the reference above. By November of 1834, however, the Whigs of Essex North had come to terms with each other, and Cushing, backed by Webster, was triumphantly elected to the first of four consecutive terms in the House of Representatives.

FROM CALEB CUSHING

F. 23. 1834

Dear Sir:

In accordance with the wish expressed in your favor of the 17th instant,[1] I transmit, by this day's mail, a list of persons in Essex North,[2] who are among the most influential, in that District, of the opponents of the present Administration.

Will you pardon me, if I say one word upon the main cause of the apparent inertness of the Legislature of Massachusetts upon the great question, which now agitates the Union?

We are paralyzed by the Antimasons. On most political questions, there seems to be perfect harmony of action between the Antimasonic & Jackson parties. They voted together, by express compact in all the elections of January. Recently, they voted together to defeat the Plurality Bill[3] in the House. The [*Boston Daily*] *Advocate* is vehemently hostile to us on many, and with us in few, political questions, even when these are totally independent of Masonry or Antimasonry.

The Antimasons profess extreme horror of voting with or for National Republican Masons; they are readily for & with Jacksonian Masons.

The Masons have surrendered their Charter. They have assented to a law severely to punish the administration of extra-judicial oaths, for which nearly all the Masons in the House actually voted. Still, *after all this*, the Antimasons are hotly pushing a *general inquisition* into Masonry, and to appearance sacrificing every thing else in order to keep up a clamor on the subject of Masonry.

But are there no practicable means of ending this miserable contention? (And could not <Mr [John Quincy] Adams, Mr [Edward] Everett, and> *you* equally respected by both parties, interpose efficaciously in the matter? I should rejoice to commit the question to your umpirage.)

(I will not trouble you with disquisition upon the subject, because you see all its bearings) <but I will write to Mr Everett & Mr Adams, to solicit and *entreat* the[m], especially the latter> Could not Mr. Adams be induced to give counsels of moderation to the Antimasons?) With perfect respect Yr ob. s.   C. C.

ALS draft. DLC.
1. See above.
2. Not found.
3. The bill proposed to settle for a plurality rather than a majority of the vote in elections for Massachusetts congressmen. At least three congressional districts, including Cushing's Essex North, had been denied representation in Washington for a considerable time because no candidate obtained over half of the vote. The bill received lengthy discussion and numerous amendments were proposed both before and after rejection; it was defeated in the House on February 3.

FROM STEPHEN WHITE

Boston March 2d 1834

My Dear Sir

The vote in the [Massachusetts] House of Representatives (307 to 125) shows the strength of parties pretty accurately I mean on the deposite question.[1] Had the Resolves as our Committee reported them, remained without amendment, the vote of the Jackson party would have been greatly diminished. The more moderate of them would have gone with us and it seemed to the majority of the Committee important that we should thus break in upon their ranks. The Anti-masons, generally speaking, went with us. Those from New Bedford mostly fled the question and those from Lynn, with one exception, voted on the Jackson side. I give you many thanks for your two letters of 23 & 25.[2] I have abstained from writing so frequently of late fearing you would feel obliged to reply more frequently than you would think convenient or desireable. Since you intimate a desire I should recommence I will resume my former habit with all the pleasure that its exercise always gives me. It was stated in debate the day the deposite resolves passed that the Branch here had that day discounted $200,000. This had much effect, though not strictly true. I take the feud to be that A[mos] and A[bbott] L[awrence] and J[ames] W[illiam] P[aige] & Co had on that day discounts in the way of renewals to meet heavy payments of Southern d[ra]fts, to even a larger amount, falling due in all March. The Young mens meeting held here last week resulted in a memorial to Congress which I have been requested to send you a copy of.[3] A Committee of 100 individuals are at work obtaining subscriptions and tomorrow it will probably be sent you with 500 signatures. The pressure is unabated in the money market.

Mr [Jeremiah] Mason is powerfully impressed with the necessity of a press at Washington. We shall make another effort to get it up if possible though A L [Abbott Lawrence?] deserves a good scolding.

Our Legislature will I think rise about the first of April. The time of their adjournment is however mere matter of conjecture. I should rejoice to be able to go to Washington but matters are so pressing here that I fear to be away.

We hope the Mass. delegation will allow Gov. Lincoln to present our Resolves and to make his first speech in so doing. Ever most truly yours

Step. White

The 10th of our Resolves, that one offered and accepted as an amendment, denounces the President personally in regard to the removal, his motives, &c. The party flew off as soon as their idol was touched.

ALS. NhHi.

1. "Resolutions of the Legislature of Massachusetts, in relation to the Currency, and the removal of the Public Deposites," *Executive Documents*, 23d Cong., 1st sess., Serial 256, Doc. No. 174. The resolutions were presented in the House of Representatives by John Quincy Adams on March 17, and by Nathaniel Silsbee in the Senate a week earlier.

2. Neither letter found.

3. The "Young mens meeting" was held in the Boston Common Council room on February 27 and its resolutions were published in the Boston *Columbian Centinel* on March 1. Its memorial, drafted after the meeting, was presented to the House by Representative Benjamin Gorham on March 17. *Executive Documents*, 23d Cong., 1st sess., Serial 256, Doc. No. 175.

FROM SAMUEL FINLEY BREESE MORSE
TO DANIEL WEBSTER AND SEVERAL OTHER MEMBERS OF CONGRESS

Mar. 7th. 1834

My dear Sir,

I perceive that the Library Committee have before them the consideration of a resolution on the expediency of employing four artists to paint the remaining four pictures on the Rotunda of the Capitol.[1] If Congress should pass a resolution in favor of the measure, I should esteem it a great honor to be selected as one of the artists. I have devoted twenty years of my life, seven of which were passed in England France and Italy, studying with special reference to the execution of works of the kind proposed, and I must refer to my professional life and character in proof of my ability to do honor to the commission and to the country.

May I take the liberty for myself to ask your favorable recommendation to those in Congress who have the disposal of the commissions? With great respect Sir Yr. mo. ob. servt.   S. F. B. Morse

Circular ALS draft, with list of proposed recipients. DLC.

1. The resolution initiated by Henry Alexander Wise on January 24, 1834, and referred to the House Committee on Public Buildings, floundered for several years. Eventually artists Robert Walter Weir, John Vanderlyn, and John Gadsby Chapman painted three of the four proposed portraits in the decade after 1837. In 1847, when Congress undertook to fill the vacant panel, Morse again lost out, this time to William Henry Powell.

FROM JAMES GORE KING

Newyork 8th. March 1834

My dear sir

I intended to have kept you informed of what was doing here—towards carrying into effect the objects of those in whose behalf others as well as myself, were sent to Washington—but the double and sometimes triple duties devolving upon me—left no time for correspondence not strictly required.

You will probably have followed our movements—up to the appointment of the Union Committee[1]—with Mr. [Albert] Gallatin as efficient and active, and not merely nominal chairman—and withall you may have been looking for our Report. I am apprized that you approved the first letter which Mr. Biddle wrote to our corresponding committee[2]—but you may not know, how very differently that letter was viewed here, —its manner and tone—as well as its conclusions, were of a nature to embarrass us exceedingly—so much so that Mr [John Austin] Stevens and myself were urged to visit Philadelphia, with a view of causing the letter to be withdrawn, on the ground that if published, (and our Committee could not but publish it)—it would be impossible to justify it to our community—disagreeing as we did as to the positions assumed for the Bank, of its being discharged from obligations to regulate the currency—because the Executive had committed an aggression upon it— of its awaiting in calmness and silence, the overthrowing of commercial order & stability, and the happening of all imaginable evils—before it interposed,—with power admitted to be all sufficient to become a rallying point and safeguard to the Nation—and finally of its being under the *necessity* of diminishing accomodations in Newyork—instead of maintaining them at least, at the present mark. It was found that the letter, having been placed beyond the control of the Directors, could not be recalled—and the efforts of Mr Stevens' & myself were directed to the only practicable result then in our power—namely—to prove that the *necessity* just alluded to—did not exist—in the condition of the Bank— and even if it did—there was a greater necessity in the actual condition of Newyork—requiring that no diminution should at this moment be attempted in the facilities from the U S. Branch. We urged, with great respect, but with equal frankness—that Newyork thro' the Union Committee was willing to declare that up to this time the course of the Bank had been beyond objection—that its curtailments had not exceeded the bounds demanded by prudence and regard to the security of the Institution—but that now it was unquestionably the strongest institution in the World—and abundantly able without the smallest risk—to grant the aid required—and if it did not do so—there must be some motive, paramount—tho' not avowed—but which would not fail to be ascribed to political effect, and if once convinced on that point—that our committee in our opinion should unanimously report—that tho, the deposites as a matter of contract—should be instantly restored—yet that an Institution capable of being influenced by such motives, under such circumstances —*ought never to be rechartered.* We stated that in Boston (as is probably well known to you)—the sentiment was gaining ground that the Bank could and should extend its aid—and here, as well as there, that sentiment was very difficult to be repressed—and unless repressed—that so far as the friends of order and good government in general, as well as of a National Bank in particular—in those two Cities, are looked to, for cooperation with others—in this eventful crisis—they would be worse than neutral—their embarassment would be a signal triumph to the opposite parties. We moreover declared that there was an atmosphere around the Directors of the U S. Bank at Philadelphia which prevented a correct vision of objects at a distance—and that the true state of feeling in Newyork city in respect to the Bank, was not known—the channels of communication were thro' those, who were no longer in sympathy and full communion with the great body of active, intelligent and influential individuals connected with commerce—that tho' there was a natural feeling that the Mother Bank should be placed, at the centre of commerce—and that two millions and a half of Capital for the great Emporium was shortcoming beyond question, of its just proportion—yet these were hardly thought about—compared with the mightier considerations of the overthrow, from political hatred, of the safeguard of the National Currency—and of the dread of the blighting effects of the fatal "Experiment." That under no possible Circumstances could the friends, in Newyork of *a* Bank and of *the* Bank—be brought again, by pressure from without, to such unanimity—and finally that all asked from the Bank was a possible extension of a half a million of dollars for sixty days, and the only astonishment we felt was, that the least demur should be made about it.

After a day's necessary delay, we were left under the full impression that our wishes would be complied with—and while the official letter was preparing to that effect, as I believe—the message of Governor [George] Wolf was received—and by the Board of Directors deemed to be of sufficient importance, to cause a postponement of the Bank's decision relative to Newyork: —and this was officially communicated to our Union Committee, instead of what was expected by us, on leaving Phila.

I will frankly state that I see no connection between the political denunciation of the Bank by Gov. Wolfe and the fiscal ability of the Bank to grant half a million of dollars to Newyork—and I much doubt if our people will be more clearsighted: but I am not so sure, that they may not see—a course of policy—dictated by other considerations than those suggested by the ability of the Institution to come forward to the relief of a suffering community.

Your Senate Chamber has been enlivened of late, by Æsop's fables— one occurs to me—of the trial between the north wind and the sun— that genius of our people renders the moral—doubly applicable and they may be turned from the right, by an attempt to coerce them to pursue it, by foul instead of fair means—by harshness instead of mildness.

Unwilling to omit any opportunity of doing service in the good cause —I have thought best to ask your interference with friends at Philadelphia provided you see matters as we do here—and I may add one consideration more—which though last is not least—I mean the effect to be produced upon our Charter Elections next month, if the Union Committee are prevented from coming out in full and strong terms, in favor of the Bank. I think it would be fatal—I know of nothing else, so certainly fatal—and I do believe if that can be made to redound to our advantage

—right would be done all round, for a more general turning out in ward meetings never occurred. You will have seen a sort of Manifesto in yesterday's Phila. papers—of the Bank—and will have observed the concluding paragraph—that owing to the present unsettled state of the currency the Bank must lessen its business.

This declaration is unfortunate—and seeing that Newyork *must* be relieved by the Bank—it seems necessary to put such relief upon the ground of temporary exception to the general rule as announced—and *in that* sense it may yet be urged most strenuously upon the Board of Directors.

Genl. [Thomas] Cadwallader[3] *accidentally* here, to day, called upon me —and I labored hard to satisfy him of the correctness of our views—and I believe he returns tomorrow fully impressed therewith. He urged me to go back with him—but I have been so much away from my private concerns of late, that I could not. On the other hand, I begged him to use his influence to induce Mr. Biddle to come here—and see & hear, for himself. The result I should not doubt if he came.[4]

I have thrown my remarks hastily together and you will at once perceive that a portion of them—namely the *political* ones, cannot and ought not to be urged to the Bank—though they tend to the greater results—and far outweigh the mere question of this or another Bank.

I do not go into detail about our views as opposed to the grounds assumed in Mr. Biddle's first letter to our Committee—nor to his manner of enforcing them—but if the Bank refuse aid to N. Y—and the Union Committee are so obliged to report—stating at same time their belief that it can do so—without the slightest risk—it will be needful in our justification before our own people—to animadvert upon said letter, as showing the motives of such refusal.

The Union Committee will not probably report, before the end of next week—which will leave but little time for your good interference— which I pray you not to delay beyond the regular course of mail, if your important avocations permit—tho' possibly you may deem this, as important an avocation as may present.

The smallness of the amount required for Newyork may surprise you —considering the importance that we attach to the obtaining it. The truth is, by allowing our Banks here to remain in debt, upon the aggregate, a half million dollars, to the Branch—will give confidence to each City Bank—and restore harmony among them all—and any step towards restoring confidence, will be more useful than throwing a mere sum of money into the market—discounts will be more steady & apprehensions will be banished.

The U. S. Bank has now about an equal amount of available funds, with that possessed [on] 1 August and owes only seven or eight millions less—in deposites and circulation—its position is not only impregnable—but such as may be used most efficiently for good or for evil—and it must now declare its course.

It must risk something whichever way it decides—important steps are seldom clear of such opposite tendencies—if it produces by its course, further distress—it runs more risk besides inflicting unutterable evils—than if it interposes, and saves the commercial interests—from utter ruin—altho' it should by so doing, make good its enemies words—that it was able to do so.

Pray write to me soon and believe me With great regard and truth Yrs faithfully   James G. King

ALS. NhD.

1. Unable to convince Biddle of the need for an expansion of loans, the New York financial community under the leadership of King and John A. Stevens helped organize a Union Committee of Bankers and Merchants with the intention of applying for aid from the Bank.

2. The committee wrote to Biddle on February 15 to ask whether the Bank would increase its loans to local New York banks and whether it planned to continue receipt and redemption of branch notes and drafts.

A week later Biddle replied that he could not increase loans and could not give a definite answer to their second query.

3. Cadwalader (1779–1841; University of Pennsylvania 1795), a Philadelphia lawyer, sometime agent for the Bank, and close confidant of Biddle.

4. Biddle eventually did come to New York on March 14 and two days later agreed to suspend curtailments there until May 1, thus ending the crisis.

TO CHARLES HENRY THOMAS

friday Eve'
Mar. 14. [1834]

Dear Henry,

At the close of a hard day's work in Court, and extremely tired, I sit down to write you, in answer to your letter of the 8th,[1] & about several other things.

I know not how much I may enjoy Marshfield, in time to come; but there are some things which being begun must be completed, & wound off.

1st. The Barn. This you will of course see done & finished, according to previous arrangement. The extreme scarcity of money *ought* to bring about some diminution of carpenters' wages: I leave Mr [Seth] Weston to do what he thinks right about that. I have no new direction to give. Let the carpenters begin the first day of May, & go right thro; & see that all requisite materials are seasonally on hand.

2. Trees.—The new part of the Belt will of course require trees. More trees are also needed, (& shrubs,) along by the sides of the Avenue; & could be well disposed of, in sundry other places.

I shall send about 300 trees from this place. They will be flowering dogwood, American limes, Glutinous acacias, &c &c. Some of these will be small. They must be mixed with other trees, & set out in various places. The dogwoods are very beautiful in flower. They must be scattered about, & a considerable number would be very pretty on Cherry Hill. Other trees Mr Dunn[2] must find in the native forests. I hope he will set out a great many small pines, where the evergreens died last summer, & in other favorable situations. In elms, too, we are rather deficient. Perhaps he may obtain some handsome ones on good terms, about Mount Blue, or Hingham. Sumacs he will find on Juniper Island, & will naturally use a good many. Some locusts & catalpas, I suppose, he will transplant from the nursery.

The trees which go from this place will be directed to [Nathaniel] Ray [Thomas].

3. Fruit trees. I shall send from this region 30 apple trees. These are of 4 or 5 sorts of early summer & fall apples. Our stock of winter apples is already good. These apple trees must be set out, wherever you can find room for them, *without taking up more land for orchard.* You must find room in vacant spots in the orchard, or the old orchard, or where the few trees stand, planted by Mr Lord,[3] near the South end of the belt; or put a few of the handsomest in the garden, or on the east side of the Avenue, near the road, or any where else, without making any new Extent of orchard ground.

I am pleased with the idea of your father's going to Mr [Jonathan] Winship,[4] for some choice trees. Let him get whatever he thinks best, especially if he could find some pear trees, likely to bear pretty soon.

He must not set out *too many* quinces. He wants to see a whole row of golden quinces, hanging down, all along the east side of the Garden. I doubt whether we can spare all that room. It is our *best place* for *peaches*, & I wish he would get a few very nice trees of that kind.

Any thing else, in the way of trees, that strikes you as proper, you will have done. How would it do to make a clump round the rock, South of the orchard?

3. [4] Plough in the kelp, as soon as practicable.

4. [5] As to the salt meadow, near Hither point, it is of little importance whether we retain more or less. Our Barn is likely, at least for the present, to be too large for our hay, so that if we keep a few acres of the marsh it will be well enough—& if we let the Dr. [John Porter?] have it it will be well enough.

5. [6] Get a deed from Mr [Charles] Wright.[5] I will send the cash short-ly. Move the wall. As some part of the wall will be very visible from the House, being on high land, Mr Dunn must make a trench, inside the wall, fill it up with meadow mud, and manure, & plant such shrubs & vines, as will run up soon, & cover the naked stones with something green. This wall ought to be made stout & stiff; tho' no higher than is absolutely necessary. Dont let it be a thin thing.

6. [7] I will send you the 150 Dlls, which you need for my affairs soon —& write you again, as soon as I can.

It is yet uncertain, whether I go home. And now, my good friend, adieu!   D. Webster

ALS. MHi.
1. Not found.
2. Not identified.
3. Not identified.
4. Winship (c. 1780–1847), a Brighton horticulturalist and proprie-tor of well-known flower gardens.
5. Webster had discussed the pur-chase of the Wright land in January and gave his approval to Thomas to buy it on February 28 (mDW 11500).

FROM ROSWELL L. COLT

Bal[timo]r[e] 14 March 1834

Dear Sir

Mr [Samuel] Jaudon asked me last Evening, if I could give you any in-formation as to the number of manufacturing Establish[men]ts that had stopped working, in consequence of the pressure of the times. I can only speak positively of those at Paterson, & its immediate neighbourhood, where alone one half of the Cotton Mills have stopped spinning. The Population of Paterson was last year over 10000 all dependant on the Mills for support. There were 43500 Spindles in use at that place, 24500 have stopped working, and my Brother will stop his two Mills of upwards of 5000 Spindles as soon as he works out his present supply of cotton. About 5100 Spindles in three neighboring Mills, have also suspended spinning and if the present state of things last 60 days longer, I see nothing but ruin for all our Cotton Establishments, and nine tenths of those in New Jersey & probably near the same proportion elsewhere, must suspend their Works—for the Commission Merchants in New York & Philadelphia, refuse to accept of consignments of Yarns, or Goods, & let the manufacturers draw at 60 days for even one half the value of their consignments, & without advances they cannot go on.

I see by the newspapers that in Connecticut & R Island they are also stopping their factories—as they are also further East; at Dover N H 1 Cotton Mill of 600 spindles has stopped work & the Cacheco Mill No 2 will stop the 15 March;

at New Market N H—one Cotton Mill of 4000 has stopped working;
at Nashua   Do.   5000   Do.
at Great Falls a large Woollen Establishment employing 200 hands
              & using yearly 300000 lbs wool has ceased operating;
at Dedham a like large Woollen Estab[lishment]   Do   Do.;
a large Cotton Mill in Wilmington Delaware has stopped working and
the Mills in this neighbourhood are only spinning about half the usual
quantity, & some of them will probaby be stopped entirely and are now
merely working out of charity to their hands.

I earnestly hope that you will succeed in your praiseworthy efforts, to
restore confidence. Let the deposits be restored to the Bank, & its charter
be extended as you propose, 5 or even 3 years, & in 24 hours, we shall
have an entire new state of things—at present, the Bank cannot with
safety, do any thing to relieve the distresses of the community, & was the
Bank U S to let out 5 Millions of Dollars, it could do no good, it would
only enable the State Banks to curtail to that amount, & throw the whole
burthen of supporting specie payments, on the Bank, with so much diminished means, & besides, unless the Public confidence is restored, by
replacing the Bank in its amicable connection with Government, & a
prospect of a continuation of its charter held out to the community, the
very extension of discount now, would add to the evil hereafter, & this all
prudent men would know, how then could this extension by the Bank, remove the panic—in truth, so long as the Deposits are under the control
of the Secretary of the Treasury, & may be used to cripple the Bank, the
Public will be alarmed—look at the returns made by the Deposit Banks
to Feby, & you will see, these deposit Banks in Boston, New York, &
Philad. return, that they hold upwards of 7 Millions of *checks* & *Notes of
Banks pay[in]g Specie*—now the custom of the Banks in these Cities is,
every morning to send in *all the Notes* they have received the day before, can one believe they have departed from their usual custom, without some given purpose, & what inducement would there be to hold rival
State Bank Notes, it is plain, that these Banks have held back U S Bank
& Branch Notes, this must be the reason why the circulation of the Bank
keeps up to so large an amount, & is a source of alarm to the Bank, for
after the wicked attack on Savannah, the Bank has every reason to fear
the Treasury, will lend itself to any mad scheme which may tend to
break it, or a Branch—it seems to me, that with this fact before them,
the Bank must curtail its discounts in New York & Philad., & yet from
the accounts we have from the Eastward today of encreased distress
there I do not know how this can be done without causing a general
stoppage of payments.

Will it be in order, in calling on the Secretary of the T[reasury] for weekly returns from the receiving Banks, to ask, that such Banks in their return of *Bank Notes and checks on hand*, Specify how many Dollars they have in Notes of the Bank U S & the Branches, & Branch *checks* & specifying what Branches the Notes are of—this would be valuable information for the Bank, & enable it to guard against any new attempt like the one made on the Savannah Branch   can this be demanded. With great respect I remain Your mo ob sr   Roswell L Colt

I know your time is taken up   do not give yourself the trouble to answer this letter.

ALS. DLC. Colt (1779–1856) was the president of the Society for the Establishment of Useful Manufactures in Paterson, New Jersey, from 1814 until his death in 1856, and a commercial merchant in New York City.

Samuel Colt, the revolver manufacturer, was his nephew. Colt's wife, Betsy Oliver, and Biddle's wife, Jane Craig, were cousins, and the two families remained on terms of intimacy.

FROM NICHOLAS BIDDLE

Phila. March 15. 1834

My Dear Sir,

I returned today from New York where I have been endeavoring to satisfy our friends and think I shall succeed. If the enemies of the Bank are overcome without much difficulty, our friends give much more anxiety. Sincerely desirous as I am of retaining their support, they sometimes are disposed to ask more than it is entirely prudent to yield—and yet it is often better to err a little than to be too right in resisting them. Boston is I believe quite satisfied.

Mr [Samuel] Jaudon has shown me this evening the copy of your proposed bill.[1] I am content with the whole of it except the section limiting the amount of reduction in the course of a year. I wish you would reconsider this which on reflection will I think appear not at all advisable. It limits nothing of the amount of circulation—of loans—of responsibilities of every kind—but it limits the power of calling in your means to pay your debts—and it limits it in a very restricted way. If sudden calls arise for funds—a panic—a specie drain from any quarter you cannot protect yourself—you cannot ask for 2 per cent every 60 days—not one per cent reduction per month. Now on our capital we receive at this moment in New York & Phila alone more than 10 per cent in the shape of our notes coming in for payment in the course of two months. Think this over and I believe you will find that the section will not work well. Yrs always   N Biddle

ALS. DLC.

1. Webster introduced his Recharter Bill on March 18. *Register of Debates*, 23d Cong., 1st sess., pp. 984–
996. He proposed that the Bank be
continued for six years and that the
deposits be restored by July 1, 1834,

but that Congress might create another bank any time after March
1836. The section to which Biddle
objected was omitted in the copy of
the bill presented to Congress. *Ibid.*,
pp. 1004–1005, and mDW 43879.

FROM JOEL ROBERTS POINSETT

Charleston
17 March 1834

My dear Sir

I send you our city paper of this morning by which you will perceive
the disturbed state of this portion of our common country. I would not
trouble you with our domestic quarrels at this time if I were not persuaded that you might aid in compromising them. The people of the interiour
of this state are exasperated to madness by the cruel persecution they
experience from the leaders of the nullification party—and if an attempt
is made to enforce the Test Oath[1] (a test of party) they will resist to the
death and this unfortunate state nearly ruined already by the effects of
our late political contest will be involved in civil war.

We understand from authority which we cannot question, that this
measure originated with Mr. Calhoun and was we know opposed by
many of his party. If he will yield to the public opinion he may prevent
bloodshed.

If it had not been for this ill judged measure party spirit would have
subsided in South Carolina. The nullifiers were in possession of the
power and we were satisfied to leave it in their hands—at least we were
decided not to agitate the public mind by renewing the struggle. On the
present question in which the whole nation takes so deep an interest we
should have been united.

I am going to Greenville in the interiour of this state to calm the troubled waters if possible. The excitement there however is so very great,
that I fear peaceful councils will not avail, if the authorities of the state
persist in enforcing the law. I believe Mr. Calhoun possesses sufficient
influence with his party to restore the Country to tranquility and as circumstances have united you politically I hope you may take sufficient interest in the peace of this state to induce you to speak to him on the subject and lead him to pursue a course more worthy of an honorable mind
towards his fellow citizens. I blush while I write this; but the interests of
the country are too dear to me to allow me to consult personal feelings.
I protest to you if I thought the Liberties of the Country could survive

the contest, be the results in other respects what they might; I would yield to the wishes and urgent entreaties of the people of my own party and lead them at once to battle. I am dear Sir respectfully & cordially Yours   J. R. Poinsett

ALS. NcU.

1. Poinsett here refers to a South Carolina statute of November 1833 which prescribed an oath giving primary allegiance to the state rather than to the United States. The oath was the new center of controversy between unionists and nullifiers until it was invalidated by the State Court of Appeals in the spring of 1834.

FROM JARED SPARKS

Cambridge, March 19th. 1834

My dear Sir,

At the solicitation of Miss Janette Taylor I promised some time ago to write to you respecting a claim, which she proposed to lay before Congress.[1] I have nothing to say, more than what you already know, but I am unwilling to neglect a promise to a lady.

Miss Taylor I have no doubt is the neice and legal heiress of [John] Paul Jones. Four or five years ago she began to write to me from Scotland about her uncle & other matters, telling me that she had his papers, & the like. But as you have seen her, you have doubtless heard her story.

When Paul Jones was out on his famous cruise in the Bon Homme Richard, his squadron took two English prizes, which were sent into Bergen, then a Danish port, and presumed to be neutral. But the King of Denmark, not yet having courage to look the British lion in the face, released these prizes to their owners, on the plea, that he had not recognized the independence of the United States. Dr. Franklin, then our ambassador in Paris, sent a remonstrance to the Danish minister of State, in which he set forth in his characteristic manner the injustice, illegality, and impolicy of the proceedings, and claimed the prizes, or their value, for the captors. The remonstrance was repeated on suitable occasions. After the war, Paul Jones was commissioned by Congress to go to Denmark and pursue the claim. But he had not the patience of a diplomatist, and in the meantime being asked by the Empress of Russia to take command of her fleet in the Black Sea, he hurried away to this new theatre of action. He returned to Paris & died. How the affair ended, in regard to the claim, I have never inquired. Miss Taylor told me that [Pierre] Landais, the mad captain who was second in command to Paul Jones, obtained some years afterwards a remuneration from Congress in consequence of these captures.[2]

The services of Paul Jones were so very important to the American cause in the revolution, that, should it appear that he had just claims against the United States, which have never been settled, both gratitude & equity would seem to prompt the payment of the debt to his heirs.

I regretted that your Washington medals[3] were not returned before your departure. They are safe, and in good keeping. Two volumes of Washington's Writings[4] have at last got through the press. When you have a respite from your great affairs of state, I hope you will find leisure to look into them, and that you will be pleased with their matter & execution. Moreover, should this be the case, I shall be gratified if you will say so when proper opportunities occur, for the undertaking has cost me more labor, expense, & trouble than can easily be imagined.

With great respect, and best wishes for a happy issue of all your important efforts to save a republic, which so many worthy patriots have bled & struggled to establish, I am, dear Sir, Your friend & most obt. st.

Jared Sparks

ALS. DLC.

1. Miss Taylor, daughter of John Paul Jones's sister, Janet, petitioned Congress in 1836 (*Executive Documents*, 24th Cong., 2d sess., Serial 301, Doc. No. 19), but it was more than a decade before Congress voted an amount in excess of $150,000 to be distributed among Jones, his officers and men, or their heirs. See *House Reports*, 30th Cong., 1st sess., Serial 524, Report No. 9.

2. On March 24, 1806, Congress passed a bill whereby Landais received $4,000, which was to be deducted ultimately from his share of the prize money in the event of any final settlement. *Annals of Congress*, 9th Cong., 1st sess., pp. 197, 838.

3. In 1827 Webster purchased eleven medals originally given to Washington by Congress. See DW to Robert Lewis, April 9, 1828, published in *MHi Proc.*, 1st Series 20 (1882–1883): 343–344; and DW to [Bushrod Washington], May 24, 1828, mDW 7092. In 1874 the medals were presented to the Massachusetts Historical Society by Peter Harvey.

4. *The Writings of George Washington* (12 vols, Boston, 1834–1837).

TO CAMPBELL PATRICK WHITE

March 22. 1834

My Dear Sir,

I feel very solicitous for the early passage of your Bill, regulating the value of silver coins.[1] There can be no objection to it, from any quarter, and its passage will certainly be of considerable importance, at the present moment. Allow me to suggest the propriety of an attempt to call it up, out of its order, as a public measure of practical importance, & such an one as is not likely to occasion long debate. If you can send the Bill to us, I will ask the Senate's immediate attention to it. I am, Dr. Sir, with much regard, Your Ob. Sert.   Danl Webster

ALS. NHi.
1. White's bill, which facilitated the use of foreign silver coin as legal tender in the United States, was not passed until mid-June.

TO CHARLES HENRY THOMAS

Washington Mar. 25. 1834

Dear Henry,

I do not give up the idea of going home, but am unable to fix, as yet, the day of departure. Yrs of the 21. was recd. this morning.[1] Make yrself easy about the $1000. If we cannot get it from Duxbury, we can find it elsewhere.

I learn, by a former letter,[2] that you have finished ploughing Winslow Hill, & have turned in 100 loads of kelp. Are those loads so large, as that you regard the field as richly manured? If not, we will set the gondola to work, & bring on muscles. I am disposed to try the methods of enriching this field, by sea manure, alone, of the two sorts; viz, sea weed, & muscle mud.

I suppose the trees, purchased here, & of which you have a list, are on the way, & will soon be at Boston. Write to [Nathaniel] Ray [Thomas] to send them down.

As I wrote you, I wish to complete the present plan, & stop there, leaving the rest to the next occupant, or the next generation. Let the Belt be filled up. If necessary & proper, let some trees be set out on the sides of the new dyke; thicken up trees a little on the sides of the avenue, & all the rest as I have written before.[3]

As to the field before the House, you will of course lay most of it down. We talked of reserving one measured acre for carrots, for Mr Morehead.[4] Do so, if you please. It will be convenient to have some little pieces of corn, near the House. You might make a strip, if you think fit, at the upper end—next to Mr Cushman's[5] pasture. All this, as you see fit. *Lay down nothing that is not* RICHLY *manured.*

The roller appears to me to be a *bad* one. It is too small. If necessary, get a larger one, & roll down all the field so that you can drop a marble from one end to the other. I like the idea of getting a good many trees from Mount Blue. We want a good deal of wild shrubbery, to be set out in some places, so as to make a thicket.

I suppose there will be no want of work. If there should be, remember that there must be a little stone work done, (very little) down at the bottom of the yellow bog pond, where we must have, you know, a little narrow, white, arched bridge, so that we may continue the walk from the belt across the brook & go round to the ice house. The English meadow, above the pond must be made as smooth & handsome as may be.

Shall we have any manure fit to top dress the faintest part of this meadow?

Enough—

I will write you again, so soon as I know when I may set out. Yrs
D Webster

ALS. MHi.
1. Not found.
2. Not found.
3. See above, March 14, [1834].
4. Most likely John Morehead (c.

1760–1836) or his son of the same
name (1784–1855), who lived nearby.
5. A reference to land owned by
Robert Cushman, or by his son, Joseph Phillips Cushman (b. 1785).

TO BENJAMIN G. WELLES

Washington Hall, April 15, 1834

My Dear Sir:

I have received your note,[1] in behalf of the Committee of Arrangements, inviting me to be present at the meeting of the Whigs of New York, this afternoon, called to celebrate their late triumph in this city. This invitation, and the expressions of regard which accompany it, demand my most grateful acknowledgments. Although circumstances do not allow me to enjoy the pleasure of seeing together those of my fellow-citizens who will be assembled at this meeting, yet I cannot altogether refrain from expressing those sentiments which the occasion naturally calls forth. So far as your triumph is local, or so far as the city of New York is alone concerned in the result, it does not become me to enter into the feelings which it excites.

But knowing that it is on an all-important question of general politics, interesting alike to the whole community, that the election has manifestly turned, I cannot but rejoice, as a citizen of the republic, at the manly, vigorous, and successful support which has been given to the Constitution, to the Laws, and the interests of the country, by this great city.[2]

The son of a father, who acted a zealous and patriotic, though humble part, in establishing the independence of the country, I have been educated from my cradle, in the principles of the WHIGS OF 1776. Riper years have enabled me to learn, that in these principles is to be found the source of our own republican liberty, as well as of all that degree of freedom which exists on the other continent.

These principles teach us that Government is a trust, that those who administer it, are but agents and servants; that offices are created, not for the benefit of the holders, but for the good of the People; and that public office is grossly abused, and its uses corrupted, when it seeks, mainly, not the benefit of the community, but its own emolument and perpetuation, and that the whole essential character of representative Government is dangerously perverted, and its true manner of operation reversed, when the opinions, which the people are expected to receive, are prescribed to them by those whom they have appointed to places of power, instead of being the spontaneous result of their own intelligence and their own patriotism.

These principles teach us also, that all political power should be subject to constitutional and legal restraint; that it is not enough that legislators and magistrates be elected by the People; but, that when elected, they must be subject, also, in the exercise of their several functions, to the rule of the Constitution and the laws. When Republicans appoint men to office, they are choosing agents, not electing masters. Miserable indeed is the condition of the community, where all power, or any unlimited power, is placed in the hands of one, in whatever form, or for whatever merits, that one may be selected.

"An elective despotism," said Mr. Jefferson, "is not the Government we fought for." I will add, it is not a Government to which the people of the United States will ever submit.

The principles of 1776, further teach us the indispensable necessity of maintaining, in the hands of the immediate representatives of the people, the control over the public revenues. In no country, and at no time, has there been found any other adequate security for liberty than the withholding both the right of taxation and the control of the public treasures from the Executive power.

This principle is fundamental, and any thing which attacks it, strikes against the foundation stone of the sacred temple of political freedom. Every appearance of encroachment, on this branch of the popular right, ought to be received by all true Whigs with unflinching spirits.

So far as I am acquainted with the sentiments of the Whigs of New York, on the present state of the country, and its deep and wide spread distress, I cordially concur in those sentiments, one and all. I think this distress has its origin, directly in injurious and disastrous measures of Government: and that the only remedy is the repeal and reversal of those measures. The laws must be re-established in their just authority, and the public treasures restored to the guardianship of the nation's Legislature, before confidence or prosperity can return.

The "Experiment" under which we are suffering, and at which the world is gazing, some with unfeigned sorrow, some with sneers at the wisdom of Republics, and all with wonder and amazement, is now felt severely by the numerous classes of those in active employments. It diminishes the value of property; it cuts off income; it prevents employment, by inspiring fears of the future in those whose business, if confidence were not destroyed, would naturally furnish employment. It ties up the hands of labor, and robs it of the bread of its mouth. The case is not one which is to be relieved, permanently, by loans of money from any quarter. What the industrious classes desire, is, not to borrow, but to earn; they ask not for bounty, but for the return of their usual occupations. They solicit no favor, they demand a right: and no right is dearer, in a Republican Government, than that of living under the protection of wise laws, steadily administered. They demand a restoration of that confidence in the Government and in the laws, which shall excite the industry, awaken the activity, and reward the honest labors of all; and in this demand I trust they will persevere, till their object be attained.

I pray you, my dear sir, to present to the Committee, and to the meeting, my hearty congratulations, and may the principles of the Whigs prevail forever! Daniel Webster.

Text from the *National Intelligencer,* April 24, 1834. Original not found. Although appointed chairman of the April 15 Castle Garden Whig victory celebration for which this letter was intended, Welles (or Wells), who was a builder by trade, remained an obscure ward politician.

1. Welles to DW, [April 15, 1834], also published in the *National Intelli-*gencer, April 24, 1834.

2. Although the anti-Jackson mayoral candidate, Gulian C. Verplanck, lost to Democrat Cornelius W. Lawrence, the voters of New York City had during the previous week elected a majority of Whig aldermen and assistant aldermen, giving the party control over appointments and financial affairs.

During the winter of 1833–1834 Nicholas Biddle used the enormous, but steadily decreasing, power of the Bank to carry on what amounted to a personal vendetta against Andrew Jackson. He tightened credit in all the major commercial cities, never doubting that the resulting hardship to the business community would be followed by such severe pressure upon the administration that the President would capitulate, restore the deposits, and accept recharter of the Bank. It was soon obvious, however, to bankers, manufacturers, merchants—indeed to businessmen of all persuasions—that their distress stemmed from Biddle's obstinacy rather than from government policies, and many began to question the wisdom of perpetuating an institution capable of such an abuse of power. Friends of the Bank became indifferent or hostile.

The tide had definitely turned by February 18 when the House voted to refer Taney's reasons for removal to the Committee of Ways and Means, chaired by James K. Polk and boasting a substantial Jackson

majority. Polk's report of March 4 laid the blame for the current eco-
nomic distress squarely upon Nicholas Biddle. Committee Reports, 23d
Cong., 1st sess., Serial 261, Report No. 312, and minority Report No.
313. Now fully in control, the Democrats pushed four key resolutions
through the House on April 4. By a vote of 134 to 82 the House declared
that the Bank should not be rechartered; by a smaller margin, 118 to
103, that the deposits should not be restored; and by an almost identical
117 to 105 vote, that state banks should be used as repositories for pub-
lic funds. Finally, by an overwhelming margin of 175 to 42, the House
authorized a seven-man committee to study the Bank's affairs and to
determine the causes of the financial distress. Appointed by Speaker
Andrew Stevenson, the committee included five Jacksonian Democrats
and only two Whigs, Edward Everett of Massachusetts and William W.
Ellsworth of Connecticut. When the committee carried its investigation
to Philadelphia, Biddle destroyed whatever case he may have had left by
refusing to testify or to permit access to the Bank's books or to its con-
gressional correspondence. The committee report on May 22 roundly
condemned the Bank for precipitating the financial crisis of the winter.
Ibid., Serial 262, Report No. 481. A separate investigation by the Senate,
documented below, pages 352–357, was too late and too weak in argu-
ment significantly to change public opinion.

TO EDWARD EVERETT

Washington April 26. '34

Dear Sir

I am obliged to you for your letter of the 23rd.[1] All things with your
name on them shall be taken care of, so as that you shall find no trouble,
in that regard.

If, in the course of yr investigation, the Com[mitt]ee should incline
to notice my name, I wish you to state, as on my authority;—
That I never had any particular or unusual accomodation from the
Bank, to the amt. of a single dollar;—
that since I went to Boston, in 1817, I have kept my account, & done my
necessary banking business at the Boston Office; & notes, bills of Exchange &c, &c, with my name on them have been collected, & discounted, &c as often as occasion required, precisely as would have been done
in the case of any other person, & not otherwise. I have reports of mortgages, standing loans, &c &c between the Bank & myself, in all which
there is not a single word of truth. I never gave the Bank any mortgage,
& never had any standing loan, or any other accomodation, except in
the way of discount of bills and notes, as at other Banks.

As to Mr [John] Connell's notes &c., they arise in a strictly professional transaction. He obtained the agency of the claims of our Boston Merchants & Insurance Offices, under the French Treaty. They made it a
condition of the bargain, that he should secure my professional services,
in all cases; & having the agency of a vast amount of other claims, Mr
Connell engaged my professional aid in the whole, as matter of contract,
& the notes were given in pursuance of this contract. That is the whole
matter. You may make any use of these facts, public or private, which
you deem proper.

I recd yr former letter,[2] at Boston. All things look exceedingly well in
N York. They can hardly fail to go right, in their further progress. I am
glad you propose writing to Col [Thomas Handasyd] Perkins. He is now
here, & will probably remain a few days longer. If the suggestion is put
to me, I shall make something like what you suggest *a condition*, to any
effort on my part. We now consider Va. as gone decidedly & strongly
agt. the President. The Protest[3] has finished the work. Did you ever see
any thing better than the Baltimore Resolutions?[4]

It will oblige me *much*, if you will keep me advised of yr proceedings,
& let me know the general temper manifested by the Com[mit]tee. We
think something of making a like Com[mitt]ee from the Senate. Yrs truly
ever   D. Webster

ALS. MHi. Published in *PC*, 2: 6.

1. Not found.

2. Not found.

3. On April 17 President Jackson
sent to the Senate a "protest" against
the resolution passed by that body
censuring his conduct in the removal
of the deposits. See *Register of De-*
bates, 23d Cong., 1st sess., pp. 1317–
1336.

4. On April 23 at a Whig meeting
in Baltimore, the President's protest
was roundly condemned in a lengthy
set of resolutions. See *Niles' Register*,
46 (May 3, 1834): 165–166.

FROM BENJAMIN T. PICKMAN, DAVID HENSHAW, CHARLES SPRAGUE, AND FRANKLIN HAVEN

Boston 28th April 1834

Sir,

With this we take the liberty of handing you a memorial, addressed
to the Congress of the United States, on the subject of the legal value of
Gold Coin & the making of foreign Coins a legal tender under suitable
regulations as to their weight & fineness.[1] The memorial as you will perceive contains the names of a very large number of our business men &
we believe expresses the individual sentiments of the mercantile community of this City. In behalf of the memorialists we would respectfully
ask you to present the memorial to the Senate & would request your aid

& that of your Colleague Mr [Nathaniel] Silsbee in the promotion of its object. We remain very respectfully Your most obt. Servts.

B T Pickman[2]
David Henshaw
Charles Sprague[3]
Franklin Haven.[4]

LS. NhHi.

1. The memorial, of "sundry inhabitants of Boston, Massachusetts, praying that the value of gold coins may be enhanced and regulated," dated April 10, 1834 (mDW 45084), was presented to the Senate by Webster on May 2.

2. Benjamin Troppan Pickman (1790–1835), merchant at 24 India Wharf, was at this time president of the Massachusetts Senate. His father, Benjamin Pickman, Jr., and Webster had served together in the state Constitutional Convention of 1820.

3. Sprague (1791–1875), former city councillor, was first associated with the Suffolk Bank of Boston, then in 1825 came to the Globe Bank, where he was cashier.

4. Haven (1804–1893) was at this time cashier of the Merchants Bank in Boston and became its president in 1836, a position he held for the next forty-six years. The bank through Haven's efforts had earlier been chosen by Kendall as one of the "pets" for government deposits. By at least 1836 or 1837 Webster and Haven had formed a close social and financial relationship: the Boston banker became an important source of political backing and of legal fees for Webster while the senator was able to bring governmental business and an occasional appointment Haven's way.

TO [SAMUEL JAUDON]

Washington May 5. 1834

Private

My dear Sir

I have been looking two or three days for Mr [John] Connell, in order to send a renewal for my drafts. The form of the papers is, if I mistake not, two drfts, 5,000 each, drawn by him, & accepted by me, payable at Boston, one of 11/14 May, the other 14/17 Do.—I intended to pay one of them, without renewal, but am not able to do so. Mr Connell has not yet arrived here. He may intend to stay some days yet, in Philadelphia. I therefore enclose two acceptances, for his signature, leaving notes to be filled by you; & if he shall be in Philadelphia, on receipt of this, please send for him, & have the signatures. When discounted, please forward proceeds to Mr [Samuel] Frothingham, requesting him to apply same to payment of exisiting acceptances. I shall write him to pass difference to my debit in acct. in his Office. You will see by above minutes, that the first becomes due the 14th. inst.

I must pray you & Mr [Joseph] Cowperthwaite to take the trouble of arranging this matter. If I live to see you once more, I will place them on some other footing.

Should Mr Connell arrive here within a day or two, I will obtain his signatures to other dr[a]fts, here, & forward them to you.

We have nothing particularly new today. No new nominations for Directors. Yrs truly   D Webster

Please let me know whether Mr Connell is in Phila. when you receive this.

When shall we see the Com[mitt]ee?[1]

ALS. NHi.
1. The select House committee in-vestigating the Bank had been in Philadelphia for the past two weeks.

TO CHARLES HENRY THOMAS

Washington May 6, '34

Dear Henry,

I recd a letter from you, some days ago,[1] by which it wd. appear that all things were going along well. What you have done with the Wood lot (Hewett) is about right. It will be easy to throw a coat of mud over the level land, between the road & the hill, next fall, & plough it in.

Some things are to be remembered

1. The barn yard must be well scooped out, & made particularly deep in the centre. The bottom must be hard; to which end it may be necessary to cover it with clay, or, perhaps, at the deepest part, with a layer of small stones or gravel, with clay over. The centre of the yard, is the point to commence the manure heap. In to this center, so soon as it's cleared, in the spring, trash, mud, &c should be occasionally thrown in, & on this heap the barn yard summer manure should be thrown, every morning. In this way, the outer parts of the yard will be kept clean, for milking, & a growing heap of manure will be rising up in the centre. This will be about right.

2. In addition to the barn yard, we must have a manure heap some-where else, where we can pile up mud, trash, muscles &c, mix-ing the mass, occasionally with stable manure, or a little lime, &c. The best place I can now think of, is on that part of the land, lately bought of Mr [Charles] Wright, which is enclosed in the little pasture. This will be a handy place to draw mud, muscles, & trash to; & pretty convenient for distribution all over the farm.

This is suggested, only, for consideration. *The making of manure is the chief business of a farmer, at least in Marshfield.*

3. The open gutter, or drain, from the sink, along behind the corn barn, is a nuisance. There must be a covered drain. It need be but small. Mr Dunn must attend to it, before hot weather comes, & let the drain run out into the pig pen, or elsewhere.

These are all the particulars I think of, at present.

We have had a very *dry* time here, & I was fearing, that, if equally dry with you, t[rees] might suffer. Tree planting, I find, succeed[s or] not, very much according to the wetness or [dry]ness of the season. We have now had a copious rain here.

Do not omit writing longer than 5 or 6 days, at one time.

We are all well. Abt. 15th inst Mrs W. & the boys take their departure.

Give my love to the family, & to the Dr [John Porter] & Ann [Thomas Porter]. Yrs   D. Webster

How many calves—and how good? Ask Capt. [John] Thomas to be kind enough to look up the Potato Memorandum,[2] made last year, & take heed thereof.

ALS. MHi.   2. See mDW 39055.
  1. Not found.

TO WILLIAM JOHN DUANE

Washington May 10. 1834

Dear Sir,

I pray you to accept my thanks for a copy of your letters to the People of the U. States,[1] in Pamphlet form, which I recd. this morning; & I avail myself of the opportunity to tender you an expression of my respect, for the independent & patriotic manner, in which you conducted yourself, in your late official station, under circumstances peculiarly embarrassing.

Although you feel, doubtless, in common with us all, great pain at the distress brought upon the Country by recent measures, it must give you heartfelt satisfaction to reflect that you firmly opposed those measures, at the first step.

You have relinquished Office; but you have not paid too dear for the conscientious discharge of duty, nor for the new & large measure of regard, manifested towards you by the American People. I am, with respect, Your ob. sert   Danl Webster

ALS. PPAmP. Published in *Pennsylvania Magazine of History and Biography*, 54 (1930): 31.
  1. *Letters, addressed to the people of the United States, in vindication of* his conduct, by Wm. J. Duane, late secretary of the Treasury (Philadelphia, 1834), in which Duane defended his conduct and related through correspondence, other docu-

mentation, and his own commentary
the events leading up to his removal

as treasury secretary in September
1833.

TO NATHAN DANE

Washington May 15th. 1834

My Dear Sir,

I have in my possession a pamphlet bearing the following title.

"An

Explanation

of the

Map

which delineates that part of the FEDERAL LANDS, comprehended between Pennsylvania West Line, the River Ohio, & Scioto, & Lake Erie;
confirmed to the UNITED STATES, by sundry tribes of Indians, in the
Treaties of 1784 & 1786, and now ready for settlement.

Salem:
Printed by Dabney & Cushing,
1787"

This is an interesting publication, especially for an anticipation, which
it contains, of the general use of Steam Boats, on the Western Rivers. I
have thought it probable you could give me information of its authorship;[1] & with a view to that inquiry I have taken the liberty to write you
this letter.

I pray you to accept the assurance of my regards & best wishes.

Danl Webster

ALS. NhD.
1. In Dane's reply of May 23, 1834
(mDW 11703), he suggested to Webster that the pamphlet might have

been written by either John Fitch or
Arthur Lee. Modern authorities at-
tribute it to Manasseh Cutler.

FROM NICHOLAS BIDDLE

Phila. May 15. 1834

My dear Sir

I duly received, read and burnt your favor—and I have since waited
for the appearance of the motion.[1] Is it abandoned?

Of one thing I am certain,—that if nothing is done this session, we
shall have a summer and fall such as have not often been experienced.
The B. U. S. will be able to stand the squall—but I really fear that the
country will suffer deeply—you and I have done what we can to prevent
it & therefore will have nothing to reproach ourselves with.

The Government Directors are a poor set. [Henry] Horn I would not confirm were I in the Senate in consequence of the extreme insolence of his publications about the Senate itself. The same remark applies to [James Nelson] Barker the Collector. Roberts Vaux you know. Mr McAllister [Charles Macalester] was a member of the Board last year, named by the Stockholders. His conduct as a Director was not approved—not from any political consideration, but entirely and exclusively from his conduct in his monied transactions with the Board—and he was omitted—very deservedly—and he ought not now to be confirmed.[2] Let me hear of the condition, and progress of these nominations as they go along. Very truly Yrs   N. B.

LC. DLC.
1. Probably a promised motion for a Bank investigation by a favorably inclined Senate committee. The motion was not actually made until June 30, by Samuel L. Southard of New Jersey.

2. Charles Macalester along with Joseph White of Baltimore and Saul Alley of New York was confirmed by the Senate on May 22 while Roberts Vaux was confirmed and Henry Horn rejected on May 28.

TO DANIEL FLETCHER WEBSTER

Washington June 5. '34

My Dear Son

I presume you will be in Boston, by the time this letter shall arrive. So soon as you shall have made a short visit to Marshfield, I wish you to proceed to Exeter with Edward. It is high time he was at school. You will take him to Mr [Peter] Chadwicks,[1] & see him provided for, as to room &c. Ask Mr Chadwick to be kind enough to take care of him, in all those respects, in which a boy needs looking after. He must, among other things, take the trouble of attending to his personal cleanliness, &c &c. In all these particulars enjoin on Edward the importance of exact & steady habits. As to any clothes, or books, or other articles, if he shall need them Mr Chadwick will see him supplied, or tell him where to obtain what he wants. You must leave him a little pocket money, & a small monthly allowance can be sent him from home. Go with him to Dr. [Benjamin] Abbott,[2] & stay in town a day or two, until he has been at school once or twice, & begins to feel a little at home.

Congress will adjourn, I think, the 30th. & I shall probably be at home the 10. or 15 July. I shall be detained here a few days, perhaps, by business with the Comm[issione]rs, & must stop a day or two on the road. Your affectionate father   D Webster

ALS. NhHi. Published in Van Tyne, p. 587.

1. Chadwick (c. 1783–1847; admitted to Phillips Exeter in 1797),

clerk of courts in Exeter, New Hampshire.

2. Abbot (1762–1849; Harvard 1788), principal of Phillips Exeter Academy, Exeter, New Hampshire, from 1788 to 1838.

TO CHARLES HENRY THOMAS

Washington
June 9. 1834
Monday 1 oclock

Dear Henry,

I recd yr letter from Hingham this morning, & Thursday one from Marshfield.[1] I have only time to give you a short answer.

I incline to buy the land, down at the Fish House, should it go *cheap*, as you suppose it will, tho' you do not mention any probable price.

There are three things, on acct. of which it might be valuable.

1. I think I can make a good oyster pond, on it; but of this I am not certain, till I look at it, & have its height &c, accurately taken. If there be any difficulty, in this respect, it would be to make the water deep and, to preserve the oysters in the winter. That, I am afraid, would be difficult.

2. It is a most excellent place for salt works. There can be no mistake about this.

3. I suppose the pasturage is worth something; and now that we have a gondola, I presume oxen & steers could readily be navigated across.

If, on the whole, it goes at a price which you think *cheap*, you may buy it.

Congress will adjourn, I presume, either June 30th, or July 7th. You say nothing in your last of the progress of the barn, shed &c. I hope the carpenters drive on well. If the barn is not done *well*, & *nice*, in every respect, & according to the plan, I fear I shall scold. For so much money, we ought to have the *precise thing*.

You say nothing abt. the well, in the yard. If you receive this at Marshfield, find time to tell us *all* about *all* things. Ann [Thomas Porter] has forgotten, I almost fear, there is any such person as Mr W.

The weather is warm. My health is pretty good, but I have been obliged to buy a cheap poor sort of a pacing saddle horse. If it seems worth it, I shall bring him home. He may do, possibly, for Mrs We[b]ster & Julia to ride sometimes. I take a pace upon him, every day.

You must get somebody to weed my corn, & let me do as much for them, next hoeing. I expect my corn will be twice as good as that at the Winslow place. Yrs   D. Webster

Before you receive this, you will see the boys & the brown horses. If F[letcher] is still with you, ask him to write me his views & ideas about Marshfield.

ALS. MHi.
  1. Neither letter found.

FROM ALBERT GALLATIN

New York 13th June 1834

Dear Sir

There is some uneasiness amongst our Banks about the delay, on the part of the Com[mitt]ee of Finance, to report on the bill from the House respecting foreign silver coins.[1] The draft of a bill which accompanied our Memorial to the Senate[2] had met with universal approbation and is all we want. I understand that it does not differ materially from the bill as amended which passed the House. I can assure you that this is a subject of extreme simplicity, & that the Mexican dollars may be taken by tale with as great safety as the Spanish which are now by law receivable in that way. Their average weight taken on various parcels amounting together to more than 200,000 dollars is 416 1/6 grains, and their fineness exceeds that of ours by almost 1/2 p%. This I may aver on my own knowledge, and you may have seen within a few days in our news papers that the same fact has lately been verified in England by authentic assays in the Mint. I am assured by persons well acquainted with the subject, that the same may be affirmed of the dollars of Peru and Chili. As to the five francs pieces, they are worth when new 93 cents & 3 mils, and were for a while legal tender here, without any inconvenience and to the advantage of the public at large. You are already aware of the necessity of the measure and that not one tenth part of the specie in our vaults consists of U. States or foreign legal coins.

The bill, which we also sent, for raising the value of the gold American coins to about their average market price,[3] would add, I believe, one or two millions of dollars to our metallic currency, and greatly facilitate a regular payment of the balances due to each other by the Banks in the same city. Perfect accuracy in fixing the true average ratio of the relative value of gold to silver is unattainable: but that of 15 to 1 established by our Mint laws is universally acknowledged to be erroneous by more than 4 p% and has of course made our gold coins an article of merchandize instead of being a part of our currency. The true ratio is from 15.6 to 15.7 to 1. That of 15.625 (or 15 5/8) to 1, which was adapted in Mr C[ampbell] White's bill & which we preserved in ours is as good as any. The only practical objection is that it will make the Sovereign or £

St. [pound sterling] equal to $4.75.6, and that our tariff regulations make it in estimating duties, worth $4.80. But this is not very material. What is important is, that the bill for that purpose, in order to ensure its passage, should be exclusively limited to that object, and that every theoretical view of the subject should be for the present be discarded.

You will render a great service to the commercial community and to the public at large by hastening the passage of both bills. I have the honour to be with great respect Dear Sir Your most obedient Servant

Albert Gallatin

ALS. Samuel J. Feigus, Uniontown, Pennsylvania.

1. The bill, House Bill 255, had been passed in the House on May 28 and was reported out with amendments by Webster's Finance Committee on June 14.

2. "Memorial of Sundry Banks of New York, Praying that certain Foreign Coins be made a legal tender, that the value of Gold Coins be regulated, and that the means of coining at the Mint be increased," *Senate Documents*, 23d Cong., 1st sess., Serial 242, Doc. No. 399, p. 4.

3. *Ibid.*, p. 3. This bill, House Bill 312, was finally passed by the Senate on June 28.

TO JOHN BRADFORD WALLACE

Washington June 14. '34

My Dear Sir

I have recd yours, & have dispatched the Speeches, according to your list.[1] If you should find a dozen more, on your own office table, when you reach Meadville, you can give them to friends, or throw them away with other rubbish, as may be most convenient.

I pray you to remember me, most kindly, to your wife & daughters; & believe me, My Dear Sir, Very cordially yours,   Danl Webster

ALS. NhD.

1. Webster is responding to Wallace's request of June 12 (mDW 11742) for copies of his speech on the President's protest against the resolutions, censuring him for removing the government deposits from the Bank of the United States. *Register of Debates*, 23d Cong., 1st sess., pp. 1663–1690.

TO EDWARD WEBSTER

Washington, June 23, 1834.

My Dear Son:

Fletcher wrote me from Exeter the next day after your arrival,[1] and informed me that you had been so fortunate as to be received at Colonel [Peter] Chadwick's, and was commencing your studies. I am glad you are so well situated, and trust you will make progress in your studies.

You are now at a most important period of your life, my dear son, soon growing up to be a young man and a boy no longer, and I feel a great anxiety for your success and happiness.

I beseech you to be attentive to all your duties, and to fulfill every obligation with cheerfulness and punctuality. Above all, remember your moral and religious concerns. Be constant at church, and prayers, and every opportunity for worship. There can be no solid character and no true happiness which are not founded on a sense of religious duty. Avoid all evil company and every temptation, and consider that you have now left your father's house and gone forth to improve your own character, —to prepare your own mind for the part you are to lead in life. All that can be done for you by others will amount to nothing unless you do much for yourself. Cherish all the good counsel which your dear mother used to give you, and let those of us who are yet alive have the pleasure of seeing you come forward as one who gives promise of virtue, usefulness, and distinction. I fervently commend you to the blessing of our Heavenly Father.

.   .   .   .

I wish you to make my best respects to Dr. [Benjamin] Abbot, and remember me to Colonel and Mrs Chadwick and their family. If I do not hear from you sooner, I shall expect to find a letter from you when I reach Boston. Your affectionate father,   Daniel Webster

P.S. Since writing this I have received your letter,[2] and am very glad to hear from you.

Give my love to your friend Upham.[3] I remember the great tree, and know exactly where your room is. Charles sends love.[4]

Incomplete text from Frank H. Cunningham, *Familiar Sketches of the Phillips Exeter Academy and Surroundings* (Boston, 1883), pp. 137–138. Original not found.

1. Not found.
2. Not found.
3. This is probably George Timothy Upham (c. 1820–1857), son of Timothy Upham of Portsmouth, who was admitted to Phillips Exeter in 1834, the same year as Edward, and later became a merchant in San Francisco.

4. Charles Brown, a servant and former slave, emancipated by Webster.

On June 30, the last day of the first session of the Twenty-third Congress, Senator Samuel L. Southard brought forth a motion that Webster's Finance Committee have leave to sit during the summer and fall recess in order to conduct an investigation of the Bank of the United States. The committee was instructed to inquire whether the Bank had violated its charter and whether public monies still in its possession were "safe," and to look into the operations of the institution since 1832 with regard to the extension and curtailment of loans and discounts, its internal exchange dealings, and its management. The resolution passed 20 to 12, with predictable Whig support for an investigation by a committee consisting of Webster, Ewing, Mangum, Tyler, and Wilkins, only the last of whom had any notable Jacksonian leanings. Senate Journal, 23d Cong., 1st sess., Serial 237, pp. 391–392.

Upon the adjournment of Congress the committee went to Philadelphia to determine the "readiness" of Biddle and the directors "to submit the books and papers of the bank to the free and unreserved inspection and examination of the committee." Committee members then went home in order to obtain information from their own and nearby states on a number of banking questions in accordance with the document below drafted by Webster. A number of the branch banks were visited. Committee members, for instance, visited the Boston branch in late August and early September. On September 13 the committee returned to Philadelphia where it pursued its investigation to completion. Throughout the half year Webster did as little as possible, leaving most of the investigation and nearly all of the writing of the report to John Tyler and Willie P. Mangum. As a well-known friend of the Bank, he followed the most prudent course. As chairman of the committee, however, Webster was able to shape the substance of the investigation and to blunt conclusions. Some indication of his effectiveness appears in his draft of Biddle's reply to the committee (printed below), which is unaltered, except for minor changes, from the letter the Bank president submitted to the committee on July 8 (also printed below). The report was read by its principal author, John Tyler, on December 18, 1834. With unimportant exceptions, the report approved of the policy and operations of the Bank.

TO NICHOLAS BIDDLE AND THE DIRECTORS OF THE BANK OF THE UNITED STATES FROM DANIEL WEBSTER, CHAIRMAN OF THE SENATE FINANCE COMMITTEE

Philadelphia, July [7th] 1834

Gentlemen,

We enclose you the copy of a Resolution, passed by the Senate of the United States on the 30th. of June, by which you will perceive it is made our duty to execute certain inquiries, respecting the Bank of the United States. These inquiries are,

1. Whether the Bank has violated its Charter;
2. Whether the monies of the United States, now remaining in the Bank are safe;
3. What has been the conduct of the Bank, since 1832, in regard to the

successive extentions & curtailments of its loans & discounts, and its dealings in domestic or internal bills of Exchange;

4. And what has been its general conduct & management since that period.

We shall enter upon these inquiries, at some period before the next meeting of Congress, & shall endeavor to obtain the most full & ample information upon all & each of the points, enumerated in the instructions of the Senate. To this end it will be necessary that the Books of the Bank should be freely subject to our inspection, and that we should be furnished with all such accounts, statements, abstracts, & exhibits, as we may deem useful & proper. The time of commencing this examination will hereafter be communicated to you; but in order to facilitate our labor, & enable us to go through it with more dispatch, when we shall again assemble, we have now to request that the following statements or tables should be made out, & forwarded as soon as convenient to the Chairman of the Committee, viz.

    I. A quarterly statement of the affairs of the Bank, and of its officers, respectively, for the several quarters of the years 1832, & 1833, & the three first quarters of 1834. This statement to contain

      1. Amount of notes discounted.

      2. Domestic bills of Exchange, purchased, or discounted

      3. Foreign bills of Exchange, purchased or discounted.

      4. Balance due from other Banks, including their notes.

      5. Balance due to other Banks.

      6. Amount of Specie; specifying how much is gold & how much silver; how much coin, & how much bullion.

      7. Amount of public Deposites

      8. Amt. of private Deposites.

   II. Statement of all the dividends of the Bank; with an account of any existing surplus fund, or contingent fund.

  III. Statement of the real estate & banking houses, held by the Bank, with an estimate of their value.

  IV. The Debt due the Bank; with an estimate, showing what part is regarded as bad, or doubtful, & what funds, if any are relied on to meet any deficiency arising from such causes.

   V. Copies of all the bye laws & rules of proceeding adopted by the Directors.

  VI. Statement of the rates of exchange, on domestic bills, at the several quarters before mentioned, between the principal distant cities, in the U.S.

AL revised draft in Webster's hand. NhHi. Published in *W & S*, 16: 236–238.

HEADS OF INQUIRY FOR MEMBERS OF THE [FINANCE] COM[MITT]EE

[c. July 7, 1834]

1. What is the circulating money; how much paper, & how much or how little coin? What denominations of coin?
2. What is the existing Banking system? How many Banks, with what capitals, & what denominations of Bills do they issue?
3. Are the bills of these Banks at par, & how widely do they circulate? Have the Banks made provision for their payment in other places, besides the Bank which issues them?
4. What is the general course of trade? & what is the course of exchange? How are remittances made, & at what rates are bills bought & sold in the great Cities?
5. How have the rates of exchange been affected, by recent measures of Govt, & how are they likely to be affected by the expiration of the Bank Charter?
6. Which are the Deposite Banks, in the State? What capital—how much public money on Deposite—how is this public money secured? Do the Deposite Banks deal in stocks? How far are they able to increase their discounts, by reason of having the public monies? Is their circulation greater, & their credit more widely extended than before? Have they, in fact, extended their discounts? At what rates do they buy & sell exchange? How largely does it appear that they deal, in internal exchange? Do they buy bills, in all parts of the Union? Do they deal in inland bills without the interaction of a broker? Obtain lists, if practicable of their rates of exchange.
7. What is effect of the late laws, in regard to the introduction of gold coin into circulation?
8. In what money are payments made at land offices? Is this money of higher value than the general circulation? If so what is the rate of premium?

AD. NhHi. Published in *W & S*, 16: 238.

TO THE COMMITTEE ON FINANCE, U.S. SENATE, FROM NICHOLAS BIDDLE
[DRAFT IN WEBSTER'S HAND]

[c. July 8, 1834]

To A B.
 C D &c.
 &c &c.
 Com[mitt]ee of Finance of the Senate
  of U. S.
Gentlemen
 Your communication of   to the President & Directors of the

Bank of the United States has been received. As the Senate has thought proper to institute an examination into the conduct & condition of the Bank, the Board of Directors will certainly oppose no obstacle to the full & free prosecution of that examination. They presume, that in inquiring whether the Bank has violated its Charter, the Committee will think it matter of common right & justice, that the nature of any supposed violation may be suggested to the Board of Directors, to the end that they may lay before the Com[mitt]ee all the evidence & all the facts respecting such supposed violation. All the Books of the Bank will be freely subject to the inspection of the Com[mitt]ee, and <requested aid yielded them> all required assistance granted to them <to facilitate> for the examination of their contents.

So far as respects itself & its own proceedings, the Bank has no secrets. There is nothing which it would not disclose, with perfect willingness & readiness; nothing, indeed, that it would not rather desire to make known. Individuals have pecuniary transactions, & private accounts, with the Bank, which in this, & in all similar institutions, are regarded as confidential. The private accounts of individuals, therefore, it is presumed, the Committee does not wish to inquire into, unless such inquiry should become necessary, in the prosecution of some <substantial> specific charge of misconduct,[1] or violation of Charter, against the Bank, should it arise. In such case, the Directors suppose they should be justified in exhibiting even private accounts, as they would be in cases of judicial proceedings. If therefore any thing be charged against the Bank, amounting to a violation of Charter, every proceeding, document, paper & voucher in the possession of the Bank, connected with the alledged violation, will be promptly delivered to the Com[mitt]ee, verified, if required, by the oaths of the proper officers. And the Directors assure themselves that the Committee will not call for private accounts, or transactions with individuals, unless for some such reason or cause as has now been mentioned.

The papers called for by the Committee will be immediately furnished, & forwarded to the Chairman; & whenever it shall be the pleasure of the Committee to proceed with the examination, the Directors will give directions to the officers of the Bank to render all such aid to the Committee as may be necessary to facilitate their own labors, & to enable them to fulfill the expectations of the Senate.

AD draft by Webster. DLC. Copy in Biddle's hand, undated, is virtually identical. Compare the letter actually sent by Biddle to the committee, below.

1. Biddle's version (mDW 9969) deletes "of misconduct" and substitutes "which might make the production material."

FROM NICHOLAS BIDDLE TO WEBSTER AND MEMBERS OF THE SENATE
FINANCE COMMITTEE

Bank of the United States
July 8. 1834

Gentlemen,

I have had the honor of receiving your letter of the 7th. which was this morning submitted to the Board of Directors.

They have instructed me to inform you in reply that they will very promptly and cheerfully give every facility within their power to the investigation you propose. Having not the least motive or wish to withhold the most complete information of all their proceedings, but on the contrary being desirous of giving to them every publicity consistent with the rights and interests of other parties, they will freely submit all their books to the inspection of the Committee and furnish every assistance which may be required. They take the liberty of suggesting that the private accounts of individuals with this Bank, as with all similar institutions are regarded as confidential, and feel full confidence the Committee will in no case make public the state of such accounts unless to do so becomes necessary by reason of some imputed misconduct or infraction of the Charter. They further suggest that if in the progress of this examination the Committee see reason to suppose that any violation of the charter of the Bank has been committed the Committee will deem it a matter of common right and justice that the nature of the alleged violation should be suggested to the Board of Directors in order that they may lay before the Committee all the facts and explanations respecting such alleged violation.

The statements requested by the Committee will be immediately prepared and forwarded to the Chairman and whenever it shall be the pleasure of the Committee to proceed the Board of Directors will be ready and willing to render every aid in the most unlimited investigation of the concerns of the Bank.

I have the honour to be Very Respectfully   N. Biddle Prest.

ALS. NhHi.

TO [SAMUEL JAUDON]

Boston July 25. 1834

My Dear Sir,

I enclose you a letter from Mr. [John] Connell.[1] In reply, I have written him[2] that he must let the dr[a]fts be renewed till fall, & have added that I suggested to you, while in Philadelphia, a mode of arranging the matter, if we could accomplish it, without stating particulars. It is of great importance to get these matters out of the Bk of U. S. I feel very anxious, on this matter, & fear I shall find a necessity even of going to Philadelphia, which I should be most desirous to avoid, for a thousand reasons.

As to the small dr[a]ft, falling due the 24./27 current, please pay it if it go on, & draw on me for the amt, at 10 d[ay]s—and send an acceptance for same sum to Mr. [Samuel] Frothingham. It gives me great pain to trouble you with these affairs. But here they are, & we must manage them as well as we can, till times turn a little better. I have means ultimately, to pay them; & that is one comfort.

Mr. Connell ought to make no difficulty in renewing the two small dr[a]fts, (5,000 each) as I indorse the renewals of the note, (10,000) which is his. If they cannot be arranged else where, they must be renewed in the Bank for a short time, say 60 or 90 d[a]ys; & in mean time I must go to Philadelphia, if necessary; though such a journey, without some known object would attract a great deal of attention. Yrs truly

D. Webster

I must depend on your kindness to write me early, on these subjects, as I shall have no *quiet* till I see they are likely to be satisfactorily disposed of. I enclose a draft for 268.17.³

ALS. NHi.   2. Not found.
    1. Not found.   3. Not found.

TO [SAMUEL JAUDON]

Boston Aug. 2. 1834

Dear Sir,

I am obliged to you for your letter of July 30th.¹ It is my wish & intention to have my name out of the Bank, & all its branches, in the course of the Summer. I think this desirable on all accounts, & I believe it can easily be accomplished.

1. Mr [John] Connells two drafts. His acceptance of my drafts, guaranteed by you, (on a separate paper) could be discounted here, & with the proceeds the outstanding acceptances paid.

2. Mr. Connells note for $10,000 indorsed by me. By a little pains, & with the assistance of friends this c[oul]d probably be discounted at some other Bank in Phila[delphi]a—either in one note or two.

3. Two or three small matters of mine in the Branch here will be paid off.

These things being done, I can take an early occasion, next Session to say, that I neither owe the Bank a dollar, nor am on any paper discounted at the Bank, for any body, to the amt. of a dollar.

In these times of the prevalence of slander & falsehood, it seems important to be able to make this declaration, on some fit occasion, in my place.

The only difficulty will be, if there be any, in regard to Mr Connell's note;—but I should think that might be easily arranged.

In a day or two, I will send you papers, for yr consideration, for carrying this plan into effect. Yrs   D Webster

ALS. NHi.   1. Not found.

TO JAMES BROOKS

Boston, Aug. 5, 1834.

My Dear Sir

I have received your letter of the 3d instant,[1] in which you say that the Portland Argus imputes to me the expression of this sentiment, viz., "Let Congress take care of the Rich, and the Rich will take care of the Poor."

The same imputation has appeared in other prints. I know not where it originated, but you are quite correct in supposing it to be an entire and utter falsehood. I never expressed any such sentiment, publicly or privately, nor anything like it, nor any thing to give the least countenance or color to such an imputation.

My dear sir, if there be any who think it important to know my sentiments on subjects of this nature, they may readily satisfy themselves, that, for the last twenty years, on all suitable occasions, I have endeavored to maintain, as great and leading political truths, that Republican Constitutions are established for the benefit of the whole People, and that all measures of government ought to be adopted with strict regard to the greatest good of the greater number; that the Laws should favor the distribution of property to the end that the number of the very rich, and the number of the poor, may both be diminished, as far as practicable, consistently with the rights of industry and property; and that all legislation in this country is especially bound to pay particular respect to the *earnings of labor*; labor being the source of comfort and independence to far the greatest portion of our people.

I thank you for the friendly feeling which has led you to desire a direct contradiction of this calumny, and am, with much true regard, your friend,   Danl Webster

Text from the *National Intelligencer*,   Published in *W & S*, 16: 241–242.
August 16, 1834. Original not found.   1. Not found.

TO SAMUEL JAUDON

Aug. 6. 1834

D Sir,

I send enclosed to you two dr[a]fts on Mr [John] Connell, for 5,000 each; two memoranda of guaranty, & a written acknowledgment & promise of indemnity to Mr Connell, signed by me.[1] If agreeable to provide, in this way, for taking up the existing acceptances, please let these papers be signed & returned (except, of course, that designed to be held by Mr. Connell[)]. It wd. be *very* agreeable to me to hear from you soon, as I desire to make a little journey, & must wait till this matter be first settled.

I am going tomorrow to see the Salem Whigs.[2] Mr. [William] McIlvaine is here, & is also going to Salem, *cum multis aliis.* Yrs truly

D. Webster

ALS. NHi.
1. Enclosures not found.
2. The following day Webster de-livered a speech at a public dinner in Salem. See *Speeches and Forensic Arguments*, 2: 401–411.

Through the efforts of younger politicians like Rufus Choate and Caleb Cushing, the Boston Atlas *was converted into a distinctive Whig organ in the latter part of 1834. For some time the* Atlas *had been an embarrassment to Webster and others because of its opposition to a National Republican and Anti-Mason coalition. The contest over the governorship the year before showed the need for accommodation with the Anti-Masons lest they drift into the Democratic camp, while vacant congressional seats and incompleted business in the state legislature lent that need a measure of urgency.*

Webster's own ambitions, at the same time, required that he have at his command a strong, vital press. Acquisition of a controlling interest in the Atlas *coincided with the appearance in the* New England Magazine *of an article—unsigned but the work of Joseph Story—entitled "Statesmen—Their Rareness and Importance" which highlighted Webster's political career and gave him glowing praise. With the help of the* Atlas *and of its dynamic young associate editor, John Osborne Sargent, the press build-up of Webster gathered momentum. Shortly before the end of the year, the* Atlas *nominated the senator as a presidential candidate (see Sargent to DW, December 17, 1834, below), and in late February 1835, in the spirit of a new coalition and the demise of older party identifications, the Webster newspaper endorsed Edward Everett as the Anti-Masonic candidate for governor.*

FROM CALEB CUSHING

Newbury Port Aug 9. 1834

Dear Sir:

Our interview with Mr [John O.] Sargent yesterday was altogether satisfactory. He is young, but manly, intelligent, & in every respect, as it seems to me, such as we could desire, except on the score of general experience. He enters, heart & soul, into all our hopes & wishes.

We were unable to do any thing in the forenoon, except to make an appointment for the afternoon; and it was so late when I left Mr Sargent that I could not conveniently apprise you of the result in person. Not knowing whether the mail is to be trusted entirely, I shall not go over the details of the conversation. Nor is it needful at present. I give you the results.

Mr [Richard] H[aughton] is the businessman; and Mr Sargent answers for him decidedly. They are to meditate on the details of the plan as I explained it; to consult with Mr [William] Sullivan, or write to Mr [Rufus] Choate or me if there should be occasion; and to be ready for a final adjustment of matters on the 20th instant at farthest. Mr Choate was obliged to leave town before our second interview; but with his concurrence I pledged our friends to two things: 1. indemnity. 2. any requisite intellectual aid, without limitation of quantity or form. Our friends in Boston can take up the matter sooner; or I will see to its completion at our meeting on the 20th: as you may decide.

We saw Mr Sullivan in Lynn, where he was awaiting us in consequence of your intimation. Very respectfully Your ob. sert.

C. Cushing

ALS. DLC. Published in part in Fuess, *Cushing*, 1: 146.

FROM CALEB CUSHING

Newbury Port Aug 10. 1834

Dear Sir:

I have just received a letter from Mr [John O.] Sargent, informing me that he has conferred with Mr H[aughton] who enters with the most perfect cordiality into all our feelings. Of course, nothing remains but the adjustment of the details, whether by me or any other gentleman, as convenience and your judgment may dictate. If you think the matter should or can be completed before the 20th, and desire my presence, I will attend your summons at any time. Meanwhile, in casting the parts for the writing to be done, please to consider my pen at your command, for whatever may be deemed within my competency; since other engagements compel me to be in Boston three quarters of the time during the coming autumn.

One thing needs your consideration. The A[tlas] has, in past times, treated unjustly the two Messrs Everett, and especially Mr. Edward Everett. I owe all possible gratitude to Mr. Everett; and Mr. [Rufus] Choate concurs with me in respect for his feeling & attachment to his interests. It would afflict me very much if he should fail to approve what we have done. It has seemed to me, however, that we do him a service in fact, since, I can not distinguish his interests from those of the general cause; and I think proper & seasonable explanation from you would make the arrangement satisfactory to his feelings. Very faithfully & respectfully Your ob. servt. C. Cushing

ALS. DLC. Published in part in Fuess, *Cushing*, 1: 147.

TO CALEB CUSHING

Boston Aug. 13. 1834

Private
My Dear Sir

I have recd your several letters of the 9th & 10th. instant,[1] & rejoice to find circumstances so promising, in regard to the A[tlas]. I am clear in opinion, that you & Mr. C[hoate] must carry thro' the arrangement. It cannot be in better hands. Our Boston friends, I am quite sure, will fully support you.

What you say of the treatment, heretofore, of Mr. E[dward] E[verett] by the Atlas, deserves much consideration. No consideration would lead me to do anything injurious to Mr. E. or which should wound his feelings. We are friends, of long standing, & I not only respect him, as a man, & admire his talents, but have a sincere personal attachment to him. I hope he will see the propriety of putting the A[tlas] under new influences; but if he should hesitate, it would create, in my mind, great doubts of the propriety of future proceeding. I could not, & would not, unjustly disregard his feelings, for the sake of any object, political or person[al]. But looking to Mr. Sargent, as the effective head, hereafter, of the paper, I confess its former course, in regard to Mr. E. did not occur to me, as furnishing an objection.

When you come up, suppose you call on him, & have a free conversation.

I shall be here, on & about the 20th. I am, Dr Sir, with true regard, Yrs D Webster

ALS. NN. Published in Fuess, *Cush-ing*, 1: 147–148.

1. See above.

TO JOHN DAVIS

Boston Aug 14. 1834

Dear Sir,

I have seen your correspondence with the Anti Masonick Com[mitt]ees[1] & have no doubt it will produce very considerable impression. There may be some Masons, so much attached to the Institution, as to be displeased with your recommendation of its abandonment; and there may be others, who wish its continuance *because* of its tendency to keep apart the Whigs & the Antimasons; but a great, a vastly great majority of the People I have no doubt, approve your views. I sincerely hope the Masons of Worcester County will adopt the suggestion, & set the example of giving up the lodges. I am persuaded, it would be extensively followed.

As to the Anti Masons, I confess I do not see how they can now, with any justice, set up a candidate in opposition to you. What could any Govr. do, more than you have done? You have supported a law for the abolition of secret oaths; & all such oaths are abolished. You have now recommended to Masons, to surrender their Charters; many of them, I trust, will follow your advice. It seems to me that reasonable & just men must see that your course has been candid, just, & conciliatory; & that there is no fair ground to oppose your re election. I have not the pleasure of much personal acquaintance with Mr [Pliny] Merrick, but his known character for honor & fairness gives me confidence, that to the extent of his example & influence, the friends of Anti Masonry will give you their support. On the other hand, I have like confidence, that Mr. [Ira] Barton, Mr [Charles] Russell,[2] & other Gentlemen of character & consideration in the County, will come forward, & agree to discontinue Masonic meetings, & Masonic lodges. Some effort, some action, some setting of an example, is all that is wanting, on either side, as it appears to me, in order to bring the great body of Whigs & Antimasons, in this State, into harmonious action. I am, My Dear, with the truest regard, yours

Danl Webster

ALS. MWA. Published in *W & S*, 16: 242–243.

1. On July 31, 1834, Pliny Merrick, chairman of the Anti-Masonic Committee for the County of Worcester, addressed a letter to Governor Davis on the subject of freemasonry. Urging that the Whigs join the attack on the Masonic institution, Merrick's letter called for a political conciliation founded on "the broad and common ground of opposition to the national administration." The letter further asked that Davis communicate to the committee his own views concerning this issue.

Davis's reply, dated August 1, equivocated, agreeing to the need for "public harmony" and a united anti-Jackson front, but criticized the Worcester group for overzealousness in pursuit of Masonry. Both letters were published, first in the Worcester *Palladium*, later in *Niles' Register*, 46 (August 23, 1834): 433–434, and attracted wide public attention.

2. Russell (b. 1793), of Princeton, Massachusetts, and a state senator from Worcester County, was a member of the Committee of Worcester County Masons which, on August 18, 1834, unanimously adopted a set of resolutions recommending the voluntary dissolution of the freemasonry. *Niles' Register*, 46 (August 30, 1834): 447–448.

FROM EDWARD D. GAZZAM

Mobile Ala Sept 20th. 1834

Dear Sir

The propriety & policy of your visiting the South *this fall*, strike me so forcibly that I should feel it as a loss of time & of occasion were I to defer any longer the communication of my views on this subject. I give them frankly & freely but if they seem to you urged with an earnestness uncalled for, I must plead in excuse the strength of my own convictions & the apprehensions I am under that you are by no means aware of the admirable opportunity which the present state of Southern feeling offers for an advantageous movement on your part.

Long continued ill health, made worse by each successive winter compelled me to seek a climate more congenial with a feeble constitution, and in accordance with my own judgment & the advice of medical & other friends I removed to this city last April, since which time I have been a quiet but not inattentive or careless observer of southern affairs. The result of my observations so far as they have a bearing on your political prospects is as I have just said, a firm conviction that your intended visit ought not to be further postponed or I should rather say that things in this quarter promise the happiest results from such a step. With the exception of some of the interior & less important parts of Alabama & Mississippi the Southern portion of the Union is in the enjoyment of *good* health. New Orleans & the other Southern cities have thus far not only escaped epidemics but throughout the summer have had such an unusual exemption from sickness as would have been remarkable at any season of the year. The Bills of Mortality for this city during the past summer & up to this day would compare advantageously with those of any of the Northern towns. So much for what concerns your personal safety.

The elections recently held in this & several of the neighboring states show conclusively that in the *South* the fortunes of "the party" are on the decline. But the people of the South are as yet entirely uncommitted on the subject of the next Presidency. Numbers may be considered as committed *against* some one of the distinguished men who have been spoken of for that office but as it regards all the others they are free to choose; for few or none are pledged or have even made up their minds in *favour* of any individual. Thus many of the Union party have said & done so much against Mr Calhoun that they might without hesitation be set down as the uncompromising opponents of that gentleman though they have not declared themselves in favour of any other. And again many of the old Jackson party though heartily ashamed of Jackson misrule could not nevertheless be brought over under any ordinary circumstances to the support of Mr Clay whom in the days of the "Bargain & Sale" clamour they were taught to distrust and whom they still consider or affect to consider all that their violent hostility & heated imagination then represented him to be. As for Mr Van Buren he has in this part of the country so little individual popularity that were it not for the peculiar position which he holds in the ranks of a drilled party it were scarce worth while attending to him. Not that he is unknown or unthought of here for the reverse is the fact, his bad eminence having gained for him in the South more positive & uniquivocal unpopularity than ever before fell to the share of any American statesman one of his predecessors in the Vice Presidency only excepted.

But as it regards yourself I may with truth observe that if there is no open & active advocacy there is no settled & confirmed hostility and on this you may rely that *at present* Public Opinion in the South in relation to the next Presidency is fairly *at sea* without a helmsman to direct its course—and furthermore that your character is more highly & more generally esteemed in the Southern states than you or your *Northern* friends are aware of. In this state in particular, considerable pains have been taken for several years past to make the people (not the reading portion, but the *crowd*) acquainted with your name & character & that too in such a way as not to excite the attention or suspicions of leading politicians. Public Opinion is not settled; it is on the open sea but such a pilot as yourself may direct its course even to the *North*. But a skilful eye is of little worth, if shut to the signs & tokens of the times, & a powerful arm will avail nothing if its strength be not put forth in the proper season. *This* is the moment for action & here is the fairest starting point. A visit from you at the present juncture would stir public opinion & give it the much needed impetus. There is just now a calm; but such an occurrence would spring a breeze and a strong and lasting one in your favour. There is ample time to make the Southern tour before the meeting of Congress & your venturing hither at *this season* would be considered a compliment to the Southern climate. It would imply a confidence in the general healthfulness of this country which would in no inconsiderable degree inhance your popularity with Southern citizens. I repeat then that this seems a most propitious period for your contemplated visit. You are not as yet an avowed, at least not a formally nominated candidate for the Chief Magistracy, but you are every where well known as the first among American Senators. In *that* character you would be received throughout the South with much respect and in many places with enthusiasm. Your presence among us would convert much of the respect now quietly & with some perhaps coldly entertained into warm & aroused sentiments of admiration. The time has come when the safest & surest course is the boldest. The *Constitutional* Whig who secures the South or any considerable portion of it will in all probability be the next President for such a candidate the Northern & Western whigs would be most ready to support. I know that Mr Clay has said to some of his friends that he would not again be a candidate but it is not yet certain that all of Mr Clays *friends* are satisfied that he should withdraw so that he may yet be the gentleman most in your way. My previous remarks respecting him were made on the supposition of *Mr Clay at home* and not Mr Clay travelling through the South & mingling freely with the people. Such an event may occur and those only who are acquainted with Southern character could form an idea of the effect which would probably ensue. But should you be the first to start for the South it would give you a decided advantage over any competitor coming after. There is in the nature of our Southern citizens a warmth of hospitality a contagious good feeling, & a sympathetic enthusiasm which would be enlisted in your behalf were you among them to look them in the face & take them by the hand. Such an opportunity as now offers for you to influence the South to your support may never again occur in favour of a Northern Statesman. Besides those who wish well to your cause there are thousands of the Jackson men who knowing their party to be on the decline would be ready to turn then from the setting to a rising sun.

Should you conclude to travel South you would probably pass through Charleston S. C. & Savannah & Augusta Geo. and these are all points which it would be advisable for you to visit. But I will not trouble you with details, my present object being to draw your attention to the importance of an immediate visit to the Southern section of the Union. I remain very respectfully Yr obt sert   Edward D. Gazzam

P.S. For reasons sufficiently obvious I shall enclose this letter to your friend Mr [Stephen] White.

ALS. DLC. The writer was probably Dr. Edward D. Gazzam (b. 1803), a Pittsburgh doctor and lawyer, who in the late 1840s and 1850s became a Free Soiler and then a Republican. He served in the Pennsylvania state Senate in 1856.

TO GEORGE WASHINGTON LAY

Boston Sept 22nd. 1834.

My dear Sir,

I congratulate you on the proceedings of the Utica Convention, and the great unanimity with which Mr. [William Henry] Seward was nominated for Governor of your State.[1]

I took the liberty of mentioning his name for that office to friends frequently, both in Washington and New York, and the only objection that I ever heard was his want of years.

I am glad this did not prevail. Mr. Seward is known out of the State as well as in it, his speeches in the Senate last winter, being the very first class of political productions, and having been extensively read. So far as I can judge no better nomination could possibly have been made.

I do not learn yet much about candidates for Congress with you. I presume that yourself and Messrs. [Philo Case] Fuller, Hazelton [Abner Hazeltine] and Whittlesea [Frederick Whittlesey] will be re-elected and that Mr. [Francis] Granger will go from Ontario. Several of our members have declined a re-election, we have to find successors to Mr. [Edward] Everett, Mr. [Benjamin] Gorham, Mr. [Isaac C.] Bates and Mr. [Rufus] Choate. It is uncertain who will fill the places of the two former gentlemen. Mr. [Leverett] Saltonstall, it is supposed, may succeed Mr. Choate and Mr. [William B.] Calhoun, Mr. Bates. We hope to send a good man from every district in the State.

I have suffered severely lately under a cold which has affected my eyes, so that I am obliged to write you by another hand. In about ten days I go to New York, to meet the members of the Committee of Finance in that city and in Philadelphia. It would give me much pleasure to hear from you at your convenience. I am, dear Sir, with very true regard, Yrs   Danl Webster

LS. DLC.

1. Earlier in September the New York Whig state convention had nominated Seward, a former Anti-Mason, but he was later defeated in the general election by the incumbent, William L. Marcy.

FROM WILLIE PERSON MANGUM

Philadelphia 24th. Septr. 1834.

My dear sir

Mr. [Thomas] Ewing & I deferred our departure from Boston a day or two, hoping to see you.

We regretted to learn that you were so much indisposed that your return from Marshfield could not be hoped for at a very early day. We endeavored to put you fully in possession of our views through your friend.

Mr. Ewing is now at Washington on the P[ost] O[ffice] Comm:—Gov. [John] Tyler is pursuing the investigation of the Bank here leisurely.

I read the news papers &c.

The officers of the Bank are making out several interesting papers—particularly a minutely detailed statement of the contraction of its operations since last fall, & the supposed necessity &c. &c.

Every facility is afforded us. We sit in the Bank house, & every requisition is promptly & cheerfully complied with.

Suggestions & intimations are reaching us from various quarters. I am sure, judging from what has appeared, that the real interest, as well as the wish of the Bank, is to court the fullest scrutiny. I believe that every thing yet looked into, is satisfactory to the members of the Comm. here. Mr. Ewing will return here in eight or ten days. I recd. a letter from him last night. He says Mr. [Samuel] Southard, is unwell. His committee go on well. They will take testimony here & in New York, when he shall come north.

We supposed that it was wholly unnecessary for you, at the *slightest sacrifice of convenience or inclination*, to come south, until we go to New York.

That will probably be in 8 or 10 days. We shall however, apprize you in advance of the precise time. It may be longer.

You may therefore in the opinion of all of us, consult freely your convenience & inclination. We shall need you at N. York & likewise 2 or 3 days in Phila. We shall not touch the *Pets* until your arrival.

You know how important it is for you to be at Baltimore.

Be pleased to make my best respects to Mrs. Webster and accept for yourself Dear Sir, the assurance of my entire respect & regard.

W. P. Mangum

Gov. T[yler] desires his best respects to Mrs. W. & yourself.

ALS. NhHi.

FROM SAMUEL FROTHINGHAM

Office Bank U. S.
Boston Sep 25. 1834

Dear Sir,

Mr. [William] Appleton had an opportunity of conversing with some of the gentlemen of the Com[mitte]e after their investigation at the Office and seems to think that one of them at least was still under an impression that the Members of our board had had an undue share of Discounts during the season of pressure following the removal of the deposits. If any such impression exists it is very desirable that it should be removed, and with this in view I have taken the liberty to present to you a few facts from our Books in relation to the subject.

The whole amount discounted for Members of our Board from 1 Octo. 1833 to Jan. 1. 1834 was

Notes dis[counte]d	$107,667.09
Domestic Bills	66,859.93
for Directors in all	174,527.02

This has already been furnished the Com[mitte]e in reply to one of their questions; but they did not require a Statement of the whole amount discounted at this Office during the same period, which would seem to be necessary in forming an opinion of the relative amount of Discounts to Directors.

The whole amount discounted during this term was—

in Notes dis[counte]d—	$1,319,559.47
Domestic Bills—	874,489.68
Whole amount Discounted	$2,194,049.15
Whole amount for Directors	174,527.02

Which gives a little short of 8 p Ct of the whole amount discounted, to Directors.

On the 20 Feb following our loan was down to the lowest point of the season and we then commenced increasing it. From this date to May 1st. we discounted

in Notes	1,490,145.84
Domestic Bills	899,269.47

Whole amount dis[counte]d from 20 feb to 1 May } $2,389,415.27

Of which was discounted for Directors as follows, viz.

in Notes	256,193.92
Domestic Bills	313,420.29

Whole amount for Directors from 20 feb to 1 May } $569,614.21

during which last period, (20 feb to 1 May) two of our Board for whose firm, we discounted the largest amounts, being agents for certain large Manufacturing establishments, had to provide means for payments of acceptances at this Office for said Factories of drafts negotiated at other branches of the Bank to the amount of $601,984.

These two periods were those of the greatest pressure and those to which the inquiries [of] the Com[mitte]e were particularly directed. I have the honor to be with great respect, Dr Sir, Your ob st.

Sam. Frothingham, Cashr.

ALS. NhHi.

TO PELEG SPRAGUE

Boston. Oct. 3. 1834

My Dear Sir,

I recd your letter this morning.[1]

It had not occurred to me that the result of the Election in Maine had rendered it indispensable for you to resign your seat in the Senate; but I suppose you look upon the election as a kind of appeal, to the People, & feel bound, by what was said in the Senate, to follow the result by resignation; altho. I do not recollect that you pledged yourself to any such course.[2] I shall—we all shall deeply deplore your resignation. The session will be important, & critical; & men on the other side, like Mr [Bedford] Brown, will doubtless not think of resigning, tho' they have as much reason for that course as you have.[3] I have not heard it suggested, by any one, that you ought to resign, or probably would. Nevertheless, it is a point fit for consideration, & in regard to which I am desirous you should act in the manner most agreeable to the honor & dignity of your own character. I am going to Philadelphia, & shall there see some of our friends of the Senate, & will learn, without formal asking, what strikes them as being proper.

On one point I am very clear. I *would not* resign to the Governor [Robert Pinckney Dunlap], nor would I give any formal notice of my intention. I would wait quietly at home, hold my peace, & a short time before the assembling of the Legislature, I would address a letter to the Legislature, & enclose it to the Governor with a request that he would lay it before the two Houses on their meeting. If you give any reasons, I think they should be short & grave. Mr [John Quincy] Adams letter, resigning his seat in the Senate, in 1807, or thereabout, is a good model. As I remember, he only said that he resigned, because the Legislature seemed to expect from him a degree of opposition to the measures of the Administration, which he could not make, consistently with his sense of public duty.[4]

I will write you again from Philadelphia, but on the present question, that is, the propriety of resigning in season for the Govr. to fill the place, I am already clear & decided. I am entirely against that.[5]

We drank your health at Concord, with as much enthusiasm as if you had beaten your opponent ten thousand votes.[6] I cannot but be obliged to you, for the kind manner in which you alluded to me in your letter to the Com[mitt]ee.[7] I need not assure you that I value your friendship & regard at a very high price. I pray kind remembrance to Mrs Sprague, & am, as always, very truly Yours   Danl Webster

I am obliged to go to Phila[delphi]a, to meet the Com[mitt]ee. If I get back in any season, I shall, *assuredly*, visit Maine.

ALS. MDuHi.
1. Not found.
2. Sprague had just lost the governorship in a statewide popular election. His Senate term would expire March 3, 1835, and with a solidly Democratic state legislature, he stood no chance of reelection. His letter of resignation, dated November 7, 1834, is in *Niles' Register*, 47 (November 29, 1834): 203.
3. The cases were not comparable. Although party divisions in North Carolina were close, Brown was subsequently reelected.
4. John Quincy Adams to the Honorable Senate and House of Representatives of the Commonwealth of

Massachusetts, June 8, 1808, in Worthington C. Ford, ed., *The Writings of John Quincy Adams* (7 vols., New York, 1913–1917), 3: 237–238.
5. In January 1835 the Maine legislature elected John Ruggles, a Democrat, to fill Sprague's unexpired term and to continue for the full term beginning March 4.
6. At a public dinner on September 30 for Senator Samuel Bell of New Hampshire.
7. The letter, not found, was undoubtedly sent to the Senate Finance Committee, the committee referred to later in the letter, which was currently investigating the Bank of the United States.

TO [?]

Boston Oct. 11. 1834
[M]y Dear Sir,
    Allow me to congratulate you, & [th]e other friends, on the triumph of correct [prin]ciples in Maryland. So complete [a] revolution was hardly to have been [e]xpected.[1] We cannot doubt that your [e]xample will have great weight, [in] neighboring states, now about holding [their?] elections.[2] Yrs truly   D. Webster

ALS. NhHi.
1. On October 6 the Whigs had gained a 62 to 18 majority over the Jacksonians in the elections for the Maryland House of Delegates. This represented a major reversal from the previous year's 45 to 35 Democratic margin.

2. New Jersey, Ohio, and Pennsylvania were to hold general elections on October 14, and New York and Massachusetts would follow in early November. By and large these early Whig expectations of victory went unfulfilled.

TO [EDWARD EVERETT]

[c. Oct 11, 1834]

Dear Sir

The results of the Maryland election furnish another opportunity for a paragraph for *Mr. Taney*. His labors have come to little.[1]

It might be said, perhaps, *inter alia*, that what Mr Webster said professed to be founded on documents—& if not well founded, was easily refuted.[2] Mr. Taney seems to have been influenced by some other motive than defense of the administration in giving a *personal* character, to the matter; as if what was publicly stated, on the strength of public documents, was a affair of *private* veracity,[3] &c &c &c Yrs   D. Webster

ALS. MHi.

1. In the Whig landslide of October 6, Taney's home county, Frederick, elected four Whig candidates in place of four Jacksonian incumbents.

2. During the Senate's investigation of the deposit system in the spring of 1834, Taney had frequently been accused of having appointed, without legislative authorization, an agent to act as liaison between the Treasury Department and the deposit banks. Although Taney had flatly denied this in an official letter to the Senate on April 11, 1834, Webster, speaking in reply to Jackson's protest on May 7, reasserted the charge, citing unspecified "official" information. This apparent disregard by Webster for existing documentation was widely attacked in the Jackson press.

3. In a speech at Salem on August 7, 1834, Webster referred to Taney as the "pliant instrument" of Jackson. *Niles' Register*, 47 (October 18, 1834): 106; but the term is missing in Webster's own text in *Speeches and Forensic Arguments*, 2: 401–411. As Taney had been rejected by the Senate as secretary of the Treasury on the previous June 24 and was therefore no longer a government official, he considered Webster's statement to be both an abuse of the senator's high station and a personal affront. Thus in a speech at Elkton, Maryland, on September 4, Taney charged Webster with having intentionally misrepresented official documents and added that he believed Webster himself to be the "pliant instrument" of the Bank. *Niles Register*, 47 (October 18, 1834): 106–108.

TO HENRY HUBBARD

Boston, November 18, 1834.

My Dear Sir:

I have received your two letters.[1] The note accompanying the last I have indorsed, and sent to the bank, where it will be doubtless discounted, according to your wishes.

Will you allow me to say, my dear sir, that I had one objection, though a trifling one, to indorsing your note. You know what stories have been circulated (and nowhere more diligently than in New Hampshire) of my pecuniary obligations to the Bank of the United States, heavy mortgages, etc., etc. Now, the truth is, that the bank never discounted or advanced to me a cent in the world, except in the ordinary way as they have done for others; and, at this moment, the indorsement of your note, and one other signed by another gentleman, constitutes nearly, if not entirely, my whole liability to the bank; and, to put an end to such slanders, and to have been enabled myself to say that the bank did not hold my name for a dollar, I should, perhaps, if you had lived here, have suggested to you the obtaining of some other name instead of my own. But, as you lived in the country, it might have been inconvenient to you; and, after all, I suppose there would be just as much libellous matter published, let the facts be one way or the other. Mr. [Samuel] Frothingham will probably write you. I hope you will find the rogue that took such liberties with your name.[2] Yours with regard   Danl. Webster

Text from Curtis, 1: 498–499. Original not found.

1. Hubbard to DW, November 2, 1834, mDW 11949; other not found. Hubbard wished to obtain a loan from the Boston branch of the Bank of the United States for $5,000. The missing letter contained a note for that amount to the Boston branch, which, as Webster indicates here, he endorsed before turning it over to the Bank.

2. Webster had received a letter purportedly from Hubbard on Octo-ber 14 in which the New Hampshire congressman requested Webster to send two $500 bills from two Boston banks allegedly to use in a court case involving the passing of bogus bills. Enclosed was a promissory note for $2,000 signed by himself and Milo G. Bliss (mDW11922). "Suspecting the whole to be a hoax or something worse," Webster sent back the letter and note on October 27 (mDW 11923). A week later Hubbard wrote to Webster to confirm his suspicions.

FROM JOHN BARNEY

Falls of Ohio Louisville Kentucky
Decr. 7th. 1834

My dear Sir

I have been highly gratified, in the rapid tour made through the West, to find, how strong a hold you have in the confidence and affections of the People.

At Cincinnati your visit is recollected with pride & your address[1] spoken of as a master piece.

The enclosed extracts cut out of an Ohio Journal[2] will show you that their friendship is animated; be pleased to return them to me after perusal directed to *Baltimore*, where I shall be in a few days—as Steam Boat Conveyance is more rapid than the Mail.

I wish to use them in Maryland.

I found Judge [John] McLean very civil and disposed to do every thing which becomes a Patriot.

In the approaching contest, he says, Men should be considered by the People but as straws to be blown out of their way, if they will not *give* way to insure success. As for himself, he will withdraw his name the moment any Candidate is agreed upon by the Party in opposition to Van Buren, & he is anxious that a decision should be made, as he considers V. B. gains strength by our division and consequent indecision. It is evident he is determined not to play a losing game, and unless he is nominated by the Party, and the friends of the other Candidates acquiesce in the nomination he will not be a Candidate.

This is as it should be. How shall we arrive at the conclusion? By nominations in the State Legislatures? or by a General Convention of all in the opposition? The time for action approaches.

My first and most ardent wishes are for your success—next the defeat & overthrow of the Heir *adopted*. Yrs ever   Jno. Barney

P.S. Do not omit to return me the enclosed to BALTIMORE.

ALS. NhD.

1. Although Webster did give a speech in Cincinnati during his western tour in the summer of 1833, it was probably never published. The *Boston Evening Transcript* of June 29, 1833, reported in a story from the *Cincinnati Gazette* that Webster's speech in the Ohio city was "extempore and there was no reporter present," but that Webster had given "encouragement" that he would furnish a copy for publication. No such copy, if one exists, has been found.

2. Enclosures missing.

TO EDWARD EVERETT

[December 8, 1834]

ROYALTY PUZZLED.—

It would seem that another Richmond is in the field, or to be brought into it, in the person of Hugh Lawson White. This worthy senator has been so true to his chief, in all & singular his measures, ends & aims, that report goes that it perplexes the occupant of the White House to decide between the Rival claims. To one, it has been "glory enough to serve under such a chief"; the other, whatever he may have said of the glory of it, has tracked his master with a never failing scent, in all his doublings, since the time when he recommended to Mr Monroe an oblivion of party, & voted for the Tariff.

[Here quote the two first Speeches, in King Lear].

Dr Sir,

You can make a readable paragraph out of the above. If you have no Shakespeare at hand, tell Charles[1] to bring you the Book.

That it is not strange that other persons, beside Mr V. B. should occasionally be mentioned, as candidates—[2]

There may be various reasons for this; there may be some of the party, no doubt there are many, with whom he is no favorite. These may naturally wish to bring forward somebody else.

And those who are for Mr [V.] B.—& who are completely pledged to him, may yet be willing to hold out an appearance of consultation, & canvass; as if it were the object to collect the sense of the party generally—whereas it is perfectly known that the K. C. & the office holders, & the whole band of pensioners & retailers are all linked to Mr. V. B.'s future.

That howsoever the Jackson jugglers may conduct their own nominations, the duty of the Whigs is plain.

They have committed themselves to the cause of the Constitution, in its original purity, & they will do nothing which may entrust it to unsafe hands.

They will support a Whig, & none but a Whig.

As to giving a preference to one Jackson man over another, & making that preference a ground of support; or as to voting for any man who has been looking with one eye to Whigs, & one to Tories;— all this is entirely out of the question.

The Whigs, while they have a most important duty to perform, have a very plain one.

They have engaged in the rescue of the Constitution from the hands of arbitrary power; & it is idle to expect that they will now give their support to any other than to one of those distinguished men, who have embarked in the same cause; staked their political futures upon it, & bearded power, in its strongest holds, in defense of the public Liberty.

AL. MHi. Although the editorial contained in this letter has not been located in any contemporary printed form, the general ideas it presents were widely circulated by the Whig press, including Webster's *Boston Atlas*, in early December 1834.

1. Identified in DW to Edward Webster, June 23, 1834, above, note 1.

2. Here and in the following paragraphs Webster on separate sheets appears to have added additional, unfinished ideas for the editorial.

FROM NICHOLAS BIDDLE

Phil. Dec 8th 1834.

My dear Sir

I have written to Mr. [John] Tyler that I wish his report to precede one I propose to make in answer to the Presidents Message.[1] I wish it for the sake of the Committee, in order that their report may have all the freshness of novelty about it instead of being forestalled by a previous publication of its Statements. I wish it too for the sake of the Bank, because I should prefer citing the opinion of an impartial Committee rather than making observations which from the Bank might appear interested. If you think so, have the goodness to make it so—even if the Committee has to report *in part* on the subject of the Bank.

There is one point I would have conversed with you about, but for my ill luck in not meeting you here. Among the documents furnished to Mr. Tyler was one showing the change in the policy of the Bank made by myself which led to the full development of its power & its usefulness. It is a very curious and very authentic document and interests me specially because really the change of the system made the Bank what it has been for the ten years past, and is my peculiar work. I should like that matter explained to the country by your Committee, so as to become historical and I will thank you therefore to take charge of it. Mr. Tyler can give you the paper & you can readily at a glance mould it properly. I pray you also to see that the report does justice to your friends in the Bank, assailed as they are by the rabble in power. With great regard Yrs   N. B.

LC. DLC.

1. Biddle did not in fact answer the charges in the President's message. He ordered instead a large printing of the Finance Committee's report. Although John Tyler, author of the report, had criticized the Bank for its practice of reprinting and disseminating congressional documents, he saw no objection to accepting a thousand copies from Biddle.

FROM NICHOLAS BIDDLE

Phila. Decr. 10. 1834

My dear Sir,

I recd tonight your favor of yesterday.[1] My letter of the 8th[2] will in part have anticipated its contents.

The points to throw out in high relief are

1. The curtailments—<which can be put in the best way by> showing that the curtailments ordered did not equal the deposits—that the curtailments effected did not equal by several million the aggregate amount of public deposits withdrawn—of private deposits which followed them—of diminished circulation—and that as soon as the Bank had put itself in safety it hastened to relieve the country. Mr Tyler has a memorandum which is conclusive on that head.

2. The exemption from all politics and the endeavors to pervert the institution by the people in power.

3. The historical development of the powers of the Bank for ten years past.

4. The Branch drafts—, French bills &c. about which Mr Tyler differs

somewhat in opinion from you as to the origin of them—but seemed inclined to consider it as settled by the Judiciary.

I wish your report would come soon as I wish to follow. Yrs   N. B.

ALS draft. DLC.   2. See above.
   1. Not found.

TO JOSEPH GALES

Sunday Morning [December 14, 1834]

Dear Sir

I have read the marked passages in the Alb'any Argus.[1] They are a tissue of falsehoods. I know not whether it be worth while to contradict the calumny. If you think it be, call over here & we will have a paragraph made.[2] Yrs   D. Webster

ALS. NN. Published in *W & S*, 16: 245.
   1. The article in question was a letter from the Washington correspondent of the *Albany Argus*, published on December 10. The passages pertaining to Webster were reprinted in the *New York Evening Post* of December 13, 1834. The *Argus* article accused Webster of having received in 1832 a fee of $20,000 from an "agent for French claims prior to 1800." The agent alluded to was James H. Causten, Washington representative for French spoliations and other claims, and agent for the

Baltimore Life Insurance Company. The fee would not have been considered irregular except that legislation recognizing these particular claims had never been passed by Congress. Webster's position as chairman of the Senate Select Committee on French Spoliations prior to 1800 made the *Argus* accusations especially damaging.
   2. See James H. Causten to Joseph Gales & William W. Seaton, December 16, 1834, below. The letter is in Webster's hand, though signed by Causten.

TO JOSEPH GALES & WILLIAM WINSTON SEATON
FROM JAMES H. CAUSTEN [IN WEBSTER'S HAND]

Washington Decr. 16. 1834

Gen[t]l[emen:]

A friend has pointed out to my notice an Article in the New York Evening Post, copied from the Albany Argus, which Article asserts that the Agent for the Claimants for indemnity for French Spoliations before 1800, had entered into a pecuniary arrangement with Mr Webster, by which he was to act as counsel for those claimants. I am, & long have been, agent for those claimants, & I know of no other agent, & no such arrangement, nor any other arrangement has been made between Mr Webster & myself. The whole statement is entirely false. Mr Webster has no personal connexion with the claims, whatsoever. He has been induced to take a part in bringing them forward, by my request, in behalf of many claimants, & after expressing an earnest desire that some other Gentleman would take the lead in the business. I feel it a duty, not only to Mr W. & myself, but to the claimants also, thus to declare the false-hood of the statement in the Albany & N York Papers.[1]

AL draft. H. Bartholomew Cox, Oxon Hill, Maryland. The letter was published in the *National Intelligencer* on December 18, 1834, signed by James H. Causten.

1. A diary entry by Causten on the same date explains the episode:

"An opponent of this class of claim (1800) and a vindictive enemy of Mr. Webster—believed to be Mr Benton—wantonly perverted intentionally a fact, for this twofold purpose.

"Mr. John Connell, who was the agent of several Insurance com-panies & individuals, who had claims under the Convention with France of July 4. 1831, then fully ratified and exchanged and a Board to audit the claims appointed, made an engagement with Mr W as counsel to advocate said claims before said Board, for a fee in hand of $10000. The engagement therefore had no reference direct or indirect to the claims then before Congress, those prior to 1800, all of which were in my agency. The turpitude of the writer of said article is manifest." mDW 12020.

TO NICHOLAS BIDDLE

Decr. 17. [1834]

My Dear Sir,

I do not see how any body here can pitch that "key note," which you truly say is so desirable to have sounded.[1] We have no *lead* here, no concert, no conference; & we have had neither, since *Mar. 1833*. Whether we shall ever have either again, is more than I know. But I assure you, My Dear Sir, that on *other* subjects & questions, not less important than this French Dispute, if people wait for a lead from Washington, they may wait till the Greek calends.

I have my opinions, in this French business, which, I am persuaded, would tally with yours; & if occasions offer, I shall express them freely; but without concert with others, (of which I see no probability) an occasion can not well be *made*.

AL. DLC.
1. This letter is in response to

Biddle's second letter of December 11, 1834, mDWs.

TO NICHOLAS BIDDLE

Decr. 17, 1834

Private

Dear Sir

The Report is finished & will be presented tomorrow or next day. The matter of *expenses*, & of the expenditures under the Vote of *1831*, is stated in as modified & qualified a form, as was possible to get it into. Our friend seemed to reserve all his cannon for those heads. In other respects, the Report will do; &, as to this, you are not much hurt.[1]

I am not altogether answerable for its *statements* & *figures*—not having compared them with the vouchers—but presume they are right.

D. W.

ALS. DLC.

1. The report was delivered by John Tyler in the Senate on the following day. *Senate Documents*, 23d Cong., 2d sess., Serial 267, Doc. No. 17. Tyler in particular objected to the practice under the Bank's resolu- tion of March 11, 1831, whereby Biddle was given authority "to cause to be prepared and circulated such documents and papers as may communicate to the people information in regard to the nature and operations of the bank" (pp. 46–48).

With the increasing number of Presidential aspirants either declaring their candidacy or receiving endorsements during the fall or early winter of 1834, John O. Sargent, associate editor of the Webster-oriented Boston Atlas, *found it necessary by December 17 "to take a decided step" and make a public endorsement of Webster. The task at hand was to persuade Whig members of the state legislature, due to convene early in January 1835, to make a formal nomination. The relevant portion of Sargent's editorial, its concluding paragraphs, is reproduced below.*

Speaking as the voice of the Atlas, *the editor thought it "obvious" that the "*People*" were "impatient" to have an antiadministration nomination for the Presidency, and thought it best to "put at their head the* BEST AND STRONGEST CHAMPION OF THEIR PRINCIPLES, *and fight under his banner the battles of the* CONSTITUTION." *But who would be best? The editorial began its list of potential contenders with Hugh Lawson White, but found him merely a "less obnoxious" supporter of the administration. The* Atlas *thought it impossible for Calhoun, coming from South Carolina, to get the nomination. A third rival, Judge John McLean, was dealt with less summarily, but his popularity both within and without Ohio was judged to be meager. Clay was the final straw man, handled respectfully but just as negatively. The Kentucky senator had lost too often to carry the party's banner another time. The impact of Sargent's declaration was less than Webster's intimates had hoped. It certainly did not slow down the nomination of McLean in Ohio later in the month nor did it speed up Webster's nomination by the Whigs in the Massachusetts legislature. Only after weeks of effort by Webster stalwarts did the three hundred and fifteen Whig members of the legislature on January 21, 1835, unanimously nominate Webster for the Presidency.*

FROM JOHN OSBORNE SARGENT

Boston Dec. 17th. 1834

Dear Sir,

You will perceive by the Atlas of this morning that we have taken the field. We have found it advisable to take a decided step—with a view of anticipating the session of the Legislature, and pressing them for an immediate. action. We *know* that [it] is idle to defer operations any longer. While the McLean presses, and Mr. [Hugh Lawson] White's friends, and Mr. Van Buren's friends are combining about their respective candidates all the forces they can command—it is useless to defer an open expression of our own sentiments. The opposition of the North are impatient for a nomination; the time for it has come. We hope that the movement may meet your views of expediency.

We propose to follow up this matter immediately; and are desirous to communicate by letter with such of your friends as you may designate in other parts of the country. It is in vain to attempt this through the intervention of third persons. Where a perfect mutual understanding, and rapidity of intercourse, are *indispensable*, it is of the utmost importance to have direct access to *principals*. You know that it can be only half done by agents and friends.

Such hints and materials as you can furnish us in relation to the State of parties, and the grounds on which the battle is to be fought, will of course render material assistance, in setting the matter properly before the public. With great respect, I remain, My Dear Sir, your mo. obdt. servant   J. O. S.

ALS draft. MHi.

EDITORIAL, *Boston Atlas*, DECEMBER 17, 1834

*   *   *   *   *

On whom then shall the choice fall? Who, under all the circumstances should be the candidate of the great WHIG PARTY? We answer without a thought of hesitation—that man is DANIEL WEBSTER. He stands before the country with the highest claims to its favor and rewards. He stands before the friends of the Constitution, as the ablest expounder and champion of that sacred charter. He stands before the friends of free principles, as the advocate of liberal opinions—as the ardent, zealous, consistent advocate of freedom—at home and abroad—in the struggling nations of Europe—in the devoted republics of South America—whenever Liberty could get a foothold, and raise her voice and banner to the people—she has heard a responsive signal from a distant land—a voice not altogether lost in the roar of a dividing ocean—and that voice has been the eloquence of WEBSTER! In times of domestic dissensions, when the great Temple of our rights and liberties, whose key-stone was *union*, seemed tottering to its foundation—whose giant arms sustained the edifice with its individual strength? When the usurpations of an aspiring Executive had prostrated the outward bulwarks of the CONSTITUTION, who stood forth the leader of the Forlorn Hope, first among the gallant band which maintained the Citadel of the Senate, and spoke stern defiance to a haughty and imperious tyrant? And in times like the present—with such powers as the Executive has now concentrated in his hands—with the Treasury and the military force—the Purse and the Sword—a menaced and impending war with an old ally—to whom do the friends of the country—the cause—and the Constitution—turn, with the firmest faith and most confident reliance?

Why then may we not unite, in the support of a man like WEBSTER, the full strength of the friends of the CONSTITUTION? It is time that the Whig candidate should take the field. Why should the friends of Mr Webster throughout the country delay any longer to present his claims to his fellow citizens?

FROM WILLIAM TAGGARD

New York 17th. Decr. 1834

My dear Sir

I intended to have written you before this time, but have delayed a little to see what would be the result of the election in Virginia, but as that is likely to be delayed, and the result not certain although much more likely to be what we wish than was feared a few weeks since,[1] and as the Legislature of Massachusetts will ere long be assembled, I have consulted with a few friends and members of the Whig General Committee, who are likely to know the probable course of the Whigs in this State. They think that as the Whigs are at present considerably in the minority here, it will be better policy, to wait the action of some of the States who have a certain and commanding majority against the measures and policy of the present administration, be it Massachusetts, Virginia or South Carolina.

There is a strong feeling towards you as the candidate most desirable in all respects if events should favor it, and render it probable that you could be elected, and it is admitted on all hands that you could command more votes in the eastern States than any other candidate, and probably more in the west than any other candidate that can be named: the only doubt about it was that Mr. Clay would be likely to carry Virginia South Carolina & Louisiana in consequence of the compromise of the Tariff question, but then again he could hardly expect to have the votes of Connecticut, Rhode Island, Vermont & Ohio—and Massachusetts would not be so cheerful now in her vote for him as heretofore—and no man so unlikely to carry the vote of. this State, Maine, Pennsylvania & New Hampshire as he. I think some one will be nominated in Virginia or South Carolina entirely acceptable to the Nullifiers or what is called ultra State Rights men—and for one I should think that desirable. The nomination then of a high minded Union man from the East, one in whose integrity they could entirely rely for an observance of the Laws, and all the rights guaranteed by the Constitution to the States would command the consideration of the Southern men, and in fact all good men, who desire a good Government, and that a Republican Government.

The more I think of it, the more am I convinced that there are 14 States that will vote against V. B. To wit Vermont 7, Massachusetts 14, Rhode Island 4, Connecticut 8, Delaware 3, Maryland 8, Virginia 23, North Cara 15, South Carolina 11, Kentucky 15, Ohio 21, Louisiana 5, Indiana 9, Illinois 5, in all 148, remaining only 138 votes and I think we may well count as doubtful, Maine 10, New Jersey 8, and I by no means think that Penns 30, & Georgia 11, could be placed to V. B. if you should be a candidate—New Hampshire 7, Tennessee 15, Mississippi 4, Alabama 7, Missouri 4 & New York 42 making to say the most of it only 79 votes for V. B.

I think his friends, that would calculate deliberately, would come to this conclusion, and if so I do not doubt but they would prefer that you should be elected rather than any other candidate that is likely to be in nomination, save and except such as Isaac Hill.

I am of the opinion as I have been for some time past, that you are the only man that can succeed against V. Buren or Jackson, and I cannot doubt but that it must and will come to that test. This affair with France is at this time in a very unhappy posture for the Whigs—but I hope it may be got rid of without war, although if need be we must meet it—for they deserve it and have for a long time, that is, the Government, but the worst of it now is I think King Louis Philip[pe] desires war to strengthen his power at home. I am most truly and sincerely Yours   Wm. Taggard

ALS. DLC. Taggard was a New York City merchant located at 29 South Street.

1. Taggard refers to the senatorial contest between Benjamin W. Leigh and William C. Rives, which Leigh ultimately won in the Virginia legislature on January 29 by four votes.

TO DANIEL DEWEY BARNARD

Washington Dec. 19. 1834

My Dear Sir

You may have noticed in the Albany Argus of the 10th. instant a Letter from Washington, in which the writer charges me with having a pecuniary interest in an important measure, now pending before Congress. Will you be kind enough to go to the Editor of the Argus, in my behalf, & ask him if he will do me the justice to inform me who is the writer of that letter?[1] I am, Dr. Sir, with true regard, Yr. obt. svt.

AL copy. DLC.

1. Barnard replied to Webster on December 24 in two separate letters (mDW 12065, 12067). In the first he reported that Edwin Croswell, editor of the *Argus*, declined to disclose the name of the letter writer; in the second, Barnard stated that Croswell made a *"quasi* apology" for publication of the letter and stated that the writer was a member of the United States House of Representatives.

Speaking to the Senate on January 12, 1835, in support of the bill for payment of claims for French spoliations prior to 1800, Webster opened with a brief denunciation of the *Argus'* charges as "false and malicious," and added from the information received in the Barnard letter that it had been written by a congressman. *Register of Debates*, 23d Cong., 2d sess., pp. 162–178. Following this speech, the *Argus* published an editorial which apologized to Webster and admitted that its correspondent had "confounded the claims prior to 1800 with those of a subsequent period, which were allowed and included in the treaty of indemnity of 1831." Reprinted in *Niles' Register*, 47 (January 31, 1835): 369–370.

TO [SAMUEL FROTHINGHAM]

Decr. 19. [1834]

D Sir,

I have yr favor of the 15.[1] Tomorrow, I intend to send you a remittance of 1500, or thereabouts. If it do not go tomorrow, (as I trust it will,) it cannot go for two or three days; but it will go.

Mr [Timothy] Fletcher[2] has a blank, by which he can renew Mr A's note. The note, you know, is secured by Stock.

The Bank Report has made Mr [Thomas Hart] Benton, & the Globe, & all the K[itchen] C[abinet] full of wrath. They say Mr Webster wrote it—now Mr W. did not write a page of it. Mr W. you know, had sense enough to leave the whole investigation to Mr. [John] T[yler] & Mr [Willie P.] M[angum]. Every thing relative to your office stands well. Nothing is said of loans to Directors, & all that is said abt. loans to members of Congress is true & just—& as it should be. The Report acquits the public men of the Country, of all sides, from any such influence over their conduct as the Bank could exert.

We have nothing new here, abt. French affairs. Our latest intelligence, is in the N. Y. papers. I am always truly Yrs   D. Webster

The Senate does not sit today, (friday) & the House is on private bills.

ALS. PHC. Published in Van Tyne, p. 190, where recipient is incorrectly identified as Nicholas Biddle.

1. Not found.

2. Fletcher (1775–1842), brother of Grace Fletcher Webster and half brother of James William Paige.

TO ISAAC P. DAVIS

Washington Decr. 20 [1834]

Scrope
Dr Sir,

I could not find Scrope[1] at Marshfield; & have written to Henry Thomas,[2] & had another search made, & cannot find him. I think he must have been in my study in town, & put away by my wife, (after a Lady's fashion) into some corner or lower shelf of the Book case, when every thing was turned upside down for a *party*.

I want the book *here*, very much indeed;—& if you will find it, & send it to me, or send me another copy, I will send you as good a pair of canvass back ducks, as ever wet their webs in the Potomac.

Suppose you take Mr Paige with you & go into the study, & make a search. If you can find it, please direct it to me, under cover to "Walter Lowrie Esqr, Secretary of the Senate."

If you cannot find it, do see if there be another copy in town.

Please forward early your papers about nails & cordage.

Nothing new respecting French affairs. Our main hope is, that the Chambers may have voted the money, before the Message shall have reached Paris. If not, I fear the day of payment will be long deferred.[3]

Mrs W. & Julia are both here, & quite well. Yrs truly   D Webster

ALS. MnHi. Included in the Ignatius P. Donnelly Papers through misidentification of addressee.

1. This is most likely *Principles of political economy, deduced from natural laws of social welfare, and applied to the present state of Britain* (London, 1833), written by George Julius Duncombe Poulett Scrope (1797–1876), an English political economist, geologist, and local his-

torian, a copy of which was in Webster's library. Scrope had also published, in 1830, *The currency question freed from mystery, in a letter to Mr. Peel, showing how the distress may be relieved without altering the standard*, which might have interested Webster.

2. DW to Thomas, December 4, 1834, mDW 11970.

3. With continued refusal of the

French Chambers to make appropriations to settle the long-standing French debt question, Jackson in his annual message of December 1, 1834, recommended passage of a law that would authorize reprisals on French property if a settlement were not soon forthcoming. The controversy both within and without the country over Jackson's handling of the matter continued for another year, and only after British mediation and a softening of Jackson's position were the payments on the debt begun, in 1836. For background on the treaty and the establishment of the Claims Commission, see above, DW to Henry Willis Kinsman, January 1, 1833, note 2.

FROM DANIEL FLETCHER WEBSTER

Hopkinton Dec 21st. 1834

My dear Father

I have been with Uncle [Timothy] Fletcher to Derry and looked about the McMurphy farm.

There are three hundred and thirty odd acres, beside the fifty that Mr. Tucker[1] claims. It is very finely timbered, over two hundred and forty acres, pitch pine, white pine and oak, about seventy acres are cleared; the land is merely decent. There is a house, a work shop, two good barns, out houses &c. &c. on the place.

I found no one ready to buy timber or wood to the amount of the first note, and was advised not to sell if I could. The Market is more than full, and a good deal of timber on the river banks, beside this they are about making a canal, near the place from Massabesick to the Merrimack, which design, if carried into effect will more than double the value of your land. The farm is about two miles from what is called the *fang* of the pond from which the canal is to run. You should do all in your power to encourage the project by taking a few shares in the stock, for it makes or unmakes by success or failure the whole profit of the purchase.

The wood standing now is worth a dollar per cord, if the canal goes it will be worth one and a half or two, merely as firewood, and the timber will be worth even more in proportion.[2]

The canal is to be four miles long, not a lock upon it, and at the end will be an inclined plain a hundred feet long or rather to descend a hundred feet into the river from the top of the bank. Massabesick is much higher than the Merrimack. The probable cost thereof will be thirty thousand. You would then have to cart the timber to the canal, from places a mile distant and so on back to the farther part, about three miles, and you have your wood at Market. As it is you must carry it four or five or sell it standing; The best way is to wait a while, have the lot surveyed and marked out into acre or five acre pieces, numbered and when the canal is decided on, sell at a good advance and pocket the profit.

I dont think you could sell at any advantage now. There are an old man and woman on the place; she is the *man* and takes care of matters, she says she could tell you several things worth knowing about the farm if she could see you. The taxes are now due and *advertized.* They amount to about fifty dollars in all, and must be paid by March the 1st. If you will send it to me I will send it to Melvin[3] who will see it attended to.

I have a plan of the farm drawn by Capt. Clarke.[4] Uncle F[letcher] will send you a copy if you wish.

This is pretty much all I know of the place. There is a brook running through it, with a couple of small mill privileges on it, which will keep two saw mills going about six months in the year. The meadows which would be flooded by damming are on the farm, so no one could complain. But I take [it] you would hardly desire to go into the milling business.

They are all well in Boston at last accounts. I had a letter from Julia which I shall answer soon. You will be very sorry and surprized to hear of the death of Wm. Kelly.[5] He died of typhus fever.

With much love to Mother and Julia if they are with you I remain yr. affectionate son   Fletcher Webster.

Mr. [Samuel B.] Walcott may not go to Salem at all, this year. He is very unwilling to leave. I have had two important cases and advised rightly.[6]   F. W.

ALS. NhHi.

1. Not identified.

2. The Massabesick Canal Company was incorporated on July 4, 1833, and the charter was amended in January 1837 so that the corporation could "make and construct a cut or sluice way sufficient to float wood, lumber and other things capable of transportation . . . from Massabesick Pond to Merrimack river." *Laws of New Hampshire; Passed November Session, 1836* (Concord, 1837), pp. 333–334.

3. Not identified.

4. Not identified.

5. William P. Kelly (1812–1834) was the son of Israel W. Kelly of Salisbury, New Hampshire, who was Webster's brother-in-law through his first marriage to Grace Fletcher.

6. At this time Fletcher was studying law with his former tutor for Harvard, Samuel B. Walcott. He was admitted to the Suffolk Bar on October 5, 1836.

FROM STEPHEN FALES

Cincinnati Decr 29th 1834

Dr Sir

The Committee, whose printed report is subjoined,[1] asked me to write you & request your aid in getting a law of Congress passed to change the location of the National Road so as to pass through Dayton & Eaton. If you have been at Dayton, you can better appreciate the reasons assigned by the Committee. I presume as a matter of course that Mr [Thomas] Ewing will be in favour of the [torn.] I have just returned from Columbus, where I have been a few weeks: The majority of members in the House of Representatives opposed to the administration of the General Government is considerable. The Senate consists of 36 members. Of these 19 are opposed to the administration, of which 19 two are nullifiers & were untill lately Jacksonians. There was considerable effort made by the friends of Judge [John] McLean to get him nominated by the Whigs for the Presidency. The effort was unsuccessful. It was thought best to wait & see upon whom the people through the country would fix. The political excitement at Columbus was not so strong this winter as it was last. I continue in the belief that McLean cannot get this State. With the old National Republican party in Ohio you are much more popular than Judge McLean. With much esteem & respect Yr friend & servt   S. Fales

ALS, with enclosed report, Printed document with MS signatures. DLC. Fales (1789–1854; Harvard 1810, A.M. 1813) was a tutor at Bowdoin College, 1811–1812, studied law under Jeremiah Mason, and went to Cincinnati in 1819 where he practiced law. On Webster's motion, he was admitted to practice before the United States Supreme Court on January 13, 1830.

1. Report of the Citizen's Committee of Montgomery and Preble Counties on the National Road, mDW 12082.

TO [EDWARD EVERETT]

[December 1834]

Dear Sir

I enclose a copy of Mr [Jacob Merritt] Howards letter,[1] having struck out some passages, & endeavored to obliterate the *names*. Please see to this last matter. I think it should be strongly stated to Mr W.[2] that it is indispensable to arrest the progress of the O[hio] nomination, &c, if any other is intended hereafter to be brought out.[3]

AL. MHi.

1. This is probably the letter of December 22, 1834, not found, which Webster refers to in his reply to Howard on January 13, 1835. See *Correspondence*, 4.

2. This is probably John Woods, Whig editor of the Hamilton, Ohio, *Intelligencer*. On August 20, 1834, Warren Dutton, Edward Everett, Abbott Lawrence, Franklin Dexter, and Rufus Choate had addressed a circular letter to Woods asking for his assistance, as a "friend of the Constitution," in promoting Webster's candidacy for President. *New England*

Quarterly, 9 (December 1936): 682–683. Although Woods had been politically intimate with Webster in years past, Everett and his associates were probably overly optimistic in expecting him to work actively to head off the nomination of his fellow Ohioan, Justice John McLean.

3. This sentence doubtless refers to the impending nomination of John McLean as a favorite-son Whig from Ohio. An informal movement for his nomination had begun in the fall of 1833, and in March 1834 he formally agreed to be a candidate. In late December, sometime after Stephen Fales left Columbus, he was officially nominated by a rump caucus of "Democratic Republicans." McLean's supporters had originally sought a nomination for him by a majority of the state legislature. By December 19, however, uncertainty as to the necessary votes prompted a decision to postpone the move until after January 1. When the nomination by McLean partisans came in late December, it was signed by only fifty-seven members of the legislature and thirty-two other prominent citizens.

Calendar, 1830–1834

(Items in italic are included in this volume.)

1830

Jan 1	*From Eliza Buckminster Lee.*
Jan 1	Draft to Mr. Gilmer for $270.45. Printed document with MS insertions. DLC. mDW 39696.
Jan 2	Draft to Mr. W. for $382.23. Printed document with MS insertions. DLC. mDW 39697.
Jan 2	From Henry Willis Kinsman. LC, Kinsman Letterbook. NhD. mDW 7418. Reports on the disposition of several promissory notes owed by DW; conjectures that the Charles River Bridge case may be carried to the Supreme Court.
Jan 2	From C. Valdez. ALS. DLC. mDW 8276. Regrets he will be unable to go to Washington until next week when he hopes to have an interview with DW.
Jan 2	From Daniel Fletcher Webster. ALS. NhHi. mDW 8278. Relates correspondence with family and friends; describes his school subjects and life in Hopkinton, Mass.
Jan 2, 4	From Henry White. ALS draft. MdHi. mDW 8281. Reports on the delayed shipment of three boxes by steamboat.
Jan 3	From William Sullivan. ALS. NhHi. mDW 8282. Offers his congratulations on DW's recent marriage.
Jan 4	From Nicholas Biddle. LC. DLC. mDWs. Reports that the board of the BUS has declared a dividend and that the entire amount of forfeited bank stock has been finally disposed of.
Jan 4	Draft to Henry Willis Kinsman for $1,500. Printed document with MS insertions. DLC. mDW 39698.
Jan 4	Petition of Harriet Carter of Boston for renewal of a pension to widows of naval officers. ADS. DNA, RG 46. mDW 42780.
Jan 4	Memorial of Jonathan Chapman, et al., asking that a drawback of 10 cents per gallon be allowed on the exportation of spirits distilled from foreign molasses. Printed document with MS signatures. DNA, RG 46. mDW 42651.
Jan 4	Petition of Thomas Davis asking to be included on the pension roll for services in the Revolutionary War. DS. DNA, RG 46. mDW 42783.
Jan 4	Petition of Thomas G. Lobdell asking for a

	remission of duties on the cargo of a reclaimed sunken ship. DS. DNA, RG 46. mDW 42703.
Jan 5	From Henry Willis Kinsman. Abstract, Kinsman Letterbook. NhD. mDW 7418. Refers to the *Massachusetts Register*.
Jan 5	From Amos Pettengill, et al. ALS. NhHi. mDW 8284. Ask DW to donate his buildings in Salisbury, N.H., for the support of the town ministry.
[Jan 6]	To Nicholas Biddle. ALS. DLC. mDW 9126. Informs Biddle of the Senate confirmation of BUS directors, and of Henry Baldwin to the Supreme Court.
Jan 6	To Jeremiah Mason. Copy. NhHi. mDW 8288. Mason, *Memoir and Correspondence*, pp. 327–328 (in part). Thanks the Masons for their congratulations on his remarriage; discusses nominations to the Supreme Court and a bill affecting the Portsmouth branch of the BUS.
Jan 6	To Henry White. ALS. MdHi. mDW 8290. Sends $7.94 for freight on three boxes from New York to Baltimore.
Jan 6	From Henry Clay. Printed. Curtis, 1: 370 (in part). Plans to spend the winter in New Orleans; discusses appointment of a Mexican ambassador.
Jan 6	From Henry Willis Kinsman. Abstract, Kinsman Letterbook. NhD. mDW 7418. Refers to the Grafton stock.
Jan 7	From Henry Willis Kinsman. Abstract, Kinsman Letterbook. NhD. mDW 7419. Encloses a letter to Dr. Thomas Sewall; refers to two packages of records pertaining to *James Boyce's Executors* v. *Felix Grundy*, 3 Peters 210 (1830).
Jan 8	Draft to Henry Willis Kinsman for $500. Printed document with MS insertions. DLC. mDW 39700.
Jan 9	*From William Aiken.* 4
Jan [10]	*To Sarah Goodridge.* 5
Jan [10]	*To Joseph Hopkinson.* 6
Jan 10	From Elbridge Gerry[, Jr.]. ALS. NhHi. mDW 8297. Relates his experiences in attempting to retain political office in Jackson's administration.
Jan 10	From Herman Le Roy. ALS. NhHi. mDW 8301. Asks DW's help in settling his long-standing Dutch claims.
Jan 11	From Daniel Le Roy. ALS. mDW 8308. Relates recent family news in New York City.
Jan 11	Draft to Samuel Frothingham for $39.93. Printed document with MS insertions. DLC. mDW 39704.
Jan 11	Draft to Henry Willis Kinsman for $650. Printed document with MS insertions. DLC. mDW 39702.

Jan 12 From Lemuel Shaw. AL. DLC. mDW 8310. Reports
Massachusetts Supreme Judicial Court divided
equally in Charles River Bridge case; wonders
whether it can be sent promptly to the U.S.
Supreme Court.

Jan 13 From Thomas March. ALS. NhHi. mDW 8313.
Discusses a continuing dispute with his brother,
Charles, and DW's role in the controversy.

Jan 14 *To Nicholas Biddle.* 7

Jan 14 From William Leete Stone. ALS. DLC. mDW 8319.
Discusses New York state politics; Jackson's
reelection chances; support of Van Buren now and
in 1836.

[Jan 15] To Warren Dutton. ALS (incomplete). NhD. mDW
8325. PC, 1: 483–484 (in part). Discusses the
executive power of removal; reports on the lack
of progress with tariff legislation, the Eaton
affair, and the Supreme Court docket.

[Jan 15] *To Joseph Hopkinson.* 8

Jan 15 *From Robert Young Hayne.* 9

Jan 15 From Henry Willis Kinsman. LC, Kinsman Letterbook. NhD. mDW 7419. Refers to various
promissory notes and drafts, giving DW an
assessment of his bank balance and reminding
him when his notes are due.

Jan 17 To Warren Dutton. ALS. NhD. mDW 8327. Thinks
it unlikely Supreme Court will hear the Charles
River Bridge case this term, but hopes counsel
will be retained immediately.

Jan 1[7] To Lemuel Shaw. ALS. MBS. mDW 8329. Discusses
the method of appeal for the Charles River Bridge
case; promises to send a blank writ of error for
Shaw to fill out.

Jan 17 To Achsah Pollard Webster. ALS. NhD. mDW 8334.
PC, 1: 484–485. Expresses his sympathy over the
ill health of her mother and relates family news
from Washington.

Jan 18 *From Joseph Healy.* 10

Jan 18 From Henry Willis Kinsman. LC, Kinsman
Letterbook. NhD. mDW 7240. Reports on
additional notes due to creditors.

Jan 18 Motion by DW to furnish judges of the Supreme
Court with a copy of the Executive Journal of the
U.S. Senate. AD. DNA, RG 46. mDW 42523.

Jan 18 Senate Finance Committee report on the petition of
Thomas G. Lobdell. AD. DNA, RG 46. mDW
42622.

Jan 18 Memorial of widows of Revolutionary officers asking
that laws granting relief to their husbands be
extended to them. DS. DNA, RG 46. mDW 42803.

Jan 18 Petition of Thomas L. Winthrop, Director of the
New England Mississippi Land Co., regarding
Yazoo claims owed by the U.S. Treasury. DS.
DNA, RG 46. mDW 42733.

Jan 19 To Charles Brickett Haddock. Printed. *PC*, 1:
485–486. Discusses plans for a volume of DW's
speeches and forensic arguments.

Jan 19 From Joseph Hopkinson. ALS. NhHi. mDW 8342.
Writes at length on the constitutionality of the
Presidential removal power.

Jan 19 From Henry Willis Kinsman. LC, Kinsman
Letterbook. NhD. mDW 7420. Reports on the
possible renewal of several outstanding promissory
notes, a case in the Court of Common Pleas, and
additional news about his Grafton stock.

Jan 21 *From James Kent.* *11*

Jan 21 From Henry Willis Kinsman. LC, Kinsman
Letterbook. NhD. mDW 7421. Reports that several
notes have been renewed; asks instructions on
others.

Jan [21?] Memorial of the inhabitants of Beverly, Mass.,
against the Sunday mails. DS. DNA, RG 46.
mDW 42811.

Jan 21 Memorial of some Boston merchants and mechanics
asking for the enactment of a measure to regulate
auctions. DS. DNA, RG 46. mDW 42654.

Jan 25 To Nicholas Biddle. ALS. PU-S. mDW 8353. *W & S*,
16: 192. Discusses recent argument before
Supreme Court in *Thornton* v. *Bank of
Washington*, 3 Peters 36 (1830); reports case
decided in favor of bank.

Jan 25 From Thomas Washington. ALS. NhHi. mDW 8355.
Asks DW to represent Mrs. Ellen Kirkman in
forthcoming Supreme Court litigation, *Kirkman* v.
Hamilton, 6 Peters 218 (1832).

Jan 26 From John Pierpont. ALS. NhHi. mDW 8374. Asks
DW to consider hiring his friend to assist him in
his legal practice, should DW move to New York
City.

Jan 30 From Henry Willis Kinsman. LC, Kinsman
Letterbook. NhD. mDW 7421. Reports on the
renewal of several notes and lists discounted
notes; other miscellaneous news.

Jan 30 Draft to Henry Willis Kinsman for $2,606.25.
Printed document with MS insertions. DLC.
mDW 39706.

Jan 31 *From Joseph E. Sprague.* *13*
[*Jan*] *To [Henry Willis Kinsman].* *14*
Feb 1 From Isaac Munroe. ALS. NhHi. mDW 8387. Van

Tyne, p. 147. Praises reply to Hayne; asks for
copies as soon as it is published.

Feb 2   To Edward Everett. AL. MHi. mDW 8389. The
Websters request Everett's company for dinner.

Feb 3   *From Nicholas Biddle.*   16

Feb 5   From Henry Alexander Scammell Dearborn. ALS.
NhHi. mDW 8393. Van Tyne, pp. 147–148.
Praises DW's "eloquent defense of New England"
in his recent speech.

Feb 6   *From Jeremiah Evarts.*   17

Feb 6   From Herman Le Roy. ALS. NhHi. mDW 8400. Is
anxious to learn financial impact of Van Staphorst
judgments on his son, Jacob. *William Konig* v.
William Bayard, et al., 1 Peters 250 (1828), and
*Gerritt Schimmelpennich and Jan Adrian Toe
Lear* v. *William Bayard, et al.,* 1 Peters 264 (1828).

Feb 7, [1830?]   To Mr. and Mrs. John Quincy Adams. AL. MHi.
mDW 8404. Accepts dinner invitation.

Feb 7   From Theodore Dwight, Jr. ALS. NhHi. mDW 8406.
Relays news of Texas and comments on Simón
Bolívar's activities in Colombia.

Feb 8   To Samuel K. Williams. ALS. National Library of
Scotland, Edinburgh. mDW 7413. Assures
Williams that Congress will give relief to widows
and orphans of men of the sloop of war *Hornet;*
thanks him for expression of feelings on reply to
Hayne.

Feb 8   From Jeremiah Mason. ALS. NhHi. mDW 8415.
Mason, *Memoir and Correspondence,* pp. 328–330
(in part). Discusses New Hampshire politics,
tracing the current state of "political depravity"
to the influence of Isaac Hill and Levi Woodbury
on local appointments.

Feb 8   Memorial of citizens of Massachusetts asking for
protection of the southern Indians (enclosed with
Samuel G. Allen, et al., to DW, Feb 15, 1830).
DS. DNA, RG 46. mDW 42996.

Feb 9   To Lemuel Shaw. ALS. MHi. mDW 8423. Goes over
some details in the appeal of the Charles River
Bridge case to the Supreme Court.

Feb 10   To Henry Willis Kinsman. ALS. NNC. mDW 8425.
Details the steps to be taken in renewal of a
$3,000 promissory note before it comes due.

Feb 12   From Henry Willis Kinsman. LC, Kinsman
Letterbook. NhD. mDW 7421. Congratulates DW
"on the eloquent & successful defence of N Engd.
Character" in his reply to Hayne; reminds him of
notes due during the month.

Feb 12   From J. W. Scott. ALS. NhHi. mDW 8427. Van

	Tyne, p. 148. Sends praise as a Yankee in South Carolina for DW's reply to Hayne.
Feb 13	From Herman Le Roy. LS. NhHi. mDW 8429. Reports on impending suits of Dutch and Swiss creditors against himself and his son as partners in Le Roy, Bayard & Company; asks DW about possible compromise settlement.
Feb 14	To Albert H. Tracy. ALS. NN. mDW 8436. Reports federal district Judge Alfred Conkling of New York is not included in pending judges' compensation bill, but expects Senator Charles E. Dudley to move that his name be added; assures Tracy he will support the amendment.
Feb 15	From Samuel G. Allen, et al. (with enclosure: Memorial of citizens of Massachusetts asking for protection of southern Indians, DS, Feb 8, 1830). LS. DNA, RG 46. mDW 43012. Submit a memorial concerning the southern Indians passed at a meeting in the Massachusetts State House, Feb 8, 1830.
Feb 15	From Henry Willis Kinsman. LC, Kinsman Letterbook. NhD. mDW 7422. Reports on the disposition of various promissory notes.
Feb 15	From Samuel Martin. ALS. NhHi. mDW 8438. Suggests revenue from sale of public lands go to post office, after the national debt has been paid, for the purpose of free postage to all.
c. Feb 16	To Edward Everett. ALS. MHi. mDW 8461. Asks if Everett would look over [Hayne's] argument of the "right of State interference" and write him "a line."
Feb 16	To Joseph Hopkinson. ALS. PHi. mDW 8440. Informs Hopkinson that the judges' compensation bill proposes to fix his salary at $2,500.
c. Feb 16	From Edward Everett. ALS. DLC. mDW 8463. Van Tyne, p. 146 (in part). Reports on the content of Hayne's reply to DW's first speech prior to its publication in the *National Intelligencer*.
Feb 16	Petition by New England Quakers asking for protection of southern Indians. ADS. DNA, RG 46. mDW 42988.
Feb 19	*From Henry Alexander Scammell Dearborn.* 17
Feb 19	From Henry R. Warfield. ALS. NhD. mDW 8446. Sees Hayne's role in the debate as a source of discord and division among the opposition; notes level of general dissatisfaction among Jackson men in Maryland.
Feb 20	From DeWitt Clinton Clarke. ALC. DLC. mDW 8450. Informs DW that he has been elected an

	honorary member of the Delphian Institute of Union College, Schenectady, N.Y.	
Feb 20	From Henry Willis Kinsman. LC, Kinsman Letterbook. NhD. mDW 7422. Reports on renewal of various promissory notes and that nothing more will probably be taken up in the Massachusetts Supreme Judicial Court until next November.	
Feb 23	From Charles King. ALS. DLC. mDW 8452. Indicates an interest by Columbia University to educate naval midshipmen in light of a resolution passed earlier in the session instructing the House Committee of Naval Affairs to look into the possibility of establishing a naval academy.	
Feb 26	To [?]. ALS. NhD. mDW 8455. Discusses the removal of Elbridge Gerry, Jr., as surveyor of the Port of Boston, and the nomination and recent confirmation of his successor, John McNiel, Jr.	
Feb 26	To [?]. ALS. Vincent E. Edmunds, Staten Island, N.Y. mDWs. Thinks debate on the process bill was never reported; his notes on the matter are of little help.	
Feb 27	*To Jeremiah Mason.*	*18*
Feb 27	From John H. Gibbon (with enclosure of printed memorial to Congress from the farmers and graziers of Philadelphia County, Pa.). ALS. NhHi. mDW 8457. Effect of tariff on farmers and graziers; asks DW to consider greater protection for those engaged in agriculture.	
Feb 27	From Henry Willis Kinsman. LC, Kinsman Letterbook. NhD. mDW 7423. Reports on various promissory notes and deposits; notifies DW that the second part of his reply to Hayne has been published in the Boston papers today.	
March 1	*From Henry Ridgley Warfield.*	*20*
March 1	Draft for $400. Printed document with MS insertions. DLC. mDW 39708.	
March 1	Petition of publishers of periodical works asking for a reduction of postage on books and pamphlets. DS. DNA, RG 46. mDW 42830.	
March 2	*To Jeremiah Mason.*	*21*
March 3	From Amos Lawrence. ALS. NhHi. mDW 8474. *PC,* 1: 489. Thanks DW for vindicating New England from "the foul aspersions cast upon it by the South."	
March 3	From Isaac Munroe. ALS. DLC. mDW 8476. Sends a letter of introduction for Charles W. Holbrook.	
March 4	*To Charles Brickett Haddock.*	*22*
March 4	From Warren Dutton. ALS. CtY. mDW 8482. Hopes	

	that DW will consider revising the "Reply" for printing in pamphlet form.	
March 4	From John Hampden Pleasants. Printed. Curtis, 1: 370 (in part). Praises DW for his speech.	
March 5	*From Samuel Atkinson.*	24
March 6	*To John Hampden Pleasants.*	25
March 8	To Warren Dutton. ALS. NhD. mDW 8493. PC, 1: 493–494. Is gratified by Dutton's commendation of his speech; describes events and personalities in the Senate on that day.	
March 8	*To Amos Lawrence.*	27
March 8	From David Daggett. ALS. DLC. mDW 8499. Thanks DW for copies of the speech and worries about the state of the Constitution under the Jacksonians.	
March 8	*From Jeremiah Mason.*	27
March 8	From Robert Walsh, Jr. ALS. NhHi. mDW 8505. Van Tyne, p. 148 (in part). Thanks DW for sending a copy of his speech which Walsh states is universally read regardless of political persuasion.	
March 9	Memorial of inhabitants of Stoneham, Mass., against the Sunday mails. DS. DNA, RG 46. mDW 42816.	
March 10	*From George Hay.*	28
March 10	From Ansel W. Ives and Joshua Leavitt. LS. DLC. mDW 8512. Extend a speaking invitation to DW from the New York City Temperance Society.	
March 10	From Henry Willis Kinsman. LC, Kinsman Letterbook. NhD. mDW 7423. Discusses the state of various promissory notes; asks for DW's minutes of evidence in Captain Peters's case, *Peters et al.* v. *Rogers et al.*, 19 Federal Cases 368 (1830), which will be argued shortly.	
March 11	*From Henry Bond.*	29
March 11	From Franklin Dexter. ALS. CtY. mDW 8518. Appreciates DW's words about his father, Samuel, in the speech, but is critical of the published preface which has a strong antisouthern tone.	
March 12	*To George Hay.*	30
March 12	To Lemuel Shaw. ALS. MHi. mDW 8525. Regrets that he will be unable to give the next bar address as the length of the congressional session is uncertain.	
March 12	From William Gaston. ALS. NhD. mDW 8528. Assures DW that among "the intelligent portion of the community" there is scarcely any difference of opinion on the substance of his speech, but is generally pessimistic about the future of the Union.	

March 20   To Enoch van Aken. ALS. NhD. mDW 8573.
                  Acknowledges honor of membership in Van
                  Aken's institute.
March 20   From Stephen Webster Marsten. ALS. DLC. mDW
                  8575. Praises DW's reply to Hayne.
March 22   To Edward Everett. AL. MHi. mDW 8579. Sends a
                  dinner invitation.
March 22   To Jacob Hall and Samuel Austin, Jr. Printed.
                  Boston Weekly Messenger, April 8, 1830. Thanks
                  them for their letter praising his services in the
                  Senate.
March 22   To John W. Taylor. ALS. NHi. mDW 8580. Thanks
                  Taylor for his kind opinions of the speech and
                  sends a copy of the large edition.
March 22   From Henry Willis Kinsman. LC, Kinsman
                  Letterbook. NhD. mDW 7424. Reports on the
                  state of several promissory notes and refers to
                  Ithamar Kellog v. *Abijah Curtis*, 9 Pickering 534
                  (1830), and *Joseph Bryant et al.* v. *Commonwealth
                  Insurance Company*, 9 Pickering 485 (1830).
March 22   From Henry R. Warfield. ALS. DLC. mDW 8582.
                  Praises DW's speech and discusses recent
                  accounts of President John Quincy Adams's
                  views about the appointment of old Federalists
                  in his administration.
March 23   To Samuel Frothingham. ALS. PHi. mDW 8586.
                  Asks Frothingham to credit a draft to his account.
March 23   Draft for $1,000. Printed document with MS
                  insertions. MeWC. mDW 39714.
March 23   Memorial from inhabitants of Boston, against the
                  transportation of mails on Sunday. DS. DNA, RG
                  46. mDW 42822.
March 23   Memorial of the inhabitants of Brighton, Mass.,
                  asking for protection of the southern Indians.
                  Printed document with MS signatures. DNA, RG
                  46. mDW 43020.
March 23   Memorial of the inhabitants of New Ipswich, N.H.,
                  asking for protection of the southern Indians.
                  DS. DNA, RG 46. mDW 43016.
March 24   To Joseph E. Sprague. Copy. NhHi. mDW 8595. Van
                  Tyne, p. 152. Asks if David Henshaw knew how
                  Boston appointments were to be disposed of before
                  President Jackson's election.
March 24   From William Plummer. ALS. NhHi. mDW 8602.
                  Sends his appreciation for DW's counsel in *John
                  V. and Thomas Wilcox* v. *Executors of Kemp
                  Plummer*, 4 Peters 172 (1830).

	publication of his speeches for *Speeches and Forensic Arguments*.
March 30	From John M. Berrien. ALS (with MS notation by DW). MWalB. mDW 8625. Asks for DW's terms for his services as counsel in the Florida cases, *United States v. Arredondo*, 6 Peters 691 (1832), and *United States* v. *Heirs of John Forbes*, 15 Peters 173 (1841).
March	Memorial of the inhabitants of Topsfield, Mass., asking for protection of the southern Indians. Printed document with MS signatures. DNA, RG 46. mDW 43039.
April 1	From Henry Willis Kinsman. Abstract, Kinsman Letterbook. NhD. mDW 7424. Refers to a promissory note due shortly.
April 2	From Lemuel Shaw. ALS. DLC. mDW 8627. Reports on the present state of the Bryant case.
April 3	To Nathan Hale. ALS. MHi. mDW 8630. Discusses congressional politics and the uncertain fate of disputed nominations like the printers.
April 3	From Samuel Hubbard. ALS. DLC. mDW 8632. Reports on the disposition of several Massachusetts cases; hopes DW will make an effort for the southern Indians and against the Sunday mails.
April 3	From Henry Willis Kinsman. LC, Kinsman Letterbook. NhD. mDW 7425. Discusses an overdue note and a stock dividend.
April 3	Draft for $51. Printed document with MS insertion. NhD. mDW 39715.
April 4	*From Benjamin Estill.* 49
April 4	From George Ticknor. Printed. Curtis, 1: 371–372. Expresses high regard for Horatio Greenough's talent in relation to a contemplated statute of Washington; encourages DW to make another important speech this session.
April 4	From George A. Waggaman. ALS. NhHi. mDW 8639. Praises DW's "unequalled exposition of the nature of the Sovereignty of the States, and their reciprocal obligations to the Union."
April 5	Memorial of Massachusetts inhabitants asking that federal subscription to the Hampshire & Hampden Canal and to the Farmington Canal Company be deferred. DS. DNA, RG 46. mDW 42947.
April 6	From William Aiken. LS. DLC. mDW 8643. Shows satisfaction with the arrangements DW and McDuffie may make on the railroad bill and hopes for early action on the measure.
April 6	From Henry Willis Kinsman. LC, Kinsman Letterbook. NhD. mDW 7425. Discusses various

	notes and refers to the occasional inquiries as to whether French claims will be taken up in Congress this session.	
April 6	From Daniel Fletcher Webster. ALS. NhHi. mDW 8645. Relates family news and his own activities.	
April 8	To George Ticknor. Printed. Curtis, 1: 372–373; misdated in *PC*, 1:533–534. Will strongly endorse Greenough if Congress should vote for a statue of Washington; elaborates on his views of Lord Byron.	
April 9	From Henry Willis Kinsman. LC, Kinsman Letterbook. NhD. mDW 7425. Discusses the current state of several promissory notes, and informs DW that the Bryant case will not be argued until June.	
April 10	To John M. Berrien. ALS. Copy. NRU. mDW 8648. Agrees to serve as counsel in the Supreme Court for Forbes, *United States* v. *Heirs of John Forbes*, 15 Peters 173 (1841), and Arredondo, *United States v. Arredondo*, 6 Peters 691 (1832), stipulating his fees.	
April 10	To Joseph Story. ALS. MHi. mDW 8651. *MHi Proc.*, 2d Series, 14 (1900–1901): 406–407. Discusses congressional business; plans to return to New England in the summer.	
April 10	From Eliza Buckminster Lee. ALS. NhHi. mDW 8655. Relates recent Boston events and looks forward to the arrival of the new Mrs. Webster in the coming months.	
April 11	From Bellamy Storer. Printed. Curtis, 1: 373–374. Mentions DW's future role as counsel in *Cincinnati* v. *Lessee of Edward White*, 6 Peters 431 (1832), and compliments him on his vindication of New England.	
April 13	To William Pope. Printed. Everett Pepperrell Wheeler, *Daniel Webster: The Expounder of the Constitution* (New York, 1905), p. 90. Views "paltry party purposes" as cause of antagonism between North and South; expresses high regard for William Wirt.	
April 13	Memorial of sundry inhabitants of Boston for protection to the Indians. Printed document with MS signatures. DNA, RG 46. mDW 43029.	
April 14	*To Jeremiah Mason.*	51
April 14	*From Joseph Lanier Williams.*	52
April 15	Motion by DW asking for the separation of the office of agent of the Treasury from the office of the fifth auditor, and for conferring further powers on the former. AD. DNA, RG 46. mDW 42525.	

April 15   Memorial of the inhabitants of Brookfield, Mass.,
asking for protection of the southern Indians.
DS. DNA, RG 46. mDW 43036.

April 16   To [Samuel Frothingham]. ALS. PPL. mDWs. Writes
"Please pass this to my credit." Endorsement
says check for $1,250 enclosed.

[April 16]   To Peleg Sprague. ALS. MDuHi. mDWs. Praises
Sprague's speech on removal of the Indians.

April 17   From Henry Willis Kinsman. LC, Kinsman
Letterbook. NhD. mDW 7426. Discusses various
notes and mentions Hill's rejection by the Senate.

April 17   *From Joseph Story.*   56

April 18   *To Henry Clay.*   58

April 19   From Louis Dwight. Printed circular with MS notes
for reply and ANS transmittal by DW. NhHi.
mDW 8679. Van Tyne, pp. 155–156. Asks a series
of questions on imprisonment for debt.

[c. April 19]   To Louis Dwight. ALS draft. NhHi. mDW 8680.
Van Tyne, pp. 156–157. Replies to several of
Dwight's questions and proposes some remedies.

April 20   From Thomas Hart Benton. ALS. NhHi. mDW
8685. Van Tyne, p. 157. Asks if DW has any
objection to the publication of his correspondence
with John Randolph in 1825 despite a verbal
agreement binding each party to contradict any
publication of it.

April 20   To Thomas Hart Benton. AL draft. NhHi. mDW
8683. Van Tyne, pp. 157–158, 171. States to
Benton that he has adhered to the agreement
and does not want to depart from it.

April 20   To Henry Willis Kinsman. ALS. Dr. Gurdon S.
Pulford, Palo Alto, Calif. mDW 8686. Discusses
various promissory notes and some legal business.

April 20   From Herman Le Roy. ALS. NhHi. mDW 8690. Is
pleased to hear that DW has had an interview
with Van Buren concerning the "Java" claim.

[April 21]   To Nathan Hale. ALS. MHi. mDW 8694. Reports
that the Massachusetts militia claims bill has
passed the Senate.

[April 22]   To Joseph Gales & William Winston Seaton. AL.
NhD. mDW 8692. Praises the articles about the
Jefferson Birthday Dinner which appeared in the
National Intelligencer.

April 24   *To Nathan Hale.*   60

April 24   To Charles Hammond. ALS. OHi. mDW 8698.
Thinks Jackson will be a candidate in 1832, but
talks encouragingly about Clay's chances and
strengths.

April 24   To John McVickar. ALS. Rev. John Brett Langstaff,
Morristown, N.J. mDWs. Sends copies of his
speeches; is critical of the application of gen-

eral rules of political economy to specific cases.

April 24	*To William Plumer, Jr.*	60
April 24	To Edward Webster. ALS. NhHi. mDW 8706. Informs Edward that his sister and stepmother will soon set out for New York and will arrive in Boston sometime next month.	
April 24	*To John Woods.*	61
April 24	From Herman Le Roy. ALS. NhHi. mDW 8713. Shares his disappointment and anxiety over the Van Staphorst legal judgments.	
[April 25]	To Edward Everett. ALS. MHi. mDW 8717. Encloses a paper to Everett which he had been unable to present to him earlier.	
April 25	From Daniel Fletcher Webster. ALS. NhHi. mDW 8719. Describes his stay in Boston on vacation from his studies in Hopkinton.	
April 26, 1830 –Jan 31, 1831	Records of the impeachment proceedings of district court Judge James H. Peck of Missouri. Printed and AD. DNA, RG 46. mDW 43120-331.	
April 27	To James Kent. Printed. Van Tyne, p. 158. Deplores the current state of affairs as a time "when public men seek low objects, and when the tone of public morals and public feeling is depressed and debased."	
April 27	From Henry Willis Kinsman. LC, Kinsman Letterbook. NhD. mDW 7427. Discusses the state of some of DW's promissory notes.	
April 27	Motion by DW in executive session to refer the nomination of Daniel D. Brodhead to the Committee of Naval Affairs with instructions. AN in DW's hand. DNA, RG 46. mDW 43102.	
April 28	From A. M. Hughes. ALS. NhHi. mDW 8722. Praises DW's speeches on Foot's Resolution and assures him that Western Tennessee "hails you as the champion of the Union."	
April 29	*From Henry Clay.*	62
April 29	From Caroline Le Roy Webster. ALS. NhHi. mDW 8738. Has arrived safely in New York City and looks forward to hearing from him.	
April 29, 1830 –Nov 5, 1831	Bill and receipt of Messrs. F. & J. Winship for the purchase of trees, $63.17. ADS. NhHi. mDW 39754.	
April 30	From Henry Willis Kinsman. LC, Kinsman Letterbook. NhD. mDW 7427. Asks whom he should retain to conduct the Delaplaine case (*Delaplaine* v. *Burnham et al.*, unreported case, U.S. Circuit Court, District of Massachusetts, October term, 1830) if it should be sent to trial soon.	
April 30	From Caroline Le Roy Webster (enclosed with	

Julia Webster to DW, April 30, 1830). ALS. NhHi. mDW 8744. Relates family news.

April 30· From Julia Webster (with enclosure: Caroline Le Roy Webster to DW, April 30, 1830). ALS. NhHi. mDW 8743. Reports on events since their arrival in New York.

April [c. 30] From John Nevers. ALS. DLC. mDW 8740. Sends a resolution of thanks from citizens of Franklin County, Mass., for the "late able vindication of the character and policy of New England . . . against the confounded and unprovoked attacks of Senators from the South and West."

[April?] To [Nathan Appleton?]. ALS. MHi. mDW 8746. Sends a new note to cover one which will soon fall due.

[April] To Henry Willis Kinsman. AL (signature removed). NhD. mDW 8747. Discusses the state of various promissory notes.

May 1 From Caroline Le Roy Webster. ALS. NhHi. mDW 8751. Writes about friends and relatives she has seen in New York.

May 2 *To Louis Dwight.*   65

May 2 From Henry Alexander Scammell Dearborn. ALS. NhHi. mDW 8755. Is apprehensive about Jackson's dismissals and new appointments to office.

May 2 From Herman Le Roy. ALS. NhHi. mDW 8767. Discusses the background of a possible future suit against him.

May 2 From Caroline Le Roy Webster. ALS. NhHi. mDW 8770. Relates the visit of some Boston friends.

May 3 From Caroline Le Roy Webster. ALS. NhHi. mDW 8772. Reports on events in New York.

May 3 From Daniel Fletcher Webster. ALS. NhHi. mDW 8775. Mentions the murder of Captain Joseph White in Salem and talks about his studies.

May 3 Bill to provide for the appointment of a solicitor of the Treasury. Printed document with MS amendments by DW and others. DNA, RG 46. mDW 42473.

May 4 From Julia Webster. ALS. NhHi. mDW 8778. Relates Caroline's social activities for the past few days.

May 4 From William Wirt. ALS. NhD. mDW 8781. Asks DW whether he thinks it "most agreeable" to try the impeachment against Judge Peck this session or the next.

May 5 To William Wirt. ALS. DLC. mDW 8782. Indicates that the Peck impeachment trial will probably start or continue into the following session of Congress.

May 5   From William Plumer. LC. DLC. mDW 8784.
           Deplores "unprincipled timeserving office-seekers"
           and the "despicable art and intrigues of designing
           demagogues," but applauds the Senate's efforts
           in rejecting many "improper nominations."

May 6   From Martin Van Buren. LC. DNA, RG 46. mDW
           55672. Acknowledges receipt at the Department
           of State of a memorial and documents of the
           owners of the ship *Esther* asking for indemnity
           from the Peruvian government.

May 6   From Caroline Le Roy Webster. ALS. NhHi. mDW
           8785. Relates social and personal activities and
           plans for moving to Boston.

May 6   Draft to DW for $1,000. Printed document with MS
           insertions. DLC. mDW 39716.

May 6   Draft for $1,000. ADS. DLC. mDW 39719.

May 7   From Caroline Le Roy Webster. ALS. NhHi. mDW
           8788. Reports on her daily activities.

May 8   To Jeremiah Mason. ALS. MHi. mDWs. Thinks it
           now likely that Amos Kendall and Mordecai M.
           Noah will be confirmed, though it will probably
           turn on Vice President Calhoun's vote.

May 8   From Peter B. Porter. ALS. NhHi. mDW 8791.
           Commends DW's speeches in reply to Hayne and
           discusses the state of politics in New York.

May 8   From Caroline Le Roy Webster. ALS. NhHi. mDW
           8793. Reports on family and social activities.

May 9   *To Warren Dutton.*   67
May 10   *To John Evelyn Denison.*   70
May 10   From Nicholas Biddle. LC. DLC mDWs. Discusses
           DW's financial affairs.

May 10   From Julia Webster (with enclosure: Caroline Le
           Roy Webster to DW, May 11). ALS. NhHi. mDW
           8806. Reports on social events in New York.

May 10   Promissory note to Richard Rush for $1,416.33
           with interest. ADS. DLC. mDW 39720.

[May 11] [1830?] To Nicholas Biddle. ALS. DLC. mDW 8810.
           Acknowledges Biddle's letter of May 10.

May 11   From Henry Willis Kinsman. LC, Kinsman
           Letterbook. NhD. mDW 7428. Reports on various
           promissory notes, and on victory of the National
           Republican ticket for state representatives in the
           Massachusetts election.

May 11   From Caroline Le Roy Webster (enclosed in Julia
           Webster to DW, May 10). ALS. NhHi. mDW 8808.
           Looks forward to DW's return and hopes he will
           "forsake congress after this term" to become
           "master of your own movements."

May 11   Motion by DW that James H. Peck file his answer
           and plea with the secretary of the Senate to the

article of impeachment of the House on or before May 25th. AD in DW's hand. DNA, RG 46. mDW 43195.

[May] 12   From Julia Webster. ALS. NhHi. mDW 8814. Relates her activities of the past two days.

May 13   From Daniel Fletcher Webster. ALS. NhHi. mDW 8816. Discusses his studies and special academic interests.

May 14   *To Nathaniel F. Williams.*   71

May 14   From Caroline Le Roy Webster. ALS, NhHi. mDW 8821. Van Tyne, pp. 579–580 (in part). Relates visits with friends.

May 15   *From Ralph Randolph Gurley.*   72

May 15   From Julia Webster. ALS. NhHi. mDW 8827. Details her recent social activities.

May 15   Memorial of the inhabitants of New Alstead, N.H., asking for protection of the southern Indians. Printed document with MS signatures. DNA, RG 46. mDW 43043.

May 18   From Alfred Smith. ALS, DNA, RG 46. mDW 42966. Sends a copy of a statement in answer to the petition of the Hampshire and Hampden Canal Companies.

May 19   To Samuel B. Walcott. AL (signature removed). MHi. mDWs. Expects to return by June at which time he would like to confer about Fletcher's "progress and his future course."

May 21   From Henry Willis Kinsman. LC, Kinsman Letterbook. NhD. mDW 7429. Is uncertain whether DW will return home before several notes are due; informs him that his federal circuit court cases have been postponed.

May 22   *To [Amos Lawrence?].*   72
May 22   *To Nathaniel F. Williams.*   73
May 24   *To James Barbour.*   74
May 24   *To Levi Lincoln.*   75
May 24   *To James Madison.*   76

May 25   From Bellamy Storer. ALS. DLC. mDW 8845. Informs DW of a case which may be tried in Ohio in June and asks him if he will visit Cincinnati at that time.

May 25   Motion by DW that the secretary notify the House that the Senate is ready to proceed on the trial of the impeachment of Judge James H. Peck. AD in DW's hand. DNA, RG 46. mDW 43195.

May 25   Motion by DW that the impeachment court adjourn until the second Monday of the next session at which time the trial will proceed; together with two deleted motions by DW ordering the Senate secretary to send a copy of Peck's answers to the

impeachment articles and notice of the Senate's
approaching adjournment as a court to the House.
AD in DW's hand. DNA, RG 46. mDW 43187.

May 27   *From James Madison.*   77

May 28   To Henry Willis Kinsman. ALS. NhHi. mDW 9470.
Van Tyne, p. 158. Advises Kinsman of the approaching ratification of the Danish treaty, and
asks him to go with Nathaniel Snelling "to the
other [insurance] offices, and secure the agency
of their claims."

May 29   *To Henry Clay.*   78

[May 29]   To [John Davis, 1761–1847?]. ALS. NN. mDW 7364.
Informs him of the passage of the judges' bill in
which his salary is fixed at $2,500.

[May 29]   To Joseph Hopkinson. ALS. PHi. mDW 8855.
Informs Hopkinson that the judges' bill has
passed and his salary as amended will be $2,500.

May 31   From the Committee of Citizens of Baltimore.
Printed. *National Intelligencer*, June 5, 1830.
Invite DW to a public dinner in his honor.

May 31   To the Committee of Citizens of Baltimore. Printed.
W & S, 16: 204. Thanks them for their invitation,
but reluctantly declines.

May 31   Motion by DW (joint resolution) that a committee
of two House and one Senate members be
appointed to prepare and report in the next session
of Congress a system of civil and criminal law
for the District of Columbia and the organization
of courts, and that the report be printed in the
recess. Printed. *Senate Journal*, 21st Cong., 1st
sess., Serial 191, p. 356.

[May 1830?]   To [Richard Smith?]. ALS. DLC. mDW 39717. Asks
for a draft on Boston in the amount of $1,000.

June 1   Draft to Dr. [Thomas] Sewall for $20. Printed
document with MS insertions. NhD. mDWs.

June 3   To Henry Willis Kinsman. ALS. MAnP. mDW 8859.
Notifies Kinsman he will be detained in New
York until Saturday.

June 3   From John Davis [1761–1847]. ALS. DLC. mDW
8861. Sends belated praise of DW's recent
congressional speeches and thanks him for his
letter on the "Judges' bill."

June 4   To [Jeremiah Mason]. ALS. NhD. mDW 8865. Van
Tyne, p. 159. Expects the administration will lose
in several state elections and reveals that Madison
has come out against nullification.

[June 5]   To Edward Everett. ALS. MHi. mDW 8869. Is
delayed in leaving New York and asks Everett to
tell friends when he is expected to arrive in
Boston.

June 7	*From Henry Clay.*	80
June 10	Draft for $1,153.17. Printed document with MS insertions. NhExP. mDW 39722.	
June 13	To Mrs. John Agg. ALS. NhD. mDW 8874. Reports on arrival in Boston.	
June 13	To John Evelyn Denison. ALS. University of Nottingham Library, Nottingham, England. mDW 8877. Writes a letter of introduction for [Francis Calley] Gray.	
June 16	From Nehemiah Eastman. ALS. DLC. mDW 8878. Discusses an arrangement to pay DW for his right in some land at New Durham, N.H.	
June 17	Draft for $1,500. Printed document with MS insertions. NN. mDW 39723.	
June 22	To William Thomas Carroll. AL (signature removed). DNA, RG 267. mDWs. Asks him to docket the case of *Leland* v. *Wilkinson* (6 Peters 317, 1832) and charge fees to J. H. Hubbard.	
June 22	To Messrs. [Francis J.] Oliver, [Thomas?] Motley, [Joseph T.] Buckingham, [?] Bradlee, [Joseph E.] Sprague, [William H.] Eliot, [Harrison Gray] Otis, [Charles P.] Curtis, and [William] Hayden, Jr. ALS. NhD. mDW 8880. Accepts an invitation to an Independence Day dinner.	
June 22	To Nathaniel F. Williams. ALS. NhD. mDW 8881. Thinks the Maryland election will have great influence on other elections and hopes Williams will keep him informed of developments.	
June 25	To John Thomas. ALS. MHi. mDW 8884. Sends word that he has returned to Boston and is glad to hear that Thomas and his family are well.	
June 27, [1830?]	From Alexander Hill Everett. ALS. DLC. mDW 8886. Desires to speak with DW on "political topics."	
June 28	To Benjamin Perkins and Theophilus R. Marvin. ALS. NhD. mDW 8888. Subscribes "with great pleasure" to their proposal to publish the speeches on the Indian Bill.	
June 28	To Joseph E. Sprague. Copy. NhHi. mDW 8891. Van Tyne, p. 160. Encourages Sprague in his project, but thinks others must do the planning.	
June 29	From James W. Webb. ALS. DLC. mDW 8892. Invites DW and Mrs. Webster to stay with him for several days on their return from Washington.	
[June?]	From Nathan Dane (enclosed in Nathan Dane to Joseph Story, June 23, 1830). AL extract. TxU. mDW 8894. Criticizes Benton's recent congressional speeches in which he gave credit to Jefferson for provisions in the Ordinance of 1787.	
July 5	From David Lawrence Morrill. ALS. DLC. mDW	

	8899. Requests copies of some of DW's pamphlet speeches.	
July 7	From Samuel L. Knapp. ALS. DLC. mDW 8901. Reports on the interest of people in having the material on DW in his *Sketches of Public Men* published as a separate pamphlet "for more extensive circulation."	
July 12	Promissory note to Robert Rogerson for $500. ADS. DLC. mDW 39724.	
July 15	From Peleg Sprague. ALS. DLC. mDW 8904. Expects the Maine state convention to nominate or strongly endorse Clay for the Presidency and asks DW for his views on "the course best to be adopted."	
July 21	*Record of Payment from Herman Le Roy to Daniel Webster.*	83
July 22	To Peleg Sprague. ALS. MDuHi. mDWs. Advises Sprague that the Maine National Republican convention should not formally nominate Clay but rather pass a resolution strongly expressing confidence in him.	
July 22	Stock certificate in William Appleton's Hamilton Manufacturing Company, of 2 shares at $1,000 each. Printed document with MS insertions. MWalB. mDW 39728.	
July 24	Promissory note to Nathan Hale for $1,500. ADS. DLC. mDW 39730.	
July 25	From James Barbour. ALS. NhHi. mDW 8908. Assesses Clay's chances for the Presidency, especially in Virginia.	
July 29	From Enoch Parsons (with legal opinion by Henry Willis Kinsman, AN). ALS. NhHi. mDW 8914. Everett Pepperrell Wheeler, *Daniel Webster: The Expounder of the Constitution* (New York, 1905), pp. 44–45. Asks for DW's legal opinion on whether a state government can tax stock of the Bank of the United States.	
[July–Aug 1830?]	To [William H.?] Gardiner. ALS. RPB. mDW 8920. Asks him to stop by for a moment before he confers with his clients.	
Aug 1	From John Davis [1761–1847]. ALS. DLC. mDW 8921. Discusses the characteristics of several species of fish.	
Aug 6	*To Joseph Story.*	83
Aug 11	To Joseph Story. Printed. PC, 1: 506. Asks Story to delay hearing date for a case in Rhode Island, so DW may finish with Knapp trial.	
[Aug 13]	To John Quincy Adams. ALS. MHi. mDW 8928. Writes a letter of introduction for William W. Irwin.	

Aug 14 Receipt for $1,000 received of Stephen White for services in the Knapp case. ADS. MHi. mDW 39732.

Aug 20 From Robert Gilchrist. ALS. NhD. mDW 8932. Asks DW to find a book for him; discusses Kentucky politics.

Aug 25 From William W. Irwin. ALS. DLC. mDW 8936. Wishes to know if DW would like to have his name placed in nomination at the Anti-Masonic party convention should they nominate a Presidential candidate.

Aug 28 From Samuel B. Walcott. ALS. NhHi. mDW 8944. Van Tyne, p. 580 (in part). Reports that Fletcher was admitted to the sophomore class at Harvard.

Aug 30 To Richard Sears. ALS. NjP. mDW 8950. Asks Sears if there is any good bird hunting at Chatham this season.

Aug 30 To [Richard Smith?]. ALS. NhD. mDW 8946. Sends an acceptance to cover a promissory note due Richard Rush in early September.

Sept 1 To Charles Henry Thomas. ALS. MHi. mDW 39023. Expects to be down at Sandwich for several days and wants a boat for hunting and fishing.

Sept 17 *From William Wallace Irwin.*   *84*

Sept 18 To John Evelyn Denison. ALS. University of Nottingham Library, Nottingham, England. mDW 8958. Writes a letter of introduction for Allyne Otis.

Sept 18 *To Joseph Story.*   *85*

Sept 20 To [the Secretary of the Suffolk Bar Association], certifying that Thomas Kemper Davis has read law in his office for the past three years. DS. MBBA. mDWs.

Oct 12 Promissory note to George Blake for $1,000. ADS. DLC. mDW 39733.

Oct 20 *To Nathaniel F. Williams.*   *85*

Oct 20 Promissory note to George Blake for $600. ADS. DLC. mDW 39735.

Oct 23 From Amos Lawrence. ALS. NhHi. mDW 8970. *PC*, 1: 507. Sends DW a service of silver plate "as a testimony of my gratitude for . . . your late efforts in the Senate."

Oct 23 To Amos Lawrence. Printed. William R. Lawrence, *Extracts from the Diary and Correspondence of the late Amos Lawrence* (Boston, 1855), p. 103. Thanks Lawrence for his present of plate as "a most gratifying evidence of your friendship."

Oct 26 To Mr. and Mrs. Edward Everett. AL. MHi. mDW 8973. The Websters invite the Everetts for dinner.

Nov 4 From Thomas T. Davis. ALS. DLC. mDW 8994.

	Informs DW that he has been elected an honorary member of the Phoenix Society of Hamilton College, Clinton, N.Y.	
Nov 5	From Lucy Jane D. Webster. ALS. NhHi. mDW 8996. Reports that her husband's health is declining, but hopes to see DW about his affairs.	
Nov 6	*From Josiah Stoddard Johnston.*	*86*
Nov 8	From Charles Marsh. ALS. NhHi. mDW 9001. Assures DW of the political views of Vermont's newly elected U.S. senator, Samuel Prentiss.	
Nov 11	*From Caleb Cushing.*	*88*
Nov 13	To Dr. Cyrus Perkins. Printed. *PC*, 1: 507–508. Sends a letter of sympathy after news of the sudden death of Dr. Perkins' son, Henry.	
Nov 15	From Dudley L. Pickman. ALS. NhHi. mDW 9005. Has been unable to see DW to ask what should be done with the Nashua drafts.	
Nov 17	To Samuel Willard Bridgham. ALS. NhD. mDW 9008. Asks for information on the background and judicial history of *Potter* v. *Gardner*, 5 Peters 718 (1831), which he will reargue in Washington.	
Nov 20	To John Farmer. ALS. NhHi. mDW 9011. Thanks Farmer for allowing him to keep a letter which was written to DW's father by W. Stickney.	
Nov 22	To Cyrus Perkins. Copy. NhHi. mDW 9015. Van Tyne, pp. 619–620. Plans to see Dr. and Mrs. Perkins on his way to Washington.	
Nov 23	To Simon Greenleaf. ALS. MH-L. mDWs. Thanks Greenleaf for the prompt payment of his fees.	
Nov 25	From John M. Berrien. ALS. MWalB. mDW 9032. Notifies DW that a $500 check has come for him for initial services in the Forbes case.	
Nov 25, 1830 –Dec 27, 1838	Daniel Webster's Cellar Book. AD. MWalB. mDW 9016.	
Nov 26, [1830?]	To [Robert C. Winthrop?]. ALS. MHi. mDW 9034. Asks him to accept a promissory note.	
Nov 28	To Richard W. Greene. ALS. MWA. mDW 9035. Has not heard from Greene and plans to leave home in a few days.	
Dec 1	To Richard W. Greene. ALS. MWA. mDW 9037. Tells Greene that he cannot consent to the brief of Whipple and Tillinghast in *Farnum et al.* v. *Blackstone Canal Corporation*, 8 Federal Cases 1059 (1830).	
Dec 1	To Joseph Story. ALS (with MS notation by Story). MWA. mDW 9040. Informs Story that the opposing lawyers in the Farnum case have sent more information in their brief than agreed upon.	

Dec 3   Promissory note to John Welles for $500. ADS. DLC.
          mDW 39737.
Dec 8   From John DeWitt, et al. ALS. DLC. mDW 9044.
          The Peithessophian and Philoclean societies of
          Rutgers College invite DW to give the next annual
          oration.
Dec 9   To Levi Lincoln. ALS. MWA. mDW 9045. Asks if
          Lincoln can suggest the names of young men who
          would be interested in becoming a farm overseer
          for Edward A. Le Roy, DW's brother-in-law, in
          Avon, N.Y.
Dec 10   Indenture between DW and Caroline Le Roy
          Webster, and Herman and Daniel Le Roy. DS.
          MHi. mDW 39835–308, and mDWs.
Dec 14   From Herman Le Roy. ALS. NhHi. mDW 9049.
          Suggests that the Bayard House legal matters
          might be redressed through chancery proceedings.
Dec 14   *From William Leete Stone.*   89
Dec 15   From Henry Willis Kinsman. LC, Kinsman Letter-
          book. NhD. mDW 7441. Discusses DW's personal
          finances; reports that Harrison Gray Otis has
          been reelected mayor of Boston with little
          opposition.
Dec 15   From Daniel Fletcher Webster. ALS. NhHi. mDW
          9054. Reports on his Harvard studies and
          vacation plans.
[Dec 16] From John M. Berrien. ALS. MWalB. mDW 38226.
          Encloses the $500 check for DW's legal services
          and desires to confer with him on the case as
          soon as possible.
Dec 17   To John DeWitt, et al. ALS. NjR. mDW 9057.
          Declines invitation to address their societies at
          Rutgers College.
Dec 17   To John H. Eaton. ALS. NjHi. mDW 9059. Sends
          a pension application.
Dec 17   *From Stephen White.*   90
Dec 18   From Henry Alexander Scammell Dearborn. ALS.
          NhHi. mDW 9063. Reacts to Jackson's recent
          Annual Message.
Dec 21   From Nicholas Biddle. LC. DLC. mDWs. Asks
          "When will you write that address?"
Dec 23   From Henry Willis Kinsman. Abstract, Kinsman
          Letterbook. NhD. mDW 7441. Sends four
          packages of papers for a case.
Dec 24   To Thomas Washington. ALS. T. mDW 9067. Asks
          Washington to send his brief for *Kirkham* v.
          Hamilton since the case depends "a good deal" on
          Tennessee state law.
Dec 24   To George Watterston. ALS. DLC. mDW 9069. Plans

	to acquire Watterston's *Gallery of American Portraits* and to distribute copies among friends.	
Dec 24	*From Daniel Fletcher Webster.*	91
Dec 25	*To Levi Lincoln.*	92
Dec 27	To [the National Republicans of Massachusetts], from DW, et al. Copy. MHi. mDW 9079. Decide it is presently inexpedient to hold a national convention to nominate a Presidential candidate; think best current policy is to convince people "of the propriety and necessity of a change of Administration."	
Dec 27	From Josiah Quincy. ALS. DLC. mDW 9085. Sends an evaluation of Fletcher as a student at Harvard.	
Dec 28	*To Nathaniel F. Williams.*	94
Dec 30	From Nicholas Biddle. LC. DLC. mDWs. Asks what the disposition of the Senate is on the Turkish treaty.	
Dec 31	To Sarah Goodridge. ALS. NhD. mDW 9090. Talks about portraits and miniatures and hopes she will finish his picture upon his return.	
Dec 31	From Charles Miner. ALS. DLC. mDW 9092. Calls DW "the most popular man in this state"; discusses national and Pennsylvania politics.	
[1830]	To Warren Dutton. ALS. NhD. mDW 9096. Discusses the content of the preface for *Speeches and Forensic Arguments*.	
[1830]	To Warren Dutton. ALS. NhD. mDW 8199. Plans a meeting with Dutton and Lemuel Shaw concerning the [Charles River Bridge] case appeal.	
[1830?]	To [Edward Everett]. ALS. MHi. mDW 9099. Asks that an enclosure be sent to [Orville?] Dewey, the "orator."	
[1830?]	To Sarah Goodridge. ALS. MHi. mDW 9100. Plans to visit and take his sister's pictures if they are completed.	
[1830?]	To Josiah S. Johnston. ALS. PHi. mDW 9102. Regrets that he will be unable to see Johnston tomorrow.	
[1830?]	The Doctrine of Nullification [Memorandum]. AD. DLC. mDW 9104. W & S, 15: 98–99.	

1831

| Jan 1 | Memorial to Committee of Claims from some citizens of New York and the New England states for a lightboat on the middle ground in Long Island Sound. DS. DNA, RG 46. mDW 43681. |

Jan 3   *From Daniel Fletcher Webster.*   *94*

Jan 3   Promissory note of William Prentiss for $250 cosigned by DW. ADS. NhD. mDW 39739.

Jan 5   From Jared Coffin. ALS. DNA, RG 59. mDW 55439. Requests DW's aid in recovery of the ship *Planter*, captured by the Portuguese in 1830.

[c. Jan 5] [1831?]   To Edward Everett. AL. MHi. mDW 9163. Wonders if his dinner acceptance written in French is correct.

Jan 6   *From J[ohn] H[eysham] Gibbon.*   *95*

Jan 10   *From Nicholas Biddle.*   *96*

Jan 11   Memorial of the inhabitants of Dunstable, Mass., asking that the rights of Indians may be protected. DS. DNA, RG 46. mDW 43013.

Jan 12   From Josiah Quincy. ALS. MHi. mDW 9130A. Sends a dozen herring for DW's use.

Jan 15   *To Nicholas Biddle.*   *97*

Jan 15   *To Albert Haller Tracy.*   *97*

Jan 18   Memorial of some merchants and manufacturers of Boston and its vicinity asking for a drawback of the duty on nails manufactured from imported iron. DS. DNA, RG 46. mDW 43686.

Jan 20   From Herman Le Roy. ALS. NhHi. mDW 9144. Is worried about the financial liability of his son, Jacob, in claims made against the Robert Bayard House.

Jan 21   Memorial of the inhabitants of Andover, Mass., asking that the rights of the Indians be protected. DS. DNA, RG 46. mDW 42718.

Jan 22   From Daniel Fletcher Webster. ALS. NhHi. mDW 9147. Van Tyne, p. 585 (in part). Writes about his school work.

Jan 23   From John Marshall. ALS. NhD. mDW 9150. Curtis, 1: 110n. Sends his thanks for a copy of DW's *Speeches and Forensic Arguments,* but recalls two speeches not included.

Jan 23   From Joseph Story. ALS. NhD. mDW 9154. Curtis, 1: 110n. Reiterates Marshall's praise of DW's volume of speeches and his disappointment over two omissions.

Jan 25   Petition of Thomas Denny asking that grain and other articles may be brought from Canada for the purpose of manufacture free of duty. ADS (with enclosures). DNA, RG 46. mDW 42670.

Jan 26   Memorial of the American Board of Commissioners for Foreign Missions of Massachusetts, asking that all treaty stipulations with Indians be faithfully observed. DS. DNA, RG 46. mDW 43045.

Jan 26   Memorial of the inhabitants of Brookfield, Mass.,

	asking that the rights of Indians be protected. DS. DNA, RG 46. mDW 43077.	
[Jan 27, 1831?]	To Lewis Williams. ALS. NcU. mDW 9156. Agrees to represent the University of North Carolina in *Pinson* v. *Ivy*, 1 Yerger 296 (Tennessee 1830).	
Jan 29	To Henry Willis Kinsman. ALS. Dr. Gurdon S. Pulford, Palo Alto, Calif. mDW 9160. Discusses notes due and explains his policy on retainers.	
Jan 29	Motion by DW to proceed with the trial of Judge James H. Peck. AD. DNA, RG 46. mDW 42527.	
Jan 30	From Nicholas Biddle. LC. DLC. mDWs. Warns DW that Benton plans "a sortie" against the BUS after the Peck impeachment trial, and encourages DW to make a speech which he promises to circulate.	
[Jan–June?]	To [George Ticknor]. Printed. Curtis, 1: 205–206 (in part). Explains the purpose of his Greek speech of 1824.	
Feb 1	From John M. Berrien. ALS. MWalB. mDW 9165. Encloses a letter from Mr. [Colin] Mitchel, a party in one of the Florida land cases.	
Feb 1	From William Reed. ALS. NhD. mDW 9167. Encloses a memorial from the American Board of Commissioners for Foreign Missions for the protection of the southern Indians.	
Feb 1	A bill for payment to John Culbertson of $333.33⅓ for service as interpreter in Eastern District of Louisiana, U.S. District Court; he asks to be officially appointed an interpreter. AD. DNA, RG 46. mDW 42491.	
[*Feb 2*]	*To [Nicholas Biddle].*	99
Feb 3	A bill regarding the jurisdiction of certain federal district courts. AD in DW's hand. DNA, RG 46. mDW 42494.	
Feb 4	*To [Nicholas Biddle].*	100
Feb 4	To Richard Smith. ALS. NhD. mDW 9174. Asks Smith to handle several banking matters for him.	
Feb 4	From Chester Harding (enclosed with DW to John H. Eaton, Feb 9, 1831). ALS. DNA, RG 94. mDWs. Desires his brother, Charles, to be appointed to West Point as a cadet.	
Feb 5	From Nicholas Biddle. LC. DLC. mDWs. Discusses Benton's attack on the BUS, and pending cases involving the Bank; tries to dissuade DW from thinking of leaving the Senate.	
Feb 5	From Stephen White. ALS. NhHi. mDW 9176. Reports on the Massachusetts legislative session, and asks about the Black Sea trade treaty and information on French claims.	
Feb 6	To Charles Brickett Haddock. ALS. NhD. mDW 9180. *PC*, 1: 508–509. Asks Haddock to arrange	

for the sale of Ezekiel Webster's interest in "The Elms"; comments on *Speeches and Forensic Arguments.*

Feb 6 From Daniel Fletcher Webster. ALS. NhHi. mDW 9184. Van Tyne, p. 581 (in part). Discusses his school work and notes his progress.

Feb 7 From Henry Alexander Scammell Dearborn. ALS. NhHi. mDW 9187. Thinks that Calhoun must denounce the current administration or he will be ruined; believes this would render the election of Clay certain.

Feb 8 To Nicholas Biddle. ALS. DLC. mDW 9195. Thinks it best to abandon pending cases until his jurisdiction bill is enacted; is optimistic of that outcome.

Feb 9 To Nicholas Biddle. ALS. DLC. mDW 9197. Reports on the progress of the jurisdiction bill.

Feb 9 To John H. Eaton (with enclosure: Chester Harding to DW, Feb 4, 1831). AN. DNA, RG 94. mDWs. Seeks appointment to West Point for Charles Harding.

Feb 9 To Samuel Frothingham. ALS. PHC. mDW 9199. Asks Frothingham to credit his bank account with the enclosure.

Feb 10 *To Nicholas Biddle.*   101

Feb 10 A bill for the relief of Martha Jefferson Randolph. AD. DNA, RG 46. mDW 42497.

Feb 12 From Harrison Gray Otis. ALS. DNA, RG 46. mDW 42601. Seeks help in securing an appropriation to rebuild the sea wall at Deer Island in Boston Bay.

Feb 14 Memorial of faculty and students of Amherst College, Mass., asking that the rights of the Indians be protected. DS. DNA, RG 46. mDW 43081.

Feb 14 Memorial of the inhabitants of Brookfield, Mass., asking that the rights of Indians may be protected. DS. DNA, RG 46. mDW 43085.

Feb 16 Motion by DW to inquire into the making of an appropriation to repair a sea wall at Boston. AD in DW's hand. DNA, RG 46. mDW 42529.

Feb 18, [1831?] To Nathaniel F. Williams. ALS. NhD. mDW 9204. Allows Williams to draw on him; was pleased to meet one of Williams' friends.

Feb 21 From Harrison Gray Otis. ALS. DLC. mDW 9206. Describes the recent storm damage done on Deer and George Islands in Boston Bay and the need for a seasonable federal appropriation for their preservation.

Feb 22 To James McFarlane Mathews. ALS. MH. mDW

	9209. Regrets that he is unable to contribute in any way to Mathews' "new & promising Institution" [New York University].	
Feb 23	To [?]. Draft with revision in DW's hand. NhHi. mDW 9211. Van Tyne, pp. 160–161. Declines to give an opinion in a forthcoming Supreme Court case (*Briscoe* v. *Commonwealth Bank of Kentucky*, 8 Peters 118, 1834).	
Feb 23	From James Kent, et al. LS. MHi. mDW 9214. *National Intelligencer*, March 29, 1831. Invite DW to a public dinner in his honor in New York at his convenience.	
Feb 23	Memorial of a convention of officers of the Massachusetts militia asking that an efficient and uniform system be adopted for the regulation and government of the U.S. militia. DS. DNA, RG 46. mDW 42746.	
Feb 24	To John Branch. ALS. DNA, RG 45. mDWs. Inquires whether Mr. Hogan's draft can now be paid.	
Feb 24	A resolution authorizing the secretary of the Senate to subscribe for 100 copies of a report of the impeachment trial of Judge James H. Peck. AD. DNA, RG 46. mDW 42533.	
Feb 25	*To Nicholas Biddle.*	102
Feb 25	*To [Henry Willis Kinsman].*	102
Feb 25	Draft to "self" for $50. Printed document with MS insertions. NN. mDW 39743.	
[*Feb 26*]	*To Nicholas Biddle.*	103
Feb 26	From William B. Calhoun (enclosed with DW to John H. Eaton, March 5, 1831). ALS. DNA, RG 94. mDWs. Asks if DW will help secure a cadetship at West Point for Chester Harding's brother, Charles.	
Feb 28	From Nicholas Biddle. LC. DLC. mDWs. Plans to follow DW's advice concerning the resignation of B. W. Richards, a BUS director, and sends a paper to help counteract Benton's attack on the BUS.	
Feb 28	Promissory note from Ford & Chapman of Clyde, N.Y., for $400. Copy in DW's hand. NhHi. mDW 9225.	
March 1	To James Kent, et al. Printed. *W & S*, 16: 207. Accepts their invitation for a public dinner in New York.	
March 1	From Timothy Walker. ALS. DLC. mDW 9227. Thanks DW for sending him copies of his speeches.	
March [1–9]	From John McLean (enclosed with DW to John H. Eaton, March 9, 1831). ALS. DNA, RG 94. mDWs.	

	Endorses the application of Charles Harding for a cadetship at West Point.
[March 3], [1831?]	To Nicholas Biddle. ALS. DLC. mDW 9229. Informs Biddle of his forthcoming Philadelphia visit.
March 5	To John H. Eaton (with enclosure: William B. Calhoun to DW, Feb 26, 1831). AN. DNA, RG 94. mDWs. Encloses a letter from William B. Calhoun regarding the nomination of Charles Harding to West Point.
March 5	Petition of Supreme Court Bar regarding fees and fee bonds. AD, signed by DW and others. DNA, RG 267. mDWs.
[c. March 5]	To the People of the United States [Editorial]. Printed. *National Intelligencer*, March 5, 1831.
March 6	To Richard Smith. ALS. PHi. mDW 9235. Discusses personal banking business.
March 7	To Nicholas Biddle. ALS. DLC. mDW 9238. Presents "a small acct for fees" for cases argued during the term.
March 8	From John Woods. ALS. DLC. mDW 9394. Looks forward to DW's western visit in the spring.
March 9	To John H. Eaton (with enclosure: John McLean to DW, March [1–9], 1831). AN. DNA, RG 94. mDWs. Encloses a letter from John McLean endorsing the application of Charles Harding for an appointment to West Point.
March 9	From Henry Willis Kinsman. Abstract, Kinsman Letterbook. NhD. mDW 7445. Reports on the disposition of several promissory notes.
March 10, [1831?]	From Henry R. Storrs. ALS. NhD. mDW 9402. Is upset over DW's recent letter, and explains his reasons for leaving Congress.
March 10	*Edward Everett to Alexander Hill Everett.*	105
March 11, [1831?]	To [Samuel Frothingham]. ALS. PHC. mDW 9406. Asks to have the enclosure credited to his bank account.
March 12	*To Joseph Gales & William Winston Seaton.*	106
March 13	From Charles Richard Vaughan. ALS. NhHi. mDW 9410. Would like DW to bring Warren Dutton to dinner.
March 15	Power of attorney to endorse and renew certain notes given by DW to Richard Smith of Washington. ADS. NhD. mDW 39744.
March 17	To [Henry Willis Kinsman]. ALS. William A. Philpott, Jr., Dallas, Texas. mDW 9413. Discusses financial matters and reports that the Charles River Bridge case will not be decided this term.
March 17	From William Prescott. ALS. NhD. mDW 9414. Asks DW's advice on two cases involving Danish claims.

March 19	Fom Isaac Munroe. ALS. DLC. mDW 9420. Informs DW of plans to establish a New York newspaper with an editor "of the old democratic stamp."
March [25, 1831?]	To Warren Dutton. ALS. NhD. mDW 10771. Plans to leave New York on Monday for Boston, and briefly describes the dinner as good and his speech as "so, so."
March 27	From Joseph Gales. Printed. Curtis, 1: 398–399 (in part). Prefers DW to any other man for the Presidency, but thinks he must go with the more popular Clay.
March 30	From Joseph Hopkinson. ALS. DLC. mDW 9424. Expects Jackson forces will be in trouble if they do poorly and sees "a mass of connected strength," the "Lovers of our Country & Constitution," who will rally in opposition throughout the country.
[April] 4	*To Henry Clay.* *106*
April 5	To Nicholas Biddle. ALS. DLC. mDW 9428. Encloses a communication from Mr. Barnet that he neglected to give Biddle earlier.
April 5	Draft for "my note" of $1,149.35. Printed document with MS insertions. NhD. mDW 39747.
April 6	*To Nathaniel F. Williams.* *108*
April 7	From Thomas Beekman. ALS. NhD. mDW 9433. Thinks that McLean may be nominated in New York in September.
April 9	*From John Sergeant.* *109*
April 9	Draft for $102.47. Printed document with MS insertions. NhD. mDW 39748.
April 16	Draft to Henry Willis Kinsman for $500. Printed document with MS insertions. DLC. mDW 39749.
April 18	Draft to Henry Willis Kinsman for $1,500. Printed document with MS insertions. DLC. mDW 39751.
April 19	*From Ambrose Spencer.* *110*
April 19	Draft to Daniel Fletcher Webster for $34.29. Printed document with MS insertions. NhD. mDW 39752.
April 20	Draft to "toll" for $6.58. Printed document with MS insertions. DLC. mDW 39753.
April 23	From Henry Willis Kinsman. Abstract, Kinsman Letterbook. NhD. mDW 7446. Encloses two promissory notes.
April 26	To Jeremiah Mason. Printed. PC, 1: 509–510. Tries to persuade Mason to move from Portsmouth to Boston.
April 26	From William L. Brent. ALS. NhD. mDW 9444. Complains that an earlier confidential letter of his to DW was widely read by others.
April 29	From Henry Willis Kinsman. Abstract, Kinsman Letterbook. NhD. mDW 7446. Encloses some notes to be signed by DW.

April 30   To William T. Carroll. AL (signature removed;
                  mutilated). DNA, RG 267. mDWs. Asks Carroll
                  to locate a book he used in the Charles River
                  Bridge case argument.
April 30   To Philip Hone. ALS. NhD. mDW 9448. Will be
                  unable to remain in New York long enough to
                  attend [a public dinner] for [James] Maury,
                  former consul at Liverpool.
May 9   To William L. Brent. ALS copy. NhD. mDW 9447.
                  Contends that there was no intended harm in
                  showing Brent's letter to others.
May 10   To Achsah Pollard Webster. ALS. NhD. mDW 9449.
                  Plans to travel to New Hampshire next week on
                  business concerning "The Elms."
May 10   *To Elisha Whittlesey.*   *112*
May 10   To John Woods. ALS. OHaBHi. mDW 9455. Fears
                  that a western trip at this time might cause
                  "injurious effects on others . . . in the present
                  state of political ferment."
May 13   *From Noah Webster.*   *113*
May 16   *To Noah Webster.*   *113*
May 18   From Freeman G. Cary. ALS. DLC. mDW 9463.
                  Informs DW of his election as an honorary
                  member of the Union Literary Society of Miami
                  University.
May 19   From Richard Rush. ALS. DLC. mDW 9465.
                  Suggests that Pennsylvania Anti-Masons will be
                  tied more to the principles of Anti-Masonry than
                  to Henry Clay.
May 25   From William L. Brent. ALS. DLC. mDW 9467.
                  Apologizes for his earlier letter and reports on
                  politics in Maryland.
June 1   From Francis Johnson. ALS (with enclosure). MHi.
                  mDW 9472. Sends information concerning the
                  bright prospects of an anti-Jacksonian victory this
                  year in Kentucky.
June 6   From John Woods. ALS. NhD. mDW 7475.
                  Anticipates antiadministration gains in the Ohio
                  election and discusses other political
                  developments.
[June 8]   To Edward Everett. ALS. MHi. mDW 9483. Will be
                  unable to attend to a certain matter until next
                  week.
[June] [11th?]   To George Ticknor. Printed. Curtis, 1: 409. Has read
                  Ticknor's review of *Speeches and Forensic
                  Arguments* in the *American Quarterly Review*;
                  thinks several points should be expanded if it is
                  reprinted.
[June 13,   To [Samuel Frothingham]. ALS. PHC. mDW 9485.
  1831?]   Discusses personal financial matters.

[June 13]	Appeal for Relief of Fayetteville, N.C., signed by DW for the Boston Committee. Printed. *National Intelligencer*, June 18, 1831.
June 14	To Achsah Pollard Webster. AL (signature removed). NhD. mDW 9486. *PC*, 1: 510. Plans to leave shortly for Boscawen and hopes she will accompany them from Nashua.
[June 16]	To George Ticknor. Printed. Curtis, 1: 409. Would like Ticknor to expand his discussion of nullification and of finance in a reprint of his review of *Speeches and Forensic Arguments*.
June 19	To Nathan Appleton. ALS. MHi. mDW 9489. Asks Appleton "the favor" to deposit $1,000 to his account as both DW and his office staff will be out of Boston for some time.
June 21	From Nicholas Biddle. LC. DLC. mDWs. Agrees to supply DW with a memorandum of arguments favoring the continuation of the BUS.
June 23	From Elisha Whittlesey. ALS. DLC. mDW 9492. Sees the effect of the cabinet "explosion" on Jackson's party as not so "great as might have been reasonably expected," but is alarmed by John Quincy Adams' shift to Anti-Masonry.
June 28	From Nicholas Biddle. ALS (with LC enclosure). DLC. mDW 9496 and mDWs. Sends DW a memorandum on arguments for the continuation of the BUS.
June 29	From Herman Le Roy. ALS. NhHi. mDW 9498. Asks if Stephen White would allow his name to be used as owner of the Bayard House which Le Roy wishes to purchase but without arousing suspicion.
July 1	To Nicholas Biddle. ALS. NhD. mDW 9501. Refutes the charge that he has represented the BUS in every case during the mid-1820s.
July 4	From John M. Berrien. ALS. MWalB. mDW 9503. Asks DW to return information about a party in Florida land claim case.
July 6	*To Joseph Warren Revere.*
July 6	From Asher Robbins. ALS. DLC. mDW 9508. Discusses possible congressional action on the Massachusetts-Rhode Island boundary dispute.
July 9	From Henry Willis Kinsman. Abstract, Kinsman Letterbook. NhD. mDW 7449. Advises DW that he has been retained in *Richardson et al. v. Alexander H. Read*.
July 12	From Richard Keese, et al. LS. DLC. mDW 9510. Invite DW to visit their ironworks and ore beds of Keeseville, N.Y. while visiting the region.
July 15	From Abraham R. Thompson. ALS. NhHi. mDW

July 6 — 114

	9513. Requests DW to give a lecture in September to the Charlestown, Mass., Lyceum.	
July 22	From Henry Wheaton. ALS. DLC. mDW 9515. Requests DW to represent him in a Pennsylvania suit with Richard Peters: *Wheaton* v. *Peters*, 8 Peters 591 (1834).	
Aug 4	From Herman Le Roy, Jr. ALS. NhHi. mDW 9519. Discusses the "intended sporting expedition" to Massachusetts.	
Aug 7	*From Stephen White.*	*114*
Aug 8	To Harriette Story White Paige. ALS. MH. mDW 9528. Sends a small present.	
Aug 8	To George Ticknor. ALS. NhD. mDW 9529. Returns Ticknor's article and reports on recent local news.	
Aug 15	From Stephen C. Phillips. ALS. NhHi. mDW 9537. Invites DW to give a lecture at the Salem, Mass., Lyceum.	
Aug 17	To George Ticknor. ALS. MHi. mDW 9541. Has sent additions to Ticknor's article; learns of Mrs. Ticknor's illness.	
Aug 17	*From William Wirt.*	*116*
Aug 17	Draft to "self" for $75. Printed document with MS insertions. NjMoHP. mDWs.	
Aug 19	*From Robert Field Stockton.*	*117*
Aug 20	*From Edward Curtis.*	*117*
Aug 25	*To [Edward Everett].*	*118*
[Aug 25]	*To Robert Field Stockton.*	*118*
Aug 25	To Charles Henry Thomas. ALS. MHi. mDW 9548. Is unable to go to Marshfield this week as planned.	
Aug 27	From Robert Buchanan (with ANS by Bellamy Storer and printed DS certificate of membership in the Cincinnati Angling Club). ALS. DLC. mDW 9550. Informs DW that he has been elected an honorary member of the Cincinnati Angling Club.	
[Aug 27]	From Bellamy Storer. ANS. DLC. mDW 9550. Is pleased to have DW associated with his friends of the Angling Club.	
Aug 28	*To [Charles Miner].*	*119*
Sept 2	From James Kent. ALS. DLC. mDW 9557. Informs DW that Major [Adam] Hoops is planning a visit to Boston.	
Sept 5	*To Nathan Hale.*	*120*
Sept 7	From Ethan Allen Crawford. ALS. NhHi. mDW 9562. *PC*, 1: 511. Asks DW when he can see him in Boston.	
Sept 8	*From Charles Miner.*	*121*
Sept 10	Certificate of legal study for Robert C. Winthrop. DS. MHi. mDW 7363.	

[c. Sept 10]	Certificate of legal study for Robert C. Winthrop. DS. NhD. mDW 9567. Differs from above.	
Sept 11	*To Nathan Appleton.*	*123*
Sept 12	To Isaac P. Davis. ALS. NhD. mDW 9572. Expects to see Davis shortly at Sandwich, Mass.	
Sept 13	*From James Buchanan.*	*125*
Sept 16	From A. Murray McIlvaine, et al. ALS by McIlvaine, signed also by others. DLC. mDW 9577. DW has been unanimously elected by the Philomathean Society of the University of Pennsylvania to deliver the annual oration.	
Sept 22	*To [Thomas Wigglesworth].*	*126*
Sept 23	From Joshua Vansant, et al. LS. NhD. mDW 9582. Ask DW to give an address at the Maryland Institute for the Promotion of Mechanic Arts.	
Sept 24	To James Buchanan. LS. PHi. mDW 9586. Curtis, 1 : 406. Is astonished by the secretary of the Treasury's construction of the Insolvent Debtors Act and encloses a separate "expression of opinion" on the matter.	
Sept 24	To James Buchanan. Copy. PHi. mDW 9589. Curtis, 1 : 405–406. Expresses surprise at the opinion of the attorney general and the construction by the secretary of the Treasury on the Insolvent Debtors Act.	
[Sept 24]	To Edward Everett. ALS. MHi. mDW 9590. Asks Everett to dine with him and friends.	
Sept 27	To Charles Henry Thomas. ALS. MHi. mDW 9592. Is uncertain whether he will visit Marshfield at the end of the week.	
Sept 28	To Thomas Wigglesworth. ALS. MHi. mDW 9602. Has decided to take the "2nd lot" and will arrange for deeds and payments.	
Oct 1	*To Nathaniel F. Williams.*	*126*
Oct 1	From M. Amoureux. ALS. DLC. mDW 9598. Fears British political intervention with the help of the "British faction" in the country.	
Oct 4	To Thomas Wigglesworth. ALS. MHi. mDW 9602. Has agreed to buy all the land at this time.	
Oct 5	*To Henry Clay.*	*128*
Oct 7	To [?]. AL draft. NhHi. mDW 9610. Van Tyne, p. 620. Denies making a charge against Congressman [James L.] Hodges.	
Oct 8	To Samuel L. Southard. ALS. NjP. mDW 9612. Thanks Southard for helping [Amos] Binney "in maintaining his rights."	
Oct 8	Draft to "my acceptance" for $1,000. Printed document with MS insertions. NjMoHP. mDWs.	
Oct 14	To Joseph Story. ALS. NhD. mDW 9614. Wishes to see Story the following day.	

[Oct 15] To Warren Dutton (with enclosure: letter of introduction for James Dutton Russell, Oct 15, 1831). ALS. NhD. mDW 9616. Asks Dutton to make several copies of the enclosure for mailing.

Oct 15 Letter of introduction for James Dutton Russell (enclosed with DW to Warren Dutton, [Oct 15], 1831). AL draft. NhD. mDW 9618.

Oct 17 From William C. Rives. ALS. DLC. mDW 9620. Discusses the treaty-making power of the government with respect to subsequent action of the Congress.

Oct 18 To Alexander H. Everett. Printed. *National Intelligencer*, Nov 2, 1831. Will be unable to attend a meeting that evening on imprisonment for debt; transmits paper giving his views on the subject.

Oct 19 From Joseph Gales. Printed. Curtis, 1:401–402. Thinks Wirt's Anti-Masonic nomination will not cause defections among Clay's supporters; believes Jackson's reelection would be better than the "rule of frantic fantaticism" under an Anti-Masonic or nullification "dynasty."

Oct 22 To Alexander Townsend. ALS. NhD. mDW 9624. Encloses letters of introduction to Nicholas Biddle and William Wirt.

Oct 24 To Nathaniel F. Williams. ALS. NhD. mDW 9627. Draws on Williams for $1,000 and reports that the Massachusetts delegates of the Friends of American Industry have left for the convention in New York.

Oct 24 *From Ambrose Spencer.*   *130*

Oct 30 *From Joseph M. White.*   *133*

[Oct] To Warren Dutton. ALS. NhD. mDW 38345. Wants Dutton to stop by to discuss a matter.

Nov 2 To Israel W. Kelly. ALS. NhHi. mDW 9637. Would like to see Kelly at "The Elms" in the morning.

Nov 5 From Augustus Alden. ALS. NhHi. mDW 9639. Relates a college anecdote.

Nov 5 From William Channing Woodbridge. Facsimile LS. NhHi. mDW 9643. Asks for DW's suggestions on methods of biblical instruction.

Nov 7 To Charles Henry Thomas. ALS. MHi. mDW 9647. Is sending down a pair of oxen from his New Hampshire farm this week.

[c. Nov 7?] To [?]. (Inscribed on "The Opinion of Daniel Webster, Esq., on the Several Questions Submitted for his Consideration in Regard to the Constitutionality of the Bank of Mississippi," printed document.) ALS. NhD. mDWs. States this opinion was drawn for the case only and does not wish it published "for the benefit or to the detriment of others."

Nov 10 From Herman Le Roy. ALS. NhHi. mDW 9651.

	Asks for DW's legal assistance in the pending Schneevoogd case and encloses a retainer.	
Nov 11	Draft for $50. Printed document with MS insertions. NhD. mDW 39756.	
Nov 14	To Charles Henry Thomas. ALS. MHi. mDW 9654. Will probably be unable to visit Marshfield this fall, but wishes to see Thomas later in the week.	
Nov 15	To Thomas Wigglesworth. ALS. MHi. mDW 9657. Discusses the legal rights of a mortgagor.	
Nov 16	*To Ambrose Spencer.*	*134*
Nov 17	Promissory note to William Hancock for $400. ADS. NjMoHP. mDWs.	
Nov 17	Conveyance of Samuel H. Hewes, et al., to DW of a tract of land in Boston for $44,966. MWalB. mDW 39757.	
Nov 17	Conveyance of DW to Thomas Wigglesworth of land for $23,964. Printed document with MS insertions. NhD. mDW 39761.	
[Nov 19, 1831?]	*From Francis Lieber.*	*135*
Nov 24	From Ambrose Spencer. Printed. Curtis, 1: 402–404. Will not attend the National Republican convention in Baltimore; believes that Clay's nomination will ensure Jackson's election.	
[Nov 27, 1831?]	To Theodore Dwight. ALS. NhD. mDW 9665. Will stay in New York until he has an opportunity to see Dwight.	
[c. Nov]	To Thomas Wigglesworth. ALS. MHi. mDW 9669. Would be glad to see him.	
Dec 4	To Nathan Appleton. ALS. MHi. mDW 9675. Requests Appleton to engage lodgings for them in Washington.	
Dec 4	To Henry Willis Kinsman. ALS. NNC. mDW 9677. Asks Kinsman to handle a personal financial matter.	
Dec 6	From Henry Willis Kinsman. Abstract, Kinsman Letterbook. NhD. mDW 7458. Lists notes payable and names of newspapers not discontinued.	
Dec 6	From Elijah Paine. ALS. NhHi. mDW 9679. Henry Wheaton desires DW to argue his case (*Wheaton* v. *Peters*, 8 Peters 591, 1834) should it come before the Supreme Court.	
Dec 9	From Henry Willis Kinsman. Abstract, Kinsman Letterbook. NhD. mDW 7458. Concerning a $1,500 check.	
Dec 9	From Henry Willis Kinsman. Abstract, Kinsman Letterbook. NhD. mDW 7458. Encloses a letter from the post office.	
Dec 10	To James William Paige. ALS. MHi. mDW 9683. Reports that his health is better.	

Dec 14	From Henry Willis Kinsman. Abstract, Kinsman Letterbook. NhD. mDW 7459. Writes "respecting Mr. [John or William?] Pratt's business."
Dec 14	From Daniel Le Roy. ALS. NhHi. mDW 9685. Asks for DW's assistance in a $3,000 claim against the War Department.
Dec 14	From Herman Le Roy. ALS. NhHi. mDW 9687. Asks for DW's opinion on the cost of legal services provided by Mr. Thomas W. Ludlow in several long-standing cases.
Dec 15	From Stephen White. ALS. NhHi. mDW 9689. Has received a $2,000 check from DW and discusses French claims.
Dec 15	Memorial of Newburyport, Mass., asking that newspapers be allowed postage free and that the price of letter postage be reduced. DS. DNA, RG 46. mDW 43751.
[Dec 16]	To Henry Willis Kinsman. ALS. NNC. mDW 9693. Requests Kinsman to have discontinued an unsolicited [newspaper] which has been sent to him.
Dec 17	*To Charles Henry Thomas.* 137
Dec 17	From Henry Willis Kinsman. Abstract, Kinsman Letterbook. NhD. mDW 7459. Sends a statement concerning the ship *Antelope.*
Dec 17	From Henry Willis Kinsman. Abstract, Kinsman Letterbook. NhD. mDW 7459. Concerning several personal financial matters.
Dec 17	*From Daniel Fletcher Webster.* 138
Dec 18	*To Nicholas Biddle.* 139
Dec 18	To Charles Henry Thomas. ALS. MHi. mDW 39043. Sends $1,000 in bills and a check for Captain John Thomas as initial payment on the Marshfield farm.
Dec 20	From Nicholas Biddle. LC. DLC. mDWs. Asks, "Have you forgotten?"
Dec 21	To [Henry Willis Kinsman]. ALS. NhHi. mDW 9702. Van Tyne, p. 719. Discusses "proofs of condemnation" in some Danish claims cases and mentions various personal financial matters.
Dec 21	To Nathaniel F. Williams. ALS. NhD. mDW 9704. Encloses a $1,000 draft on Williams and plans to see him in Baltimore on the weekend.
Dec 22	To Joseph Gales. ALS. CLU. mDW 9706. Invites Gales to dine with several "Western Gentlemen" who were delegates to the National Republican convention.
Dec 22	From Levi Woodbury. LC. DNA, RG 45. mDWs. Has

	referred DW's letter to the accounting officer of the Navy Department.
Dec 22	A bill for the financial aid of Martha Jefferson Randolph. AD. DNA, RG 46. mDW 43338.
Dec 23	To James William Paige. Printed. *PC*, 1: 511–512. Plans to be in the Maryland courts as counsel for the railroad, *Chesapeake and Ohio Canal Co. v. Baltimore and Ohio R. R. Co.*, 4 Gill & Johnson 1 (Maryland, 1832).
Dec 23	From Nicholas Biddle. LC. DLC. mDWs. Wants to enlist DW as "an opponent for our adversary" [Thomas Hart Benton].
Dec 23	From Daniel Le Roy. ALS. NhHi. mDW 9708. Asks what course to follow if the War Department refuses his $3,000 Charleston claim.
Dec 24	To [Henry Willis Kinsman]. ALS. NjP. mDW 9710. Gives Kinsman directions in handling various promissory notes.
Dec 24	From Henry Willis Kinsman. Abstract, Kinsman Letterbook. NhD. mDW 7459. Discusses DW's personal financial affairs.
Dec 25	From Julia Webster. ALS. NhHi. mDW 9713. Reports on family news in New York.
Dec 27	From Daniel Le Roy. ALS. NhHi. mDW 9716. Is in agreement with DW's method of resolving his claim, provided a better settlement can be made.
[1831]	To Nathan Hale. ALS. MHi. mDW 38437. Likes the plan for [Mount Auburn Cemetery] and would be glad to help "carry it into effect."
[1831]	To George Ticknor. Printed. Curtis, 1: 409–410. Encloses autobiographical material to 1816, and discusses his early experiences in the House of Representatives.
[1831]	To [George Ticknor]. AN. DLC. mDW 9720. Memorandum on Phi Beta Kappa oration and other early addresses.
[1831]	To Thomas Wigglesworth. ALS. MHi. mDW 9721. Would like to meet where they can view the "plan."
[1831]	To Thomas Wigglesworth. ALS. MHi. mDW 9723. Thinks a group of men would be interested in taking up the land.
[1831]	The Currency [Memorandum]. Printed. Curtis, 1: 140–141, 147–148, 150.
[1831–1832]	To [Nathan Hale]. ALS. MHi. mDW 38430. Discusses the renewal of promissory notes, and praises his article which DW urges him to send to Clay and Sergeant.

1832

Jan 1   From Edward Webster. ALS. NhHi. mDW 9736. Relates family and school news.

Jan 3   *To James William Paige.*   *140*

Jan 3   To Charles Henry Thomas. ALS. MHi. mDW 9739. Acknowledges that he has received the deed for the Marshfield farm.

Jan 4   From Thomas Hart Benton. ALS. MHi. mDW 9746. Van Tyne, p. 169. Asks DW for his reaction to a recent published report of a personal disagreement John Randolph had with DW in the 1824–1825 session of Congress.

Jan 4   To Thomas Hart Benton. ALS copy. NhHi. mDW 9741. Van Tyne, p. 169. Denies that he is responsible or that he gave any authorization for the publication of the story.

Jan 4   From Thomas Hart Benton. ALS. NhHi. mDW 9748. Van Tyne, pp. 169–170. Asks DW publicly to contradict the story according to the verbal agreement made earlier.

Jan 4   To Sarah Goodridge. ALS. NhD. mDW 9742. Encourages her to come South during the congressional session to paint portraits.

Jan 4   To Henry Willis Kinsman. AL (signature removed). NNC. mDW 9744. Asks Kinsman to include two promissory notes among the "payables."

Jan 5   To Thomas Hart Benton. ALS draft. NhHi. mDW 9750. Van Tyne, p. 170. Denies that there was ever a verbal agreement between Randolph and himself.

Jan 5   From Thomas Hart Benton (with enclosures: Benton to DW, April 20, 1830, ALS copy; DW to Benton, April 20, 1830, copy). ALS. NhHi. mDW 9755. Van Tyne, pp. 170–171. Sends DW a copy of the agreement not to publish and the verbal agreement to contradict stories about the Randolph disagreement with DW.

Jan 5   To Richard Smith. ALS. InU. mDW 9753. Asks if Smith will discount a draft from the Bank of Mississippi.

Jan 5   From Warren Ransom Davis (with enclosure: clipping from New York *Commercial Advertiser*, dated Washington, Dec 26, 1831). ALS. NhHi. mDW 9760. Encloses a copy of the published account of the Webster-Randolph controversy.

Jan 6   To [Thomas Hart Benton]. AL draft. NhHi. mDW 9763. Van Tyne, pp. 171–172. Again denies the extent to which Benton wishes to apply the

agreement and notes Randolph has not
contradicted recent remarks made in a speech.

Jan 6	*From Nicholas Biddle.*	*140*
Jan 6	From Henry Willis Kinsman. Abstract, Kinsman Letterbook. NhD. mDW 7460. Concerning a promissory note for $600.	
Jan 6, 183[2]	From [Henry Willis Kinsman]. AL draft. NhHi. mDW 9769. Sends Danish claims documents and materials, and discusses the problems of procuring evidence.	
Jan 7	To Charles Henry Thomas (with enclosure: sketch for a quitclaim deed, Daniel Bassett to DW, AD draft). ALS. MHi. mDW 9772. Wishes to pay off Bassett's mortgage on the Marshfield arm.	
Jan 7	From Joseph May (with enclosure: petition of May in behalf of the estate of Col. Nehemiah Freeman). ALS. DNA, RG 46. mDW 43737. Asks DW to present the enclosed petition to the Senate at his earliest convenience.	
Jan 7	Petition of Joseph May, administrator of the estate of Col. Nehemiah Freeman, that the balance due to the estate be paid by the United States (enclosed with May to DW, Jan 7, 1832). ADS. DNA, RG 46. mDW 43734.	
Jan 8	*To Nicholas Biddle.*	*141*
[Jan 8]	To Henry Clay. ALS. DLC. mDW 9783-A. Discusses Clay's proposed tariff resolutions and tells him that a BUS charter renewal memorial will be introduced shortly.	
Jan 8	To Mrs. George Ticknor. Printed. *PC*, 1:512–513. Sends his condolence on the recent death of her brother, William H. Eliot.	
Jan 8	From Thomas Hart Benton. ALS. NhHi. mDW 9780. Van Tyne, pp. 172–173. States that DW's letter "contains matter which I deem it indispensably necessary to refer to Mr. Randolph."	
Jan 8	*From Henry Clay.*	*141*
Jan 9	To Thomas Hart Benton. ALS copy. NhHi. mDW 9784. Van Tyne, p. 173. Tells Benton he considers the matter closed.	
[Jan 9]	To Nicholas Biddle. ALS. DLC. mDW 9785. Sends a list of the senators chosen as the select committee for the BUS renewal memorial.	
[Jan 9]	*To Nicholas Biddle.*	*141*
Jan 9	Motion that the memorial of the president and directors of the Bank of the United States for renewal of their charter be referred to a select committee. AD. DNA, RG 46. mDW 43364.	
Jan 11	To Virgil Maxcy. ALS. DLC. mDW 9789. Asks for copies of the record in the Mitchel (*Colin*	

Mitchel v. *United States*, 9 Peters 711, 1835; 15 Peters 52, 1841) and Arredondo cases.

Jan 11   From Nicholas Biddle. LC. DLC. mDWs. Is unable to come to Washington at this time, but will send Horace Binney to discuss with DW "whatever information may be needed."

Jan 11   From Henry Willis Kinsman. Abstract, Kinsman Letterbook. NhD. mDW 7460. Concerning the Colby land.

Jan 11   From Henry Willis Kinsman. Abstract, Kinsman Letterbook. NhD. mDW 7460. Memorandum of payables.

Jan 12   From Henry Willis Kinsman. Abstract, Kinsman Letterbook. NhD. mDW 7460. Concerning Dr. [David] Osgood and land on Summer Street, Boston.

Jan 14   From Henry Willis Kinsman. ALS. NhHi. mDW 9791. Discusses the disposition of DW's promissory notes and refers to the Danish claims.

Jan 16   To Henry Willis Kinsman. ALS. NNC. mDW 9794. Discusses Dr. David Osgood's interest in buying some of his land at High and Summer Streets, Boston.

Jan 16   From John Hazlehurst Boneval Latrobe. ALS. NhHi. mDW 9796. Thanks DW for sending him a facsimile first edition of Shakespeare.

Jan 17   From Josiah Quincy (enclosed with DW to Lewis Cass, Jan 30, 1832). ALS. DNA, RG 94. mDWs. Writes to DW about Charles Harding, brother of artist Chester Harding, and his interest in an appointment as a cadet to West Point.

Jan 17   From Elkanah Watson. ALS. DLC. mDW 9798. Asks DW's support for internal improvements in his region.

Jan 17   Memorial of some inhabitants of Boston, Mass., asking that the postage on newspapers be reduced. Printed document with MS signatures. DNA, RG 46. mDW 43755.

Jan 19   To Lewis Cass. ALS. MiU-C. mDW 9802. Writes a letter of introduction for Herman Lincoln of the Boston Baptist Missionary Auxiliary.

Jan 20   *To Stephen White.*   142

Jan 23   To Nathaniel F. Williams (with ANS reply to Williams from James H. McCulloch). ALS. NN. mDW 9804. Asks Williams to find out how many vessels have cleared Baltimore port and what cargoes they took with them to the British West Indies since the trade was reopened.

Jan 23   To James Worthen. ALS. NhD. mDW 9806.

	Expresses his "excessive mortification at the non-representation" of Worthen's northern Essex County, Mass., district in Congress.	
Jan 24	*To John Quincy Adams.*	*144*
Jan [24]	*From John Quincy Adams.*	*144*

Jan 24   From Abbott Lawrence (enclosed with DW to Lewis Cass, Jan 30, 1832). ALS. DNA, RG 94. mDWs. Asks for DW's help in placing Charles Harding in West Point as a cadet.

Jan 24   From Edward Webster. ALS. NhHi. mDW 9813. Writes about family and school news.

Jan 26   To [Henry Willis Kinsman]. ALS. Dr. Gurdon S. Pulford, Palo Alto, Calif. mDW 9816. Asks Kinsman to send his brief for *Carrington* v. *Merchants Insurance Co.*, 8 Peters 495 (1834), as well as Franklin Dexter's, "if he would so far oblige me as to give it to you."

Jan 27   To Ezekiel F. Chambers. ALS. MHi. mDW 39306. Can send his whole speech [on the Van Buren nomination] to Joseph Gales by the afternoon "if you think it desirable."

Jan 28   From Henry Willis Kinsman. Abstract, Kinsman Letterbook. NhD. mDW 7460. Respecting several promissory notes.

Jan 28   Promissory note to Peters, Pond & Co. for $1,000. ADS. NjMoHP. mDWs.

Jan 30   To Lewis Cass (with enclosures: Josiah Quincy to DW, Jan 17, and Abbott Lawrence to DW, Jan 24, 1832). ALS. DNA, RG 94. mDWs. Encloses letters and commends Harding's application to Cass's "favorable regard."

Jan 30   To [Henry Willis Kinsman]. ALS. NhD. mDW 9818. Sends instructions concerning promissory notes for February.

Jan 30   From John S. Tyler. ALS. NhHi. mDW 9820. Thanks DW for a copy of military documents and asks to be kept informed of various measures before Congress.

Jan 30   From Edward Webster. ALS. NhHi. mDW 9824. Writes about family news.

Jan   Memorial of some citizens of Boston, Mass., asking for recharter of the BUS. Printed document with MS signatures. DNA, RG 46. mDW 43760.

Feb 1   From Lewis Cass. LC. DNA, RG 94. mDWs. Has received DW's of Jan 30, and will give every consideration to Harding's candidacy for West Point.

Feb 1   From Henry Willis Kinsman. Abstract, Kinsman Letterbook. NhD. mDW 7460. Encloses Franklin Dexter's notes on the Carrington case.

RG 46. mDW 43637. Claims DW holds no shares
of BUS stock and his name must have been
mistaken for Daniel Weld.

Feb 13   Report of the Joint Committee on the Celebration
of the Centennial Birthday of George Washington.
ADS and ALS. DNA, RG 46. mDW 43832.

Feb 13   Petition of Ebenezer Dorr asking that the act for
the relief of certain insolvent debtors may be
extended to him. DS. DNA, RG 46. mDW 43725.

Feb 14   To Samuel Frothingham. ALS. NhD. mDW 9858.
Encloses a check for $800 and requests that it not
be paid with the S. W. [Stephen White?] credit
if DW's account is good.

Feb 14   To Messrs. Josiah S. Johnston, George A.
Waggaman, Nathaniel Silsbee, and Edward
Everett. AN. MHi. mDW 9856. Regrets that he
cannot accept their invitation on Sunday.

Feb 15   From Nicholas Biddle. LC. DLC. mDWs. Wants to
put an undisclosed matter "to right."

Feb 16   From William McIlvaine (enclosed with Documents
pertaining to the select Senate committee inquiry
into the memorial for charter renewal of the
BUS, March 12, 1832). ALS. DNA, RG 46. mDW
43635. Claims that DW holds no shares of stock
in the BUS according to the Bank's books.

Feb 17   From James Barbour. ALS. DLC. mDW 9860. Curtis,
1: 424n–425n. Discusses his role in Congress in
debate over the British Colonial Trade Act of 1823
in light of the controversy over the Van Buren
nomination.

Feb 17   From Daniel Le Roy. ALS. NhHi. mDW 9866.
Reports that Herman Le Roy, Sr.'s health is
worsening; fears "his end is not far distant."

Feb 18   To Henry Willis Kinsman. ALS. NhD. mDW 9868.
Discusses some business matters and advises
Kinsman that he "had better make . . .
calculations to visit the West, in the spring."

Feb 18   *To Levi Lincoln.*   152

Feb 18   To William McIlvaine. ALS. PP. mDW 9874. Thinks
it presently unimportant to correct the error of
the name in the letter to the Treasury secretary,
but would like the means of correcting it.

Feb 18   From Henry Willis Kinsman. LC, Kinsman
Letterbook. NhD. mDW 7461. Concerning various
personal financial matters.

Feb 22   To John H. B. Latrobe. Printed. *Harper's New
Monthly Magazine*, 64 (Feb 1882): 431.
Informs Latrobe that his Washington Centennial
Birthday Dinner speech, based on his notes made
available for Latrobe's own use, "*did* come off."

Feb 23   From Henry Willis Kinsman. ALS. NhHi. mDW
              9876. Lists "payables" for March and inquires
              about news on the outcome of the Danish claims
              cases before the commission.
Feb 25   *From Daniel Fletcher Webster.*   *153*
Feb 27   From Stephen White. ALS. NhHi. mDW 9882.
              Discusses the sale of lands on Summer Street
              and his delay in departing for Washington.
Feb 27   Memorial of the citizens of Columbia County, N.Y.,
              asking for the abolition of slavery in the District
              of Columbia. DS. DNA, RG 46. mDW 43697.
Feb 27   Memorial of Inhabitants of Greene County, N.Y.,
              asking for the abolition of slavery in the District
              of Columbia. DS. DNA, RG 46. mDW 43694.
Feb 27   Memorial of the inhabitants of New Bedford, Mass.,
              asking for the abolition of slavery in the District
              of Columbia. DS. DNA, RG 46. mDW 43700.
Feb 27   Memorial of inhabitants of Norton, Mass., asking
              for the abolition of slavery in the District of
              Columbia. Printed document with MS signatures.
              DNA, RG 46. mDW 43691.
Feb 27   Memorial to the Committee on Manufactures of
              some citizens asking that duty on coal may not
              be reduced. Printed document with MS signatures.
              DNA, RG 46. mDW 43728.
Feb 27   Documents relating to the apportionment of
              representatives among the several states,
              according to the fifth census. AD. DNA, RG 46.
              mDW 43565.
Feb 28   To Austin E. Wing. Copy. DNA, RG 46. mDW
              43822. Asks for Wing's opinion of "the general
              character" of Judges William Woodbridge and
              James D. Doty of Michigan Territory.
Feb [28]   *From John Quincy Adams.*   *155*
Feb 28   From Ford & Chapman. ALS. NhHi. mDW 9895.
              Regarding a note of theirs sent by DW for
              collection.
Feb 28   From Austin E. Wing. Copy. DNA, RG 46. mDW
              43823. Replies that Judges Woodbridge and Doty
              command "a high reputation" in Michigan
              Territory; thinks both should be reappointed.
Feb 28   Memorial of citizens of Somerset, Mass., asking
              that slavery be abolished in the District of
              Columbia. Printed document with MS signatures.
              DNA, RG 46. mDW 43774.
Feb   Memorial of merchants and others of Nantucket,
              Mass., asking that the duty on foreign palm,
              olive, and other oils may not be reduced. ADS.
              DNA, RG 46. mDW 43731.
March 4   From Daniel Fletcher Webster. ALS. NhHi. mDW

	9920. Reports on family news and college activities.	
March 5	*To Hiram Ketchum.*	*157*
March 5	To James William Paige. Printed. *PC*, 1:514. Congratulates Paige on the birth of his daughter.	
March 5	From Henry Willis Kinsman. Abstract, Kinsman Letterbook. NhD. mDW 7462. Respecting a promissory note.	
March 6	From Henry Willis Kinsman. LC, Kinsman Letterbook. NhD. mDW 7462. Encloses "payables" from April through June 13, and discusses his arrangements for the journey to St. Louis.	
March 6	Statement concerning the ratio of representation under the fifth census. AD, part in DW's hand. DNA, RG 46. mDW 43563–43564, 43585–43586.	
March 8	Memorial of the New England Anti-Slavery Society asking for the abolition of slavery in the District of Columbia. DS. DNA, RG 46. mDW 43772.	
March 8	Memorial of some inhabitants of Troy, Mass., asking that slavery be abolished in the District of Columbia. Printed document with MS signatures. DNA, RG 46. mDW 43768.	
March 9	Promissory note to pay E. & H. Raymond of New York $1,000. ADS. NhD. mDW 39766, 40665.	
March 10	To James William Paige. Printed. *PC*, 1: 514–515. Reports on Mrs. Webster's arrival at Washington and is anxious to see Stephen White shortly.	
March 10	From Nicholas Biddle. LC. DLC. mDWs. Asks DW to "inspirit" Dallas's work on the Bank bill to counteract any efforts to postpone the measure.	
March 11	From Daniel Fletcher Webster. ALS. NhHi. mDW 9925. Van Tyne, pp. 582–583 (in part). Reports on his college activities; justifies failure to meet his father's expectations.	
March 12	Documents pertaining to the select Senate committee inquiry into the memorial for charter renewal of the BUS (with enclosures: William McIlvaine to DW, Feb 16, 1832; Samuel Frothingham to DW, Feb 13, 1832). AD and ALS. DNA, RG 46. mDW 43603.	
March 14	To John Quincy Adams. ALS. MHi. mDW 9929. Writes a letter of introduction for Messrs. Starr and Lane of Ohio.	
March 14	*From Ambrose Spencer.*	*158*
March 15	From Herman Le Roy. ALS. NhHi. mDW 9936. Has discovered legal restraint to sale of the Bayard house, purchased earlier by DW.	
March 19	*From Bellamy Storer.*	*160*
March 19	From Stephen White. ALS. NhHi. mDW 9942.	

<table>
<tr><td></td><td>Informs DW of his expected departure date for Washington along with news from Boston.</td></tr>
<tr><td>March 20</td><td>To James William Paige. ALS. MH. mDW 9946. Asks Paige to plant some nuts from an American horse chestnut tree and to have Edward Webster take care of them.</td></tr>
<tr><td>March 20</td><td>Report of the select committee on the bill concerning relief for Martha Jefferson Randolph. AD. DNA, RG 46. mDW 43478.</td></tr>
<tr><td>March 23</td><td>To Charles Henry Thomas.   161</td></tr>
<tr><td>c. March 23</td><td>"The President, Nominating a Vice President!" [Editorial]. AD. NhD. mDW 9899.</td></tr>
<tr><td>March 24</td><td>To Joseph Gales & William Winston Seaton. ALS. NhD. mDW 9952. Expects to receive shortly from Boston additional funds for the printing of the Supreme Court opinions in Samuel A. Worcester v. Georgia, 6 Peters 515 (1832).</td></tr>
<tr><td>March 26</td><td>To Charles Henry Thomas. ALS. MHi. mDW 9954. Has been "reading and thinking about trees" for his Marshfield estate.</td></tr>
<tr><td>March 26</td><td>From Henry Willis Kinsman. Abstract, Kinsman Letterbook. NhD. mDW 7463. Concerning a draft of Mr. Raymond.</td></tr>
<tr><td>March 28</td><td>To the Marquis de Lafayette. ALS. MHi. mDW 9958. Writes a letter of introduction for Jonathan Mason Warren, son of Dr. John Warren of Boston.</td></tr>
<tr><td>March 28</td><td>To William C. Rives. ALS. MHi. mDW 9960. Writes a letter of introduction for Jonathan Mason Warren.</td></tr>
<tr><td>March 28</td><td>To Aaron Vail. ALS. NHi. mDW 9962. Letter of introduction for Jonathan Mason Warren.</td></tr>
<tr><td>March 29</td><td>From Julia Webster. ALS. NhHi. mDW 9963. Reports on school subjects and the recent visit of the Whites.</td></tr>
<tr><td>[March 31]</td><td>To Warren and Elizabeth Cutts Dutton. ALS. NhD. mDW 10028. Sends news that the Whites have arrived in Washington.</td></tr>
<tr><td>April 2</td><td>To Charles Henry Thomas. ALS. MHi. mDW 9972. Sends $200 for expenditures and the deed to the Marshfield estate.</td></tr>
<tr><td>April 2</td><td>From Henry Willis Kinsman. Abstract, Kinsman Letterbook. NhD. mDW 7463. Acknowledges receipt of DW's letters.</td></tr>
<tr><td>April 3</td><td>To James Strong. ALS. NhPoS. mDWs. Is unable to predict outcome of the French Spoliation Bill in Congress.</td></tr>
<tr><td>April 3</td><td>From Henry Willis Kinsman. Abstract, Kinsman Letterbook. NhD. mDW 7463. Informs DW of the discounting of Raymond's acceptance.</td></tr>
<tr><td>[April 4]</td><td>The Imprisonment of Missionaries in Georgia</td></tr>
</table>

	[Editorial]. AD. NhD. mDW 9974. *National Intelligencer*, April 5, 1832 (with additions).	
April 5	*From Theodore Dwight.*	*162*
April 5	Reports of the Select Committee on the House bill for the apportionment of representatives according to the fifth census. Printed document and AD (in DW's and others' handwriting). DNA, RG 46. mDW 43501.	
April 6, [1832?]	To [Nicholas Biddle?]. ALS. NN. mDW 39279. Tells him not to come until he has further word.	
April 6	To James William Paige. ALS. MHi. mDW 9981. Discusses the sale of lots on Summer Street and the Whites' activities in Washington.	
April 10	To Thomas C. Hambly (from Henry Clay, DW, and Edward Everett). Printed. *National Intelligencer*, April 21, 1832 (in part). Deny attending a caucus with the judges of the Supreme Court in which they urged them to decide against Georgia in the Cherokee case on political grounds.	
April 10	To Henry Willis Kinsman. ALS. Dr. Gurdon S. Pulford, Palo Alto, Calif. mDW 9985. Asks for another copy of the list of "payables" which he has mislaid, and mentions the Gray, and Peters, Pond & Co. cases.	
April 10	From Hugh Mercer. Printed. *PC*, 1: 515–518. Writes at length about his father, Hugh Mercer, the Revolutionary general.	
April 10	Promissory note to pay Peters, Pond & Co. $1,000. ADS. NPV. mDW 39767.	
April 11	*From Harrison Gray Otis.*	*164*
April 13	Documents relating to the Apportionment Bill. AD. DNA, RG 46. mDW 43587.	
April 14	From Henry Willis Kinsman. Abstract, Kinsman Letterbook. NhD. mDW 7463. Concerning a promissory note.	
[April 14]	The Bank Committee [Editorial]. AD. NhD. mDW 9995. Printed. *National Intelligencer*, April 17, 1832.	
April [14–20]	From Henry Willis Kinsman. Abstract, Kinsman Letterbook. NhD. mDW 7464. Concerning Peters, Pond & Co.	
April 16	To Charles Henry Thomas. ALS. MHi. mDW 9997. Asks about the arrival of the trees and the work on the house; would like an account of Henry's activities around the estate.	
April 18	To William Gaston. ALS. NcU. mDW 9999. *W & S*, 16: 219. Asks for Gaston's opinion on the constitutional question in [DW's apportionment] report.	

April 19   To Nicholas Biddle. ALS. DLC. mDW 10001. Writes
            a letter of introduction for Stephen White.
April 19   From Ralph Huntington (enclosed with DW to
            Lewis Cass, April 23, 1832). ALS. DNA, RG 94.
            mDWs. Thanks DW for helping to secure a
            cadetship at West Point for Alexander Huntington
            Clapp.
April 19   From Stephen White. ALS. NhHi. mDW 10003.
            Thanks DW for his hospitality during his family's
            visit to Washington.
[c. April 19]   Prostitution of Office [Editorial]. AD. NhD. mDW
            10029. *National Intelligencer*, April 19, 1832.
April 20   To John Quincy Adams. ALS. MHi. mDW 10006.
            Dispatches a book to Adams sent by Mrs. Hannah
            Lee of Boston with an extract of her accompany-
            ing note.
April 20 [1832?]   To Nicholas Biddle. ALS. DLC. mDW 10875. In-
            forms Biddle that Senator George Poindexter will
            be in Philadelphia and thinks he "would probably
            like to know him" if not already acquainted.
April 21   From David Daggett. ALS. DLC. mDW 10007. Sees
            nothing unconstitutional in DW's apportionment
            plan.
April 21   From James Kent. AL (signature removed). DLC.
            mDW 10009. Curtis, 1: 427. Is impressed with
            DW's report on the Apportionment Bill and sees
            nothing unconstitutional in its argument.
April 21   From Daniel Fletcher Webster. ALS. NhHi. mDW
            10011. Van Tyne, p. 583 (in part). Writes about
            school subjects and news of the family.
April 22   From John Quincy Adams. LC. MHi. mDW 10014.
            Is pleased to accept Mrs. Lee's memoir of Hannah
            Adams and is fully satisfied with her reasons for
            using an extract from one of his father's letters
            without his previous consent.
April 22   *From James Kent.*   *168*
April 23   To Lewis Cass (with enclosure: Ralph Huntington
            to DW, April 19, 1832). ALS. DNA, RG 94.
            mDWs. Sends testimonials in behalf of Alexander
            Huntington Clapp's application for admission to
            West Point.
April 23   Conveyance of John Thomas' Marshfield farm to DW
            for $3,650. Printed document with MS insertions.
            NhD. mDW 39770.
April 24   To James William Paige. Printed. *PC*, 1: 518. Asks
            for Harriette's advice on the color of the lining
            for his chaise.
April 25   From Lewis Cass. LC. DNA, RG 94. mDWs. Informs
            DW that he has received his letter and enclosures
            regarding Alexander Huntington Clapp.

April 27   To James Kent. ALS. DLC. mDW 10017. William Kent, ed., *Memoirs and Letters of James Kent* (Boston, 1898), p. 207. Thanks Kent for his letters on his apportionment report, but is uncertain about the prospects of its success.

April 27   To Charles Henry Thomas. ALS. MHi. mDW 10019. Plans to return to Boston for a short stay on May 2, and expects to see Thomas at that time.

April 27   From Hugh Mercer, ALS. DLC. mDW 10023. Asks DW to take some copies of a eulogium to New York and Boston to be sold there in bookstores.

April 30   To James William Paige. ALS. MH. mDW 10025. Plans to be in Boston in several days.

[April]   Memorandum to Nathan Appleton. AN. MHi. mDW 10401. Van Tyne, p. 174. Concerning the care of letters received while DW is away, especially those regarding apportionment.

May 8   To Charles Henry Thomas. ALS. MHi. mDW 10036. Plans to leave for New York [from Boston] tomorrow.

May 11   To Nathan Appleton. ALS. MHi. mDW 10038. Is expected to return to Washington [from New York] in several days and reports on Boston news.

May 11   *From Joseph Tinker Buckingham.*   *169*

May 14   To Nicholas Biddle. ALS. DLC. mDW 10048. Sends an enclosed bill of $1,000 for fees and services at the last term of the Supreme Court.

May 14   *To Nicholas Biddle.*   *171*

May 16   To Nicholas Biddle. ALS. DLC. mDW 10053. Expects the Bank Bill will be taken up next week in the Senate.

May 16   To [Henry Willis Kinsman]. ALS. NBLiHi. mDW 10055. Sends a list of "payables."

May 16   From Hugh Mercer. ALS. DLC. mDW 10059. Thanks DW for his advice on selling copies of the eulogium.

May 19   To Charles Henry Thomas. ALS. MHi. mDW 10061. Discusses various expenditures and places a limit on them for the Marshfield estate.

May 19   From Nicholas Biddle. LC. DLC. mDWs. Asks DW to arrange to have a suite for him at Gadsby's tomorrow night.

May [19–21]   From Henry Willis Kinsman. Abstract, Kinsman Letterbook. NhD. mDW 7465. Discusses promissory notes and French claims.

May 25   From William W. Stone (with enclosure: Resolutions of Boston meeting on tariff, Printed document). ALS. NhHi. mDW 10065. Advocates continuation of the minimum principle rather than an increase on woolen duties.

May 25	Draft to Henry W. Kinsman for $588. Printed document with MS insertions. NjMoHP. mDW 39772.	
May 27	*From Jeremiah Mason.*	*172*
May 28	From Henry Willis Kinsman. Abstract, Kinsman Letterbook. NhD. mDW 7465. Encloses unsigned promissory note for George Blake.	
May 28	Amendment by DW for continuation of exclusive benefits and privileges to the BUS upon the payment by the Bank of a bonus of $150,000 a year. Printed. *Senate Journal*, 22d Cong., 1st sess., Serial 211, p. 305.	
May 30	From Henry Willis Kinsman. Abstract, Kinsman Letterbook. NhD. mDW 7465. Encloses letter from Israel Thorndike, Esq.	
May 31	From J. Johnson. ALS. NhHi. mDW 10078. Asks DW to send a statement of his unpaid fees in *United States* v. *Saline Bank of Virginia*, 1 Peters 100 (1828).	
May 31	From Henry Whitney. ALS. NhHi. mDW 10079. Asks DW to help maintain present duties on glass.	
June 1	From Josiah Knapp. ALS. MHi. mDW 10091. Asks DW to handle his French spoliation claims.	
June 2, [1832?]	To Charles Henry Thomas. ALS. MHi. mDW 39048. Asks Thomas to send barrels of pork and beef as the session of Congress may last until August.	
[June 3]	*To Joseph Gales & William Winston Seaton.*	*174*
[June 5]	To John Middleton Clayton. ALS. DLC. mDW 9826. Thinks they cannot agree to an amendment to limit to 5 per cent the rate of interest charged on BUS loans or discounts.	
June 5	To James Kent. ALS. DLC. mDW 10097. William Kent, ed., *Memoirs and Letters of James Kent* (Boston, 1898), p. 235. Sends praise of Kent's recent speech at Washington Irving's dinner.	
June 5	To James William Paige. ALS. MHi. mDW 10098. Thinks the Bank Bill will pass Congress, but is unsure what Jackson will do; expects he will fail of reelection should he veto the measure.	
June 8	To Harrison Gray Otis. ALS. MHi. mDW 10104. Is confident a tariff bill will pass and has hopes it will be a good one.	
June 8	From Henry Willis Kinsman. Abstract, Kinsman Letterbook. NhD. mDW 7466. Concerning personal financial matters.	
[June 11]	To Mr. and Mrs. Edward Everett. AL. MHi. mDW 10106. Regrets that he is unable to accept their dinner invitation on Wednesday.	
June 11, [1832?]	To [John Wingate] Weeks. ALS. NhHi. mDW 10108.	

June 24 From Gabriel Mead. ALS. DLC. mDW 10135.
Discusses problems in the pending tariff bill.

June 27 From Henry Willis Kinsman. Abstract, Kinsman
Letterbook. NhD. mDW 7468. Sends an "account
of notes &c."

June 27 From Abraham Van Vechten. LS. NhHi. mDW 10144.
Van Tyne, p. 174. Asks DW for his views on efforts
to reconcile Anti-Masons and National Republicans
to defeat Jackson.

June 27 From Thomas Washington. ALS. DLC. mDW 10147.
Encloses $200 of his $300 fee for legal services
in *Kirkham* v. *Hamilton* (6 Peters 20, 1832)

June 28 *To [Stephen White].* *181*

June 28 From Herman Le Roy. ALS. NhHi. mDW 10154.
Writes of the cholera in New York and Caroline
Le Roy Webster's departure for Boston.

June 29 From Daniel Le Roy. ALS. NhHi. mDW 10156.
Invites DW to stay at his house in New York on
his way home from Washington.

June 30 *To Isaac P. Davis.* *182*

[June] To Nathan Appleton. ALS. MHi. mDW 10158. *MHi
Proc.*, 1st Series (1860–1862): 278. Praises
Appleton's speech of May 30 on the tariff.

[June 1832?] From John MacKay (enclosed with MacKay to
John Quincy Adams, n.d.). ALS. NhHi. mDW
38704. Asks DW to help maintain the duty on
pianofortes.

[July 1] To [Edward Everett]. ALS. MHi. mDW 10160. Asks
Everett to sign a [note], and wants him to come
by for a talk.

July 2 *To Isaac P. Davis.* *182*

July 2 *To Abraham Van Vechten.* *183*

[July 3] From Seth A. Raulet, et al. LS. NhHi. mDW 10168.
Call to DW's attention the effect a tariff reduction
as presently contemplated would have on the
brush industry.

[c. July 4] *To [Nicholas Biddle].* *184*

July 4 From James W. Webb. ALS. DLC. mDW 10175. Is
worried about Biddle's overconfidence and
explains plans to arrange for a loan from Biddle
after the Bank veto.

July 5 To Thomas Cadwalader. ALS. DLC. mDW 10177.
McGrane, *Correspondence of Nicholas Biddle*, p.
193 (in part). Thinks Biddle's personal efforts in
Washington have helped immeasurably in the
passage of the Bank bill.

July 7 To John Quincy Adams. ALS. MHi. mDW 10179.
Van Tyne, p. 176. Returns Adams's letters on the
tariff bill, and thinks the House will have to

	agree to the Senate woolen amendment if it is to pass.	
[July 7]	To Nathan Hale. ALS. MdHi. mDW 10182. *W & S*, 16: 179. Reports that the Tariff Bill has passed to engrossment in the Senate though many important amendments have been made.	
[July 7]	To [Harrison Gray Otis]. ALS. MHi. mDW 10185. Informs him the Tariff Bill has been amended and engrossed; lists certain items affected by or omitted in the Senate version.	
[July 7]	To Nathaniel F. Williams. ALS. NhD. mDW 10187. Reports the Tariff Bill engrossed with indigo set at 15 percent ad valorem.	
[July 8]	Tariff [Editorial]. AD. NhD. mDW 10189. *National Intelligencer*, July 10, 1832 (in altered form).	
[July 10]	*To Nicholas Biddle.*	*186*
July 12	To William Allen. ALS. NhD. mDW 10211. Would be pleased to represent Allen (*Allen v. McKean*, 1 Fed. Cases 489, 1833) if his case "should fall within the range of my ordinary practice."	
July 13	*From James Watson Webb.*	*186*
July 21	*To [Joseph Story].*	*186*
July 25	From Samuel Fessenden. ALS. NhD. mDW 10218. Invites DW to a dinner in honor of Maine's U.S. senators.	
July 25	From Henry Willis Kinsman. Abstract, Kinsman Letterbook. NhD. mDW 7469. Encloses list of notes due from July 31 to September 29.	
July 28	From Ambrose Spencer. ALS. DLC. mDW 10220. Reports that the New York National Republican convention has nominated the same candidates as did the Anti-Masons, in order to defeat the Democrats.	
[July]	From [Harrison Gray Otis]. Press copy (incomplete). MHi. mDW 10222. Discusses the Tariff Bill as passed by the House.	
Aug 1	From Simon Greenleaf. ALS. DLC. mDW 10226. Asks DW if he has any objection to William Allen moving from Maine in order to bring his suit into federal jurisdiction.	
[Aug 5?]	To Stephen White. ALS. NhHi. mDW 10228. *PC*, 1: 521–523. Discusses the yacht White presented to DW and talks about a location for White's marine villa.	
Aug 7	From Thomas Washington (enclosed in DW to Edward Everett, Aug 24, 1832). LS. MHi. mDW 10249. Reports on an invention useful in mitigating the effects of cholera.	
Aug 11	From Nicholas Biddle. LC. DLC. mDWs. Is impatient	

	to receive DW's speech on the President's veto of the Bank Bill.	
Aug 11	From Simon Greenleaf. ALS. NjMoHP. mDW 9531. Relates the background in the Allen controversy with Bowdoin College.	
Aug 12	To Stephen White. ALS. NhHi. mDW 10232. *PC*, 1: 520–521. Discusses their vacation plans together at Marshfield, Chatham, and White's house at Cherry Hill from August to October.	
Aug 16	Draft to R. T. for $30. Printed document with MS insertions. ICN. mDWs.	
Aug 17	To Stephen White. ALS. NhHi. mDW 10236. *PC*, 1: 523–524. Reports on the arrival of *Calypso*, DW's yacht, and looks forward to White's visit in several days.	
Aug 18	To Stephen White (with enclosure: Caroline Le Roy Webster to White, Aug [18]). ALS. NhHi. mDW 10240. *PC*, 1: 524. Invites White's daughters to stay at Green Harbor and to remain there during DW's and White's visit to Chatham.	
Aug 20	To Nicholas Biddle. ALS. DLC. mDW 10243. Sends a portion of his speech on the President's veto of the Bank Bill and asks for corrections and amendments.	
[Aug 22?]	To Edward Everett. ALS. MHi. mDW 10245. Asks to borrow Everett's Washington Book which lists members of Congress.	
Aug 24	To Edward Everett (with enclosure: Thomas Washington to DW, Aug 7, 1832). ALS. MHi. mDW 10246. Sends Washington's letter, and with Everett's concurrence, thinks the letter ought to come before the medical faculty.	
Aug 24	*From John Marshall.*	*187*
Aug 25	To Nicholas Biddle. ALS. DLC. mDW 10254. Sends the remainder of his speech on the Bank veto.	
Aug 27	*From Henry Clay.*	*188*
[Aug 1832?]	To [Edward Everett]. ALS. MHi. mDW 10259. Encloses letters to Everett.	
Sept 6	To Nicholas Biddle. ALS. DLC. mDW 10261. Sends the "last words" of his speech on the Bank veto.	
Sept 8	From Charles Onion. ALS. NhHi. mDW 10262. Sends information about Virginia creeper and "Rhododendron Maximum."	
Sept 10	To [Stephen White]. ALS. NhHi. mDW 10264. Van Tyne, pp. 713–714. Asks to postpone their stay at Cherry Hill until next week.	
Sept 11	From Samuel P. Lyman. ALS. DLC. mDWs. Asks if DW plans to publish his speech on the Bank veto as it is needed to counter the effect of the veto message in coming elections.	

[Sept 12]	To Stephen White. ALS. NhHi. mDW 10268. Will come to Cherry Hill as soon as Mrs. Webster's health improves.
Sept 14	To Stephen White. ALS. NhHi. mDW 10269. *PC*, 1: 525–526. Mrs. Webster's health is better, and they plan to leave the following Monday.
[c. Sept 22]	To Nicholas Biddle. ALS. DLC. mDW 38256. Will write shortly on Bank affairs at the Boston BUS branch and encloses two confidential letters respecting conditions there.
Sept 24	*To Nicholas Biddle* (1).
Sept 24	*To Nicholas Biddle* (2).
Sept 24	To Samuel P. Lyman. ALS. MiU-C. mDW 10278. Reports that his speech on the veto message has been published and hopes it will do some good during the election campaign.
Sept 25	To Simon Greenleaf. ALS. MH-L. mDWs. Discusses the legal strategy for the forthcoming Allen case.
Sept 27	From Isaac Cox Barnet. ALS. DLC. mDW 10279. Discusses notarizing documents in France.
Sept 27	*From Nicholas Biddle.*
Sept 27	From Ambrose Spencer. ALS. N. mDW 10281. Expects the Anti-Masons to do well in New York, and thinks all anti-Jackson electoral votes may have to be given to Wirt.
Sept 29	To Joseph Gales & William Winston Seaton. AL. NhD. mDW 10285. Sends under separate cover an editorial ["To the People of the United States"] for publication.
Sept 29	To Levi Lincoln. ALS. MHi. mDW 10287. Declines Lincoln's invitation to stay with him during the Worcester convention; is hopeful of Clay's chances.
Sept 29	To Peleg Sprague. ALS. MDuHi. mDW 10291. Does not plan to visit Maine on legal business as reported in the newspapers.
Oct 1	*To Nicholas Biddle.*
Oct 4	*From Nicholas Biddle.*
Oct 6	"To the People of the United States" [Editorial]. Printed. *National Intelligencer*, Oct 6, 1832.
Oct 8, 1832 –Sept 9, 1833	Memorandum of itemized professional fees. Printed. *PC*, 1: 297–298. Notes: "A very poor year's work. Nullification kept me out of the Supreme Court all last Winter."
Oct 15	From Robert R. Hunter. ALS. MHi. mDW 10299. Plans to submit copies of documents for DW's consideration before instituting a suit against sixteen Boston insurance companies.
Oct 16	From Reuben Dimond Mussey, et al. LS. DLC. mDW 10301. DW has been elected first president of

Dartmouth Alumni, and correspondents request him to give a speech to their society at the next commencement.

Oct 22   To Nicholas Biddle. ALS. DLC. mDW 10303. Says his Worcester speech has been "*shockingly printed*"; will send a corrected copy in the next post.

Oct 22   *To Henry Clay.*   *193*

Oct 24   To [?]. ALS. Carlos B. Wright, Riverside, R.I. mDW 10308. Hopes to be at his house by next Tuesday.

Oct 26   From Philip Richard Fendall. ALS. NhHi. mDW 10309. Regrets that the Worcester convention did not meet earlier so that DW's speech might have been better circulated before the election; discusses the "catastrophe" of the national union newspaper.

Oct 29   To Edward Everett. ALS. MHi. mDW 10311. *MHi Proc.*, 2d Series, 15 (1901–1902): 208. Is glad to know Everett intends to write an article on Judge Story.

Oct 29   *To James Kent.*   *195*

Oct 29   From Abner Phelps. ALS (with AN in DW's hand). NhHi. mDW 10316. If DW would "favour" him with an interview, "it would on my part be very acceptable."

Oct 29   To Abner Phelps. ALS. NhHi. mDW 10318. Would be able to see Phelps this evening.

Oct 29   From James Strong. ALS. NhHi. mDW 10320. Hopes Wirt will withdraw so as not to harm Clay's chances which would be lost if election goes to the House.

Oct 31   *From James Kent.*   *195*

Nov 1   From Joseph Kent. ALS. NhD. mDW 10327. Thanks DW for a copy of the Worcester speech; is assured New York will be lost to Jackson; comments on Clay and Wirt.

Nov 2   *From John Brooks.*   *197*

[c. Nov 2–7]   To [Agent of John Brooks]. ANS. NhHi. mDW 10332. Authorizes Ray Thomas to receive cattle from Princeton, Mass.

[c. Nov 3]   To Edward Everett (with AN enclosure: outline of Story's judicial career). ALS. MHi. mDW 10405. *MHi Proc.*, 2d Series, 15 (1901–1902): 209. Asks in what way he can help Everett in his forthcoming article about Judge Story.

[c. Nov 3]   To [Edward Everett] (enclosed with DW to Everett, c. Nov. 3, 1832). AN. MHi. mDW 10408. Discusses Judge Story's judicial career and publications.

[c. Nov 4]   To [Edward Everett]. ALS. MHi. mDW 10410.

	Writes a short sketch of three of Judge Story's opinions.	
Nov 5	To [?] Livingston. ALS. N. mDW 10333. Refuses to take a case for which his compensation is contingent rather than certain.	
Nov 7	To John Quincy Adams. ALS. MHi. mDW 10335. Van Tyne, p. 178. Discounts rumors that Adams is going to be put up in opposition to DW for the U.S. Senate.	
Nov 7	From Joshua Peirce. ALS. NhHi. mDW 10337. Sends DW a descriptive list of his tree and plant order along with planting instructions.	
Nov 7	From Abraham G. Stevens. ALS. NhHi. mDW 10342. Sends by Benjamin Shaw an order of livestock for Marshfield.	
Nov 9	From John J. Crittenden. ALS. NjMoHP. mDW 10343. Thanks DW for a copy of Worcester speech; is positive Clay electors have won in Kentucky and is waiting for Ohio and "decisive" vote of Pennsylvania.	
Nov 12	From Thomas Eskridge. ALS. NhHi. mDW 10346. Sends $100 fee for DW's opinion concerning the deed of John Perkins to Benjamin S. Bynam.	
Nov 15	From Nicholas Biddle. LC. DLC. mDWs. Asks DW and Abbott Lawrence to compose a list of nominees for the board of directors of the Boston BUS.	
Nov 18	To Nicholas Biddle. ALS. DLC. mDW 10348. Will receive a letter from Lawrence and himself in the next post.	
Nov 19	*To Nicholas Biddle.*	*197*
Nov 22	To John Andrews. ALS. PHi. mDW 10357. Concerning private banking business and his life insurance policy.	
Nov 23	From Nicholas Biddle. LC. DLC. mDWs. Informs DW he has received his letter of Nov 19.	
Nov 25	From Joseph L. Williams. ALS. NhD. mDW 10359. Regards Georgia's nullification more "venal" than South Carolina's; is in "the deepest melancholy" over Jackson's reelection.	
Dec 1	Bill of sale of farm articles bought by DW from Charles Henry Thomas. ANS. NhHi. mDW 39777.	
Dec 1	Memorandum of articles in house and farm at Marshfield. AN. NhHi. mDW 39780.	
[c. Dec 4, 1832?]	From Francis C. Gray. Requests DW's presence at a Faneuil Hall meeting next Tuesday "in support of the constitution & the Law." ALS draft. DLC. mDW 11005.	
Dec 7	Stock certificate for four shares of the Merrimack Manufacturing Company. Printed document with	

	MS insertions. MWalB. mDW 39783.	
Dec 8	To Thomas Wren Ward. ALS. MHi. mDW 10363. Invites Ward to let him handle his Neapolitan claims.	
Dec 10	*To Levi Lincoln.*	200
Dec 11	Promissory note to Caleb Pratt for $400 with interest. ALS. PHi. mDW 39785.	
Dec 11	Bill to provide for claims due to certain American citizens for spoliations committed on their commerce before Sept 30, 1808 ("French claims"). Printed document (with some MS insertions in DW's hand). DNA, RG 46. mDW 43341.	
Dec 15	To Edward Everett. ALS. DNA, RG 94. mDWs. Asks Everett to help Russell Soley receive a cadetship to West Point.	
Dec 16	From Joel Henry Dyer. ALS. NhHi. mDW 10368. Enlists DW's aid to determine whether his father was eligible for a military pension.	
Dec 20	*From Charles Brickett Haddock.*	200
Dec 23	From George Bancroft. ALS. NhHi. mDW 10377. The town of Northampton, Mass., sends its gratitude for DW's efforts against nullification.	
Dec 24	To Nicholas Biddle. ALS. DLC. mDW 10379-A. Plans to go to Philadelphia shortly to see Biddle.	
Dec 26	From John Fuller. ALS. NhHi. mDW 10380. Asks for DW's help in finding a job.	
Dec 27	To Peter Chardon Brooks. ALS. NhD. mDW 10384. Will serve as agent for French Spoliation claims *"provided I am to be concerned, as under the Spanish Treaty."*	
Dec 27	*To Joseph Story.*	201
Dec 27	From Benjamin F. French. ALS. NhHi. mDW 10392. Has uncovered a manuscript volume of the proceedings of the Stamp Act Congress and asks whether it should be placed in the Washington Archives.	
Dec 27	From Henry Willis Kinsman. Abstract, Kinsman Letterbook. NhD. mDW 7475. Concerning personal financial matters.	
Dec 27	From Henry Willis Kinsman. Abstract, Kinsman Letterbook. NhD. mDW 7475. Concerning General Henry A. S. Dearborn's note.	
Dec 27	From Josiah Quincy. ALS. MH. mDW 10387. Gives DW additional information about his French claim.	
Dec 29	From Henry Willis Kinsman. Abstract, Kinsman Letterbook. NhD. mDW 7475. Sends, under cover to Walter Lowrie, secretary of the Senate, memorials and supporting evidence respecting French claims.	

Dec 29	From Henry Willis Kinsman. Abstract, Kinsman Letterbook. NhD. mDW 7476. Sends additional French claims documents.
Dec 31	From Nicholas Biddle. LC. DLC. mDWs. Discusses the list of nominations for Bank directors and possible future actions of the House Ways and Means Committee.
Dec 31	From Caroline Le Roy Webster (enclosed with Caroline Le Roy Webster, et al., to DW, Jan 1, 1833). ALS. NhHi. mDW 10395. Van Tyne, p. 584 (in part). Reports on family and social news from Boston.
Dec	Petition of inhabitants of Marshfield and Duxbury, Mass., asking that an appropriation be made for placing a spar buoy on Sunken Rock in Green Harbor. DS. DNA, RG 46. mDW 43683.
Dec [?]	To Thomas Wigglesworth. ALS. MHi. mDW 10399. Is sorry to have inconvenienced Wigglesworth and hopes to render an equivalent service to him on some future occasion.
[1832]	To Warren Dutton. ALS. NhD. mDW 10403. Hopes the Duttons will take lodgings here.
[1832?]	To Abraham G. Stevens. Printed. W & S, 16: 679. Asks Stevens to look after the needs of Thomas Davis during his stay in the Franklin, N.H., area.
[1832?]	To Stephen White. ALS. NhHi. mDW 10259. PC, 1: 524–525. Assures White "it is not often that good wine is under any roof where I am without my knowing it."

1833

Jan 1	To [?] Edwards. AL. NN. mDW 10416. Asks Edwards to reply to the writer of the enclosed letter.	
Jan 1	*To Henry Willis Kinsman.*	203
Jan 1	From Mrs. John Fuller. ALS. NhHi. mDW 10421. Discusses her husband's disappointment at not seeing DW and asks for DW's assistance in helping him find a job from his "friends of affluent Circumstances."	
Jan 1	From Henry Willis Kinsman. Abstract, Kinsman Letterbook. NhD. mDW 7477. Informs DW about a promissory note and a claims memorial.	
Jan 1	From Joshua C. Oliver. ALS. NhHi. mDW 10424. Thinks Fuller has reformed and should be given another chance.	
Jan 1	From Caroline Le Roy Webster (including ANS greetings from Edward, Julia, Daniel Fletcher	

Webster, and [Hannah Cornell Newbold?];
enclosed with Caroline Le Roy Webster to DW,
Dec 31, 1832). ALS. NhHi. mDW 10398. Van
Tyne, p. 585 (in part). Reports on her few New
Year's Day activities.

[Jan 2]   To Thomas Kemper Davis. ALS. NhD. mDW 10428.
Asks about a case discussed in a letter from Louis
Leroy of North Carolina which DW received last
summer.

Jan 3   To John Fuller. ALS draft. NhHi. mDW 10430. Van
Tyne, p. 742. Has written to Dr. Cyrus Perkins in
Fuller's behalf; thinks he can "restore" himself
by "exemplary good conduct."

Jan 3   To [Joshua C. Oliver]. AL draft. NhHi. mDW 10432.
Van Tyne, pp. 741–742. Describes Fuller's
"misconduct" while a teller at the Boston BUS
branch.

Jan 3   To [Dr. Cyrus Perkins]. ALS. NhHi. mDW 10435.
Recommends John Fuller for a job as a writer or
accountant.

Jan 3   *To William Sullivan.*   204

Jan 3   From Henry Willis Kinsman. Abstract, Kinsman
Letterbook. NhD. mDW 7477. Sends letter
concerning memorials for claims.

Jan 3   From Caroline Le Roy Webster. ALS. NhHi. mDW
10442. Reports on family and social news.

Jan 4   *To Warren Dutton.*   205

Jan 4   To Henry Willis Kinsman. ALS. Dr. Gurdon S.
Pulford, Palo Alto, Calif. mDW 10451. Encloses a
summary of the Danish claims and desires
additional evidence in the French claim cases.

Jan 4, [1833?]   To Henry Willis Kinsman. ALS. NhD. mDW 38686.
Asks Kinsman to report every day or two on the
"general feeling" of the members of the
Massachusetts legislature.

Jan 4   To Charles Henry Thomas. ALS. MHi. mDW 10454.
Discusses plans for a bath and boat house at
Marshfield.

[Jan 5]   To Edward Everett. ALS. MHi. mDW 10459. Asks
about the strength of parties [in the
Massachusetts legislature].

Jan 5   To Messrs. Edward Everett, et al. ALS. MHi. mDW
10457. Accepts with pleasure their invitation for
dinner on Tuesday.

Jan 5   To Arthur Livermore. Printed. PC, 1: 530. Thinks
"the danger of immediate collision" over
nullification "has assumed a less threatening
aspect," but is less certain about the outcome on
the tariff.

Jan 5   From Henry Willis Kinsman. Abstract, Kinsman

	Letterbook. NhD. mDW 7477. Sends three additional claims memorials.
Jan 6	From Peter Chardon Brooks. ALS. H. Bartholomew Cox, Oxon Hill, Md. mDW 10461. Discusses French claims and DW's fee, and the continuing controversy over the Charles River Bridge case.
Jan 8	From Nicholas Biddle. LC. DLC. mDWs. Assures DW about the "Three per cents," and inquires about the French indemnity payments.
Jan 8	From Nicholas Biddle. LC. DLC. mDWs. Understands that Hartman Kuhn declines to serve as a director, and should he know in advance the replacement, "it would perhaps enable us to exclude some very bad selection which is now probable."
Jan [8-9]	From Henry Willis Kinsman. Abstract, Kinsman Letterbook. NhD. mDW 7477. Discusses notes and inquires about the Danish commissioners.
Jan 9, [1833?]	To [Henry Willis Kinsman]. ALS. NNC. mDW 38684. Discusses his current "payables" and other financial arrangements.
Jan [9-10]	From Henry Willis Kinsman. Abstract, Kinsman Letterbook. NhD. mDW 7478. Returns the list of Danish claims allowed and sends a printed list of representatives in the General Court.
[Jan 10]	Motion by DW that Indian treaties should contain no stipulation for the payment of Indian debts to Indian traders. AD in DW's hand. DNA, RG 46. mDW 43826.
Jan 11	*To Nicholas Biddle.*
Jan 11	To Henry Willis Kinsman. ALS. NhHi. mDW 10475. Discusses the lack of progress in disposing of Danish claims before the commission.
Jan 11	To Charles Henry Thomas. ALS. MHi. mDW 10476. Thinks the time is right for "laying the *ice*" and buying old hay for compost.
Jan 12	To Henry Willis Kinsman. ALS. Dr. Gurdon S. Pulford, Palo Alto, Calif. mDW 10478. Will send $500 or $600 on Monday.
Jan 12	Petition of James Patrick asking for a pension in consideration of a disability created while employed in the revenue service in 1832 (with enclosures). DS. DNA, RG 46. mDW 43744.
Jan 14	From Nicholas Biddle. LC. DLC. mDWs. Sees no objection to Peter Wager as a government director; has asked John Sergeant to make DW an associate whenever possible, but for now "our only causes of quarrel are in the Executive Departments, not in the Courts."
Jan 14	From Henry Willis Kinsman. Abstract, Kinsman

206

Letterbook. NhD. mDW 7478. Sends more information about claims cases.

Jan 15   To Warren Dutton. Printed. *PC*, 1: 530–531. Thinks Jackson will shortly send a communication on nullification and doubts a new tariff bill will pass.

Jan 15   From Henry Willis Kinsman. Abstract, Kinsman Letterbook. NhD. mDW 7478. Reports on DW's reelection in the Massachusetts House of Representatives.

Jan 16   From Henry Willis Kinsman. Abstract, Kinsman Letterbook. NhD. mDW 7478. Tells DW that the vote for him in the Massachusetts Senate was unanimous.

Jan 16   Credentials of DW's election to the U.S. Senate signed by Levi Lincoln, governor of Massachusetts. ADS. DNA, RG 46. mDW 43794.

Jan 17   From Henry Willis Kinsman. Abstract, Kinsman Letterbook. NhD. mDW 7478. Has borrowed $1,500 from Mr. Samuel Frothingham.

Jan 18   To Theodore Dwight. AL. NhD. mDW 10481. Thinks it "improbable" any tariff bill will pass this session and wonders what South Carolina will do after February 1.

Jan 18   *To [Stephen White].*   207

Jan 18   From Henry Willis Kinsman. Abstract, Kinsman Letterbook. NhD. mDW 7478. Sends a copy of the joint report of resolutions of the Massachusetts legislature regarding the tariff.

Jan 19   From Henry Willis Kinsman. Abstract, Kinsman Letterbook. NhD. mDW 7478. Reports on promissory notes, the Boston assessments, the Providence Railroad, and the tariff.

Jan 19   Draft to Caroline Le Roy Webster for $50. Printed document with MS insertions. NjMoHP. mDW 39790.

Jan [19–24]   From Henry Willis Kinsman. Abstract, Kinsman Letterbook. NhD. mDW 7478. Discusses a claims memorial and Nathan Hale's note for $1,000.

Jan 21   From John Evelyn Denison. Printed. Curtis, 1: 466–467. Thinks nullification will be settled without violence, and asks DW to "enlighten" him on the voting ballot and American experiments in prison discipline.

Jan 22   To Charles Henry Thomas. ALS. MHi. mDW 10488. Writes about the plans for the boat house.

Jan 23   To [Henry Willis Kinsman, et al.]. ADS. OYMHi. mDW 10490. Declares that they are all qualified as justices of the peace to administer oaths by the law of Massachusetts.

Jan 23   To Edward Livingston. ALS. DNA, RG 59. mDWs.

	Sends papers and application of Thomas Dimmock to be consul at St. Thomas.
Jan 23	To Charles A. Parker. ALS. MH. mDW 10491. Informs Parker that Congress will be unable to handle his father's claim this session.
Jan 23	To Charles Henry Thomas. ALS. MHi. mDW 10494. Returns the boat house plan and suggests several alterations.
Jan 24	From Timothy Pitkin. ALS. NhD. mDW 10495. Comments on the protective system and nullification, and other political issues.
Jan 25	To Henry Willis Kinsman. ALS. NhHi. mDW 10502. Discusses defects in French claims memorials and returns them for corrections.
Jan 25	From Jesse Hawley. ALS. NhHi. mDW 10504. Suggests a revenue tariff with specific changes in the duties in order to conciliate North and South.
Jan 25	From Edward Livingston. LC. DNA, RG 59. mDW 55673. Informs DW that there is no vacancy in the U.S. consulate at St. Thomas.
[Jan 26]	To Edward Everett. 209
Jan 26	From Levi Lincoln. ALS. NhHi. mDW 10509. Sends the resolutions of the Massachusetts legislature on the tariff.
[Jan 27]	To Joseph Hopkinson. 209
[Jan 28]	To [James Kent]. ALS. NNC. mDW 10518. Sends a copy of [Jackson's "Force Bill"] message and rejoices "most heartily, in seeing the truth taught, from high places."
Jan 28	From Henry Willis Kinsman. Abstract, Kinsman Letterbook. NhD. mDW 7479. Concerning Nathan Hale's note of $1,000 which is to be renewed for $500.
Jan 29	To Warren Dutton. ALS. NhD. mDW 10519. Tells Dutton to come in mid-February to help prepare a second argument for the Charles River Bridge case.
[c. Jan 29]	From John Lindsey (enclosed with Joseph A. Merrill, et al., to DW, Jan 29, 1833). ALS. NhHi. mDW 10523. Is authorized by Bishop Elijah Hedding to secure DW's legal services.
Jan 29	From Joseph A. Merrill, et al. (with enclosure: John Lindsey to [DW], [c. Jan 29, 1833]). ALS. NhHi. mDW 10521. Request DW's legal counsel in the trial of Rev. Ephraim H. Avery.
Jan 30	From Louis Leroy (with enclosure of statement of facts in controversy with B. F. Copeland, AD copy). ALS. NhHi. mDW 10524. Renders a detailed account of the background of the controversy.

Jan 31   To Joseph Hopkinson. ALS. PHi. mDW 10533. Discusses the Tariff Bill before the House; thinks the "only *real* danger" now is that "Congress may surrender to S. Carolina all she claims."

[c. Jan 31]   To Henry Willis Kinsman. ALS. NhHi. mDW 10535. W & S, 16: 225–226. Discusses two Danish claims cases.

Jan 31   From Henry Willis Kinsman. Abstract, Kinsman Letterbook. NhD. mDW 7479. Acknowledges receipt of claims memorials to be corrected.

[Jan]   To Edward Everett. ALS. MHi. mDW 10538. Offers Everett a bottle of his "good Boston" Madeira.

[Jan 1833?]   Principles [Notes on the Tariff Controversy]. AD. MHi. mDW 10412. W & S, 15: 104–105.

Feb 3   To [Joseph Hopkinson]. ALS. PHi. mDW 10540. Reiterates the impropriety of John McLean's electioneering for the Presidency from the Supreme Court bench and his preference for Van Buren in a contest between them; will attempt to answer Calhoun should he speak in the Senate.

Feb 3   From Joseph Hopkinson. ALS. MHi. mDW 10544. Is alarmed by the policy of a compromise tariff in light of southern nullification activities.

Feb 4   To [Peter Paul Francis?] Degrand. ALS. KyU. mDW 10550. Will do what he can to see an unidentified bill passed in the Senate.

Feb 4   To Joseph Hopkinson. ALS. PHi. mDW 10551. Asks Hopkinson to send the enclosed "Extract of a letter from Washington" to the editor of the *Gazette of the United States.*

Feb 4   *From Charles Miner.*   210

Feb [4–5]   From Henry Willis Kinsman. Abstract, Kinsman Letterbook. NhD. mDW 7479. Informs DW of notes due in February.

Feb 5   To Henry Willis Kinsman. ALS. NhHi. mDW 10556. W & S, 16: 226–227. Discusses defective memorials among the French claims which they are handling.

Feb 5   *From Henry Clay.*   211

Feb 6   *From Joseph Hopkinson.*   211

Feb 6   From Anna Lloyd. ALS. NhHi. mDW 10562. Asks DW's support of her nephew's application to become a midshipman.

Feb 7   *To Joseph Hopkinson.*   212

Feb 7   To Julia Webster. ALS. M. mDW 10571. Discusses the art of writing, congressional business, and Julia's activities.

Feb 7   From Henry Willis Kinsman. Abstract, Kinsman Letterbook. NhD. mDW 7480. Sends information about railroad stock.

Feb 8	From Nicholas Biddle. LC. DLC. mDWs. Sends a report of a BUS committee vindicating the Bank from the charges preferred against it by the administration.
Feb 8	From Henry Willis Kinsman. Abstract, Kinsman Letterbook. NhD. mDW 7480. Writes about information in another claims case.
Feb 8	From Henry Willis Kinsman. ALS. NhHi. mDW 10574. Has received a memorandum of decision in several French claims cases and has corrected defects in others.
[Feb 9]	To Nathan Appleton. ALS. ICHi. mDW 10576. Relates the current state of congressional business and fears that the House will pass a new tariff bill.
Feb 9	*To Joseph Hopkinson.* 213
Feb 11	To Charles Henry Thomas. ALS. MHi. mDW 10584. Asks Thomas to get Mr. [Charles] Baker's terms for sale of some pasture land.
Feb 11	From Henry Willis Kinsman. ALS. NhHi. mDW 10586. Discusses the lack of proof in the Otis case and reports on other claims.
Feb [11–15]	From Henry Willis Kinsman. Abstract, Kinsman Letterbook. NhD. mDW 7480. Writes about General Henry A. S. Dearborn's note.
Feb 12	Bill to modify the Act of July 14, 1832, and other acts imposing duties on imports (with AD Senate select committee amendments). AD. DNA, RG 46. mDW 43348.
Feb [14]	Resolution by DW regarding adjustments to the tariff. AD. DNA, RG 46. mDW 43366.
Feb 15	To [Edward Everett]. ALS. MHi. mDW 10593. Van Tyne, p. 179. Asks for Everett's "thoughts" on Clay's tariff measure.
[Feb 15]	*To Joseph Hopkinson.* 214
Feb 15	From Henry Willis Kinsman. Abstract, Kinsman Letterbook. NhD. mDW 7480. Sends word about a promissory note and a package containing two claims memorials.
Feb 16	From Henry Willis Kinsman. Abstract, Kinsman Letterbook. NhD. mDW 7480. Informs DW that he owes Mr. Samuel Frothingham about $2,000.
[Feb 17]	*To Nathan Appleton.* 216
Feb 18	From Francis Preston Blair. ALS. MoHi. mDW 10691. Asks how soon DW can furnish a copy of his speech in reply to Calhoun as "it is a matter of interest with some of my friends."
Feb 18	*From Harrison Gray Otis.* 217
Feb 20, 183[3]	From Henry Willis Kinsman. AL draft. NhHi. mDW

	Requests Frothingham to credit his account for $1,500 with the enclosure.
Feb 28	To Edward Livingston (from John M. Berrien, Joseph M. White, and DW). ALS by Berrien, signed also by DW. DNA, RG 59. mDWs. Discuss new information on Spanish law applicable to the Forbes case now pending in Supreme Court.
[March 1, 1833?]	To James William Paige. ALS. MHi. mDW 10737. Reports that he is suffering from another "violent cold" and notes the House's extended business on the Tariff Bill that day.
March 1	From Henry Willis Kinsman. Abstract, Kinsman Letterbook. NhD. mDW 7481. Encloses a French claims memorial.
March 2	*From Henry Clay.* 221
March 2	From Henry Willis Kinsman. Abstract, Kinsman Letterbook. NhD. mDW 7481. Writes about Dr. [Cyrus] Perkins' draft.
March 3	From Julia Webster. ALS. NhHi. mDW 10741. *PC,* 1: 531–532. Reports on family and social news in Boston and thanks DW for a present he has sent.
[March 4, 1833?]	To [George M.] Grouard. ALS. MHi. mDW 38414. Has looked over the corrections for a printed version of his speech and wants to adopt most of them.
March 4	From Henry Willis Kinsman. Abstract, Kinsman Letterbook. NhD. mDW 7481. Writes about a promissory note.
March 8	To Ether Shepley. ALS. NhD. mDW 10744. Will probably be unable to attend the circuit court at Portland in May.
March 9	To Julia Webster. Printed. *PC,* 1: 532–533. Plans to leave Washington in about a week and remain in Philadelphia on business for several days.
[March 11]	To Joseph Gales. ALS. ICHi. mDW 10746. Invites Gales to dine with him and friends tomorrow.
March 11, [1833?]	To [George M.] Grouard. ALS. PWb. mDWs. Returns the proofs and hopes to see the revision shortly as he plans to leave town.
March 13	To Nicholas Fish. ALS. DLC. mDW 10748. Encloses a letter from the secretary of the Navy.
March 13	To Charles Henry Thomas. ALS. MHi. mDW 10750. Is glad to hear he has concluded the land deal with [Charles] Baker and informs Thomas of his current plans.
March 15	*From James Madison.* 222
March 15	From William B. Reed, et al. (with enclosure of report of a committee of the Franklin Institute,

	AD copy). ALS by Reed, signed also by others. DLC. mDW 10759. Invite DW to give the annual public discourse at the Franklin Institute.	
[*March 21?*]	*To [Edward Livingston].*	225
March 22	From Joshua Peirce (with enclosure of bill from Peirce, AD). ALS. NhHi. mDW 10773. Has sent the plants and trees ordered by DW.	
March 23	From Thomas March (with AN abstract of reply by DW, March 25). ALS. NhHi. mDW 10776. Asks DW to help resolve differences with his brother Charles.	
March 24	To Samuel Jaudon. ALS. NHi. mDW 10778. Would like to hear from Mr. [Thomas Wren?] Ward before leaving New York.	
March 24	To [Henry Willis Kinsman]. ALS. NhHi. mDW 10780. W & S, 16: 227. Reports that a Danish claim has been allowed, and asks for the power of substitution to receive the awards in this and another case.	
March 25	To Thomas March (abstract reply to March's letter of March 23). AN. NhHi. mDW 10777. Concludes that he will not get involved in the controversy.	
March 25	*From Joel Roberts Poinsett.*	227
March 26	From Henry Willis Kinsman. Abstract, Kinsman Letterbook. NhD. mDW 7482. Writes about drafts and notes.	
[*March 27*]	*To [Nicholas Biddle].*	228
March 27	To Joseph Hopkinson. ALS. PHi. mDW 10786. Tells Hopkinson that he has written to [Levi] W[oodbury].	
[March 27]	To [Samuel Jaudon]. AL. NHi. mDW 10788. Is not surprised that Mr. W[ard?] declined; will arrange to have someone in Boston draw on Jaudon for DW so their names will not "appear on the same paper."	
March 27	To Levi Woodbury (with ANS abstract of reply dated March 29, 1833). ALS. DLC. mDW 10791. Encloses Hopkinson's letter requesting Woodbury to consider his son for an appointment as a [midshipman?].	
March 27	*From Nathan C. Brownell, William B. Breed, and Stephen Whitney.*	228
March 27	*From Eli S. Davis.*	233
March 27	From John E. Wool. ALS. N. mDW 10807. Thanks DW for copies of his speech in reply to Calhoun, and hopes the country will "place you where many, very many, would be more than glad to see you."	
[*March 28*]	*To Nicholas Biddle.*	234
March 28	To Samuel Frothingham. ALS. ICN. mDW 10810.	

Asks Frothingham to credit his account for $5,000
and discusses an outstanding bill of exchange.

[March 28]   To Jonathan Goodhue. ALS. NNS. mDW 10812.
                Writes letter of introduction for John W. Taylor.

March 28   To Samuel Jaudon. ALS. NHi. mDW 10814.
                Contemplates seeing Mr. W[ard?] upon his return
                to New York.

March 28   To Henry Willis Kinsman. ALS. NNC. mDW 10816.
                Discusses the renewal and settlement of several
                promissory notes.

March 28   To Charles Henry Thomas. ALS. MHi. mDW 10818.
                Is delayed in leaving New York; discusses the
                financial arrangements for the new Marshfield
                land he has bought.

March 29   From Levi Woodbury (abstract reply to DW's letter
                of March 27). ANS. DLC. mDW 10791. Regrets
                that there is no vacancy for Hopkinson's son;
                candidates from Pennsylvania are numerous.

[March]   To Nicholas Biddle. AL fragment. DLC. mDW
                10890. Plans to stay in New York for about two
                weeks in anticipation of using the *"earliest
                opportunity"* to see Edward Livingston.

April 1   *To John Ellis Wool.*   234
April 1   From Henry Willis Kinsman. Abstract, Kinsman
                Letterbook. NhD. mDW 7482. Writes about Mr.
                [?] Lawrence's case in Worcester.

April 1   *From Benjamin Franklin Perry.*   235
April 3   From Henry Willis Kinsman. Abstract, Kinsman
                Letterbook. NhD. mDW 7482. Encloses a stock
                certificate of the Boston and Providence Railroad
                Company for seventy-five shares.

[April 4]   To Henry Willis Kinsman. ALS. Dr. Gurdon S.
                Pulford, Palo Alto, Calif. mDW 10827. Is delayed
                in New York on business, but makes necessary
                arrangements concerning a Worcester, Mass.,
                case to be heard later in the month.

April 7   *To [Nicholas Biddle].*   236
April 8   *To [Nicholas Biddle].*   237
April 8   To the Marquis de Lafayette. ALS. NIC. mDW
                10833. Writes a letter of introduction for
                [Samuel?] Greele.

April 8   *From Nicholas Biddle.*   238
April 9   To Simon Greenleaf. ALS. MH-L. mDWs. Thinks his
                services in the Allen case "would cost more than
                they would be worth" to Dr. Allen.

April 9   To Charles Henry Thomas. ALS. MHi. mDW 10836.
                Has arrived home in Boston and asks Thomas to
                come and see him.

April 9   *From Mathew Carey.*   238
April 10   To David A. Hall. ALS. NhD. mDW 10846. Notes

had with Van Buren about the Vice President's future plans.

April 30   To William Drayton, et al. LS. MBBS. mDW 10889. Has received their printed circular and has "great pleasure in contributing [$10] towards the truly National object which it suggests."

[May 6]   To Edward Everett. ALS. MHi. mDW 10896. Asks if Everett has some spare copies of DW's "late" speeches.

May 7   *To Joel Roberts Poinsett.*   248

May 8   To Joseph Hopkinson. ALS. PHi. mDW 10902. Will talk to Livingston about Hopkinson's son; has altered plans for western trip.

May 10   From James Gordon Bennett. ALS. CSmH. mDW 10905. Asks DW if he would be counsel in suits against the editors and proprietors of the *New York Standard* and the *New York Post.*

May 10   From Nicholas Biddle. LC. DLC. mDWs. Has learned that Livingston will be in Philadelphia on May 13 and urges DW to come there before starting his western tour.

May 12   *From Joseph Hopkinson.*   249

May 13   To James Gordon Bennett. ALS. NhD. mDW 10910. Would be glad to handle Bennett's contemplated suits provided they did not interfere with his congressional obligations next spring.

May 13   To Mathew Carey. LS. The John Rylands Library, Manchester, England. mDW 10915. Van Tyne, pp. 182–183. Hopes that Carey will not be discouraged from continuing to write and circulate his popular tracts on the Constitution and the attempts at nullification.

May 14   To Hugh McCulloch. Typed copy. InU. mDW 10917. Writes a letter of reference to McCulloch for his use while visiting and eventually settling in the West.

May 14   *From Benjamin Franklin Perry.*   250

May 15   To the Marquis de Lafayette. ALS. InU. mDW 10922. Writes a letter of introduction for William Burns, a New York merchant.

May 16   *From John Bolton.*   251

May 17   *To John Bolton.*   252

May 22   From Henry Willis Kinsman. Abstract, Kinsman Letterbook. NhD. mDW 7485. Encloses a blank power to receive payment of drafts.

May 24   From Benjamin F. Pepoon. ALS. NhHi. mDW 10935. Thanks DW for his contribution to their cause.

May 24   *From Joel Roberts Poinsett.*   253

May 28   *Memorandum of visit to Edward Le Roy's farm.*   254

May 30   From John Pringle Jones. ALS by Jones, signed also by others. DLC. mDW 10945. Invites DW to address the Law Academy of Philadelphia.

May 30   Memorial from sundry citizens of Massachusetts asking that an academy be instituted for the instruction of mariners. DS. DNA, RG 46. mDW 44603.

[May]   From Mathew Carey. AL (incomplete). DLC. mDW 10947. Reiterates the financial cost and lack of honor for all his work in behalf of the protective tariff.

[May–June] Objects [Memorandum of political aims]. AD. NhHi. mDW 10977. Van Tyne, p. 183.

June 1   *To John G. Camp, and others.*   255

June 1   Promissory note to James W. Burdett for $600. ADS. DLC. mDW 39787.

June 2, [1833?] To Albert H. Tracy. ALS. NN. mDW 39087. Would like to see Tracy this morning for his advice in a matter.

June 3   Promissory note to Richard D. Tucker for $500. ADS. DLC. mDW 39793.

June 6   From William Armstrong, et al. LS. DLC. mDW 10955. Invite DW to come to Nashville, Tenn., on his western tour.

June 8   From Henry Willis Kinsman. Abstract, Kinsman Letterbook. NhD. mDW 7487. Writes about money for Fletcher Webster, Charles Henry Thomas, and T. F. Le Roy.

June 10   To Henry Clay. ALS. DLC. mDW 10963. Colton, *Henry Clay*, p. 366. Tells Clay it is uncertain whether he will get to Lexington.

June 10   From Henry Willis Kinsman. Abstract, Kinsman Letterbook. NhD. mDW 7488. Encloses the opinion in a case.

June 10   From Henry Willis Kinsman. Abstract, Kinsman Letterbook. NhD. mDW 7488. Encloses a confidential letter.

June 15   From Morgan Neville. Printed. *National Intelligencer*, June 25, 1833. Invites DW to a public dinner in Cincinnati on June 19.

June 15   To Morgan Neville. Printed. *National Intelligencer*, June 25, 1833. Accepts the June 19 Cincinnati dinner invitation.

June 17   *From Henry Clay.*   257

June 19   *From John Test.*   258

June 21   From John McLure. ALS. DLC. mDW 10971. Reports that the cholera epidemic in Wheeling, Va., has subsided so that DW can safely pass through on his return from Ohio.

June 22	*To Henry Clay.*	258
June 26	To Citizens of Lancaster, Ohio. Printed. *Boston Courier*, July 11, 1833. Declines their invitation for a public dinner, but thanks them for their remarks on "my public service in favor of the Union."	
June 28	Promissory note to Nathan Hale for $700. ADS. DLC. mDW 39795.	
June 29	From Samuel F. Vinton. ALS. NhD. mDW 10974. Is disappointed that DW returned by an interior route and missed seeing thouands of friends along the Ohio.	
July 1	To Daniel Fletcher Webster. Printed. *PC*, 1: 538. Advises Fletcher on the preparation of his Harvard class oration.	
July 2	From Henry Willis Kinsman. Abstract, Kinsman Letterbook. NhD. mDW 7488. Writes about French claims.	
July 4	From James Ross, et al. Printed. *Speeches and Forensic Arguments*, 2:213. Wish to honor DW with some form of public tribute such as a public dinner.	
July 5	To James Ross, et al. Printed. *Speeches and Forensic Arguments*, 2:214. Expresses his thanks for the cordial reception he has received in Pittsburgh.	
July 5	*To Daniel Fletcher Webster.*	259
July 6	From Nathan Wright. LC abstract. DLC. mDW 10981. Encloses a statement of one legal case and an argument in another.	
July 12	From John R. Thompson. ALS. NhHi. mDW 10983. Encloses a $100 retainer for legal services in any future case involving the Delaware and Raritan Canal, and Camden & Amboy Railroad and Transportation Companies.	
July 19	To Nicholas Biddle. ALS. DLC. mDW 10985. Writes a letter of introduction for Edward Curtis.	
July 19	From Jeremiah Smith. ALS. MHi. mDW 10987. Sends a letter of introduction for J. H. Abbot, who wishes to start a school for young ladies in Boston.	
July 24	From James Lynch and A. Williams (with enclosure: DS invitation from James Lynch, et al.). ALS by Williams, signed also by Lynch. DLC. mDW 10991. Invite DW to deliver the 1833 annual address at the American Institute in New York City.	
[July 25]	To Edward Everett. ALS. MHi. mDW 10994. Has just returned to Boston and his Court Street office, and would be glad to see Everett today.	

July 27   From Benjamin F. Hallett. ALS. DLC. mDW 10996.
        Encloses the resolutions of Anti-Masonic members
        of the Massachusetts legislature.

July 29   From Samuel Atkinson. ALS. DLC. mDW 10999.
        Reports on the course of the wind in his region.

July 31   From Benjamin Ruggles. ALS. NhD. mDW 11001.
        Is disappointed that DW did not visit St.
        Clairsville, Ohio, on his western tour.

Aug 3   To James Lynch and A. Williams. ALS draft. DLC.
        mDW 11007. Regrets that he will be unable to
        address the American Institute in October.

Aug 3   To [Thomas Grubb McCullough]. ALS. NhD. mDW
        11009. Is thankful for kindnesses received at
        Chambersburg, Pa., while on his western tour.

Aug 3   To Nathaniel F. Williams. ALS. NhD. mDW 11011.
        Concerning DW's personal financial matters.

[*Aug 5*]   *To Edward Everett.*   260

Aug 6   To [?]. ALS. NhD. mDW 11015. Has received a $50
        retainer and assures correspondent that the case
        will be defended "by competent counsel, & [the]
        best made of it that can be."

Aug 6   *To Ezekiel Forman Chambers.*   260

Aug 6   *To [John Renshaw Thomson].*   261

[*Aug 7*]   To Edward Everett (with enclosure: "Another Judge
        in Nomination," AD draft, in Everett's hand,
        revised by DW). ALS. MHi. mDW 11024. Has
        made some changes in the manuscript and hopes
        to be able to see the revision this evening.

Aug 7   From Nicholas Biddle. LC. DLC. mDWs. Requests
        DW "to make Jack Downing write a letter about
        the Bank," and notes that the "universal diffusion
        and the actual power of those letters is
        marvellous."

[*Aug 8*]   To [Edward Everett]. ALS. MHi. mDW 11033. Has
        altered Everett's article and thinks it is "just the
        thing."

Aug 8   To [Edward Everett]. ALS. MHi. mDW 11034.
        Thinks Everett's suspicion about an unidentified
        man is well founded.

Aug 9   *From Edward Everett.*   262

Aug 10   To Elihu Chauncey. ALS. MHi. mDW 11041. Writes
        a letter of introduction for Edward Everett, who
        "possesses our full confidence."

[Aug 10?]   To [Edward Everett]. ALS. MHi. mDW 11042.
        Thnks it prudent to postpone the article for
        several days; would like to see a similar article
        appear in the *United States Gazette* in
        Philadelphia.

Aug 10   *To Samuel P. Lyman.*   265

Aug 10   *To Albert Haller Tracy.*   266

Aug 10   To Nathaniel F. Williams. ALS. NhD. mDW 11052. Encloses a draft for $1,000 payable to Henry P. Williams and has drawn $1,000 on Nathaniel F. Williams.

Aug 11   To James Bell. ALS. Burton L. Bruce, Nashua, N.H. mDWs. Thinks it very unlikely he will be able to attend in October the postponed trial in the Exeter court.

[Aug 11]   *To Edward Everett.*   267

Aug 11   From Dutee J. Pearce. ALS. NhHi. mDW 11062. Appeals to DW for help against the strong opposition to his reelection to Congress.

Aug 12   To George Edmund Badger. LC. Nc-Ar. mDW 11065. Will be pleased to be retained for the state of North Carolina in a pending Supreme Court case (*Lattimer* v. *Poteet*, 14 Peters 77, 1840).

Aug 12   *From Rufus Choate.*   269

Aug 12   *From Henry Alexander Scammell Dearborn.*   270

[Aug 13]   To [Edward Everett]. ALS. MHi. mDW 11054. Advises Everett that [the article] would best be put in the *United States Gazette.*

[Aug 13]   To [Edward Everett]. ALS. MHi. mDW 11077. Baltimore friends have arrived; will send Everett a letter at New Haven later in the week.

Aug 13   *To [Edward Everett].*   272

Aug 13   *From Nicholas Biddle.*   273

Aug 13   From John Brooks. ALS. NhHi. mDW 11080. Sends a bill for a yoke of four-year-old oxen, and asks whether DW is interested in two two-year-old steers he has mentioned before.

Aug 16   From William Bradford Reed. ALS. NhD. mDW 11083. Wishes to know the date in October that DW has fixed for his "discourse" to the Franklin Institute in Philadelphia.

Aug 17   To [Henry Willis Kinsman]. ALS. NhD. mDW 11086. Asks Kinsman to handle several notes falling due this week and to send the invitation from the Pittsburgh Committee, when it arrives, to Joseph T. Buckingham.

Aug 17   From Josiah Quincy. ALS. NhD. mDW 11090. Tells DW that a special meeting of the Harvard Board of Overseers will have to be called in order to approve an honorary LL.D. degree for Edward Livingston, a nomination made at DW's suggestion.

Aug 18   From Samuel P. Lyman. ALS draft. MiU-C. mDWs. Has decided to visit Boston at DW's invitation and will arrive Aug 27; discusses his initial efforts to win support for DW's presidential candidacy in New York state.

Aug 21	From Thomas Chambers. ALS. DLC. mDW 11094. Expresses his delight in DW's visit to Chambersburg, Pa., on his tour.	
Aug 23	*From Edward Cutts, Jr.*	273
Aug 24	To Elihu Chauncey. ALS. MHi. mDW 11100. Writes a letter of introduction for Edward Everett, who wishes to talk "on public matters."	
Aug 24	To Samuel Jaudon. ALS. MHi. mDW 11101. Writes a letter of introduction for Edward Everett, who wishes to converse on "sundry matters" with DW's "full confidence."	
Aug 25	To Edward Everett. ALS. MHi. mDW 11102. Encloses the letters to Chauncey and Jaudon; has received letters from Washington, Utica, and Buffalo written "in very friendly spirits."	
[Aug 27]	To Samuel P. Lyman. ALS. MiU-C. mDWs. Informs Lyman that dinner will be at 3 o'clock.	
Aug 27	To Samuel P. Lyman. ALS. MiU-C. mDWs. Hopes Lyman received his note of this morning and that he will be able to come for dinner at 3 o'clock.	
Aug 27	Draft to John Brooks for $102. Printed document with MS insertions. GU. mDW 39797.	
[*Aug 28*]	*To [Edward Everett].*	275
Aug [28]	To Mr. and Mrs. Edward Everett (from Caroline Le Roy Webster). AL in DW's hand. MHi. mDW 11106. Requests the Everetts' company to meet a small party on Friday evening.	
Aug 28	To Dutee J. Pearce. ALS. DLC. mDWs. Thinks that a written endorsement for Pearce would be improper and may do "more harm than good."	
[Aug 30]	To Edward Everett. ALS. MHi. mDW 11108. Writes that Samuel P. Lyman would like to see Everett later this morning at Tremont House.	
Aug 30	*From Nicholas Biddle.*	275
Aug 31	To Mrs. Edward Everett. AL in Caroline Le Roy Webster's hand. MHi. mDW 11110. Regret they will be unable to accept an invitation the following Tuesday.	
Sept 2, 1833 –Aug 20, 1834	Account with Timothy Fletcher for office and sundry expenditures. AD. NhHi. mDW 39798–39801, 39827–39829.	
Sept 3	To Jeremiah Smith. Copy. NhHi. mDW 11112. Van Tyne, pp. 186–187. Writes a letter of introduction for Matthew St. Clair Clarke of Chambersburg, Pa.	
Sept 6	From Rufus Choate. ALS. DLC. mDW 11114. Discusses libel case between Rev. Mr. [George B.] Cheever and Deacon [John?] Stone.	
Sept [9?]	To [Josiah Quincy]. ALS. MH. mDW 11116. Informs Quincy that he has just received his letter of Aug	

17 which followed him in his "wanderings."

Sept 10, [1833?] To Samuel Frothingham. ALS. PHC. mDW 11117. Asks to be informed should Mr. Welles's note for $2,500 come due shortly.

Sept 12 Promissory note to Nathan Hale for $900. ADS. DLC. mDW 39802.

Sept 14 From [Elisha Whittlesey]. AL (incomplete). DLC. mDW 11118. Thinks DW might contribute more as Marshall's successor; doubts his Presidential prospects because of prejudice against New England in the southern and southwestern states.

Sept 17 To Samuel Jaudon. ALS. NHi. mDW 11122. Returns an acceptance in exchange for two others of $2,500 each.

Sept 20 From George Corbin Washington. ALS. DLC. mDW 11124. Would like to sell the Washington papers currently held by Jared Sparks to satisfy his creditors.

Sept 24 From George Corbin Washington. ALS. DLC. mDW 11129. Wishes DW to handle the matter of the Washington papers in a private, indirect manner without public disclosure of his financial situation.

Sept 25 To Elisha Whittlesey. ALS. OClWHi. mDW 11130. Categorically states that he would refuse any judicial position offered and disagrees that McLean is the "only one competent" to oppose Van Buren.

Sept 26 To Henry Alexander Scammell Dearborn. ALS. NhD. mDW 11134. Thanks Dearborn for letting him see the letters and agrees with him that "our people here lack *courage*, & *decision*."

Sept 26 *To Samuel Jaudon.* 275

Sept 26, 183[3?] Draft to Mr. S[amuel] F[rothingham] for $1,500. Printed document with MS insertions. DLC. mDW 39804.

Sept 27 Promissory note to George Blake for $1,700. ANS. DLC. mDW 39806.

Sept 30 *To John Davis.* 276

Sept 30 From Henry Willis Kinsman. Abstract, Kinsman Letterbook. NhD. mDW 7490. Encloses notes to be endorsed.

Sept 30 From Richard Rush. ALS. DLC. mDW 11140. Thanks DW for a copy of his Pittsburgh speech.

Sept 1833 Memoranda of professional fees. MS notebook in
–April [1837] DW's hand. MWalB. mDW 11142.

Oct 3 From Jules von Wallenstein. ALS. NhHi. mDW 11157. Introduces a Mr. Parker, an American merchant in Rio de Janeiro, and relates events in Brazil.

Oct 6   From Henry Willis Kinsman. Abstract, Kinsman
Letterbook. NhD. mDW 7490. Encloses a note
to be endorsed.

Oct 11   To Edward Everett. ALS. MHi. mDW 11161.
Comments on political news and looks forward
to Everett's speech on agriculture at Brighton.

Oct 12   To Emeline C. Webster Lindsly. ALS. DMaM. mDW
11166. Asks her to give an enclosed letter to
Mrs. Thompson, DW's landlady, concerning his
lodgings for the next session.

Oct 12   Draft to Mr. [Daniel?] Colby for $300. Printed
document with MS insertions. DLC. mDW 39808.

Oct 14   Draft to "my draft" for $150. Printed document
with MS insertions. DLC. mDW 39809.

Oct 15   Draft for $500. Printed document with MS
insertions. DLC. mDW 39810.

Oct 16   Draft to Henry Willis Kinsman for $20. Printed
document with MS insertions. DLC. mDW 39811.

Oct 17   To Dr. Benjamin Shurtleff. ALS. MBBS. mDW
11169. Asks for information on the blood lines of
two heifers he bought yesterday.

[Oct 17]   To Charles Henry Thomas. ALS. MHi. mDW 39026.
Informs Thomas that he has purchased some
heifers and plans to return to Marshfield
shortly.

Oct 17   Draft to Mr. [Henry Willis] K[insman] for $500.
Printed document with MS insertions. DLC. mDW
39812.

Oct 18   *From Benjamin Shurtleff.*   277

Oct 23   Draft to "A. B." for $6.00. Printed document with
MS insertions. DLC. mDW 39813.

Oct 24   Draft to "my note" for $31.50. Printed document
with MS insertions. DLC. mDW 39814.

Oct 26   To Israel W. Kelly. Printed. *W & S*, 16: 234–235.
Has sold a lot for less than Kelly's valuation;
expects Kelly and Captain Abraham G. Stevens
in Boston before his departure for Washington.

Oct 26   To Achsah Pollard Webster. ALS. NhD. mDW
11171. Van Tyne, pp. 586–587. Invites her down
to Boston before he starts out for New York and
Washington.

Oct 26   From Thomas Handasyd Perkins, et al. LS. NhHi.
mDW 11173. Would like to place a marble bust
of DW in some public institution because of his
services to the country.

Oct 26   Draft to J. T. [B?] [Joseph T. Buckingham?] for
$172.00. Printed document with MS insertions.
DLC. mDW 39815.

Oct 27   *To John Gorham Palfrey.*   278

	Does not want to start in "new & great controversies unless it shall be made quite an object for me to do so."	
Nov 29	To Emeline C. Webster Lindsly. ALS. DMaM. mDW 11194. Asks Mrs. Lindsly to notify his landlady, Mrs. Thompson, that they have been delayed in New York by illness.	
Dec 4	*From Stephen White.*	*281*
[Dec 6]	To Edward Everett. ALS. MHi. mDW 11200. Asks Everett to stop by this morning for a few minutes.	
Dec 6	To Nathaniel F. Williams. ALS. NhD. mDW 11202. Sends Williams an acceptance for $1,000.	
Dec 7	From George Edmund Badger. ALS. DLC. mDW 11204. Inquires about the proper fee to DW for handling the North Carolina case (*Lattimer* v. *Poteet*, 14 Peters 77, 1840).	
Dec 7	Promissory note to Daniel Colby for $1,500. ADS. DLC. mDW 39824.	
Dec 8	From Henry Willis Kinsman. Abstract, Kinsman Letterbook. NhD. mDW 7493. Writes about claims and receipt of $500.	
[Dec 9]	To Nathaniel F. Williams. ALS. NhD. mDW 11208. Fears "an angry & stormy session" of Congress.	
Dec 9	From Nicholas Biddle. LC. DLC. mDWs. Encloses copies of the BUS memorial for DW and Horace Binney, and asks them to decide on the most appropriate time to present them.	
Dec 9	From Henry Willis Kinsman. Abstract, Kinsman Letterbook. NhD. mDW 7493. Encloses [Daniel] Colby's note.	
Dec 9	From Henry Willis Kinsman. Abstract, Kinsman Letterbook. NhD. mDW 7493. Sends claims papers.	
Dec 10	Bill for the satisfaction of claims due American citizens for spoliations committed on commerce before Sept 30, 1800 ("French claims"). Printed Document with MS insertions. NhHi. mDW 43852.	
Dec 10	Memorial of some citizens of Cincinnati asking that the United States purchase stock of the Portland & Louisville Canal and the canal be made free for navigation. Printed document with MS signatures. DNA, RG 46. mDW 45124.	
[Dec 11]	*To Nicholas Biddle.*	*282*
Dec 11	From Henry Willis Kinsman, Abstracts, Kinsman Letterbook. NhD. mDW 7493. Sends claims papers.	
Dec 11	From [Henry Willis Kinsman]. AL. NhHi. mDW 11212. Writes about a complication with a Neapolitan claimant.	

Dec 11   Draft to "myself" for $500. Printed document with
                MS insertions. PHi. mDW 39826.
Dec 12   To Charles Henry Thomas. ALS. MHi. mDW 11214.
                Wants to be kept informed of activities in
                Marshfield weekly and discusses sundry details.
[Dec 13]   *To Edward Everett.*   284
Dec [13]   To Edward Everett. AL. MHi. mDW 11220. Requests
                his company for dinner next Tuesday.
Dec [13]   To Edward Everett. LS. MHi. mDW 11222. Has
                mistakenly asked Everett to dinner on Tuesday
                instead of Wednesday.
Dec 13, [1833?] To Nathan Hale. ALS. MHi. mDW 11224.
                Concerning Hale's personal financial transactions
                with DW.
Dec 14, [1833?] To Charles Henry Thomas. ALS. MHi. mDW 11226.
                Discusses and asks about Thomas's activities in
                Marshfield.
Dec 15   *From Nicholas Biddle.*   285
Dec 17   To William Allen. LS. DLC. mDW 11229. Will be
                unable to have dinner with his friends tomorrow
                because of the death of his landlady, Mrs.
                Thompson.
Dec 17   To Edward Everett. LS. MHi. mDW 11231. Will be
                unable to have dinner with his friends tomorrow
                because of the death of his landlady.
Dec 17   From Samuel Yorke Atlee. ALS. NhHi. mDW 11233.
                Asks DW whether the executive in a republican
                government ought to be invested with a pardoning
                power.
Dec 17   From Henry W. Conrad. ALS. DLC. mDW 11237.
                States that DW's stand last winter in the Senate
                and his "subsequent declarations" while on tour
                in support of Jackson have made "a deep
                impression" on Pennsylvania Democrats.
Dec 18   *To [Joseph Hopkinson].*   285
Dec 18   Motion by DW that that part of the President's
                message of Dec 3 relating to financial matters be
                referred to the Committee on Finance. *Senate
                Journal*, 23d Cong., 1st sess., Serial 237, p. 50.
Dec 19   *To Nicholas Biddle.*   286
Dec 19   To Henry Willis Kinsman. ALS. Dr. Gurdon S.
                Pulford, Palo Alto, Calif. mDW 11246. Asks
                Kinsman to settle for payment of a promissory
                note with a third party for T. Savage of
                Hampton, Va.
[Dec 20]   To Edward Everett. ALS. MHi. mDW 11248. Asks
                Everett to stop by on his way to the House of
                Representatives.
[Dec 20]   To Edward Everett. ALS. MHi. mDW 11250. Tells

Everett not to make a special trip later in the day
to see him.

Dec 20   *From Nicholas Biddle.*   287
[Dec 21]   *To Nicholas Biddle, with enclosure from Webster to
           Biddle.*   288
Dec 21   *To [Stephen White].*   288
Dec 21   From Henry Willis Kinsman. Abstract, Kinsman
           Letterbook. NhD. mDW 7493. Writes about
           Birkhead and Company v. *Savage.*
[Dec 22]   To Nicholas Biddle. ALS. DLC. mDW 11305. States
           that future events will "make the path of duty
           plain" regarding the nominations of the
           government Bank directors.
Dec 23   To Edward Everett. AL. MHi. mDW 11260. The
           Websters invite Everett for dinner next
           Wednesday.
Dec 23   From Nicholas Biddle. LC. DLC. mDWs. Is more
           convinced that the government nominees for
           Bank director ought to be rejected.
Dec 23   From Henry Willis Kinsman. Abstract, Kinsman
           Letterbook. NhD. mDW 7494. Reminds DW of
           payment of mortgage suit to Taylor and
           acknowledges receipt of DW's letter about *Savage*
           v. *Cox.*
Dec 23   Motion by DW in relation to preventing accidents
           on board steam vessels. AD in DW's hand. DNA,
           RG 46. mDW 43911.
Dec 24   To Mr. and Mrs. John Quincy Adams. AL. MHi.
           mDW 11262. Accepts their invitation for dinner
           on Thursday, Jan 2.
Dec 24   To Charles Henry Thomas (with ALS enclosures
           from Caroline Le Roy Webster and Fletcher
           Webster). ALS. NhD. mDW 11264. *Old-Time New
           England,* 44 (Fall 1953): 58. Congratulates
           Thomas on his marriage and discusses details of
           Thomas's work.
Dec 24   *From Alexander Hill Everett.*   290
Dec 25   To Samuel Frothingham. ALS. NhExP. mDW
           11272. Concerning DW's personal financial
           affairs with Thomas Handasyd Perkins.
Dec 25   To [Samuel Frothingham]. ALS. ICHi. mDW 11273.
           Concerning DW's personal financial affairs.
Dec 25   *From Nicholas Biddle.*   292
Dec 25   *From Joseph Story.*   292
Dec 26   To Henry Willis Kinsman. ALS. NNC. mDW 11275.
           Asks Kinsman to try to help renew a note for a
           Mr. Hunt and informs him that he will shortly be
           "put in funds."
Dec 26   To Roger B. Taney. Copy. DNA, RG 206. mDWs.
           Asks for an account of cases in which process

of distress has been issued under the Treasury
Act of 1820.

Dec 26   From Henry Willis Kinsman. ALS draft. NhHi.
mDW 11278. Requests a copy of a memorial
previously filed with the Claims Commission and
inquires about a defect in another.

Dec 26   Bill for the relief of George Chinn. Printed
document. DNA, RG 46. mDW 43933.

Dec 30   To James White. ALS. NN. mDW 11291. Informs
White that there is nothing new to report
concerning his case (*King* v. *White*, unreported
U.S. Supreme Court case, file #1673, 1836).

Dec 30   From Henry Alexander Scammell Dearborn. ALS.
NhHi. mDW 11293. Is hopeful for the formation
of a "constitution" party before the close of the
congressional session and reports on the tight
money situation in Boston.

Dec 30   From Henry Willis Kinsman. Abstract, Kinsman
Letterbook. NhD. mDW 7494. Sends several
abstracts of claims.

Dec [30–31]   From Henry Willis Kinsman. Abstract, Kinsman
Letterbook. NhD. mDW 7494. Sends information
about several other claims.

Dec 30   From John D. Mahon. ALS. NhHi. mDW 11297.
Asks DW's opinion on "what lapse of time will
operate as a Bar to suits founded on simple
contracts."

Dec 30   From Stephen White. ALS. NhHi. mDW 11299.
Writes that Massachusetts Jacksonians are
watching to see what DW does with the Taney
nomination, but they fear removal of the deposits
may drive him into opposition.

Dec 31   To [Henry Willis Kinsman]. ALS. NjP. mDW 11302.
Discusses business matters and personal finances,
and mentions that he is "daily looking for funds,
here, from two sources; but, as yet, they come
not."

Dec 31   To Samuel N. Sweet. Copy. NhHi. mDW 11304.
W & S, 16: 235. Tells Sweet he made no speech
on the occasion to which he refers, but that he
may be thinking of his speech on the character of
Washington delivered in 1832.

Dec 31   Bill to authorize the secretary of the Treasury to
compromise the claims of the United States
against the late firm of Minturn & Champlin, and
their securities. AD. DNA, RG 46. mDW 43858.

[1833]   To [John Thomas]. "Memorandum of Potatoes." AL.
            MHi. mDW 39056, 39060.
[1833]   To John Thomas. "Further memorandum about
            Potatoes." AL. MHi. mDW 39055, 39057–39059,
            39061.
[1833?]   To Isaac P. Davis. ALS. CSmH. mDW 11307. Would
            be pleased to have the Davises visit Marshfield.
[1833?]   To [Edward Everett]. ALS. MHi. mDW 11310. Asks
            for Everett's signature on a bank order.
[1833?]   To [Edward Everett]. ALS. MHi. mDW 11311. Asks
            for Everett's advice on the amount he should
            contribute in response to a circular.
[1833?]   To [Edward Everett]. ALS. MHi. mDW 11312.
            Inquires about the President's alleged comparison
            of the Massachusetts claim with "the case of So.
            Carolina."
[1833?]   To Richard Smith. ALS. MHi. mDW 11313. Asks
            Smith to handle several financial matters.
[1833?]   To Charles Henry Thomas. ALS. MHi. mDW38988.
            Is reluctant to build a barn with the cost of
            lumber so high.
[1833?]   Memorandum concerning Boston provision
            merchants. AD. NhHi. mDW 11315. Van Tyne,
            pp. 646–647.
[1833–1835] To Samuel T. Armstrong. ALS. MHi. mDW 38203.
            Regrets that he will be unable to keep a dinner
            engagement with Armstrong.
[?]   Power of attorney to DW for Sicilian claims. Blank
            copy, endorsed by DW. MWalB. mDW 11318.

1834

Jan 1   To James Reeside. Printed. *Senate Documents*, 23d
            Cong., 2d sess., Serial 268, Doc. No. 86, p. 300.
            Writes that he is acquainted with Stephen
            Heartwell and recommends him for employment.
Jan [1?]   From Henry Willis Kinsman. Abstract, Kinsman
            Letterbook. NhD. mDW 7495. Sends abstracts in
            several claims cases.
Jan 2   *To Nicholas Biddle.*   298
Jan 2   Bill for partial governmental appropriations for
            1834 with Senate Committee on Finance
            amendments in DW's hand. ADS, and printed
            document with MS insertions. DNA, RG 46. mDW
            43937.
Jan 3   To Simon Greenleaf. ALS. MH-L. mDWs. Writes a
            letter of introduction for a Mr. Walker, from

	Charleston, S.C., a student at Harvard Law School.	

Jan 3   From James W. Webb. ALS. DLC. mDW 11330. Discusses the Presidential prospects of several contenders.

Jan 4   To Charles Henry Thomas. ALS. MHi. mDW 11324. Sends funds to pay outstanding bills and wants to buy all the lumber before money becomes scarce.

Jan [5]   To [Henry Willis Kinsman]. ALS. NNC. mDW 11328. Discusses French claims and his current financial arrangements.

[*Jan 7*]   *To [Nicholas Biddle].*   299

[Jan 7, 1834?]   To Nicholas Biddle. ALS. DLC. mDW 10103. Has been listening to Horace Binney's speech, which he thinks quite "able" and will produce "*some* effect."

Jan 7   To Eleazar Lord. ALS. CtHC. mDW 11334. Thanks him for his suggestions on a manuscript.

[Jan 8]   To Edward Everett. ALS. MHi. mDW 11335. Asks if Everett would find out what the House Committee of Ways and Means did with "our" amendment to the appropriations bill.

Jan 8   *To [Levi Lincoln].*   299

Jan 8   To Charles Henry Thomas. Printed. *Old-Time New England,* 44 (Fall 1953): 56, 60 (two separate excerpts). Advises Henry on the "dressing" of the ground with kelp.

Jan 8   *From Nicholas Biddle.*   301

Jan 8   From John Henderson. ALS. DLC. mDW 11337. Asks for congressional assistance by granting public lands for the building of a railroad through parts of Louisiana and Mississippi.

Jan 8   From Henry Willis Kinsman. Abstract, Kinsman Letterbook. NhD. mDW 7495. Lists votes for governor in Massachusetts Senate.

Jan 9   From Henry Willis Kinsman. Abstract, Kinsman Letterbook. NhD. mDW 7495. Lists votes for governor and lieutenant governor and writes about "payments."

Jan 9   *From Stephen White.*   302

Jan 10   *To Charles Henry Thomas.*   304

Jan 10   *To Stephen White.*   305

Jan 10   From Clement Dorsey. ALS. NhD. mDW 11350. Relates a story about why Jackson was opposed to the BUS; praises DW's report on the Bank.

Jan 11   To [Henry Willis Kinsman]. ALS. NhHi. mDW 11354. Van Tyne, pp. 720–721. Thinks the French Spoliations Bill now "will assuredly pass the

Senate," and therefore wants to move immediately
to "obtain the agency of the greater part of the
interest, in our region."

Jan 11   *From Levi Lincoln.*   307
Jan 11   From Ambrose Spencer. ALS. DLC. mDW 11366. Is
          worried by Jackson's attempts "to concentrate all
          power in himself."
Jan 11   Resolutions of a meeting of citizens of Boston,
          relative to the state of the currency and in favor
          of restoring the deposits to the BUS. Printed
          document. DNA, RG 46. mDW 44628.
Jan 12   *From Nathan Appleton.*   310
Jan 13   *To [Henry Willis Kinsman] .*   310
[Jan 13] To [Stephen White]. ALS. NhD. mDW 11379. Thinks
          it a mistake of the Henshaw Democrats to
          assume from his lack of visible opposition to
          Jackson that he will acquiesce in the succession
          of Van Buren as President or that he does not
          find his Bank policy "utterly repugnant."
Jan 13   From Perez Morton. ALS. NhHi. mDW 11375. Asks
          advice on his French spoliation claims, and on
          compensation for his Revolutionary War service.
Jan 14   *From John McLure.*   311
Jan 15   Bill making an appropriation for the naval service
          for 1834. Printed document. DNA, RG 46. mDW
          43953.
Jan 15   Motion by DW relative to the transfer of the public
          money from the BUS to the state banks. AD in
          DW's hand. DNA, RG 46. mDW 43913.
Jan 15   Draft for $1,000 from Richard Smith. Printed
          document with MS insertions. DLC. mDW
          39835/1.
Jan 15   Memorial of the clerks of the Navy Yard,
          Charlestown, Mass., asking for an increase of
          compensation. AD. DNA, RG 46. mDW 45096.
[Jan 16] To [Edward Everett]. AL. MHi. mDW 11383. Thinks
          Everett's article well written and plans to follow
          it up soon with one of his own.
Jan 17   To Nathan Appleton. ALS. MHi. mDW 11385. Van
          Tyne, p. 187. Sees no majority in the House for
          restoration of deposits; plans speech "to repel
          certain foolish inferences drawn from my
          silence."
Jan 17   To Henry Willis Kinsman. ALS. NNC. mDW 11388.
          Asks Kinsman to pick up his $500 fee in *Rhode
          Island v. Massachusetts* (12 Peters 657, 1838)
          to pay off several notes.
Jan 17   From Henry Willis Kinsman. ALS copy. NhHi. mDW
          11390. Has secured the agency of Peter Chardon

	Brooks's French claims, but has agreed to the assistance of Edward Brooks in their preparation.
Jan 17	Resolutions adopted at a meeting of the citizens of New Bedford, Mass., relative to the embarrassments in the monied operations of the country (enclosed with Alden Bradford, et al., to DW, Jan 18). Printed document. DNA, RG 46. mDW 45014.
Jan 18	To Mr. and Mrs. John Quincy Adams. AN. MHi. mDW 11394. Accepts with pleasure their dinner invitation for Thursday.
Jan 18	To Edward Everett. AL. MHi. mDW 11395. Invites Everett to dinner the following evening with Chief Justice Marshall and others.
Jan 18	To Charles Henry Thomas. ALS. MHi. mDW 11397. Sends additional funds to buy land, pay for lumber, and possibly purchase a pair of oxen.
Jan 18	From Alden Bradford, William R. Rodman, and James Howland, 2d (with enclosure: Resolutions of New Bedford, Mass., citizens, Jan 17). Printed letter with MS signatures. DNA, RG 46. mDW 45018. Seek cooperation of Massachusetts representatives and senators in affording relief to the New Bedford citizens.
Jan 20	From James Blair. ALS. DLC. mDW 11399. Wishes some assurance from DW that he would not vote with Clay and Calhoun to repeal the Force Bill.
Jan 20	Petition of John Etheridge, clerk to the commandant of the Navy Yard at Washington, seeking payment of certain arrears of his salary. ADS. DNA, RG 46. mDW 45098.
[Jan 21]	To Edward Everett. ALS. MHi. mDW 11401. Van Tyne, p. 188. Notifies Everett that the Senate passed his motion to limit application of the contingent fund of the congressional printing office.
Jan 21	From John H. Ostrom. ALS. DLC. mDW 11403. Encloses a list of names from the Utica, N.Y., area for mailings of newspapers and public documents.
Jan 21	*From Stephen White.* 312
Jan [22?]	From Joseph Kent. ALS. DLC. mDW 11411. Presents DW with the gift of a cane cut from the birthplace of George Washington.
Jan 23	Report of the Senate Committee on Finance on the House resolution for a conference on the government appropriations in 1834. AD in DW's hand. DNA, RG 46. mDW 44207.
Jan 24	Motion by DW that the secretary of the Treasury lay before the Senate a statement on the condition

	of the deposit banks. AD in DW's hand. DNA, RG 46. mDW 43915.
Jan 24	From Caleb Cushing. Printed. Fuess, *Cushing*, 1: 135–136 (in part). Praises DW's speech in condemnation of the removal of the deposits and awaits his report of the Committee on Finance.
Jan 24	From George C. Washington. ALS. DLC. mDW 11413. Thinks only DW's help can settle "this vexed question of Bank & deposits."
Jan 24	From James Wilson. ALS. NhD. mDW 11416. Discusses the effects of Jackson's policy toward the Bank and hopes for compromise so that the institution might be preserved.
Jan 25	To James White. ALS. NhD. mDW 11420. Discusses preliminary arrangements in *King et al.* v. *Mitchell et al.* (unreported U.S. Supreme Court case, #1748, 1834) and urges White to come as soon as possible.
Jan 26	*From Nathaniel Prime.*
[Jan 27]	To Edward Everett. ALS. MHi. mDW 11426. Expects shortly to hear in reply to a letter sent to Governor John Davis.
Jan 27	Report by DW for the joint congressional committee concerning amendments to the government appropriations bill for 1834. AD. DNA, RG 46. mDW 45155.
Jan 28	To Charles Henry Thomas. ALS. MHi. mDW 11428. Sends $400 to pay bills and discusses farm chores and need for a road improvement.
Jan 28	From Willard Phillips (with AN abstract of reply by DW). ALS. NhHi. mDW 11432. Asks redress for the government's default on a contract for a steam engine.
[c. Jan 28]	To [Willard Phillips]. AN (abstract reply). NhHi. mDW 11434. Will not fail to take care of claim if it comes to the Senate.
Jan 29	To Henry Willis Kinsman. ALS. Dr. Gurdon S. Pulford, Palo Alto, Calif. mDW 11435. Discusses his present financial situation.
Jan 30	From Richard Bond (enclosed with John Bingham to DW, Feb 1, and petition of Isaiah Rogers and Richard Bond asking payment for plans for the contemplated New York custom house, Feb [1]). ALS. DNA, RG 46. mDW 44596. Seeks DW's help in securing compensation for plans destroyed in the Treasury building fire.
Jan 31	From Hugh Birckhead. ALS. DLC. mDW 11437. Deplores Jackson's removal of deposits and looks forward to seeing DW's report [of Feb 5].
[Jan–Feb?]	To John [Osborne] Sargent (sent under cover to

313

Thomas B. Curtis). ALS. MHi. mDW 11441. *MHi Proc.*, 45 (1911): 159. Thinks Stephen C. Phillips will be the probable successor to Rufus Choate in the House of Representatives.

Feb 1   *From James Blair.*   314

Feb 1   From John Bingham (with enclosures: Richard Bond to DW, Jan 30, and petition of Isaiah Rogers and Richard Bond asking for payment for plans for the contemplated New York custom house, Feb [1]). ALS. DNA, RG 46. mDW 44594. Encloses Bond's letter asking compensation for a building design consumed in the Treasury building fire.

Feb [1]   Petition of Isaiah Rogers and Richard Bond, architects of Boston, to be paid for plans, drawings, and specifications for the contemplated custom house at New York (enclosed with Richard Bond to DW, Jan 30, and John Bingham to DW, Feb 1). ADS. DNA, RG 46. mDW 44592.

Feb 2   *To Nathan Appleton.*   315

Feb 3   Bill making appropriations for the revolutionary and other pensioners of the United States for 1834. Printed document. DNA, RG 46. mDW 43971.

[Feb 3]   Webster's future course on the removal of deposits [Editorial]. AD. NhD. mDW 11449. *National Intelligencer*, Feb 4, 1834.

Feb 3   *From Henry Willis Kinsman.*   315

[Feb 4]   To Joseph Gales & William Winston Seaton. ALS. NhD. mDW 11459. Sends alterations for his Feb 4 speech on the removal of deposits.

Feb 5   Report on the removal of deposits relative to the report of Secretary Taney of Dec 3, 1833, and Clay's second resolution of Dec 26, 1833. AD, in part in DW's hand. DNA, RG 46. mDW 44218.

Feb 6   From Henry Alexander Scammell Dearborn. ALS. NhHi. mDW 11461. Sends praise and encouragement for DW's speeches on the removal of deposits.

Feb 8   From William W. Swaine (with enclosure: memorial of officers of New Bedford, Mass., banking institutions, Feb [8]). ALS. DNA, RG 46. mDW 45033. *Senate Documents*, 23d Cong., 1st sess., Serial 239, Doc. No. 127, pp. 3–4. Asks DW for congressional aid during the current economic distress.

Feb [8]   Memorial of the officers of the several banking institutions of New Bedford, Mass., complaining of the pecuniary distress of the community, and asking that relief may be speedily granted (enclosed with William W. Swaine to [DW], Feb 8). DS. DNA, RG 46. mDW 45023.

Feb 9 From Henry Charles Carey. ALS. ViU. mDWs. Discusses publication of William J. Duane's correspondence with the President and others.

Feb 9 From William Smith. ALS. DLC. mDW 11465. Has abandoned sugar production for cotton in Louisiana because of the reduction of duty; warns DW it will be to his political discredit to align with Calhoun and Clay.

Feb 14 From Nicholas Biddle. LC. DLC. mDWs. Thinks that a plan of "compromise," a Bank charter of four to six years, would be supported at Harrisburg.

Feb 14 From David Stone. ALS. DLC. mDW 11478. Asks help in behalf of G. C. Johnson for the settlement of debts of the Shawnee Indians which were not provided for in a treaty with the government.

Feb 15 To James Trecothick Austin. ALS. NhD. mDW 11482. Expects one house to vote for and the other against on the deposit question next week and thinks some proposition will follow for the continuance of the present Bank.

Feb 16 To [Henry Willis Kinsman]. ALS. NNC. mDW 11483. Writes that French claims are "going on pretty well" and expects the Neapolitan Commission to resume in March.

Feb 17 From Henry Willis Kinsman. Abstract, Kinsman Letterbook. NhD. mDW 7996. Writes about Francis C. Gray's claims.

Feb 17 From George Ryan, et al. ALS. NhHi. mDW 11488. Report that their memorials against the removal of deposits were never presented to the Senate by Samuel McKean and ask DW to do so.

Feb 19 Motion that the Finance Committee be instructed to inquire into the probable effect of the present state of commercial affairs on the revenue of the United States. AD in DW's hand. DNA, RG 46. mDW 43917.

Feb 20 To James H. Causten. ALS. NhD. mDW 11493.

	Asks Causten to pick up his French claims documents.	
Feb 22	From P. S. Michler, et al. LS. DLC. mDW 11495. Send a memorial for recharter of the BUS and restoration of deposits.	
Feb 23	*From Caleb Cushing.*	323
Feb 24	Resolutions of the building mechanics of Philadelphia disapproving the measures of the executive in removing the deposits from the BUS. DS. DNA, RG 46. mDW 44633.	
Feb 26, [1834?]	To Mr. and Mrs. John Quincy Adams. AN. MHi. mDW 38154. Accepts their dinner invitation for March 6.	
Feb 27	Memorial of 866 inhabitants of Northampton County, Pa., complaining of the pecuniary distresses and asking for relief. Printed document with MS insertions. DNA, RG 46. mDW 45047.	
Feb 27	Memorial of 303 inhabitants of the county of Warren, N.Y., complaining of the pecuniary distress of the community, and asking that relief may speedily be granted. DS. DNA, RG 46. mDW 45036.	
Feb 28	To Nicholas Biddle. ALS. DLC. mDWs. Thinks that Governor's Wolf's message to the Pennsylvania legislature will postpone relief and that it would be imprudent to bring forth the Bank recharter bill at this time.	
Feb 28	To Charles Henry Thomas. ALS. MHi. mDW 11500. Gives his approval to buy the Wright land, but cautions that money is scarce "and grows *scarcer.*"	
Feb 28	To Samuel B. Walcott. ALS. MHi. mDWs. Praises Walcott's efforts to abolish the practice of secret attachment of real estate in Massachusetts.	
Feb 28	From Robert Harris. ALS. NhD. mDW 11502. Lauds DW's remarks on the removal of deposits and thinks the country's views are coming around to support restoration.	
Feb 28	Motion that the secretary of the Treasury lay before the Senate the monthly returns of the BUS, from Aug 1833 to Feb 1834. AD in DW's hand. DNA, RG 46. mDW 43919.	
[Feb]	To [Edward Everett]. AL. MHi. mDW 11505. Discusses plans for a meeting that DW would like Everett to arrange.	
Feb	Memorial and resolutions of the citizens of Worcester, Mass., asking for the recharter of the BUS. Printed document with MS signatures. DNA, RG 46. mDW 44747.	

Feb   Memorial of sundry citizens of New York, asking
       for extension of the right to writ of error in
       actions arising under the patent laws where the
       matter in dispute exceeds $500. Printed document
       with MS signatures. DNA, RG 46. mDW 45091.

Feb   Resolutions and memorial of a meeting of the
       inhabitants of Brooklyn, N.Y., for restoration of
       deposits to the BUS. DS. DNA, RG 46. mDW
       44652.

March 1   To Henry Willis Kinsman. ALS. NNC. mDW 11512.
       Discusses the difficulty of getting money "for
       fees or anything else."

March 1   To Anthony McCoy. ALS. NhD. mDW 11515. Will
       be glad to receive resolutions and memorials on
       the questions which "so much agitate the
       country" and hopes that public sentiment will
       compel the administration to offer relief.

March 1   Statement of Ebenezer Webster, of Portland, Me.,
       regarding charges against the appointment of
       Albert Smith. ADS. DNA, RG 46. mDW 45137.

March 2   *From Stephen White.*   324

[March 3]   To Edward Everett. ALS. MHi. mDW 11522.
       Encloses $600 and asks Everett to see Rufus
       Choate's important letter from Pennsylvania.

March 4   Draft to Henry Willis Kinsman for $300. Printed
       document with MS insertions. NhD. mDW
       39835/3.

March 6   From A[lfred] W. Haven (with enclosure: John W.
       Langdon to John Haven, March 4, 1834, and with
       AN to [Henry Willis Kinsman] in DW's hand,
       [March 12, 1834]). ALS. NhHi. mDW 11524.
       Inquires about spoliation claims of the Portsmouth,
       N.H., Athenaeum.

March 7   From James Kent. ALS. MeHi. mDW 11528. Praises
       DW's "devoted patriotism," but is discouraged
       with the present state of affairs in the country.

March 7   *From Samuel Finley Breese Morse.*   326

March 8   From Henry A. Bullard. ALS. NhD. mDW 11532.
       Reports on Whig election victories in Louisiana
       and the financial distress felt in the South.

March 8   *From James Gore King.*   326

March 8   Memorial of the people of Lynn, Mass., in favor of
       the BUS. Printed document with MS signatures.
       DNA, RG 46. mDW 44723.

March 9   From Henry Alexander Scammell Dearborn (with
       enclosure: Dearborn to Orin Fowler, March
       8, 1834). ALS. NhHi. mDW 11547. Sends his
       views on Jackson and republican government.

March 10   From Henry Willis Kinsman. Abstract, Kinsman
       Letterbook. NhD. mDW 7496. Writes about

	T[erle?] Savage v. Thomas B. Smith (a Kinsman case, unreported, Massachusetts Supreme Judicial Court, March term, 1834) and Deacon [Daniel?] Colby's note.	
March 10	Memorial of inhabitants of Utica, N.Y., asking for the restoration of the deposits and recharter of the BUS. Printed document (incomplete). DNA, RG 46. mDW 44954.	
March 11	To Samuel P. Lyman. ALS. MiU-C. mDW 11559. Tells Lyman of his suggestions to "rescue" New York from a "monied influence" in his Senate speech of yesterday.	
[c. March 11]	A Bill to allow further time to the BUS to close its business (enclosed in a letter from Samuel Jaudon to Nicholas Biddle, March 11, 1834). AD draft in DW's hand and Jaudon's. DLC. mDWs.	
[March 12]	To [Henry Willis Kinsman] (forwarding A[lfred] W. Haven to DW, March 6; John W. Langdon to John Haven, March 4, with AN to [Henry Willis Kinsman] in DW's hand, [March 12]). ALS. NhHi. mDW 11561. Asks Kinsman to notify Mr. Alfred W. Haven that all claims papers of the Portsmouth Athenaeum which he has received have been filed with the commission.	
March 12	To Eliza Buckminster Lee. Copy. NhHi. mDW 11563. PC, 2: 4–5. Reports on family news from Washington.	
March 14	To Charles Henry Thomas.	330
March 14	From Roswell L. Colt.	332
March 14	From John Welles. ALS. DLC. mDW 11577. Would like to know whether Maryland and Pennsylvania farmers use plaster or gypsum on their lands as they used to for improved crop production.	
March 15	From Nicholas Biddle.	334
March 15	From J. W. P. ALS. NhHi. mDW 11583. Agrees with DW about the indispensability of the BUS and refutes arguments against a national bank.	
March 15	Memorial of the inhabitants of Brockport, N.Y., against the removal of the deposits and in favor of the recharter of the BUS. Printed document with MS signatures. DNA, RG 46. mDW 44975.	
March 17	Bill making appropriations for the support of the army for the year 1834. Printed document with AD amendments in DW's hand. DNA, RG 46. mDW 43973.	
March 17	Memorial of the inhabitants of Adams, Mass., asking for the restoration of the deposits to the BUS. Printed document with MS signatures. DNA, RG 46. mDW 44825.	
March 17	From Stephen Oliver, et al. ALS by Oliver also	

March 24   Memorial from the inhabitants of Ontario County,
  –April[?]   N.Y., asking for restoration of deposits and
                rechartering the BUS. DS. DNA, RG 46. mDW
                44836.

March 25   *To Charles Henry Thomas.*   *338*

[March 26]   To Nicholas Biddle. ALS. DLC. mDW 11607. Tells
                Biddle that he tabled his Bank recharter motion
                in order not to delay debate and decision on
                Clay's resolutions.

[March 26]   To Joseph Gales & William Winston Seaton. ALS.
                NhD. mDW 11611. Will not pay "what may well
                be paid by another."

March 27,   To Charles Henry Thomas. ALS. MHi. mDW 11613.
  [1834?]   Expects to be in Boston on April 4 and wants to
                meet him there.

March 27   To John D. Williams. ALS. OMC. mDW 11615.
                Thanks Williams for his letter outlining the "great
                advantages from the cheapness of internal
                exchange."

March 29   Memorial of inhabitants of Muncy, Creek
                Township, Lycoming County, Pa., in favor of
                restoring the deposits and rechartering the BUS.
                DS. DNA, RG 46. mDW 44751.

March 29   Memorial of inhabitants of Borough of Muncy,
                Lycoming County, Pa., in favor of restoring the
                deposits and rechartering the BUS. Printed
                document with MS insertions. DNA, RG 46. mDW
                44754.

March 31   From Lewis Cass. LC. DNA, RG 107. mDW 57169.
                Sends a report on the services of the Indiana
                militia companies and requests an appropriation
                of $300 for them.

April 4   From Lewis Cass. LC. DNA, RG 107. mDW 57170.
                Requests an appropriation of $700 for a company
                of the Indiana militia.

April 4   Memorial and resolutions of the citizens of Detroit
                in favor of the restoration of the deposits and
                the recharter of the BUS. DS. DNA, RG 46. mDW
                44929.

April 5   Promissory note to Richard D. Tucker for $500.
                ADS. DLC. mDW 39835/4.

April 10   Memorial of sundry inhabitants of Boston, Mass.,
                asking that the value of gold coins may be raised,
                and that foreign coins may be made legal tender.
                DS. DNA, RG 46. mDW 45084.

April 11   To William King. ALS. MeHi. mDW 11617. Is
                delighted by the results of the Portland and
                Bangor, Me., elections, and regards the state's
                September elections as *"immensely* important."

[April 13,   To Charles Henry Thomas. ALS. MHi. mDW 38960.

[April]   To Edward Everett. Printed. *PC*, 2: 5. Expects his
           speech to be ready for printing on Monday.

May 2   Motion by DW in executive proceedings that the
           secretary of the Senate be authorized to give
           extracts from the executive journal of Senate
           proceedings in relation to the nomination and
           renomination of the directors of the BUS for
           1834. AD in DW's hand. DNA, RG 46. mDW
           45141.

May 3   From Henry Willis Kinsman. Abstract, Kinsman
           Letterbook. NhD. mDW 7497. Encloses Herman
           LeRoy's note for $3,000, paid, and discusses
           several others.

May 5   To Jacob M. Howard. LS. MiD-B. mDW 11648.
           Acknowledges receipt of the memorial of citizens
           of Detroit asking for restoration of deposits.

May 5   *To [Samuel Jaudon].*   *344*

May 5   From Peter W. Radcliff, et al. (with enclosure:
           Resolution of Brooklyn Whigs, May 2, 1834).
           ALS. NhHi. mDW 11653. Praise DW and the
           U.S. Senate for efforts [to restore the deposits].

May 6   *To Charles Henry Thomas.*   *345*

May 6   From Joseph Coolidge, Jr. (with enclosure: Sir
           John Withers Audry to Coolidge, March 31, 1834).
           Copy. NhHi. mDW 11662. Sends Audry's letter
           which praises DW's *Speeches and Forensic
           Arguments*.

May 6   Motion by DW for an opinion of the attorney
           general relative to the transfer of appropriations.
           AD. DNA, RG 46. mDW 43921.

May 8   Resolutions of a meeting of the citizens of Columbia,
           Pa., against the removal of the deposits and in
           favor of rechartering the BUS. DS. DNA, RG 46.
           mDW 44956.

May 9   To Edward Everett. ALS. MHi. mDW 11668. Van
           Tyne, p. 189. Doubts whether Everett's House
           committee investigating the Bank can meet as a
           secret committee unless it was originally
           constituted as such.

May 10   *To William John Duane.*   *346*

[May 10]   To [Samuel Jaudon]. ALS. NHi. mDW 11672.
           Encloses the Connell checks which "must be kept
           as cool as possible" until word from the French
           Chamber of Deputies; thinks the Bank correctly
           handled the select House committee in their
           investigation.

May 10   To John A. Stevens. ALS. RNHi. mDW 11673.
           Would like to hear from Stevens "confidentially"
           concerning the "heavy blow" dealt to custom

house officers by the House in its appropriations
bill.

May 10   Memorial of sundry citizens of Tompkins County,
N.Y., opposed to the measures of the executive,
and asking for a restoration of the currency.
Printed document with MS signatures, copied.
DNA, RG 46. mDW 44999.

May 11   To Charles Henry Thomas. ALS. MHi. mDW 39034.
Asks about the progress of improvements at
Marshfield and informs him of his family's
summer plans.

May 12   To Sarah Goodridge. ALS. MHi. mDW 11675.
Concerning a financial matter and the plans of
the Websters to return to Boston.

May 12   From Henry Willis Kinsman. Abstract, Kinsman
Letterbook. NhD. mDW 7497. Writes about
several promissory notes.

May 12   Bill making appropriations for the civil and
diplomatic expenses of government for 1834.
Printed document with MS amendments. DNA,
RG 46. mDW 44000.

May 12   Bill for the relief of Aaron and Enoch Baldwin,
owners of the brig *Despatch* and cargo, for
discriminating duties on a British vessel. AD.
DNA, RG 46. mDW 43862.

May 12   Memorial of farmers, manufacturers and others of
Mifflin County, Pa., against the removal of
deposits and in favor of the recharter of the BUS.
Printed document with MS signatures, copied.
DNA, RG 46. mDW 44906.

May 12   Memorial of the Merchants, Manufacturers, Traders,
and Mechanics of Rochester, N.Y., attributing
the derangement of the currency to the removal
of public money from the BUS, and asking that
measures of relief may be speedily adopted.
Printed document with MS signatures. DNA, RG
46. mDW 45075.

May 13   From Frederick A. Taft (with enclosure: Memorial
of inhabitants of Dedham, Mass., remonstrating
against the renewal of John Ames's patent). ALS.
DNA, RG 46. mDW 45119. Asks DW to present
to the Senate the enclosed memorial opposed to
the extension of John Ames's patent.

May [13]   Memorial of the inhabitants of Dedham, Mass.,
remonstrating against the renewal of the patent
of John Ames. Printed document with MS
insertions and signatures. DNA, RG 46. mDW
45115.

May 13   Memorial of certain citizens of Massachusetts,
remonstrating against the renewal of the patent

	of John Ames for an improvement in the machinery for making paper. Printed document with MS insertions and signatures. DNA, RG 46. mDW 45111.	
May 13	Resolutions of a meeting of the citizens of Mercer County, Pa., disapproving measures of the executive and the removal of deposits from the BUS. AD. DNA, RG 46. mDW 44988.	
May 14	From George E. Badger. ALS. DLC. mDW 11677. Sends $1,000 for DW's fee in the North Carolina case (*Lattimer* v. *Poteet*, 14 Peters 4, 1840).	
May 14	From Hector Craig. LS. DNA, RG 46. mDW 44452. Printed. *Senate Documents*, 23d Cong., 1st sess., Serial 243, Doc. No. 435, pp. 5–6. Thinks great injustice will be done if the Senate should pass the bill received from the House affecting port weighers, inspectors, and collectors, and naval officers, and surveyors.	
May 15	*To Nathan Dane.*	*347*
May 15	*From Nicholas Biddle.*	*347*
May 15	From Denis Prieur (with enclosure: resolutions of New Orleans City Council, April 26, 1834). ALS. NhHi. mDW 11682. Sends resolutions asking DW to be legal counsel in the Supreme Court (*New Orleans* v. *Armas and Cucullu*, 9 Peters 223, 1835).	
[May 16]	To Edward Everett. ALS. MHi. mDW 11687. Asks Everett to come to the Senate to have a short conversation.	
May 16	To Samuel Jaudon. ALS. NHi. mDW 11689. Sees "much objection" to Thomas S. Russell's nomination as U.S. consul at Valparaiso, Chile, and thinks it will be fully weighed before confirmation.	
May 16	To Henry Willis Kinsman. ALS. MBNU. mDWs. Plans to send some money in about a week.	
May 16	To John Woods. ALS. OHaBHi. mDW 11691. Thinks that "we must fight a general battle against the common enemy" until the fall elections are over.	
May 16	From William M. Muzzey, et al. LS. DLC. mDW 11694. Ask DW to attend their first anniversary meeting of the Philadelphia Young Men's Society.	
May 16	Bill making appropriations for the Indian Department for 1834. Printed document. DNA, RG 46. mDW 43947.	
[May 17]	To [Edward Everett]. ALS. MHi. mDW 11698. Asks Everett to write to Stephen Fales of Cincinnati, a constant writer and "warm friend" of DW's.	
May 17	To Virgil Maxcy (from DW and Charles G. Loring). LS. DNA, RG 206. mDWs. Discusses a statement	

of counter claims filed by the defendant in *United States* v. *Amos Binney, Administrator* (pending U.S. Circuit Court case, District of Massachusetts, 1834) which DW asks to be admitted in evidence without objection to its competency in order to avoid a great waste of time and labor.

May 17   From Nicholas Biddle. LC. DLC. mDWs. Lists reasons why Charles Macalester should not be confirmed a government director.

May 19   From [Alexander Brown & Sons?]. LC. DLC. mDW 11700. Send particulars of a post office check returned protested from New Orleans.

May 20   From [Alexander Brown & Sons?]. LC. DLC. mDW 11702. Will send a copy of correspondence with the President but do not want it made public.

May 20   From Samuel Swartwout. LS. DNA, RG 46. mDW 44456. *Senate Documents*, 23d Cong., 1st sess., Serial 243, Doc. No. 435, pp. 7–8. Asks that Congress not reduce the compensation for port collectors and cites statistics in New York.

May 20   Promissory note to Thomas Swann for $1,500. ADS. CCC. mDW 39835/6.

May 21   To Paschal Franchot. Typed copy. Original owned by G. McMeurtrie Godley, Morris, N.Y. mDWs. Reports that he has presented in the Senate Franchot's county petition asking for relief from the present "great pecuniary distresses."

May 21   Memorial of sundry inhabitants of Pittsford, Monroe County, N.Y., against the removal of the deposits and in favor of the renewal of the charter of the BUS. DS. DNA, RG 46. mDW 44964.

May 23   From Nathan Dane. ALS. DLC. mDW 11703. Suggests that a pamphlet which interests DW might have been written by John Fitch or Arthur Lee.

May 23   From Henry Willis Kinsman. Abstract, Kinsman Letterbook. NhD. mDW 7498. Writes about Nathan Hale's notes.

May 23   From Henry Willis Kinsman. Abstract, Kinsman Letterbook. NhD. mDW 7498. Discusses the case *Savage* v. *Smith*.

May 24   To George E. Badger. ALS. Nc-Ar. mDW 11708. Acknowledges receipt of the $1,000 draft for his legal fee.

May 24   To William M. Muzzey, et al. LS. John H. Freund, New York, N.Y. mDW 11709. Regrets that he cannot attend the Philadelphia Young Men's Society's first anniversary meeting.

May 24   To Mrs. John A. Washington. ALS. Patty W.
                Washington, Alexandria, Va. mDW 11710. Writes
                a letter of introduction for Mr. [Abbott?]
                Lawrence.
May 25   To R. H. Moulton. ALS. NcU. mDW 11712. Is
                unable to find a document on the subject of
                removals which Moulton desires, but suggests he
                write to John Holmes in Maine.
May 28   From Nicholas Biddle. LC. DLC. mDWs. Discusses
                the impending failure of a business concern
                [Union Bank of Baltimore?], but does not wish
                to have the Bank intervene.
May 28   Bill to repeal certain provisions of "An act to alter
                and amend the several acts imposing duties on
                imports," approved July 14, 1832. Printed
                document with MS amendment. DNA, RG 46.
                mDW 43864; 43886.
May 28   Report of the Committee on Finance by DW on the
                case of Pierre Menard and Louis Vallé for the
                return of certain duties. AD in DW's hand. DNA,
                RG 46. mDW 44311.
May 30   From Henry Willis Kinsman. Abstract, Kinsman
                Letterbook. NhD. mDW 7498. Writes about
                promissory notes.
May 30   From Roger B. Taney. LS. DNA, RG 46. mDW
                44460. *Senate Documents*, 23d Cong., 1st sess.,
                Serial 243, Doc. No. 435, p. 9. Encloses a copy of
                a letter from the collector of the Port of New
                York, Samuel Swartwout.
May 30   Bill regulating the value of certain foreign silver
                coins within the United States. Printed document
                with AD amendments in DW's hand. DNA, RG
                46. mDW 43993.
June 2, [1834?] To [Edward Everett]. ALS. MHi. mDW 11722. Asks
                Everett to endorse a note.
June 2   To S. S. Schmucker, et al. LS. PGC. mDWs. Is
                unable to accept their invitation to speak at
                Gettysburg College on July 4.
June 2   Draft for $1,616.50. Printed document with MS
                insertions. InU. mDWs.
June 2   Bill for the relief of William D. Ross, overcharged
                on the rate of duty while importing Canadian
                scrap iron. AD. DNA, RG 46. mDW 43865;
                43888.
June 4   From Henry Willis Kinsman. Abstract, Kinsman
                Letterbook. NhD. mDW 7498. Encloses a copy of a
                letter to T[erle?] Savage [re *Savage v. Smith*?].
June 4   From Henry Willis Kinsman. Abstract, Kinsman
                Letterbook. NhD. mDW 7498. Sends a memorial
                concerning the President's protest.

June 5	To Lewis Cass. LS. DNA, RG 107. mDW 57166. Asks for a detailed estimate of contingent expenses for the War Department.
June 5	To Louis McLane. LS. DNA, RG 59. mDW 55441. Asks for a detailed estimate of contingent expenses for the State Department.
June 5	*To Daniel Fletcher Webster.* 348
June 5	To Levi Woodbury. LS. DNA, RG 45. mDWs. Asks for a detailed estimate of contingent expenses for the Navy Department.
June 5	From Henry Willis Kinsman. Abstract, Kinsman Letterbook. NhD. mDW 7499. Encloses a Neapolitan claims memorial.
June 5	From Henry P. Phillips. ALS. NhHi. mDW 11725. Thinks that the Senate should not confirm Andrew Stevenson as minister to Great Britain.
June 6	From Louis McLane. ALS. DNA, RG 46. mDW 44443. Encloses a detailed estimate of the contingent expenses of the State Department.
June 6	From Levi Woodbury. LS. DNA, RG 46. mDW 44415. Encloses a listing of contingent expenses for the Navy Department for 1833.
[June 7]	To Joseph Gales & William Winston Seaton. ALS. NhD. mDW 11727. Sends part of his remarks on the Harrisburg Memorial [June 3] and will send the rest by tomorrow.
June 7	To Nathaniel F. Williams. ALS. NhD. mDW 11729. Assures Williams that he will send the $1,000 within a week.
June 8	To Samuel Jaudon. ALS. NHi. mDW 11731. Thinks there will be no new developments in the House concerning the Bank for the balance of the session.
June 8	To Samuel Jaudon. ALS. NHi. mDW 11733. Asks Jaudon to accept and sign a draft for $2,500 and send it to Samuel Frothingham.
June 9	*To Charles Henry Thomas.* 349
June 9	From Lewis Cass. ALS. DNA, RG 46. mDW 44421. Encloses a listing of contingent expenses for 1833 of the various bureaus of the War Department.
[c. June 9]	To [Samuel Jaudon]. AL. NHi. mDW 11734. Encloses a copy of the last statement of the Bank of Metropolis and asks Jaudon to keep the information confidential.
[June 11]	To Nathaniel F. Williams. ALS. NhD. mDW 11738. Encloses a draft for $1,000 and asks him to accept a bill of exchange.
June 11	From Nicholas Biddle. LC. DLC. mDWs. Would like to come to Washington for a short stay, but

	wonders if it is politically advisable at this time.	
June 12	From Nicholas Biddle. LC. DLC. mDWs. Thinks it would be beneficial to pass Clay's resolutions.	
June 12	From Benjamin T. Pickman. ALS. NhHi. mDW 11740. Expresses the interest among Boston memorialists to have the House bill passed regarding foreign silver coins.	
June 12	From John B. Wallace. ALS. DLC. mDW 11742. Applauds DW's speech on the President's protest and requests that DW send it to the Pennsylvanians listed in the letter.	
June 12	Report of the Committee on Finance on the bill entitled "An act making appropriations for the civil and diplomatic expenses of government for the year 1834." AD, with insertions in DW's hand. DNA, RG 46. mDW 44313.	
June 13	*From Albert Gallatin.*	350
June 13	From John B. Manchester. ALS. NhHi. mDW 11744. Requests a copy of DW's speech on the President's protest.	
June 13	From Charles S. Wingfield. ALS. DLC. mDW 11746. Finds DW's arguments in the protest speech "unanswerable."	
June 14	*To John Bradford Wallace.*	351
June 14	From Mathew Carey, et al. LS. MHi. mDW 11750. Invite DW to attend a dinner in Philadelphia on July 4.	
June 14	From Henry Willis Kinsman. Abstract, Kinsman Letterbook. NhD. mDW 7499. Sends materials in claims cases.	
June 14	Bill making appropriations for Indian annuities and other similar objects for 1834. Printed document with MS additions. DNA, RG 46. mDW 43961.	
June 15	To [Nicholas Biddle]. ALS. DLC. mDWs. Encourages Biddle to visit Washington.	
June 15	From Robert Gilchrist. ALS. NhHi. mDW 11753. Discusses local and state politics in Kentucky.	
June 17	From Lewis Cass. Printed. *Committee Reports*, 23d Cong., 2d sess., Serial 276, Report No. 59, p. 21. Sends documents relevant to Dr. Henry Gale's claim to title of Pea Patch Island in the Delaware River.	
June 17	From Henry Willis Kinsman. Abstract, Kinsman Letterbook. NhD. mDW 7499. Concerning Nathan Hale's notes.	
June 17	From Peter Oxenbridge Thacher. ALS. DLC. mDW 11757. Praises DW's protest speech and discusses the Bank and deposits questions.	
June 18	From John Morrow. ALS. DLC. mDW 11761. Asks	

	DW to send copies of reports or other documents that would "enlighten the people here."
June 19	From Samuel Black, et al. LS by Black, signed for others. DLC. mDW 11763. Citizens of the first Pennsylvania congressional district "opposed to Executive usurpation" invite DW to their July 4 celebration.
June 19	From John Cooper. ALS. DLC. mDW 11765. Thanks DW for a copy of his speech on the President's protest and states that he subscribes to its sentiments.
June 20	From Lewis Cass. LC. DNA, RG 107. mDW 57172. Encloses a report of the quartermaster general.
June 20	From James F. Conover. ALS. DLC. mDW 11767. Asks permission to dedicate to DW his digest index of Ohio, Indiana, and Illinois reports.
June 20	From James McDowell and James Lee. ALS by McDowell, signed also by Lee. DLC. mDW 11770. Send a copy of the proceedings of the Democratic Republicans of Washington County, Pa., regarding the protest.
June 21	To Mrs. Thomas Ewing. Typed copy. DLC. mDW 11773. Sends her a "little volume" and his good wishes.
June 21	From James Gibson, Jr. ALS. NhHi. mDW 11774. Asks DW for a copy of his speech on the protest.
June 22	From Littleton W. Tazewell. ALS. ViU. mDWs. Praises speech DW has sent (President's protest, May 7?); discusses his election as governor, and Virginia politics.
June 23	*To Edward Webster.* 351
June 23	From John Davis [1761–1847]. ALS. DLC. mDW 11776. Asks DW if he will pick up some money owed by a Washington bookseller and praises his efforts in the "present crisis."
June 23	Bill regulating the value of certain foreign gold coins within the United States. Printed document with MS insertions. DNA, RG 46. mDW 44075.
June 23	Bill concerning the standards and quality of gold coins of the United States. Printed document. DNA, RG 46. mDW 44081.
June 24	From John Gilmore. ALS. NhHi. mDW 11780. Thanks DW for a copy of the protest speech and thinks it contains sound views on the Constitution and principles of government.
June 25	Joint resolutions offered on the occasion of the death of General Lafayette. AD. DNA, RG 46. mDW 43908.
June 25	To Thomas W. Ward. ALS. MHi. mDW 11782. Doesn't think anything likely to occur before the

	end of the session "to affect the present state of things materially."
June 25	From Henry Willis Kinsman. Abstract, Kinsman Letterbook. NhD. mDW 7499. Concerning notes and drafts.
June 25	From Henry Willis Kinsman. Abstract, Kinsman Letterbook. NhD. mDW 7499. Discusses evidence in French claims cases.
June [25]	From John B. McPherson and Thaddeus Stevens. LS. DLC. mDW 11784. Ask if DW might return home through Gettysburg, Pa., and partake in a public dinner there.
June 26	From Virgil Maxcy. LC. DNA, RG 206. mDWs. Declines to accept DW's statement of counterclaims in *United States* v. *Amos Binney, Administrator* as valid without a thorough examination of sources.
June 26	From John Phelps. NhHi. mDW 11787. Thanks DW for a copy of the protest speech and condemns the "depravity in high places" of the administration.
June 27	Report of the Committee on Finance on the bill entitled "An act regulating the deposit of the money of the United States in certain local banks." AD, in part in DW's hand. DNA, RG 46. mDW 44324.
June 28	Motion by DW that the June 9 resolution of the Senate, appropriating Fridays and Saturdays for the consideration of bills exclusively, be rescinded. Printed. *Senate Journal*, 23d Cong., 1st sess., Serial 237, p. 367.
June 30	To Robert Gilmore. ALS. NhD. mDW 11791. Sends the autographs of Lords [Edward] Thurlow and [Alexander Wedderburn] Loughborough in a judicial opinion concerning the will of Benning Wentworth.
June 30	From Robert Gilchrist. ALS. NhHi. mDW 11793. Sends several enclosures and writes about local politics and politicians.
June 30	Memorial of certain citizens of Boston in response to the antibank memorial from that city. DS. DNA, RG 46. mDW 45109.
June 30	Memorial of sundry inhabitants of Massachusetts remonstrating against the renewal of the patent of John Ames. Printed document with MS insertions and signatures. DNA, RG 46. mDW 45120.
[June 1834?]	To [Daniel Fletcher Webster]. ALS. MHi. mDW 39181. Sends some money and plans to write Henry Willis Kinsman to tell him to give whatever

July 18 From Henry Willis Kinsman. Abstract, Kinsman Letterbook. NhD. mDW 7500. Notifies DW that Nicholas Biddle has arrived and that the John Connell acceptances are due.

July 18 From Henry Willis Kinsman. Abstract, Kinsman Letterbook. NhD. mDW 7500. Concerning letters.

July 19 From Henry Willis Kinsman. Abstract, Kinsman Letterbook. NhD. mDW 7500. Concerning the Le Roy draft.

July 21 To Churchill C. Cambreleng. ALS. Charles J. Tannenbaum, New York, N.Y. mDW 11816. Expects that *New Orleans* v. *United States*, 10 Peters 662 (1836), will be reargued next winter in the Supreme Court.

July 22 From William B. McClure. ALS. DLC. mDW 11817. Sends DW a copy of his speech at Pittsburgh on July 4.

July 23 To Edward Coles. LS. NjP. mDW 11819. Tells Coles that it was the evidence laid before the Senate which led him to vote against confirmation of Andrew Stevenson.

July 25 *To [Samuel Jaudon].*   *357*

July 27 To Caleb Cushing. ALS. DLC. mDW 11823-a. Will be in Boston next week at which time he would like to see Cushing.

July 28 From Henry Hubbard. ALS. DLC. mDW 11824. Asks for DW's help in obtaining a loan from the Boston BUS for $5,000.

[July 31] To Edward Everett. ALS. MHi. mDW 11828. Asks Everett to come now to see him if he can.

Aug 1 To Edward Everett. ALS. MHi. mDW 11834. Encloses a note for $1,600 which he asks Everett to endorse.

Aug 1 From Joseph Tuckerman. ALS. NhHi. mDW 11836. Would like eight copies of DW's "Forensic Exercises" [*Speeches and Forensic Arguments?*] to send to eight prominent Englishmen.

Aug 1 Draft to "my acceptance" for $800. Printed document with MS insertions. DLC. mDW 39835/10.

Aug 2 Draft for $275. Printed document with MS insertions. DLC. mDW 39835/11.

Aug 2 Draft to "note" for $700. Printed document with MS insertions. DLC. mDW 39835/12.

Aug 2 *To [Samuel Jaudon].*   *358*

Aug 4 Draft to James Foster, cashier, for $100. Printed document with MS insertions. DLC. mDW 39835/13.

Aug 5 *To James Brooks.*   *359*

Aug 6	*To Samuel Jaudon.*	*360*
Aug 6	To James M. Rix. LS. MH. mDW 11842. Regrets that he has run out of copies [of a speech?].	
Aug 6	Draft to Asa Gilson for $151.28. Printed document with MS insertions. DLC. mDW 39835/18.	
Aug 6	Draft to "my acceptance" for $500. Printed document with MS insertions. DLC. mDW 39835/16.	
Aug 6	Draft to "self" for $30. Printed document with MS insertions. DLC. mDW 39835/15.	
Aug 6	Draft to N[athaniel] R[ay] Thomas for $27.02. Printed document with MS insertions. DLC. mDW 39835/19.	
Aug 9	*From Caleb Cushing.*	*361*
Aug 10	*From Caleb Cushing.*	*361*
Aug 10	From Samuel P. Lyman. ALS draft. MiU-C. mDWs. Asks DW to speak at a joint fair of the Mechanics Association and the Oneida County Agricultural Society in October; thinks his appearance there will greatly enhance his electoral appeal in New York state.	
Aug 13	*To Caleb Cushing.*	*362*
Aug 13	Draft to R[oswell] L. Colt for $94. Printed document with MS insertions. DLC. mDW 39835/20.	
Aug 14	*To John Davis.*	*363*
Aug 14	Draft to "self" for $30. Printed document with MS insertions. DLC. mDW 39835/21.	
Aug 15	Draft to "my note" for $750. Printed document with MS insertions. DLC. mDW 39835/22.	
Aug 20	To Edward Webster. AL (signature removed). NhHi. mDW 11862. Van Tyne, p. 588. Encloses money for expenses at Exeter and expects to see him home at the end of the week.	
Aug 20	From Samuel Jaques. ALS. NhHi. mDW 11864. Sends a pig and some South Down sheep at DW's request.	
Aug 21	To Charles Henry Thomas. ALS. MHi. mDW 11866. Asks Thomas to lay out the work for men to mow and plow the land.	
Aug 21	Draft to "A. B." on Aug 23 for $1,000. Printed document with MS insertions. DLC. mDW 39835/23.	
Aug 21	Draft to "A. B." for $30. Printed document with MS insertions. DLC. mDW 39835/24.	
Aug 21	Draft to "note" for $600. Printed document with MS insertions. DLC. mDW 39835/26.	
Aug 21	Draft for $137.50. Printed document with MS insertions. DLC. mDW 39835/25.	
Aug 22	Draft to Mr. [Samuel] Frothingham for $1,050.	

Printed document with MS insertions. DLC. mDW 39835/27.

Aug 22   Draft to "Insurance" for $86.50. Printed document with MS insertions. DLC. mDW 39835/28.

Aug 23   To George W. Lay. ALS. DLC. mDW 11868. Tries to dissuade Lay from leaving Congress; is pleased with the correspondence between Governor John Davis and the Massachusetts Anti-Masons, and with political developments in Maine and the West.

Aug 25   To John Quincy Adams. AL. MHi. mDW 11872. Invites Adams to dinner on Thursday.

Aug 25   From John G. Gamble (with postscript from James G. King to DW, Aug 26, 1834). ALS. DLC. mDW 11874. Discusses DW's private opinion on the authority of territorial legislatures to create banks and the power of Congress to repeal territorial law.

Aug 26   To John Gorham Palfrey. ALS. MH. mDW 11878. Thinks Palfrey has "misremembered" who borrowed a book of his.

Aug 26   Draft to "A[B?]" for $150. Printed document with MS insertions. DLC. mDW 39835/30.

Aug 26   Draft to "Mount Auburn" [Cemetery?] for $60. Printed document with MS insertions. DLC. mDW 39835/29.

[Aug 27] To Edward Everett. ALS. MHi. mDW 11880. Asks Everett to dine with him and the Senate Finance Committee tomorrow.

Aug 27   Draft to Henry Soule for $600. Printed document with MS insertions. DLC. mDW 39835/31.

Aug 29   To James G. King. Printed. *Executive Documents*, 26th Cong., 2d sess., Serial 385, Doc. No. 111, p. 278. Sees no legal limitation on the power of Congress to repeal territorial laws.

Aug 29   Draft to "J. T. B." [Joseph T. Buckingham?] for $500. Printed document with MS insertions. DLC. mDW 39835/33.

Aug 29   Draft to "my check" for $1,500. Printed document with MS insertions. DLC. mDW 39835/35.

Aug 29   Draft to "Mr. Reed" for $70. Printed document with MS insertions. DLC. mDW 39835/34.

Aug 29   Draft to "self" for $20. Printed document with MS insertions. DLC. mDW 39835/32.

Aug 30   From Nicholas Biddle. Printed. *Senate Documents*, 23d Cong., 2d sess., Serial 267, Doc. No. 17, p. 176. Encloses papers requested by DW for the Finance Committee investigation of the Bank.

Aug 30   Draft for $30. Printed document with MS insertions. DLC. mDW 39835/36.

Sept 6	From Noah Webster. Copy. MHi. mDW 11882. *American Historical Review*, 9 (October 1903): 96–104. Writes a long letter regarding events in New England from the Revolution to the Hartford Convention, viewing the latter as benign and justifiable.	
Sept 20	*From Edward D. Gazzam.*	*364*
Sept 22	*To George Washington Lay.*	*367*
[Sept 22]	To Harriette Story White Paige. ALS. NhD. mDW 11903. Warns her not to fail to bring down "the pattern for a shirt bosom" as his wife wants him "to look like your husband."	
Sept 24	*From Willie Person Mangum.*	*367*
Sept 25	*From Samuel Frothingham.*	*368*
Sept 29	Copy of a deed to Benjamin Morrill from DW for land in Boscawen, N.H. ADS copy. NhD. mDW 39835-37.	
Oct 3	*To Peleg Sprague.*	*370*
Oct 7	To Willie P. Mangum. ALS. NcD. mDW 11912. Shanks, *Mangum Papers*, 2: 219–220. Reports that he has been unwell for several weeks and that he plans to join the committee in New York shortly.	
Oct 7	From Henry Willis Kinsman. Abstract, Kinsman Letterbook. NhD. mDW 7501. Reports verdict in *United States* v. *Leavitt et al.* (unreported U.S. Circuit Court case, District of Massachusetts, verdict, Sept term, judgment, Dec term, 1834).	
Oct 8	To Willie P. Mangum. ALS. DLC. mDW 11914. Shanks, *Mangum Papers*, 2: 220: Asks for the exact day the committee plan to come to New York.	
Oct 9	To Willie P. Mangum (with enclosure: AN extract, Thomas Ewing to DW, n.d.). ALS. DLC. mDW 11915. Shanks, *Mangum Papers*, 2: 220–221. Notifies Mangum that Ewing will be unable to go to New York until Nov 1, and asks whether he should come now or wait.	
[c. Oct 9]	From Thomas Ewing (enclosed with DW to Mangum, Oct 9). AN extract. DLC. mDWs. Shanks, *Mangum Papers*, 2: 221: Wishes to postpone his trip to New York until the Post Office Committee meets there on Nov 1.	
Oct 11	*To [?].*	*371*
[c. *Oct 11*]	*To [Edward Everett].*	*372*
Oct 11	Draft to E. Dyer & Co. for $60. Printed document with MS insertions. NjP. mDW 39835/39.	
Oct 12	To [Samuel L. Southard]. ALS. NjP. mDW 11917. Is looking forward to seeing Southard in Boston	

	on Oct 20 and asks for the first results in the New Jersey elections.
Oct 13	To William Woodbridge. LS. MiD-B. mDW 11920. Writes a letter of introduction for Dr. [Arthur L.?] Porter of New Hampshire, who plans to make his residence in Michigan.
Oct 14	From Henry Hubbard [forgery] (with copy of promissory note, signed by Henry Hubbard and Milo G. Bliss, for $2,000, and copy of DW's reply of Oct 27, 1834). Copy. mDW 11922. Asks DW to accept the enclosed note for $2,000 and send two "genuine" $500 bills from two Boston banks for use in a case at trial.
Oct 14	From Abraham G. Stevens (to DW under cover to Timothy Fletcher). ALS. NhHi. mDW 11925. Encloses a list of livestock which will be delivered to Cambridge on Saturday night.
Oct 14	Draft to "self" for $25. Printed document with MS insertions. DLC. mDW 39835/40.
Oct 15	From Henry Willis Kinsman. Abstract, Kinsman Letterbook. NhD. mDW 7502. About Deacon Colby's note.
Oct 15	From Henry Willis Kinsman. Abstract, Kinsman Letterbook. NhD. mDW 7502. Concerning overdrafts.
Oct 16	From Benjamin W. Dwight, Jr., and Anson S. Miller. LS. DLC. mDW 11928. Inform DW that he has been selected an honorary member of the Phi Gamma Alpha Society of Hamilton College.
Oct 16	From Timothy Fletcher (with enclosure: Abraham G. Stevens to DW, Oct 14). ALS copy. NhHi. mDW 11930. Encloses Stevens's letter.
Oct 18	Draft to Henry W. Kinsman for $5,000. Printed document with MS insertions. DLC. mDW 39835/41.
Oct 18	Draft to Henry Willis Kinsman for $260. Printed document with MS insertions. DLC. mDW 39835/43.
Oct 20	Draft to Mrs. [Caroline Le Roy] Webster for $100. Printed document with MS insertions. NhD. mDW 39835/45.
Oct 27	To Benjamin W. Dwight, Jr., and Anson A. Miller. Draft. DLC. mDW 11934. W & S, 16: 243. Thanks the Phi Gamma Alpha Society of Hamilton College for making him an honorary member.
Oct 27	To Henry Hubbard (with enclosure: copy of Hubbard to DW, Oct 14, and copy of a promissory note for $2,000). Copy. DLC. mDW 11923.

Suspects the contents of Hubbard's letter "a hoax, or something worse" and returns it to him.

Oct 27   From Gulian C. Verplanck. ALS. George Arms, Albuquerque, N.M. mDW 11937. Writes a letter of introduction for William A. Lawrence and A. R. Wyckoff of New York City who come to Boston "on a subject of great interest here."

[Oct 29]   To Edward Everett. ALS. MHi. mDW 11942. Sends Everett [a book?] for his consideration.

Oct 29   To Richard W. Greene. LC. MH-BA. mDWs. Offers to see the mill owners on Saturday should they come to see him (re: *Mann et al.* v. *Wilkinson et al.*, 16 Federal Cases 637, November term, 1835).

Oct 29   To Peleg Sprague. ALS. MDuHi. mDWs. Appeals again to Sprague not to resign his seat in the Senate.

Oct 30   Draft to "reviews &c." for $10. Printed document with MS insertions. DLC. mDW 39835/46.

Nov 2   To Charles Henry Thomas. ALS. MHi. mDW 11944. Informs Thomas of his schedule during November and lays out directions on the management of the Marshfield farm.

Nov 2   From Henry Hubbard. ALS. NhD. mDW 11949. Confirms DW's suspicion that the letter of Oct 14 was a forgery and asks him to endorse his note for $5,000 to the Boston BUS.

Nov 4   To Willie P. Mangum. ALS. DLC. mDW 11953. Shanks, *Mangum Papers*, 2: 223–224. Thinks it advisable that the committee not try to assemble again until the reconvening of Congress.

Nov 4   From Henry Willis Kinsman. Abstract, Kinsman Letterbook. NhD. mDW 7503. Encloses a $1,700 note payable to DW's order and endorsed by George Blake.

Nov 5   Promissory note to Edward Everett for $1,200. ADS. PHi. mDW 39835/47.

Nov 6   To Charles Henry Thomas. ALS. MHi. mDW 39040. Has decided to return home before going to New Bedford and will arrive on Monday morning.

Nov 6   From Peleg Sprague. ALS. DLC. mDW 11955. Plans to resign from the U.S. Senate but will attend the session until January when the Maine legislature meets.

Nov 7   From Henry Willis Kinsman. Abstract. Kinsman Letterbook. NhD. mDW 7503. Concerning Mr. [Daniel?] Wild's note.

Nov 9   To Cyrus Perkins. ALS. NhD. mDW 11959. Van Tyne, pp. 621–622. Encloses letters of

	introduction for Perkins's use while abroad in Europe.	
Nov 10	From Henry Willis Kinsman. Abstract, Kinsman Letterbook. NhD. mDW 7504. Writes about the election.	
[Nov 18]	To Edward Everett. ALS. MHi. mDW 11962. Returns a manuscript finding fault only in its being of "too great kindness & partiality."	
Nov 18	*To Henry Hubbard.*	372
[Nov 18]	To Lewis Tappan. AL draft. DLC. mDW 11964. Thinks Tappan mistaken about passages between lots of the Summer–High Street property in Boston.	
Nov 27	To John Tyler. ALS. DLC. mDW 11965. Shanks, *Mangum Papers*, 2: 224. Sends papers to Tyler on account of the possible delay of his arrival in Washington.	
Dec 2	To Samuel Frothingham. ALS. PHC. mDW 11967. Asks Frothingham to discount a note and credit his account.	
Dec 2	To James William Paige. ALS. MnU. mDW 11968. Reports on arrival in New York after stormy trip by boat.	
Dec 4	To Charles Henry Thomas. ALS. MHi. mDW 11970. Asks Henry to search for a book by [G. Poulett] Scrope which he left behind in Marshfield.	
Dec 4	From Charles L. Telford and Daniel Gilmore. ALS by Telford or Gilmore for both. NhHi. mDW 11972. Write that DW has been elected the annual orator for the Erodelphian Society at Miami University in Oxford, Ohio.	
Dec 6	To Benjamin Kellogg. ALS. DLC. mDW 11974. States that it would be inconvenient to take his case since he does not practice law in New York.	
Dec 6	From James F. Conover. ALS. DLC. mDW 11976. Asks DW if he has received the copy of his digest index of midwestern law reports that he gave to Mr. Le Roy in New York.	
Dec 7, [1834?]	To Mrs. John Agg. ALS. NhD. mDW 11978. Reports on his and his family's activities since the beginning of July.	
Dec 7	*From John Barney.*	373
[Dec 8]	*To Edward Everett.*	374
Dec 8	To Zachariah Eddy, et al. Copy. NhHi. mDW 11991. States that no ill feeling exists between him and Francis Baylies, congressman from the Bristol district, and thinks his election important for the state and country.	
Dec 8	*From Nicholas Biddle.*	375

Dec 9   To [Samuel Frothingham]. ALS. NhHi. mDW 11998.
        Hopes that the money [French spoliations] will be
        voted upon before Jackson's message reaches
        France.

Dec 9   Bill to provide for the satisfaction of claims due to
        certain American citizens for French spoliations
        committed on their commerce prior to Sept 30,
        1800. Printed document with some MS alterations.
        DNA, RG 46. mDW 43892.

Dec 9   Memorial of sundry citizens of Boston asking for
        the allowance of drawback on the exportation of
        cordage manufactured from imported hemp. DS.
        DNA, RG 46. mDW 45952.

Dec 10   To Nicholas Biddle. ALS. DLC. mDW 11999. Assures
        Biddle that the Senate Finance Committee report
        on the Bank will be "satisfactory."

Dec 10   To John Whipple. ALS. NN. mDW 12001. Does not
        know when *Leland* v. *Wilkinson* will be reargued
        in Rhode Island U.S. circuit court. Case later
        reappealed to U.S. Supreme Court and appears
        in Appellate Case File #1861 (1836).

Dec 10   From Francis Baylies. ALS. NhD. mDW 12003.
        Thanks DW for his letter and thinks his prospects
        in the election are good.

Dec 10   *From Nicholas Biddle.*   376

Dec 10   From Stephen White. ALS. NhHi. mDW 12006.
        Discusses the impact of a French war on shipping
        and cotton; writes about some personal affairs.

[c. Dec 11–16] To [Nicholas Biddle]. AL. DLC. mDW 38257.
        Describes the various sections of the forthcoming
        report on the Bank.

Dec 11   To James William Paige. ALS. NhHi. mDW 12009.
        Van Tyne, pp. 189–190. Believes that there is not
        great haste to go to war with France, but thinks
        she has acted "cavalierly."

Dec 11   From Nicholas Biddle. LC. DLC. mDWs. Thinks
        that the subject of Bank expenses in the
        forthcoming report should be suppressed or
        reduced to a minimum.

Dec 11   From Nicholas Biddle. LC. DLC. mDWs. Desires
        DW to present his views on French affairs to
        political associates throughout the country.

Dec 11   Motion by DW that so much of the President's
        message of Dec 2 as relates to the subject be
        referred to the Committee on Finance. Printed.
        Senate Journal, 23d Cong., 2d sess., Serial 265, p.
        35.

Dec 12   Petition of Mary A. Patrick, widow of Captain
        Matthew A. Patrick, asking for the amount of pay

	corresponding to the brevet rank of the deceased. AD. DNA, RG 46. mDW 46001.	
Dec 13	From Albert Picket, Sr., et al. ALS. NhHi. mDW 12013. Invite DW to Cincinnati to deliver the annual address for the association of teachers.	
[Dec 14]	*To Joseph Gales.*	377
Dec 14	To Timothy Fletcher from Henry Willis Kinsman. Conveys DW's instructions that Fletcher go to Brookline and personally give notice to quit to a Mr. Jones.	
Dec 16	*To Joseph Gales & William Winston Seaton from James H. Causten [in DW's hand].*	377
Dec 17	*To Nicholas Biddle.*	378
Dec 17	*To Nicholas Biddle.*	378
[Dec 17]	To Edward Everett. ALS. MHi. mDW 12027. Asks Everett to look over two letters and comment upon them.	
Dec 17	To Samuel Frothingham. ALS. PHC. mDW 12029. Has received Frothingham's letter and enclosure of a check for $2,000.	
Dec 17	*From John Osborne Sargent.*	380
Dec 17	*Excerpt from Boston Atlas.*	380
Dec 17	*From William Taggard.*	381
Dec 18	To Nicholas Biddle. ALS. DLC. mDW 12037. Describes the initial reaction to the Bank report in the Senate.	
Dec 18	To Warren Dutton. ALS. NhD. mDW 12039. Expects the Charles River Bridge case to be the first cause for argument; has heard nothing more of Judge Duvall's resignation, and thinks Wayne of Georgia will replace William Johnson on the bench.	
Dec 18	To Charles L. Telford and Daniel Gilmore. Photocopy. DLC. mDWs. Thanks them for the honor of election as orator of their society, but regrets he will be unable to attend.	
Dec 19	*To Daniel Dewey Barnard.*	383
[Dec 19]	To Edward Everett. ALS. NHi. mDW 12044. Sends a letter from Governor John Davis and his reply, and asks for Everett's comments.	
Dec 19	*To [Samuel Frothingham].*	383
Dec 20	*To Isaac P. Davis.*	384
[Dec 21]	To [Edward Everett]. ALS. MHi. mDW 12050. Asks Everett to stop by for a moment.	
Dec 21	To Edward Everett. ALS. MHi. mDW 12053. Asks Everett if he would send some books to his niece.	
Dec 21	To Charles Henry Thomas. ALS. MHi. mDW 39005. Is sending back with Henry Willis Kinsman some canvass back ducks, and asks that Dr. Porter	

	and Hugh Peterson see them before they are cooked.	
Dec 21	*From Daniel Fletcher Webster.*	*385*
[Dec 23]	To Edward Everett. ALS. MHi. mDW 12059. Asks Everett if he would come to the Senate for a moment.	
Dec 23	From George C. Washington. ALS. NhD. mDW 12061. Discusses the resolution before Congress to appropriate $25,000 for the George Washington papers.	
Dec 23	Resolutions reported from the Joint Committee on Arrangements for the delivery of the oration on the death of General Lafayette. AD. DNA, RG 46. mDW 45144.	
Dec 24	From Daniel Dewey Barnard. ALS. DLC. mDW 12065. Reports that Edwin Croswell, editor of the *Albany Argus*, declines to disclose the name of the writer from Washington whose letter appeared in the Dec 10 issue.	
Dec 24	From Daniel D. Barnard. ALS. DLC. mDW 12067. States, in addition, that Croswell made a *"quasi* apology" for publication of the letter and that the letter writer is a member of the House of Representatives.	
Dec 24	From Daniel Fletcher Webster. ALS. NhHi. mDW 12069. Van Tyne, pp. 588–589. Writes about family and personal news.	
Dec 26	To Ellen Kelly. ALS. NhHi. mDW 12073. Van Tyne, p. 622. Expresses his sympathy upon hearing of the death of her brother William.	
Dec 26	From John Halkett. ALS. DNA, RG 59. mDW 55444. Recommends some honorable notice be given a British naval captain who stopped the piracy of an American ship.	
Dec 28	To Warren Dutton. ALS. NhD. mDW 12075. Advises Dutton not to come to Washington, as the Charles River Bridge case will not be argued; does not plan to resign from the Senate.	
Dec 28	From Julia Webster. ALS. NhHi. mDW 12078. Writes about her school work and news of family and friends.	
Dec 29	*From Stephen Fales.*	*386*
Dec 29	From [Henry Willis Kinsman.]. AL draft. NhHi. mDW 12084. Writes about the Neapolitan claims of Stephen White and others.	
[*Dec*]	*To [Edward Everett].*	*387*
Dec [?]	From [Anonymous]. ALS. NhHi. mDW 12087. Sends his views on the salaries of the principals in the custom house department.	
[1834]	To Warren Dutton. ALS. NhD. mDW 12091.	

	Encloses a letter from Mr. C.; would like to see Dutton before he writes to him.
[1834?]	To Edward Everett. ALS. MHi. mDW 12093. Notifies Everett that Elihu Chauncy has come to Boston to see friends and stay several days.
[1834?]	To Edward Everett. ALS. MHi. mDW 12094. Would be pleased to confer with Everett or others if any good might result from a meeting.
[1834?]	To Edward Everett. ALS. MHi. mDW 12097. Expects to have speech ready for publication by Monday.
[1834?]	To [Timothy Fletcher]. ALS. NhHi. mDW 12098. Asks Fletcher to pick up some supplies in Boston and send via stage.
[1834?]	To [Timothy Fletcher]. ALS. NhHi. mDW 12100. Requests he fetch some supplies and send them down to Marshfield via stage.
[1834?]	To John Thomas. ALS. MHi. mDW 39053. Tells Thomas that great effort must be taken to water the trees during the current drought.
[1834?]	To Campbell Patrick White. ALS. NHi. mDW 12102. Will see him later this morning.
[1834]	Circular appeal for financial aid to the *Annals of Education*. ADS by DW, et al. DLC. mDW 12104.

Index

The following abbreviations are used: BUS, Bank of the United States; DW, Daniel Webster. The entry for Webster is confined to personal details, avocations, feelings, opinions, political information not readily located elsewhere, and writings and speeches. The reader is referred to specific entries within the main Index for the major information on Webster's political activities. The entries for Boston, New York, and Washington are selective.

Page-entry numbers between 389 and 507 refer to material in the Calendar. Numbers set in bold-face type indicate pages where individuals are identified. Individuals identified in the *Dictionary of American Biography* are denoted by an asterisk immediately following the name. Those identified in the *Biographical Directory of the American Congress* are denoted by a dagger.

1. Bibb's middle name is in doubt. The DAB gives Mortimer; BDAC gives Motier; DLC card catalog gives Minos. The birth record entered a long time after the event in the family Bible, the certificate of election to Congress, and the official oath upon his becoming secretary of the Treasury give only the middle initial.